Lecture Notes in Artificial Intelligence 9862

Subseries of Lecture Notes in Computer Science

More information about this series at http://www.springer.com/series/1244

Matteo Baldoni · Amit K. Chopra
Tran Cao Son · Katsutoshi Hirayama
Paolo Torroni (Eds.)

PRIMA 2016: Principles and Practice of Multi-Agent Systems

19th International Conference
Phuket, Thailand, August 22–26, 2016
Proceedings

Springer

Editors
Matteo Baldoni
Dipartimento di Informatica
Università degli Studi di Torino
Turin
Italy

Amit K. Chopra
Computing and Communications
Lancaster University
Lancaster
UK

Tran Cao Son
Department of Computer Science
New Mexico State University
Las Cruces, NM
USA

Katsutoshi Hirayama
Graduate School of Maritime Sciences
Kobe University
Kobe
Japan

Paolo Torroni
Dept. di Informatica: Sci. e Ingegneria
Universitá di Bologna
Bologna
Italy

ISSN 0302-9743 ISSN 1611-3349 (electronic)
Lecture Notes in Artificial Intelligence
ISBN 978-3-319-44831-2 ISBN 978-3-319-44832-9 (eBook)
DOI 10.1007/978-3-319-44832-9

Library of Congress Control Number: 2016948231

LNCS Sublibrary: SL7 – Artificial Intelligence

Printed on acid-free paper

This Springer imprint is published by Springer Nature
The registered company is Springer International Publishing AG Switzerland

The original version of the cover and title page was revised:
The conference title is updated. Title of the conference
is updated from PRIMA 2016: Princiles and Practice
of Multi-Agent Systems to PRIMA 2016: Principles
and Practice of Multi-Agent Systems.
The Erratum to the book frontmatter is available
at 10.1007/978-3-319-44832-9_28

Preface

Welcome to the proceedings of the 19th International Conference on Principles and Practice of Multi-Agent Systems (PRIMA 2016) held in Phuket, Thailand, during August 22–26, 2016.

Started as an Asia-Pacific workshop in 1998 and run as a full conference since 2009, PRIMA has become one of the leading and influential scientific conferences for research on multi-agent systems. Each year, PRIMA brings together researchers, developers, and practitioners from academia and industry to showcase research in several domains, ranging from foundations of agent theory and engineering aspects of agent systems, to emerging interdisciplinary areas of agent-based research. Previous successful editions were held in Nagoya, Japan (2009), Kolkata, India (2010), Wollongong, Australia (2011), Kuching, Malaysia (2012), Dunedin, New Zealand (2013), Gold Coast, Australia (2014), and Bertinoro, Italy (2015).

The 2016 edition was a special one for a number of reasons. (1) To foster a larger Asia-Pacific community, it was co-located with the 14th Pacific Rim International Conference on Artificial Intelligence (PRICAI 2016). (2) To foster interdisciplinarity, we ran a *social science* track, whose accepted papers will be fast-tracked into the *Journal of Artificial Societies and Social Simulation*. (3) To foster student participation, we ran a special *student session* track. Student authors of accepted papers received free registration for the conference.

We received 50 full paper submissions from 22 countries. Each submission was carefully reviewed by at least three members of the Program Committee (PC) composed of 107 prominent international researchers. The review period was followed by PC discussions moderated by Senior Program Committee (SPC) members. The PRIMA SPC has been part of the PRIMA reviewing scheme since 2010, and this year it included 21 members. At the end of the reviewing process, in addition to the technical reviews, each paper received a summary meta-review by an SPC member. The PC and SPC were truly international, involving researchers from 28 countries.

PRIMA 2016 accepted 17 full papers, giving an acceptance rate of 34 %; 16 papers are included in this volume. Moreover, the volume contains three extended abstracts, accepted for the presentation in the social science track, and nine promising early innovation short papers. Further, we accepted seven submissions for the student session track. In addition to paper presentation sessions, the conference also ran a workshop, a mini-school, and three keynote talks.

We would like to thank all the individuals, institutions, and sponsors who supported PRIMA 2016. We thank the authors for submitting high-quality research papers, confirming PRIMA's reputation as a leading international conference in multi-agent systems. We are indebted to our SPC and PC members and additional reviewers for writing insightful reviews and recommendations for the submissions. We are grateful to members of the PRIMA 2016 Organizing Committee, who worked behind the scenes to make PRIMA 2016 successful. These include the social science track chair, Michael Mäs; workshop chairs, Jamal Bentahar and Masayuki Numao; publications chair, Neil Yorke-Smith; publicity chairs, Nadin Kökciyan and Tenda Okimoto; mini-school chairs, Bo An and William Yeoh; Web chair, Federico Capuzzimati; finance chairs, Chutima Beokhaimook, Choermath Hongakkaraphan, and Nongnuch Ketui; and the local organizing chairs, Jantima Polpinij, Virach Sortlertlamvanich, Thepchai Supnithi, Nattapong Tongtep, and Rattana Wetprasit. We thank Enrico Pontelli, Pradeep Varakantham, Makoto Yokoo, and Aditya Ghose for holding tutorials in the mini-school; we also thank Jörg P. Müller, Phan Minh Dung, and Toru Ishisa for the keynotes. Special thanks to some individuals who have consistently supported this conference, in particular the senior advisers of PRIMA 2016, Aditya Ghose, Guido Governatori, and Makoto Yokoo.

We are grateful to Elsevier's *Artificial Intelligence* and the International Foundation for Autonomous Agents and Multiagent Systems for sponsoring PRIMA 2016. We thank the journal of *Autonomous Agents and Multi-Agent Systems*, ACM *Transactions on Autonomous and Adaptive Systems, Fundamenta Informaticae*, and the *International Journal of Agent-Oriented Software Engineering* for agreeing to fast track selected papers. We also thank EasyChair for the use of their conference management system. Finally, we thank Springer for publishing the conference proceedings.

We hope you enjoy the proceedings!

August 2016
Matteo Baldoni
Amit Chopra
Tran Cao Son
Katsutoshi Hirayama
Paolo Torroni

Organization

General Chairs

Katsutoshi Hirayama	Kobe University, Japan
Paolo Torroni	University of Bologna, Italy

Program Chairs

Matteo Baldoni	University of Torino, Italy
Amit K. Chopra	Lancaster University, UK
Tran Cao Son	New Mexico State University, USA

Social Science Track Chair

Michael Mäs	University of Groningen, The Netherlands

Workshop Chairs

Jamal Bentahar	Concordia University, Canada
Masayuki Numao	Osaka University, Japan

Publication Chair

Neil Yorke-Smith	American University of Beirut, Lebanon

Publicity Chairs

Nadin Kökciyan	Bogazici University, Turkey
Tenda Okimoto	Kobe University, Japan

Mini-School Chairs

Bo An	Nanyang Technological University, Singapore
William Yeoh	New Mexico State University, USA

Web Chair

Federico Capuzzimati	University of Turin, Italy

Financial Chairs

Chutima Beokhaimook	Rangsit University, Thailand
Choermath Hongakkaraphan	SIIT, Thammasat University, Thailand
Nongnuch Ketui	RMUTL, Nan, Thailand

Local Organizing Chairs

Jantima Polpinij	Mahasarakham University, Thailand
Virach Sortlertlamvanich	SIIT, Thammasat University, Thailand
Thepchai Supnithi	NECTEC, Thailand
Nattapong Tongtep	PSU, Thailand
Rattana Wetprasit	PSU, Thailand

Secretary Generals

Thatsanee Chareonporn	Burapa University, Thailand
Kiyota Hashimoto	PSU, Thailand
Choermath Hongakkaraphan	SIIT, Thammasat University, Thailand

Senior Advisers

Aditya Ghose	University of Wollongong, Australia
Guido Governatori	Data61, Australia
Makoto Yokoo	Kyushu University, Japan

Senior Program Committee

Bo An	Nanyang Technological University, Singapore
Tina Balke	University of Surrey, UK
Cristina Baroglio	University of Turin, Italy
Rafael H. Bordini	FACIN-PUCRS
Stephen Cranefield	University of Otago, New Zealand
Hoa Khanh Dam	University of Wollongong, Australia
Mehdi Dastani	Utrecht University, The Netherlands
Paul Davidsson	Malmö University, Sweden
Yves Demazeau	CNRS, France
Frank Dignum	Utrecht University, The Netherlands
Rino Falcone	ICST–CNR, Italy
Zhi Jin	Peking University, China
Felipe Meneguzzi	Pontifical Catholic University of Rio Grande do Sul, Brazil
Marco Montali	Free University of Bozen-Bolzano, Italy
Enrico Pontelli	New Mexico State University, USA

Sebastian Sardina	RMIT University, Australia
Tony Savarimuthu	University of Otago, New Zealand
Da Yang	Jilin University, China
Makoto Yokoo	Kyushu University, Japan
Michael Winikoff	University of Otago, New Zealand
Jie Zhang	Nanyang Technological University, Singapore

Program Committee

Thomas Ågotnes	University of Bergen, Norway
Stéphane Airiau	LAMSADE – Université Paris-Dauphine, France
Huib Aldewereld	Delft University of Technology, The Netherlands
Natasha Alechina	University of Nottingham, UK
Wagdi Alrawagfeh	Memorial University of Newfoundland, Canada
Leila Amgoud	IRIT – CNRS, France
Alexander Artikis	University of Piraeus and NCSR Demokritos, Greece
Fatma Başak Aydemir	Utrecht University, The Netherlands
Chiara Bassetti	ISTC-CNR, Italy
Salem Benferhat	Cril, CNRS UMR8188, Université d'Artois, France
Jamal Bentahar	Concordia University, Canada
Olivier Boissier	Mines Saint-Etienne, France
Elise Bonzon	LIPADE - Universite Paris Descartes, France
Nils Bulling	Delft University of Technology, The Netherlands
Patrice Caire	University of Luxembourg
Cristiano Castelfranchi	ICST–CNR, Italy
Qingliang Chen	Jinan University, China
Massimo Cossentino	National Research Council of Italy
Stefania Costantini	University of L'Aquila, Italy
Stephen Cranefield	University of Otago, New Zealand
Célia Da Costa Pereira	Université Nice Sophia Antipolis, France
Dave De Jonge	Western Sydney University, Australia
Nirmit Desai	IBM T.J. Watson Research Center
Frank Dignum	Utrecht University, The Netherlands
Juergen Dix	Clausthal University of Technology, Germany
Esra Erdem	Sabanci University, Turkey
Moser Fagundes	Instituto Federal do Rio Grande do Sul, Brazil
Michael Fisher	University of Liverpool, UK
Nicoletta Fornara	Università della Svizzera Italiana, Switzerland
Katsuhide Fujita	Tokyo University of Agriculture and Technology
Amineh Ghorbani	Delft University of Technology, The Netherlands
Guido Governatori	Data61, Australia
Akin Gunay	Nanyang Technological University, Singapore
The Anh Han	Teesside University, UK
James Harland	RMIT University, Australia
Koen Hindriks	Delft University of Technology, The Netherlands
Xiaowei Huang	University of Oxford, UK

Athirai A. Irissappane	Nanyang Technological University, Singapore
Fuyuki Ishikawa	National Institute of Informatics, Japan
Wojtek Jamroga	Polish Academy of Sciences, Poland
Yichuan Jiang	Southeast University, China
Anup Kalia	North Carolina State University, USA
Sabrina Kirrane	Vienna University of Economics and Business, Austria
Yasuhiko Kitamura	Kwansei Gakuin University, Japan
Andrew Koster	Samsung Research Institute, Brazil
Jérôme Lang	LAMSADE, France
Joao Leite	NOVA LINCS, Universidade Nova de Lisboa, Portugal
Churn-Jung Liau	Academia Sinica, Taipei, Taiwan
Chanjuan Liu	Peking University, China
Fenrong Liu	Tsinghua University, Bejing, China
Yuan Liu	Nanyang Technological University, Singapore
Brian Logan	University of Nottingham, UK
Emiliano Lorini	IRIT, France
Xudong Luo	Sun Yat-sen University, China
Marco Lützenberger	Technische Universität Berlin/DAI Labor, Germany
Patrick MacAlpine	University of Texas at Austin, USA
Samhar Mahmoud	King's College London, UK
Elisa Marengo	Free University of Bozen-Bolzano, Italy
Viviana Mascardi	University of Genoa, Italy
Shigeo Matsubara	Kyoto University, Japan
Toshihiro Matsui	Nagoya Institute of Technology, Japan
John-Jules Meyer	Utrecht University, The Netherlands
Roberto Micalizio	University of Turin, Italy
Tsunenori Mine	Kyushu University, Japan
Marco Montali	Free University of Bozen-Bolzano, Italy
Pavlos Moraitis	LIPADE, Paris Descartes University, France
Zeinab Noorian	Ryerson University, Canada
Timothy Norman	University of Aberdeen, UK
Andrea Omicini	Università di Bologna, Italy
Nir Oren	University of Aberdeen, UK
Julian Padget	University of Bath, UK
Maurice Pagnucco	The University of New South Wales, New Zealand
Odile Papini	LSIS UMR CNRS 7296, France
Simon Parsons	King's College London, UK
Fabio Patrizi	Free University of Bozen-Bolzano, Italy
Duy Hoang Pham	Posts and Telecommunications Institute of Technology, Vietnam
Jeremy Pitt	Imperial College London, UK
Enrico Pontelli	New Mexico State University, USA
David Pynadath	University of Southern California, USA
Franco Raimondi	Middlesex University, UK

Surangika Ranathunga	University of Moratuwa, Sri Lanka
Alessandro Ricci	University of Bologna, Italy
Juan Antonio Rodriguez Aguilar	IIIA-CSIC, Spain
Luigi Sauro	University of Naples Federico II, Italy
Vadim Savenkov	Vienna University of Economics and Business (WU), Austria
Torsten Schaub	University of Potsdam, Germany
Claudia Schulz	Imperial College London, UK
Francois Schwarzentruber	École normale supérieure de Rennes, France
Sandip Sen	University of Tulsa, USA
Murat Sensoy	Ozyegin University, Turkey
Carles Sierra	IIIA-CSIC, Barcelona, Spain
Leandro Soriano Marcolino	University of Southern California, USA
Leon Sterling	Swinburne University of Technology, Australia
Yuqing Tang	Carnegie Mellon University, USA
Michaël Thomazo	Inria, France
Andreea Urzica	University Politehnica of Bucharest, Romania
Leon van der Torre	University of Luxembourg
Wamberto Vasconcelos	University of Aberdeen, UK
Harko Verhagen	Stockholm University, Sweden
Serena Villata	CNRS Sophia-Antipolis, France
Mirko Viroli	Università di Bologna, Italy
Kewen Wang	Griffith University, Australia
Michael Winikoff	University of Otago, New Zealand
Brendon J. Woodford	University of Otago, New Zealand
Nitin Yadav	RMIT University, Australia
William Yeoh	New Mexico State University, USA
Logan Yliniemi	University of Nevada, USA
Neil Yorke-Smith	American University of Beirut, Lebanon
Fabio Zambetta	RMIT University, Australia

Additional Reviewers

Albert, Michael	Küster, Tobias	Ribino, Patrizia
Andres, Benjamin	Lefèvre, Claire	Ricca, Francesco
Balbo, Flavien	Montagna, Sara	Sabuncu, Orkunt
De Vos, Marina	Morales, Javier	Seidita, Valeria
Dennis, Louise	Najjar, Amro	Shams, Zohreh
Fioretto, Ferdinando	Noriega, Pablo	Sperati, Valerio
Galdi, Clemente	Okimoto, Tenda	Stawowy, Michele
Gavanelli, Marco	Pesenti Gritti, Armando	Tamassia, Marco
Knobbout, Max	Pianini, Danilo	Zhan, Jieyu

Contents

Social Science Extended Abstracts

Invited Papers

Intercultural Collaboration and Support Systems:
A Brief History

Toru Ishida

Department of Social Informatics, Kyoto University, Kyoto, 606-8501, Japan
ishida@i.kyoto-u.ac.jp

Abstract. At the beginning of the new millennium, we proposed the concept of *intercultural collaboration* where participants with different cultures and languages work together towards shared goals. Because intercultural collaboration is a new area with scarce data, it was necessary to execute parallel experiments in both in real fields as well as in research laboratories. In 2002, we conducted a one-year experiment with Japanese, Chinese, Korean and Malaysian colleagues and students to develop open-source software oriented towards machine translation. From this experiment, we understood the necessity of a language infrastructure on the Internet that could create customized multilingual environments for various situations. In 2006, we launched *the Language Grid* project to realize a federated operation of servers for language services. Using the Language Grid, we worked with a nongovernmental organization since 2011 to support knowledge communications between agricultural experts in Japan and farmers in Vietnam via their children. We observed that a large community emerged to utilize these nonmature machine translation technologies. During these experiences, by facing different types of difficulties, we gradually came to understand the nature of intercultural collaboration. Problems are *wicked* and not easily defined because of their nested and open networked origin. Fortunately, multiagent technologies can be applied to model and simulate intercultural collaboration so as to predict the difficulties and to prepare a better support systems. In this paper, we provide a brief history of the research and practice as regards intercultural collaboration and support systems.

1 Intercultural Collaboration

Immediately after September 11 in 2001, we started research on *intercultural collaboration*.[1] We were strongly motivated to utilize technologies to enhance communications among people in different cultures. While the Internet allows people to be linked together regardless of location, language remains the biggest barrier: only 25.9 % of the Internet population speaks English. The remainder is divided between other European and Asian

---

[1] There was no such concept at that time. We created the word "intercultural collaboration" by adding *goals* to *intercultural communication*, so that researchers in computer science can participate to advance methodologies and technologies to support multi-language and multi-cultural communities.

M. Baldoni et al. (Eds.): PRIMA 2016, LNAI 9862, pp. 3–19, 2016.
DOI: 10.1007/978-3-319-44832-9_1

languages.[2] However, it is not possible for anyone to learn the languages needed to access all possible information on the Internet. In particular, Asian people are not taught neighboring languages. Only a small portion of the Japanese population understand Chinese or Korean and vice versa. People learn English to collaborate, but often cannot think in English: serious barriers to intercultural collaboration exist, because the collaboration often requires the elaboration of new ideas. Therefore, communication in real intercultural situations is rather complex. For example, conversations between Chinese and Japanese are often done in English with the aid of written Chinese characters. As there is no simple way to solve this problem directly, it is necessary to combine different approaches. Learning English as a second language is one way, but learning other languages and respecting different cultures are also important. Since one cannot master all languages, the use of machine translation and other existing technologies on the Internet is a viable solution.

Intercultural collaboration is a goal-directed group activity. The research target emphasizes collaboration rather than communication. Therefore, we can clearly identify research objectives. Goal-directed group activities can be evaluated both qualitatively and quantitatively, and thus attract researchers with both socio-cultural and technological backgrounds. Culture and its effects on human cognition and behaviors have been intensively studied in sociology [7], psychology [17, 22] and linguistics [2]. Some of their research findings are confirmed in collaboration environments by laboratory experiments [24, 32]. Various technologies to bridge cultural and language gaps have been tried out and their effectiveness and limitations have been analyzed, e.g., pictogram communication to avoid language communications [1, 26], and machine translation to cope with language barriers [34, 35]. We can combine findings and ideas including social psychological analyses, collaboration support technologies, and case studies by field workers.

The research area of intercultural collaboration will become essential in a world in which physical borders disappear rapidly and people and cultures are more and more on the move and in contact. To understand how humans manage language and cultural issues, researchers should join and observe intercultural activities. However, sites related to intercultural activities are often far from research laboratories (both geographically and mentally). Workshops and conferences have been started for mutual learning between researchers and field workers [3, 10].

2   ICE2002: Getting Started with Machine Translation

We conducted *Intercultural Collaboration Experiment* in 2002 (ICE2002) among Asian universities.[3] Since the experiment pursued collaboration among heterogeneous groups across country borders, participants never saw each other and communicated only in

---

[2] Internet World Users by Language - Top 10 Languages, Internet World Stats, Miniwatts Marketing Group, 30 June 2015, retrieved from http://www.internetworldstats.com/stats7.htm.

[3] In this project, 32 students from Kyoto University (Japan), Shanghai Jiaotong University (China), Seoul National University and Handong University (South Korea), and University of Malaya (Malaysia) jointly developed software over the Internet.

their mother languages supported by machine translation. Given the dramatic Internet penetration in Asian countries, an intercultural collaboration support system that overcomes the language differences had to be developed. Differing from face-to-face communications, machine translation services can be easily applied to computer mediated communications. This approach drastically increases the potential for intercultural collaboration by lowering the language barrier.

Although natural language processing researchers had rigorously studied machine translation for years, translation quality was not adequate for wide application to actual worksites. The preceding studies evaluated the machine translation of written documents, and do not take into account the interaction factor for refining translation quality. We, on the other hand, applied machine translation to human-to-human collaboration, and tried to analyze the interactive translation refinement procedures implemented among humans and machines.

Figure 1 shows the participants of ICE2002. In this trial, multilingual discussions were established among the participants. These tools incorporate translation services for Chinese, Japanese, Korean, Malay, and English; a multilingual bulletin board system was utilized as a daily discussion space, and a multilingual Web browser enabled participants to share documents in their own languages. To explore the possibilities and limitations of machine translation technologies, communications during the experiment were restricted to just those tools.

Fig. 1. ICE2002 participants

The experiment had two tracks. The first track was conducted from May to July, and the second one from October to December. To synchronize software developments in different countries, each track was divided into two 4-week-phases. In *Software Design Phase*, collaboration software was designed. The goal of this phase was to submit a system design proposal to implement software. In *Software Implementation Phase*, software based on the design proposal was to be implemented. The goal of this phase was to complete and release a collaboration tool.

In ICE2002, collaboration software consisting of Web-based email, SMS, search engine, was proposed the outcome of the multinational teams. We observed how participants achieved the goal with communications in a noisy media. To analyze translation-mediated collaboration on multilingual tools, conversation and content analyses were conducted. We soon realized that users were adapting to the machine translators. Students tried to repair their input sentences so that the machine translators would produce better translations. Though the students exhibited significant flexibility in adapting to the machines, since the mental models of the machine translators were basically unavailable to the students, the students' behavior was sometimes humorous.[4] By investigating the interaction among users and machine translators, we confirmed two repair patterns as follows [23].

- *Self-initiated repair* or *user adaptation to machine translation*: People adapt themselves to machine translation capability to convey remarks properly to other team members. Before posting a message, the poster would repeated alter the input text to improve the translation results.
- *Other-initiated repair* or *collaborative translation*: Even if a translation was imperfect, people worked out the intentions of other members' remarks. The collaborative repair process is initiated by a message receiver's reaction.

During the experiment, we confirmed the above *repair patterns* in the process of eliminating translation errors. In particular, we explored other-initiated repair, and establish protocols for collaborative translation by monolinguals with machine translators [20]. We also realized that machine translation indeed supported intercultural collaborative works. We decided to further explore the approach to use machine translation in the context of collaboration. At the same time, we understood how difficult it is to create a comprehensive intercultural collaboration environment. The next section explains our attempts to develop a language infrastructure for intercultural collaboration.

3   The Language Grid: Building a Language Service Infrastructure

3.1   From Language Resources to Language Services

To increase the accessibility and usability of language resources (dictionaries, parallel texts, part-of-speech taggers, machine translators, etc.), we proposed the *Language Grid*,[5] which wraps existing language resources as atomic services and enables users to compose new services by combining the atomic services. We believe that *fragmentation*

---

[4] Japanese students input Japanese sentences with many personal pronouns such as "I" and "you" so that the machine translators would generate better results, though Japanese do not often use personal pronouns in their conversations.

[5] The concept was first presented in a keynote speech at SAINT 2006 [9], and later in a book published in 2011 [12].

and recombination[6] is the key to creating a full range of customized language environments for different types of user communities.

Our slogan is "from language resources to language services." To allow users to create their own language services that can be combined with other services, we take the service-oriented approach, where each language resource is wrapped as a language service. For example, data like multilingual dictionaries and parallel texts can be wrapped to form atomic language services that can translate words or sentences. However, those atomic services are not restricted to just a simple retrieval function: a parallel text service can return the translation of a sentence that is similar to the input sentence. Wrapping software like machine translators is straightforward, but even human interpreters can be wrapped as translation services. Users do not have to distinguish machines from human translation services other than by their quality of services: machine translators can provide faster services while human interpreters return higher quality translations.

The next step is to combine atomic language services to create new services. Figure 2 illustrates the process of combining a variety of atomic services for Japanese agricultural experts to translate their knowledge for Vietnamese farmers. To translate Japanese sentences into Vietnamese, we first need to cascade Japanese-English and English-Vietnamese translators, because there is no direct translator handling Japanese to Vietnamese. To replace words output by machine translators with the words in multilingual dictionaries specific to agriculture, part-of-speech taggers are necessary to divide the input sentences into parts. We can train *example-based machine translators* with

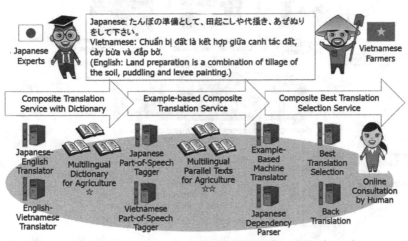

☆ Multilingual Dictionary for Agriculture is provided by NPO Pangaea, Japan National Agriculture Research Center, Vietnam MARD. Entry Number: 3,099 (Sep. 2014)
☆☆ Multilingual Parallel Texts for Agriculture is provided by NPO Pangaea, Japan National Agriculture Research Center, Vietnam MARD. Entry Number: 2,485 (Sep. 2014)

Fig. 2. Language service composition

---

[6] The concept *fragmentation and recombination* appeared in *e-topia* written by William J. Mitchell.

Japanese-Vietnamese parallel texts. We then have different types of translators and face the problem of determining which one is the best: example-based machine translators can create high quality translation only when they trained with similar sentences. We may use back-translation, say Japanese-Vietnamese-Japanese translation, to compare original and back-translated Japanese sentences, and select the translator that can produce back-translated sentences most similar to the original ones. In spite of all these efforts, if the quality of translation is still insufficient, the Japanese experts may use human translation services.

3.2   Service Grid Architecture

A variety of language resources already exist online. However, difficulties often arise when people try to use those language resources in their intercultural activities; the confusing web of complex contracts, intellectual property rights, and non-standard application interfaces make it difficult for users to create customized language services that support intercultural activities. Since many language resources have usage restrictions, it is difficult for users to negotiate with every language resource provider when combining several resources for their purpose. To improve the accessibility and usability of existing language resources, the Language Grid illustrated in Fig. 3 reduces the negotiation costs related to intellectual property rights.

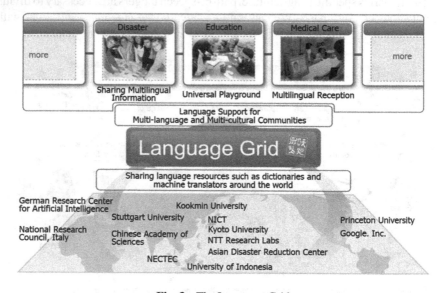

Fig. 3.   The Language Grid

We need to allow users to easily create new language services by combining existing ones. The Language Grid[7] allows users to register services and share them. Let us define the infrastructure that supports the formation of service-oriented collective intelligence, the *service grid*.[8] Major stakeholders fall into three categories: *service providers, service users, and service grid operators*. Service providers provide language services such as machine translators, part of speech taggers, dependency parsers, dictionaries and parallel texts. Service users invoke registered language services as needed for their intercultural activities. Service grid operators manage and control language resources and services. For institutional design, we considered the following issues of the stakeholders:

- How to protect the intellectual property rights of service providers and to motivate them to provide services to the service grid. To this end, service providers should be allowed to define for what purposes their services can be used and the usage rights.
- How to encourage a wide variety of activities of service users to increase their satisfaction. To this end, service users should be allowed to run application systems that employ the services permitted for such use.
- How to reduce the load on service grid operators while allowing them to globally extend their service grids. To this end, *federated operation* is to be facilitated, where several operators collaboratively operate their service grids by connecting them in a peer-to-peer fashion.

We organized this project based on collaboration between researchers in various universities and research institutes and potential users in nonprofit and nongovernmental organizations. Participatory design and action research methodologies are being employed during the project. Software development, applications in real communities, and institutional design for federated operation are all related, and thus performed in parallel.[9] It has become one of the most advanced service infrastructures for intercultural collaboration.

Various service computing technologies have been developed to enable the collaboration needed among language services. *Language service ontology* is a technology to define standard language service interfaces in a hierarchical way so that end users are provided with simple interfaces while professionals can access more complex interfaces [6]. *Horizontal service composition* was invented to select the best atomic service from a set of atomic services to instantiate a desired workflow.[10] We apply constraint optimization algorithms to select the appropriate services and thus satisfy quality of service (QoS) requirements [4]. *Context-aware service composition* was proposed to coordinate

---

[7] The word *grid* is defined as "a system or structure for combining distributed resources; an open standard protocol is generally used to create high quality services." Our approach, applying the grid concept to ensure the collaboration of language services, has not been tried before.

[8] Service grid is a generic term meaning a framework where "services are composed to meet the requirements of a user community within constraints specified by the resource provider [14]."

[9] As a result, we took only two years to start its operation. Around 30 organizations joined in December 2007 to share language resources.

[10] Contrary, *vertical service composition* generates workflows based on AI planning technologies.

multiple translations to determine the meanings of words consistently [18, 28]. *Service supervision*, on the other hand, is a runtime technology to monitor and modify the processes of composite services [27]. Furthermore, by monitoring existing language services, a *policy-aware parallel execution method* of atomic services was invented for users to adapt to the operation policies of service providers [31].

Table 1. Language service list

Service category	Service type	Number of services
Translation	Translation Service	32
	Domain-Specific Translation Service	5
	Multilingual Mixed Document Translation Service*	0
	Back Translation Service	3
	Multi-hop Translation Service	2
	Translation Selection Service	1
Paraphrase	Paraphrasing Service*	0
	Transliteration Service*	0
Dictionary	Multilingual Dictionary Service	17
	Multilingual Dictionary Service with Longest Match	34
	Concept Dictionary Service	19
	Pictogram Dictionary Service	2
	Multimedia Dictionary Service*	0
	Multilingual Glossary Service*	0
	Dictionary Creation Support Service*	0
Corpus	Parallel Corpus Service	40
	Dialog Parallel Corpus Service	1
	Template Parallel Corpus Service	5
Analysis	Morphological Analysis Service	19
	Named Entity Tagging Service	1
	Dependency Parsing Service	4
	Morphemese Dependency Parsing Service	1
	Similarity Calculation Service	6
	Quality Estimation Service	1
	Language Identification Service	5
	Text Summarization Service	2
	Keyphrase Extraction Service	4
Speech	Text To Speech Service	4
	Speech Recognition Service	2
Other	Structural Alignment Creation Service*	0
Meta Service	Service Management Service	1

(Service types marked * are currently under development.)

As of February 2015, 170 groups in 22 countries had joined to share more than 200 language services as listed in Table 1. However, we still need to collect language resources for so called *low resource languages*. Automatic generation algorithms have been studied to create dictionaries between minor languages from existing dictionaries [33].[11]

3.3 Federated Operation

The operation model we designed reflects the intentions of user groups around the world like research institutes and nonprofit and nongovernmental organizations. Nonprofit and nongovernmental organizations and public sectors became the major users, but universities are using the Language Grid more intensively; researchers and students who are working on services computing, text analysis, computer-supported cooperative work, and multilingual communication are using language services to attain their research goals.

From our operation experience over several years, we have gained many insights. Because the operation center in Kyoto cannot reach local organizations in other countries, over 70 % of participating organizations are local. Since we need global collaboration to solve language issues in local communities, this imbalance should be rectified: the operators need to be dispersed into different organizations globally and to collaborate with each other. The *federated operation model* [21] was invented to realize such collaboration. Reasons to drive federated operation include not only the limited number of users that a single operator can handle, but also the locality caused by geographical conditions and application domains.

There are two types of federated operation. One is *centralized affiliation*, where the operators form a federal association to control the terms of affiliation based on mutual agreement. This yields flexibility in deciding affiliation style, but incurs high cost in maintaining the federal association. The other is *decentralized affiliation*, which allows a service grid user to create and become the operator of a new service grid that reuses the agreements set by the first service grid.[12] This type of operation promotes the formation of peer-to-peer networks by operators. Since the formation of peer-to-peer networks by the operators is flexible and maintenance costs are avoided, we adopted the decentralized affiliation since it suits research organizations like universities and research institutes.

Using the Language Grid, various kinds of intercultural activities have been implemented at hospital reception desks, local schools, shopping streets, and so on. To enable each multi-cultural community to develop its own multi-language environment, we take the participatory design approach, where collaboration among humans and technologies is the key for creating customized multi-language environments [15]. In other words, we could develop customized language environments for intercultural collaboration by

---

[11] For example, the algorithm enables users to create a Uyghur-Kazakh dictionary from Uyghur-Chinese and Kazakh-Chinese dictionaries.

[12] Sometimes it is impossible for different service grids to use exactly the same agreements. A typical problem is the governing law. For international affiliation, a possible idea is to adopt a common law like New York State law, but operators may wish to adopt the governing law of their own locations.

mirroring the approach taken by humans in creating and diffusing domain specific words and dictionaries.

Another important aspect of the Language Grid is to encourage the collaboration of widely separated people. The joint research conducted with Tsinghua University's smart classroom is a typical achievement [25]. We rebuilt the smart classroom as a collection of pervasive computing services to allow easier connection of the smart classrooms. The Language Grid then quickly realized the *open smart classroom*, which connects classrooms in different countries.

The *service grid server software* has been released as open source software. Using this source code, universities and research institutes can operate any kind of service grid not only for language services but also for services in other domains. We are now in the process of creating a network of operation centers to cover Asian languages. The Bangkok operation center in Thailand opened in October 2010 to provide a collection of atomic services including a Thai-English dictionary and machine translator, Thai text-to-speech tagger, and morphological analysis utilities. Those services can be accessed by users of the Kyoto operation center.[13] The service grid software has been selected as a basis of *Open Language Grid*, where Asian, US and EU projects are going to share open-source language resources.[14]

4   YMC-Viet: Forming a Community to Utilize Nonmature Technologies

We have been participating in an agriculture support project in Vietnam with rice harvesting experts since 2011. The project aims at designing new services for multi-language knowledge communication via the Internet. The goal is to transfer agriculture knowledge from Japanese experts to Vietnamese farmers in rural areas with low literacy rate, to increase rice productivity, and to decrease the environmental burdens caused by excess use of agrichemicals. The motivation of Japanese experts, who work for the Japan International Cooperation Agency to support developing countries, in using information technology is that they cannot physically travel to all rural areas that need their advice.[15]

There exists a huge gap between Japanese experts and Vietnamese farmers, not only in agricultural knowledge but also language and culture. Furthermore, the farmers have difficulties in using computers and indeed in reading/writing messages. Therefore, as shown in Fig. 4, a *youth-mediated communication (YMC) model* was proposed and applied to bridge the gaps in knowledge, language, and cultures [19]. In the YMC model,

---

[13] Jakarta and Urumqi operation centers have just started at the University of Indonesia and Xinjiang University.

[14] The Language Application Grid (LAPPS Grid) project in the US adopts the service grid server software described in this section.

[15] The project consists of our team in Kyoto University for providing the multilingual collaboration environment, NPO Pangaea for educating children and conducting experiments, University of Tokyo and Mie University for providing agricultural knowledge, Vietnam National University for local arrangements, and MARD/DARD for planning and controlling the whole process of the project.

the children received training at a local community center, and then acted as mediators between the Vietnamese farmers (parents) and the Japanese experts. The YMC model is a breakthrough idea for gap bridging, but it exposes another difficulty in communi- cation: the computer literacy and background knowledge of children determine the boundaries of agricultural knowledge communication. To cope with all the problems, we formed a project with a variety of stakeholders: agricultural experts and language processing experts in universities, farmers and their children, nongovernmental organ- izations targeting the education of children in developing countries, and Vietnamese national and local ministries.

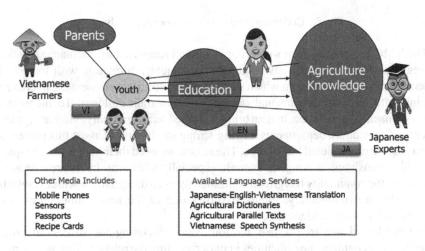

Fig. 4. Youth mediated communication

At the beginning, we designed services for knowledge transfer from Japanese experts to Vietnamese children, where the experts are service providers and the children are customers. Multi-language knowledge communication services were developed and managed in the project [13]. These services were realized based on the different moti- vations of various stakeholders. The nongovernmental organization staff working in the field were motivated to educate the children. Soon after the project started, however, we observed that the experts became more and more motivated by obtaining field data from the children: a complementary service was added where the children are service providers and the experts are customers. Meanwhile, the local government highly praised the project because they found that it became easier for them to form commun- ities in low literacy areas. Figure 5(a) shows a child collecting field data, and Fig. 5(b) shows the local government officers involved in helping the children to read the experts' advice.

(a)   (b)

Fig. 5. Collecting field data/reading expert's advice

The YMC project has been well recognized and supported by Vietnamese national and regional governments. It has resulted in community formation with local stakeholders and researchers, among which staffs from the local government are in charge of working with the nongovernmental organizations to train children. To increase the quality of machine translation, human bridgers joined our community. They are typically students of agriculture departments, having strong motivation to assist this project and also to acquire professional knowledge. The reason we need their help is that the quality of machine translation is not good enough, especially when translators are cascaded.[16] In this way, the community has grown continuously even though the machine translation technologies are rudimentary. Figure 6 shows one of the new communities which includes various stakeholders.

We conducted one trial a year for four years.[17] During the successful project, however, we recognized the difficulties in understanding the relationships among newly created services and existing services. Here is one episode.

One of the goals of this project is to reduce the amount of agrichemicals by enhancing knowledge communication among agricultural experts and farmers. Employees of the local government became heavily involved in the project by helping farmers' children to learn information technology. However it was found that local government workers usually work part-time, and they normally have second jobs, such as selling agrichemicals and fertilizers to farmers.

Moreover, it is also difficult to estimate the effects of services. Here is another episode.

This project aims at increasing the yield of rice. One project member, an agricultural expert, recognized the lack of nitrogen in this particular rice field, and suggested the use of a little more

---

[16] For Japanese-Vietnamese translation, two translators, Japanese-English and English-Vietnamese, are cascaded using English as a pivot, because there is not enough data to create a direct translator between Japanese and Vietnamese. Since machine translators expect correct input, human bridgers are requested to post-edit translated sentences in the pivot language.

[17] We conducted experiments 2011/02–2011/03, 2012/10–2013/01 and 2013/09–2014/01 in Thien My, Vinlong Province, and 2013/09–2014/01 and 2014/02–2014/03 in Dong Thanh, Vinlong Province. Both villages are located near Can Tho City in the Mekong Delta.

fertilizer. The farmers did not follow this advice, since they believe bugs would gather from neighboring fields, if they increased the amount of fertilizer.

These episodes shows how difficult it is to shape the problem and design services in a single project. We need a new methodology to deal with the unexpected interdependency of problems and services by widening the scope of stakeholders and forming a sustainable problem-solving organization that will continue the process of service design.

5 Modeling and Simulation: Predicting Difficulties in Intercultural Collaboration

We have been modeling intercultural collaboration based on the findings acquired through field activities. Culture itself has been modeled in various ways. Hofstede proposed *cultural dimensions* based on a large scale survey [7]. Agent models to simulate cultures has been proposed [8]. This section, describes a model for service design to support practical activities in intercultural collaboration.

Service can be seen as the fundamental basis of exchange; *the organizations, markets and society are concerned with the exchange of service* [16]. We think this view can be effectively modeled using multiagent systems. We first introduce a role playing game and a participatory simulation, in which humans and software agents are connected. We then propose a gaming simulation, which applies participatory simulation to role playing games.

Fig. 6. Various stakeholders in YMC

Role playing games (RPGs) are a well-known multiagent approach, where stakeholders participate in a game and mutually confirm their decisions on a game board. There are several ways to utilize RPG:

- For consensus building, RPG enables stakeholders to compromise and reach an optimal decision for the community by representing and sharing individual decisions on a game board.
- For system design, team members can learn the requirements and environments of the systems to be designed by simulating the decision processes of various stakeholders.
- For field analysis, a more accurate model of the decision processes of the community can be obtained by observing stakeholder decisions during RPG sessions.

Let us illustrate the process of modeling players' decision making. An initial model is created from relevant literature and surveys. RPG sessions are conducted using a board game that represents the players' environment. The decision making process can be understood based on the logs obtained during the game. The reasons behind the decisions made in the RPG are exposed by interviewing the players after the game. Finally, the decision making model is refined by analyzing the RPG log data and the interviews. Running the RPG several times can improve the obtained models [30].

Multiagent simulations are getting popular as a method of micro simulation in various research areas. In multiagent simulations, agent behaviors are determined by scenarios, which can either be described by programming languages or scenario description languages with embedded decision-making models. The scenario processor interprets agent scenarios and requests agents in a virtual space to perform sensing and acting functions. *Participatory simulations* have been invented as an extension of multiagent simulations. We can easily extend multiagent simulations to yield participatory simulations by replacing some of the scenario-guided agents with human-controlled avatars [11]. A participatory simulation consists of (1) *agents* for modeling users, (2) *avatars* to represent human subjects, (3) *scenarios* for modeling interactions, (4) *human subjects* to control avatars, (5) *virtual space* to represent real space, and (6) a *monitor* to visualize simulations underway in the virtual space. In this situation, human subjects and agents can cooperate in performing a simulation. Just as with video games, human subjects can join the simulation by controlling avatars via joy sticks, mice, or other input devices. To analyze simulation results, we monitor the entire process of the simulation by visualizing the virtual space. Recording human behavior is useful for analyzing the simulation results and for improving the agent decision making models.

Gaming simulation can be conducted by fusing participatory simulation with RPG [29]. Although RPG requires all the stakeholders to participate in the game, this not always practical in design processes. It is more efficient if a small design team conducts the simulations to understand the nature of problems and services at the early stage of design. We actually tried a gaming simulation to predict difficulties in YMC-Viet (described in the previous section). Since we can execute only one field experiment a year, problems in support systems should be detected as much as possible in advance. One of the advantages of gaming simulations is that they provide seamless design activities from a design team to all stakeholders. Moreover, it is easy to deal with situations where additional services are required or conflicts occur among new and existing services. Those advantages come from the fact that multiagent simulations are a type of micro simulation [5].

Let us summarize an approach to design support systems for intercultural collaboration. Especially in the early stage of design, it is necessary to understand the problems in the community, and propose services that can solve the problems. However, designing services in the field is always difficult due to the interdependency between problems and their evolution over time. Therefore, developing a continuous problem solving process is as important as solving currently known problems. In other words, the key to support intercultural collaboration is to provide a design process and form a flexible team that can support the process. In this context, we propose a multiagent approach including role playing games, participatory simulations and gaming simulations as a basis of experiments for designing support systems with various stakeholders. In intercultural collaboration, designers cannot always completely understand the complex relations and behaviors of stakeholders. The purpose of running gaming simulations is to design services for intercultural collaboration by understanding the interdependencies of existing services, and to reach agreement on the design of future services. We have to be careful, however, when interpreting the results of gaming simulations. We should be sensitive to what is important and what is not in the results from simulations. Since simulation results depend on participating stakeholders and agent models, result validity should be confirmed both in the field and theoretically.

To end this paper, we suggest the next step to model agents that can not only support a specific culture, but also recognize the differences among cultures, and differences among the understanding of cultural differences. There exists work that clarifies the asymmetry among the recognition of cultural differences. For example, paper reported how people in the US, Japan and China feel about the cultural differences in punctuality.[18] In terms of how Japanese perceive the approach of Americans and Chinese to punctuality, 67.0 % of the Japanese in the US perceive the cultural difference to be significant, while 72.2 % of those in China claim the same feeling. In contrast, 50.3 % of Americans perceive the cultural difference to significant, while only 29.3 % of Chinese say the same. The results reveal that most Japanese feel there are strong cultural differences in the approaches to punctuality, much more than Americans or Chinese, and more importantly there exists a difference in recognizing the cultural differences.

Acknowledgments. This work could not have been conducted without the collaboration of a number of colleagues and students. The work was partially supported by a Grant-in-Aid for Scientific Research (S) (24220002, 2012–2016) from Japan Society for the Promotion of Science (JSPS).

---

[18] There are many interesting examples listed in Hiroko Nishida's book on *intercultural communication friction in Japanese companies operating in the US and Chinese market*, published in 2007. The book is written in Japanese.

References

1. Cho, H., Ishida, T., Takasaki, T., Oyama, S.: Assisting pictogram selection with semantic interpretation. In: Bechhofer, S., Hauswirth, M., Hoffmann, J., Koubarakis, M. (eds.) ESWC 2008. LNCS, vol. 5021, pp. 65–79. Springer, Heidelberg (2008)
2. Deutscher, G.: Through the Language Glass: Why the World Looks Different in Other Languages. Macmillan, London (2010)
3. Fussell, S.R., Hinds, P., Ishida, T. (eds.): Proceedings of the Second International Workshop on Intercultural Collaboration. ACM (2009)
4. Ben Hassine, A., Matsubara, S., Ishida, T.: A constraint-based approach to horizontal web service composition. In: Cruz, I., Decker, S., Allemang, D., Preist, C., Schwabe, D., Mika, P., Uschold, M., Aroyo, L.M. (eds.) ISWC 2006. LNCS, vol. 4273, pp. 130–143. Springer, Heidelberg (2006)
5. Gilbert, N., Troitzsch, K.: Simulation for the Social Scientist. Open University Press, London (1999)
6. Hayashi, Y., Declerck, T., Buitelaar, P., Monachini, M.: Ontologies for a global language infrastructure. In: International Conference on Global Interoperability for Language Resources, pp. 105–112 (2008)
7. Hofstede, G., Hofstede, G.J., Minkov, M.: Cultures and Organizations: Software of the Mind, 3rd edn. McGraw-Hill, London (2010)
8. Hofstede, G.J., Pedersen, P.: Synthetic cultures: intercultural learning through simulation games. Simul. Gaming 30(4), 415–440 (1999)
9. Ishida, T.: Language grid: an infrastructure for intercultural collaboration. In: IEEE/IPSJ Symposium on Applications and the Internet, pp. 96–100 (2006)
10. Ishida, T., Fussell, S.R., Vossen, P.T.J.M. (eds.): Proceedings of the First International Workshop on Intercultural Collaboration. Springer, Berlin (2007)
11. Ishida, T., Nakajima, Y., Murakami, Y., Nakanishi, H.: Augmented experiment: participatory design with multiagent simulation. In: International Joint Conference on Artificial Intelligence, pp. 1341–1346 (2007)
12. Ishida, T. (ed.): The Language Grid: Service-Oriented Collective Intelligence for Language Resource Interoperability. Springer, Berlin (2011)
13. Kita, K., Takasaki, T., Lin, D., Nakajima, Y., Ishida, T.: Case study on analyzing multi-language knowledge communication. In: International Conference on Culture and Computing (2012)
14. Krauter, K., Buyya, R., Maheswaran, M.: A taxonomy and survey of grid resource management systems for distributed computing. Softw. Pract. Experience 32(2), 135–164 (2002)
15. Lin, D., Murakami, Y., Ishida, T., Murakami, Y., Tanaka, M.: Composing human and machine translation services: language grid for improving localization process. In: International Conference on Language Resources and Evaluation (2010)
16. Lusch, R., Vargo, S.: Service-Dominant Logic: Premises, Perspectives, Possibilities. Cambridge University Press, Cambridge (2014)
17. Masuda, T., Nisbett, R.E.: Attending holistically versus analytically: comparing the context sensitivity of Japanese and Americans. J. Pers. Soc. Psychol. 81(5), 922 (2001)
18. Matsuno, J., Ishida, T.: Constraint optimization approach to context based word selection. In: International Joint Conference on Artificial Intelligence, pp. 1846–1851 (2011)
19. Mori, Y., et al.: Youth mediated communication - agricultural technology transfer to illiterate farmers through their children. In: World Conference on Computers in Agriculture (2012)

20. Morita, D., Ishida, T.: Collaborative translation by monolinguals with machine translators. In: International Conference on Intelligent User Interfaces, pp. 361–366 (2009)
21. Murakami, Y., Tanaka, M., Lin, D., Ishida, T.: Service grid federation architecture for heterogeneous domains. In: IEEE Ninth International Conference on Services Computing, pp. 539–546 (2012)
22. Nisbett, R.: The Geography of Thought: How Asians and Westerners Think Differently… and. Simon and Schuster, New York (2010)
23. Nomura, S., Ishida, T., Yamashita, N., Yasuoka, M., Funakoshi, K.: Open source software development with your mother language: intercultural collaboration experiment 2002. Int. Conf. Hum.-Comput. Interact. **4**, 1163–1167 (2003)
24. Setlock, L.D., Fussell, S.R., Neuwirth, C.: Taking it out of context: collaborating within and across cultures in face-to-face settings and via instant messaging. ACM Conference on Computer Supported Cooperative Work, pp. 604–613 (2004)
25. Suo, Y., Miyata, N., Morikawa, H., Ishida, T., Shi, Y.: Open smart classroom: extensible and scalable learning system in smart space using web service technology. IEEE Trans. Knowl. Data Eng. **21**(6), 814–828 (2009)
26. Takasaki, T., Mori, Y.: Design and development of a pictogram communication system for children around the world. In: Ishida, T., Fussell, S., Vossen, P. (eds.) IWIC 2007. LNCS, vol. 4568, pp. 193–206. Springer, Heidelberg (2007)
27. Tanaka, M., Murakami, Y., Lin, D., Ishida, T.: Service supervision for service-oriented collective intelligence. In: IEEE International Conference on Services Computing, pp. 154–161 (2010)
28. Tanaka, R., Murakami, Y., Ishida, T.: Context-based approach for pivot translation services. In: International Joint Conference on Artificial Intelligence, pp. 1555–1561 (2009)
29. Tsunoda, K., Hishiyama, R.: Design of multilingual participatory gaming simulations with a communication support agent. In: ACM International Conference on Design of Communication, pp. 17–25 (2010)
30. Torii, D., Ishida, T., Bousquet, F.: Modelling agents and interactions in agricultural economics. In: International Joint Conference on Autonomous Agents and Multiagent Systems, pp. 81–88 (2006)
31. Trang, M.X., Murakami, Y., Ishida, T.: Policy-aware parallel execution in service composition. In: IEEE Transactions on Services Computing (2016, to appear)
32. Wang, H.C., Fussel, S.F., Setlock, L.D.: Cultural difference and adaptation of communication styles in computer-mediated group brainstorming. In: ACM Conference on Human Factors in Computing Systems, pp. 669–678 (2009)
33. Wushouer, M., Lin, D., Ishida, T., Hirayama, K.: A constraint approach to pivot-based bilingual dictionary induction. ACM Trans. Asian Low-Resour. Lang. Inf. Process. **15**(1), Article 4 (2015)
34. Yamashita, N., Ishida, T.: Effects of machine translation on collaborative work. In: International Conference on Computer Supported Cooperative Work, pp. 515–523 (2006)
35. Yamashita, N., Inaba, R., Kuzuoka, H., Ishida, T.: Difficulties in establishing common ground in multiparty group using machine translation. In: ACM Conference on Human Factors in Computing Systems, pp. 679–688 (2009)

Argumentation for Practical Reasoning: An Axiomatic Approach

Phan Minh Dung$^{(\boxtimes)}$

Asian Institute of Technology, Khlong Luang, Thailand
dung.phanminh@gmail.com

Abstract. An argument system could be viewed as a pair of a set of argument and a binary attack relation between arguments. The semantics of argumentation rests on the acceptability of arguments and the structure of arguments and their attack relations. While there is a relatively good understanding of the acceptability of arguments, the same can not be said about their structure and attack relations. In this paper, we present an axiomatic analysis of the attack relations of rule-based argument systems by presenting a set of simple and intuitive properties and showing that they indeed determine an uniquely defined common attack relations for rule-based argument systems.

1 Introduction

People of all walks of life get involved in argumentation on a daily basis. Arguing could be viewed as one of the most intellectual important activities of humans during their entire lives. Peoples of different cultures, countries, times often have different arguments based on different world views, rules, norms, conventions, beliefs and assumptions ect. For example, Harry Potter's arguments are based on the "science" of witch crafts and vampires while the Inca peoples in the pre-Columbus time believed in human sacrifices. Despite their often distinctly "incomparable" arguments, humans could understand each other (if they make an effort). How could it be possible?

Humans may have different ways to build their arguments but they all share *similar ways of drawing conclusions* from a given set of arguments. Such "similar ways" seem to be captured by an old saying **"he/she who laughs last laughs best"** that seems to be understood and employed by every rational human being. The saying could be viewed in fact as an **common mechanism** for drawing conclusions from conflicting arguments. Research on argumentation could be viewed as efforts to understand the structure and dynamics of this common mechanism.

Example 1. Consider a dialogue between a boy and his parents.

- Father to Boy: *Stop playing play with the ipad as you have not finished your homework yet.*
- Boy to Father: *Come on Dad ! There is no school tomorrow.*

© Springer International Publishing Switzerland 2016
M. Baldoni et al. (Eds.): PRIMA 2016, LNAI 9862, pp. 20–39, 2016.
DOI: 10.1007/978-3-319-44832-9_2

– Father to Boy: *Well, today is not a school holiday.*
– Boy to Mother: *Mum, I do not need to do my homework because there is no school tomorrow, right ?*
– Father to Mother: *Of course he needs to do it.*
– Mother to both Son and Father: *Guys, I have things to do. Sort out your quarrel by yourself.*

In essence the dialogues is about which of the following two arguments should be accepted:

Boy's argument B: *No school tomorrow, no homework.*

Father's argument F: *There is school today, hence homework.*

Arguments B, F attack each other and obviously neither father nor son gives up their argument. In other words, their sets of accepted arguments are $\{F\}, \{B\}$ respectively. As the mother refuses to be partisan, her set of accepted arguments is empty.

This simple dialogue reveals a fundamental issue in practical argumentation:

Different agents will get different conclusions (or semantics) from a same set of arguments.

In other words, a central issue in practical argumentation is the question: *What arguments do rational people accept in an exchange of arguments and how do we know that some of them could be the "consensus" of the "debate"?*

or more formally, *Can we provide a formal model of argument systems for practical reasoning ?*

At its most abstraction, an argument system could be viewed as an argumentation framework [23] consisting of a set of arguments and a binary attack relation between them. Though simple, argumentation frameworks are powerful enough to provide a sophisticated account of the acceptance of arguments representing different ways peoples could draw conclusions from exchanges of arguments.

While there is a good understanding about the acceptability of arguments due to an extensive amount of research [2,4,5,10,15,23,26], more need to be done to gain a better understanding about the structure of arguments and their attack relations. In experimental domains like experimental medicine, arguments often have no internal structure as the purpose of the experiments is to uncover the underlining rules [32]. In contrast, arguments in commonsense reasoning and legal domains are often based on rules [6,20]. In both medicine and legal domains as well as in commonsense reasoning, one could easily imagine arguments based on both complex rules and uncertainties. The complex structure of arguments often lead to challenging questions about the structure of their attack relations.

In this paper, we will first give an overview of the works on the acceptability of arguments wrt abstract argumentation. The main part of the paper is focused on rule-based argument systems as they are the most researched instances of abstract argumentation. We conclude with a discussion on probabilistic argumentation.[1]

---

[1] The materials in Sects. 4, 5, 6 are from a recent paper [19]. The materials in Sects. 7, 8 are new.

There are extensive research on rule-based systems (see for example [9,11, 17,28,29,35,36,38–40]). Distinct semantics have been proposed that could lead to contradictory answers to the same query as the following example illustrates.

Example 2. Consider a knowledge base K (adapted from [11,12,18]), consisting of three defeasible rules

$$d_1 : Dean \Rightarrow Professor \quad d_2 : Professor \Rightarrow Teach \quad d_3 : Administrator \Rightarrow \neg Teach$$

and two strict rules

$$r : Dean \rightarrow Administrator \quad r' : \neg Administrator \rightarrow \neg Dean$$

with $d_1 \prec d_3 \prec d_2$.[2]

Suppose we know some Dean. The question is *whether the dean teaches.*

Proposed approaches in literature deal with this example differently. Modgil and Prakken [35] in their influential ASPIC+ framework proposed four attack relations where one of them leads to semantics with respect to which *the dean does not teach* while the other three as well as the prominent non-argument-based approach of Brewka and Eiter [11] lead to conclusion that *the dean does teach.*

The example illustrates the need to establish general principles for characterizing and evaluation of possible semantics for rule-based systems.

2   Abstract Argumentation

An abstract argumentation framework [23] is defined simply as a pair $AF = (AR, att)$ where AR is a set of arguments and $att \subseteq AR \times AR$ and $(A, B) \in att$ means that A *attacks* B.

A set of argument S attacks (or is attacked by) an argument A (or a set of arguments R) if some argument in S attacks (or is attacked by) A (or some argument in R); S is *conflict-free* if it does not attack itself. A set of arguments S *defends* an argument A if S attacks each attack against A.

S is *admissible* if S is conflict-free and defends each argument in it. A *complete extension* is an admissible set of arguments containing each argument it defends. A *preferred extension* is a maximal admissible set of arguments. A *stable extension* is a conflict-free set of arguments that attacks every argument not belonging to it.

It is well-known that both preferred and stable extensions are complete but not vice versa.

The *characteristic function* of AF is defined by

$$F_{AF}(S) = \{A \mid A \in AR, S \text{ defends } A\}.$$

Since F_{AF} is a monotonic function, there exists a least fixed point of F_{AF}. The grounded extension is defined as the least fixed point of F_{AF}.

---

[2] $d \prec d'$ means that d is less preferred than d'.

As complete extensions coincide with conflict-free fixed points of F_{AF}, the grounded extension is also the least complete extension.

Example 1 can be represented as an argumentation framework (AR, att) where $AR = \{F, B\}$ and $att = \{(F, B), (B, F)\}$.

There are two preferred extensions that are also stable: $\{F\}, \{B\}$. There are three complete extensions $\emptyset, \{F\}, \{B\}$. The grounded extension is hence empty.

Conceptually, the grounded extension represents an agent who is skeptical in its reasoning where other extensions represent agents who are credulous.

In Example 1, both father and son stick to their guns. The mother, who does not want to get drawn into the discussion as none of the presented arguments could be accepted without any bias, represents a skeptical reasoner.

3 Defeasible Knowledge Bases

In this section, we recall the basic notions and notations on knowledge bases from [18]. We assume a non-empty set $\mathcal{L}$ of ground atoms (also called a positive literal) and their classical negations (also called negative literals). A set of literals is said to be *contradictory* iff it contains an atom a and its negation $\neg a$. We distinguish between *domain atoms* representing propositions about the concerned domains and *non-domain atoms* of the form ab_d representing the non-applicability of defeasible rules d (even if the premises of d hold).

We distinguish between strict and defeasible rules as often done in the literature [18,27,28,35,36,41]. A *defeasible* (resp. *strict*) rule r is of the form $b_1, \ldots, b_n \Rightarrow h$ (resp. $b_1, \ldots, b_n \rightarrow h$) where $b_1, \ldots, b_n$ are domain literals and h is a domain literal or an atom of the form ab_d. The set $\{b_1, \ldots, b_n\}$ (resp. the literal h) is referred to as the *body* (resp. *head*) of r and denoted by bd(r) (resp. hd(r)).

Definition 1. *1. A **rule-based system** is a triple $\mathcal{R} = (RS, RD, \preceq)$ where*
  (a) RS is a set of strict rules,
  (b) RD is a set of defeasible rules, and
  (c) $\preceq$ is a transitive relation over RD representing the preferences between defeasible rules, whose strict core is $\prec$ (i.e. $d \prec d'$ iff $d \preceq d'$ and $d' \npreceq d$ for $d, d' \in RD$.)
*2. A **knowledge base** is defined as a pair $K = (\mathcal{R}, BE)$ consisting of a rule-based system $\mathcal{R}$, and a set of ground domain literals BE, the base of evidence of K, representing unchallenged observations, facts ect..*
For convenience, knowledge base K is often written directly as a quadruple $(RS, RD, \preceq, BE)$ where RS, RD, $\preceq$ or BE of K are often referred to by $RS_K, RD_K, \preceq_K$ or BE_K respectively.

Definition 2. *Let $K = (RS, RD, \preceq, BE)$ be a knowledge base. An **argument** wrt K is a proof tree defined inductively as follows:*

1. For each $\alpha \in BE$, $[\alpha]$ is an argument with conclusion α.

2. *Let r be a rule of the forms $\alpha_1, \ldots, \alpha_n \to / \Rightarrow \alpha$, $n \geq 0$, from $RS \cup RD$ and $A_1, \ldots, A_n$ be arguments with conclusions α_i, $1 \leq i \leq n$, respectively. Then $A = [A_1, \ldots, A_n, r]$ is an argument with **conclusion** α and **last rule** r denoted by **cnl(A)** and **last(A)** respectively.*

3. *Each argument wrt K is obtained by applying the above steps 1, 2 finitely many times.*

Example 3. Consider a rule-based system $\mathcal{R}$ whose sets of rules are from Example 2 together with a precedence relation consisting of just $d_2 \prec d_3$. Suppose we know some dean who is also a professor.

The considered knowledge base is represented by $K = (RS, RD, \preceq, BE)$ with $RS = \{r, r'\}$, $RD = \{d_1, d_2, d_3\}$, $\preceq = \{(d_2, d_3)\}$ and $BE = \{D, P\}$.[3]

Relevant arguments can be found in Fig. 1 where $A_1 = [[D], d_1]$, $A_2 = [A_1, d_2]$, $A_2' = [[P], d_2]$, $A_3 = [[[D], r], d_3]$.

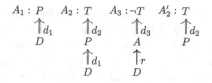

Fig. 1. Dean example

Notation 1. *The set of all arguments wrt a knowledge base K is denoted by $\mathbf{AR_K}$. The set of the conclusions of arguments in a set $S \subseteq AR_K$ is denoted by* **cnl(S)**.

A **strict argument** *is an argument containing no defeasible rule. An argument is* **defeasible** *iff it is not strict. A defeasible argument A is called* **basic defeasible** *iff $last(A)$ is defeasible.*

For any argument A, the set of defeasible rules appearing in an argument A is denoted by $\mathbf{dr}(A)$. The set of last defeasible rules in A, denoted by $\mathbf{ldr}(A)$, is $\{last(A)\}$ if A is basic defeasible, otherwise it is equal $ldr(A_1) \cup \ldots \cup ldr(A_n)$ where $A = [A_1, \ldots, A_n, r]$.

An argument B is a **subargument** *of an argument A iff $B = A$ or $A = [A_1, \ldots, A_n, r]$ and B is a subargument of some A_i. B is a proper subargument of A if B is a subargument of A and $B \neq A$.*

Definition 3. *Let K be a knowledge base.*

1. *The* **closure** *of a set of literals $X \subseteq \mathcal{L}$ wrt knowledge base K, denoted by $CN_K(X)$, is the union of X and the set of conclusions of all strict arguments wrt knowledge base $(RS_K, RD_K, \preceq_K, X_{dom})$ with X_{dom} (the set of all domain literals in X) acting as a base of evidence.*

---

[3] D,P,T,A stand for Dean, Professor , Teach and Administrator respectively.

X is said to be **closed** iff $X = CN_K(X)$. X is said to be **inconsistent** iff its closure $CN_K(X)$ is contradictory. X is **consistent** iff it is not inconsistent. We also often write $X \vdash_K l$ iff $l \in CN_K(X)$.

2. K is said to be **consistent** iff its base of evidence BE_K is consistent.

As the notions of closure, consistency depend only on the set of strict rules in the knowledge base, we often write $X \vdash_{RS} l$ or $l \in CN_{RS}(X)$ for $X \vdash_K l$ or $l \in CN_K(X)$ respectively.

Definition 4. *Let $\mathcal{R} = (RS, RD, \preceq)$ be a rule-based system and $K = (\mathcal{R}, BE)$ be a knowledge base.*

1. *$\mathcal{R}$ and K are said to be* closed under transposition *[13] iff for each strict rule of the form $b_1, \ldots, b_n \to h$ in RS s.t. h is a domain literal, all the rules of the forms $b_1, \ldots, b_{i-1}, \neg h, b_{i+1}, \ldots, b_n \to \neg b_i$, $1 \le i \le n$, also belong to RS.*
2. *$\mathcal{R}$ and K are said to be* closed under contraposition *[36, 37] iff for each set of domain literals S, each domain literal λ, if $S \vdash_{RS} \lambda$ then for each $\sigma \in S$, $S \setminus \{\sigma\} \cup \{\neg\lambda\} \vdash_{RS} \neg\sigma$.*
3. *$\mathcal{R}$ and K are said to satisfy the* self-contradiction property *[21] iff for each minimal inconsistent set of domain literals $X \subseteq \mathcal{L}$, for each $x \in X$, it holds: $X \vdash_{RS} \neg x$.*

Lemma 1. *[18] Let $\mathcal{R}$ be a rule-based system that is closed under transposition or contraposition. Then $\mathcal{R}$ satisfies the property of self-contradiction.*

Definition 5. *(Attack Relation) An* attack relation *for a knowledge base K is a relation $att \subseteq AR_K \times AR_K$ such that there is no attack against strict arguments, i.e. for each strict argument $B \in AR_K$, there is no argument $A \in AR_K$ such that $(A, B) \in att$.*

For convenience, we often say A attacks B wrt att for $(A, B) \in att$.

3.1 Basic Postulates

We recall the postulates of consistency and closure from [13] and of subargument closure from [1, 34, 35]. For simplicity, we combine the postulate of closure and the postulate of subargument closure into one.

Definition 6. *Let att be an attack relation for a knowledge base K.*

- *att is said to satisfy the* **consistency postulate** *iff for each complete extension E of (AR_K, att), the set $cnl(E)$ of conclusions of arguments in E is consistent.*
- *att is said to satisfy the* **closure postulate** *iff for each complete extension E of (AR_K, att), the set $cnl(E)$ of conclusions of arguments in E is closed and E contains all subarguments of its arguments.*

For ease of reference, the above two postulates are often referred to as **basic postulates**.

4   Sufficient Properties for Basic Postulates

As the basic postulates are more about the "output" of attack relations rather than about their structure, we present below two simple properties about the structure of attack relation that ensures the holding of the basic postulates. We first introduce some simple notations.

We say A *undercuts* B (at B') if B' is basic defeasible and $cnl(A) = ab_{last(B')}$. We say A **rebuts** B (at B') iff B' is a basic defeasible subargument of B and the conclusions of A and B' are contradictory.

We say A *directly attacks* B if A attacks B and A does not attack any proper subargument of B.

An argument A is said to be **generated by** a set S of arguments iff all basic defeasible subarguments of A are subarguments of arguments in S. For an example, let $S = \{B_0, B_1\}$ (see Fig. 2). Let consider A_0. The set of basic defeasible subarguments of A_0 is $\{[d_0]\}$. It is clear that $[d_0]$ is a subargument of B_0. Hence A_0 is generated by S. Similarly, A_1 is also generated by S.

Definition 7. *(Strong Subargument Structure) Attack relation att is said to satisfy the property of strong subargument structure for K iff for all $A, B \in AR_K$, followings hold:*

1. *If A undercuts B then A attacks B wrt att.*
2. *A attacks B (wrt att) iff A attacks a basic defeasible subargument of B (wrt att).*
3. *If A directly attacks B (wrt att) then A undercuts B (at B) or rebuts B (at B).*

We present the first result showing that strong subargument property is sufficient to guarantee the postulate of closure.

Lemma 2. *Let att be an attack relations for knowledge base K satisfying the property of strong subargument structure. Then att satisfies the postulate of closure.*

Proof. (Sketch) From condition 2 in Definition 7, it follows that each attack against an argument generated by complete extension E is an attack against E. The lemma holds obviously.   □

A set S of arguments is said to be *inconsistent* if the set of the conclusions of its arguments, $cnl(S)$, is inconsistent. We introduce below a new simple property of inconsistency resolving.

Definition 8. *(Inconsistency Resolving) We say attack relation assignment att satisfies the inconsistency-resolving property for K iff for each finite set of arguments $S \subseteq AR_K$, if S is inconsistent then S is attacked (wrt att(K)) by some argument generated by S.*

As we will show later, the inconsistency-resolving property is satisfied by common conditions like closure under transposition, or contradiction or the property of self-contradiction.

Example 4. Consider the basic knowledge base K consisting of just the rules appearing in arguments in Fig. 2. The set $S = \{B_0, B_1\}$ is inconsistent. The argument A_0 is generated by S. Let $att = \{(X, Y) \mid X$ rebuts $Y\}$. It is obvious that S is attacked by A_0. It is clear that att is inconsistency-resolving.

$$A_0 : \neg b \quad A_1 : \neg a \quad B_0 : c \quad B_1 : \neg c$$
$$\uparrow r_0 \qquad \uparrow r_1 \qquad \uparrow r_2 \qquad \uparrow r_3$$
$$a \qquad\quad b \qquad\quad a \qquad\quad b$$
$$\uparrow d_0 \qquad \uparrow d_1 \qquad \uparrow d_0 \qquad \uparrow d_1$$

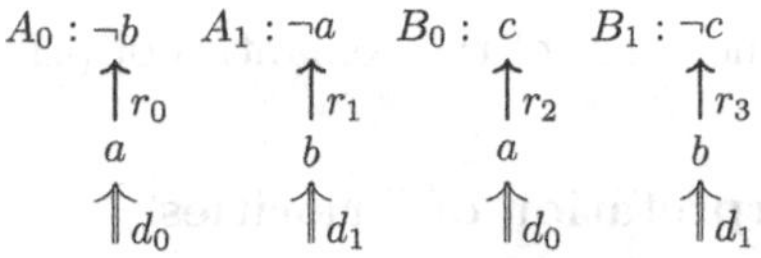

Fig. 2. Generated arguments

We present now the first important result.

Theorem 1. *Let att, att' be attack relations for knowledge base K.*

1. *If $att \subseteq att'$ and att is inconsistency-resolving for K then att' is also inconsistency-resolving for K;*
2. *If att satisfies the strong subargument structure and inconsistency-resolving then att satisfies the postulate of consistency.*

Proof. (Sketch) Assertion 1 follows easily from the definition of inconsistency-resolving. We only need to show assertion 2. From condition 2 in Definition 7, it follows that each argument generated by a complete extension E belongs to E. Therefore, if E is inconsistent then E is not conflict-free. Since E is conflict-free, E is hence consistent. □

5   Regular Attack Relation Assignments

In general, attack relations satisfying the basic postulates do not capture the semantics of prioritized rules. To see this point, consider a simple knowledge base consisting of exactly two defeasible rules $d_0 : \Rightarrow a$ and $d_1 \Rightarrow \neg a$ with $d_0 \prec d_1$. There are only two arguments A_0, A_1 as given in Fig. 3.

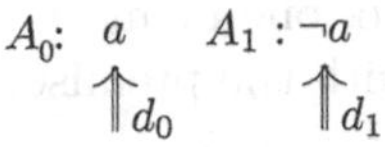

$$A_0 : a \quad A_1 : \neg a$$
$$\uparrow d_0 \qquad \uparrow d_1$$

Fig. 3. Effective rebuts

The attack relation $att = \{(A_0, A_1), (A_1, A_0)\}$ has two extensions $E_i = \{A_i\}$, $i = 0, 1$. It is obvious that E_0 satisfies both properties of inconsistency-resolving and strong subargument structure. As the prime purpose of the preference of

d_1 over d_0 is to rule out extension E_0, attack relation att does not capture the expected semantics.

Dung[18,24] has proposed several simple and natural properties referred to as ordinary properties, to capture the intuition of prioritized rules. We recall and adapt them below. We also motivate and explain their intuitions. We also present two novel concepts of regular attack relations and regular attack relation assignments that lie at the heart of the semantics of prioritized rules.

5.1   A Minimal Interpretation of Priorities

We first recall from [18] the effective rebut property stating a "minimal interpretation" of a preference $d_0 \prec d_1$ that in situations when both are applicable but accepting both d_0, d_1 is not possible, d_1 should be preferred.

Definition 9. *(Effective Rebut) We say that attack relation att satisfies the* effective rebut property *for a knowledge base K iff for all arguments $A_0, A_1 \in AR_K$ such that each A_i, $i = 0, 1$, contains exactly one defeasible rule d_i (i.e. $dr(A_i) = \{d_i\}$), and A_0 rebuts A_1, it holds that A_0 attacks A_1 wrt att iff $d_0 \not\prec d_1$.*

In Fig. 3, the effective rebut property dictates that A_1 attacks A_0 but not vice versa.

5.2   Propagating Attacks

Example 5. Consider the knowledge base in Example 3.

While the effective rebut property determines that A_3 attacks A_2' (see Fig. 1) but not vice versa (because $d_2 \prec d_3$), it does not say whether A_3 attack A_2.

Looking at the structure of A_2, A_2', we can say that A_2 is a weakening of A_2' as the undisputed fact P on which A_2' is based is replaced by a defeasible belief P (supported by argument A_1). Therefore if A_3 attacks A_2' then it is natural to expect that A_3 should attack A_2 too.

The above analysis also shows that attacks generated by the effective rebut property, could be propagated to other arguments based on a notion of weakening of arguments. We recall this notion as well as the associated property of attack monotonicity from [18] below.

Let $A, B \in AR_K$ and $AS \subseteq AR_K$. Intuitively, B is a weakening of A by AS if B is obtained by replacing zero, one or more premises of A by arguments in AS whose conclusions coincide with the premises.

Definition 10. *B is said to be* **a weakening of** *A by AS iff*

1. *$A = [\alpha]$ for $\alpha \in BE$, and ($B = [\alpha]$ or $B \in AS$ with $cnl(B) = \alpha$), or*
2. *$A = [A_1, \ldots, A_n, r]$ and $B = [B_1, \ldots, B_n, r]$ where each B_i is a weakening of A_i by AS.*
By $A \downarrow AS$ we denote the set of all weakenings of A by AS.

For an illustration, consider again the arguments in Fig. 1. It is clear that $[P] \downarrow \{A_1\} = \{[P], A_1\}$, $A_2' \downarrow \{A_1\} = \{A_2', A_2\}$.

The attack monotonicity property states that if an argument A attacks an argument B then A also attacks all weakening of B. Moreover if a weakening of A attacks B then A also attacks B.

Definition 11. *(Attack Monotonicity) We say attack relation* att *satisfies the property of attack monotonicity for knowledge base K iff for all $A, B \in AR_K$ and for each weakening C of A for each weakening D of B, the following assertions hold:*

1. *If $(A, B) \in att$ then $(A, D) \in att$.*
2. *If $(C, B) \in att$ then $(A, B) \in att$.*

We next recall the link-oriented property in [18] which is based on an intuition that attacks are directed towards links in arguments implying that if an argument A attacks an argument B then it should attack some part of B.

Definition 12. *(Link-Orientation) We say that attack relation att satisfies the property of link-orientation for K iff for all arguments $A, B, C \in AR_K$ such that C is a weakening of B by $AS \subseteq AR_K$ (i.e. $C \in B \downarrow AS$), it holds that if A attacks C (wrt att) and A does not attack AS (wrt att) then A attacks B (wrt att).*

In real world conversation, if you claim that my argument is wrong, I would naturally ask which part of my argument is wrong. The link-oriented property could be viewed as representing this intuition.

Example 6. Consider again arguments in Fig. 1. Suppose d_2 is now preferred to d_3 (i.e. $d_3 \prec d_2$). The effective rebut property dictates that A_3 does not attack A_2'. Does A_3 still attack A_2 ? Suppose A_3 attacks A_2. Since A_3 does not attack A_1 that is a subargument of A_2, we expect that A_3 should attack some other part of A_2. In other words, we expect that A_3 attacks A_2'. But this is a contradiction to the effective rebut property stating that A_2' attack A_3 but not vice versa. Hence A_3 does not attack A_2.

In other words, the link-orientation property has propagated the "non-attack relation" between A_3, A_2' to a "non-attack relation" between A_3, A_2.

We present below a novel concept of regular attack relations.

Notation 2. *For ease of reference, we refer to the properties of inconsistency-resolving, strong subargument structure, effective rebuts, attack monotonicity and link-orientation as* **regular properties**.

Definition 13. *(Rgular Attack Relation) An attack relation is said to be* **regular** *iff it satisfies all regular properties.*

5.3   Attack Relation Assignments: Propagating Attacks Across Knowledge Bases

While regular attack relations are natural and intuitive, they are still not sufficient for determining an intuitive semantics of prioritized rules. The example below illustrates this point.

Example 7. Consider a knowledge base K_0 obtained from knowledge base K in Example 3 by revising the evidence base to $BE = \{D\}$. It is clear that arguments A_1, A_2, A_3 belong to AR_{K_0} while A_2' is not an argument in AR_{K_0}.

As A_2' does not belong to AR_{K_0}, the effective rebuts property does not "generate" any attacks between arguments in AR_{K_0}. How could we determine the attack relation for K_0?

As both A_2, A_3 belong to AR_K, AR_{K_0} and the two knowledge bases K_0, K have identical rule-based system, we expect that the attack relations between their common arguments should be identical. In other words, because A_3 attacks A_2 wrt K (see Example 5), A_3 should attack A_2 also wrt K_0. This intuition is captured by the context-independence property [18] linking attack relations between arguments across the boundary of knowledge bases.

The example also indicates that attack relations of knowledge bases with the same rule-based system should be considered together. This motivates the introduction of the attack relation assignment in Definitions 14, 15.

Definition 14. *Let $\mathcal{R} = (RS, RD, \preceq)$ be a rule-based system. The class consisting of all consistent knowledge bases of the form $(\mathcal{R}, BE)$ is denoted by $\mathcal{C}_{\mathcal{R}}$.*

A rule-based system $\mathcal{R}$ is said to be **sensible** iff the set $\mathcal{C}_{\mathcal{R}}$ is not empty. *From now on, whenever we mention a rule-based system, we mean a sensible one.*

Definition 15. *(Attack Relation Assignment) An attack relation assignment atts for a rule-based system $\mathcal{R}$ is a function assigning to each knowledge base $K \in \mathcal{C}_{\mathcal{R}}$ an attack relation $atts(K) \subseteq AR_K \times AR_K$.*

We next recall the context-independence property stating that the attack relation between two arguments depends only on the rules appearing in them and their preferences.

Definition 16. *(Context-Independence) We say attack relation assignment atts for a rule-based system $\mathcal{R}$ satisfies the property of context-independence iff for any two knowledge bases $K, K' \in \mathcal{C}_{\mathcal{R}}$ and for any two arguments A, B from $AR_K \cap AR_{K'}$, it holds that $(A, B) \in atts(K)$ iff $(A, B) \in atts(K')$*

The context-independence property is commonly accepted in many well-known argument-based systems like the assumption-based framework [8,25], the ASPIC+ approach [35,37].

We can now present a central result, the introduction of the regular attack relation assignments.

Definition 17. *(***Regular Attack Relation Assignments***) An attack rela-tion assignment atts for a rule-based system $\mathcal{R}$ is said to be* **regular** *iff it satis-fies the property of context-independence and for each knowledge base $K \in \mathcal{C}_{\mathcal{R}}$, $atts(K)$ is regular.*
The set of all regular attack relation assignments for $\mathcal{R}$ is denoted by $RAA_{\mathcal{R}}$.

For attack relation assignments $atts, atts'$, define $atts \subseteq atts'$ iff $\forall K \in \mathcal{C}_{\mathcal{R}}$, $atts(K) \subseteq atts'(K)$.

5.4 Minimal Removal Intuition

A key purpose of introducing priorities between defeasible rules is to remove certain undesired attacks while keeping the set of removed attacks to a minimum. The following very simple example illustrates the idea.

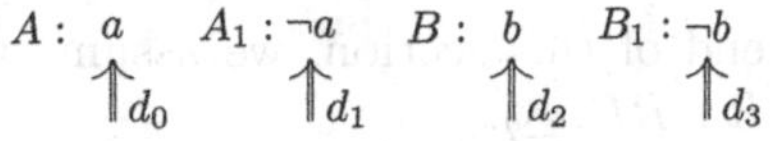

$$A : a \qquad A_1 : \neg a \qquad B : b \qquad B_1 : \neg b$$
$$\uparrow d_0 \qquad \uparrow d_1 \qquad \uparrow d_2 \qquad \uparrow d_3$$

Fig. 4. Minimal removal

Example 8. Consider a knowledge base consisting of just four defeasible rules and four arguments A, A_1, B, B_1 as seen in Fig. 4. Without any preference between the rules, we have A, A_1 attack each other. Similarly B, B_1 attack each other.

Suppose that for whatever reason d_3 is strictly less preferred than d_2 (i.e. $d_3 \prec d_2$). The introduction of the preference $d_3 \prec d_2$ in essence means that the attack of B_1 against B should be removed, but it does not say anything about the other attacks. Hence they should be kept, i.e. the attacks that should be removed should be kept to a minimum.

Let $\mathcal{R}$ be a rule-based system and $K \in \mathcal{C}_{\mathcal{R}}$. The *basic attack relation assign-ment* for $\mathcal{R}$, denoted by $Batts$ is defined by: $\forall K \in \mathcal{C}_{\mathcal{R}}$, $Batts(K) = \{(A, B) \mid A$ undercuts or rebuts B$\}$. Further let atts be a regular attack relation assignment. From the strong subargument structure property, it is clear that $atts \subseteq Batts$. $\forall K \in \mathcal{C}_{\mathcal{R}}$, the set $Batts(K) \setminus atts(K)$ could be viewed as the set of attacks removed from $Batts(K)$ due to the priorities between defeasible rules.

Combining the "minimal-removal intuition" with the concept of regular attack relation assignment suggests that the semantics of $\mathcal{R}$ should be captured by regular attack relations atts such that $\forall K \in \mathcal{C}_{\mathcal{R}}$, the set $Batts(K) \setminus atts(K)$ is minimal, or equivalently the set $atts(K)$ is maximal. As we will see in the next section, such maximal attack relation assignment indeed exists.

6 The Upper Semilattice of Regular Attack Relation Assignments

6.1 Preliminaries: Semilattice

We introduce the concept of semilattice. A partial order[4] $\leq$ on a set S is a **upper-semilattice** (resp. **lower-semilattice**) [16] iff each subset of S has a supremum (resp. infimum) wrt $\leq$. The supremum (resp. infimum) of a set $X \subseteq S$ of a upper (resp. lower) semilattice S is often denoted by $\sqcup X$ (resp. $\sqcap X$) and the upper (resp. lower) semilattice is often denoted as a triple $(S, \leq, \sqcup)$ (resp. $(S, \leq, \sqcap)$).

It follows immediately that each upper (resp. lower) semilattice S has an unique greatest (resp. least) element denoted by $\sqcup S$ (resp. $\sqcap S$).

6.2 Semilattice Structure of $RAA_{\mathcal{R}}$

From now on until the end of this section, we assume an arbitrary but fixed rule-based system $\mathcal{R} = (RS, RD, \preceq)$.

Let $\mathcal{A}$ be a non-empty set of attack relation assignments. Define $\sqcup \mathcal{A}$ by:

$\forall K \in \mathcal{C}_{\mathcal{R}}: \quad (\sqcup \mathcal{A})(K) = \bigcup \{ atts(K) \,|\, atts \in \mathcal{A} \}$

The following simple lemma and theorem present a deep insight into the structure of regular attack assignments.

Lemma 3. *Let $\mathcal{A}$ be a non-empty set of regular attack relation assignments. The $\sqcup \mathcal{A}$ is also regular.*

Proof. (Sketch) The proof is not difficult though rather lengthy as we just need to check in a straightforward way for each regular property. $\qquad \Box$

It follows immediately.

Theorem 2. *Suppose the set $RAA_{\mathcal{R}}$ of regular attack relation assignments is not empty. Then $(RAA_{\mathcal{R}}, \subseteq, \sqcup)$ is an upper semilattice.* $\qquad \Box$

Definition 18. *Suppose the set $RAA_{\mathcal{R}}$ of all regular attack relation assignments for $\mathcal{R}$ is not empty. The **canonical attack relation assignment** of $\mathcal{R}$ denoted by $\mathbf{Att}_{\mathcal{R}}$ is defined by:* $\mathbf{Att}_{\mathcal{R}} = \sqcup RAA_{\mathcal{R}}$.

Even though in general, regular attack relation assignments (and hence the canonical one) may not exist (as the Example 9 below shows), they exist under natural conditions that we believe most practical rule-based systems satisfy, like the property of self-contradiction or closure under transposition or contraposition as proved in Theorem 3 below.

---

[4] a reflexive, transitive and antisymmetric relation.

Example 9. Consider a rule-based system $\mathcal{R}$ consisting of $d_0 :\Rightarrow a$ $d_1 :\Rightarrow b$
$r : a \to \neg b$ and $d_0 \prec d_1$. Suppose atts be a regular attack relation assignment
for $\mathcal{C_R}$. Let $K = (\mathcal{R}, \emptyset)$. The arguments for K are given in Fig. 5. From the
property of effective rebut, it is clear that $(A, B) \notin att(K)$. Hence $atts(K) = \emptyset$.
The inconsistency-resolving property is not satisfied by $atts(K)$, contradicting
the assumption that atts is regular. Therefore there exists no regular attack
relation assignment for $\mathcal{C}_K$.

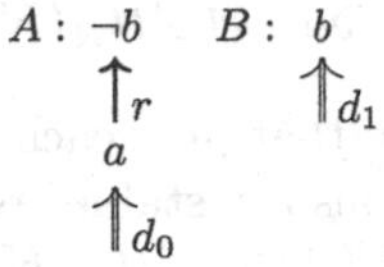

$$A : \neg b \quad B : b$$
$$\uparrow r \qquad \uparrow d_1$$
$$a$$
$$\uparrow d_0$$

Fig. 5. Non-existence of regular assignments

It turns out that a special type of attack relations, the normal attack relations
introduced in [18] is regular if the rule-based systems is closed under transposition or contraposition or self-contradiction.

Let K be a knowledge base and $A, B \in AR_K$. We say that A *normal-rebuts*
B (at X) iff A rebuts B (at X) and there is no defeasible rule $d \in ldr(A)$ such
that $d \prec last(X)$.

The *normal attack relation assignment* [18] $atts_{nr}$ is defined by: For any
knowledge base $K \in \mathcal{R}$ and any arguments $A, B \in AR_K$, $(A, B) \in atts_{nr}(K)$ if
and only if A undercuts B or A normal-rebuts B.

We present below a central result.

Theorem 3. *Suppose the rule-based system $\mathcal{R}$ satisfies the self-contradiction
property. Then the normal attack relation assignment $atts_{nr}$ is regular and the
canonical assignment $Att_\mathcal{R}$ exists and $atts_{nr} \subseteq Att_\mathcal{R}$.*

Proof. (Sketch) From Theorem 2 and the definition of the canonical attack relation, we only need to show that $atts_{nr}$ is regular.

It is straightforward to show that for each $K \in \mathcal{C_R}$, the attack relation $atts_{nr}(K)$ satisfies the properties of strong subargument structure, attack
monotonicity, effective rebuts and link-orientation. Further it is also obvious
that $atts_{nr}$ satisfies the context-independence property. Let $K \in \mathcal{C_R}$. We show
that $atts_{nr}(K)$ satisfies the inconsistency-resolving property. Let $S \subseteq AR_K$ s.t.
S is inconsistent. Let S' be the set of all basic defeasible subarguments of S
and S_0 be a minimal inconsistent subset of S'. Let $A \in S_0$ s.t. last(A) is
minimal (wrt $\prec$) in $\{last(X) \mid X \in S_0\}$. From the self-contradiction property,
$cnl(S_0) \vdash \neg hd(last(A))$. We could then construct an argument B such that B
attacks A and all basic defeasible subarguments of B are subarguments of arguments in S_0.   □.

It follows immediately

Lemma 4. *Suppose the rule-based system $\mathcal{R}$ satisfies the self-contradiction property. For each $K \in \mathcal{C}_{\mathcal{R}}$ and all $A, B \in AR_K$ such that A rebuts B (at B) and $(A, B) \notin Att_{\mathcal{R}}(K)$, there is $d \in ldr(A)$ such that $d \prec last(B)$.*

Though the normal and canonical attack relations do not coincide in general, they are equivalent in the sense that they have identical sets of stable extensions.

Theorem 4. *Suppose the rule-based system $\mathcal{R}$ satisfies the property of self-contradiction. Then for each $K \in \mathcal{C}_{\mathcal{R}}$, $E \subseteq AR_K$ is a stable extension wrt $atts_{nr}(K)$ iff E is a stable extension wrt $Att_{\mathcal{R}}(K)$.*

Proof. (Sketch) We first show that for each $atts \in RAA_{\mathcal{R}}$, each stable extension of $(AR_K, atts(K))$ is also a stable extension of $(AR_K, atts_{nr}(K))$. Hence each stable extension of $(AR_K, Att_{\mathcal{R}}(K))$ is also stable extension of $(AR_K, atts_{nr}(K))$. The theorem follows then from Lemma 5 below. □

Lemma 5. *Let $atts, atts'$ be regular attack relation assignments for $\mathcal{R}$ such that $atts \subseteq atts'$. Then*

1. *each stable extension of $(AR_K, atts(K))$ is a stable extension of $(AR_K, atts'(K))$; and*
2. *each stable extension of $(AR_K, atts(K))$ is a stable extension of $(AR_K, Att_{\mathcal{R}}(K))$.*

Proof. (Sketch) (1) Let E be a stable extension of $(AR_K, atts(K))$. It is clear that E attacks each argument in $AR_K \setminus E$ wrt $atts'(K)$. If E is not conflict-free wrt $atts'(K)$, E is inconsistent (since both $atts, atts'$ have the same set of undercuts) and hence not conflict-free wrt atts(K) (a contradiction). Hence E is conflict-free (and hence stable) wrt $atts'(K)$. (2) Follows immediately from (1) and the definition of $Att_{\mathcal{R}}$. □

7   Credulous Cumulativity of Regular Semantics

A key property satisfied by many argument-based and non-argument-based approaches to reasoning with prioritized rules is the credulous cumulativity property [18] stating intuitively that if some beliefs in your belief set are confirmed in the reality then your belief set will not change because of it.

A set $S \subseteq \mathcal{L}$ is said to be a *belief set* of knowledge base K wrt an attack relation assignment atts iff there is a stable extension E of $(AR_K, atts(K))$ such that $S = cnl(E)$.

Definition 19. *(Credulous Cumulativity) We say attack relation assignment atts satisfies the property of credulous cumulativity for $\mathcal{R}$ if and only if for each $K \in \mathcal{C}_{\mathcal{R}}$, for each belief set S of K wrt atts and for each finite subset $\Omega \subseteq S$ of domain literals, $K + \Omega = (RS_K, RD_K, \prec_K, BE_K \cup \Omega)$ belongs to $\mathcal{C}_{\mathcal{R}}$, and S is a belief set of $K + \Omega$ wrt atts.*

For an illustration, consider again Example 2. Suppose $\{D, P, T\}$ is a belief set of K. Then the property of credulous cumulativity dictates that $\{D, P, T\}$ is also a belief set of $K + \{P\} = (RS_K, RD_K, \prec_K, \{D, P\})$. We state now an important result of this paper.

Theorem 6. *The credulous cumulativity property is satisfied by all regular attack relation assignments.*

Proof. (Sketch) Let $atts \in RAA_\mathcal{R}$, $K \in \mathcal{C_R}$ and E be a stable extension of $(AR_K, atts(K))$, $S = cnl(E)$ and $\Omega \subseteq S$ be a finite set of domain literals. Further let $K' = K + \Omega$ and $E' = \{X \in AR_{K'} \mid \exists Y \in E, AS \subseteq E \text{ s.t. } cnl(AS) \subseteq \Omega \text{ and } Y \in X \downarrow AS \}$. It is clear that $E \subseteq E'$ and $cnl(E) = cnl(E')$ and $BE \cup \Omega \subseteq S$. We show that E' is a stable extension of $(AR_{K'}, att(K'))$ by showing that it is conflict-free and attacks each argument not belonging to it. The theorem follows from the fact that $cnl(E) = cnl(E')$.   □

Attack relation assignments satisfying the credulous cumulativity property together with all other regular properties except the inconsistency resolving one are defined as ordinary attack relation assignments in [18]. Theorem 5 implies directly that regular attack relation assignments are ordinary.

8   The Lower SemiLattice Structure of Value-Based Semantics

The value-based approaches to argumentation [3,7,35–37] define the semantics of defeasible knowledge bases by first defining a preference relation between arguments and then using the preference relation to define attack relation between arguments. We show in this section that the preference relations between arguments have a lower semilattice structure and hence a least one that characterizes the common semantics.

We first introduce a new operator about a "structured intersection" of relations that is needed to characterize the structure of preference relations between arguments.

Any relation $R \subseteq X \times X$ over a set X could be decomposed into a disjoint union of a **strict core**, denoted by R_{st} and **symmetric core**, denoted by R_{sy} as follows: $R = R_{st} \cup R_{sy}$ where $R_{st} = \{(a, b) \in R \mid (b, a) \notin R\}$ and $R_{sy} = \{(a, b) \in R \mid (b, a) \in R\}$.

For any relations $R, R' \subseteq X \times X$, we introduce a **"strong intersection"**-operator $R \sqcap R'$ by: $R \sqcap R' = (R_{st} \cap R'_{st}) \cup (R_{sy} \cap R'_{sy})$.

Further define a partial order $R \ll R'$ by: $R \ll R'$ iff $R_{st} \subseteq R'_{st}$ and $R_{sy} \subseteq R'_{sy}$.

Definition 20. *An* **argument preference assignment** *(or* **ap-assigment** *for short) for a rule-based system $\mathcal{R}$ is a function Γ assigning to each knowledge base $K \in \mathcal{C_R}$, a relation $\sqsubseteq_{\Gamma,K} \subseteq AR_K \times AR_K$ (whose strict core is $\sqsubset_{\Gamma,K}$) representing a preference relation between arguments in AR_K where strict arguments are not strictly less preferred than any other arguments.*

Definition 21. *Let Γ an ap-assignment defined for $\mathcal{R}$. The* **attack relation assignment derived from** Γ *and denoted by* $\mathbf{atts}_\Gamma$, *is defined by: For each $K \in \mathcal{C}_\mathcal{R}$ and all $A, B \in AR_K$, $(A, B) \in atts_\Gamma(K)$ iff A undercuts B or A rebuts B (at B') and $A \not\sqsubseteq_{\Gamma,K} B'$.*

Definition 22. *An ap-assignment Γ is* **regular** *for $\mathcal{R}$ iff its derived attack relation assignment $atts_\Gamma$ is regular.*

The set of all regular ap-assignments for $\mathcal{R}$ is denoted by $AP_\mathcal{R}$.

Notation 3. *The "strong intersection"-operator is expanded for non-empty set $\mathcal{P}$ of ap-assignments and denoted by $\sqcap\mathcal{P}$ as follows: $(\sqcap\mathcal{P})(K) = \sqcap\{\Gamma(K) \mid \Gamma \in \mathcal{P}\}$.*

For ap-assignments Γ_0, Γ_1, we write $\Gamma_0 \ll \Gamma_1$ iff for each $K \in \mathcal{C}_\mathcal{R}$, $\Gamma_0(K) \ll \Gamma_1(K)$.

It is easy to see that $\Gamma_0 \ll \Gamma_1$ implies $att_{\Gamma_1} \subseteq att_{\Gamma_0}$. The following lemma shows that the "strong intersection" forms an infimum operation for regular ap-assignments.

Lemma 6. *Let $\mathcal{P}$ be a non-empty set of regular apr-assignments for $\mathcal{R}$. Then $\sqcap\mathcal{P}$ is regular.*

Proof. (Sketch) It is not difficult to see that the equation $atts_{\sqcap\mathcal{P}} = \sqcup\{atts_\Gamma \mid \Gamma \in \mathcal{P}\}$ holds. The regularity of $\sqcap\mathcal{P}$ follows from lemma 3.   □

It follows immediately from Lemma 6.

Theorem 6. *If $AP_\mathcal{R}$ is non-empty then $(AP_\mathcal{R}, \ll, \sqcap)$ forms a lower semilattice with $CA_\mathcal{R} = \sqcap AP_\mathcal{R}$ being the least regular ap-assignment for $\mathcal{R}$ and is referred to as the* **canonical ap-assignment**.   □

9   Discussion and Conclusions

Regular properties interact. While the attack monotonicity and link-prientation properties propagate respectively the attack relations and non-attack relations within the boundary of a knowledge base, context-independence propagates the attack (and non-attack) relations across knowledge base boundaries.

A more liberal notion of unrestricted rebut where a basic defeasible argument could directly attack a non-basic defeasible argument is studied in [13,14]. Intuitively an unrestricted rebut is a rebut against a set of defeasible rules without explicitly rebutting any individual rule in it. It would be interesting to see how this notion of rebut interacts with the regular properties.

It is often necessary to combine normative reasoning with causal and probabilistic reasoning in practical reasoning.

Example 10. (see [22]) John sues Henry for the damage caused to him when he drove off the road to avoid hitting Henry's cow. John's argument is:

J: *Henry should pay for the damage because Henry is the owner of the cow and the cow caused the accident.*

Henry counter-attacks by stating that,

H_1: *John was negligent, for evidence at the accident site shows that John was driving fast.*
H_2: *The cow was mad and the madness of the cow should be viewed as a force-majeure.*

John's argument is based on a common norm (or law) that owners are responsible for the damages caused by their animals. Henry's first argument is based on the causal relationship between John's fast driving and the accident. Henry's second argument is based on the legal concept of force-majeure and the probability of the event of a cow getting mad. Can John win the case?

The chance of John winning the case depends on how probable the judge considers Henry's arguments. Suppose the judge dismisses the madness of the cow as improbable, then the probability of Henry's second argument is 0. Therefore the chance for John to win depends on the probability of Henry's first argument. Suppose the judge considers the probability that John was driving fast to be 0.4, then the probability for John's argument to stand is 0.6, and John would win the case. However, if the judge considers the probability of the event "John's driving fast" to be 0.7, then Henry would win the case because the probability for John's argument to stand is 0.3 only.

Dung and Thang developed a probabilistic argumentation framework in [22] to model applications involving both causal and norm-based reasoning as illustrated in this example. Other works include [30,31,33].

Acknowledgements. Many thanks to Matteo Baldoni, Amit K. Chopra, Tran Cao Son, Katsutoshi Hirayama, Paolo Torroni for the invitation to include this paper in the proceedings of Prima2016.

References

1. Amgoud, L.: Postulates for logic-based argumentation systems. Int. J. Approximate Reasoning **55**(9), 2028–2048 (2014)
2. Amgoud, L., Cayrol, C.: Integrating preference ordering into argument-based reasoning. In: Proceedings of ESQUARU-FAPS (1997)
3. Amgoud, L., Cayrol, C.: Infering from inconsistency in preference-based argumentation framework. Int J. Autom. Reasoning **29**(2), 197–215 (2002)
4. Baroni, P., Giacomin, M.: Semantics of abstract argument systems. In: Simari, G., Rahwan, I. (eds.) Argumentation in Artificial Intelligence. Springer, New York (2009)
5. Bench-Capon, T.J.M., Atkinson, K.: Abstract argumentation and values. In: Simari, G., Rahwan, I. (eds.) Argumentation in Artificial Intelligence. Springer, New York (2009)

6. Bench-Capon, T.J.M., Prakken, H., Sartor, G.: Argumentation in legal reasoning. In: Simari, G., Rahwan, I. (eds.) Argumentation in Artificial Intelligence. Springer, New York (2009)
7. Bench-Capon, J.M.T.: Persuasion in practical argument using value-based argumentation frameworks. J. Log. Comput. **13**(3), 429–448 (2003)
8. Bondarenko, A., Dung, P.M., Kowalski, R.A., Toni, F.: An abstract, argumentation-theoretic approach to default reasoning. Artif. Intell. **93**, 63–101 (1997)
9. Brewka, G.: Preferred subtheories: an extended logical framework for default reasoning. In: Proceedings of IJCAI 1989, pp. 1043–1048. Morgan Kaufmann, Burlington (1989)
10. Brewka, G., Dunne, P.E., Woltran, S.: Relating the semantics of abstract dialectical framework and standard AF. In: Proceedings of IJCAI (2011)
11. Brewka, G., Eiter, T.: Preferred answer sets for extended logic programs. Artif. Intell. **109**, 297–356 (1999)
12. Brewka, G., Niemelä, I., Truszczynski, M.: Preferences and nonmonotonic reasoning. AI Mag. **29**(4), 69–78 (2008)
13. Caminada, M., Amgoud, L.: On the evaluation of argumentation formalisms. Artif. Intell. **171**, 286–310 (2007)
14. Caminada, M., Modgil, S., Oren, N.: Preferences and unrestricted rebut. In: Proceedings of Comma 2014 (2014)
15. Cayrol, C., Doutre, S., Mengin, J.: On decision problems related to the preferred semantics for argumentation frameworks. J. Log. Comput. **13**(3), 377–403 (2003)
16. Davey, B.A., Priestley, H.A.: Introduction to Lattices and Order. Cambridge University Press, Cambridge (2002)
17. Delgrande, J.P., Schaub, T., Tompits, H.: A framework for compiling preferences in logic programs. Theory Pract. Logic Program. **3**(2), 129–187 (2003)
18. Dung, P.M.: An axiomatic analysis of structured argumentation with priorities. Artif. Intell. **231**, 107–150 (2016)
19. Dung, P.M.: A canonical semantics for structured argumentation with priorities. In: Baroni, P. (ed.) Proceedings of Comma 2016. IOS Press (2016)
20. Dung, P.M., Sartor, G.: The modular logic of private international law. Artif. Intell. Law **19**, 233–261 (2011)
21. Dung, P.M., Thang, P.M.: Closure and consistency and logic-associated argumentation. J. Artif. Intell. Res. **49**, 79–109 (2014)
22. Dung, P.M., Thang, P.M.: Towards (probabilistic) argumentation for jury-based dispute resolution. In: COMMA, pp. 171–182 (2010)
23. Dung, P.M.: On the acceptability of arguments and its fundamental role in nonmonotonic reasoning, logic programming and n-person gamescceptability of arguments and its fundamental role in nonmonotonic reasoning, logic programming and n-person games. Artif. Intell. **77**(2), 321–358 (1995)
24. Dung, P.M.: An axiomatic analysis of structured argumentation for prioritized default reasoning. In: Proceedings of ECAI 2014 (2014)
25. Dung, P.M., Kowalski, R.A., Toni, F.: Assumption-based argumentation. In: Simari, G., Rahwan, I. (eds.) Argumentation in Artificial Intelligence. Springer, New York (2009)
26. Gabbay, D.M.: Equational approach to argumentation networks. Argument Comput. (2012)
27. Garcia, A.J., Simari, G.R.: Defeasible logic programming: an argumentative approach. TPLP **4**(1–2), 95–138 (2004)

28. Gelfond, M., Son, T.C.: Reasoning with prioritized defaults. In: Dix, J., Moniz Pereira, L., Przymusinski, T.C. (eds.) LPKR 1997. LNCS (LNAI), vol. 1471, pp. 164–223. Springer, Heidelberg (1998)

29. Pearl, J. Geffner, H.: Conditional entailment: bridging two approaches to default reasoning. Artif. Intell. in, 990 ?44 (1992)

30. Hunter, A.: Probabilistic qualification of attack in argument argumentation. Int. J. Approximate Reasoning **55**(1), 607–638 (2014)

31. Hunter, A., Thimm, M.: Probabilistic argument graphs for argumentation lotteries. In: Computational Models of Argument (COMMA 2014). IOS Press (2014)

32. Hunter, A., Williams, M.: Aggregating evidence about positive and negative effects of treatments. Artif. Intell. Med. **56**, 173–190 (2012)

33. Li, H., Oren, N., Norman, T.J.: Probabilistic argumentation frameworks. In: Modgil, S., Oren, N., Toni, F. (eds.) TAFA 2011. LNCS, vol. 7132, pp. 1–16. Springer, Heidelberg (2012)

34. Martinez, D.C., Garcia, A.J., Simari, G.R.: On acceptability in abstract argumentation frameworks with an extended defeat relation. In: Bench-Capon, T.J.M., Dunne, P.E. (eds.) Proceedings of International Conference on "Computational Models of Arguments". IOS Press (2006)

35. Modgil, S., Prakken, H.: A general account of argumentation with preferences. Artif. Intell. **197**, 361–397 (2013)

36. Modgil, S., Prakken, H.: The aspic+ framework for structured argumenttion: a tutorial. J. Arguments Comput. **5**, 31–62 (2014)

37. Prakken, H.: An abstract framework for argumentation with structured arguments. J. Arguments Comput. **1**, 93–124 (2010)

38. Prakken, H., Sartor, G.: Argument-based extended logic programming with defeasible priorities. J. Appl. Non-Class. Logics **7**(1), 25–75 (1997)

39. Rintanen, J.: Lexicographic priorities in default logics. Artif. Intell. **106**, 221–265 (1998)

40. Schaub, T., Wang, K.: A comparative study of logic programs with preferences. In: Proceedings of IJCAI 2001. Morgan Kaufmann, Burlington (2001)

41. Vreeswijk, G.: Abstract argumentation systems. Artif. Intell. **90**, 225–279 (1997)

Regular Papers

Argumentation-Based Semantics
for Logic Programs with First-Order Formulae

Phan Minh Dung[1]($\boxtimes$), Tran Cao Son[2], and Phan Minh Thang[3]

[1] Department of Computer Science, Asian Institute of Technology,
Klong Luang, Thailand
dung.phanminh@gmail.com
[2] Department of Computer Science, New Mexico State University,
Las Cruces, NM, USA
[3] Department of Computer Science, Burapha University International College,
Bangsaen, Thailand

Abstract. This paper studies different semantics of logic programs with first order formulae under the lens of argumentation framework. It defines the notion of an *argumentation-based answer set* and the notion of an *argumentation-based well-founded model* for programs with first order formulae. The main ideas underlying the new approach lie in the notion of a *proof tree* supporting a conclusion given a program and the observation that proof trees can be naturally employed as arguments in an argumentation framework whose stable extensions capture the program's well-justified answer semantics recently introduced in [23]. The paper shows that the proposed approach to dealing with programs with first order formulae can be easily extended to a generalized class of logic programs, called programs with *FOL-representable atoms*, that covers various types of extensions of logic programming proposed in the literature such as weight constraint atoms, aggregates, and abstract constraint atoms. For example, it shows that argumentation-based well-founded model is equivalent to the well-founded model in [27] for programs with abstract constraint atoms. Finally, the paper relates the proposed approach to others and discusses possible extensions.

1 Introduction

Answer set semantics for logic programs [12] is one of the most widely adopted semantics for logic programs—i.e., logic programs that allow negation as failure in the body of the rules. It is a natural extension of the minimal model semantics of positive logic programs to the case of normal logic programs. Answer set semantics provides the theoretical foundation for *answer set programming* [16,18] which has proved to be useful in several applications such as diagnosis, bioinformatics, planning, etc. (see, e.g., [1–3,6,11,14]).

A set of atoms S is an *answer set* of the program Π if S is the minimal model of the positive program Π^S (the *reduct of Π with respect to S*), obtained from the *Gelfond-Lifschitz transformation* by (*i*) removing from Π all the rules whose

© Springer International Publishing Switzerland 2016
M. Baldoni et al. (Eds.): PRIMA 2016, LNAI 9862, pp. 43–60, 2016.
DOI: 10.1007/978-3-319-44832-9_3

body contains a negation as failure literal *not b* which is false in S (i.e., $b \in S$); and (*ii*) removing all the negation as failure literals from the remaining rules.

One of the most interesting properties of answer sets that can be derived from the above definition is that each atom in an answer set is *non-circular justifiable*, i.e., for each atom a there exists a proof tree for a that does not involve a in any of the proof step.

The successes of answer set programming (ASP) and the needs for a more expressive and simple modeling language led to several extensions of the language such as weight constraint atoms [19], aggregates atoms (e.g., [10,20]), abstract constraint atoms (e.g., [17,25]), logic programs with first order formulae (e.g., [4,23]). The notion of an answer set has been extended to various extensions of logic programming and one of the contentious issue in this endeavor is related to the circular justifiability of atoms belonging to an answer set. This problem has been discussed extensively in the literature and can be seen in the following example.

Example 1. Consider the program Π_1 with aggregates discussed in [23]:

$$p(1) \leftarrow \tag{1}$$
$$p(2) \leftarrow p(-1). \tag{2}$$
$$p(-1) \leftarrow \text{SUM}(\{X : p(X)\}) \geq 1. \tag{3}$$

where $\text{SUM}(\{X : p(X)\}) \geq 1$ represents an aggregate atom; informally, it is true in an interpretation I if $\Sigma_{p(x) \in I} x \geq 1$. This program has an answer set $\{p(1), p(2), p(-1)\}$ according to [10] but does not admit any answer set according to many other definitions (e.g., [20,23,25]). The issue of this answer set, as discussed in [23], lies in that $p(2)$ is circular justified by the sequence $p(2) \Leftarrow p(-1) \Leftarrow \text{SUM}(\{X : p(X)\}) \geq 1 \Leftarrow p(2)$.   ◊

It is easy to see that the five Herbrand interpretations of the above program $\{p(2)\}$, $\{p(2), p(1)\}$, $\{p(2), p(-1)\}$, $\{p(2), p(1), p(-1)\}$, and $\{p(1)\}$, where elements not belonging to an interpretation are assumed to be false, are the only ones satisfying the atom $\text{SUM}(\{X : p(X)\}) \geq 1$. Let us denote with λ the atom $\text{SUM}(\{X : p(X)\}) \geq 1$ and C_λ be the collection of rules:

$$\lambda \leftarrow p(2), \neg p(1), \neg p(-1). \tag{4}$$
$$\lambda \leftarrow p(2), p(1), \neg p(-1) \tag{5}$$
$$\lambda \leftarrow p(2), p(-1), \neg p(1). \tag{6}$$
$$\lambda \leftarrow p(2), p(1), p(-1). \tag{7}$$
$$\lambda \leftarrow p(1), \neg p(2), \neg p(-1). \tag{8}$$

These rules basically provide the definition for the atom $\text{SUM}(\{X : p(X)\}) \geq 1$, i.e., they define when it is true. Let Π_λ be the program obtained from Π_1 by replacing $\text{SUM}(\{X : p(X)\}) \geq 1$ with λ. It is easy to check that the program $\Pi_\lambda \cup C_\lambda \cup \{\neg p(X) \leftarrow \text{ } not \text{ } p(X) \mid X \in \{1, 2, -1\}\}$ does not have an answer set. As such, it is reasonable to conclude that Π_1 is inconsistent. This argument is similar to the one used in [24] to show that Π_1 is inconsistent, i.e., Π_1 does not have an answer set.

It is interesting to observe that if we were to construct a SLD-proof[1] for $p(-1)$ given the program Π_1 assuming that *not p* implies $\neg p$ (i.e., assuming the negation-as-failure rule or NAF rule) we will eventually have to make use of the rules in C_λ. For example, a proof tree using (8) is depicted in Fig. 1(left); a proof tree using (5) is depicted in Fig. 1(right) where T_1 denotes a proof tree for $p(-1)$. It is easy to verify that every tree supporting $p(-1)$ from any set of assumptions, which is a subset of $\{not\ p(1),\ not\ p(2),\ not\ p(-1)\}$, under the program Π_1 is inconsistent in the sense that it assumes that $p(-1)$ is false ($not\ p(-1)$) to conclude that $p(-1)$ is true. In fact, the dependence discussed in [23] can be extracted from these proof trees.

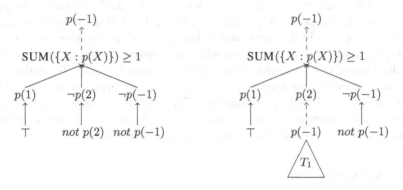

Fig. 1. Possible proof trees for $p(-1)$

It is not difficult to see that a proof tree constructed from a given program—informally defined as above—represents an argument supporting the conclusion of the literal at its root. Furthermore, there can be several arguments constructible from a program. The question is then which arguments should be *acceptable*, a central question in the studies of argumentation framework.

It is worth noticing that argumentation framework is another line of research that has its root in the study of logic programming and nonmonotonic reasoning. In fact, the landmark paper [9] originated from a paper studying the acceptability semantics of logic programming [8]. The proposed argumentation framework in [9] laid the foundation for the development of several argumentation-based theories and applications. Within logic programming, it has been showed in [9] that different semantics of argumentation frameworks such as grounded extensions and stable extensions correspond to the well-founded and answer set semantics of normal logic programs. In a recent paper, [22] showed that the 3-valued stable model of logic programming [21] can also be viewed as a semi-stable labeling of a corresponding assumption-based argumentation framework [5].

---

[1] SLD stands for "selective linear **definite**" (see, e.g., [15]).

Can argumentation-based semantics be extended to more generalized logic programs? The main purpose of this paper is to investigate different semantics of logic programs with first order formulae under the view of argumentation framework. The advantages of this study are twofold. First, it shows that the traditional approach to studying the semantics of logic programs using argumentation framework can be generalized to more generalized programs. Second, it allows for the definition of the well-founded semantics for programs with first order formulae that has not been studied thus far. To the best of our knowledge, this is the first time the notion of a well-founded model for logic programs with first order formulae is discussed.

To summarize, the paper contributes to both areas of logic programming and argumentation framework. Regarding logic programming, the paper proposes to consider proof trees as arguments and to use different semantics of argumentation framework as the semantics of the original program. The paper then extends the proposed approach to a generalized class of logic programs, called programs with FOL-representable atoms, which covers several extensions of logic programs such as programs with aggregates, programs with abstract constraint atoms, and programs with weight constraint atoms. Regarding argumentation framework, the paper demonstrates that its principle is applicable in various extensions of logic programming. The equivalent results in this paper indicate that argumentation-based semantics can be used as a means to study different approaches to defining semantics of those extensions.

2   Background

In this section, we review the basics of argumentation framework and logic programs with first order formulae.

2.1   Argumentation Framework

An abstract *argumentation framework* (AF) [9] AF is a pair $(Args, Atts)$ where $Args$ is a set of abstract entities called arguments and $Atts \subseteq Args \times Args$ is the attack relation between arguments. An argument $a \in Args$ attacks an argument $b \in Args$ if $(a, b) \in Atts$. a is called an attacker of b if a attacks b. The set of arguments $S \subseteq Args$ *attacks* b if there exists $a \in S$ such that a attacks b. a (respectively S) *defends* an argument c against its attacker b if a (respectively S) attacks b. S is *conflict free* if it does not attack itself. S is *admissible* if it is conflict free and defends against every of its attackers. The *characteristic function* of AF is defined by

$$F_{AF}(S) = \{a \mid a \in Args, S\text{defends } a\}.$$

Since F_{AF} is a monotonic function, the sequence

$$F_{AF}(\emptyset), F_{AF}(F_{AF}(\emptyset)), \ldots, F_{AF}^n(\emptyset) = \underbrace{F_{AF}(\ldots F_{AF}(F_{AF}(\emptyset))), \ldots}_{n \ times}$$

converges to its least fixpoint, denoted by $lfp(F_{AF})$. By this definition, it is easy to see that $lfp(F_{AF})$ is unique.

Given an $AF = (Args, Atts)$, a conflict free set of arguments $S \subseteq Args$ is a *stable extension* of AF if it attacks each argument $A \notin S$; a *grounded extension* of AF if $S = lfp(F_{AF})$; and a *preferred extension* of AF if it is a subset-maximal admissible set of AF. The focus of this paper is the two semantics associated with stable and grounded extensions of argumentation framework.

2.2   Logic Programs with FOL-Formulae

Let $\Sigma = (\mathcal{C}, \mathcal{P}, \mathcal{F})$ be a signature with finite set of constants $\mathcal{C}$, finite set of predicate symbols $\mathcal{P}$, and finite set of function symbols $\mathcal{F}$. We assume that $\mathcal{P}$ contains two 0-ary symbols $\top$ and $\bot$, denoting *truth* and *falsity* respectively. Let L_Σ be the first-order logic language with equality over Σ. We will make use of the usual notions in first-order logic (FOL) such as term, atom, literal, interpretation, satisfaction of a formula w.r.t. an interpretation etc. without precise definition. We refer the readers to [15, 23] for detail.

A *logic program with FOL-formulae* is a finite set of rules of the form $\phi \leftarrow \psi$ where ϕ and ψ are classical first order logic formulae in L_Σ such that $\phi \neq \top$ and $\psi \neq \bot$. For a rule $r = \phi \leftarrow \psi$, $head(r)$ and $body(r)$ denote ϕ and ψ respectively. When ϕ is an atom and ψ is a conjunction of literals, we say that the rule is a *normal rule*. A program is *normal* if every of its rules is normal.

Given a program Π, H_Π denotes the Herbrand base of Π excluding $\top$ and $\bot$. For a program Π, $ground(\Pi)$ denotes the set of ground instantiations of rules in Π using the set of constants occurring in Π. By an interpretation of Π, we mean a Herbrand interpretation. In this paper, we will assume that $ground(\Pi)$ is finite.

A *partial interpretation* of Π is a pair (P, Q) such that $P, Q \subseteq H_\Pi$ and $P \cap Q = \emptyset$. Given a Herbrand interpretation I of Π, we denote with $\neg I^-$ the set $\{\neg a \mid a \in H_\Pi \setminus I\}$ and say that I satisfies a rule $r \in ground(\Pi)$ if $I \cup \neg I^- \models body(r)$ implies $I \cup \neg I^- \models head(r)$ ($\models$ denotes the usual logical entailment relation). I *satisfies* a program Π (or I is a *model* of Π) if it satisfies every rule in $ground(\Pi)$.

Let Π be a program with FOL-formulae and I be an interpretation of Π. Let $f\Pi^I$ be the program obtained from $ground(\Pi)$ by (i) eliminating all the rules whose bodies are not satisfied by I; and (ii) adding the negative literals in $\neg I^-$ as constraints to the resulting program. For two first order theories O and N, let $T_\Pi(O, N) = \{head(r) \mid r \in ground(\Pi), O \cup N \models body(r)\}$. A model I of a program Π is a *well-justified answer set* of Π if $lfp(T_{f\Pi^I}(\emptyset, \neg I^-)) \cup \neg I^- \models a$ for every $a \in I$ where $lfp(T_{f\Pi^I}(\emptyset, \neg I^-))$ denotes the least fixpoint of the function $T_\Pi(., \neg I^-)$.

Example 2. Consider the program from [23]:

$$a \vee (\neg b \wedge c) \leftarrow \neg a \wedge (\neg c \vee c).$$
$$d \leftarrow c.$$

Let us call the program Π_2. It is easy to see that $I = \{c, d\}$ is a model of Π_2 since $\neg I^- = \{\neg a, \neg b\}$ and for each rule r in Π_2, $I \cup \neg I^- \models body(r)$ and $I \cup \neg I^- \models head(r)$. It is also easy to see that $f\Pi_2^I$ consists of Π_2 together with the clause $\neg a \leftarrow$. $\Diamond$

Observe that the interpretation $I' = \{a, d\}$ is also a model of Π_2. However, d cannot be justified by this model. It can be seen that only I is considered as a well-justified answer set of Π_2.

3   Argumentation Framework and Logic Programs with FOL-Formulae

In this section, we define different semantics for logic programs with FOL formulae. In the following, whenever we refer to a program, we mean a logic program with FOL formula whose signature is assumed to be known.

3.1   Argumentation-Based Semantics for Logic Programs with FOL Formulae

Let Π be a program and L_Π be the set of ground formulae formed over H_Π. We extend the program Π (and hence, $ground(\Pi)$) with rules: (i) $\bot \leftarrow a \wedge \neg a$, denoted by $\mathbf{F}_a$, for each atom a in H_Π; (ii) $\neg a \leftarrow not\ a$, denoted by $\mathbf{A}_a$, where not is the default negation and is not a symbol in the language of Π for each atom a in H_Π. Intuitively, $\mathbf{F}_a$ indicates that if both a and $\neg a$ are provable then Π is inconsistent as it derives falsity; $\mathbf{A}_a$ encodes the negation-as-failure rule that says that if a is not provable then $\neg a$ can be concluded.

Definition 1 (Proof Tree).   A *proof tree* (or *tree*) for a formula σ w.r.t. a program Π is a finite tree with nodes labelled by formulae in $L_\Pi \cup \{\top, \bot\} \cup \{not\ a \mid a \in H_\Pi\}$ such that

1. the root is labelled by σ;
2. for every node N labelled by φ if N is not a leaf node and has n children, labelled by $\varphi_1, \ldots, \varphi_n$ then one of the following conditions is satisfied:
   - $\varphi_1 \wedge \ldots \wedge \varphi_n \models \varphi$; or
   - $\varphi \leftarrow \varphi_1 \wedge \ldots \wedge \varphi_n$ is in $ground(\Pi)$.
3. a leaf of the tree must be either $\top$ or $not\ a$ for some $a \in H_\Pi$.

Intuitively, a tree represents a possible derivation of the formula at its root given the rules of the program and the assumptions made at its leaves. The formula labeled an interior node is either a logical consequence of the conjunction of formulae labeled its children (first case of Item 2) or it is the head of a ground rule whose body is the conjunction of formulae labeled its children (second case of Item 2).

For a tree T and a node N in T, $label(N)$ denotes the formula that labels N. The *conclusion* of a tree T, denoted by $Concl(T)$, is the formula labelling its root. The support of a tree T, denoted by $Support(T)$, is the set $\{label(N) \mid N$ is a leaf, $label(N) \neq \top\}$. A tree T is *strict* if $Support(T) = \emptyset$. For a set of trees S, $Concl(S) = \{Concl(T) \mid T \in S\}$.

Example 3. In Fig. 2, we can see different types of nodes:

- the node whose label is $a \vee (\neg b \wedge c)$ whose connections to their children are dashed lines are constructed from rules in the program (constructed using the second case in Item 2 of Definition 1, via $a \vee (\neg b \wedge c) \leftarrow \neg a \wedge (\neg c \vee c)$ of Π_2).
- the node whose label is $\neg a$ with a unique child whose label is *not a* (constructed using the second case in Item 2 of Definition 1, via the rule A_a)
- the node whose label is the valid formula $\neg c \vee c$ with a unique child whose label is $\top$ (constructed using the first case in Item 2 of Definition 1).

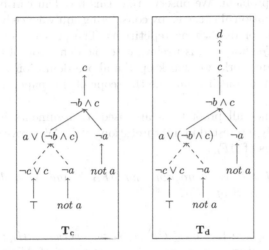

Fig. 2. Two possible proof trees for program in Example 2

Observe that for each $a \in H_\Pi$, we can create a tree whose conclusion is $\neg a$ and whose set of supports is $\{not\,a\}$ (Fig. 3) using the rule A_a. Abusing the notation, we will refer to this tree as A_a.

Fig. 3. A_a – NAF-Tree

Definition 2 (Induced AF). Let Π be a program. The argumentation framework induced by Π, $AF_\Pi = (Args_\Pi, Atts_\Pi)$, is defined as follows:

- $Args_\Pi$ is the set of all proof trees whose roots are labeled with elements in $H_\Pi \cup \{\neg a \mid a \in H_\Pi\} \cup \{\top, \bot\}$.
- $Atts_\Pi = \{(A, B) \mid not\ Concl(A) \in Support(B)\}$, i.e., $A \in Args_\Pi$ attacks an argument $B \in Args_\Pi$ if and only if $not\ Concl(A) \in Support(B)$.

In general, the set of arguments and the set of attacks of AF_Π can be infinite since there are infinitely many formulae that can be constructed from $L_\Pi \cup \{\top, \bot\} \cup \{\,not\ a \mid a \in H_\Pi\}$ and repetitions are allowed in the construction of proof trees. For instance, if we replace $\neg b \wedge c$, the formula associated with the child of the root of the tree $\mathbf{T}_c$ in Fig. 2, by $(\neg b \wedge c) \wedge (a \vee \neg a)$, then we will receive a new proof tree for c; or, if we replace the child $not\ a$ of $\neg a$ by the tree $\mathbf{A}_a$, then we also receive a new proof tree for c. This property is important from the computational aspect, i.e., any system for computing different semantics of logic programs with FOL-formulae as defined in Definitions 4–5 will need to deal with this problem. We observe that this problem can be dealt with by tightening the definition above, e.g., by considering equivalence between formulae as a single formula or disallowing repetitions. The presence of infinitely many arguments isn AF_Π, however, is irrelevant to the definition of the semantics of argumentation framework, we will keep the above definition as it. Addressing this issue is important but it is outside the scope of this paper and we leave this as a future task.

Observe that not all proof trees are used as arguments in AF_Π. This is because we are only interested in interpretations of Π. We prove some properties of stable extensions of AF_Π.

Proposition 1. *Let Π be a program and AF_Π be the AF induced by Π. For every stable extension S of AF_Π,*

1. *$\top \in Concl(S)$;*
2. *if $\bot \in Concl(S)$ then $\{a, \neg a\} \subseteq Concl(S)$ for every $a \in H_\Pi$;*
3. *if $\bot \in Concl(S)$ then S is the only stable extension of AF_Π; and*
4. *if $\bot \notin Concl(S)$ then for every atom $a \in H_\Pi$, $\{a, \neg a\} \setminus Concl(S)$ is a singleton.*

Proof.

1. The first item is trivial since $\top$ is a single node tree whose support is empty and hence cannot be attacked.
2. If $\bot \in Concl(S)$ then there exists a tree $T \in S$ with $\bot = Concl(T)$. Since $\bot \models \varphi$ for any formula φ, we can easily construct a tree T_φ with $Concl(T_\varphi) = \varphi$ and $Support(T_\varphi) = Support(T)$. Since T is not attacked by S, T_φ is not attacked by S. Hence $T_\varphi \in S$. Restricting φ to literals of the program, we get the conclusion of the proposition.
3. Assume that there exists a stable extension S' of AF_Π and $S' \neq S$. Consider some $T \in S \setminus S'$. S' attacks T implies that $Support(T) \neq \emptyset$. Assume that $not\ a \in Support(T)$. Since $\bot \in S$ then from the previous item, we have that S contains a tree T_a such that $a = Concl(T_a)$. It means that T_a attacks T, i.e., S is not conflict free. Contradiction.

4. Assume the contrary. There are two cases:
   - $\{a, \neg a\} \setminus Concl(S) = \emptyset$. This means that S contains two trees T_a and $T_{\neg a}$ such that $Concl(T_a) = a$ and $Concl(T_{\neg a}) = \neg a$. From these two trees, we can construct a tree $T_\perp$ as in Fig. 4. Obviously, this tree is not attacked by S since its set of supports is $Support(T_a) \cup Support(T_{\neg a})$ and S is conflict free by definition. In other words, $T_\perp \in S$ because S is a stable extension, i.e., $\perp \in Concl(S)$. Contradiction.
   - $\{a, \neg a\} \setminus Concl(S) = \{a, \neg a\}$. This means that S does not contain any tree T with $Concl(T) = a$. As such, S does not attack the tree $\mathbf{A}_a$. Since S is a stable extension, $\mathbf{A}_a \in S$ which implies that $\neg a \in Concl(S)$. A contradiction with the assumption that $\{a, \neg a\} \setminus Concl(S) = \{a, \neg a\}$. $\square$

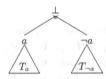

Fig. 4. Tree $T_\perp$

The above proposition shows that programs consisting of arguments supporting $\perp$ would have a single stable extension, if one exists. Intuitively, such programs should not be used in making conclusions, especially programs with strict proof trees supporting contradictory conclusions. We characterize this class of programs as *incoherent* as follows.

Definition 3 (Coherent Programs). A program Π is said to be *incoherent* if there are strict arguments supporting both a and $\neg a$ for some $a \in H_\Pi$ in its induced argumentation framework AF_Π.

Π is *coherent* if it is not incoherent.

It is easy to check that $\Pi_3 = \{a \leftarrow \top.\ \ \neg a \leftarrow \top.\}$ is incoherent. Coherent programs satisfy the following property.

Proposition 2. *Let Π be a program. It holds that*

1. *If Π is coherent then $Concl(S)$ is consistent for each stable extension S of AF_Π.*
2. *If there is a stable extension S of AF_Π such that $Concl(S)$ is consistent then Π is coherent.*

Proof. The first item follows from the second and fourth items of Proposition 1 and the fact that if Π is incoherent then $\perp \in Concl(S)$ for every stable extension S. The second item follows immediately from the first item. $\square$

Proposition 2 suggests that it is reasonable to focus on coherent programs. In fact, all normal logic programs as defined in [12] are coherent since they do not allow classical negation. As such, *from now on if nothing is explicitly stated, by a program we mean a coherent program.* Having defined the argumentation framework of a program Π, we now define answer sets.

Definition 4 (Argumentation-Based Answer Set). Let Π be a program and $AF_\Pi = (Args_\Pi, Atts_\Pi)$ be the AF induced by Π. An interpretation I of Π is an *argumentation-based answer set* (or *AB-answer set*, for short) of Π if there exists a stable extension S of AF_Π such that $I \cup \neg I^- \cup \{\top\} = Concl(S)$.

The above definition is in line with the recently adopted convention in defining answer sets which requires that answer sets are consistent sets of literals. It also indicates that a program might not have an AB-answer set. In that case we say that the program is inconsistent. Generalizing the result on well-founded model of normal logic programs in [9], we next define well-founded model for programs with FOL formulae.

Definition 5 (Argumentation-Based Well-Founded Model). Let Π be a program and $AF_\Pi = (Args_\Pi, Atts_\Pi)$ be the AF induced by Π. A partial interpretation (P, Q) of Π is the *argumentation-based well-founded model* (or *AB-well-founded model*) of Π if $P \cup \{\neg a \mid a \in Q\} \cup \{\top\} = Concl(S)$ where S is the grounded extension of AF_Π.

Intuitively, if (P, Q) is the well-founded model of Π, then P (Q) is the collection of atoms that are true (false) given Π. It is worth noticing that the notion of a well-founded model for logic programs with first-order formulae has not been defined in the literature.

It follows directly from the property of grounded extension and stable extensions of argumentation framework that the well-founded model is unique and every AB-answer set contains the AB-well-founded model.

Proposition 3. *Let Π be a program. Then, the AB-well-founded model of Π, (P, Q), always exists and is unique; and for every AB-answer set I of Π, $P \subseteq I$ and $Q \subseteq H_\Pi \setminus I$.*

Finally, it is not difficult to derive from the results of Theorems 49 and 50 in [9] that, for normal programs, the above defined AB-answer sets and AB-well-founded model coincide with the classical stable models (as in [12]) and well-founded model (as in [26]). In this sense, this paper lifts the work in [9] to logic programs with FOL-formula.

3.2   Argumentation-Based Answer Sets Are Well-Justified

In this section we will focus on the well-justified provability of elements in an AB-answer set. In the following, we make use of terminologies related to trees such as ancestor, subtree, path, etc. without definitions. For precise definitions, the readers are referred to [7]. A pair of two different nodes N and N' in a tree T is a *cycle* if $label(N) = label(N')$ and N is an ancestor of N'. T is *circular* if it has a cycle; *non-circular* if it does not have a cycle. We prove some properties related to the non-circularity of trees.

Lemma 1. *For each tree T, there exists a non-circular tree T' such that $Concl(T) = Concl(T')$ and $Support(T') \subseteq Support(T)$.*

Proof. Let $k = 0$ and $T_k = T$. If T_k is non-circular then the proposition is proved. Otherwise, T_k has a cycle (N, N'). Clearly, replacing the subtree rooted at N by the subtree rooted at N' in T_k results in a tree T_{k+1} that has at least one cycle less than T_k and $Concl(T_k) = Concl(T_{k+1})$ and $Support(T_k) \subseteq Support(T_{k+1})$. Furthermore, the number of nodes of T_{k+1} is less than the number of nodes of T_k. As such, there exists a finite n such that T_n is non-circular. Clearly, we have that $Concl(T) = Concl(T_n)$ and $Support(T_n) \subseteq Support(T)$. □

Lemma 2. *Let Π be a program and $AF_\Pi = (Args_\Pi, Atts_\Pi)$ be the AF induced by Π. Let S be a stable extension of AF_Π. For each $T \in S$ there exists a non-circular T' in S such that $Concl(T') = Concl(T)$.*

Proof. It follows from Lemma 1 that there exists a non-circular T' such that $Concl(T) = Concl(T')$ and $Support(T') \subseteq Support(T)$. We will show that T' belongs to S. Assume that $T' \notin S$. Since S is a stable extension of AF_Π, S attacks T'. Since $Support(T') \subseteq Support(T)$, S attacks T. Contradiction because S is conflict free and $T \in S$. □.

The above lemmas allow us to prove an important property of AB-answer sets.

Theorem 1. *Let Π be a program and I be an AB-answer set of Π. Then, for each atom $a \in I$, there exists a non-circular proof tree T such that $Concl(T) = a$ and $\{\neg b \mid not\ b \in Support(T)\} \subseteq \neg I^-$.*

Proof. I is an argumentation-based answer set of Π iff there exists a stable extension S of AF_Π such that $I \cup \neg I^- \cup \{\top\} = Concl(S)$. This implies that there exists some tree in $T' \in S$ such that $Concl(T') = a$. It follows from Lemma 2 that there exists a non-circular $T \in S$ such that $Concl(T) = Concl(T')$. Since S does not attack T, it means that each $\mathbf{A}_b$. where $not\ b \in Support(T)$ belongs to S, i.e., $\{\neg b \mid not\ b \in Support(T)\} \subseteq Concl(S)$. By the definition of I, we can conclude that $\{\neg b \mid not\ b \in Support(T)\} \subseteq \neg I^-$. □.

To prove the non-circularity of AB-answer sets, we need some additional notations. Let T be a tree. The level of a node N, denoted by $l(N)$, in T is defined as follows: (*i*) if N is a leaf then $l(N) = 0$; (*ii*) if N is not a leaf then $l(N) = 1 + \max\{l(i) \mid i$ is a child of $N\}$. The level of a tree T is defined by the level of its root and is denoted by $l(T)$. For a program Π and its induced AF_Π, let S be a stable extension of AF_Π. The level of S, denoted by $l(S)$, is defined as $\max\{l(T) \mid T \in S\}$. The *kernel* of S, denoted by $k(S)$, is the collection of trees in S such that $Concl(S) = Concl(k(S))$ and for each $z \in Concl(S)$ there exists a unique $T \in k(S)$ such that $z = Concl(T)$, $l(T) = \min\{l(T') \mid T' \in S, Concl(T') = z\}$.[2] For each stable extension S of AF_Π, let $\langle S_i \rangle_{i=0}^{l(S)}$ be the sequence of literals $S_i = \{Concl(T) \mid T \in k(S), l(T) = i\}$.

---

[2] Intuitively, a tree T belongs to the kernel of S if T belongs to S and the level of T is minimal wrt trees in S supporting the same conclusion.

Proposition 4. *Let Π be a program and $AF_\Pi = (Args_\Pi, Atts_\Pi)$ be the AF induced by Π. Let S be a stable extension of AF_Π and $0 \leq i \leq l(S)$. Then, for every tree $T \in k(S)$ such that $Concl(T) \in \bigcup_{0 \leq j < i} S_j$, T does not contain any node whose label is $z \in S_t$ for $t \geq i$.*

Proof. Suppose the contrary. Consider $T_z \in k(S)$ such that $Concl(T_z) = z$. It implies that T contains a subtree T' such that $Concl(T') = z$. It is easy to see that $T' \in S$. Since $l(T') < l(T) < i = l(T_z)$, it means that $T_z \notin k(S)$. This is a contradiction.   □

A consequence of the above proposition is that each tree with level i in the kernel of a stable extension of AF_Π can be constructed using only literals that were the conclusions of trees whose levels are smaller than i. This demonstrates that AB-answer sets are indeed well-justified. Theorem 2 in Subsect. 5.1 formalizes this result in precise terms.

4   Programs with FOL-Representable Atoms

Since the construction of a proof tree makes use of logical inference (first case of Item 2 of Definition 1), it is easy to see that AB-answer sets are preserved under equivalent transformations. This stipulates that the notion of AB-answer sets can be extended to allow extended atoms whose truth values can be defined via a formula in the language of the given program. In fact this is true for many well-known extensions of logic programs such as weight constraint atoms (e.g., [19]), aggregates (e.g., [10]), or abstract constraint atoms (e.g., [17]). Let us quickly review some basic notions of these types of extensions of logic programming.

- A weight constraint atoms [19] of a program Π is of the form $l \ [p_1 : q_1 = w_1, \ldots, p_n : q_n = w_n] \, u$ where l and u are two real numbers such that $l \leq u$, p_i is either a or $not\ a$ for some atom $a \in H_\Pi$, q_i is an atom in H_Π, and w_i is a real number. $p_i : q_i$ is called a *conditional literal*. Given a weight constraint atom C and an interpretation I, the weight of the formula $[p_1 : q_1 = w_1, \ldots, p_n : q_n = w_n]$, denoted by $W(C)$, is calculated[3] and C is declared to be true w.r.t. I if $l \leq W(C) \leq u$.
- An aggregate atom (e.g., [10]) of a program Π is of the form $f(S) \prec T$ where T is a term, $\prec \in \{=, <, >, \leq, \geq\}$, and $f(S)$ is an aggregate term with f is an aggregate function symbol ($\#\mathtt{count}, \#\mathtt{sum}, \ldots$) and S is a set term. In fact, following this syntax the aggregate atom in Π_1 is written as $\#\mathtt{sum}\{X : p(X)\} \geq 1$. Given an aggregate atom $f(S) \prec T$ and an interpretation I, the set term S is evaluated and the value for $f(S)$ is calculated; the atom is true w.r.t. T if the evaluation of $f(S) \prec T$ returns true.
- An abstract constraint atom (e.g., [17,25]) of a program Π is of the form (D, C) where C is a set of subsets of H_Π and D is a subset of H_Π. (D, C) is true w.r.t. an interpretation I if $I \cap D \in C$.

---

[3]   Precise formula for computing $W(C)$ is not really important for the discussion. It can be found in [19].

In short, each of these extensions to logic program starts by defining the syntax of a new type of atoms and associating a method for evaluating the truth value of a new atom w.r.t. an interpretation. Usually, this method allows for the identification of all interpretations of the program that satisfies the atom, i.e., each atom a is associated with a set $\mathcal{I}_a$ of interpretations satisfying a. As such, we can identify a with $t_a = \bigvee_{I \in \mathcal{I}_a} (\bigwedge_{b \in I} b \wedge \bigwedge_{b \notin I} \neg b)$ and $\neg a$ with $\neg t_a$. As an example, the aggregate atom $\lambda = \mathrm{SUM}(\{X : p(X)\}) \geq 1$ in Example 1 is associated to the formula $t_\lambda = \bigvee_{i=1}^{5}(I_i \wedge \neg I_i^-)$ where $I_1, \ldots, I_5$ are the five interpretations satisfying λ detailed in Sect. 1.

The method of evaluation of extended atoms is then used to define when a rule (or a program with extended syntax) is satisfied given an interpretation which, in turn, is used in defining answer sets although the approach to define the semantics of programs with these new types of atoms might be different (e.g., by using a two step definition similar to the original definition of answer sets [10], or using a mathematical operator [17,20], etc.). The key distinction between previous approaches in dealing with these extensions lies in the requirement whether or not t_a needs to be proved or can be assumed. For examples, the approaches in [20,23,25] seem to require that the formulae related to the extended atoms are provable; on the other hand, the approaches in [10,17] seem to allow they to be assumed.

It is easy to recognize that the approach developed in the previous section requires provability of the conclusions. As it turns out, it can be easily adapted to any of the proposed extensions of logic programs. Instead of generalizing the approach for each extension separately, we next propose a generalization of the AB-semantics which can be instantiated to each of the above discussed extensions of logic programs. Given a signature $\Sigma = (\mathcal{C}, \mathcal{P}, \mathcal{F})$. An expression of the form $\gamma[\alpha]$ where γ is a 0-ary predicate symbol that does not occur in the language L_Σ and $\alpha \in L_\Sigma$ is called a *FOL-representable atom* w.r.t. Σ. Intuitively, the formula α is a definition of γ in the language over Σ. For instance, $(\mathrm{SUM}(\{X : p(X)\}) \geq 1)[t_\lambda]$ is a FOL-representable atom over the language of Π_1.

Definition 6. Let $\Sigma = (\mathcal{C}, \mathcal{P}, \mathcal{F})$ be a signature and Γ be a set of FOL-representable atoms w.r.t. Σ. A *program with FOL-representable atoms* over (Σ, Γ) is a set of rules of the form $\psi \leftarrow \phi$ where $\psi \in L_\Sigma$ and ϕ is a formula in the language over the signature $\Sigma' = (\mathcal{C}, \mathcal{P} \cup \{\gamma \mid \gamma \in \Gamma\}, \mathcal{F})$.

We will now extend the notion of AB-semantics to programs with FOL-representable atoms.

Definition 7. Let Π be a program with FOL-representable atoms over (Σ, Γ) and Π' be Π extended with the set of rules $\{\gamma \leftarrow \alpha \mid \gamma[\alpha] \in \Gamma\} \cup \{\neg\gamma \leftarrow \neg\alpha \mid \gamma[\alpha] \in \Gamma\}$. Let $\Lambda = \{\lambda \mid \lambda[\alpha] \in \Gamma\}$. We define (*i*) an interpretation I of Π is an AB-answer set of Π iff there exists some $\Lambda_p \subseteq \Lambda$ such that $I \cup \Lambda_p$ is an AB-answer set of Π'; and (*ii*) a partial interpretation (P, Q) of Π is the AB-well-founded model of Π iff there exists some $\Lambda_p, \Lambda_n \subseteq \Lambda$ such that $\Lambda_p \cap \Lambda_n = \emptyset$ and $(P \cup \Lambda_p, Q \cup \Lambda_n)$ is the AB-well-founded model of Π'.

Intuitively, the semantics of programs with FOL-representable atoms is defined by transforming them to programs with FOL-formulae without extended features. By adding $\gamma \leftarrow \alpha$ and $\neg\gamma \leftarrow \neg\alpha$ to the original program, we essentially add rules to the construction of proof trees which allow for the derivation of FOL-representable atoms. The former (latter) rule allows for the conclusion of γ ($\neg\gamma$). The usefulness of this definition is illustrated in the next section.

5   Related Work and Discussion

The paper relates to works that extend the answer set semantics to more generalized logic programs and that study semantics of logic programs using argumentation. The main distinctions between our approach and previous approaches to defining semantics of logic programs using argumentation such as [5,9,13,22] lie in our focus on generalized logic programs and the explicit use of the notion of a proof tree. Due to the space limitation, we will focus our discussion on the properties of the AB-semantics. Specifically, we show that AB-answer set semantics (resp. AB-well-founded model) is equivalent to well-justified answer set semantics for programs with FOL-formula [23] (resp. well-founded model for programs with abstract constraint atoms [27]). We note that these results, together with the results in [23,27], show that the argumentation-based answer set (Definition 4) is equivalent to a number of previously defined semantics for various extensions of logic programs such as aggregates, description logics, or abstract constraint atoms.

5.1   Well-Justified Answer Sets for Logic Programs with FOL-formulae

The relationship between well-justified answer sets and AB-answer sets is proved in the next theorem.

Theorem 2. *Let Π be a program with FOL formulae. I is a well-justified answer set of Π iff I is an argumentation-based answer set of Π.*

Proof. Let I be a well-justified answer set of Π. Let S be the set of trees in AF_Π such that for every $T \in S$, $Support(T) \subseteq \{not\ b \mid b \notin I\}$. Because I is an answer set of Π, we can show that S is conflict free. Furthermore, for every $a \in I$, there exists a tree $T \in S$ such that $Concl(T) = a$. This also implies that S attacks every T' such that $Support(T') \setminus \{not\ b \mid b \notin I\} \neq \emptyset$, i.e., S attacks every T' does not belonging to it. Hence, S is a stable extension of AF_Π. This implies that I is an argumentation-based answer set of Π.

Let I be an argumentation-based answer set of Π and S be the stable extension of AF_Π. For a tree T and a rule $r \in ground(\Pi)$, r is applicable in T if r is used in the construction of T (in the second condition of Item 2, Definition 1). It is easy to see that $f\Pi^I$ is the set of rules in $ground(\Pi)$ applicable in S. By induction over the levels of trees in the kernel of S and Proposition 4, we can show that $lfp(T_{f\Pi^I}(\emptyset, \neg I^-)) \cup \neg I^- \models a$ for every $a \in I$. It means that I is a well-justified answer set of Π.   □

5.2 Well-Founded Semantics for Programs with Abstract Constraint Atoms

Well-Founded Semantics for programs with abstract constraint atoms [27] is
defined for programs consisting of rules of the form

$$a \leftarrow A_1, \ldots, A_k, \neg A_{k+1}, \ldots, \neg A_m$$

where a is an atom and A_i's are abstract constraint atoms, each is of the form
(D, C), D is a set of atoms and $C \subseteq 2^D$. Let S, J be two sets of atoms such
that $S \cap J = \emptyset$. The S-prefixed power set $S \uplus J$ is $\{S' \mid S \subseteq S' \subseteq S \cup J\}$. $S \uplus J$
is maximal in an abstract constraint atom $A = (D, C)$ if $S \uplus J \subseteq C$ and there
exists no $S' \uplus J' \subseteq C$ such that $S \uplus J \subset S' \uplus J'$. It has been shown that each
$A = (D, C)$ can be represented by an $A' = (D, C^*)$ such that C^* is a set of
maximal prefixed power sets in A.

Let $X = (P, Q)$ be a partial interpretation of Π and $A = (D, C^*)$ be an
abstract constraint atom in abstract representation. X satisfies A, written $X \models
A$, if for some $S \uplus J \in C^*$, $S \subseteq P$ and $D \setminus (S \cup J) \subseteq Q$. X falsifies A, written
$X \Vdash A$, if for every $S \uplus J \in C^*$, $S \cap Q \neq \emptyset$ or $D \setminus (S \cup J) \cap Q \neq \emptyset$. X
satisfies (resp. falsifies) $\neg A$ if X falsifies (resp. satisfies) A. X satisfies (resp.
falsifies) a set Z if it satisfies (resp. falsifies) every member of Z. A set of atoms
U is an unfounded set of Π with respect to X iff, for any $a \in U$ and any
$r \in ground(P)$ with $head(r) = a$, either (i) for some $\neg A \in body(r)$, $X \Vdash \neg A$; or
(ii) for some $A = (D, C^*) \in body(r)$, for any $S \uplus J \in C^*$, either $U \cap S \neq \emptyset$ or
$X \Vdash S \cup \{\neg z \mid z \in (D \setminus (S \cup J))\}$. For a program Π, we define

$$T_\Pi(X) = \{head(r) \mid r \in \Pi, X \text{ satisfies } body(r)\}$$
$$U_\Pi(X) = \text{the greatest unfounded set of } \Pi \text{ w.r.t. } X$$
$$W_\Pi(X) = (T_\Pi(X), H_\Pi \setminus U_\Pi(X))$$

$lfp(W_\Pi)$ is defined as the well-founded model of Π.

A program with abstract constraint atoms Π can be viewed as a program with
FOL-representable atoms Π^* where each abstract constraint atom $A = (D, C^*)$
is replaced by λ_A whose FOL-representation is $\lambda_A[\alpha(D, C^*)]$ and $\alpha(D, C^*) =
\bigvee_{S \uplus J \in C}(\bigwedge_{p \in S} p \wedge \bigwedge_{n \in D \setminus (S \cup J)} \neg n)$. Let $\Lambda(\Pi) = \{\lambda_{A[\alpha(D, C^*)]} \mid A = (D, C^*) \text{ is}$
an abstract constraint atom in $\Pi\}$. The relationship between the well-founded
model of Π and the AB-well-founded model of Π^* is proved in the next theorem.

Theorem 3. *For a program with abstract constraint atoms Π, (P, Q) is its well-
founded model iff there exists a pair (A_p, A_n) such that $A_p, A_n \subseteq \Lambda(\Pi)$, $A_p \cap
A_n = \emptyset$, and $(P \cup A_p, Q \cup A_n)$ is the AB-well-founded model of Π^*. In addition,
$(P, Q) \models \alpha(D, C^*)$ for every $\lambda_{A[\alpha(D, C^*)]} \in A_p$ and $(P, Q) \models \neg \alpha(D, C^*)$ for every
$\lambda_{A[\alpha(D, C^*)]} \in A_n$.*

Proof. (Sketch) Let AF_{Π^*} be the argumentation framework induced by the
program Π^*. Let $G^i = \{T \mid T \in lfp(F_{AF_{\Pi^*}}), l(T) = i\}$. We can prove by
induction over i that (i) if $a \in H_\Pi$ then $a \in W_\Pi^i(\emptyset)$ iff there exists a tree

$T_a \in G^i$ such that $Concl(T_a) = a$; (ii) for every $A = (D, C^*)$, $W_{\Pi}^i(\emptyset) \models A$ iff there exists a tree $T_{\lambda_{A[\alpha(D,C^*)]}} \in G^i$ such that $Concl(T_{\lambda_{A[\alpha(D,C^*)]}}) = \lambda_A$; and (iii) for every $A = (D, C^*)$, $W_{\Pi}^i(\emptyset) \models \neg A$ iff there exists a tree $T_{\neg \lambda_{A[\alpha(D,C^*)]}} \in G^i$ such that $Concl(T_{\lambda_{A[\alpha(D,C^*)]}}) = \neg \lambda_A$. This proves the theorem.   □

6   Conclusions

In this paper, we defined different argumentation-based semantics for programs with FOL-formulae. The key idea behinds our approach lies in the notion of a proof tree. We proved that the proposed semantics captured the well-justified semantics for programs with FOL-formulae defined in [23] and the well-founded semantics for programs with abstract constraint atoms defined in [27]. To the best of our knowledge, this is the first proposal of argumentation-based semantics for generalized programs that exhibits this equivalence. The proposed framework also sheds new light on the answer set semantics for various extensions of logic programs in the literature by showing that they can be viewed as programs with FOL-formulae extended with FOL-representable atoms, indirectly providing a means for comparison among approaches to defining semantics of logic programs with extensions. Finally, we note that our focuses in this paper is on the two most well-known semantics of logic programs as well as the most recently introduced semantics. Due to the results in [9,22], we expect that similar results for 3-valued stable models and complete extensions can be established. In addition, the results established in Theorems 2–3 and the results in [23,27] show that equivalence between AB-defined semantics and other approaches in the literature such as [20,24] can also be established. This will be reported in the future extended version of the paper.

Finally, we note that the paper focuses on the development of argumentation-based semantics for logic programs with FOL-formulae. It does not address question relating to the computation of the semantics. For example, how to construct arguments (or proof-trees) of a program?; is the set of arguments always infinite?; etc. We leave this for the future work.

References

1. Balduccini, M., Gelfond, M., Watson, R., Nogueira, M.: The USA-Advisor: a case study in answer set planning. In: Eiter, T., Faber, W., Truszczyński, M. (eds.) LPNMR 2001. LNCS (LNAI), vol. 2173, pp. 439–442. Springer, Heidelberg (2001)
2. Baral, C.: Knowledge Representation, Reasoning, and Declarative Problem Solving with Answer Sets. Cambridge University Press, Cambridge (2003)
3. Baral, C., Provetti, A., Son, T.C. (eds.): Theory and Practice of Logic Programming Special Issue on Answer Set Programming, vol. 3. Cambridge Univeristy Press, Cambridge (2003)
4. Bartholomew, M., Lee, J., Meng, Y.: First-order extension of the FLP stable model semantics via modified circumscription. In: IJCAI 2011, pp. 724–730. IJCAI/AAAI (2011)

5. Bondarenko, A., Dung, P.M., Kowalski, R.A., Toni, F.: An abstract, argumentation-theoretic approach to default reasoning. Artif. Intell. **93**, 63–101 (1997)
6. Olinham, B., Pontelli, E., Son, T.C., Wright, B.: Cdaostore: a phylogenetic repository using logic programming and web services. In: Gallagher, J.P., Gelfond, M. (eds.) Technical Communications, ICLp 2011, pp. 200–210 (2011)
7. Cormen, T., Leiserson, C., Rivest, R., Stein, C.: Introduction to Algorithms, 2nd edn. MIT Press, Cambridge (2001)
8. Dung, P.M.: An argumentation-theoretic foundations for logic programming. J. Log. Program. **22**(2), 151–171 (1995)
9. Dung, P.M.: On the acceptability of arguments and its fundamental role in non-monotonic reasoning, logic programming and n-person games. Artif. Intell. **77**, 321–357 (1995)
10. Faber, W., Leone, N., Pfeifer, G.: Recursive aggregates in disjunctive logic programs: semantics and complexity. In: Alferes, J.J., Leite, J. (eds.) JELIA 2004. LNCS (LNAI), vol. 3229, pp. 200–212. Springer, Heidelberg (2004)
11. Gebser, M., Guziolowski, C., Ivanchev, M., Schaub, T., Siegel, A., Thiele, S., Veber, P.: Repair and prediction (under inconsistency) in large biological networks with answer set programming. In: KR 2010, pp. 497–507. AAAI Press (2010)
12. Gelfond, M., Lifschitz, V.: The stable model semantics for logic programming. In: LPICS, pp. 1070–1080 (1988)
13. Kakas, A., Mancarella, P.: Generalized stable models: a semantics for abduction. In: Proceedings of ECAI-90, pp. 385–391 (1990)
14. Lifschitz, V.: Answer set programming and plan generation. Artif. Intell. **138**(1–2), 39–54 (2002)
15. Lloyd, J.: Foundations of Logic Programming. Springer, Berlin (1987). Second, extended edition
16. Marek, V., Truszczyński, M.: Stable models and an alternative logic programming paradigm. In: The Logic Programming Paradigm: A 25-Year Perspective, pp. 375–398 (1999)
17. Marek, V.W., Niemelä, I., Truszczynski, M.: Logic programs with monotone abstract constraint atoms. TPLP **8**(2), 167–199 (2008)
18. Niemelä, I.: Logic programming with stable model semantics as a constraint programming paradigm. Ann. Math. Artif. Intell. **25**(3,4), 241–273 (1999)
19. Niemelä, I., Simons, P., Soininen, T.: Stable model semantics for weight constraint rules. In: LPNMR, pp. 315–332 (1999)
20. Pelov, N., Denecker, M., Bruynooghe, M.: Partial stable models for logic programs with aggregates. In: Lifschitz, V., Niemelä, I. (eds.) LPNMR 2004. LNCS (LNAI), vol. 2923, pp. 207–219. Springer, Heidelberg (2003)
21. Przymusinski, T.: Stable semantics for disjunctive programs. New Gener. Comput. **9**(3,4), 401–425 (1991)
22. Schulz, C., Toni, F.: Logic programming in assumption-based argumentation revisited - semantics and graphical representation. In: AAAI 2015, pp. 1569–1575. AAAI Press (2015)
23. Shen, Y., Wang, K., Eiter, T., Fink, M., Redl, C., Krennwallner, T., Deng, J.: FLP answer set semantics without circular justifications for general logic programs. Artif. Intell. **213**, 1–41 (2014)
24. Son, T.C., Pontelli, E.: A constructive semantic characterization of aggregates in answer set programming. Theory Pract. Logic Program. **7**(03), 355–375 (2007)
25. Son, T.C., Pontelli, E., Tu, P.H.: Answer sets for logic programs with arbitrary abstract constraint atoms. In: AAAI (2006)

26. Van Gelder, A., Ross, K., Schlipf, J.: The well-founded semantics for general logic programs. J. ACM **38**(3), 620–650 (1991)
27. Wang, Y., Lin, F., Zhang, M., You, J.: A well-founded semantics for basic logic programs with arbitrary abstract constraint atoms. In: AAAI (2012)

Resistance to Corruption of General Strategic Argumentation

School of Engineering and Information Technology, University of New South Wales,
Canberra, ACT 2600, Australia
michael.maher@unsw.edu.au

Abstract. [16,18] introduced a model of corruption within strategic
argumentation, and showed that some forms of strategic argumentation
are resistant to two forms of corruption: collusion and espionage. Such
a model provides a (limited) basis on which to trust agents acting on
our behalf. However, that work only addressed the grounded and stable
argumentation semantics. Here we extend this work to several other well-
motivated semantics. We must consider a greater number of strategic
aims that players may have, as well as the greater variety of semantics.
We establish the complexity of several computational problems related
to corruption in strategic argumentation, for the aims and semantics we
study. From these results we identify that strategic argumentation under
the aims and semantics we study is resistant to espionage. Resistance
to collusion varies according to the player's aim and the argumentation
semantics, and we present a complete picture for the aims and semantics
we address.

1 Introduction

When agents are acting on our behalf – whether they are human or software –
there is a problem of trust: are these agents acting in our best interests? [16,18]
addressed this problem when the agents engage in strategic argumentation, similar to legal disputation or negotiation, by adapting ideas of [3] on voting resistance to manipulation. That work formulated a notion of resistance to corruption, where corruption may be collusion of the two nominally opposed agents,
or espionage by one agent by gaining illicit knowledge of her opponent's arsenal
of arguments.

However, [18] addressed only two semantics for argumentation: the grounded
and stable semantics. While these are sensible semantics, they each have flaws:
the grounded semantics employs a drastic notion of scepticism, while the stable
semantics is empty for some argumentation frameworks. Many semantics have
been proposed that avoid these problems (see [2]).

Furthermore, the nature of the grounded and stable semantics is such that
some variations in the (nominal) strategic aims of an agent collapse for these
semantics. Consequently, [18] only addresses a limited range of strategic aims.
This narrowness of the semantics and strategic aims addressed makes it difficult

© Springer International Publishing Switzerland 2016
M. Baldoni et al. (Eds.): PRIMA 2016, LNAI 9862, pp. 61–75, 2016.
DOI: 10.1007/978-3-319-44832-9_4

to see how resistance to corruption extends to other semantics and aims. In this paper we extend the analysis to a broader range of semantics and strategic aims. In the process we identify and correct an error in [18].

[18] analyses resistance to corruption via three computational problems: the Desired Outcome problem, which must be solved at each move of the strategic argumentation game; the Winning Sequence problem, which must be solved to exploit collusion among agents; and the Winning Strategy problem, which must be solved to exploit illicit knowledge of the opponent's arguments. In addressing a wider range of both semantics and aims, we find it convenient to introduce a further problem, the Aim Verification problem, to verify that an aim is achieved in a given argumentation framework.

Resistance to corruption is, essentially, the idea that if the computational complexity of exploiting corruption is greater than the complexity of simply playing the strategic argumentation game, then that is a disincentive to corruption. Thus, we will need to establish the complexity of the Desired Outcome problem (which is key to the complexity of playing the game) and the Winning Sequence and Winning Strategy problems, for each of the semantics we address. Like [3], the complexity comparison relies on the commonly-believed assumption that the polynomial complexity hierarchy does not collapse.

In the next section we present background information on abstract argumentation and complexity theory. Following that, we formally define strategic argumentation and the variety of desired outcomes that a player might wish to achieve. Following sections address, respectively, the Aim Verification, Desired Outcome, Winning Sequence, and Winning Strategy problems. Finally, building on this work, we establish under which aims and argumentation semantics strategic argumentation is resistant to corruption.

The proofs of the results in this paper are substantial, and there is no room to present them here. However, the surrounding text of the main results provides some discussion of how they are proved.

2   Background

2.1   Abstract Argumentation

This work is based on abstract argumentation in the sense of [7], which addresses the evaluation of a static set of arguments. An *argumentation framework* $\mathcal{A} = (S, \gg)$ consists of a finite set of arguments S and a binary relation $\gg$ over S, called the attack relation. If $(a, b) \in \gg$ we write $a \gg b$ and say that a attacks b. The semantics of an argumentation framework is given in terms of *extensions*, which are subsets of S.

Given an argumentation framework, an argument a is said to be *accepted* in an extension E if $a \in E$, and said to be *rejected* in E if some $b \in E$ attacks a. The set of rejected arguments in E is denoted by E^-. An argument that is neither accepted nor rejected in E is said to be *undecided* in E. An extension E is *conflict-free* if the restriction of $\gg$ to E is empty. An argument a is *defended* by E if every argument that attacks a is attacked by some argument in E.

An extension E of $\mathcal{A}$ is *stable* if it is conflict-free and for every argument $a \in S \backslash E$ there is an argument in E that attacks a. An extension E of $\mathcal{A}$ is *complete* if it is conflict-free and, $a \in E$ iff a is defended by E.

The set of complete extensions forms a lower semi-lattice under the containment ordering, and many semantics can be defined directly in terms of this semi-lattice. The least complete extension under the containment ordering exists and is called the *grounded* extension. The *preferred* extensions are the maximal complete extensions under the containment ordering. The *semi-stable* extensions are the complete extensions that are maximal under the containment ordering of $E \cup E^-$. The *eager* extension is the maximal complete extension contained in all semi-stable extensions. These are not necessarily the original definitions of these extensions, but they are equivalent definitions.

A semantics is defined to be a set of extensions: the grounded semantics consists only of the grounded extension, the complete semantics is the set of complete extensions, the stable semantics is the set of stable extensions, etc. Each semantics expresses a criterion for what arguments can coherently be accepted together, given an argumentation framework. Each extension in the semantics represents a "reasonable" adjudication, according to that criterion, of the arguments in the argumentation framework.

We identify some classes of semantics. A semantics is *unitary* if every argumentation framework has a single extension under the semantics. The grounded, ideal and eager semantics are unitary.

The semantics in this paper are all sets of complete extensions, but we need to identify a more specific class of semantics. Any semantics σ in this class is determined solely by the semi-lattice of complete extensions. That is, there is a function based only on the order-theoretic structure of the semi-lattice that defines the set of σ-extensions.

Definition 1. *We say a semantics σ is* completist *if all σ-extensions are complete. A semantics σ is* strongly *completist if it is completist and the set of σ-extensions is determined by the semi-lattice structure of the complete extensions.*

Among the completist semantics are the grounded, preferred, stable, semi-stable, ideal, eager, and complete semantics. The grounded semantics is also strongly completist because it is the least complete extension under the containment ordering. Similarly, the preferred, semi-stable, ideal, eager, and complete semantics are strongly completist, because they can be defined structurally, as is done above. On the other hand, the stable semantics is not strongly completist. Stable extensions are defined by a property of the individual extension, rather than by a structural property within the semi-lattice of complete extensions, and it turns out there is no equivalent structural definition.

Proposition 1. *The stable semantics is completist, but not strongly completist.*

2.2 Complexity

We can view each complexity class of interest as a set of decision problems. We assume the reader has knowledge of the polynomial complexity hierarchy (see, for example, [15]) but there are some additional complexity classes both within and beyond the hierarchy that we need. D^p (D^p_2) is the class of problems that can be expressed as the conjunction of a problem in NP and a problem in coNP (respectively Σ^p_2 and Π^p_2). We use PTIME to refer to the class of problems solvable in polynomial time. The following describes the containment relation among complexity classes between the first and second levels of the polynomial hierarchy.

$$PTIME \subseteq NP, coNP \subseteq D^p \subseteq \Delta^p_2 \subseteq \Sigma^p_2, \Pi^p_2$$

PSPACE is the class of decision problems solvable in polynomial space. It contains the entire polynomial hierarchy PH.

As usual, the notation $\mathcal{C}^{\mathcal{D}}$, where $\mathcal{C}$ and $\mathcal{D}$ are complexity classes, refers to the class of problems that can be decided by an algorithm of complexity $\mathcal{C}$ with calls to a $\mathcal{D}$ oracle.

There are several prominent decision problems in abstract argumentation. For any semantics σ:

- The *Verification problem* asks, given an argumentation framework $\mathcal{A}$ and a set of arguments S, is S a σ-extension?
- The *Credulous Acceptance problem* asks, given $\mathcal{A}$ and an argument a, is there a σ-extension containing a?
- The *Sceptical Acceptance problem* asks, given $\mathcal{A}$ and an argument a, do all σ-extensions contain a?
- The *Non-emptiness problem* asks, is there a σ-extension of $\mathcal{A}$ that is non-empty?

Table 1 summarizes complexity results for these problems under a variety of completist semantics, drawn from [6–10,12]. For a complexity class $\mathcal{C}$, $\mathcal{C}$-c denotes $\mathcal{C}$-completeness.

Table 1. Complexity of several argumentation reasoning problems under selected completist semantics

	Credulous acceptance	Sceptical acceptance	Verification	Non-emptiness
Grounded	in PTIME	in PTIME	in PTIME	in PTIME
Stable	NP-c	coNP-c	in PTIME	NP-c
Complete	NP-c	in PTIME	in PTIME	NP-c
Preferred	NP-c	Π^p_2-c	coNP-c	NP-c
Semi-stable	Σ^p_2-c	Π^p_2-c	coNP-c	NP-c
Eager	Π^p_2-c	Π^p_2-c	D^p_2-c	Π^p_2-c

The complexities in Table 1 are all within the polynomial hierarchy. To address counting aims in strategic argumentation we need to consider the complexity class PP and related classes. Roughly, PP is the class of decision problems that have more accepting paths than rejecting paths. A complete problem for PP is to decide whether a given Boolean formula is satisfied by more than half of the assignments to its variables. NP^{PP} lies between the polynomial hierarchy and PSPACE, that is, $PH \subseteq NP^{PP} \subseteq PSPACE$.

The *counting polynomial-time hierarchy* [23] is an extension of the polynomial hierarchy that also involves the complexity class PP. Complete problems for classes in the counting polynomial hierarchy are satisfiability problems for a class of quantified Boolean formulas involving the quantifiers ∃ (existential), ∀ (universal), and C (counting) [22,23]. The formula $CX\,\psi$, where X is a set of Boolean variables and ψ is a formula with free variables X, can be interpreted as: "for more than half of the assignments to X, ψ evaluates to True". Thus these complete problems are an extension of the class of QBF satisfiability problems.

Toda [21] proved a powerful theorem relating PP and the conventional polynomial hierarchy PH. He showed $PP^{PH} \subseteq PTIME^{PP}$, which suggests that PP is more powerful as an oracle than as a base of computation. The next lemma is a consequence of Toda's theorem. It shows that some parts of the counting polynomial hierarchy collapse. We will need it in determining the complexity of the Desired Outcome problem for some aims under the preferred and semi-stable semantics.

Lemma 1. *Let C be a complexity class contained in the polynomial hierarchy PH (i.e. $C \subseteq PH$). Then $PTIME^{PP^C} = PTIME^{PP}$ and $NP^{PP^C} = NP^{PP}$. More generally, for any complexity class $\mathcal{D}$ in the polynomial hierarchy $\mathcal{D}^{PP^C} = \mathcal{D}^{PP}$.*

3 Strategic Argumentation

Strategic argumentation provides a simple model of dynamic argumentation. Originally [14] it was formulated for a concrete argumentation system based in a defeasible logic, but we will use the model of [18] which is defined in terms of abstract argumentation. In strategic abstract argumentation, players take turns to add arguments to an argumentation framework. At each turn, the player adds arguments so that the argumentation framework is in a desired state. We refer to such states interchangeably as *desired outcomes* or *strategic aims* of the player. A player loses the strategic argumentation game when she is unable to achieve her desired outcome. In general, both players can win if the argumentation reaches a state that is desired by both players, but in this paper we consider an adversarial setting where the players' aims are mutually exclusive.

Strategic abstract argumentation is formalized as follows [18]. We assume there are two players, a proponent P and her opponent O. A *split argumentation framework* $(\mathcal{A}_{Com}, \mathcal{A}_P, \mathcal{A}_O, \gg)$ consists of three sets of arguments: $\mathcal{A}_{Com}$ the arguments that are common knowledge to P and O; $\mathcal{A}_P$ the arguments available to P, and $\mathcal{A}_O$ the arguments available to O; and an attack relation $\gg$ over

$\mathcal{A}_{Com} \cup \mathcal{A}_P \cup \mathcal{A}_O$. $\mathcal{A}_P$ is assumed to be unknown to O, and $\mathcal{A}_O$ is unknown to P. Each player is aware of $\gg$ restricted to the arguments they know. We assume that P's desired outcome is that a distinguished argument a is accepted, in some sense, while O's aim is to prevent this. a is said to be the *focal* argument. Starting with P, the players take turns in adding sets of arguments to $\mathcal{A}_{Com}$ from their available arguments, ensuring that their desired outcome is a consequence of the resulting argumentation framework[1]. As play continues, the set of arguments that are common knowledge $\mathcal{A}_{Com}$ becomes larger. When a player is unable to achieve her aim when it is her turn to play, she loses.

It might seem that a better choice would distinguish a set S of arguments since, in concrete argumentation, there may be several arguments for the same proposition. However we now show that, by a slight expansion of the argumentation framework, a single argument can represent a set of arguments. (The construction involves additional arguments a and a', where a' attacks a, and all arguments in the set attack a'.) Thus there is no loss of generality in having a single focal argument.

Proposition 2. *Let $\mathcal{A} = (A, \gg)$ be an argumentation framework, and let $S \subseteq A$ be a set of arguments, any one of which is sufficient to establish a desired proposition. Then there is an expansion $\mathcal{A}'$ of $\mathcal{A}$ including a new argument a such that, in any strongly completist semantics σ,*

1. *E is a σ-extension of $\mathcal{A}$ iff $E = E' \cap A$ and E' is a σ-extension of $\mathcal{A}'$*
2. *for every σ-extension E' of $\mathcal{A}'$, a is accepted in E' iff for some $s \in S$, s is accepted in $E = E' \cap A$*
3. *for every σ-extension E' of $\mathcal{A}'$, a is rejected in E' iff for every $s \in S$, s is rejected in $E = E' \cap A$*

Furthermore, these statements hold true for the stable semantics.

[18] addresses only the grounded semantics, which is unitary, and the stable semantics, in which no argument is undecided. When the semantics σ admits multiple extensions and admits extensions where the status of some arguments is undecided, players have a greater range of strategic aims related to the distinguished argument a and the σ-extensions. The aims considered in this paper are:

1. **Existential:** a is accepted in at least one σ-extension
2. **Universal:** a is accepted in all σ-extensions
3. **Unrejected:** a is not rejected in any σ-extension
4. **Uncontested:** a is accepted in at least one σ-extension and is not rejected in any σ-extension
5. **Plurality:** a is accepted in more σ-extensions than it is rejected
6. **Majority:** a is accepted in more σ-extensions than it is not accepted
7. **Supermajority:** a is accepted in at least twice as many σ-extensions than it is not accepted

---

[1] Each player's move is a normal expansion [4].

Of these aims, the middle three (unrejected, uncontested, and plurality) did not appear in [18]. Some of these aims seem related to proof standards in Carneades [13], although those proof standards are designed for a concrete argumentation language. Each of the first four of these aims corresponds to a disjunction of justification statuses in [24], while the remaining three will be called *counting aims*.

In addition to these aims, a player may wish to "spoil" or prevent such aims from being achieved. Such aims are the negation of the above aims. For example, the negation of the uncontested aim aims to have a not accepted in any extension or have a rejected in some extension. Recall that, in this paper, player O's aim is to prevent P's desired outcome; thus O's aim is the negation of P's aim.

A player with a negative attitude towards a may have a dual aim to the above aims. By the *dual* of an aim we mean an aim that exchanges the role of acceptance and rejection in the definition of the aim. Thus, for example, the dual of the uncontested aim is the aim to have a rejected in at least one extension and not accepted in any extension. Duality is useful in simplifying proofs about the complexity of the Aim Verification problem.

Some of the dual aims coincide with the negation of other aims. For example, the dual of the unrejected aim is the same as the negation of the existential aim. Thus there is an algebraic structure to the aims. Additional aims – such as universal rejection, which is the dual of the universal aim – are needed to fill out the algebra. We will restrict attention to the above listed aims, which we think are the most natural.

In general, all these aims are distinct. However, for a unitary semantics σ (such as the grounded semantics) this variety of aims collapses: all the above aims – except the unrejected aim – collapse into one, that a is accepted in the σ-extension. For the stable semantics, assuming the semantics is not empty, the universal, unrejected, and uncontested aims are identical, as are plurality and majority.

In strategic argumentation, an argument played by P (say) may attack other arguments in $\mathcal{A}_P$, which might otherwise have been used later to attack arguments played by O. Thus the game truly is strategic in nature[2]. Furthermore, it is preferable, in general, to play as few arguments as possible, to retain as much strategic advantage as possible from the confidentiality of the arguments available. However, the strategic argumentation model discussed here omits more refined aspects of play, such as opponent modelling, to focus on the fundamental issues. Nevertheless, our complexity results give a lower bound on the complexity of problems incorporating opponent modelling, for example.

We now turn to the computational problems that arise in strategic argumentation, both those that arise from normal play, and those that arise from exploiting corrupt behaviour. For convenience, we formulate these problems as decision problems.

---

[2] For a similar argumentation game, results of [20] suggest games are strategy-proof only under very constraining conditions.

4   Aim Verification

The problem of verifying that an aim is satisfied by some state of strategic argumentation is a fundamental part of each move in a game, and of the exploitation of corrupt behaviour. The problem becomes more complex as we deal with a greater range of semantics and aims. For this reason, we introduce it as a separate computational problem.

The Aim Verification Problem

> **Instance.** An argumentation framework $(\mathcal{A}_{Com}, \gg)$, an argumentation semantics, and an aim.
> **Question.** Is the aim satisfied under the given semantics by the given argumentation framework?

The structure provided by the negation and dual operations is reflected in the complexity of aim verification, which greatly simplifies establishing the complexity of aim verification for our range of aims.

Proposition 3. *Let x be an aim concerning an argument a. Let $\bar{x}$ be x's negation, and $x^\dagger$ be x's dual.*

- *The complexity of the Aim Verification problem for $\bar{x}$ is the complement of the complexity of the Aim Verification problem for x.*
- *Under any completist semantics, the Aim Verification problem for $x^\dagger$ and the Aim Verification problem for x, have the same complexity wrt membership and hardness for complexity classes in the polynomial counting hierarchy.*

Aim verification for the existential (respectively, universal) aim is credulous (respectively, sceptical) acceptance. Verification of the unrejected aim is the complement of the existential rejection aim which, as we have seen (Proposition 3) has the same complexity as the existential aim (that is, credulous acceptance). Thus the complexity of the unrejected aim is the complement of the complexity of the existential aim. The uncontested aim is the conjunction of the existential aim and the unrejected aim. Using these facts, and existing work on complexity of abstract argumentation problems as presented in Table 1, identification of the complexity of the Aim Verification problem is straightforward for many aims. However, the plurality, majority and supermajority aims – although themselves closely related – require significantly more work.

Theorem 1. *The complexity of Aim Verification for P is as stated in Table 2.*

Similar results were obtained by [11] for essentially the uncontested aim (called weak acceptance there).

In this paper we assume that the aim of O is to prevent P from achieving her aim. Thus the aim of O is the negation of the aim of P and, by Proposition 3, the complexity of aim verification for O is the complement of the complexity of aim verification for P. For example, using Table 2, aim verification for O under the preferred semantics when P has the existential aim is coNP-complete.

Table 2. Complexity of aim verification problem for selected strategic aims and semantics

	Grounded	Stable	Complete	Preferred	Semi-stable	Eager
Existential	in PTIME	NP-c	NP-c	NP-c	Σ_2^p-c	Π_2^p-c
Universal	in PTIME	coNP-c	in PTIME	$\Pi_?^p$-c	Π_2^p-c	Π_2^p-c
Unrejected	in PTIME	coNP-c	coNP-c	coNP-c	Π_2^p-c	Σ_2^p-c
Uncontested	in PTIME	coNP-c	D^p-c	D^p-c	D_2^p-c	Π_2^p-c
Plurality	in PTIME	PP-c	PP-c	in PP^{NP}	in PP^{NP}	Π_2^p-c
Majority	in PTIME	PP-c	PP-c	in PP^{NP}	in PP^{NP}	Π_2^p-c
Supermajority	in PTIME	PP-c	PP-c	in PP^{NP}	in PP^{NP}	Π_2^p-c

5 Desired Outcome

The Desired Outcome problem [18] is the problem that a player must solve at each step of a strategic abstract argumentation game. It requires identifying a move in the strategic argumentation game that would achieve the player's desired outcome.

The Desired Outcome Problem for P

Instance. A split argumentation framework $(\mathcal{A}_{Com}, \mathcal{A}_P, \mathcal{A}_O, \gg)$ and a desired outcome for P.
Question. Is there a set $I \subseteq \mathcal{A}_P$ such that P's desired outcome is achieved in the argumentation framework $(\mathcal{A}_{Com} \cup I, \gg)$?

The complement of this problem is also of interest, because it addresses the question: has P lost?

The Desired Outcome Problem for O is similar.

There is a straightforward relationship between the Desired Outcome problem and the Aim Verification problem: solving the DO problem involves choosing a move and verifying that the aim is satisfied by the move. This leads to the following result.

Proposition 4. *Fix an argumentation semantics σ, and let $\mathcal{C}$ be a complexity class.*

1. *Suppose the Aim Verification problem for σ and a given aim is in $\mathcal{C}$. Then the Desired Outcome problem with the aim is in $NP^{\mathcal{C}}$.*
2. *Suppose the Aim Verification problem for σ and a given aim is in $NP^{\mathcal{C}}$. Then the Desired Outcome problem with the aim is also in $NP^{\mathcal{C}}$. Furthermore, if the Aim Verification problem is $NP^{\mathcal{C}}$-complete, then so is the Desired Outcome problem.*

The above proposition gives us upper bounds for each of the Desired Outcome problems, and matching lower bounds for some of them. The lower bounds

Table 3. Complexity of the desired outcome problem for P, for selected aims and semantics. (Results for grounded and stable semantics are essentially due to [18].)

	Grounded	Stable	Complete	Preferred	Semi-stable	Eager
Existential	NP-c	NP-c	NP-c	NP-c	Σ_2^p-c	Σ_3^p-c
Universal	NP-c	Σ_2^p-c	NP-c	Σ_3^p-c	Σ_3^p-c	Σ_3^p-c
Unrejected	NP-c	Σ_2^p-c	Σ_2^p-c	Σ_2^p-c	Σ_3^p-c	Σ_2^p-c
Uncontested	NP-c	Σ_2^p-c	Σ_2^p-c	Σ_2^p-c	Σ_3^p-c	Σ_3^p-c
Plurality	NP-c	NP^{PP}-c	NP^{PP}-c	NP^{PP}-c	NP^{PP}-c	Σ_3^p-c
Majority	NP-c	NP^{PP}-c	NP^{PP}-c	NP^{PP}-c	NP^{PP}-c	Σ_3^p-c
Supermajority	NP-c	NP^{PP}-c	NP^{PP}-c	NP^{PP}-c	NP^{PP}-c	Σ_3^p-c

for stable semantics provide matching lower bounds for some aims under the preferred semantics. The remaining matching lower bounds can be obtained by adapting the corresponding construction for the Aim Verification problem.

Theorem 2. *The complexity of the Desired Outcome problem for P is as stated in Table 3.*

Note that we do not have a characterization of the complexity of the Aim Verification problem for the counting aims under the preferred and semi-stable semantics but, nevertheless, have a characterization for the corresponding Desired Outcome problems. This comes about through the use of Lemma 1. By Proposition 4 and Theorem 1 these Desired Outcome problems lie in $NP^{PP^{NP}}$. By Lemma 1, this class is equal to NP^{PP}. Finally, the problem for the stable semantics provides a lower bound to both the preferred and semi-stable semantics.

6   Winning Sequence

In the case of collusion between P and O to ensure that (say) P wins, the players must arrange a sequence of moves that satisfy the rules of the game and leads to P winning. This sequence must give the appearance of being normal play. In particular, O cannot simply "give up" and fail to make a move – such behaviour would open her to charges of incompetence or corruption. Instead, she must exhaust her possible moves.

The Winning Sequence Problem for P

> **Instance.** A split argumentation framework $(\mathcal{A}_{Com}, \mathcal{A}_P, \mathcal{A}_O, \gg)$ and a desired outcome for P.
> **Question.** Is there a sequence of moves such that P wins?

Because the losing player must protect her reputation (and, perhaps, her licence to act as an agent), the players must collude on a sequence of moves

Table 4. Complexity of the winning sequence problem for P for selected aims and semantics. (Results for grounded and stable semantics are essentially due to [18], except for the existential aim under the stable semantics.)

	Grounded	Stable	Complete	Preferred	Semi-stable	Eager
Existential	Σ_2^p-c	Σ_3^p-c	Π_3^p-c	Σ_3^p-c	Σ_3^p-c	Σ_3^p-c
Universal	Σ_2^p-c	Σ_2^p-c	Σ_2^p-c	Σ_3^p-c	Σ_3^p-c	Σ_3^p-c
Unrejected	Σ_2^p-c	Σ_2^p-c	Σ_2^p-c	Σ_2^p-c	Σ_3^p-c	Σ_4^p-c
Uncontested	Σ_2^p-c	Σ_2^p-c	Σ_3^p-c	Σ_3^p-c	Σ_3^p-c	Σ_3^p-c
Plurality	Σ_2^p-c	$NP^{NP^{PP}}$-c	$NP^{NP^{PP}}$-c	$NP^{NP^{PP}}$-c	$NP^{NP^{PP}}$-c	Σ_3^p-c
Majority	Σ_2^p-c	$NP^{NP^{PP}}$-c	$NP^{NP^{PP}}$-c	$NP^{NP^{PP}}$-c	$NP^{NP^{PP}}$-c	Σ_3^p-c
Supermajority	Σ_2^p-c	$NP^{NP^{PP}}$-c	$NP^{NP^{PP}}$-c	$NP^{NP^{PP}}$-c	$NP^{NP^{PP}}$-c	Σ_3^p-c

that can be defended as normal play. This is a source of the complexity of the Winning Sequence problem.

The Winning Sequence problem can be solved by the following algorithm:

Nondeterministically choose $n < \min\{|\mathcal{A}_P|, |\mathcal{A}_O|\}$. Nondeterministically choose sets $S_1, T_1, S_2, \ldots, T_{n-1}, S_n$ where $S_i \subseteq \mathcal{A}_P$ and $T_i \subseteq \mathcal{A}_O$. Verify that after each S_i move P's aim is satisfied, and that after each T_i move O's aim is satisfied. Verify that the following fails: there is $T_n \subseteq \mathcal{A}_O$ such that in the resulting argumentation framework O's aim is achieved.

This is a polynomially bounded nondeterministic computation, using as oracles verification of the aims for P and O and the (complement of the) Desired Outcome problem for O. From the complexity of these oracles we obtain upper bounds on the complexity of the Winning Sequence problem. To obtain lower bounds it suffices to consider winning sequences of length 1.

Theorem 3. *The complexity of the Winning Sequence problem for P is as stated in Table 4.*

Note that the Winning Sequence problem for P with the existential aim under the stable semantics is Σ_3^p-complete, and not Σ_2^p-complete as stated in [18]. The problem is in Σ_3^p, using the above algorithm. Completeness is by reduction of satisfiability of $\exists\forall\exists$ QBF formulas. This error affects one of the conclusions of [18]: with the existential aim under the stable semantics strategic argumentation is, in fact, resistant to collusion.

7   Winning Strategy

In the case of espionage, one player, say P, knows her opponent's arguments $\mathcal{A}_O$ and desires a strategy that will ensure P wins, no matter what moves O makes. A *strategy* for P in a split argumentation framework $(\mathcal{A}_{Com}, \mathcal{A}_P, \mathcal{A}_O, \gg)$ is a function from a set of common arguments to the set of arguments to be played in the next move. A sequence of moves $S_1, T_1, S_2, T_2, \ldots$ resulting in common arguments $\mathcal{A}_{Com}^{P,1}, \mathcal{A}_{Com}^{O,1}, \mathcal{A}_{Com}^{P,2}, \mathcal{A}_{Com}^{O,2}, \ldots$ is *consistent with* a strategy s for P if, for every j, $S_{j+1} = s(\mathcal{A}_{Com}^{O,j}, \mathcal{A}_P)$. A strategy for P is *winning* if every valid sequence of moves consistent with the strategy is won by P.

The Winning Strategy Problem for P

> **Instance.** A split argumentation framework $(\mathcal{A}_{Com}, \mathcal{A}_P, \mathcal{A}_O, \gg)$ and a desired outcome for P.
> **Question.** Is there a winning strategy for P?

The following result shows that the Winning Strategy problem is PSPACE-complete for all completist semantics and all the aims discussed in this paper.

Theorem 4. *Consider any completist semantics for abstract argumentation, and any of the above aims for P.*
The Winning Strategy problem is PSPACE-complete.

It is straightforward that this problem is in PSPACE. To show it is PSPACE-hard we build on the proof of PSPACE-hardness for the grounded semantics [17]. All argumentation frameworks in the construction in that proof are well-founded in the sense of [7]. Consequently, these argumentation frameworks have a single complete extension [7]. Thus all completist semantics are identical on such argumentation frameworks. The result then follows.

8   Resistance to Corruption

The idea of *resistance* is due to [3] which formulated the notion that a voting system is resistant to manipulation if the complexity of determining the right actions to achieve a manipulation is NP-hard. Thus manipulation requires greater computational effort than simply voting (which is polynomial), under the commonly-believed assumption that PTIME $\neq$ NP. (If PTIME = NP then the polynomial hierarchy collapses.) [16,18] adapted this idea to strategic argumentation, formulating that it is resistant to collusion if the complexity of choosing

Table 5. Resistance to collusion to ensure P wins, for several aims and semantics.

	Grounded	Stable	Complete	Preferred	Semi-stable	Eager
Existential	Resistant	Resistant	Resistant	Resistant	Resistant	
Universal	Resistant		Resistant			
Unrejected	Resistant					Resistant
Uncontested	Resistant		Resistant	Resistant	Resistant	
Plurality	Resistant	Resistant	Resistant	Resistant	Resistant	
Majority	Resistant	Resistant	Resistant	Resistant	Resistant	
Supermajority	Resistant	Resistant	Resistant	Resistant	Resistant	

the right collusive actions (i.e. the complexity of the Winning Sequence problem) is greater than the complexity of making a single move (i.e. the Desired Outcome problem), under the assumption that the polynomial hierarchy does not collapse. Similarly, strategic argumentation is resistant to espionage if the complexity of the Winning Strategy problem is greater than the complexity of the Desired Outcome problem.

However, a player must make a sequence of moves in strategic argumentation, and so we propose a slightly stronger notion of resistance, where the complexity $\mathcal{D}$ of the Desired Outcome problem is replaced by $\text{PTIME}^{\mathcal{D}}$, which is the complexity of a deterministic algorithm incorporating the solving of a polynomial number of Desired Outcome problems. This makes no difference to the results in [16,18], but it seems a more accurate representation of the concept of resistance.

In the case of espionage, we must compare the cost of solving a sequence of Desired Outcome problems for P against that of solving the Winning Strategy problem. Our modified formulation of resistance has no effect since the Winning Strategy problem is PSPACE-hard for all aims and semantics. Thus, in every case, strategic argumentation is resistant to espionage. However, the "distance" between the complexity of normal play and of the Winning Strategy problem for the counting aims appears less than for the other aims (that is, the other aims are low in the polynomial hierarchy whereas even NP^{PP} contains the entire polynomial hierarchy).

For collusion, the question of resistance is more complicated. First, we must specify whether the collusion is to make P or O win, since the complexity of the Winning Sequence problem is different, in general, for the two players. We have assumed the collusion supports P. We must require that the complexity of the Winning Sequence problem is greater than the complexity of both players' normal play, since both players are colluding. The resistance to collusion in favour of P is expressed in Table 5. It turns out that our modified formulation of resistance has no effect on these results.

There are some clear patterns in Table 5. The counting aims are resistant to collusion, except under the eager semantics. It seems reasonable to expect that other non-unitary semantics will also have this property. The existential aim is also resistant to collusion, again except for the eager semantics. On the other hand, the universal aim is not resistant to collusion, except under the grounded and complete semantics. This contrast arises indirectly from the complexity of the Aim Verification problem for O, which tends to be an existential (i.e. Σ) complexity for P's universal aim, with the Desired Outcome problem having the same complexity. The Desired Outcome problem for P has a greater complexity, which matches the complexity of the Winning Sequence problem for P. and a universal complexity (i.e. Π) for P's existential aim. (The Aim Verification problem for the universal aim is in PTIME for both the grounded and complete semantics, which helps explain these exceptions.) The uncontested aim is closely related to the existential aim which explains its resistance. In the two semantics where strategic argumentation with the uncontested aim is not resistant to collusion the uncontested aim is identical to the universal aim.

9   Conclusions

We have established the complexity of several computational problems related to strategic argumentation, for a variety of semantics and strategic aims. We identified an algebraic structure underlying the aims, and exploited it to simplify proofs. We have shown that strategic argumentation is resistant to espionage under all semantics and aims. We have also identified those cases where strategic argumentation is resistant to collusion. We outlined some causes for patterns in resistance which suggest that these patterns will hold for other semantics.

These results extend to some concrete argumentation formalisms, using the same methods [17] as used in [18]. In particular, they apply to the ASPIC family of languages [19], flat assumption-based argumentation [5], and the ambiguity-blocking defeasible logics in the **DL** framework [1].

References

1. Antoniou, G., Billington, D., Governatori, G., Maher, M.J.: A flexible framework for defeasible logics. In: AAAI/IAAI, pp. 405–410. AAAI Press/The MIT Press (2000)
2. Baroni, P., Caminada, M., Giacomin, M.: An introduction to argumentation semantics. Knowl. Eng. Rev. **26**(4), 365–410 (2011). http://dx.doi.org/10.1017/S0269888911000166
3. Bartholdi, J.J., Tovey, C.A., Trick, M.A.: The computational difficulty of manipulating an election. Soc. Choice Welf. **6**(3), 227–241 (1989)
4. Baumann, R., Brewka, G.: Expanding argumentation frameworks: enforcing and monotonicity results. In: COMMA, pp. 75–86 (2010)
5. Bondarenko, A., Dung, P.M., Kowalski, R.A., Toni, F.: An abstract, argumentation-theoretic approach to default reasoning. Artif. Intell. **93**, 63–101 (1997)
6. Dimopoulos, Y., Torres, A.: Graph theoretical structures in logic programs and default theories. Theor. Comput. Sci. **170**(1–2), 209–244 (1996). http://dx.doi.org/10.1016/S0304-3975(96)80707-9
7. Dung, P.M.: On the acceptability of arguments and its fundamental role in nonmonotonic reasoning, logic programming and n-person games. Artif. Intell. **77**(2), 321–358 (1995)
8. Dunne, P.E.: The computational complexity of ideal semantics. Artif. Intell. **173**(18), 1559–1591 (2009). http://dx.doi.org/10.1016/j.artint.2009.09.001
9. Dunne, P.E., Bench-Capon, T.J.M.: Coherence in finite argument systems. Artif. Intell. **141**(1/2), 187–203 (2002). http://dx.doi.org/10.1016/S0004-3702(02)00261-8
10. Dunne, P.E., Dvořák, W., Woltran, S.: Parametric properties of ideal semantics. Artif. Intell. **202**, 1–28 (2013). http://dx.doi.org/10.1016/j.artint.2013.06.004
11. Dvořák, W.: On the complexity of computing the justification status of an argument. In: Modgil, S., Oren, N., Toni, F. (eds.) TAFA 2011. LNCS, vol. 7132, pp. 32–49. Springer, Heidelberg (2012)
12. Dvořák, W., Woltran, S.: Complexity of semi-stable and stage semantics in argumentation frameworks. Inf. Process. Lett. **110**(11), 425–430 (2010). http://dx.doi.org/10.1016/j.ipl.2010.04.005

13. Gordon, T.F., Walton, D.: Proof burdens and standards. In: Rahwan, I., Simari, G. (eds.) Argumentation in Artificial Intelligence, pp. 239–260. Springer, Heidelberg (2009)

14. Covernatori, G., Olivieri, F., Scannapieco, S., Rotolo, A., Cristani, M.: Strategic argumentation is NP-complete. In: Proceedings of the European Conference on Artificial Intelligence, pp. 399–404 (2014)

15. Johnson, D.S.: A catalog of complexity classes. In: Handbook of Theoretical Computer Science, Volume A: Algorithms and Complexity, pp. 67–161. Elsevier (1990)

16. Maher, M.J.: Complexity of exploiting privacy violations in strategic argumentation. In: Proceedings of the Pacific Rim International Conference on Artificial Intelligence, pp. 523–535 (2014)

17. Maher, M.J.: Relating concrete argumentation formalisms and abstract argumentation. In: Technical Communications of International Conference on Logic Programming (2015)

18. Maher, M.J.: Resistance to corruption of strategic argumentation. In: AAAI Conference on Artificial Intelligence (2016)

19. Prakken, H.: An abstract framework for argumentation with structured arguments. Argument Comput. **1**, 93–124 (2010)

20. Rahwan, I., Larson, K., Tohmé, F.A.: A characterisation of strategy-proofness for grounded argumentation semantics. In: Boutilier, C. (ed.) IJCAI, pp. 251–256 (2009)

21. Toda, S.: PP is as hard as the polynomial-time hierarchy. SIAM J. Comput. **20**(5), 865–877 (1991). http://dx.doi.org/10.1137/0220053

22. Torán, J.: Complexity classes defined by counting quantifiers. J. ACM **38**(3), 753–774 (1991). http://doi.acm.org/10.1145/116825.116858

23. Wagner, K.W.: The complexity of combinatorial problems with succinct input representation. Acta Inf. **23**(3), 325–356 (1986). http://dx.doi.org/10.1007/BF00289117

24. Wu, Y., Caminada, M.: A labelling-based justification status of arguments. Stud. Logic **3**(4), 12–29 (2010)

Spread of Cooperation in Complex Agent Networks Based on Expectation of Cooperation

Ryosuke Shibusawa, Tomoaki Otsuka, and Toshiharu Sugawara[✉]

Department of Computer Science and Communications Engineering,
Waseda University, Tokyo 1698555, Japan
{r.shibusawa,t.otsuka}@isl.cs.waseda.ac.jp, sugawara@waseda.jp

Abstract. This paper proposes a behavioral strategy called expectation of cooperation with which cooperation in the prisoner's dilemma game spreads over agent networks by incorporating Q-learning. Recent advances in computer and communication technologies enable intelligent agents to operate in small and handy computers such as mobile PCs, tablet computers, and smart phones as delegates of their owners. Because the interaction of these agents is associated with social links in the real world, social behavior is to some degree required to avoid conflicts, competition, and unfairness that may lead to further inefficiency in the agent society. The proposed strategy is simple and easy to implement but nevertheless can spread over and maintain cooperation in agent networks under certain conditions. We conducted a number of experiments to clarify these conditions, and the results indicate that cooperation spread and was maintained with the proposed strategy in a variety of networks.

1 Introduction

Humans can be seen as self-interested and individually rational but often pursue social benefits on the basis of, for example, altruism and reciprocity. This kind of behavior is selected to avoid/resolve social dilemmas such as conflicts between (groups of) humans and the existence of free riders. On the other hand, with recent advances in computer and networking technologies, many computerized services are proposed in which computer software programs called agents, which work as delegates of companies, organizations, and individuals, act for assistance, advices and tutorial role towards their owners/people in a given context or ambient. Because the interaction between agents occurs on the basis of social connectivity in the real and virtual worlds, the behaviors of certain agents directly or indirectly affects the behaviors of other agents, and finally their effect returns to the original agents. Hence, agents' decisions made only from the self-interested and local viewpoints often result in non-cooperative behavior resulting in conflicts that may cause loss for both sides. To avoid such conflicts, agents should take into account not only local benefits but also collective benefits; such socially cooperative behavior may be the non-best choice from a short-term and local viewpoint but will bring better results eventually in the long term.

T. Sugawara—This work is supported by KAKENHI (No. 25280087).

A number of studies have been conducted to identify what maintains socially cooperative behavior. One notable and traditional study was the evolution of cooperation in public goods games by Axelrod [1] whose game structure is intrinsically an n-person prisoner's dilemma (PD) game. His paper investigated the conditions in which cooperation emerged in norm and meta-norm games, which are public goods games with punishment. Although the PD game has a fundamental structure of social interaction between agents, normal self-interested agents cannot evolve cooperation because defection is a unique Nash equilibrium. Thus, many researches focused on the mechanism/features for learning and/or emergence of cooperation in PD games between two persons (agents) [13] or in agent networks [9,19]. For example, Moriyama et al. [13] proposed Q-learning with subjective utility that could lead to cooperative behaviors in two-person PD games. Matsuda [9] showed that cooperation was evolved in agent networks with high probability by introducing a number of zealous cooperators, which almost always select cooperation, into the networks. However, the way to introduce these mechanisms into agents, which are computational entities, is not obvious and may not be practical. We believe that computationally tractable and/or conceptually reasonable methods that lead to cooperative behavior in the agent network are still to be investigated.

The contribution of this paper is the proposal of the simple behavioral strategy called *expectation of cooperation* with which (the norm of) cooperation in the PD games emerges or spreads over agent networks under a certain condition. The basic concept behind the proposed strategy is that agents are socially rational to some extent, meaning that they know that mutual cooperation is better for both sides, so they hope it, but they also know that the benefit can be reaped only when all agents select the cooperation strategy. Furthermore, agents can observe others' strategies only when they play the games and do not have an option to interact with the partner agents before the games (as in [4]). In our framework, they perform pairwise PD games between neighbors in an agent network and learn which strategy, cooperation (C) or defection (D), is better through Q-learning with ε-greedy method $(0 < \varepsilon \ll 1)$. They may learn to select D in normal situations since it is the equilibrium strategy. However, when they happen to select (C, C), the agents with the expectation of cooperation behavioral strategy try cooperation by selecting C a few times in the hope that all agents (or at least, all agents in their neighborhood) begin to cooperate. We then experimentally show that the expectation of cooperation strategy fosters cooperation in the whole network, although it is simple and easy to implement.

This paper is organized as follows. We describe related work in Sect. 2. Section 3 discusses the model of pairwise PD game in the agent network and explains the models of networks used in our experiments. Then, we propose expectation of cooperation behavioral strategy and ensemble strategy decision based on Q-values in Sect. 4. Section 5 experimentally shows that the proposed strategy can evolve, spread, and maintain cooperation. We then investigate the conditions under which cooperation spreads in the agent society by varying the number of times for challenging cooperation called cooperation persistence after encountering mutual cooperation and the initial situations in a variety of networks. Particularly, we show that the agents in the network generated by connecting nearest neighbor (CNN) model relatively easily establish and maintain cooperation, although a few agents learn that defection is better for their own utilities.

2   Related Work

Many studies on cooperation in PD games have been conducted in economics, computational biology, sociology and computer science (e.g., [6,14,19]). A notable report by Nowark [14] explains the five rules for evolving cooperation observed in human society and biological systems (using the evolutionary game framework). For example, indirect reciprocity is likely to develop cooperation under the assumption that the agents that selected cooperative behavior are conveyed to others and thereby get the good reputations [15]. In addition, Rockenbach and Milinski [17] investigated how to combine reputation building and costly punishment to sustain cooperation.

A number of studies focused on the rules or mechanisms other than those of Nowark [14] and on variations of PD games for the evolution of cooperation. Ohdaira and Terano [16] experimentally showed that when the agents discard the best choice and select the second-best strategy, they develop cooperation with high probability (but not in all cases) in PD games between two groups of agents using the evolutionary game. Li and Yong [7] proposed a variation of the PD game, called the quantum PD game, by introducing quantum strategy (they also call an agent with this strategy a *super cooperator*) based on entanglement degrees that represent the relationship between players. They then showed that quantum strategy wins the defector-dominated world in a scale-free network [8].

Recently, Matsuda [9] indicated that a small fraction of perfect and imperfect zealous cooperators (i.e., they keep cooperating) facilitates the emergence of cooperation in social dilemma situations. He insisted that this phenomenon was not included in the five rules [14] but was a case for the cascading phenomena observed in experimental studies in human social networks [3]. We believe that our proposed strategy is also another form of cascading where agents are not usually cooperative but hope for emergence of cooperative behavior in the local areas when they have encountered cooperation. Xianyu [25] reported that agents' adaptive expectations through communication prior to each game improve (but oscillate) the frequency of cooperation of PD games in complex networks. Our proposed strategy is also based on an expectation but only from a simple behavioral strategy with local interaction.

On the other hand, multi-agent system research focused on how coordinated behaviors emerge or are learned in agent networks. For example, Sen and Airiau proposed a framework for the emergence of norms for coordination games through social learning and showed that norms could arise in agent networks of complete graphs [18]. Villatoro et al. [23] discussed the situation in which main and local norms co-exist in certain networks, such as small-world networks, and the entire network does not converge to a single norm. Thus, they proposed two instruments, *rewiring* and *observation*, to facilitate convergence in the whole networks. Sugawara [21] studied the emergence and stability of norm for the conflicting situation that was described by using Markov game and intrinsically n type of anti-coordination game from the long-term viewpoint. Yu et al. [26] proposed a collective learning framework in which agents decide their behaviors based on majority voting together with their neighbor agents; thus, this mechanism imitates human relationships in society to some extent. Shibusawa and Sugawara [20] introduce the learning method by taking into account the *influential weight* with which a larger community affects other smaller communities. They experimentally show that their method succeeded in showing the emergence of norms in the networks where a certain method [26] could not. However, these works tried to have all agents learn norms using reinforcement learning to share one of Nash equilibria of coordination games. None of these focus on cooperation in PD games in which cooperation is not a Nash equilibrium, so it is unstable in the society of self-interested agents.

Of course, a number of studies have discussed the emergence of cooperation in PD games in the context of multi-agent systems (e.g., [10,11,13]). Hao and Leung [4] also studied the emergence of cooperation in a rational agent society with a number of influencer agents (IAs) that are usually added intentionally and take pre-defined actions to achieve certain desirable goals. They also assumed that agents had the option to know the type of partner (rational agent or IA) and ask the partner to decide the joint action. They found that IAs could facilitate cooperation in pairwise PD and anti-coordination games. However, we assume that all agents are of the same type and follows a shared simple rule in our paper. Matlock and Sen [10] proposed a number of tag-based mechanisms [5] for coordination in multi-agent systems, and they analyzed them and showed that some of them enhanced the evolution of cooperation in evolutionary computation of PD games by multiple agents [11]. Moriyama [12] proposed a utility-based Q-learning in which agents have an emotional mechanism deriving subjective utilities from objective rewards, and they learn Q-values using the utilities. Then, they proposed the evolutionary mechanism for deciding subjective utilities to facilitate cooperation in iterated PD games [13]. However, these researches assumed iterated PD games between two agents or two groups of agents and did not discuss emergence of cooperation (except Hao and Leung [4]), meaning that almost all agents in the society follow the same strategy for cooperation. On the other hand, this paper proposes a simple behavioral strategy with Q-learning to spread cooperation over a variety of agent networks through local interactions.

3   Model and Agent Networks

3.1   Prisoner's Dilemma Game

$A = \{0, \ldots, n-1\}$ is the set of n agents that are connected with a network, called an *agent network* and denoted by graph $G = (A, E)$, where E is the set of (undirected) links. The set of neighbors of agent $i \in A$ is denoted by N_i and is defined as

$$N_i = \{j \in A \mid (i,j) \in E\}$$

Now, all the agents in the agent network play pairwise PD games with their neighbors in a *round* with a random order. The PD game is described by the following payoff matrix:

	C	D
C	R,R	S,T
D	T,S	P,P

where $T > R > P > S$ and $2R > T+S$ are satisfied. Let $S_{tr} = \{C, D\}$ be the set of strategies that the agents can adopt. It is known that the (unique) equilibrium of the PD game is D, so their rational strategy is D for both sides; thereby, they are likely to receive P. Obviously, the joint action (C, C) is preferable but is not stable since they may have an incentive to change to D to receive more payoffs. Of course, other agents also reason in the same way, so they finally select joint action (D,D) if they do not have another rule to follow.

3.2   Network Structures

The structure of the agent network reflects the relationships of social interactions of agents based on real-world connectivity, such as a social network in human society, the topology of the Internet, and the distributed computer systems running on the Internet. Thus, a number of networks have been proposed to characterize the structures of these social interactions. In this section, we describe the models that generate networks used in our experiments below.

Barabasi-Albert Model. The Barabasi-Albert (BA) model [2] generates scale-free networks by using a mechanism called *preferential attachment*, in which when a new link is created, an agent (node) i connects to another agent j with a probability proportional to its degree. BA networks are characterized by the parameter *new link number*, $M(> 0)$, and are created as follows. The initial graph (A, E) is defined as a complete graph consisting of M agents. When a new agent i is added to A, i generates M links to the agents selected from A with probability $d_j / \sum_{k \in A \setminus \{i\}} d_k$, where d_j is the degree of node $j \in A$ in the network. This process is iterated until the required number of agents is reached.

Connecting Nearest Neighbor Model. The connecting nearest neighbor (CNN) model has the small-world property, a large cluster coefficient, and scale-free property. It is parametrized by *conversion probability*, $0 < u < 1$, expressing the probability of converting a potential link of the current network (A, E) into an actual link, where the potential link is defined as

$$\{(i, j) \notin E \mid \exists k \in A \text{ s.t. } k \in N_i \cap N_j\}.$$

Starting with a complete graph of a single or a few agents, networks are created by iteratively performing the following rules [22].

1. With probability $1 - u$, a new node i is added to the graph, the edge from i to the existing node j selected randomly from A is created, and A is set to $A \cup \{i\}$. At this time, a number of potential links from the neighbors of j and i ⟶⟶ ⟶⟶⟶⟶⟶⟶

2. With probability u, one random⟶⟶ ⟶⟶⟶⟶⟶⟶ ⟶⟶⟶⟶⟶⟶ link is converted into an actual link, so the converted link belongs to E.

CNN networks often characterize structures of friendships in social network media, so they are important to understand the interaction in social media and applications based on human networks.

We also examine complete graphs (or complete-graph networks) of A in the experiments presented in Sect. 5 for comparison.

4   Proposed Method

4.1   PD Games with Combined Strategy Decision Based on Q-Values

For a given agent network $G = (A, E)$, we assume that all pairs of agents in E play the PD game once in a single round in random order. Therefore, $|E|$ games are played in a round. Agent i decides its strategy by the *combined strategy decision with Q-value* (or simply the *combined strategy decision*) with ε-greedy method for all neighbors. More specifically, i has the Q-value, $Q^i(s, j)$, for the strategy $s \in S_{tr}$ and neighbor agent $j \in N_i$ at the t-th round, and it is updated by

$$Q^i_t(s, j) = (1 - \alpha_i) \cdot Q^i_{t-1}(s, j) + \alpha_i \cdot r^i_{j, t-1},$$

where $r^i_{j, t-1}$ is the payoff received after the latest PD game with j at round $t-1$, and α_i is the parameter for the learning rate of agent i.

At the beginning of the t-th round, agent i identifies its strategy, $s^i(t)$, so that the following condition is satisfied.

$$s^i(t) = \arg \max_{s \in S_{tr}} p^i(s), \tag{1}$$

where $p^i(s)$ is the preference function for combined strategy decision. In our experiments, we define it as a majority voting, i.e.,

$$p^i(s) = \sum_{j \in N_i} \delta(s, s^i_j(t - 1)) \tag{2}$$

$$s^i_j(t - 1) = \arg \max_{s \in S_{tr}} Q^i_{t-1}(s, j), \tag{3}$$

where $\delta(s, s') = 1$ if $s = s'$; otherwise it is zero. Then, i selects strategy $s^i(t)$ with probability $1 - \varepsilon$ and selects it randomly from S_{tr} with probability ε. Since $|S_{tr}| = 2$, another strategy would be selected with probability $\varepsilon/2$. Note that if more than one maximum values exist in Eq. (1) or Eq. (3), they are selected randomly. We call strategy $s^i(t)$ as the *preferred strategy* of i at the t-th round.

4.2   Expectation of Cooperation Strategy

Agents with the proposed behavioral strategy, called the *expectation of cooperation strategy*, are assumed to know that collective cooperative behavior is better than defection, so they expect (hope for) it when interacting with their neighbors, but they also know that it is fruitless if other local agents do not cooperate. We introduce the positive integer, L, which represents the term of *cooperation persistence*. Agent i also has the parameter $l_i(\geq 0)$ to express the remaining number of times for persisting cooperation, i.e., when $l_i = 0$, i selects the preferred strategy in accordance with the result of the combined strategy decision described above, but while $l_i > 0$, i causes cooperation persistence in the hope of cooperation in the local environment. The initial value of l_i is set to zero.

If agents i and j happen to mutually select cooperation, (C, C), they will individually set l_i and l_j to L and enter the term for persisting cooperation in the hope of (local) emergence of cooperation. Thus, i (and j) persist cooperation in at least the next L PD games (not rounds) with their neighbors (so i hardly has a chance to play the game with j again in the next L games), and l_i is decremented by one after each game. However, if i encounters joint (C, C) again, l_i is set to L and the term for persisting cooperation is prolonged. It is obvious that if the cooperation persistence, L, is large, agents continue to select C, and if $L = 0$, it is the PD games with normal Q-learning, so all agents tend to select D, which is the Nash equilibrium. We are interested in the smallest value of L that leads to (almost) total cooperation.

Agents whose preferred strategy is C are defined as the *normative cooperative agents*, or simply *NC agents*. Note that $s^i(t) = C$ for $t \geq \exists T_0$ indicates that i stably learned that C (cooperation) was better with combined strategy decision based on Q-values, so i was likely to select C even when $l_i = 0$. According to the definition in Yu et al. [26], let us define the emergence of cooperation when more than 90 % of agents are NC. On the other hand, even if agent i is not NC, i may cooperate due to the expectation of cooperation behavioral strategy due to the mutual cooperation with the neighbor agents. We call the *spread of cooperation* when more than 90 % of agents continuously take cooperation, C.

5   Experiments and Results

5.1   Cooperation in Agent Networks

We evaluated our strategy using the three types of agent networks described in Sect. 3.2. In all the experiments below, we define the payoff matrix as $T = 5$, $R = 3, P = 1$, and $S = 0$. Note that cooperation persistence, $L = 0$, is identical to only the strategy with combined strategy decision. The learning rate α ($= \alpha_i$ for $\forall i \in A$) is set to 0.1, and ε for the ε-greedy strategy is set to 0.05. The data described below is the mean values of 20 independent trials.

In the first experiment, we investigated whether cooperation spread or emerged, and if so, how many agents selected strategy C by varying the value

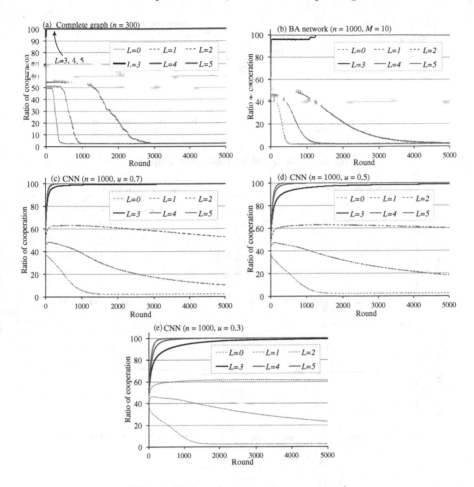

Fig. 1. Ratios of cooperation per round.

of cooperation persistence, L. We first show the results when the agent network is represented by complete graphs because the structure is canonical and the derived results must be the basis for comparison. We set the number of agents $|A|$ to three hundred.

Figure 1(a) plots the ratios of agents per round that select cooperation, C, because they are in term of cooperation persistence or their $Q(C)$ is larger than $Q(D)$. Note that the initial values of $Q_0^i(s, j)$ for $\forall i \in A$ and $\forall j \in N_i$ is set to 0. We can see that when $L \leq 2$, cooperation could not spread over the society of agents with the expectation of cooperation strategy but did spread when $L \geq 3$.

Note that we also conducted the same experiment for the agents with only expectation of cooperation strategy without the combined strategy decision with Q-values, so agent i selects D with probability $1 - \varepsilon$ and C or D randomly with probability ε when $l_i = 0$. In this case, no cooperation spread nor emerged even when $L = 5$.

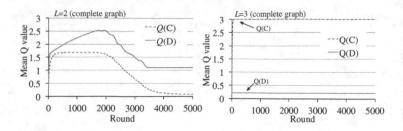

Fig. 2. Mean Q values (complete graph).

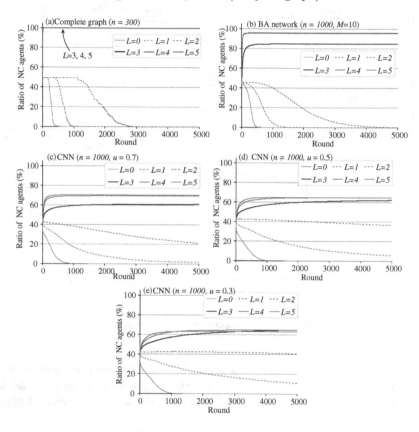

Fig. 3. Number of NC agents.

We investigated the same experiments for the CNN and BA networks in which the number of agents were one thousand ($|A| = 1,000$). The results are shown in Fig. 1(b)–(e). Interestingly, these graphs show the same gap between $L = 2$ and 3, i.e., when the cooperation persistence is larger than or equal to 3, cooperation spread, although their convergence speeds were slightly low. Note that when $L \leq 2$, the ratios of cooperation reached 2.5 % due to the ε-greedy selection where $\varepsilon = 0.05$. We do not show it here, but in Watts-Strogatz (WS) networks with a rewiring probability of 0.1 [24], cooperation emerged when $L \geq 3$ as well.

5.2   Distribution of Preferred Strategies

We investigated the mean Q values, $Q_t(C)$ and $Q_t(D)$, in all agents and the ratios of agents in which the preferred strategy is cooperation ($s^i(t) = C$), where

$$Q_t^i(s) = \sum_{j \in N_i} Q_t^i(s, j) / |N_j|$$

and

$$Q_t(s) = \sum_{i \in A} Q_t^i(s) / |A|$$

for $\forall s \in S_{tr}$.

We plotted the values of $Q_t(s)$ in Fig. 2 (we omit the subscript t in this figure) and the ratios of NC agents in Fig. 3(a) when the networks are complete graphs. These figures indicate that when $L = 2$, $Q_t(C)$ became large, but $Q_t(D)$ increased more quickly. In such a society dominated by defection strategy, cooperation always received lower utility, and higher utility was given to adversary agents, so agents hardly ever selected cooperation. When $L = 3$, cooperation spread more quickly and emerged in all agents. Actually, $Q_t(C)$ immediately became 3, but $Q_t(D)$ stayed at around 0.2. Thus, they tended to mutually select cooperation, so they continued to expect cooperation around them (and *vice versa*). Because all agents were connected to each other in a complete graph, anyone's cooperation directly affected the strategies of other agents. Therefore, convergence was very fast. As for the results, when $L \geq 3$, all agents learned that C was better than D only within approximately ten rounds and became NC agents. (the preferred strategy was $s^i(t) = C$ for $t \geq 10$ and $\forall i \in A$) as shown in Fig. 3(a). Thus, we can say that the norm for cooperation emerged successfully when $L \geq 3$. When $L \leq 2$, half of the agents seemed to cooperate initially, but agents gradually learned that $Q_t^i(D)$ was higher and finally tended to select defection.

However, this situation is slightly different from those in other networks. Figure 3(b)–(e) indicate the ratios of NC agents when the agent networks are BA and CNN. Although Fig. 1(b)–(e) show that cooperation spread over the networks when the cooperation persistence, L, was larger than or equal to three, all agents did not learn that cooperation was better in these networks. For example, when $L = 3$, around 82 % of the agents in BA networks and 60 % of the agents in CNN networks were NC agents, and the other agents preferred D to C ($s^i(t) = D$). In this sense, we cannot say that the norm for cooperation emerged. As an example, we show the distributions of NC agents in a CNN network ($u = 0.3$) of a certain experimental trial in Fig. 4, where filled (open) nodes are NC (non-NC) agents. This figure indicates that non-NC agents (open nodes) exist sparsely. However, a considerable number of agents learned that

Filled nodes indicate NC agents.
Open nodes indicate non-NC agents.

Fig. 4. Distribution of NC agents in a CNN network ($u = 0.3$).

cooperation (C) was better than defection (D), and under this environment, the expectation of cooperation behavioral strategy regulated and maintained the cooperative society.

5.3   Effect of Initial Strategy on Emergence

The ratios of NC agents and of cooperation in networks seemed to depend on the ratios of cooperation in the first round (initial strategies) due to the characteristics of expectation of cooperation behavioral strategy since the joint action (C, C) by a pair of agents forced them to cooperate individually for the next L rounds. In the experiment described above, $Q(C) = Q(D) = 0$, so fifty percent of the agents preferred cooperation ($s^i(0) = C$), and the other agents preferred defection ($s^i(0) = D$) on average. In the next experiment (Exp. 2), we set the Q-values, $Q(C) = Q(D) = 0$, like in the previous experiment, but we assumed that agents selected C as the initial preferred strategy, $s^i(0)$, with probability R_C ($0 \leq R_C \leq 0.5$, so the other agents selected D with probability $1 - R_C$). Note that $R_C = 0$ means the initial agent networks that were dominated by defection, which is the equilibrium strategy, because $Q_1^i(D, j) > Q_1^i(C, j)$ for

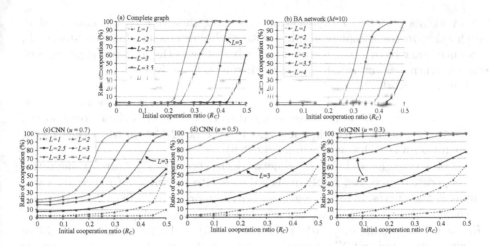

Fig. 5. Ratios of cooperation with various initial cooperation rates.

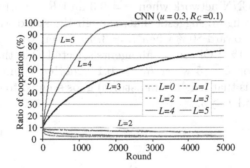

Fig. 6. Ratios of cooperation.

$\forall i \in A$ and $\forall j \in N_i$ after the first play in the initial round. Parameter R_C is called the *initial cooperation rate*. Note that many of the studies mentioned in Sect. 2 usually started their experiments from fair or random initial states, which correspond to $R_C = 0.5$ in our experiments.

Figure 5(a)–(e) plotted the ratios of cooperation at the 5000th round when R_C was varied. We added the curves for $L = 2.5$ and 3.5 for more detailed investigation. Note that when L is not an integer, it is selected probabilistically; for example, if $L = 2.5$, agents initially select 2 or 3 with the same probability. Instead, we omitted the curves for $L = 0$ and 5 since these results are obvious from the others. When the agent network is a complete graph (Fig. 5(a)), the ratios of cooperation sharply increase to 100 % with increasing initial cooperation rate, R_C. For example, the curve for $L = 3$ indicated that all agents selected C after all when $R_C = 0.45$, but approximately half of the agents and none of the agents selected C when $R_C = 0.40$ and $R_C = 0.35$, respectively. When the initial cooperation ratio was small, the experiment started from the situation in which many agents preferred D. Furthermore, since agents were tightly connected to each other in the complete graph, relatively larger cooperation persistence, L, was necessary to overturn the situation where D was the majority strategy, but the overturn was immediate if R_C reached a sufficiently large number. For the BA agent network, the graph in Fig. 5(b) indicates characteristics similar to those of the complete graphs, but slightly larger initial cooperation ratios than those in complete-graph networks were required so that all agents chose cooperation, C. Note that in this network, a few agents were not NC even when the ratio of cooperation was 100 % as shown in Fig. 3(b).

On the other hand, in the CNN networks as shown in Fig. 5(c)–(e), the ratios of cooperation increased gently in accordance with the values of R_C; when u was smaller, the curves were more gentle. Furthermore, even when R_C was small, a considerable number of agents selected C; for example, when $L = 3$ and $R_C = 0.1$, approximately 76 % (when $u = 0.3$) and 43 % (when $u = 0.5$) of agents cooperated in CNN networks. We think that this is the characteristic of CNN networks, and we will discuss it in Sect. 5.4. Figure 6 plots the ratios of cooperation in the CNN network when $u = 0.3$ and $R_C = 0.1$ to see how cooperation spread. This figure suggests that, though the speed was low, the ratios gradually increased toward 80 % when $L = 3$. However, when $L = 2$, the ratios stayed at less than 10 %.[1] Of course, all agents selected D in the complete-graph and BA networks for $L \leq 5$ when $R_C = 0.1$. Another common characteristic observable in Fig. 5 is that (slightly indistinct) gaps seemed to exist between the curves of $L \leq 2.5$ and $L \geq 3$.

5.4   Discussion

Our experimental results indicate that the proposed behavioral strategy, expectation of cooperation, with combined strategy decision based on Q-values, enabled agents to behave cooperatively in the social dilemma situations characterized by PD games. The experimental results also suggested that, to spread cooperation, $L = 3$ or more is enough in many types of networks. Agents that are programs running on a variety of computational devices, such as servers, mobile PCs, and smart phones, as delegates of humans may encounter a variety of social dilemma situations. Cooperation is better for socially rational decision-making. However, separate cooperation is not possible; agents' neighbors also have to cooperate. One important feature of our proposed strategy is that it is quite easy to implement. We also believe that its semantic meaning described in Sect. 4.2 is reasonable to regulate the behavior of agents as delegates. These features are beneficial and essential for actual applications of multi-agent systems in the real world.

We think that the expectation of cooperation strategy is another type of cooperative behavior cascade observed in human social networks [3], which states that individuals are affected by group members' cooperative contribution to the

---

[1] When $L = 2.5$, the ratios increased, but the emergence speed was extremely low.

future interaction with other individuals, and this effect persists for some periods and spreads via personal links. Matsuda [9] showed that a small number of zealots, which are zealous cooperators in an agent network, induced cooperation at the population level. He also pointed out that induced cooperation by zealots is similar to the cascading phenomenon [9]. Such zealous cooperators can be witnessed in, for example, team sports, charity, and military services [9]. Although this theory is quite curious from the viewpoints of sociology and computational biology, it is not easy to justify the implementation of zealous cooperators into agents in computer systems applications. On the other hand, in our proposed method, the non-NC agents exist but they are surrounded by majority of NC agents as shown in Fig. 4. Thus, their cooperative activities are cascaded to other neighboring agents, and cooperation spreads and is regulated in all agent finally. We believe that agents with our proposed strategy are more acceptable and reasonable to implement than those with the model of zealots [9].

Another related work to discuss here is the influencer agents (IAs) in the PD games by Hao and Leung [4], since IAs select socially rational actions. In their framework, the agent can have an additional option of asking its game partner to make the decision for both agents (joint action pair), apart from choosing an action from its action set S_{tr}. Thus, when an IA decides their joint actions, it always select socially optimal actions as the joint action pair. However, we assume that any agents have no chances for asking to decide joint actions, and instead, try to select cooperation a few times only when they can expect local cooperative behavior.

Our experiments show that spread of cooperation is more likely to occur in the CNN network. We believe that it came from the high cluster coefficient values, so small local communities in CNN networks started to cooperate, and this socially rational behavior gradually spread via weaker links. Because the CNN network often reflects the social connectivity between persons [22], it is advantageous. Recent applications of multi-agent systems are, for example, collections of agents running on individual smart phones/tablet PCs and their interactions usually occur on the basis of social connectivity between them. An appropriate strategy for attempting to find and establish mutual cooperation effectively should be implemented in such socially interactive programs, and the proposed strategy could be useful in these applications.

We also have a number of issues to investigate further. For example, if a few agents changed to self-interested behaviors or agents that do not follow the behavioral strategy are added after cooperation spread or emerged, they can exploit more utilities from other agents, and finally cooperation will dissolve. We think that we have to introduce another mechanism to avoid and/or detect such agents, such as learning behaviors of individuals or some mechanisms to eliminate/lower the incentive to defect; we need to study this topic more.

6   Conclusion

We proposed the expectation of cooperation behavioral strategy with combined strategy decision based on Q-values and showed that cooperation in the prisoner's dilemma game spread over agent networks with this strategy and learning. Because normal self-interested agents cannot select "cooperation" for their utilities, we introduced this strategy to induce, spread, and maintain cooperation in the whole networks. In this strategy, we assume that agents know that cooperation is required to avoid wasteful conflict and unfairness from the social viewpoint, but its benefit can only be obtained by mutual (or entire) cooperation. Expectation of cooperation strategy forces agents to keep cooperating for a short time to make sure that their local agents have started to cooperate. Our experiments indicate that the expectation of cooperation strategy induces spread or emergence of cooperation under the appropriate initial conditions and with the appropriate length of cooperation persistence.

We have a few issues for future study; one issue is the detection of defection after cooperation spreads as described in Sect. 5.4. Another is to examine the proposed strategy in an evolving network where nodes are replaced, added, or eliminated over time.

References

1. Axelrod, R.: An evolutionary approach to norms. Am. Polit. Sci. Rev. **80**(4), 1095–1111 (1986)
2. Barabasi, A.L., Albert, R.: Emergence of scaling in random networks. Science **286**, 509–512 (1999)
3. Fowler, J.H., Christakis, N.A.: Cooperative behavior cascades in human social networks. Proc. Natl. Acad. Sci. (PNAS) **107**(12), 5334–5338 (2010)
4. Hao, J., Leung, H.: Achieving social optimality with influencer agents. In: Glass, K., Colbaugh, R., Ormerod, P., Tsao, J. (eds.) Complex 2012. LNICST, vol. 126, pp. 140–151. Springer, Heidelberg (2013)
5. Holland, J.H., Holyoak, K.J., Nisbett, R.E., Thagard, P.R.: Induction: Processes of Inference, Learning, and Discovery. MIT Press, Cambridge (1986)
6. Jiang, Y., Jiang, J.C.: Understanding social networks from a multiagent perspective. IEEE Trans. Parallel Distrib. Syst. **25**(10), 2743–2759 (2014)
7. Li, A., Yong, X.: Entanglement guarantees emergence of cooperation in quantum prisoner's dilemma games on networks. Nat. Sci. Rep. **4**(6286) (2014)
8. Li, A., Yong, X.: Emergence of super cooperation of prisoner's dilemma games on scale-free networks. PLoS ONE **10**(2) (2015)
9. Masuda, N.: Evolution of cooperation driven by zealots. Nat. Sci. Rep. **2**(646) (2012)
10. Matlock, M., Sen, S.: Effective tag mechanisms for evolving coordination. In: Proceedings of the 6th International Joint Conference on Autonomous Agents, Multiagent Systems, AAMAS 2007, pp. 251:1–251:8. ACM, New York (2007)
11. Matlock, M., Sen, S.: Effective tag mechanisms for evolving cooperation. In: Proceedings of the 8th International Conference on Autonomous Agents and Multiagent Systems, AAMAS 2009, vol. 1, pp. 489–496 (2009)
12. Moriyama, K.: Utility based Q-learning to maintain cooperation in prisoner's dilemma games. In: Proceedings of the IEEE/WIC/ACM International Conference on Intelligent Agent Technology, IAT 2007, Washington, DC, USA, pp. 146–152 (2007)

13. Moriyama, K., Kurihara, S., Numao, M.: Evolving subjective utilities: prisoner's dilemma game examples. In: Proceedings of the 10th International Conference on Autonomous Agents and Multiagent Systems, AAMAS, vol. 1, pp. 233–240 (2011)
14. Nowak, M.A.: Five rules for the evolution of cooperation. Science **314**(5805), 1560–1603 (2006)
15. Nowak, M.A., Sigmund, K.: Evolution of indirect reciprocity. Nature **437**, 1291–1298 (2005)
16. Ohdaira, T., Terano, T.: Cooperation in the prisoner's dilemma game based on the second-best decision. J. Artif. Soc. Soc. Simul. **12**(4) (2009)
17. Rockenbach, B., Milinski, M.: The efficient interaction of indirect reciprocity and costly punishment. Nature **444**, 718–723 (2006)
18. Sen, S., Airiau, S.: Emergence of norms through social learning. In: International Joint Conference on Artificial Intelligence (IJCAI-07), pp. 1507–1512 (2007)
19. Shi, D.-M., Yang, H.-X., Hu, M.-B., Du, W.-B., Wang, B.-H., Cao, X.-B.: Preferential selection promotes cooperation in a spatial public goods game. Phys. A: Stat. Mech. Appl. **388**(21), 4646–4650 (2009)
20. Shibusawa, R., Sugawara, T.: Norm emergence via influential weight propagation in complex networks. In: Proceedings of the Europea Network Intelligence Conference (ENIC), IEEE Xplore, pp. 30–37, September 2014
21. Sugawara, T.: Emergence and stability of social conventions in conflict situations. In: International Joint Conference on Artificial Intelligence (IJCAI-11), pp. 371–378 (2011)
22. Vázquez, A.: Growing network with local rules: preferential attachment, clustering hierarchy, and degree correlations. Phys. Rev. E **67**(5), 056194 (2003)
23. Villatoro, D., Sabater-Mir, J., Sen, S.: Social instruments for robust convention emergence. In: Proceedings of the Twenty-Second International Joint Conference on Artificial Intelligence - Volume One, IJCAI 2011, pp. 420–425. AAAI Press (2011)
24. Watts, D., Strogatz, S.: Collective dynamics of 'small-world' networks. Nature **393**, 440–442 (1998)
25. Xianyu, B.: Prisoner's dilemma game on complex networks with agents' adaptive expectations. J. Artif. Soc. Soc. Simul. **15**(3), 3 (2012)
26. Yu, C., Zhang, M., Ren, F., Luo, X.: Emergence of social norms through collective learning in networked agent societies. In: Proceedings of the 12th International Joint Conference on Autonomous Agents and Multi-Agent Systems, pp. 475–482 (2013)

Semantic Reasoning with Uncertain Information from Unreliable Sources

Murat Şensoy[1]([✉]), Lance Kaplan[2], and Geeth de Mel[3]

[1] Department of Computer Science, Ozyegin University, Istanbul, Turkey
murat.sensoy@ozyegin.edu.tr
[2] US Army Research Lab, Adelphi, MD 20783, USA
[3] IBM T. J. Watson Research Center, Hawthorne, NY, USA

Abstract. Intelligent software agents may significantly benefit from semantic reasoning. However, existing semantic reasoners are based on Description Logics, which cannot handle vague, incomplete, and unreliable knowledge. In this paper, we propose $\mathcal{S}$DL-Lite which extends DL-Lite$_R$ with subjective opinions to represent uncertainty in knowledge. We directly incorporate trust into the reasoning so that the inconsistencies in the knowledge can be resolved based on trust evidence analysis. Therefore, the proposed logic can handle uncertain information from unreliable sources. We demonstrate how $\mathcal{S}$DL-Lite can be used for semantic fusion of uncertain information from unreliable sources and show that $\mathcal{S}$DL-Lite reasoner can estimate the ground truth with a minimal error.

1 Introduction

Information is collected from diverse sources such as sensors, agents, and humans. However, such information is inherently uncertain — i.e., information can be vague, incomplete, and unreliable. The vagueness is related to the fuzziness of propositions addressed in the information, e.g., the weather is *cold*; incompleteness is related to lack of evidence about truth of propositions, e.g., the road *may be* closed; and reliability may be related to the consistency of information and trustworthiness of sources.

The Semantic Web (SW) stands as a promising set of technologies for knowledge representation and reasoning. Typically in SW, Description Logics (DLs)

Research was sponsored by the U.S. Army Research Laboratory and the U.K. Ministry of Defence and was accomplished under Agreement Numbers W911NF-06-3-0001 and W911NF-14-1-0199. The views and conclusions contained in this document are those of the author(s) and should not be interpreted as representing the official policies, either expressed or implied, of the U.S. Army Research Laboratory, the U.S. Government, the U.K. Ministry of Defence or the U.K. Government. The U.S. and U.K. Governments are authorized to reproduce and distribute reprints for Goverment purposes notwithstanding any copyright notation hereon. Dr. Şensoy thanks to the U.S. Army Research Laboratory for its support under grant W911NF-14-1-0199 and The Scientific and Technological Research Council of Turkey (TUBITAK) for its support under grant 113E238.

© Springer International Publishing Switzerland 2016
M. Baldoni et al. (Eds.): PRIMA 2016, LNAI 9862, pp. 92–109, 2016.
DOI: 10.1007/978-3-319-44832-9_6

based representations are preferred as they allow decidable reasoning. Unfortunately, classical DLs assumes the knowledge to be crisp, complete, and reliable. Even though there are several fuzzy and probabilistic extensions of DLs, still incompleteness and unreliability of the knowledge cannot be handled by DL reasoners.

In the vision of SW, trust plays an important role, since the knowledge may come from unreliable sources [1]. There has been several efforts to integrate SW with trust modelling. However, none of these efforts incorporate trust into DL based reasoning; instead, they use trust models to filter information from unreliable sources before reasoning. Therefore, current DL-based reasoners do not consider reliability in information explicitly as they are already assumed to reliable. In this paper, we propose $\mathcal{S}$DL-Lite which extends DL-Lite$_R$ with subjective opinions to allow representation of vagueness and incompleteness in information. ABox and TBox axioms in an $\mathcal{S}$DL-Lite knowledge base are annotated with subjective opinions that represent *belief*, *disbelief*, and *uncertainty* in a particular axiom. We formalise how inconsistencies between subjective opinions about ABox axioms can be defined. We then use constraint optimisation techniques to resolve the inconsistencies through trust-evidence analysis.

The proposed approach has two main contributions. First, it explicitly incorporates uncertainty modelling into DL-based reasoning. Second, it exploits domain constraints defined in TBox to detect inconsistencies among ABox assertions from unreliable sources. Then, these inconsistencies are used to revise trust in the information. Lastly, the information is fused to come up with a model approximating the ground truth. Thus, this paper not only proposes a knowledge representation formalism and reasoning mechanisms, but also an information fusion framework for uncertain semantic information. Through a case study and experimental evaluations, we have shown that $\mathcal{S}$DL-Lite can combine uncertain information from unreliable sources and approximates the ground truth with minimal errors.

The rest of the paper is organized as follows. We begin by introducing preliminary information about DL-Lite$_R$, subjective opinions, and trust in Sect. 2. Section 3 describes how we extended DL-Lite$_R$ with subjective opinions. In Sect. 4, we explain how inconsistencies are detected and resolved, and how models are calculated. In Sect. 6, we present a case-study and evaluate our approach. Lastly, we discuss our approach with respect to existing literature and conclude the paper in Sect. 7 by highlighting future research directions.

2   Preliminaries

2.1   DL-Based Ontologies

The complexity of logical entailment in most of the Description Logics is Exp-time [2]. Calvanese *et al.* [4] proposed DL-Lite, which can express most features in UML class diagrams with a low reasoning overhead – i.e., data complexity of AC$_0$ for ABox reasoning. It is for this reason that we base our model on DL-Lite$_R$

(to be referred to as DL-Lite in the rest of the paper); below we provide a brief formalisation of DL-Lite to ground the subsequent presentation of our model.

A DL-Lite knowledge base $\mathcal{K} = (\mathcal{T}, \mathcal{A})$ consists of a TBox $\mathcal{T}$ and an ABox $\mathcal{A}$. Axioms of the following forms compose $\mathcal{K}$: (a) *class inclusion axioms*: $B \sqsubseteq C \in \mathcal{T}$ where B is a basic class $B := \mathsf{A} \mid \exists R \mid \exists R^-$, C is a general class $C := B \mid \neg B \mid C_1 \sqcap C_2$, A is a named class, R is a named property, and R^- is the inverse of R; (b) *role inclusion axioms*: $R_i \sqsubseteq P \in \mathcal{T}$ where $P := R_j \mid \neg R_j$; and (c) *individual axioms*: $B(\mathsf{a}), R(\mathsf{a}, \mathsf{b}) \in \mathcal{A}$ where a and b are named individuals. Description Logics have a well-defined model-theoretic semantics, which are provided in terms of interpretations. An *interpretation* $\mathcal{I}$ is a pair $(\Delta^{\mathcal{I}}, \cdot^{\mathcal{I}})$, where $\Delta^{\mathcal{I}}$ is a non-empty set of objects and $\cdot^{\mathcal{I}}$ is an *interpretation function*, which maps each class C to a subset $C^{\mathcal{I}} \subseteq \Delta^{\mathcal{I}}$ and each property R to a subset $R^{\mathcal{I}} \subseteq \Delta^{\mathcal{I}} \times \Delta^{\mathcal{I}}$.

Using a trivial normalisation, it is possible to convert class inclusion axioms of the form $B_1 \sqsubseteq C_1 \sqcap C_2$ into a set of simpler class inclusions of the form $B_1 \sqsubseteq B_i$ or $B_1 \sqsubseteq \neg B_j$, where B_1, B_i, and B_j are basic concepts [4]. For instance, during normalisation, $B_1 \sqsubseteq B_2 \sqcap \neg B_3$ is replaced with $B_1 \sqsubseteq B_2$ and $B_1 \sqsubseteq \neg B_3$. In Table 1, we define semantics over a normalised TBox for our variant of DL-Lite — $\mathcal{S}$DL-Lite.

2.2 Subjective Opinions

Dempster-Shafer Theory (DST) [11] offers a means to characterise an agent's view of the state of world by assigning *basic probability masses* to subsets of truth assignments of propositions in the logic. In DST, a *binomial opinion* about a proposition x is represented by a triple $w_x = (b_x, d_x, u_x)$ which is derived from the basic probability masses assigned to subsets of truth assignments of the language. In the opinion w_x, b_x, also denoted by $b(w_x)$, is the belief about x — the summation of the probability masses that entail x; d_x, also denoted by $d(w_x)$, is the disbelief about x — the summation of the probability masses that entail $\neg x$; and u_x, also denoted by $u(w_x)$, is the uncertainty about x — the summation of the probability masses that neither entail x nor entail $\neg x$. The constraints over the probability mass assignment function require that $b_x + d_x + u_x = 1$ and $b_x, d_x, u_x \in [0, 1]$. When a more concise notation is necessary, we use (b_x, d_x) instead of (b_x, d_x, u_x), since $u_x = 1 - b_x - d_x$. The negation over an opinion w_x is defined as $\neg(b_x, d_x, u_x) = (d_x, b_x, u_x) = (b_{\neg x}, d_{\neg x}, u_{\neg x})$ [7].

Definition 1. Let $w_1 = (b_1, d_1, u_1)$ and $w_2 = (b_2, d_2, u_2)$ be two opinions about the same proposition. We call w_1 a *specialisation* of w_2 ($w_1 \preceq w_2$) iff $b_2 \leq b_1$ and $d_2 \leq d_1$ (implies $u_1 \leq u_2$). Similarly, we call w_1 a *generalisation* of w_2 ($w_2 \preceq w_1$) iff $b_1 \leq b_2$ and $d_1 \leq d_2$ (implies $u_2 \leq u_1$).   ∎

An agent i's opinion about a proposition x is denoted by $w_x^i = (b_x^i, d_x^i, u_x^i)$. This opinion w_x^i may not be *directly* used by another agent j. Agent j could have a view of the reliability or competence of i with respect to x. Shafer [11] proposed a discounting operator $\otimes$ to normalise the belief and disbelief in w_x^j based on the degree of trust j has of i with respect to x, i.e., t_i^j. The normalised opinion is $w_x^i \otimes t_i^j = (b_x^i \times t_i^j, d_x^i \times t_i^j)$.

The trustworthiness of information sources can be modelled using Beta probability density functions [8]. A Beta distribution has two parameters $(r_i^j + 1, s_i^j + 1)$, where r_i^j is the amount of positive evidence and s_i^j is the amount of negative evidence for the trustworthiness agent i agent has for agent j. The degree of trust t_j^i is then computed as the expectation value of the Beta distribution: $t_i^j = (r_i^j + 1)/(r_i^j + s_i^j + 2)$

In the rest of the paper, we assume that subjective opinions about various propositions are received from diverse information sources and added to the knowledge base after being discounted based on the trustworthiness of their sources.

3   Adding Subjective Opinions to **DL-Lite** Axioms

In this section, we introduce how we associate subjective opinions with axioms.

3.1   TBox Axioms

Let X and Y be two atomic classes (or roles). In DL-Lite, the relationships between the classes (or roles) are asserted using TBox axioms such as $X \sqsubseteq Y$, i.e., X is a sub-class of Y, in other words, all instances of X also instances of Y. We can associate these TBox axioms with opinions as well. For instance, $X \sqsubseteq Y$: $w_{y|x}$ represents a TBox axiom with the associated opinion. In DL-Lite, all asserted TBox axioms are assumed logically true. DL-Lite does not allow negation on the left hand side of class inclusion axioms, Therefore, in a DL-Lite KB, we can only have the following TBox axioms over X and Y: (i) $X \sqsubseteq Y$, (ii) $X \sqsubseteq \neg Y$, (iii) $Y \sqsubseteq X$, and (iv) $Y \sqsubseteq \neg X$. If a DL-Lite KB contains only the axiom $X \sqsubseteq Y$, but none of the other three, we can assume the following opinions with the axioms: $X \sqsubseteq Y$:$(1,0)$, $X \sqsubseteq \neg Y$:$(0,1)$, $Y \sqsubseteq X$:$(0,0)$, and $Y \sqsubseteq \neg X$:$(0,1)$, where the opinions $(1,0)$, $(1,0)$, and $(0,0)$ refers to logical *true*, logical *false*, and *complete uncertainty*, respectively.

In this paper, we propose to associate opinions with ABox and TBox axioms explicitly. For example, we can assert $X(o)$:$(0.7, 0.2)$, i.e., the object o is an instance of X with belief 0.7 and disbelief 0.2 (the remaining 0.1 is uncertainty). Similarly, we can assert $X \sqsubseteq \neg Y$:$(0.6, 0.1)$, which means that our belief and disbelief for the proposition "X and Y are disjoint classes" are 0.6 and 0.1, respectively; and the remaining 0.3 is our uncertainty about this axiom. This opinion implies the following opinions as well: $X \sqsubseteq Y$:$(0, 0.6)$, $Y \sqsubseteq X$:$(0, 0.6)$, and $Y \sqsubseteq \neg X$:$(0.6, 0.1)$. Let us note that $X \sqsubseteq Y \equiv \neg Y \sqsubseteq \neg X$ and $X \sqsubseteq \neg Y \equiv Y \sqsubseteq \neg X$. Therefore, our opinion for $X \sqsubseteq \neg Y$ is taken directly as our opinion for $Y \sqsubseteq \neg X$. Disbelieving $X \sqsubseteq Y$ is equivalent to believing one of the following distinct propositions:

1. X and Y are disjoint classes, i.e., $X \sqsubseteq \neg Y$.
2. Set of Y's instances (S_Y) is a proper subset of X's instances (S_X), i.e., $S_Y \subset S_X$.
3. The previous cases do not hold, but X and Y have some common instances, i.e., $S_Y \setminus S_X \neq \emptyset$, $S_X \setminus S_Y \neq \emptyset$, and $S_X \cap S_Y \neq \emptyset$.

Therefore, our belief in $X \sqsubseteq \neg Y$ becomes a lower bound for the amount of our disbelieves in $X \sqsubseteq Y$ and $Y \sqsubseteq X$. Let us formalize the relationships between opinions about TBox axioms using the following axioms over X and Y:

- $X \sqsubseteq Y{:}(b_{y|x}, d_{y|x})$
- $X \sqsubseteq \neg Y{:}(b_{\bar{y}|x}, d_{\bar{y}|x})$
- $Y \sqsubseteq X{:}(b_{x|y}, d_{x|y})$
- $Y \sqsubseteq \neg X{:}(b_{\bar{x}|y}, d_{\bar{x}|y})$

Then, due to the logical relationships between these axioms, we have the following constraints on the opinions associated with them:

- $b_{\bar{y}|x} = b_{\bar{x}|y}$ and $d_{\bar{y}|x} = d_{\bar{x}|y}$
- $d_{y|x} \geq b_{\bar{y}|x}$ and $d_{x|y} \geq b_{\bar{y}|x}$
- $b_{y|x} \leq d_{\bar{y}|x}$ and $b_{x|y} \leq d_{\bar{y}|x}$
- $b_{y|x} + b_{\bar{y}|x} \leq 1$, since $b_{\bar{y}|x} + d_{\bar{y}|x} \leq 1$

If these constraints are not satisfied, the TBox becomes inconsistent. Existing TBox axioms can be combined to create new TBox axioms. That is, we can combine $X \sqsubseteq Z{:}(b_{z|x}, d_{z|x})$ and $Z \sqsubseteq Y{:}(b_{y|z}, d_{y|z})$ to calculate $X \sqsubseteq Y{:}(b_{y|x}, d_{y|x})$ using the multiplication operator of SL [7]: $b_{y|x} = b_{z|x}b_{y|z}$ and $d_{y|x} = d_{z|x} + d_{y|z} - d_{z|x}d_{y|z}$.

Let us note that, we may derive different opinions for the same TBox axiom by combining different existing axioms. If we derive several opinions for the same axiom, we only keep the one with the highest belief value. For example, let us have $X \sqsubseteq Z{:}(0,1)$, $Z \sqsubseteq Y{:}(1,0)$, $X \sqsubseteq C{:}(1,0)$, and $C \sqsubseteq Y{:}(0.5, 0.1)$. Then, we derive $(0,1)$ and $(0.5, 0.1)$ for $X \sqsubseteq Y$; we chose $(0.5, 0.1)$ as the opinion for $X \sqsubseteq Y$ if no direct opinion is asserted for it.

Given any two concepts or roles X and Y, we can have or derive at most three TBox axioms $X \sqsubseteq Y{:}(b_{y|x}, d_{y|x})$, $Y \sqsubseteq X{:}(b_{x|y}, d_{x|y})$, and $X \sqsubseteq \neg Y{:}(b_{\bar{y}|x}, d_{\bar{y}|x})$. Regarding these axioms, we restrict $\mathcal{SDL}$-Lite so that one of $b_{\bar{y}|x}$, $b_{y|x}$, or $b_{x|y}$ is zero. This restriction on $\mathcal{SDL}$-Lite is enforced to facilitate efficient reasoning support.

3.2   ABox Axioms

In this work, we assume that information sources provide their opinions about ABox axioms. Then, these opinions are discounted by the trustworthiness of these sources. Lastly, the discounted opinions are associated with the ABox axioms and asserted into an $\mathcal{SDL}$-Lite knowledge base. For the sake of clarity, we assume that there is a single opinion for each ABox axiom; that is, there is only one source that provides opinion about a specific ABox axiom. We will release this assumption later.

The ABox axiom $X(o)$ can be considered as the proposition "the object o is an instance of X". Similarly, the ABox axiom $R(o_1, o_2)$ can be considered as the proposition "the object o_1 has relation R with another object o_2". We can use the notations $X(o){:}(b, d)$ and $R(o_1, o_2){:}(b, d)$ to associate the ABox axioms with the related opinions. Let us assume that a source s provide opinion w_x^s about this axiom. Then, we assert $X(o){:}(w_x^s \otimes t_s)$ in the knowledge base, where t_s is the trust in the source and $w_x^s \otimes t_s$ is the discounted opinion.

The asserted opinions can be used with TBox axioms to derive inferred opinions for ABox axioms. Given an ABox assertion $\Theta{:}(b,d)$, an inferred opinion for Θ is denoted as (b',d') such that $b' \geq b$ and $d' \geq d$; the inferred opinions satisfy all domain constraints enforced by TBox axioms.

TBox axioms put domain constraints on inferred opinions for ABox axioms. Let us assume we have ABox assertions $X(o){:}(b_x,d_x)$ and $Y(o){:}(b_y,d_y)$. Then, opinions about TBox axioms relating X and Y constrain inferred opinions for $X(o)$ and $Y(o)$. In order to calculate inferred opinions, we use deduction over subjective opinions. Subjective Logic uses deduction operator to infer new opinions using conditional opinions based on probability theory. Let x and y be binary propositions referring to $X(o)$ and $Y(o)$, respectively. and assume we want to infer probability of y from that of x. For this purpose, we use marginalization over x in the joint probability distribution as follows:

$$p(y) = p(x)p(y|x) + p(\bar{x})p(y|\bar{x})$$

where $\bar{x}$ is another binary proposition equivalent to $\neg x$. SL extends this approach for subjective opinions to get the following constraints for the inferred opinion (b_y',d_y') [7]:

$$b_y' \geq b_x'b_{y|x} + d_x'b_{y|\bar{x}}$$
$$d_y' \geq b_x'b_{\bar{y}|x} + d_x'b_{\bar{y}|\bar{x}} = b_x'b_{\bar{y}|x} + d_x'b_{x|y}$$

where (b_x',d_x') is the inferred opinion for x; $b_{y|x}$ refers to the belief in the TBox axiom $X \sqsubseteq Y$; $b_{y|\bar{x}}$ refers to the belief in $\neg X \sqsubseteq Y$; $b_{\bar{y}|x}$ refers to the belief in $X \sqsubseteq \neg Y$; and $b_{\bar{y}|\bar{x}}$ (same as $b_{x|y}$) refers to the belief in $Y \sqsubseteq X$. Since DL-Lite does not allow negation at the left-hand side of class inclusion axioms, we have to assume $(b_{y|\bar{x}},d_{y|\bar{x}}) = (0,0)$.

Given ABox assertions $X(o){:}(b_x,d_x)$ and $Y(o){:}(b_y,d_y)$, we have the following constraints for the inferred opinions (b_x',d_x') and (b_y',d_y').

$$b_y' \geq b_y \text{ and } b_y' \geq b_x'b_{y|x} \tag{1}$$
$$b_x' \geq b_x \text{ and } b_x' \geq b_y'b_{x|y} \tag{2}$$
$$d_y' \geq d_y \text{ and } d_y' \geq b_x'b_{\bar{y}|x} + d_x'b_{x|y} \tag{3}$$
$$d_x' \geq d_x \text{ and } d_x' \geq b_y'b_{\bar{y}|x} + d_y'b_{y|x} \tag{4}$$

While deriving constraints above, we take X and Y as classes. We can derive the same set of constraints for the case that X and Y are roles (i.e., relations). In this case, ABox axioms will be in the form $X(o_1,o_2)$ and $Y(o_1,o_2)$. Let us note that, when X and Y are roles, $X \sqsubseteq Y$ implies $\exists X \sqsubseteq \exists Y$, where $\exists X$ and $\exists Y$ are classes.

The class expression $\exists R$ refers to a class of objects with relation R. If $(1,0)$ is the opinion for ABox axiom $R(o,o_1)$, then $(1,0)$ is the inferred opinion for $\exists R(o)$

and $\exists R^-(o_1)$. That is, inferred opinions for ABox axioms about R are used to infer opinions for ABox axioms about $\exists R$. Let us assume we want to determine the inferred opinion (b', d') for the ABox axiom $\exists R(o)$ and have inferred opinions $\langle (b'_1, d'_1), \ldots, (b'_n, d'_n) \rangle$ for ABox axioms $\langle R(o, o_1), \ldots, R(o, o_n) \rangle$. Then, we have the constraints

$$b' \geq max(b'_1, \ldots, b'_n) \text{ and } d'_1, \ldots, d'_n \geq d' \tag{5}$$

since, the belief in $\exists R(o)$ cannot be less than the belief in $R(o, o_i)$ and the disbelief in $R(o, o_j)$ cannot be less than the disbelief in $\exists R(o)$ for any i and j. Similarly, inferred opinions $\langle (b'_1, d'_1), \ldots, (b'_n, d'_n) \rangle$ for $\langle R(o_1, o), \ldots, R(o_n, o) \rangle$ imply (b', d') for $\exists R^-(o)$ such that $b' \geq max(b'_1, \ldots, b'_n)$ and $d'_1, \ldots, d'_n \geq d'$.

3.3   Semantics of $\mathcal{S}$DL-Lite

In this section, we formalize the semantics of $\mathcal{S}$DL-Lite using interpretations. Let $\mathcal{W}$ be the set of all possible subjective binary opinions. A subjective interpretation is a pair $\mathcal{I} = (\Delta^\mathcal{I}, \cdot^\mathcal{I})$ where the domain $\Delta^\mathcal{I}$ is a non-empty set of objects and $\cdot^\mathcal{I}$ is a subjective interpretation function, which maps:

- an individual a to an element of $\mathsf{a}^\mathcal{I} \in \Delta^\mathcal{I}$,
- a named class A to a function $\mathsf{A}^\mathcal{I} : \Delta^\mathcal{I} \to \mathcal{W}$,
- a named property R to a function $R^\mathcal{I} : \Delta^\mathcal{I} \times \Delta^\mathcal{I} \to \mathcal{W}$.

Table 1. Semantics of subjective DL-Lite

Syntax	Semantics
$\top$	$\top^\mathcal{I}(o) = (1, 0, 0)$
$\bot$	$\bot^\mathcal{I}(o) = (0, 1, 0)$
$\exists R$	$b((\exists R)^\mathcal{I}(o_1)) \geq max \bigcup_{\forall o_2} \{b(R^I(o_1, o_2))\}$ and
	$d((\exists R)^\mathcal{I}(o_1)) \leq min \bigcup_{\forall o_2} \{d(R^I(o_1, o_2))\}$
$\neg B$	$(\neg B)^\mathcal{I}(o) = \neg B^\mathcal{I}(o)$
$\neg R$	$(\neg R)^\mathcal{I}(o_1, o_2) = \neg R^\mathcal{I}(o_1, o_2)$
R^-	$(R^-)^\mathcal{I}(o_2, o_1) = R^\mathcal{I}(o_1, o_2)$
	$\forall o \in \Delta^\mathcal{I},$
$B_x \sqsubseteq B_y : w_{y\|x}$	$b(B_x^\mathcal{I}(o)) \times b_{y\|x} \leq b(B_y^\mathcal{I}(o))$
$B_x \sqsubseteq \neg B_y : w_{\bar{y}\|x}$	$b(B_y^\mathcal{I}(o)) \times b_{\bar{y}\|x} + d(B_y^\mathcal{I}(o)) \times b_{y\|x} \leq d(B_x^\mathcal{I}(o))$
$B_y \sqsubseteq B_x : w_{x\|y}$	$b(B_y^\mathcal{I}(o)) \times b_{x\|y} \leq b(B_x^\mathcal{I}(o))$
$B_y \sqsubseteq \neg B_x : w_{\bar{y}\|x}$	$b(B_x^\mathcal{I}(o)) \times b_{\bar{y}\|x} + d(B_x^\mathcal{I}(o)) \times b_{x\|y} \leq d(B_y^\mathcal{I}(o))$
$R_i \sqsubseteq R_j : w_{j\|i}$	$\forall o_1, o_2 \in \Delta^\mathcal{I},$
$R_i \sqsubseteq \neg R_j : w_{\bar{j}\|i}$	$b(R_i^\mathcal{I}(o_1, o_2)) \times b(w_{j\|i}) \leq b(R_j^\mathcal{I}(o_1, o_2))$
$\cdots$	$b(R_j^\mathcal{I}(o_1, o_2)) \times b_{\bar{j}\|i} + d(R_j^\mathcal{I}(o_1, o_2)) \times b_{j\|i} \leq d(R_i^\mathcal{I}(o_1, o_2))$
	$\cdots$
$B(\mathsf{a}):w_1, \ldots, w_n$	$\forall w_i \in \{w_1, \ldots, w_n\},\ b(w_i) \leq b(B^\mathcal{I}(\mathsf{a}^\mathcal{I}))$ and $d(w_i) \leq d(B^\mathcal{I}(\mathsf{a}^\mathcal{I}))$
$R(\mathsf{a}, \mathsf{b}):w_1, \ldots, w_n$	$\forall w_i \in \{w_1, \ldots, w_n\},\ b(w_i) \leq b(R^\mathcal{I}(\mathsf{a}^\mathcal{I}, \mathsf{b}^\mathcal{I}))$ and $d(w_i) \leq d(R^\mathcal{I}(\mathsf{a}^\mathcal{I}, \mathsf{b}^\mathcal{I}))$

To provide a semantics for $\mathcal{S}$DL-Lite, we extend interpretations of DL-Lite class and property descriptions, and of axioms under unique name assumption. The semantics are presented in Table 1. The interpretation functions for ABox axioms map the axioms to the inferred opinions described in the previous section. Therefore, $B^{\mathcal{I}}(o)$ and $R^{\mathcal{I}}(o_1, o_2)$ refer to inferred opinions.

An $\mathcal{S}$DL-Lite knowledge base $\mathcal{K}$ $(\mathcal{J}, \mathcal{A})$ is consistent it and only it it has a model. A model of $\mathcal{K}$ is an interpretation of $\mathcal{K}$ that satisfies the constraints in Table 1. A consistent $\mathcal{K}$ may have many models, but only one of them is the most general model with respect to the partial ordering of opinions in Definition 1. In the next section, we describe how to compute the most general model of a $\mathcal{S}$DL-Lite knowledge base.

4   Computing the Most General Model

In the previous section, we describe the constraints on inferred opinions. These constraints are only set lower and upper bounds for the inferred believes and disbelieves. In this section, we explain how to efficiently calculate of *the most general* inferred opinions about ABox axioms. For this purpose, we introduce the concept of *value sets* for inferred believes and disbelieves. The value set for b' (i.e., $V_{b'}$) is the set of values constituting the lower bound for b'. That is, it contains all of the lower bounds enforced by the domain constraints listed in Sect. 3.3. For instance, given only Eqs. 1–4, we can construct the value sets:

$$V_{b'_x} = \{b_x, b'_y b_{x|y}\}, V_{d'_x} = \{d_x, b'_y b_{\bar{y}|x} + d'_y b_{y|x}\}$$
$$V_{b'_y} = \{b_y, b'_x b_{y|x}\}, V_{d'_y} = \{d_y, b'_x b_{\bar{y}|x} + d'_x b_{x|y}\}$$

While a single value set contain only lower bounds, the value sets together may represent both the upper and lower bounds for the inferred opinions.

We can calculate an inferred opinion for the ABox axiom $X(o)$ by picking the maximum values within the related value sets, i.e., $(max(V_{b'_x}), max(V_{d'_x}))$. The calculated opinion would be the most general inferred opinion, since for any other inferred opinion (b''_x, d''_x) for $X(o)$, we have $b''_x \geq b'_x$ and $d''_x \geq d'_x$. Although the calculation of the most general opinion looks simple, it may require a recursive procedure since each value set may contain references to inferred opinions about other ABox axioms. For instance, calculation of b'_x may involve calculation of b'_y, because $V_{b'_x}$ contains $b'_y b_{x|y}$.

In a value set, each reference to belief or disbelief of an inferred opinion can be taken as a variable, e.g., b'_y appearing in $V_{b'_x}$ is a variable. The domain of each such variable is the corresponding value sets. e.g., b'_y takes values from $V_{b'_y}$. Therefore, we can convert a value set into a set of ground literals by iteratively replacing each variables with the set of values in its corresponding value set; however, while doing so, we omit cycles. This is called *unfolding* a value set and use $\psi(\cdot)$ to denote a function that unfolds value sets. Algorithm 1 summarizes a simple implementation of the unfolding function.

The algorithm takes a value set V_γ as input. Then, for its each element δ that contains a variable β (line 1), we replace δ with a set of elements derived from the value set of β (lines 2–9). For each element α in V_β, we add a new element to V_γ if it does not have any cycle; the new element is computed using the function $replace(\beta, \alpha, \delta)$ (line 4–7). This function replaces β with α in the statement δ and returns the resulting statement. Given a value set (e.g., $V_{b'_x}$), this algorithm recursively replaces any reference to an inferred opinion (e.g., b'_y) in the value set with all possible values from related value set (e.g., $V_{b'_y}$). While doing so, if a cycles is detected in some terms, these terms are removed (line 5 of Algorithm 1). For instance, $\psi(V_{b'_x}) = \{b_x, b_y b_{x|y}\}$, where we do not have $b'_x b_{y|x} b_{x|y}$, since it contains the cycle $(b'_x b_{y|x} b_{x|y})$. Similarly, we have $\psi(V_{b'_y}) = \{b_y, b_x b_{y|x}\}$. Also, $\psi(V_{d'_x})$ is calculated as below, where $0 \in \{b_{y|x}, b_{x|y}, b_{\bar{y}|x}\}$.

$$\psi(V_{d'_x}) = \{d_x, b_y b_{\bar{y}|x} + d_y b_{y|x}, b_x b_{y|x} b_{\bar{y}|x} + d_y b_{y|x},$$
$$b_y b_{\bar{y}|x} + (b_x b_{\bar{y}|x} + d_x b_{x|y}) b_{y|x}, b_x b_{y|x} b_{\bar{y}|x} + (b_x b_{\bar{y}|x} + d_x b_{x|y}) b_{y|x}\}$$

Algorithm 1. The unfolding function $\psi(\cdot)$ for value sets

---

function $\psi(V_\gamma)$
1: **while** $\delta \in V_\gamma$ **and** (δ includes β) **and** ($\beta \equiv b'_\tau$ **or** $\beta \equiv d'_\tau$) **do**
2:     $V_\gamma = V_\gamma \setminus \{\delta\}$
3:     **for** $\alpha \in V_\beta$ **do**
4:         $\delta' = replace(\beta, \alpha, \delta)$
5:         **if** $\delta' \neq 0$ **and** δ' **has no cycle then**
6:             $V_\gamma = V_\gamma \cup \{\delta'\}$
7:         **end if**
8:     **end for**
9: **end while**
10: **return** V_γ

While a value set V_γ has references to other inferred beliefs (e.g., b'_y) or disbeliefs (e.g., b'_y), the unfolded value set $\psi(V_\gamma)$ contains only asserted beliefs (e.g., b_y) or disbeliefs (e.g., d_y). Moreover, as shown in Theorem 1, $max(V_\gamma) = max(\psi(V_\gamma))$, therefore we can easily calculate the most general inferred opinions using unfolded value sets. For instance, the most general (b'_x, d'_x) is calculated as $(max(\psi(V_{b'_x})), max(\psi(V_{d'_x})))$.

Theorem 1. For any γ representing an inferred belief or disbelief, $max(V_\gamma)$ is equivalent to $max(\psi(V_\gamma))$ for an SDL-Lite knowledge base.

Proof: To prove this, it is enough to show that removing terms with cycles does not change the answer of $max(\psi(V_\gamma))$. We can show this in two steps. We show that this is true when i) γ is an *inferred belief* (e.g., b'_x) and ii) γ is an *inferred disbelief* (e.g., d'_x).

Case I: Let us assume that γ is an inferred belief such as b'_x. If we encounter a cycle in a term while unfolding $V_{b'_x}$, this term may look like

$(b'_{c_i} b_{c_i|c_n} \cdots b_{c_j|c_i} b_{c_i|c_k} \cdots b_{x|c_0})$. Replacing b'_{c_i} with the terms from $V_{b'_{c_i}}$ does not change the maximum value in the unfolded value set $\psi(V_{b'_x})$, because, for each term $\Delta \in V_{b'_{c_i}}$, the unfolded set already contains $\Delta \times (b_{c_i|c_k} \cdots b_{x|c_0})$, which is greater than $\Delta \times (b_{c_i|c_n} \cdots b_{c_j|c_i} b_{c_i|c_k} \cdots b_{x|c_0})$.

Case II: Let us assume that γ is an inferred disbelief such as d'_x. Let us assume that a term in $V_{d'_x}$ lead to cycles as we unfold it. This term may be in the form of $(b'_y b_{\bar{y}|x} + d'_y b_{y|x})$. The first part of the term, i.e., $b'_y b_{\bar{y}|x}$, cannot lead to a cycle, since $\mathcal{S}$DL-Lite does not allow negation at left hand side of TBox axioms, e.g., we cannot have $\neg Y \sqsubseteq Z$. Therefore, a cycle can be led only by the second part of the term, i.e., $d'_y b_{y|x}$. this term may look like $\Omega + (d'_{c_i} b_{c_i|c_n} \cdots b_{c_j|c_i} b_{c_i|c_k} \cdots b_{x|c_0})$, where Ω represents summation of all belief terms, i.e. terms that contain only belief values. The cycle contains $b_{c_i|c_n} \cdots b_{c_j|c_i} b_{c_i|c_k}$ and each term $b_{c_u|c_v}$ in the cycle is greater than zero. The cycle implies that $b_{c_v|c_u}$ must be greater than zero[1] as well; hence, $b_{\bar{c}_u|c_v} = 0$ due to the restrictions in $\mathcal{S}$DL-Lite. Therefore, replacing d'_{c_i} with the terms from $V_{d'_{c_i}}$ does not add any term to Ω. As in *Case I*, replacing d'_{c_i} with the terms from $V_{d'_{c_i}}$ does not change the maximum value in the unfolded value set $\psi(V_{d'_x})$, because, for each term $\Delta \in V_{d'_{c_i}}$, the unfolded set already contains $\Omega + \Delta \times (b_{c_i|c_k} \cdots b_{x|c_0})$, which is greater than $\Omega + \Delta \times (b_{c_i|c_n} \cdots b_{c_j|c_i} b_{c_i|c_k} \cdots b_{x|c_0})$. ∎

Once, we unfold value sets, we can compute the most general inferred opinions about ABox axioms by picking the maximum values in the value sets. For instance, the most general inferred opinion for $Y(o)$ is computed as $(max(\psi(V_{b'_y})), max(\psi(V_{d'_y})))$, where $V_{b'_y}$ and $V_{d'_y}$ are value sets for the ABox axiom $Y(o)$. The most general inferred opinions for an $\mathcal{S}$DL-Lite knowledge base satisfy all of the constraints listed in Table 1. These opinions construct the most general model of the knowledge base.

The worst-case time complexity of Algorithm 1 is exponential in the size of TBox and ABox. In an $\mathcal{S}$DL-Lite knowledge base, each element of a value set is summation of weighted variables, e.g., $b'_y b_{\bar{y}|x} + d'_y b_{y|x}$. It is possible to have unfolded value sets in polynomial time if value sets are composed of only monomials; a monomial is a polynomial which has only one term. This is the case when one of $b_{\bar{y}|x}$ or $b_{y|x}$ is always zero. In this case, each non-zero term in the unfolded value set is in the form $b_{x_1} b_{x_n|x_{n-1}} \cdots b_{x_2|x_1}$ or $d_{x_1} b_{x_n|x_{n-1}} \cdots b_{x_2|x_1}$. Let us assume that we derived opinions, e.g., $(b_{y|x}, d_{y|x})$, for all possible concept or role inclusions $X \sqsubseteq Y$ in the TBox as described in Sect. 3.1. As described before, $b_{x_n|x_1} \geq b_{x_n|x_{n-1}} \cdots b_{x_2|x_1}$; therefore we can exclude $b_{x_1} b_{x_n|x_{n-1}} \cdots b_{x_2|x_1}$ in the unfolded value set, since it may already contain $b_{x_1} b_{x_n|x_1}$. Based on this observation, we can compose an unfolded value set directly in $O(|\mathcal{A}| \times |\mathcal{T}|^2)$, where $\mathcal{A}$ and $\mathcal{T}$ are sizes of ABox and TBox, respectively.

---

[1] Note that $b_{x|z}, b_{z|y}, b_{y|x} > 0$ imply that $b_{z|x} \geq b_{z|y} b_{y|x} > 0$ as explained in Sect. 3.1.

5 Handling Inconsistencies

An SDL-Lite ABox is populated with uncertain and unreliable knowledge from diverse information sources. That is why inconsistencies may exist in the knowledge. In this section, we describe how to detect and resolve inconsistencies through trust revision.

An SDL-Lite ABox is inconsistent if there is no valid inferred opinion for any ABox axiom τ. That is, $max(\psi(V_{b'_\tau})) + max(\psi(V_{d'_\tau})) > 1$. This is possible if and only if $\exists c_i, c_j$ such that $c_i \in \psi(V_{b'_\tau})$, $c_j \in \psi(V_{d'_\tau})$, and $(c_i + c_j) > 1$. We call each such $(c_i + c_j)$ as a *source of inconsistency*. If there is no source of inconsistency, the knowledge base is consistent. Once we unfold all value sets using Algorithm 1, it is trivial to find all sources of inconsistency if there exists any.

Each *source of inconsistency* is a linear combination of belief and disbelief values from different opinions. For instance, consider the unfolded value sets for $V_{b'_x}$ and $V_{d'_x}$, where $b_y b_{x|y} \in \phi(V_{b'_x})$ and $b_x b_{y|x} b_{\bar{y}|x} + d_y b_{y|x} \in \phi(V_{d'_x})$. The summation $\mu_0 = b_y b_{x|y} + b_x b_{y|x} b_{\bar{y}|x} + d_y b_{y|x}$ is a source of inconsistency if $\mu_0 > 1$. Each source of inconsistency μ_i is related to a set of opinions O_i from ABox. For instance, the source of inconsistency μ_0 mentioned above is related to the opinions $O_0 = \{w_y, w_x\}$. For convenience, we write a source of inconsistency μ_i as

$$\mu_i = \sum_{w_j \in O_i} c_{ij} \times b(w_j) + \hat{c}_{ij} \times d(w_j)$$

where c_{ij} and $\hat{c}_{ij}$ are the coefficients of belief and disbelief in the opinion w_j in the summation representing the source inconsistency, respectively. When μ_0 is taken as an example, we have $c_{0y} = b_{x|y}$, $\hat{c}_{0y} = b_{y|x}$, $c_{0x} = b_{y|z} b_{\bar{y}|x}$, and $\hat{c}_{0x} = 0$. A source of inconsistency μ_i can be resolved by discounting the related opinions O_i. Therefore, resolving the source of inconsistency μ_i can be formalized as finding an extra discounting factor $0 \le \eta_j \le 1$ for each opinion $w_j \in O_i$ such that

$$\sum_{w_j \in O_i} c_{ij} \times b(w_j \otimes \eta_j) + \hat{c}_{ij} \times d(w_j \otimes \eta_j) = \sum_{w_j \in O_i} c_{ij} \times b(w_j) \times \eta_j + \hat{c}_{ij} \times d(w_j) \times \eta_j \le 1$$

Let us note that opinions in an ABox are collected from information sources. These opinions are discounted based on the trustworthiness of their sources before being added to the ABox. Therefore, each opinion w_j in the ABox of an SDL-Lite knowledge base is actually based on another opinion w_j^ℓ received from an information source ℓ and $w_j = w_j^\ell \otimes t_\ell$, where t_ℓ is the trustworthiness of ℓ. Discounting w_j with η_j means discounting the original opinion w_j^ℓ with $t_\ell \times \eta_j$, because $w_j \otimes \eta_j = w_j^\ell \otimes (t_\ell \times \eta_j)$. Also, discounting w_j^ℓ with $t_\ell \times \eta_j$ implies reducing the trust in the opinion w_j^ℓ from t_ℓ to $t_\ell \times \eta_j$. That is, additional discounting of w_j with η_j corresponds to *revising* the trustworthiness of w_j^ℓ as $t_\ell \times \eta_j$ by speculating about the trustworthiness of the source ℓ regarding w_j^ℓ. In other words, even though the trustworthiness of ℓ is t_ℓ based on the existing evidence $\langle r_\ell, s_\ell \rangle$, it becomes $t_\ell \times \eta_j$ for this specific opinion; therefore, $t_\ell \times \eta_j$ effectively becomes the trust in w_j^ℓ. Below, we propose a metric to measure how much we may need to speculate about the trustworthiness of ℓ regarding w_j^ℓ.

To decrease trust from t_ℓ to $t_\ell \times \eta_j$, we need additional negative evidence, which is called *speculative evidence* and designated by ρ_ℓ. Our intuition is that it is less likely for a trustworthy source to present additional negative *speculative evidence* than it is for an untrustworthy one, and thus the receipt of such evidence should be tempered by $(\bar{t}_\ell)^\kappa$. Here, $\bar{t}_\ell = 1 - t_\ell$ represents the *distrust* that we have in the source ℓ – i.e., the likelihood that we will receive additional negative evidence given our experiences with the source. The calibration constant $\kappa \geq 0$ enables us to vary the influence that prior experience has on our prediction that a source will present negative evidence in the future. If $\kappa = 0$, for example, we assume that all sources are equally likely to provide negative evidence. We set κ to 2 in our implementation in this paper. Using the trust model in Sect. 2.2, we obtain:

$$t_\ell \times \eta_j = \frac{r_\ell + 1}{r_\ell + s_\ell + 2} \times \eta_j = \frac{r_\ell + 1}{s_\ell + r_\ell + 2 + \rho_\ell.(\bar{t}_\ell)^\kappa}$$

$$= \frac{r_\ell + 1}{r_\ell + s_\ell + 2 + \rho_\ell.(\frac{s_\ell + 1}{r_\ell + s_\ell + 2})^\kappa}$$

Rearranging this for ρ_ℓ yields:

$$\rho_\ell = \frac{\nu_\ell}{\eta_j} - \nu_\ell \quad \text{where} \quad \nu_\ell = \frac{(r_\ell + s_\ell + 2)^{\kappa+1}}{(s_\ell + 1)^\kappa} \tag{6}$$

We can choose different η_j values, each of which may lead to different amount of evidence that should be speculated.

To resolve a source of inconsistency, we may discount more than one opinion. An $\mathcal{SDL}$-Lite knowledge base becomes consistent if we resolve all sources of inconsistencies by discounting involved opinions. Using the metric derived above, we can compute total amount of speculative evidence necessary to discount these opinions. Therefore, given the chosen discounting factors, we can compute the total amount of speculative evidence necessary to resolve inconsistencies; discounting an opinions corresponds to revising its trustworthiness.

In this section, we introduce a method to choose the best discounting factors to resolve inconsistencies. Our approach is based on minimizing the total amount of speculative evidence used while revising trust in the involved opinions. Let us assume we have the following n sources of inconsistencies to resolve:

$$\sum_{w_j \in O_1} c_{1j} \times b(w_j) + \hat{c}_{1j} \times d(w_j) > 1 \ \dots \ \sum_{w_i \in O_n} c_{ni} \times b(w_i) + \hat{c}_{ni} \times d(w_i) > 1$$

For each opinion $w_k \in O_1 \cup \dots \cup O_n$, we aim to find the optimum discounting factor η_k given the constant $\nu_{k'}$ that is derived from trust evidence about the source of w_k. To determine optimum discounting factors for these opinions, we construct the following optimization problem with a non-linear objective function and linear constraints.

$$\text{minimize} \quad \sum_{w_k \in O_1 \cup \cdots \cup O_n} \frac{\nu_{k'}}{\eta_k} - \nu_{k'}$$

$$\text{suchthat} \quad 0 < \eta_k \leq 1 \text{ for each } w_k \in O_1 \cup \cdots \cup O_n$$

$$\text{and} \quad \sum_{w_j \in O_1} c_{1j} \times b(w_j) \times \eta_j + \hat{c}_{1j} \times d(w_j) \times \eta_j \leq 1, \ldots,$$

$$\sum_{w_i \in O_n} c_{ni} \times b(w_i) \times \eta_i + \hat{c}_{ni} \times d(w_i) \times \eta_i \leq 1.$$

The objective function presented here is convex. The convex property of the objective function guarantees that any local minima is also the global minimum. Existing convex optimization techniques can be used to solve this problem to estimate the best discounting factors. In this work, we used the gradient-decent algorithm [3] for this purpose.

6   Implementation and Evaluation

We implemented a reasoner for $\mathcal{S}$DL-Lite in Java. The reasoner computes the most general model of the knowledge base when presented with a $\mathcal{S}$DL-Lite knowledge base. We recall that the QL fragment of OWL is equivalent to DL-Lite$_R$. Thus, an OWL-QL ontology can be taken as a $\mathcal{S}$DL-Lite knowledge base where each axiom is implicitly associated with opinion $(1, 0)$. Furthermore, we can explicitly associate arbitrary opinions with axioms using annotation properties. For this purpose, we have created an annotation property opinion that allowed us to annotate any ABox or TBox axioms with opinions. To represent information sources, we use the class InformationSource and to denote trust opinions about these sources we create the data type property trust. Using these three entities, we can easily build an $\mathcal{S}$DL-Lite knowledge base with a standard ontology development tool.

Table 2. Information sources and their trustworthiness from the viewpoint of MIL

Source	Description	Trust evidence (i.e., $\langle r, s \rangle$ pairs)	Degree of trust
LC	Local civilian sources	$\langle 4, 0 \rangle$	0.83
LP	Local police sources	$\langle 10, 3 \rangle$	0.786
CMIL	Collaborating military forces	$\langle 50, 5 \rangle$	0.89
SIES	Seismic sensors of MIL	$\langle 100, 3 \rangle$	0.96

6.1   Case-Study: Semantic Multi-modal Sensor Fusion with $\mathcal{S}$DL-Lite

Let us now introduce a scenario to demonstrate how reasoning in $\mathcal{S}$DL-Lite works. Consider a region in which insurgents are active and where civilian groups are in need of support. An NGO operating in the region has identified a safe zone Z and aims to bring relief to the injured in village V by transporting them to the safe zone. There is only one road r05 between Z and V, but there is conflict between groups G_1 and G_2 within the region. As part of a multi-national peace effort,

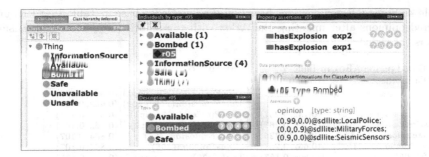

Fig. 1. Creating an $\mathcal{S}$DL-Lite ontology in the Protege for the scenario.

Table 3. An $\mathcal{S}$DL-Lite knowledge base for the scenario.

$\mathcal{S}$DL-Lite TBox	Opinion
$hasExplosion \sqsubseteq hasProblem$	$(1,0)$
$\exists hasExplosion \sqsubseteq Unsafe$	$(0.9,0)$
$\exists hasProblem \sqsubseteq Unavailable$	$(0.8,0)$
$Bombed \sqsubseteq \exists hasExplosion$	$(1,0)$
$Available \sqsubseteq \neg Unavailable$	$(1,0)$
$Safe \sqsubseteq \neg Unsafe$	$(1,0)$

$\mathcal{S}$DL-Lite ABox	Opinions from Information Sources	
$hasExplosion(\text{r05}, \text{exp1})$	$(1,0)@\text{LC}$	
$hasExplosion(\text{r05}, \text{exp2})$	$(0.9,0.05)@\text{LP}$	
$Safe(\text{r05})$	$(0.9,0)@\text{CMIL}$	
$Bombed(\text{r05})$	$(0,0.9)@\text{CMIL};$	$(0.99,0)@\text{LP}$
$Available(\text{r05})$	$(0,0.95)@\text{LP};$	$(0.8,0.1)@\text{LC}$

MIL and CMIL operate within the region, and part of their remit is to protect and support NGOs. The resources available to CMIL include Unmanned Aerial Vehicles (UAVs). MIL acts as liaison to the NGO, and has intelligence from the information sources listed in Table 2 along with models of the trustworthiness of these sources. MIL collects the following pieces of information from the sources in the area:

1. LC reports an *explosion* on road r05 with opinion $(1,0)$;
2. LP reports another *explosion* on r05 with opinion $(0.9, 0.05)$;
3. CMIL informed MIL that r05 is *safe* with opinion $(0.9, 0)$;
4. LP reports that r05 is *bombed* with opinion $(0.99, 0)$;
5. CMIL informed MIL that r05 is *not bombed* with opinion $(0.9, 0)$;
6. LP reports that r05 is *not available* with opinion $(0.95, 0)$;
7. LC reports that r05 is *available* with opinion $(0.8, 0.1)$.

The collected intelligence is converted to the $\mathcal{S}$DL-Lite knowledge base in Table 3. This knowledge base can be represented as an ontology as shown in Fig. 1 where annotation property `opinion` is used to associate opinions with the axioms.

In Table 4, we tabulate two sets of inferred opinions. Table 4(a) shows the inferred opinions for the knowledge base in Table 3. These opinions indicate that the road (a) is mostly safe but may not be available; and (b) is most probably not bombed as these axioms have a higher amount of disbelief – i.e., disbelief around 0.8. The main reason for these inferred opinions is the reports from CMIL, which is regarded highly trustworthy based on over 50 past evidence. The conflicting reports from LP and LC with those of CMIL are discounted further by the reasoner to resolve inconsistencies. Even though the trust values for LP and LC are also

Table 4. Some inferred opinions based on the knowledge base in Table 3 (at left) and inferred opinions after updating the ABox with the additional opinion from seismic sensors (at right).

(a) Based on the ABox in Table 3

SDL-Lite ABox	Inferred Opinions
$hasExplosion(r05, exp1)$	$(0.167, 0.725)$
$hasExplosion(r05, exp2)$	$(0.132, 0.725)$
$hasProblem(r05, exp2)$	$(0.132, 0.267)$
$hasProblem(r05, exp1)$	$(0.167, 0.267)$
$\exists hasExplosion(r05)$	$(0.265, 0.725)$
$\exists hasProblem(r05)$	$(0.662, 0.267)$
$Safe(r05)$	$(0.806, 0.167)$
$Unsafe(r05)$	$(0.167, 0.806)$
$Available(r05)$	$(0.334, 0.662)$
$Unavailable(r05)$	$(0.662, 0.334)$
$Bombed(r05)$	$(0.146, 0.806)$

(b) After receiving $Bombed(r05): (0.9, 0)@\mathtt{SEIS}$

SDL-Lite ABox	Inferred Opinions
$hasExplosion(r05, exp1)$	$(0.835, 0.107)$
$hasExplosion(r05, exp2)$	$(0.662, 0.107)$
$hasProblem(r05, exp1)$	$(0.835, 0.107)$
$hasProblem(r05, exp2)$	$(0.662, 0.107)$
$\exists hasExplosion(r05)$	$(0.864, 0.107)$
$\exists hasProblem(r05)$	$(0.864, 0.107)$
$Safe(r05)$	$(0.081, 0.835)$
$Unsafe(r05)$	$(0.835, 0.081)$
$Available(r05)$	$(0.134, 0.835)$
$Unavailable(r05)$	$(0.835, 0.134)$
$Bombed(r05)$	$(0.864, 0.107)$

high around 0.8, the amount of evidence used to calculate these trust values are much less than that of CMIL. Therefore, the opinions from LP and LC are discounted further when they are conflicting with the opinions from CMIL based on the optimisation techniques proposed in Sect. 5.

In Table 4(b), we show the inferred opinions for the case when the MIL received an additional opinion $(0.9, 0)$ for $Bombed(r05)$ from its seismic sensors. The trustworthiness of these sensors is 0.96 and computed based on over 100 past evidence. The report received from the sensors conflict with the opinions from CMIL. In this case, it is more meaningful to discount the opinions from CMIL significantly to resolve inconsistencies. Hence, the opinions of LP and LC are not be discounted significantly any more when they are conflicting with the opinions from CMIL. The resulting inferred opinions indicate that the road is most likely bombed, thus unsafe, and unavailable as all of these inferred opinions have belief masses over 0.8.

6.2   Evaluation

We have evaluated the SDL-Lite reasoner on a set of randomly generated ontologies, each is an extension of the ontology in our case study. These ontologies have around 1000 TBox axioms and a variable size of ABox. While the TBox axioms represent domain constraints, the ABox assertions represent the knowledge about the current state of the world. In our evaluations, we know the ground truth about the current state of the world. However, the Abox assertions in the ontologies are generated by collecting opinions from 100 information sources. At least 90 % of these sources are malicious; they sense the ground truth but deliberately provide misleading opinions. However, the remaining 10 % provides their genuine opinions about the ground truth with some noise.

We have trust opinions about each information source. In trust literature, it is emphasized that malicious agents may change their identities to white-wash their low reputation. Similarly, these agents may build up some trust through a small number of positive interactions with others before mislead them. Therefore, in our evaluations, we assume that malicious agents build some reputation with small number of positive evidence between 2 and 8; therefore, the opinions about their trustworthiness are in the form $(b_t, 0)$ where $0.5 \leq b_t \leq 0.8$. On the other hand, the trust opinions about the reliable sources are in the form (b_t, d_t) where $0.8 \leq b_t \leq 0.9$ and $d_t \leq 0.1$.

The reasoner does not know which sources are malicious. Given a randomly generated $\mathcal{SDL}$-Lite ontology, the reasoner calculates the value sets and discover inconsistencies. Lastly, it resolves the inconsistencies to compute a model of the knowledge base. The generated model can be considered as the fusion of the opinions provided by diverse unreliable sources. To resolve inconsistencies we use three methods: (i) the *evidence-based* method of Sect. 5 that considers trust evidence in addition to trustworthiness of the sources, (ii) a *trust-based* method that gradually discounts conflicting opinions relative to the trustworthiness of their source until all inconsistencies are resolved, (iii) *random* method that gradually discounts randomly selected opinions until all inconsistencies are resolved.

We generated ontologies randomly with approximately 1000 TBox axioms and ABox axioms of sizes varying between 300–1000. For each setting, we repeated our evaluations five times and report their average with standard deviations. Figure 2 shows *mean absolute error* in the inferred opinions for various methods of resolving inconsistencies in $\mathcal{SDL}$-Lite knowledge bases. The error is calculated based on the ground truth. The figure indicates that using only trust for resolving inconsistencies could be misleading; the error varies between 0.2 and 0.3 for different sizes of ABox. On the other hand, using evidence analysis, the error can be reduced to 0.1. Randomly selecting opinions to discount for resolving inconsistencies leads to an error above 0.5. Our evaluations indicate that $\mathcal{SDL}$-Lite reasoner combines various opinions from diverse sources with different trust evidence to successfully estimate the ground truth. This success is in the face of malicious sources.

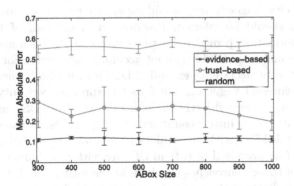

Fig. 2. Mean absolute error vs. ABox size.

Figure 3 shows the time spend for ABox reasoning with respect to different numbers of ABox assertions and inconsistencies. Reasoning time may vary significantly for different sizes of ABox. It takes around four seconds to reason with

300 ABox assertions and 4000 inconsistencies; however, it takes less than 440 seconds to reason with 1000 ABox assertions and 60000 inconsistencies.

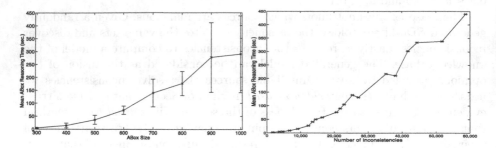

Fig. 3. ABox reasoning time in seconds vs. size (at left) and number of inconsistencies (at right).

7   Discussion

Any statements on the Web must be considered as claims instead of facts until the trust in the information is established. This is also be true for the Semantic Web [1]. That is why trust is an important component of the SW vision along with ontologies, logics, and so on. In this paper, we aim allow reasoning with uncertain information from unreliable sources in the SW. For this purpose, we extend DL-Lite$_R$ – a very useful DL constituting the logic behind OWL-QL.

DL-Lite$_R$ is a tractable subset of DLs with a large number of application areas. Its scalability makes it very useful especially for the settings where large amount of data should be queried. However, in a network of heterogeneous sources, any information provided by the sources could be uncertain, incomplete, and even conflicting. DL-Litecannot accommodate such information. Some researchers such as Straccia have extended DL-Lite with fuzzy membership values, which can represent vagueness but fails to express uncertainty in a broader sense [4]. However, we use subjective opinions derived from DST and Subjective logic that explicitly takes into account *uncertainty* and *belief ownership* [7].

Qi *et al.* extended DLs with uncertainty reasoning with probabilistic logic [9], and Benferhat *et al.* proposed to extend DL-Lite with possibilistic reasoning [6], however, none of these approaches can handle the misleading information from malicious sources, because they do not consider trust during reasoning. Gobeck and Halaschek [5] present belief revision for OWL-DL, which is based on trust degrees to remove conflicting statements from a knowledge base. However, as the authors point out, the proposed algorithm is not guaranteed to be optimal. In our work, we embed statement retraction implicitly into the opinion revision procedure with a global optimal criteria which is grounded on a Beta distribution formalisation of trust.

In our previous work [10], we extended a simpler DL that does not allow role hierarchies and disjoint roles. Unlike this work, in the previous work, TBox axioms are certain and only ABox assertions are associated with uncertainty. Furthermore, each ABox axioms could be associated with only one opinion, which is a significant limitation for realistic applications. In this work, we propose a much more expressive language that allows role hierarchies, uncertain TBox axioms, and multiple opinions about the same ABox axioms. Our empirical evaluations and analysis indicate that our approach allows semantic reasoning to combine uncertain information from unreliable sources and approximate the ground truth during reasoning using the trust evidence about the information sources. As a future work, we plan to study query answering and explore how more expressive DLs can be extended with subjective opinions.

References

1. Artz, D., Gil, Y.: A survey of trust in computer science and the Semantic Web. Web Semant.: Sci. Serv. Agents World Wide Web **5**(2), 58–71 (2007)
2. Baader, F., McGuiness, D.L., Nardi, D., Patel-Schneider, P.: Description Logic Handbook: Theory, Implementation and Applications. Cambridge University Press, Cambridge (2002)
3. Boyd, S., Vandenberghe, L.: Convex Optimization. Cambridge University Press, New York (2004)
4. Calvanese, D., Giacomo, G., Lembo, D., Lenzerini, M., Rosati, R.: Tractable reasoning and efficient query answering in description logics: the DL-lite family. J. Autom. Reason. **39**(3), 385–429 (2007)
5. Golbeck, J., Halaschek-Wiener, C.: Trust-based revision for expressive web syndication. J. Logic Comput. **19**(5), 771–790 (2009)
6. Gómez, S.A.: Reasoning with inconsistent possibilistic description logics ontologies with disjunctive assertions. J. Comput. Sci. Technol. **15** (2015)
7. Jøsang, A.: Subjective Logic. Springer, Heidelberg (2016)
8. Jøsang, A., Ismail, R.: The beta reputation system. In: Proceedings of the 15th Bled Electronic Commerce Conference e-Reality: Constructing the e-Economy, pp. 48–64 (2002)
9. Qi, G., Pan, J.Z., Ji, Q.: Extending description logics with uncertainty reasoning in possibilistic logic. In: Mellouli, K. (ed.) ECSQARU 2007. LNCS (LNAI), vol. 4724, pp. 828–839. Springer, Heidelberg (2007)
10. Sensoy, M., Fokoue, A., Pan, J.Z., Norman, T.J.: Reasoning about uncertain information and conflict resolution through trust revision. In: Proceedings of 12th International Joint Conference on Autonomous Agents and Multiagent Systems (AAMAS), pp. 837–844 (2013)
11. Shafer, G.: A Mathematical Theory of Evidence. Princeton University Press, Princeton (1976)

A Collaborative Framework for 3D Mapping Using Unmanned Aerial Vehicles

Patrick Doherty[1]([✉]), Jonas Kvarnström[1], Piotr Rudol[1], Marius Wzorek[1], Gianpaolo Conte[1], Cyrille Berger[1], Timo Hinzmann[2], and Thomas Stastny[2]

[1] Department of Computer and Information Science,
Linköping University, Linköping, Sweden
patrick.doherty@liu.se
[2] Autonomous Systems Lab, ETH Zurich, Zurich, Switzerland

Abstract. This paper describes an overview of a generic framework for collaboration among humans and multiple heterogeneous robotic systems based on the use of a formal characterization of delegation as a speech act. The system used contains a complex set of integrated software modules that include delegation managers for each platform, a task specification language for characterizing distributed tasks, a task planner, a multi-agent scan trajectory generation and region partitioning module, and a system infrastructure used to distributively instantiate any number of robotic systems and user interfaces in a collaborative team. The application focusses on 3D reconstruction in alpine environments intended to be used by alpine rescue teams. Two complex UAV systems used in the experiments are described. A fully autonomous collaborative mission executed in the Italian Alps using the framework is also described.

Keywords: Emergency and disaster management · Robotics and multi-robot systems · Human-robot interaction · Distributed planning and collaboration · Teamwork · Unmanned aircraft systems · Middleware and interaction protocols

1 Introduction

Emergency Informatics is an emerging multi-disciplinary scientific field that *"addresses the information processes (real-time collection, analysis, distribution and visualization) for the prevention, preparedness, response and recovery from emergencies"* [1]. In this context, emergencies range from local events to large scale catastrophes. An important and essential aspect of emergency informatics is collaboration and cooperation, where people interact with technical systems either directly or remotely, people interact with people through technical systems, and people interact with remote environments through technical systems such as ground or aerial robots.

This discipline targets highly complex problems characterized by multiple information interdependencies, temporal and spatial scales and latencies, nonlinear behavior and the rarity of optimal solutions to the many problems involved.

© Springer International Publishing Switzerland 2016
M. Baldoni et al. (Eds.): PRIMA 2016, LNAI 9862, pp. 110–130, 2016.
DOI: 10.1007/978-3-319-44832-9_7

Consequently, an integrated systems of systems approach to the development of technical systems interacting with emergency responders with the goal of saving lives becomes paramount.

The purpose of this paper is to present an overview of an integrated system of systems of heterogeneous autonomous unmanned aerial vehicles that collaborate with each other and with human responders at a high level of autonomy with the specific application goal of generating 3D models of operational environments. These models serve as the basis for the initial level of a dynamic information system through which additional semantic information about the operational environment can be dynamically added and used by first responders. The framework is more general, but the focus in this paper will be on a particular application.

The major components in the system that will be described in this paper are:

- A **Delegation Framework** – This is a speech act based system allowing agents and humans to collaborate by delegating tasks to each other, one-to-one and recursively.
- **Task Specification Trees** – This is the basic construct for representing complex tasks, both declaratively for formal analysis and procedurally as part of the implementation of the delegation framework.
- A **Planning Module** – This module contains a task planner and includes specialized modules associated with the scanning applications that include a scan trajectory generation module and a region partitioning module for distributed scanning.

Each component will be described at an adequate level of detail, both formally and pragmatically, and additional focus will be placed on the integration of these components into a system of systems showing how human responders interact with this technology. Although this paper is applied in nature, emphasis will also be placed on the formal foundations for each of the components. The system itself has been deployed using real UAV (unmanned aerial vehicle) platforms and can be used for relatively complex scanning missions, not only for 3D surface reconstruction, but also for search and rescue. For this paper, we will focus on using a rotor-based and a fixed-wing UAV, but the system is general enough to be used on most any robotic system. The prototype software instantiation of these components is currently being developed for use in the EU project SHERPA ([2], www.sherpa-project.eu), which focuses on the use of heterogeneous robot teams that assist alpine rescuers in the Italian alps in search and rescue missions.

Paper Outline. Section 2 begins by describing the basic collaborative mission cycle between humans and robotic systems. Section 3 provides an overview of the complex collaborative 3D reconstruction mission that will be the focus of this paper. Additionally, the two UAV platforms used in the mission will be described. Section 4 describes the delegation framework itself. This section also includes a description of Task Specification Trees. Section 5 provides an overview of task planning and its integration with the delegation system. Section 6 then describes

the application-specific scan trajectory algorithms in addition to a region partitioning algorithm. Section 7 provides the experimental results generated for the
collaborative scanning mission described in the paper.

2   Basic Collaborative Mission Cycle

In any emergency response situation, rescue operators will have access to static
interfaces such as ground stations consisting of laptops or stationary PCs in
addition to more portable systems such as touch screen devices or smart phones
that can be used anywhere in the field. Such devices are set up to provide
cognitively efficient multi-modal interfaces to human-robot teams involved in
the emergency response. For example, in the scanning mission described below,
the goal is to rapidly provide 3D reconstructions of salient regions by setting up
missions through such interfaces.

An operator should be able to request help from its team by simply marking
a region on a map in the interface and stating that a 3D re-construction of the
region is required. From the operator perspective, it is not important how that
is accomplished nor what or how many robotic systems are involved. What is
important is that this can be done efficiently within a reasonable span of time
and in the right format so that the rest of the team can use the mission output
to make better decisions and save lives.

Figure 1 shows the mission process which begins with an operator specifying a
3D reconstruction mission. Internally, this high-level request is transformed into
a *goal request* in the form of a Task Specification Tree (TST, Sect. 4) representing
the goal. This transformation can be achieved dynamically using automated
planning techniques, or by using generic TST templates that can be instantiated
appropriately.

The setup and execution of the mission represented by the goal request TST
should now be *delegated* to one or more participating team members. The TST is
therefore given to the local Delegation Module, which initiates a distributed delegation process (Sect. 4.2) where agents interact through their delegation modules
(Fig. 2) using interaction protocols based on speech acts. The process recurses
through the tree, filtering potential contractors for each node relative to their
capabilities and setting up auctions to determine the platform most fit to be
delegated each node. Both mission requirements and platform capabilities can
be represented as constraint formulas, and a constraint problem corresponding
to the TST and its allocation to agents is incrementally constructed and solved
during delegation. Systems may also call other internal functionalities such as
motion planners to determine if they can successfully contribute to the goal in
question. The net result of the distributed delegation process, if successful, is a
new TST representing the collaborative scanning plan resulting from successful
delegation. This plan can be sent back to the original human operator for final
confirmation, or it can be executed directly as all systems involved have their
parts scheduled.

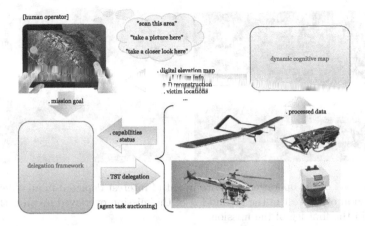

Fig. 1. Mission Process. A goal request is broadcast via the Delegation Module. Platforms with available capabilities reply and a delegation process ensues among each of the platforms' delegation modules. If successful, the net result is a joint plan to execute. Upon execution, raw and processed data can be stored locally or globally. During the mission or upon its completion the human operator can access the results via specialized interfaces.

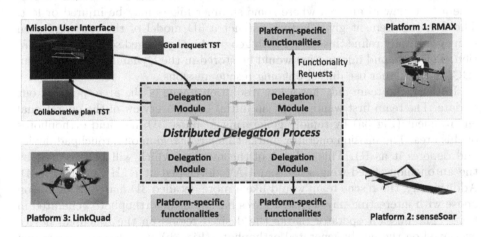

Fig. 2. Overview of the distributed delegation process.

During the mission, the robotic systems involved could stream sparse 3D models to ground stations for real-time visualization or store these models locally for access in a distributed semantic map structure called a Dynamic Cognitive Map (DCM) [2]. The intent is that during the progression of a rescue operation, additional geo-tagged information could be added to this distributed knowledge structure which could be queried by team members for both static and dynamic information related to the operation in progress.

Fig. 3. (a) Part of the operational environment of interest depicted in an older photo. (b) Sub-region of interest in the second leg of the mission overlayed on an orthophoto generated in the first leg of the mission.

3   A Collaborative 3D Reconstruction Mission

We will now provide additional details regarding the collaborative 3D reconstruction experiment mentioned above. Imagine that an alpine rescue team, consisting of a number of human operators and robotic systems, has been tasked to provide a first-view of an area where some summer hikers may be injured or lost. The first requirement given is to construct a 3D model of the area and then to incrementally refine this model with geographically tagged semantic information. This data and information would be stored in the Dynamic Cognitive Map (DCM) for further use during ongoing rescue missions.

Initially, the team only has a low resolution image of the area, possibly out of date. The team first wants to get an initial larger overview of the operational environment (Fig. 3a) by rapidly generating a sparse 3D map and orthophotos of this area. The mission operator marks this larger region on a touchpad device and denotes it as R1. This is leg 1 of the mission, which will be executed by the autonomous fixed-wing senseSoar UAV developed at ETH Zurich (Fig. 4). Additionally, the rescue team would like a more detailed 3D map of a subregion dense with interesting physical structures based on the orthophoto generated in leg 1. The mission operator marks the desired region on the touchpad device overlayed on the newly generated orthophoto (Fig. 3b), and denotes this region

Fig. 4. (a) The senseSoar solar-powered UAV, developed at ETH Zurich. (b) Modular sensor pod for onboard processing and visual-inertial sensing.

as R2. This is leg 2 of the mission, which will be executed by an autonomous Yamaha RMAX helicopter developed at Linköping University (Fig. 5).

Below, we describe the robotic systems that will be used in the mission tests in detail:

SenseSoar. A hand-launchable, solar-powered, fixed-wing UAV developed in the Autonomous Systems Lab (ASL) at ETH Zurich as a versatile platform for long-endurance sensing and mapping missions (Fig. 4a). The senseSoar is 5 kg, with a 3.1 m wingspan and an inverted V-tail configuration. Light-weight sensors and avionics are coupled with a Pixhawk Autopilot for fully autonomous attitude stabilization and waypoint navigation. A modular sensor pod containing forward-oblique and nadir facing visible light cameras, a visual-inertial sensor, and an onboard processing unit is integrated in the fuselage for vision-based 3-D mapping (Fig. 4b).

RMAX. The helicopter platform is based on a slightly modified unmanned RMAX helicopter manufactured by the Yamaha Motor Company (Fig. 5). The RMAX has a rotor diameter of 3.1 m, a 21 horsepower engine, a maximum take-off weight of 94 kg and a payload capability of about 30 kg. It includes a customized avionics system developed at Linköping University. The avionics box includes two Intel NUC i7 computers, a 2.4 GHz WiFi data link, and an Ethernet video server.

The basic sensor suite used for autonomous navigation includes a fiber optic tri-axial gyro system and a tri-axial accelerometer system, an RTK GNSS

Fig. 5. The RMAX helicopter platform with the avionics box attached below the platform and the laser scanner facing downward mounted on a vibration isolated support placed under the helicopter nose. The color and thermal video cameras are mounted on a pan/tilt unit below the avionic box. The GNSS antenna is mounted on the helicopter tail boom.

positioning system and an infrared altimeter used for automatic landing. Additionally, a color and a thermal video camera, as well as a class 1 SICK LMS511 PRO 2D laser scanner, are integrated on board the platform. The laser scanner's maximum range is 80 m and the maximum scanning field of view is 190°.

In the remaining sections, the generic components in our delegation framework will be described in the context of this mission in order to provide concrete insight into the proposed framework, its theoretical basis and its real-life implementation. We will also describe functionalities specific to 3D reconstruction missions.

4   The Delegation Framework

The experimental mission must be *delegated* to suitable participants. Castelfranchi and Falcone [3,4] provide an informal discussion about delegation as a social concept building on a BDI model where agents have beliefs, goals, intentions, and plans [5]. The Delegation Framework discussed in [6] extends these ideas with a formal characterization of delegation in terms of speech acts [7,8] and interaction protocols that implicitly update the belief states of the delegator and contractor. It also supports a concrete delegation *process* using Delegation Modules for each participating agent in a team, resulting in a software architecture for specifying, generating and executing collaborative multi-agent plans to achieve complex goals such as those of the mission above.

The delegation process is based on a recursive algorithm that conceptually sends speech act requests of the type Delegate(A, B, *Task*, *Context*), where agent A wants to delegate *Task* to agent B given a *Context* specified as a set of constraints. This could include temporal constraints, restrictions on flight altitudes and velocities, required resolution intervals for various sensors, etc. Agents can be humans or robots. Tasks and missions to delegate are represented as Task Specification Trees (TSTs). While TSTs are declaratively specified, platforms participating in their execution must provide a procedural counterpart capable of interpreting and executing this specification. Internal nodes represent control statements such as sequential and concurrent execution, while leaf nodes can represent domain-specific tasks such as scanning a region.

The current implementation of the Delegation Module (DM, Fig. 6) is based on ROS, Robot Operating System. The TST Factory is used for creating TST nodes and linking them to ancestors and descendants across agents. The TST Executor Factory provides all platform-specific functionality for a node and is consequently instantiated differently for each platform type. It also provides declarative constraints for each node type supported by a platform, representing execution conditions required by the platform itself as opposed to those imposed by a mission. For example, a constraint may define the maximum take-off time for a platform or specify that it can only generate point clouds of a certain resolution. The Delegation Manager is responsible for managing the distributed delegation process and consequently also communicates with other agents. Finally, a constraint solver is used to generate concrete parameter bindings and to verify that all tasks are allocated to platforms capable of executing them.

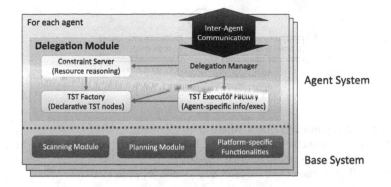

Fig. 6. The Delegation Module

4.1 Task Specification Trees

Task Specification Trees provide a very expressive means of declaratively specifying tasks to be delegated to a team of collaborating agents. Inner tree nodes can specify standardized control structures such as sequences (S), concurrency (C), conditionals (IF) and loops (WHILE), which are directly supported by the Delegation Module. Leaf nodes specify potentially domain-specific tasks to be executed. Such tasks are viewed as elementary and indivisible from the point of view of a delegator, but contractors can choose to elaborate and *expand* them into subtasks through calls to general task planners or problem-specific functionalities during the delegation process.

Every node has a set of named *parameters*, such as the destination of a fly-to task. Parameters can be given specific values or can be subject to *constraints* in a general constraint language [6]. Such constraints represent the GOP's mission requirements.

Mission Example. The delegation process requires a goal request TST. For the 3D reconstruction mission we choose to represent this at a high level of abstraction using scan-map tasks intended to be elaborated with further detail by the agents involved. This allows scan trajectory generation to be adapted to each type of platform in a decentralized manner. Therefore the following small and deceptively simple goal request TST shown in Fig. 7 is generated by the user interface, defining a sequence (S) of scan-map tasks, one for each of the regions (R1 and R2) in the mission. Parameters to these tasks include the desired result (3D point clouds, visual images, object identification, ...), resolution requirements, and requirements for information streaming and storage.

Formal Semantics. TSTs, including control structures and constraints, are given a strict formal semantics through composite actions in TALF, Temporal Action Logic with Fixpoints [9]. Temporal composite actions have the following syntactic form:

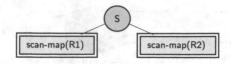

Fig. 7. Goal request TST

C-ACT ::= $[\tau, \tau']$ with $\bar{x}$ do TASK where ϕ
TASK ::= $[\tau, \tau']$ ELEMENTARY-ACTION-TERM | $[\tau, \tau']$ COMPOSITE-ACTION-TERM |
          (C-ACT; C-ACT) | (C-ACT || C-ACT) |
          if $[\tau]\psi$ then C-ACT else C-ACT | while $[\tau]\psi$ do C-ACT

Here, "with $\bar{x}$ do TASK where ϕ" declares a (possibly empty) sequence of variables $\bar{x}$ for use in a constraint formula ϕ related to the given TASK. Such formulas range over all variables in the scope of the formula, which corresponds directly to those parameters and variables that are declared in a given TST node and all of its ancestors. The task must be executed during the given temporal interval $[\tau, \tau']$. For inner nodes, τ and τ' are bounded by constraints relating subtask parameters to subtask durations. The agent executing a task is specified as a parameter to each action term. Before task allocation, this can be an unconstrained agent variable. Note that ELEMENTARY-ACTION-TERM represents a call to an elementary task such as **fly-to**(uav, x, y), whose preconditions, effects and constraints can also be modeled in TALF. COMPOSITE-ACTION-TERM, in contrast, represents a call to a named *composite* action. Semicolon represents sequencing, while || represents potentially concurrent execution.

Task Specification Tree structures can be translated directly to composite actions in TALF, which in turn can be translated to formulas in a fixpoint logic [9] whose expressivity is above that of first-order logic yet allows relatively efficient inference techniques. We emphasize that this translation is mainly used to provide a formal task semantics, and the actual implementation does not require theorem proving.

4.2   The Delegation Process

When a Task Specification Tree has been generated, the user interface can call its local Delegation Manager to initiate the distributed delegation process. This process implements the conceptual Delegate(*A, B, Task, Context*) speech act through an interaction protocol with two phases [6]: First, tasks are provisionally allocated to agents capable of performing them while satisfying all mission constraints. Second, the task allocation and a corresponding constraint solution is accepted or rejected by the operator.

First Phase. The root node of a TST is always a control node and can be handled by any agent. For simplicity we will assume this is delegated to the agent initiating the delegation process. The interaction protocol therefore begins by sending a CALL-FOR-PROPOSAL speech act to this agent [10], indicating the task to be delegated together with the constraint context. From the contractor's point of view, the remainder of the first phase of the protocol can be characterized using the DELEGATE-FIRST-PHASE procedure below. A concrete example will follow.

```
1:  procedure DELEGATE-FIRST-PHASE(task T, constraint set C)
2:     if basic capabilities for root(T) are missing then reply REFUSE
3:     Add constraints and parameters specified in root(T) to C
4:     Add platform-specific constraints for root(T) to C
5:     if C is inconsistent then reply REFUSE
6:     if root(T) is a leaf and this platform wants to expand it then
7:        Expand root(T), adding new children
8:     for every child c_i of root(T) corresponding to a subtree T_i do
9:        Broadcast a REQUEST to find P = potential contractors with capabilities
           for c_i
10:       Perform auction for c_i among P, and sort P accordingly
11:       nondeterministically choose p ∈ P :
12:          (T_i', C) ← p.DELEGATE-FIRST-PHASE(T_i, C)
13:          replace T_i with T_i' in T
14:    Provisionally commit to the delegation
15:    reply PROPOSE(T, C)
```

An agent can only be allocated a tree T if it can execute the root of T. The agent therefore begins by verifying that it has the necessary fundamental capabilities: All agents can coordinate a sequence (S), while only some are able to **fly**. If capabilities are missing, the agent immediately responds using a REFUSE speech act.

The agent must also verify that it can execute the task given the specified parameters and constraints. The currently accumulated set of constraints C is therefore augmented with (1) any mission constraints specific to $\text{root}(T)$, corresponding to a **where** clause, (2) a constraint for each node parameter that was given a specific value outside of the constraints, and (3) any platform-specific execution constraints that this agent has for the given node type, retrieved from the local TST Executor Factory. For example, different UAV platforms have different flight envelopes which must be consistent with mission requirements. If the resulting constraint set is inconsistent, the agent cannot accept the delegation and must reply REFUSE. Otherwise delegation *may* be possible, contingent on the successful delegation of all children. These children may already exist or may be generated dynamically through a potentially platform-specific expansion procedure provided by the TST Executor Factory.

For each child c_i, associated with a subtree T_i, a REQUEST for potential participants will be broadcast. This request is accompanied by a specification of the required capabilities for c_i, which allows replies (sent as INFORM speech acts) to be filtered. An auction process is then initiated where each potential contractor is REQUESTed to bid for the task in question. Each bid is also returned through an INFORM speech act.

Bids are used to prioritize potential contractors, but backtracking may be needed if a choice that is good for one part of the TST has negative consequences for other parts of the tree. For brevity we describe this backtracking using the standard notion of non-deterministic choice, where each such choice point is in fact a point to which the algorithm can backtrack in case of future failures. However, note that agents are called in the order determined by the auction. In this context, failures are reported through REFUSE speech acts, both in the cases discussed above and in case all possible contractors for a child node REFUSE a delegation attempt.

When a child has been provisionally delegated, its subtree may contain expanded nodes, and the nodes of the resulting tree are associated with execution constraints defined by the contractor(s) that were allocated parts of this tree. The expanded tree and updated set of constraints are returned in line 15 and the corresponding values returned from a recursive delegation call are handled in lines 12–13.

When the first phase of delegation succeeds (line 14), the platform also *provisionally* commits to the delegated task before it PROPOSEs a solution to the caller. The commitment is provisional both because we may backtrack over the commitment and because no delegation is final until the original delegator has received a proposed solution and accepted it. This allows a ground operator to determine whether a mission instantiation is acceptable or whether an alternative needs to be sought.

Second Phase. If the mission is accepted, an ACCEPT speech act is distributed to all callers, also specifying a concrete constraint solution to be used during execution. Alternatively, if the mission is rejected, a REJECT speech act is distributed.

Mission Example. In the example, the goal TST is provided as input to the ground operator's delegation module, which starts by attempting to delegate the top node to itself through CALL-FOR-PROPOSAL initiating a call to DELEGATE-FIRST-PHASE.

The delegation process then searches for agents capable of handling the unallocated children of the root. The GOP's delegation module makes a broadcast to acquire all scan-map-capable agents on the team in the GOP's communication range. Two agents respond, the RMAX and the senseSoar. An auction is set up to determine a suitable contractor for scan-map(R1). The cost function for this node type is based on a combination of time requirements and fuel usage. The senseSoar is equipped with visual cameras and scans an area quickly, but the time required for 3D reconstruction rises quickly with the desired resolution. The RMAX uses a laser scanner, and while it flies somewhat more slowly, the results are processed quickly even at higher resolutions. As scan-map(R1) specifies a large area to be scanned, but the resolution required is comparatively low, the senseSoar returns the best bid.

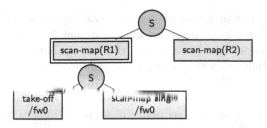

Fig. 8. TST after initial expansion in the senseSoar system.

The delegation module therefore first tries to delegate scan-map(R1) to the senseSoar. This node allows a team of platforms to be assigned to the same area and can partition scan regions according to the capabilities of those platforms (Sect. 6). Partitioning must be performed during delegation rather than execution, to ensure that each platform involved can verify its ability to scan the subregion it is assigned. After this, the scan-map node can expand to specify the concurrent execution of several scanning sub-mission. In this particular mission the team was limited to one member and partitioning was not necessary. Nevertheless the senseSoar expands the node to a sequence of actions suitable for scanning using a single platform, as shown in Fig. 8.

The expanded TST is then recursively delegated. Constraints generated during expansion ensure that the *same* platform will both take off and perform the single platform scanning task. In the general case, generated subtasks can also be delegated to additional agents that can assist in achieving the overall goal of the expanded node.

While the RMAX can take off autonomously, the light-weight senseSoar requires human assistance. Therefore, when delegated a take-off node, the senseSoar expands this to an assist-take-off node that can only be executed by human agents (included in Fig. 9). When this node is recursively delegated, the auction gives the highest priority to the fixed-wing operator, who has a personal Delegation Module running on a user interface device. Delegation to an operator always asks for confirmation that the human is willing and able to take on the task at

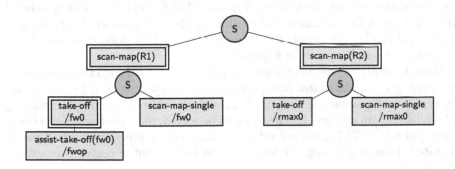

Fig. 9. Fully expanded collaborative plan TST.

the desired time. Modeling take-off as a *potentially* expandable node ensures that only the platform itself needs to know whether it is capable of taking off autonomously, or under which conditions this is possible.

Verifying the ability to scan a region using scan-map-single requires generating a scan trajectory (Sect. 6.1) and verifying through constraints that this trajectory can be flown in the desired manner. Then, an agent can choose to expand the node into a subtree including a sequence of flight actions or to provide a more complex trajectory-following implementation for the scan-map-single node itself. The latter option results in greater freedom to make choices during execution and was chosen for this mission.

Once the first subtree is successfully provisionally delegated, a similar process ensues for the rightmost leaf node, scan-map(R2). Here the operator desires a high-resolution scan of a smaller area and the auction results in the RMAX being at the top of the list. The GOP's delegation module therefore tries to delegate scan-map(R2) to the RMAX.

As both delegations succeed, the net result is that an expanded *collaborative plan TST* (Fig. 9) where all nodes are allocated to participating agents is proposed to the GOP's delegation module. The GOP can view and approve the plan, after which the approval is transmitted to the participating agents, which then store the TST structures and their associated constraint instantiations and commit to executing the TST at the desired time. Each system will execute its part of the mission TST relative to timing and other constraints that have been checked for consistency in the delegation phase. The results will be shown in Sect. 7.

5   The Planning Module: Motion and Task Planning

When using unmanned aerial or ground vehicles, *motion planning* is essential for successful execution and is used in several ways. First, when a motion-related TST node is delegated, the contractor's platform-specific constraints for this task require the existence of a feasible motion plan that is collision-free relative to available obstacle information. A motion planner must then be called to verify feasibility. Moreover, the generated motion plan must be analyzed in order to generate bounds on execution times. For the RMAX, bounds can be generated either through a fast estimation algorithm or through simulated step-by-step execution of the low-level control system. When the TST node is executed, the generated motion plan must be followed.

Though the 3D reconstruction mission was generated through template-based expansion, general *automated task planning* can also be essential for many mission types. Task planning is integrated through the use of a goal node specifying a planning domain and problem instance to be solved. Such goal nodes can occur at any point in a TST, allowing missions to be partly pre-specified and partly generated through planning. These nodes can be handled in one of two ways.

Planning First. As TSTs are sufficiently expressive to represent the output of most automated planners, existing single- or multi-agent planners can easily be integrated. When a goal node is reached, a planner capable of handling the given planning domain language is called and its output is converted into a subtree attached under the goal node. The delegation module then proceeds to recursively delegate the new TST nodes.

Planning Integrated. By adapting a planner to the use of delegation, new actions can be integrated and delegated as soon as they are generated. This has the advantage of immediately testing the feasibility of each action and can therefore reduce the need for backtracking due to plans that cannot be delegated. At the same time, any backtracking caused by the planner itself will trigger backtracking in delegation. Therefore this option is mainly feasible for planners that only cause a limited amount of backtracking. The RMAX uses the planner TFPOP [6,11] for this purpose. TFPOP is a knowledge-rich multi-agent planner whose search algorithm can be guided through additional domain information provided by domain experts. This type of approach has proven orders of magnitude faster than standard planners in many domains, and is particularly appropriate given the need to communicate with other agents when backtracking occurs.

6   Collaborative Scanning and Region Partitioning

Partitioning. Though not used in the example mission, scan-map may specify a team of agents that should collaborate to scan a single region. The contractor coordinates this task, partitioning the region according to the team members' capabilities.

The relative *size* of each subregion can be calculated by determining approximately how large an area can be scanned by each participant in any given period of time. The most significant parameters involved in this calculation can be summarized as follows:

- How quickly can and should the participant fly? This depends on the physical flight envelope of the platform, but also on the characteristics of the sensors being used as well as the desired density and quality of the scan results. For example, a LIDAR sensor may produce a certain number of scan lines per second, and the faster an aircraft flies, the longer the distance between two such lines on the ground. The desired scan quality then restricts the range of permitted air speeds.
- How wide are the "strips" that can be covered by the sensors in question during a single flight? This depends on field of view restrictions but also on resolution requirements and the range of possible altitudes, which can in turn depend on other mission constraints.

If each team member i can scan an area of a_i per time unit, then it should be assigned a partition whose proportional size is $a_i / \sum_k a_k$ of the area of the entire

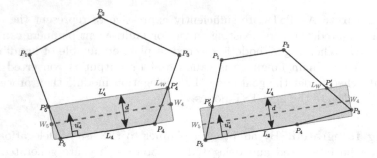

Fig. 10. How to generate one scan strip along the longest edge of a polygon $\mathcal{P}$.

polygon. We then apply a polygon decomposition algorithm [12] to generate sub-polygons of this size, *anchored* in locations calculated from the starting position of each participating UAV.

The expansion of scan-map for multiple participants is very similar to the one shown in Fig. 8, the only difference being that scan-map is followed by a concurrency (C) node whose children consist of one sequence subtree for each platform involved. The scan-map-single node in each such subtree specifies the same mission parameters as the original scan-map node except that the team consists of one specific participant and the scan region is set to its subregion. Consequently each individual member will first take off and then scan its specific partition.

6.1   Scan Trajectory Generation

Scan trajectories can follow patterns such as spirals, expanding squares and lawnmower patterns. For 3D reconstruction, flying in straight lines generally yields more uniform results. It is also important to reduce the number of turns, especially when using fixed-wing aircraft, as turns do not contribute to data collection. We therefore define a trajectory generator that in each step generates a *flight line* along the longest side of the remaining region to be scanned. For rectangles, this results in a lawn mower pattern.

Notation. A polygon $\mathcal{P}$ is defined in terms of a sequence of vertices $\langle P_1 ... P_n \rangle \in \mathbb{R}^n$. Figure 10 shows two examples with $n = 5$ vertices. We introduce the following notation: By $\bar{k}$, we mean $((k-1) \bmod n) + 1$. Thus, assuming $n = 5$, we have $P_{\overline{n+1}} = P_1$, ensuring that indexes can "wrap around". L_i is the infinite line going through the points P_i and $P_{\overline{i+1}}$. Figure 10 shows a finite segment of each line. $d_i = dist(P_i, P_{\overline{i+1}})$ is the linear distance between P_i and $P_{\overline{i+1}}$. For example, d_5 is the distance between P_5 and $P_{\bar{6}} = P_1$.

Algorithm. Trajectories are generated by a recursive algorithm *generate-trajectory*($\mathcal{P}$) that returns a list of flight line coordinates.

(1) Select the scan direction to be parallel to a longest segment L_s of the polygon $\mathcal{P}$, so that $\forall i.d_i \leq d_s$. In both polygons in Fig. 10, line L_4 is the unique longest segment.

(2) Let $\vec{u_s}$ be a vector perpendicular to L_s, pointing toward the interior of the polygon $\mathcal{P}$ (see Fig. 10). Let d be the desired distance between flight lines, taking into account the need for overlap, and let the infinite line L'_s be the translation of L_s in the direction $\vec{u_s}$ by the distance d. Then L_s and L'_s provide two of the edges for the "effective" (non-overlapping) part of a scan strip as highlighted in Fig. 10. Let L_W be the translation of L_s in the direction $\vec{u_s}$ by the distance $\frac{d}{2}$. A finite segment of this line will be followed by the UAV while scanning.

(3) We now want to find two waypoints W_j and W_{j+1} representing the start and end of the new flight line. As illustrated for $W_j = W_4$ and $W_{j+1} = W_5$ in Fig. 10, these can be situated the border of $\mathcal{P}$, to ensure that no part of the polygon is missed.

(3a) Suppose L'_s intersects $\mathcal{P}$ in *two* points, P'_s and $P'_{\overline{s+1}}$, as is the case for L'_4, P'_4 and P'_5 in Fig. 10. We can always find W_{j+1} by considering the "leftmost" point among $P_{\overline{s+1}}$, $P'_{\overline{s+1}}$ and any polygon vertices that may intervene between these two points on the polygon (in this case none). A similar situation applies at P'_s, the other end of L'_s, where P_3 intervenes between P_4 and P'_4 and is the rightmost of these points.

We therefore take the set of all such points, project them orthogonally onto L_s, and select two maximally distant points as W_j and W_{j+1} defining a new flight line $[W_j, W_{j+1}]$. When the flight line is flown, a strip corresponding to the rectangle of width d highlighted in blue will be effectively covered, while information is received from a wider rectangle to ensure overlap and compensate for any lack of precision in following the flight line. The rectangle of width d should now be removed from the polygon $\mathcal{P}$, resulting in a new polygon $\mathcal{P}'$ representing the region that remains to be covered.

$\mathcal{P}'$ is created by removing all the vertices in $\mathcal{P}_{s \to s+1}$, replacing them with P'_s and $P'_{\overline{s+1}}$. The first polygon of Fig. 10 then becomes $\langle P_1, P_2, P_3, P'_4, P'_5 \rangle$, while the second polygon becomes $\langle P_1, P_2, P'_4, P'_5 \rangle$, having fewer vertices than before. Then *generate-trajectory* is called for the new polygon (unless it is empty).

(3b) Suppose instead that L'_s has less than two intersections with the polygon $\mathcal{P}$. Then the remaining part of the polygon will be completely covered after generating this last scan strip. In this case, all vertexes from $\mathcal{P}$ are projected onto L_W, after which the two most distant points are selected as endpoints for the new flight line.

This procedure generates a set of flight lines $\{(W_0, W_1), ... (W_{m-1}, W_m)\}$, which the aircraft can cover in any order. Typically, a helicopter would follow them in the order they are defined, but for a fixed wing it might be better to skip a flight line and then come back to it later in order to accommodate a need for a larger turning radius.

7   Experiment Results: Collaborative 3D Reconstruction

Our experiments took place in Isollaz, Italy, in the region depicted in Fig. 3, at an altitude of 800 m. One of the missions tested and executed has been described in detail in previous sections of this paper together with the integrated functionalities required to do such a complex mission. For both legs of the mission, the delegation, planning, TST generation, and flight executions were fully autonomous. The intent was to generate 3D models of various resolutions for input into the Dynamic Cognitive Map where the models and data could then be used to support alpine rescue teams. Additionally, orthophoto mosaics, individual images and partial semantic classification of the operational environment were also generated from the raw data collected by the two UAVs. The missions tested were part of an evaluation demonstration for the EU project SHERPA (www.sherpa-project.eu).

Since this is an application overview paper, we only summarize the experimental results here, focusing on the integrated framework required for such missions and less on the sensor and fusion aspects. The companion paper [13] presents several collaborative UAV flights from two different locations with diverse terrain (Motala, Sweden and Isollaz, Italy). The distributed reconstructions generated from the optical camera of the fixed-wing and the Lidar of the rotary-wing UAV reveal a relative geo-referencing offset in the range of up to few meters and a slight rotational misfit. Consequently, the companion paper focuses on minimizing the rotational and translational misalignment of the point-clouds. In particular, the performance of classical point-cloud alignment methods such as Iterative Closest Point (ICP) variants [14–17] are compared to a novel probabilistic data association approach (PDA) [18] that was designed to register dense to sparse point-clouds: In contrast to ICP, PDA associates a point in the source point cloud with a set of points in the target cloud and, in simulation, demonstrated lower misalignment errors [18]. For quantitative results concerning convergence of initial configurations and misalignment errors in the real-world experiments we refer to [13].

Figure 11 depicts the scan trajectories generated for the RMAX to scan Region 2 in the second leg of the mission. Similar patterns used by the senseSoar and its internal path planner are also generated to scan Region 1 in the first leg of the mission. Each platform uses its own motion planning system. The lawn mower pattern generated by the RMAX is specific to the mission constraints and optimizes paths relative to the sensor constraints of the platform. The objective is to provide 100 % coverage of an allocated region at a required resolution. Figure 12 shows the first strip of the point-cloud generated by the laser scanner mounted on the RMAX. Figure 13 shows the point-cloud generated by the optical camera of the senseSoar using Pix4D software (pix4d.com).

One of the challenges of these missions is in their distributed nature where different robotic platforms collect different types of data using different sensors with different resolutions for data collection. For such diverse models and data, different fusion and association techniques would be required at many different levels of abstraction to provide a consistent model in the dynamic cognitive map.

Fig. 11. 3D view of the generated scan pattern for the RMAX and Region 2. The green lines represent the region to scan. The purple lines indicating the lawnmower pattern are marked with differing altitudes. (Color figure online)

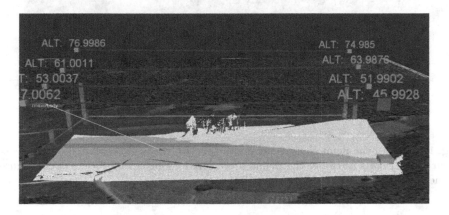

Fig. 12. The first strip of the point-cloud generated by the laser mounted on the RMAX.

For instance, Fig. 14 shows a point cloud strip collected by the RMAX. This has to be fused and aligned with the pointcloud generated by the senseSoar from its collection of images, as shown in Fig. 15 which is generated using Pix4D software. Queries now made to the DCM for 3D models of regions could then be done seamlessly, where consistently aligned combinations of low and high resolution data would be output. Once raw data and DEM models are generated and stored in the DCM, one could then begin to build semantically tagged abstractions on top of these 3D models. For instance, using LAStools (http://www.cs.unc.edu/~isenburg/lastools/), the semantic classifications shown in Figs. 16 and 17 were generated for region 2.

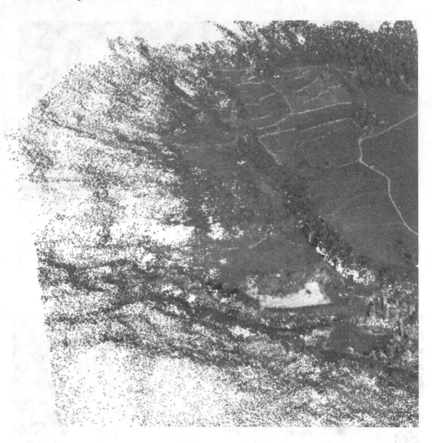

Fig. 13. Part of the point-cloud generated by the RGB camera mounted on the sens-eSoar using Pix4D software; the points are colored by pixel intensities. (Color figure online)

Fig. 14. First strip of point-cloud generated by the Laser mounted on the RMAX, including some trees. The pointcloud is colored by height. (Color figure online)

Fig. 15. RMAX strip of point-cloud aligned with the senseSoar point-cloud using Pix4D software.

Fig. 16. Color coded semantic classification: vegetation: green, terrain: brown, gray: unclassified (Color figure online)

Fig. 17. Filtered semantic classification: vegetation: green (Color figure online)

8   Conclusions

This paper has presented a multi-purpose multi-agent/robotic infrastructure that has been deployed and field tested for collaborative 3D mapping applications. It includes a great variety of specific functionalities studied formally in the multi-agent community. The novelty here is that many of these functionalities, although grounded formally, have been instantiated procedurally in a highly complex, integrated, scalable, collaborative framework for interacting robotic systems. Although only two robots and two humans have been used in the experiment, one can easily add additional robotic systems to a team in a modular and transparent manner. There is much additional research to do in terms of extending the current functionalities and in ensuring the robustness of the infrastructure. The system here can be described as a mature prototype with great potential to push state-of-the-art in multi-agent systems.

Acknowledgments. This work is partially supported by the Swedish Research Council (VR) Linnaeus Center CADICS, the ELLIIT network organization for Information and Communication Technology, the Swedish Foundation for Strategic Research (CUAS Project, SymbiKCloud Project), the EU FP7 project SHERPA (grant agreement 600958), and Vinnova NFFP6 Project 2013-01206.

References

1. Murphy, R.R.: A national initiative in emergency informatics. In: Computing Community Consortium, version 1, 3 November 2010
2. Marconi, L. et al.: The SHERPA project: smart collaboration between humans and ground-aerial robots for improving rescuing activities in alpine environments. In: IEEE International Symposium on Safety, Security, and Rescue Robotics (SSRR) (2012)
3. Castelfranchi, C., Falcone, R.: Toward a theory of delegation for agent-based systems. Robot. Auton. Syst. **24**, 141–157 (1998)
4. Falcone, R., Castelfranchi, C.: The human in the loop of a delegated agent: the theory of adjustable social autonomy. IEEE Trans. Syst. Man Cybern. Part A: Syst. Hum. **31**(5), 406–418 (2001)
5. Cohen, P., Levesque, H.: Intention is choice with commitment. Artif. Intell. **42**(3), 213–261 (1990)
6. Doherty, P., Heintz, F., Kvarnström, J.: High-level mission specification and planning for collaborative unmanned aircraft systems using delegation. Unmanned Syst. **1**(1), 75–119 (2013)
7. Austin, J.L.: How to Do Things with Words. Harvard University Press, Cambridge (1975)
8. Searle, J.R.: Speech Acts: An Essay in the Philosophy of Language. Cambridge University Press, Cambridge (1969)
9. Doherty, P., Kvarnström, J., Szalas, A.: Temporal composite actions with constraints. In: Proceedings of the 13th International Conference on Principles of Knowledge Representation and Reasoning (KR), pp. 478–488. AAAI Press (2012)
10. FIPA-ACL, FIPA Communicative Act Library Specification. Foundation for Intelligent Physical Agents (2002)
11. Kvarnström, J.: Planning for loosely coupled agents using partial order forward-chaining. In: Proceedings of the 21st International Conference on Automated Planning and Scheduling (ICAPS), pp. 138–145. AAAI Press (2011)
12. Hert, S., Lumelsky, V.: Polygon area decomposition for multiple-robot workspace division. Int. J. Comput. Geom. Appl. **8**, 437–466 (1998)
13. Hinzmann, T., Stastny, T., Conte, G., Doherty, P., Rudol, P., Wzorek, M., Gilitschenski, I., Galceran, E., Siegwart, R.: Collaborative 3D reconstruction using heterogeneous unmanned aerial vehicles. In: International Symposium on Robotics (2016)
14. Besl, P.J., McKay, N.D.: A method for registration of 3-D shapes. IEEE Trans. Pattern Anal. Mach. Intell. **14**, 239–256 (1992)
15. Chen, Y., Medioni, G.: Object modelling by registration of multiple range images. Image Vis. Comput. **10**, 145–155 (1992)
16. Zhang, Z.: Iterative point matching for registration of free-form curves and surfaces. Int. J. Comput. Vis. **13**, 119–152 (1994)
17. Segal, A., Haehnel, D., Thrun, S.: Generalized-ICP. In: Proceedings of Robotics: Science and Systems, Seattle, USA, June 2009
18. Agamennoni, G., Fontana, S., Siegwart, R.Y., Sorrenti, D.G.: Point clouds registration with probabilistic data association. IEEE (2016, submitted)

Heuristics on the Data-Collecting Robot Problem with Immediate Rewards

Zhi Xing[(✉)] and Jae C. Oh

Electrical Engineering and Computer Science, Syracuse University, Syracuse, USA
{zxing01,jcoh}@syr.edu

Abstract. We propose the Data-collecting Robot Problem, where robots collect data as they visit nodes in a graph, and algorithms to solve it. There are two variations of the problem: the delayed-reward problem, in which robots must travel back to the base station to deliver the data collected and to receive rewards; and the immediate-reward problem, in which the reward is immediately given to the robots as they visit each node. The delayed-reward problem is discussed in one of the authors' work. This paper focuses on the immediate-reward problem. The solution structure has a clustering step and a tour-building step. We propose Progressive Gain-aware Clustering that finds good quality solutions with efficient time complexity. Among the six proposed tour-building heuristics, Greedy Insertion and Total-Loss algorithms perform best when data rewards are different.

Keywords: Adversary route planning · Multi-robot systems · Autonomous systems

1 Introduction

With the increasing popularity of autonomous robots, human operators are gradually being replaced by robots in many tasks such as driving, package delivery, and image/video surveillance. In addition, robots are becoming smaller and cheaper, which makes multi-robot missions more realistic than ever. A solution utilizing specialized robots that can finish tasks through coordination and cooperation is almost always a better choice than using a single super robot that may finish the same task alone, due to the increased scalability and robustness.

These facts motivated us to formulate and propose the Data-collecting Robot Problem (DRP), in which an unspecified number of autonomous robots can be used to collect digital data. Although many multi-agent routing problems have been studied as variants of the Vehicle Routing Problem (VRP) [12], these problems assume that agents are, to our best knowledge, humans or human operated, implicitly assuming that the assigned tasks are completed with certainty. In contrast, unexpected events may destroy robots and terminate assigned tasks. This practical aspect is generally not considered in the VRP research community. Unlike existing formulations of the VRPs, in our problem formulation, the

© Springer International Publishing Switzerland 2016
M. Baldoni et al. (Eds.): PRIMA 2016, LNAI 9862, pp. 131–148, 2016.
DOI: 10.1007/978-3-319-44832-9_8

probabilities of robots breaking down and the value of the robots are explicitly modeled. The value of a robot can be the hardware cost of the robot or the strategic importance of the robot quantified by a real number. Therefore, the objective of the proposed algorithms is to generate a routing plan that maximizes the expected reward with the optimal number of robots. To our best knowledge, these two aspects, i.e., *risks* and *value of lost robots*, of DRP are unique to any other existing VRP formulations.

We divide the DRP to two classes: the delayed-reward and the immediate-reward problems. In the delayed-reward problem, robots must travel back to the base to receive rewards. Applicable scenarios of this problem include tangible or intangible objects collections. A problem that requires robots to collect tangible objects can be modeled as an instance of the delayed-reward problem. Note that even if the "objects" to be collected are intangible, the problem can be an instance of the delayed-reward problem; an example is digital data collection without communication capability [8], which requires all robots to return to the base to deliver the digital data collected to the base. In the immediate-reward problem, robots receive a reward as they visit a location of interest. An applicable scenario of this problem is the digital data collection problems with full communication capability. Delivery problems can also be formulated this way because as soon as a delivery is made to a location, the task is accomplished and the reward associated with the task is received.

This paper presents a solution to the immediate-reward problem. The solution consists of two steps: (1) clustering for the number of robots and (2) tour building for a single robot. We introduce the Progressive Gain-aware Clustering (PGC) and compare it with a naive clustering approach. Six tour building heuristics are proposed and compared.

This paper is organized as follows: Sect. 2 lists the contributions of our work, Sect. 3 discusses related work and provides a mathematical formulation of DRP, Sect. 4 describes the proposed algorithms, Sect. 5 evaluates various combinations of the proposed algorithms, and Sect. 6 presents a conclusion and future directions.

2   Contribution

The contributions of our work include:

- introducing the Data-collecting Robot Problem (DRP), which explicitly models the value of robots and the risk of losing robots,
- providing formalizations of two classes of the DRP: the delayed-reward and the immediate-reward DRPs,
- introducing heuristics for clustering and tour-building steps for solving DRP,
- showing that the Greedy Insertion (GI) and Total-Loss (TL) algorithms have the top performance among tour-building algorithms, and
- showing that the Progressive Gain-aware Clustering (PGC) algorithm produces quality results with a better time complexity.

3   Background

This section discusses problems that are related to the DRP and explain why the DRP is a new problem. We also provide mathematical formulations of DRP.

3.1   Related Work

A large volume of literature exists on route planning problems such as the Traveling Salesman Problems (TSPs) and the Vehicle Routing Problems (VRPs). In [7], several variations of the TSPs with profits are defined. The objective function may be the maximization of the collected total profit (Orienteering Problem), the minimization of the total traveling cost (Prize-Collecting TSP) or the optimization of a combination of both (Profitable Tour Problem). Traditionally, except for the Orienteering Problem, these problems assume a single-tour solution for only one vehicle [1]. Archetti et al. [1] use the term *VRPs with profits* to refer to the class of problems involving multiple vehicles.

The above problems are *company centric* because they maximize the payoff for the party that executes the plan. Some problems are *customer centric*, which means that the average satisfaction rate of all customers is the most important requirement. The Minimum Latency Problem (MLP) is a general formulation for such a goal with variations such as: the traveling repairman's problem, the delivery man problem, the cumulative TSP, the cumulative capacitated vehicle problem, TSP with cumulative costs, and the school bus driver problem. [9] gives a comprehensive taxonomy of MLP problems in many different parameters such as the characteristics of nodes, arcs, the depot, vehicles, etc. However, no taxonomy is given to understand the problems that deal with *tangible goods* verses *intangible goods*, as we discuss the DRP in this paper.

Furthermore, most of the problems studied in the VRP literature do not consider the value of the vehicles or the risk of losing them. As mentioned above, the value of a vehicle can be the monetary cost of the vehicle or strategic importance of the vehicle, quantified by a real number. An interesting exception is the Cash-in-Transit VRP [11], which takes into account the values carried by the vehicle and the risk of the vehicles being robbed. However, since the risk is modeled as an integer constraint, it is not optimized as an objective and there's no uncertainty involved in executing plans. Also in CIT, all the customers must be visited, however, in our problem, as long as the reward is maximized, not all customers are to be visited.

In DRP, robots are deployed to collect items available at each location in a large area. Because we consider these robots to be UAVs, robots can travel from one location to another through the straight-line route between them. This assumption makes the problem environment a fully connected graph. The data can be photograph, video, temperature, etc. The robots are set off from a base station, where they need to return.

We further divided the DRP problem in two categories: the delayed-reward and the immediate-reward problems. The delayed-reward problem requires all robots to return to the base station to receive rewards for bringing back data collected. This could be the case when communication is not available so that data cannot be transmitted during a mission. In the immediate-reward problem, each time a robot visits a node successfully, the robot will receive the reward associated with the node because full data communication is available.

In both delayed and immediate-reward problems, there is always a risk of mechanical breakdown, which destroys the robot. The objective is to find a plan to collect as many data items from different locations as possible to maximize rewards from the collected data. In order to find such a plan, an algorithm must minimize the risk of losing robots. This means that the algorithm must find an optimal number of robots to use and a sequence of sites for each of these robots to visit. The delayed-reward formulation of DRP is studied in [8]. In this paper, we mainly focus on the immediate-reward formulation.

The closest work to the immediate-reward DRP is the discounted-reward TSP problem studied in [3], where the reward a robot can get from a location is discounted by the distance it has to travel to reach there. However, in their work, the robot does not have to return to the base and its value is not considered, which makes the reward always positive. In DRP, the expected reward from a location is discounted due to the uncertainty of robot's breakdown along the route, and due to the value of the robot, the reward can be negative. The Multiple Agents Maximum Collection Problem [6] is similar to the discounted-reward TSP in the sense that the rewards decreases over time. However, the reward function is linear and it doesn't consider the agent's value either.

3.2 Mathematical Formulation

The world is modeled as a complete undirected graph $G = (V, \mathcal{D}, \alpha, \beta, \psi)$. $V = \{0, 1, \ldots\}$ is the set of nodes, where 0 represents the base station and the others represent the locations of interest. $\mathcal{D} : V \times V \to \mathbb{R}^+$ is a symmetric distance function, i.e., $\mathcal{D}(u, v) = \mathcal{D}(v, u)$ is the distance between nodes u and v. $\mathcal{D}$ satisfies the triangle inequality. The value of a robot is α. Data collected from location $v \in V$ has a value of $\beta(v)$. The probability of a robot successfully traversing one unit distance is ψ, so if a robot traverses from node u to v for $u, v \in V$, the probability of success is $\psi^{\mathcal{D}(u,v)}$.

We assume that data at a location is collected only once, which means there is no extra gain by visiting the same node redundantly. Since G is a complete graph that satisfies the triangle inequality, visiting an extra node before a target node always decreases the expected gain.

A tour $t = (v, \ldots, 0)$ for $v \in V \setminus \{0\}$ is a vector of distinct nodes. A robot starts a tour at node 0, then sequentially visit all the nodes in the vector, which leads it back to 0 eventually. The objective is to find a plan T consisting a set of tours, that maximizes the sum of the expected rewards of all the tours. Suppose $\mathcal{D}_t(u, v)$ is the distance between u and v along tour t, $P_t(u, v) = \psi^{\mathcal{D}_t(u,v)}$ is the probability of the robot successfully traveling from u to v along tour t. We use $P_t(v)$ to denote $P_t(0, v)$. Let $|T|$ be the cardinality of T, and let $t \setminus \{0\}$ be the *subtour* excluding the final returning edge. We assume that there are unlimited number of robots at disposal, and the nodes can be left unvisited. Therefore, in addition to generating the tours, the planning involves deciding the number of robots to deploy and which nodes to visit.

The objective function of the delayed-reward problem is expressed as:

$$\max \sum_{t \in T} \left(\sum_{v \in t \setminus \{0\}} P_t(0)\beta(v) - (1 - P_t(0))\alpha \right) \tag{1}$$

In the immediate-reward problem, we assume that data collection and transmission are instantaneous. Therefore, the optimal strategy is always to upload the data right after collecting it. If the robot is at u, the expected marginal gain from v is $\psi^{\mathcal{D}(u,v)}\beta(v)$, regardless of which nodes are visited after v. Without loss of generality, let $\beta(0) = \alpha$ so that $P_t(0)\alpha = P_t(0)\beta(0)$. Then the objective function for this problem becomes:

$$\max \sum_{t \in T} \left(\sum_{v \in t \setminus \{0\}} P_t(v)\beta(v) - (1 - P_t(0))\alpha \right)$$
$$= \max \sum_{t \in T} \left(\sum_{v \in t} P_t(v)\beta(v) - \alpha \right) = \max \left(\sum_{t \in T} \sum_{v \in t} P_t(v)\beta(v) - |T|\alpha \right) \tag{2}$$

The immediate-reward formulation is the focus of this paper. In this formulation, the inner summation term in Eq. 2 is referred to as the (expected) *gain* (of rewards) from the visiting nodes in a tour t; the expected cost due to the risk of losing a robot on t is referred as the *cost* of the tour; and the difference between the gain from all the nodes in a tour and the cost of the tour is referred as the *reward* of the tour.

4   Algorithm

4.1   Clustering for the Number of Robots

For a thorough discussion of the effects of the number of robots, refer to [8]. In that work, one important observation is that robots are reluctant to visit a node that is too faraway, because there is a higher chance of breaking down as they travel to the node and therefore the expected reward would be negligible or even negative. However, if there is a cluster of nodes that are equally faraway, a robot may visit all of them because the high cost due to the initial long edge to the cluster is effectively distributed among all the nodes within the cluster. Therefore, clustering methods should be used to find these clusters. After clustering, the problem is reduced to a single-robot problem. Each cluster is assigned to one robot and a tour covering *all* the nodes in each cluster is generated for one robot.

We use the Bottom-up Hierarchical Clustering, also known as Agglomerative Clustering, employed in [8] to determine the number of robots needed. Starting from single-node clusters, each iteration finds the best merge that gives the

---

Algorithm 1. Clustering Algorithm *Cluster*

Input: $G, \mathcal{R}$ // G: the world model, $\mathcal{R}$: a cluster evaluation function
Output: S // a set of clusters
1: $S \leftarrow \emptyset$
2: **for all** $v \in V \setminus \{0\}$ **do**
3:     $S \leftarrow S \cup \{v\}$
4: **loop**
5:     $C_i^* \leftarrow \emptyset,\ C_j^* \leftarrow \emptyset$
6:     $\Delta^* \leftarrow 0$ // the highest difference in reward
7:     **for all** $C_i \in S$ **do**
8:       **for all** $C_j \in S, j > i$ **do**
9:         $\Delta \leftarrow \mathcal{R}(C_i \cup C_j) - \mathcal{R}(C_i) - \mathcal{R}(C_j)$
10:        **if** $\Delta > \Delta^*$ **then**
11:          $\Delta^* \leftarrow \Delta,\ C_i^* \leftarrow C_i,\ C_j^* \leftarrow C_j$
12:     **if** $\Delta^* = 0$ **then**
13:       **break**
14:     $S \leftarrow S \setminus \{C_i^*, C_j^*\} \cup \{C_i^* \cup C_j^*\}$
15: **return** S

---

highest increase in total reward. Formally, if $\mathcal{R}^*(C_i)$ is the maximum reward a robot can get from cluster C_i, and $C_i \cup C_j$ is the merged cluster, then at each step we merge C_i and C_j that give the maximum positive value $\mathcal{R}^*(C_i \cup C_j) - \mathcal{R}^*(C_i) - \mathcal{R}^*(C_j)$, until there's no more positive merge values. The base node, 0, is excluded from this process. See Algorithm 1 for more details. The algorithm takes as input an evaluation function $\mathcal{R}$, which can be $\mathcal{R}^*$ or a function that estimates $\mathcal{R}^*$. Suppose the time complexity of $\mathcal{R}$ is $O(m)$, where m is a polynomial expression as we show later in this section, and there are n nodes in the graph. This procedure has $O(mn^3)$ operations. However, since the evaluation of one pair of clusters is completely independent of another, parallelism can be easily achieved, which, in the best case, is $O(m + n^3)$.

The only way to get $\mathcal{R}^*(C_i)$ is to find the optimal tour visiting all the nodes in cluster C_i for a single robot, which is a variant of the NP-hard MLP [2]. Therefore, instead of trying to find the optimal tour, we propose six tour-building heuristics, and use the tours built by the heuristics as estimations of the optimal tour. In addition, we also propose an efficient clustering heuristic that uses k Minimum Spanning Tree (k-MST) to estimate the expected reward of a cluster without explicitly building a tour.

4.2 Heuristics for Building Tours

A *partial tour* is a vector of nodes $(0, \ldots, v)$ for $v \in V$ that defines an acyclic ($v \neq 0$) or a cyclic ($v = 0$) path starting from node 0. Given a partial tour t, $t \oplus_i u$ is a new partial tour extended by inserting node u *after* the i-th node of t, $\rho(t)$ is the reward of t, defined as the gain from all the nodes in t, and $|t|$ is the total number of nodes, including the starting 0, in t. The *marginal reward* of an

---

Algorithm 2. Tour-Building Algorithm $BuildTour_\mathcal{K}$

Input: G, C // G: the world model, C: a cluster of nodes
Output: t // a tour contains all the nodes in C
1: $t \leftarrow \emptyset$
2: while $C \neq \emptyset$ do
3:      $u, i \leftarrow \mathcal{K}(C, t)$ // subroutine $\mathcal{K}$ returns a node and an insertion position
4:      $t \leftarrow t \oplus_i u$ // insert node u after position i of t
5:      $C \leftarrow C \setminus \{u\}$
6: **return** t

---

extended partial tour is calculated as the difference between its reward and the original's.

The tour-building heuristics are *incremental* in the sense that they build a tour by assigning one node at a time. All these six heuristics share the same algorithmic structure described in Algorithm 2. The difference is the subroutine for choosing a node for insertion and the insertion position given a partial tour and a set of unassigned nodes. The subroutine is denoted as $\mathcal{K}$ (subscript of $BuildTour_\mathcal{K}$) in Algorithm 2.

The Naive Greedy (NG) Algorithm ($BuildTour_{\mathcal{K}_{NG}}$). This simple heuristic picks the next node solely based on the marginal reward. Formally, to assign the next node, the algorithm calculates the marginal reward of visiting u next

$$\pi_t^{NG}(u) = \rho(t \oplus_{|t|} u) - \rho(t) \tag{3}$$

for all unassigned node u in the cluster, and picks the maximum u with $\pi_t^{NG}(u)$. The insertion position is always $|t|$, which means it always appends a node at the end of a partial tour. This is an $O(n^2)$ operation for a cluster of n nodes.

The One-Step-Ahead (OSA) Algorithm. This heuristic considers one more step than NG. Namely, it calculates:

$$\pi_t^{OSA}(u) = \max_{v \neq u} \left(\rho(t \oplus_{|t|} u \oplus_{|t|+1} v) - \rho(t) \right) \tag{4}$$

for all unassigned u and v, and picks the u with highest $\pi_t^{OSA}(u)$. The insertion position is always $|t|$. Notice that node v is used only for the evaluation of node u, there is no guarantee in that the next step actually picks node v. This is an $O(n^3)$ operation for a cluster of n nodes.

The Total-Loss (TL) Algorithm. This heuristic calculates the sum of all the "losses" that visiting a node u incurs, and picks the u that minimizes this total loss. The loss from a node v incurred by visiting $u \neq v$ is defined as:

$$\delta_t(u, v) = \left(\rho(t \oplus_{|t|} v) - \rho(t) \right) - \left(\rho(t \oplus_{|t|} u \oplus_{|t|+1} v) - \rho(t \oplus_{|t|} u) \right) \tag{5}$$

where $\rho(t \oplus_{|t|} v) - \rho(t)$ is the marginal reward of appending v to t, while $\rho(t \oplus_{|t|} u \oplus_{|t|+1} v) - \rho(t \oplus_{|t|} u)$ is the marginal reward of appending v to $t \oplus_{|t|} u$.

The difference of these two signifies the *minimum reduction* in the marginal reward of appending v to a partial tour caused by appending u first. For each assignment, TL calculates:

$$\pi_t^{\mathrm{TL}}(u) = \sum_{v \neq u} \delta_t(u, v) \tag{6}$$

for all the unassigned u and v, and picks the u with the minimum $\pi_t^{\mathrm{TL}}(u)$. The insertion position is always $|t|$. This takes $O(n^3)$ operations for a cluster of size n.

The Gain-Minus-Loss (GML) Algorithm. This heuristic calculates the difference of gain (marginal reward) and loss; then it uses only the minimum loss instead of the total. For each assignment, the algorithm calculates:

$$\pi_t^{\mathrm{GML}}(u) = \pi_t^{\mathrm{NG}}(u) - \min_{v \neq u} \delta_t(u, v) \tag{7}$$

for all unassigned u and v, and picks the u with the maximum $\pi_t^{\mathrm{GML}}(u)$. The insertion position is always $|t|$. This is an $O(n^3)$ operations for a cluster size n.

The Loss-Per-Gain (LPG) Algorithm. This heuristic considers both gain and *total* loss by taking the ratio of the total loss to the gain. For each assignment, the algorithm calculates:

$$\pi_t^{\mathrm{LPG}}(u) = \frac{\pi_t^{\mathrm{TL}}(u)}{\pi_t^{\mathrm{NG}}(u)} \tag{8}$$

for all the unassigned u, and picks the u with the minimum $\pi_t^{\mathrm{LPG}}(u)$. The insertion position is always $|t|$. This is an $O(n^3)$ operation for a cluster of n nodes.

The Greedy Insertion (GI) Algorithm. This algorithm is a single-robot variation of the Sequential Greedy Algorithm (SGA) proposed in [5][1]. At each step, GI assigns the next node by trying out all the possible insertions of all the unassigned nodes, and picks the one with the highest marginal reward. However, for each partial tour, this algorithm calculates the reward of the corresponding cyclic partial tour, which appends node 0 at the end and sets $\beta(0) = \alpha$ (see Sect. 3.2). Formally, given the partial tour t, inserting node u *after* the i-th node of t gives a marginal reward:

$$\pi_t^{\mathrm{GI}}(u, i) = \rho(t \oplus_i u \oplus_{|t|} 0) - \rho(t \oplus_{|t|} 0) \tag{9}$$

At each assignment, the algorithm calculates $\pi_t^{\mathrm{GI}}(u, i)$ for all the unassigned u and all the integral $i \in [1, |t|]$, and chooses the u and i with the maximum $\pi_t^{\mathrm{GI}}(u, i)$. This is an $O(n^3)$ operation for a cluster of n nodes.

Other than GI, all these algorithms build a partial tour by inserting nodes at the end, and therefore can be adopted for online planning. Since GI needs to

---

[1] The reward function in our problem does not satisfy the Diminishing Marginal Gain property, so the performance guarantee of SGA doesn't hold.

Algorithm 3. PGC Merging Algorithm *PGCMerge*

Input: G, $(C_i, e_i, l_i, g_i, c_i, \mathcal{L}_i)$, $(C_j, e_j, l_j, g_j, c_j, \mathcal{L}_j)$ // G: the world model, $(C_i, e_i, l_i,$
    $g_i, c_i, \mathcal{L}_i)$: data structure of C_i, see Sect. 4.3
Output: $(C_{ij}, e_{ij}, l_{ij}, g_{ij}, c_{ij}, \mathcal{L}_{ij})$ // data structure of C_{ij}
1: $C_{ij} \leftarrow C_i \cup C_j$
2: **if** $\mathcal{D}(0, e_i) > \mathcal{D}(0, e_j)$ **then**
3:     $\mathbf{swap}(i, j)$
4: $e_{ij} \leftarrow e_i$, $d \leftarrow +\infty$
5: **for all** $v_i \in C_i$ **do**
6:     **for all** $v_j \in C_j$ **do**
7:        **if** $\mathcal{D}(v_i, v_j) < d$ **then**
8:           $d \leftarrow \mathcal{D}(v_i, v_j)$, $v_i^* \leftarrow v_i$, $v_j^* \leftarrow v_j$
9: $\mathcal{L}_{ij} \leftarrow \mathcal{L}_i \cup \mathcal{L}_j \cup \{\{v_i^*, v_j^*\}\}$
10: $H \leftarrow \{(\mathcal{D}(v_i^*, v_j^*), v_j^*)\}$ // min-heap as BFS queue, sorted on the edge length
11: $M \leftarrow C_i$ // the visited nodes
12: $l_{ij} \leftarrow l_i$, $g_{ij} \leftarrow g_i$
13: **while** $H \neq \emptyset$ **do**
14:     $d, v \leftarrow H.\mathbf{pop}$ // the top of H
15:     $l_{ij} \leftarrow l_{ij} + d$, $g_{ij} \leftarrow g_{ij} + \psi^{\mathcal{D}(0, e_{ij}) + l_{ij}} \beta(v)$, $M \leftarrow M \cup \{v\}$
16:     **for all** $u \in \mathcal{L}_j(v), u \notin M$ **do**
17:        $H \leftarrow H \cup \{(\mathcal{D}(u, v), u)\}$
18: $c_{ij} \leftarrow (1 - \psi^{\mathcal{D}(0, e_i) + \mathcal{D}(0, e_j) + l_{ij}}) \alpha$
19: **return** $(C_{ij}, e_{ij}, l_{ij}, g_{ij}, c_{ij}, \mathcal{L}_{ij})$

---

insert node at any position of a partial tour and the robot cannot change the path already taken, it can only be used offline.

With a small modification (see Sect. 5), the above tour-building algorithms can be used as the input function $\mathcal{R}$ in Algorithm 1 to evaluate cluster merging. All of the algorithms except NG have $O(n^3)$ time. Fortunately, all the $O(n^3)$ algorithms can reduce the time complexity by at most a factor of n using parallelism, because the evaluation of one candidate node is independent of another.

4.3   The Progressive Gain-Aware Clustering Algorithm (PGC)

PGC has a better time complexity than the naive clustering. Based on the technique of using rooted k-MST to approximate the optimal solution of MLP [3,4], PGC estimates the reward obtainable from a cluster without building a tour. Algorithm 3 shows the merging procedure. The complete algorithm is in Algorithm 4, which follows a similar structure as the clustering algorithm.

The data structures associated with an existing cluster C_i are: (1) an entry node e_i which is the closest node to the base node in the cluster; (2) an estimated gain g_i from all the nodes in the cluster; (3) an estimated cost c_i due to the risk of losing the robot; (4) an adjacency list $\mathcal{L}_i$ that keeps track of the Minimum Spanning Tree (MST) of the nodes in the cluster, where $\mathcal{L}_i(v)$ is the list of neighbors of node v in the MST; and (5) a total length l_i that is the sum of all the edge lengths in the MST. For the rest of this section, subscript ij is used to

Algorithm 4. PGC Algorithm PGC

Input: G // the world model
Output: S // a set of clusters
1: $S \leftarrow \emptyset$
2: **for all** $v \in V \setminus \{0\}$ **do**
3: $\quad C_v \leftarrow \{v\}, \; e_v \leftarrow v, \; l_v \leftarrow 0, \; g_v \leftarrow \psi^{\mathcal{D}(0,v)}\beta(v), \; c_v \leftarrow (1 - \psi^{2\mathcal{D}(0,v)})\alpha, \; \mathcal{L}_v \leftarrow \emptyset$
4: $\quad S \leftarrow S \cup C_v$
5: **loop**
6: $\quad C_i^* \leftarrow \emptyset, \; C_j^* \leftarrow \emptyset, \; C_k^* \leftarrow \emptyset, \; \Delta^* \leftarrow 0$
7: $\quad$ **for all** $C_i \in S$ **do**
8: $\qquad$ **for all** $C_j \in S, j > i$ **do**
9: $\qquad\quad (C_k, \ldots, g_k, c_k, \ldots) \leftarrow PGCMerge((C_i, \ldots, g_i, c_i, \ldots), (C_j, \ldots, g_j, c_j, \ldots))$
10: $\qquad\quad \Delta \leftarrow (g_k - c_k) - (g_i - c_i) - (g_j - c_j)$
11: $\qquad\quad$ **if** $\Delta > \Delta^*$ **then**
12: $\qquad\qquad \Delta^* \leftarrow \Delta, \; C_i^* \leftarrow C_i, \; C_j^* \leftarrow C_j, \; C_k^* \leftarrow C_k$
13: $\quad$ **if** $\Delta^* = 0$ **then**
14: $\qquad$ **break**
15: $\quad S \leftarrow S \setminus \{C_i^*, C_j^*\} \cup \{C_k^*\}$
16: **return** S

---

denote a variable associated with cluster $C_i \cup C_j$. For example, C_{ij} is $C_i \cup C_j$ and e_{ij} is the entry node of C_{ij}.

Given C_i and C_j, the estimated reward before merging is computed trivially as $g_i - c_i + g_j - c_j$. But the computation of the estimated reward after merging is more complicated. The first step is to choose the entry node $e_{ij} \in \{e_i, e_j\}$ of C_{ij} to be the one that is closer to the base node. Without loss of generality, assume $e_{ij} = e_i$. Then the algorithm obtains $\mathcal{L}_{ij}$ by merging $\mathcal{L}_i$ and $\mathcal{L}_j$ and adding the shortest edge that connects nodes $v_i \in C_i$ and $v_j \in C_j$. To compute g_{ij}, we perform a breadth-first search (BFS) starting from node v_i on the MST of C_{ij}, with all the nodes in C_i marked as visited, l_{ij} set to l_i and g_{ij} set to g_i. At each iteration, the shortest edge that connects the visited subtree to an unvisited node is picked. Its length is added to l_{ij}, and the unvisited node on the edge, say v, is marked as visited. Assume at this point there are n visited nodes, then l_{ij} is the total edge length of the n-MST of C_{ij} rooted at node e_{ij}, which can be used as a lower-bound of the n-th node's latency in the optimal minimum-latency tour of C_{ij} starting from node e_{ij}. After adding this edge, g_{ij} is increased by $\psi^{\mathcal{D}(0,e_{ij})+l_{ij}}\beta(v)$, where ψ is the probability of the robot successfully traveling one unit distance, and $\beta(v)$ is the reward of node v. At last, the estimated cost is calculated as $c_{ij} = (1 - \psi^{\mathcal{D}(0,e_i)+\mathcal{D}(0,e_j)+l_{ij}})\alpha$, where α is the value of the robot, and the estimated reward is $g_{ij} - c_{ij}$.

Finding the closest nodes v_i and v_j is $O(n^2)$ for two clusters of size n each; BFS is $O(n)$ as the graph is a tree. Other operations are constant. Therefore, merging takes $O(n^2)$.

For the whole algorithm, assume the graph contains N nodes. During one merge iteration, where all the clusters are pair-wise evaluated and the best pair is merged, regardless of how many clusters are there: each *node* is paired with each

---

Algorithm 5. $BuildTour_{\mathcal{K}} + Cluster$

Input: G // the world model
Output: T // a plan of tours
1: $T \leftarrow \emptyset$
2: $S \leftarrow Cluster(G, BuildTour_{\mathcal{K}}')$ // $BuildTour_{\mathcal{K}}'$ returns the reward of the built tour
3: **for all** $C \in S$ **do**
4:     $t \leftarrow BuildTour_{\mathcal{K}}(G, C)$, $T \leftarrow T \cup \{t\}$
5: **return** T

Algorithm 6. $BuildTour_{\mathcal{K}} + PGC$

Input: G // the world model
Output: T // a plan of tours
1: $T \leftarrow \emptyset$, $S \leftarrow PGC(G)$
2: **for all** $C \in S$ **do**
3:     $t \leftarrow BuildTour_{\mathcal{K}}(G, C)$, $T \leftarrow T \cup \{t\}$
4: **return** T

---

of the $O(N)$ nodes outside its own cluster exactly once for finding v_is and v_js; each node is visited $O(N)$ times in all the BFS's; and there are $O(N)$ constant operations. Therefore, one iteration is $O(N^2)$ and the whole algorithm is $O(N^3)$. Note that, given an $O(n^2)$ evaluation function $\mathcal{R}$, a similar argument, which considers nodes instead of clusters, can be made for the clustering algorithm in Algorithm 1. It makes the overall time complexity of Algorithm 1 $O(N^4)$ instead of $O(N^5)$.

5   Evaluation

We run experiments with two clustering algorithms, the naive clustering algorithm (NC) in Algorithm 1 and PGC in Algorithm 4, combined with each of six tour-building heuristics (NG, OSA, TL, GML, LPG and GI) in Algorithm 2. Therefore, there are 12 different combinations of clustering and tour-building algorithms (2×6). The tour-building-NC combinations are detailed in Algorithm 5, where $BuildTour_{\mathcal{K}}'$ is the variation of $BuildTour_{\mathcal{K}}$ that still uses $\mathcal{K}$ to build tours but returns the reward of the built tour instead of the tour itself. The tour-building-PGC combinations are in Algorithm 6.

For each combination, we run experiments with different robot values and different variances in node rewards, which is also referred to as *node variance*. For each combination of clustering and tour building, robot value, and node variance, we experiment on 100 uniformly random graphs within the world size 100×100. The success rate ψ is fixed to 0.99. The results are averaged from the 100 runs. Since the problem is NP-hard, computing the optimal solution is infeasible. Therefore we compare the solutions given by our algorithms.

Section 5.1 compares the performance (*quality of solution*) of the tour-building heuristics when they are combined with NC with node reward drawn from a integral uniform distribution from 4 to 6. Section 5.2 shows the results

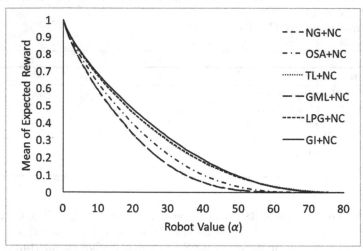

(a) Normalized mean of expected reward.

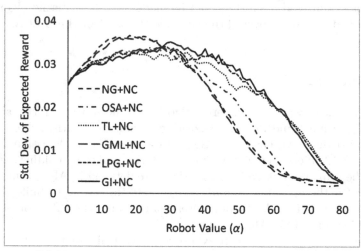

(b) Normalized standard deviation of expected reward.

Fig. 1. The performance of tour-building algorithm combined with NC. Node rewards range from 4 to 6.

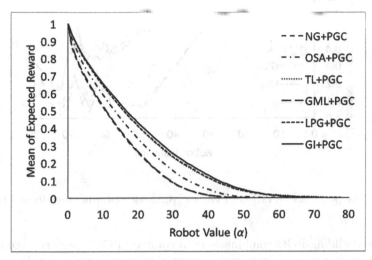

(a) Normalized mean of expected reward.

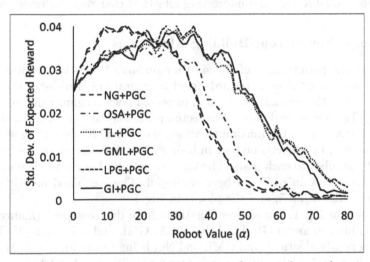

(b) Normalized standard deviation of expected reward.

Fig. 2. The performance of tour-building algorithm combined with PGC. Node rewards range from 4 to 6.

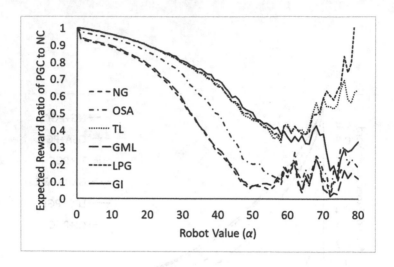

Fig. 3. The performance ratio of PGC to NC. Node rewards range from 4 to 6.

of the tour-building-PGC combinations to compare PGC's performance against NC, when node reward drawn from a integral uniform distribution from 4 to 6. Finally, Sect. 5.3 discusses the interesting effects of changing the node variance.

5.1   Comparison of Tour-Building Algorithms

To evaluate the performance of the six tour-building heuristics, we use NC for clustering and draw the node rewards from a integral uniform distribution from 4 to 6, then plot the normalized mean of expected reward against different robot values (α). The normalized mean of expected reward is the ratio of the mean in an experimental setting to the maximum, which is obtained in the setting where the robot value is 0, i.e. there is no cost in losing robot, and therefore the best plan is to send one robot to each node. The value of standard deviation is normalized by the same factor in order to be meaningful. The combined algorithms are described in Algorithm 5, and the plot is in Fig. 1.

As shown in Fig. 1, the six combinations have different performances. The order from high to low is GI, TL, LPG, OSA, GML and NG, with GI, TL and LPG being nearly identical, and GML and NG being nearly identical. Although, as shown in Sect. 5.3, the difference between GI, TL and LPG becomes more obvious when the data variance becomes larger. The standard deviation is *relatively* large for larger robot values for all the algorithms. This indicates that when the robot value is high, the algorithms are less stable. One possible reason is that, due to the high cost of losing robot, even a small difference in distance can change the decision made by an algorithm.

GI being the best is not surprising, because insertion-based construction methods generally perform better than nearest-neighbor heuristics [10]. All the other five construction methods are only able to look ahead by appending new

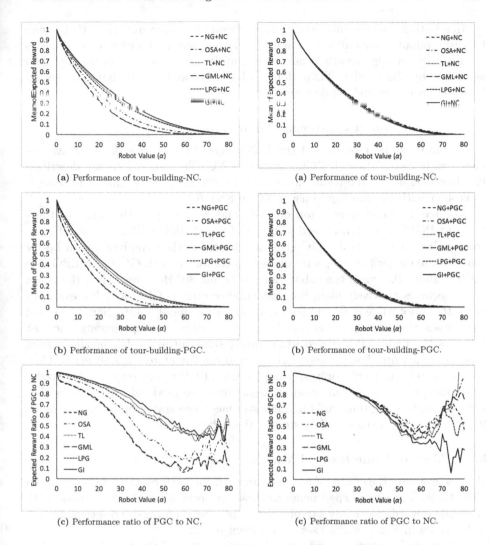

(a) Performance of tour-building-NC.   (a) Performance of tour-building-NC.

(b) Performance of tour-building-PGC.   (b) Performance of tour-building-PGC.

(c) Performance ratio of PGC to NC.   (c) Performance ratio of PGC to NC.

Fig. 4. Node rewards range from 1 to 9.   **Fig. 5.** Node rewards are all 5.

nodes to the end of a partial tour. Therefore, they are intuitively less powerful than any nearest-neighbor heuristics that adjust tours in various places. Consequently, it is surprising that TL, which takes only losses into account, performs almost as well as GI. Since NG and OSA consider the gain from the immediate next steps, and LPG and GML consider both gain and loss, this result indicates that the immediate loss, which is caused by robot traveling extra distance that discounts future gains, has more impact on the overall performance the immediate gain.

In addition, one advantage of a "look-ahead" heuristic like TL is that it can be easily adopted for online planning, in cases where nodes of interest appears dynamically, or edge length is not known until the robot reaches a node. And as shown by the results, TL performs almost as well as GI that requires all information before making decisions.

5.2   Comparison of Clustering Algorithms

To evaluate the performance of the PGC algorithm, we run the same experiments as in Sect. 5.1, with PGC instead of NC. The algorithms are described in Algorithm 6, and the results are shown in Fig. 2; the performance ranking is consistent with the ranking in using NC in Sect. 5.1.

To give a clearer comparison of PGC and NC, we plot the ratios of tour-building-PGC's expected reward to those of tour-building-NC, against different robot values (α) in Fig. 3. PGC gives good results when combined with better tour building algorithms. Specifically, when combined with GI, TL or LPG, the ratio is above 0.8 when the robot value is below 30. However, when the robot value becomes relatively high, the performance ratio is fairly low. For example, when the robot value is around 60, the ratio is only about 0.4. It should be noted that, when the robot value is very high, above 60 in our experiments, the cost becomes too high that the algorithms rarely send out any robot at all. In such cases, the measures have a large variance and are therefore less indicative. They are included in the results only for completeness. PGC's performance downgrades when low-performance tour-building algorithms are used, which indicates that a better performing tour-building heuristic has more stable performance and is less sensitive to the choice of clustering algorithm.

5.3   Effect of Node Reward Variance

We also evaluate the effects of node variance on the performance of the proposed algorithms. The same experiments as those in Sects. 5.1 and 5.2 are done with the node rewards randomly sampled from integral uniform distributions from 1 to 9, shown in Fig. 4, and all set to 5, shown in Fig. 5.

Interestingly, when the difference in performance of the tour-building algorithms varies in accordance with the node variance. Namely, as seen in Fig. 4, when node variance becomes larger, the difference in performance becomes larger, and vice versa in Fig. 5.

With respect to the performance of PGC, as shown in Figs. 4(b), (c) and 5(b), (c), the result is similar to that of in Sect. 5.2. Namely, PGC performs well for low robot values (< 30) but bad for high robot values (30 to 60). In addition, comparing across node variances, PGC performs better for larger node variance.

6   Conclusion and Future Work

This paper proposes the Data-collecting Robot Problem where values of robots and the risk of losing robots are explicitly modeled. The objective is to maximize the expected reward of a plan (a set of tours). The expected reward is determined by both the gain from visiting nodes and loss of robots. We give two formulations of the problem: the delayed-reward and the immediate-reward formulations. Solutions for the immediate-reward formulation are presented.

Six tour-building heuristics are proposed and compared. Among them, GI performs the best, followed closely by TL. However, since GI modifies a partial tour at any point, it cannot be used for online planning. TL, on the other hand, builds a tour by appending nodes at the end of a partial tour, so it can be adopted for online planning and we empirically prove that it performs almost as good as GI. We also propose PGC heuristic for clustering. With a better time complexity, this algorithm approximates the naive clustering algorithm well for low robot values, and it does better when node variance becomes larger. In addition, we discover that the most important factor in maximizing the reward is the immediate loss. Another interesting observation is that the difference of performance among tour-building algorithms increases as the data variance increases.

For future work, we would like to further investigate the effects of data variance. We are also interested in the online versions of DRP, in which nodes appear dynamically. TL seems to be a starting point. To make the problem more realistic, we also plan to add energy consumptions as an additional cost, and consider the cost due to congestion. Another direction is modeling uncertainty from robot's movement. This involves abstracting the underlying uncertainty to a high-level cost parameter that can be used in route planning. The problem formulations in this paper can address this to a certain degree, but more elaborate modeling is necessary.

Acknowledgement. We thank Mahmuda Rahman and Jeff Hudack for reviewing drafts of this paper and providing valuable suggestions.

References

1. Archetti, C., Feillet, D., Hertz, A., Grazia Speranza, M.: The capacitated team orienteering and profitable tour problems. J. Oper. Res. Soc. **60**, 831–842 (2009)
2. Blum, A., Chalasani, P., Coppersmith, D., Pulleyblank, B., Raghavan, P., Sudan, M.: The minimum latency problem. In: Proceedings of the 26th Symposium on Theory of Computing, STOC, p. 9 (1994)
3. Blum, A., Chawla, S., Karger, D.R., Lane, T., Meyerson, A., Minkoff, M.: Approximation algorithms for orienteering and discounted-reward TSP. SIAM J. Comput. **37**(2), 653–670 (2007)
4. Chaudhuri, K., Godfrey, B., Rao, S., Talwar, K.: Paths, trees, and minimum latency tours. In: Proceedings - 44th Annual IEEE Symposium on Foundations of Computer Science, FOCS, pp. 36–45. IEEE (2003)
5. Choi, H.L., Brunet, L., How, J.P.: Consensus-based decentralized auctions for robust task allocation. IEEE Trans. Robot. **25**(4), 912–926 (2009)
6. Ekici, A., Retharekar, A.: Multiple agents maximum collection problem with time dependent rewards. Comput. Ind. Eng. **64**(4), 1009–1018 (2013)
7. Feillet, D., Dejax, P., Gendreau, M.: Traveling salesman problems with profits: an overview. Transp. Sci. **39**, 188–205 (2001)

8. Hudack, J., Oh, J.: Multi-agent sensor data collection with attrition risk. In: Proceedings - The 26th International Conference on Automated Planning and Scheduling, ICAPS (2016)
9. Moshref-Javadi, M., Lee, S.: A taxonomy to the class of minimum latency problems. In: Proceedings - IIE Annual Conference, pp. 3896. Institute of Industrial Engineers-Publisher (2013)
10. Rosenkrantz, D.J., Stearns, R.E., Lewis, P.M.: An analysis of several heuristics for the traveling salesman problem. In: Ravi, S.S., Shukla, S.K. (eds.) Fundamental Problems in Computing: Essays in Honor of Professor Daniel J. Rosenkrantz, pp. 45–69. Springer Science & Business Media, Dordrecht (2009)
11. Talarico, L., Sörensen, K., Springael, J.: Metaheuristics for the risk-constrained cash-in-transit vehicle routing problem. Eur. J. Oper. Res. **244**(2), 457–470 (2015)
12. Toth, P., Vigo, D.: Vehicle Routing: Problems, Methods, and Applications, vol. 18. Society for Industrial and Applied Mathematics, Philadelphia (2014)

Verifying Real-Time Properties of Multi-agent Systems via SMT-Based Bounded Model Checking

Agnieszka M. Zbrzezny[✉] and Andrzej Zbrzezny

IMCS, Jan Długosz University, Al. Armii Krajowej 13/15,
42-200 Częstochowa, Poland
{agnieszka.zbrzezny,a.zbrzezny}@ajd.czest.pl

Abstract. We present a satisfiability modulo theories based bounded model checking (SMT-based BMC) method for timed interpreted systems (TIS) and for properties expressible in the existential fragment of a Real-Time Computation Tree Logic with epistemic components (RTECTLK). We implemented the standard BMC algorithm and evaluated it for two multi-agent systems: a timed train controller system and a timed generic pipeline paradigm. We used the Z3 solver.

1 Introduction

The formalism of *interpreted systems* (IS) was introduced in [8] to model multi-agent systems (MAS) [19], which are intended for reasoning about the agents' epistemic and temporal properties. The formalism of timed interpreted systems (TIS) [22] extends IS to make the reasoning possible about not only temporal and epistemic properties, but also about real-time aspects of MASs. The previous ten years in the area of MASs have seen significant research in verification procedures, which automatically evaluate whether a MAS reaches its intended specifications.

Model checking [4] is an automatic verification technique for concurrent systems such as: digital systems, distributed systems, real time systems, multi-agent systems, communication protocols, cryptographic protocols, concurrent programs, and many others. To be able to check automatically whether the system satisfies a given property, one must first create a model of the system, and then describe in a formal language both the created model and the property.

One of the main technique here is *symbolic model checking* [4]. Unfortunately, because of the agents' intricate nature, the practical applicability of model checking is firmly limited by the "state-space explosion problem" (i.e., an exponential growth of the system state space with the number of agents). To reduce this issue, various techniques, including the SAT- and BDD-based bounded model checking (binary decision diagrams based BMC) [10,15,18], have been advanced.

Partly supported by National Science Centre under the grant No. 2014/15/N/ST6/05079.

M. Baldoni et al. (Eds.): PRIMA 2016, LNAI 9862, pp. 149–167, 2016.
DOI: 10.1007/978-3-319-44832-9_9

These have been effective in permitting users to handle bigger MASs, however it is still hard to check MASs with numerous agents. The point of this paper is to help beat this inadequacy by employing SMT-solvers (i.e., *satisfiability modulo theories* tools for deciding the satisfiability of formulae in a number of theories) [2].

Bounded model checking for multi-agent systems is a symbolic model checking method designed for finding counterexamples, and whose main idea is to consider a model curtailed to a specific depth to search for an execution (or a set of executions) of a system under consideration of some length k, which constitutes a counterexample for a tested property. It uses a reduction of the problem of truth of a temporal formula [6] (an epistemic formula [8], doxastic formula [12], and deontic formula [14]) in a model of MAS to the problem of satisfiability of formulae. The reduction is achieved by a translation of the transition relation and a translation of a given property to a quantifier-free first-order formula. It should be emphasised that for a given temporal logic, bounded model checking is mainly used to disprove safety properties and to prove liveness properties.

A version of the SAT-based BMC method for specifications expressed in RTECTLK, and MASs modelled by interleaved interpreted systems (the interpreted system with the asynchronous semantics (interleaving semantics)), in which agents have time-limits or other explicit timing constraints to accomplish intended goals, has been published in [21].

The original contributions of the paper are as follows. First, we propose a SMT-based BMC technique for TIS and for RTECTLK. Second, we report on the implementation of the proposed BMC method as a new module of a verification system, and evaluate it experimentally by means of a modified *generic pipeline paradigm* [17] and a modified *train controller system*.

We do not compare our results with other model checkers for MASs, e.g. MCMAS [13] or MCK [9], simply because they do not support the RTECTLK language and the timed interpreted systems.

Scheme of the Paper. The rest of the paper is organised as follows. In the next section we briefly present the theory of the timed interpreted systems and the RTECTLK language. In Sect. 3 we present our SMT-based BMC method and an example of translation to SMT. In Sect. 4 we experimentally evaluate the performance of our SMT-based BMC encoding. We conclude with a brief discussion in Sect. 5.

2   Preliminaries

Timed Interpreted Systems (TIS) were proposed in [22] to extend interpreted systems (ISs) in order to make possible reasoning about real-time aspects of MASs. In the formalism of interpreted systems, each agent is characterised by a set of local states and by a set of local actions that are performed following a local protocol. Given a set of initial states, the system evolves in compliance with an evolution function that determines how the local state of an agent changes as a function of its local state and of the other agents actions. The evolution of all the agents local states describes a set of runs and a set of reachable states. These can be used to interpret formulae involving temporal operators, epistemic operators to reason about what agents know.

2.1 Timed Interpreted Systems

Let $\mathbb{N}$ be a set of natural numbers, and $\mathbb{N}_+ = \mathbb{N}\backslash\{0\}$. We assume a finite set $\mathbb{X}$ of variables, called *clocks*. Each clock is a variable ranging over a set of non-negative natural numbers. For $x \in \mathbb{X}$, $\bowtie \in \{<, \leq, =, >, \geq\}$, $c \in \mathbb{N}$ we define a set of clock constraints over $\mathbb{X}$, denoted by $\mathcal{C}(\mathbb{X})$, The constraints are conjunctions of comparisons of a clock with a time constant c from the set of natural numbers $\mathbb{N}$, generated by the following grammar:

$$\mathfrak{cc} := \mathbf{true} \mid x \bowtie c \mid \mathfrak{cc} \wedge \mathfrak{cc}.$$

A clock valuation v of $\mathbb{X}$ is a total function from $\mathbb{X}$ into the set of natural numbers. The set of all the clock valuations is denoted by $\mathbb{N}^{\mathbb{X}}$. For $\mathbb{X}' \subseteq \mathbb{X}$, the valuation which assigns the value 0 to all clocks is defined as: $\forall_{x \in \mathbb{X}'} v'(x) = 0$ and $\forall_{x \in \mathbb{X}\backslash\mathbb{X}'} v'(x) = v(x)$. For $v \in \mathbb{N}^{\mathbb{X}}$, $succ(v)$ is the clock valuation of $\mathbb{X}$ that assigns the value $v(x) + 1$ to each clock x. A clock valuation v satisfies a clock constraint $\mathfrak{cc}$, written as $v \models \mathfrak{cc}$, iff $\mathfrak{cc}$ evaluates to true using the clock values given by v.

Let $\mathcal{A} = \{1, \ldots, n\}$ denote a non-empty and finite set of agents, and Ev be a special agent that is used to model the environment in which the agents operate, and $\mathcal{AP} = \bigcup_{i \in \mathcal{A} \cup \{Ev\}} \mathcal{AP}_i$ be a set of atomic formulae, such that $\mathcal{AP}_{i_1} \cap \mathcal{AP}_{i_2} = \emptyset$ for all $i_1, i_2 \in \mathcal{A} \cup \{Ev\}$.

A *timed interpreted system* is a tuple

$$\mathbb{TIS} = (\{L_i, Act_i, \mathbb{X}_i, P_i, \mathcal{V}_i, \mathcal{I}_i, \iota_i\}_{i \in \mathcal{A} \cup \{Ev\}}, \{t_i\}_{i \in \mathcal{A}}, \{t_{Ev}\}),$$

where:

- L_i is a non-empty set of *locations* of the agent i,
- $\iota_i \subseteq L_i$ is a non-empty set of initial locations,
- Act_i is a non-empty set of *possible actions* of the agent i, $Act = Act_1 \times \ldots \times Act_n \times Act_{Ev}$ is the set of *joint actions*,
- $\mathbb{X}_i$ is a non-empty set of *clocks*,
- $P_i : L_i \rightarrow 2^{Act_i}$ is a *protocol function*,
- $t_i : L_i \times L_{Ev} \times \mathcal{C}(\mathbb{X}_i) \times 2^{\mathbb{X}_i} \times Act \rightarrow L_i$ is a (partial) *evolution function* for agents,
- $t_{Ev} : L_{Ev} \times \mathcal{C}(\mathbb{X}_{Ev}) \times 2^{\mathbb{X}_{Ev}} \times Act \rightarrow L_{Ev}$ is a (partial) *evolution function* for environment,
- $\mathcal{V}_i : L_i \rightarrow 2^{\mathcal{AP}_i}$ is a *valuation function* assigning to each location a set of atomic formulae that are assumed to be true at that location,
- $\mathcal{I}_i : L_i \rightarrow \mathcal{C}(\mathbb{X}_i)$ is an *invariant function*, that specifies the amount of time the agent i may spend in a given location.

It is assumed that locations, actions and clocks for the environment are "public", which means that all the agents know a current location, an action, and a clock valuation of the environment.

We also assume that if $\epsilon_i \in P_i(\ell_i)$, then $t_i(\ell_i, \ell_{Ev}, cc_i, X, (a_1, \ldots, a_n, a_{Ev})) = \ell_i$ for $a_i = \epsilon_i$, any $cc_i \in \mathcal{C}(X_i)$, and any $X \subseteq X_i$. Each element t of t_i is denoted by $<\ell_i, \ell_{Ev}, cc_i, X', a, \ell_i'>$, where ℓ_i is the source location, ℓ_i' is the target location, a is an action, cc is the enabling condition for t_i, and $X' \subseteq X_i$ is the set of clocks to be reset after performing t. An invariant condition allows the TIS to stay at the location ℓ as long as the constraint $\mathcal{I}_i(\ell_i)$ is satisfied. The guard cc has to be satisfied to enable the transition.

2.2 Timed Model

For a given TIS let the symbol $S = \prod_{i \in \mathcal{A} \cup \{Ev\}} (L_i \times \mathbb{N}^{X_i})$ denote the non-empty set of all *global states*. Moreover, for a given global state $s = ((\ell_1, v_1), \ldots, (\ell_n, v_n), (\ell_{Ev}, v_{Ev})) \in S$, let the symbols $l_i(s) = \ell_i$ and $v_i(s) = v_i$ denote, respectively, the local component and the clock valuation of agent $i \in \mathcal{A} \cup \{Ev\}$ in s. Now, for a given TIS we define a *timed model* (or a *model*) as a tuple $\mathcal{M} = (Act, S, \iota, T, \mathcal{V})$, where:

- $Act = Act_1 \times \ldots \times Act_n \times Act_{Ev}$ is the set of all the joint actions,
- $S = \prod_{i \in \mathcal{A} \cup \{Ev\}} (L_i \times \mathbb{N}^{X_i})$ is the set of all the *global states*,
- $\iota = \prod_{i \in \mathcal{A} \cup \{Ev\}} (\iota_i \times \{0\}^{X_i})$ is the set of all the *initial* global states,
- $\mathcal{V} : S \to 2^{\mathcal{AP}}$ is the valuation function defined as $\mathcal{V}(s) = \bigcup_{i \in \mathcal{A} \cup \{Ev\}} \mathcal{V}_i(l_i(s))$,
- $T \subseteq S \times (Act \cup \{\tau\}) \times S$ is a transition relation defined by action and time transitions. For $\tilde{a} \in Act$:

1. action transition: $(s, \tilde{a}, s') \in T$ (or $s \xrightarrow{\tilde{a}} s'$) iff for all $i \in \mathcal{A} \cup \{Ev\}$, there exists a local transition $t_i(l_i(s), cc_i, X', \tilde{a}) = l_i(s')$ such that $v_i(s) \models cc_i \wedge \mathcal{I}(l_i(s))$ and $v_i'(s') = v_i(s)[X' := 0]$ and $v_i'(s') \models \mathcal{I}(l_i(s'))$ ($v_i(s)[X' := 0]$) denotes the clock valuation which assigns 0 to each clock in X' and agrees with $v_i(s)$ over the rest of the clocks.
2. time transition $(s, \tau, s') \in T$ iff for all $i \in \mathcal{A} \cup \{Ev\}$, $l_i(s) = l_i(s')$ and $v_i'(s') = v_i(s) + 1$ and $v_i'(s') \models \mathcal{I}(l_i(s'))$.

A *path* π in $\mathcal{M}$ is a sequence $\pi = (s_0, s_1, \ldots)$ of states such that $(s_0, \tau, s_1) \in T$ holds and for each $i > 0$, either $(s_i, \tilde{a}_i, s_{i+1}) \in T$ or $(s_i, \tau, s_{i+1}) \in T$, and if $(s_i, \tilde{a}_i, s_{i+1}) \in T$ holds, then $(s_{i+1}, \tau, s_{i+2}) \in T$ holds.

Observe that the above definition of the path ensures that the first transition is the time one, and between each two action transitions at least one time transition appears.

The set of all the paths starting at $s \in S$ is denoted by $\Pi(s)$, and the set of all the paths starting at an initial state is denoted by $\Pi = \bigcup_{s^0 \in \iota} \Pi(s^0)$. Moreover, for $a \in Act \cup \{\tau\}$, we sometimes write $s \xrightarrow{a} s'$ instead of $(s, a, s') \in T$. Eventually, for $s \in S$ and $a \in Act \cup \{\tau\}$, the set of direct *a-successors* of s is defined as: $Post(s, a) = \{s' \in S | s \xrightarrow{a} s'\}$, and the set of direct successors of s is defined as $Post(s) = \bigcup_{a \in Act \cup \{\tau\}} Post(s, a)$.

Given a TIS, one can define for any agent i the *indistinguishability* relation $\sim_i \subseteq S \times S$ as follows: $s \sim_i s'$ iff $l_i(s') = l_i(s)$ and $v_i(s') = v_i(s)$.

We assume the following definitions of epistemic relations: $\sim_\Gamma^E \stackrel{def}{=} \bigcup_{i \in \Gamma} \sim_i$, $\sim_\Gamma^C \stackrel{def}{=} (\sim_\Gamma^E)^+$ (the transitive closure of $\sim_\Gamma^E$), $\sim_\Gamma^D \stackrel{def}{=} \bigcap_{i \in \Gamma} \sim_i$, where $\Gamma \subseteq \mathcal{A}$.

2.3   Abstract Model

The set of all the clock valuations is infinite which means that a model has an infinite set of states. We need to abstract the proposed model before we can apply the bounded model checking technique. Let c_i be the largest constant appearing in any enabling condition or state invariants of agent i, and $v, v' \in \mathbb{N}^{|\mathbb{X}|}$ be two clock valuations. We say that $v \simeq_i v'$ iff the following condition holds for each $x \in \mathbb{X}_i$:

$$v(x) > c_i \text{ and } v'(x) > c_i \text{ or } v(x) \leq c_i \text{ and } v'(x) \leq c_i \text{ and } v(x) = v'(x).$$

Next, we define the relation $\simeq$ as follows: $v \simeq v'$ iff $v \simeq_i v'$, for every $i \in \mathcal{A} \cup \{Ev\}$. Obviously, $\simeq$ is an equivalence relation. It is easy to see that equivalent clock valuations satisfy the same clock constraints that occur in TIS. Basing on this observation one can define the *abstract model* for TIS. Namely, let $\mathbb{D}_i = \{0, \ldots, c_i + 1\}$, and $\mathbb{D} = \bigcup_{i \in \mathcal{A} \cup \{Ev\}} \mathbb{D}_i^{\mathbb{X}_i}$. For any $v \in \mathbb{D}$ let us define the successor $succ(v)$ of v as follows: for each $x \in \mathbb{X}$,

$$succ(v)(x) = \begin{cases} v(x) + 1, & \text{if } x \in \mathbb{X}_i \text{ and } v(x) \leq c_i, \\ v(x), & \text{if } x \in \mathbb{X}_i \text{ and } v(x) > c_i. \end{cases}$$

Now, one can define the *abstract model* as a tuple $\widehat{\mathcal{M}} = (Act, \widehat{S}, \widehat{\iota}, \widehat{T}, \widehat{\mathcal{V}})$, where $\widehat{S} = \prod_{i \in \mathcal{A} \cup \{Ev\}} (L_i \times \mathbb{D}_i^{\mathbb{X}_i})$ $\widehat{\iota} = \iota$, $\widehat{\mathcal{V}} = \mathcal{V}|_{\widehat{S}}$, and $\widehat{T} \subseteq \widehat{S} \times (Act \cup \{\tau\}) \times \widehat{S}$ is a transition relation defined by action and time transitions. For $\tilde{a} \in Act$:

1. action transition: $(\widehat{s}, \tilde{a}, \widehat{s}') \in \widehat{T}$ iff $\forall_{i \in \mathcal{A}} \exists_{\phi_i \in \mathcal{C}(\mathbb{X}_i)} \exists_{\mathbb{X}_i' \subseteq \mathbb{X}_i} (t_i(l_i(\widehat{s}), \phi_i, \mathbb{X}_i', \tilde{a}) = l_i(\widehat{s}')$ and $v_i \models \phi_i \wedge \mathcal{I}(l_i(\widehat{s}))$ and $v_i'(\widehat{s}') = v_i(\widehat{s})[\mathbb{X}_i' := 0]$ and $v_i'(\widehat{s}') \models \mathcal{I}(l_i(\widehat{s}')))$
2. time transition: $(\widehat{s}, \tau, \widehat{s}') \in \widehat{T}$ iff $\forall_{i \in \mathcal{A} \cup \{Ev\}} (l_i(\widehat{s}) = l_i(\widehat{s}'))$ and $v_i(\widehat{s}) \models \mathcal{I}(l_i(\widehat{s}))$ and $succ(v_i(\widehat{s})) \models \mathcal{I}(l_i(\widehat{s})))$ and $\forall_{i \in \mathcal{A}} (v_i'(\widehat{s}') = succ(v_i(\widehat{s}')))$ and $(v_{Ev}'(\widehat{s}') = succ(v_{Ev}(\widehat{s})))$.

Given the abstract model one can define for any agent i the indistinguishability relation $\sim_i \subseteq \widehat{S} \times \widehat{S}$ as follows: $\widehat{s} \sim_i \widehat{s}'$ iff $l_i(\widehat{s}') = l_i(\widehat{s})$ and $v_i(\widehat{s}') = v_i(\widehat{s})$.

In the following paragraph and in the following two lemmas we assume that $\mathcal{M}$ is the timed model for a timed interpreted system TIS, and $\widehat{\mathcal{M}}$ is the abstract model for $\mathcal{M}$ such that for each $i \in \mathcal{A} \cup \{Ev\}$, $max(\mathbb{D}_i) = c_i$.

It is easy to see that for each $v \in \mathbb{N}^{\mathbb{X}}$ there exist unique $u \in \mathbb{D}$ such that $u \simeq v$. Indeed, for $x \in \mathbb{X}_i$ let $u(x) = v(x)$ if $v(x) \leq c_i$, and $u(x) = c_i + 1$

otherwise. Clearly, $u \simeq v$. It is also easy to see that for each $v \in \mathbb{N}^X$ and $u \in \mathbb{D}$, $v \simeq u$ implies $succ(v) \simeq succ(u)$.

The following two lemmas state that the timed and the abstract model for $\mathbb{TIS}$ are trace-equivalent. Both the lemmas can be proven by straightforward induction on j.

Lemma 1. *For each path π in $\mathcal{M}$ there exist a path $\widehat{\pi}$ in $\widehat{\mathcal{M}}$ such that $\forall j \geq 0 \; \widehat{\pi}(j) \simeq \pi(j)$.*

Lemma 2. *For each path $\widehat{\pi}$ in $\widehat{\mathcal{M}}$ there exist a path π in $\mathcal{M}$ such that $\forall j \geq 0 \; \pi(j) \simeq \widehat{\pi}(j)$.*

In fact it is easy to prove that the timed model and the abstract model for $\mathbb{TIS}$ are bisimulation-equivalent. Let us recall from [1] the definition of a bisimulation. Let $\mathcal{M}_i = (Act_i, S_i, \iota_i, T_i, \mathcal{V}_i)$, $i = 1, 2$ be timed models.

Definition 1. *Let $\mathcal{M}_i = (Act_i, S_i, \iota_i, T_i, \mathcal{V}_i)$, $i = 1, 2$ be timed models. A bisimulation for $(\mathcal{M}_1, \mathcal{M}_2)$ is a binary relation $\mathcal{R} \subseteq S_1 \times S_2$ such that*

- *for every $s \in \iota_1$, there exists $s_2 \in \iota_2$ such that $(s_1, s_2) \in \mathcal{R}$, and for every $s_2 \in \iota_2$, there exists $s_1 \in \iota$ such that $(s_1, s_2) \in \mathcal{R}$*
- *for all $(s_1, s_2) \in \mathcal{R}$ it holds:*
  1. *$\mathcal{V}(s_1) = \mathcal{V}(s_2)$*
  2. *if $s_1' \in Post(s_1)$ then there exists $s_2' \in Post(s_2)$ with $(s_1', s_2') \in \mathcal{R}$*
  3. *if $s_2' \in Post(s_2)$ then there exists $s_1' \in Post(s_1)$ with $(s_1', s_2') \in \mathcal{R}$.*

$\mathcal{M}_1$ and $\mathcal{M}_2$ are bisimulation-equivalent (bisimilar for short), if there exists a bisimulation $\mathcal{R}$ for $(\mathcal{M}_1, \mathcal{M}_2)$.

For a given timed model $\mathcal{M}$ and the abstract model $\widehat{\mathcal{M}}$ of $\mathcal{M}$ let us define a binary relation $\mathcal{R} \subseteq S \times \widehat{S}$ in the following way: $(s_1, s_2) \in \mathcal{R}$ iff $s_1 \simeq s_2$. Obviously, $\mathcal{R}$ is a bisimulation for $(\mathcal{M}, \widehat{\mathcal{M}})$. As a result from this fact we obtain the following lemma.

Lemma 3. *Let $\mathcal{M}$ be a timed model and $\widehat{\mathcal{M}}$ be the abstract model of $\mathcal{M}$. Then, $\mathcal{M}$ and $\widehat{\mathcal{M}}$ are bisimilar.*

2.4   RTECTLK

Multi-agent Systems (MAS) formalisms are typically built on extensions of computational tree logic (CTL). For the purposes of this paper we consider specifications given in the RTECTLK language built from a set of propositional formulae $p \in \mathcal{AP}$, and a set of agents $i \in \mathcal{A}$. An existential fragment of the soft real-time CTL (RTECTL) [7] is a propositional branching-time temporal logic with bounded operators, which was introduced to permit specification and reasoning about time-critical correctness properties. The RTECTLK [21] language is an epistemic soft real-time computation tree logic that is the fusion [3] of the two underlying languages: RTECTL and $S5_n$ for the knowledge operators [8].

Syntax of RTECTLK. Let $\mathcal{AP}$ be a set of atomic formulae, $\mathcal{A}$ a set of agents, and I be an interval in $\mathbb{N}$ of the form: $[a, b)$ and $[a, \infty)$, for $a, b \in \mathbb{N}$. Hereafter by **left**(I) we denote the left end of the interval I, i.e., **left**(I) $= a$, and by **right**(I) the right end of the interval I, i.e., **right**$([a, b)) = b - 1$ and **right**$([a, \infty)) = \infty$.

Let $p \in \mathcal{AP}$, $i \in \mathcal{A}$, and $\Gamma \subseteq \mathcal{A}$. The set of RTECTLK formulae is defined by the following grammar:

$$\varphi := \textbf{true} \mid \textbf{false} \mid p \mid \neg p \mid \varphi \wedge \varphi \mid \varphi \vee \varphi \mid \textbf{EX}\varphi \mid \textbf{E}(\varphi \textbf{U}_\textbf{I}\varphi) \mid \textbf{EG}_\textbf{I}\varphi \mid$$
$$\overline{\textbf{K}}_i\varphi \mid \overline{\textbf{D}}_\Gamma\varphi \mid \overline{\textbf{E}}_\Gamma\varphi \mid \overline{\textbf{C}}_\Gamma\varphi$$

$\textbf{U}_\textbf{I}$ and $\textbf{G}_\textbf{I}$ are the operators, resp., for bounded "Until" and "Always". The formula $\textbf{EG}_\textbf{I}\alpha$ is read as "there exists a computation such that α always holds in the interval I" and the formula $\textbf{E}(\alpha \textbf{U}_\textbf{I}\beta)$ is read as "there exists a computation such that β holds in the interval I at least in one state and always earlier α holds". The other basic bounded temporal operators can be introduced as usual:

$$\textbf{E}(\alpha \, \textbf{R}_\textbf{I} \, \beta) \stackrel{def}{=} \textbf{E}(\beta \, \textbf{U}_\textbf{I} \, (\alpha \wedge \beta)) \vee \textbf{EG}_\textbf{I}\beta, \qquad \textbf{EF}_\textbf{I}\alpha \stackrel{def}{=} \textbf{E}(\textbf{true}\textbf{U}_\textbf{I}\alpha).$$

$\overline{\textbf{K}}_i$ is the operator dual for the standard epistemic modality K_i ("agent i knows"), so $\overline{\textbf{K}}_i\alpha$ is read as "agent i does not know whether or not α holds". Similarly, the modalities $\overline{\textbf{D}}_\Gamma, \overline{\textbf{E}}_\Gamma, \overline{\textbf{C}}_\Gamma$ are the diamonds for $D_\Gamma, E_\Gamma, C_\Gamma$ representing distributed knowledge in the group Γ, "everyone in Γ knows", and common knowledge among agents in the group Γ.

Semantics of RTECTLK. As the semantics for the timed model and the semantics for the abstract model are identical we shall present only the semantics for the abstract model. Let $\widehat{\mathcal{M}} = (Act, \widehat{S}, \widehat{\iota}, \widehat{T}, \widehat{\mathcal{V}})$ denote the abstract model. An abstract path $\widehat{\pi}$ in the abstract model is a sequence $\widehat{s}_0 \xrightarrow{b_1} \widehat{s}_1 \xrightarrow{b_2} \widehat{s}_2 \xrightarrow{b_3} \ldots$ of transitions such that for each $i > 1$, $b_i \in Act \cup \{\tau\}$ and $b_1 = \tau$ and for each two consecutive transitions at least one of them is a time transition. The set of all the abstract paths starting at $\widehat{s} \in \widehat{S}$ is denoted by $\widehat{\Pi}(\widehat{s})$, and the set of all the abstract paths starting at an abstract initial state is denoted by $\widehat{\Pi} = \bigcup_{\widehat{s}^0 \in \widehat{\iota}} \widehat{\Pi}(\widehat{s}^0)$.

For the group of epistemic modalities we also define the following. If $\Gamma \subseteq \mathcal{A}$, then $\sim_\Gamma^E \stackrel{def}{=} \bigcup_{i \in \Gamma} \sim_i$, $\sim_\Gamma^C \stackrel{def}{=} (\sim_\Gamma^E)^+$ (the transitive closure of $\sim_\Gamma^E$), and $\sim_\Gamma^D \stackrel{def}{=} \bigcap_{i \in \Gamma} \sim_i$.

A RTECTLK formula φ is *true* in the abstract model $\widehat{\mathcal{M}}$ (in symbols $\widehat{\mathcal{M}} \models \varphi$) iff $\widehat{\mathcal{M}}, \widehat{s}^0 \models \varphi$ for some $\widehat{s}^0 \in \widehat{\iota}$ (i.e., φ is true at some abstract initial state of the abstract model $\widehat{\mathcal{M}}$). For every $\widehat{s} \in \widehat{S}$ the relation $\models$ is defined inductively as follows:

- $\widehat{\mathcal{M}}, \widehat{s} \models p$ iff $p \in \widehat{\mathcal{V}}(\widehat{s})$,
- $\widehat{\mathcal{M}}, \widehat{s} \models \neg p$ iff $p \notin \widehat{\mathcal{V}}(\widehat{s})$,
- $\widehat{\mathcal{M}}, \widehat{s} \models \alpha \wedge \beta$ iff $\widehat{\mathcal{M}}, \widehat{s} \models \alpha$ and $\widehat{\mathcal{M}}, \widehat{s} \models \beta$,

- $\widehat{\mathcal{M}}, \widehat{s} \models \alpha \vee \beta$ iff $\widehat{\mathcal{M}}, \widehat{s} \models \alpha$ or $\widehat{\mathcal{M}}, \widehat{s} \models \beta$,
- $\widehat{\mathcal{M}}, \widehat{s} \models \mathbf{EX}\alpha$ iff $(\exists \widehat{\pi} \in \widehat{\Pi}(\widehat{s}))(\widehat{\mathcal{M}}, \widehat{\pi}(1) \models \alpha)$,
- $\widehat{\mathcal{M}}, \widehat{s} \models \mathbf{E}(\alpha \mathbf{U}_I \beta)$ iff $(\exists \widehat{\pi} \in \widehat{\Pi}(\widehat{s}))(\exists m \in I)[\widehat{\mathcal{M}}, \widehat{\pi}(m) \models \beta$
  and $(\forall j < m)\widehat{\mathcal{M}}, \widehat{\pi}(j) \models \alpha]$,
- $\widehat{\mathcal{M}}, \widehat{s} \models \mathbf{EG}_I \alpha$ iff $(\exists \widehat{\pi} \in \widehat{\Pi}(\widehat{s}))$ such that $(\forall m \in I)[\widehat{\mathcal{M}}, \widehat{\pi}(m) \models \alpha]$,
- $\widehat{\mathcal{M}}, \widehat{s} \models \overline{K}_i \alpha$ iff $(\exists \widehat{s}' \in \widehat{S})(\widehat{s} \sim \widehat{s}'$ and $\widehat{\mathcal{M}}, \widehat{s}' \models \alpha)$,
- $\widehat{\mathcal{M}}, \widehat{s} \models \overline{Y}\alpha$ iff $(\exists \widehat{s}' \in \widehat{S})(\widehat{s} \sim \widehat{s}'$ and $\widehat{\mathcal{M}}, \widehat{s}' \models \alpha)$, where $\overline{Y} \in \{\overline{D}_\Gamma, \overline{E}_\Gamma, \overline{C}_\Gamma\}$,
  and $\sim \in \{\sim_\Gamma^D, \sim_\Gamma^E, \sim_\Gamma^C\}$.

We end the section by defining the notions of validity and the model checking problem. Namely, a RTECTLK formula φ is *valid* in $\widehat{\mathcal{M}}$ (denoted $\widehat{\mathcal{M}} \models \varphi$) iff $\widehat{\mathcal{M}}, \widehat{\iota} \models \varphi$, i.e., φ is true at the abstract initial state of the abstract model $\widehat{\mathcal{M}}$. The *model checking problem* asks whether $\widehat{\mathcal{M}} \models \varphi$.

From the fact that the timed model and the abstract model for TIS are bisimulation-equivalent it follows that the same formulae are true in both the models.

We state the following theorem:

Theorem 1. *Let $\mathcal{M}$ be the timed model, φ an RTECTLK formula, and $\widehat{\mathcal{M}}$ be the abstract model of $\mathcal{M}$. Then, $\mathcal{M} \models \varphi$ iff $\widehat{\mathcal{M}} \models \varphi$.*

3   SMT-based Bounded Model Checking

In this section we present an outline of the bounded semantics for RTECTLK and define a SMT-based BMC for RTECTLK, which is based on the BMC encoding presented in [21]. The main difference between the SAT-based encoding and the SMT-base encoding is the representation of symbolic states, and symbolic actions. In effect, the SMT-based encoding is the generalisation of the propositional encoding.

RTECTLK formulae can be checked by BMC on an abstract model instead of on the original model. The model checking for this class of formulae is decidable. The complexity of standard SMT-based BMC is double exponential [5].

The SMT-based BMC is based on the notion of the bounded semantics, the definition of which requires the concept of k-paths and loops.

3.1   Bounded Semantics

Let $\widehat{\mathcal{M}} = (Act, \widehat{S}, \widehat{\iota}, \widehat{T}, \widehat{V})$ be an abstract model and $k \geq 0$. A k-path $\widehat{\pi}_k$ in $\widehat{\mathcal{M}}$ is a finite sequence of abstract states $(\widehat{s}_0, \ldots, \widehat{s}_k)$ such that $(\widehat{s}_j, \widehat{s}_{j+1}) \in \widehat{T}$ for each $0 \leq j < k$. By $\widehat{\Pi}_k(\widehat{s})$ we denote the set of all the k-paths starting at $\widehat{s}$ in $\widehat{\mathcal{M}}$, and $\widehat{\Pi}_k = \bigcup_{\widehat{s} \in \widehat{S}} \widehat{\Pi}_k(\widehat{s})$. A k-path $\widehat{\pi}_k$ is a (k, l)-*loop* iff $\widehat{\pi}_k(l) = \widehat{\pi}_k(k)$ for some $0 \leq l < k$; note that (k, l)-loop $\widehat{\pi}$ generates the infinite path of the following form: $\zeta \cdot \theta^\omega$ with $\zeta = (\widehat{\pi}(0), \ldots, \widehat{\pi}(l - 1))$ and $\theta = (\widehat{\pi}(l), \ldots, \widehat{\pi}(k - 1))$. Since in the bounded semantics we consider finite prefixes of paths only, the satisfiability of all the temporal operators depends on whether a considered k-path is a loop. Thus, as customary, we introduce a function $loop : \widehat{\Pi}_k \to 2^{\mathbb{N}}$, which identifies these k-paths that are loops. The function is defined as: $loop(\widehat{\pi}_k) = \{l \mid 0 \le l < k$ and $\widehat{\pi}_k(l) = \widehat{\pi}_k(k)\}$.

Definition 2. *Given are a bound $k \in \mathbb{N}$, an abstract model $\widehat{\mathcal{M}}$, and RTECTLK formulae α, β. $\widehat{\mathcal{M}}, \widehat{s} \models_k \alpha$ denotes that α is $k-true$ at the abstract state $\widehat{s}$ of $\widehat{\mathcal{M}}$. The relation $\models_k$ is defined inductively as follows:*

- $\widehat{\mathcal{M}}, \widehat{s} \models_k \textbf{true}, \widehat{\mathcal{M}}, \widehat{s} \not\models_k \textbf{false}$,
- $\widehat{\mathcal{M}}, \widehat{s} \models_k p$ *iff* $p \in \widehat{\mathcal{V}}(\widehat{s})$,
- $\widehat{\mathcal{M}}, \widehat{s} \models_k \neg p$ *iff* $p \notin \widehat{\mathcal{V}}(\widehat{s})$,
- $\widehat{\mathcal{M}}, \widehat{s} \models_k \alpha \vee \beta$ *iff* $\widehat{\mathcal{M}}, \widehat{s} \models_k \alpha$ *or* $\widehat{\mathcal{M}}, \widehat{s} \models_k \beta$,
- $\widehat{\mathcal{M}}, \widehat{s} \models_k \alpha \wedge \beta$ *iff* $\widehat{\mathcal{M}}, \widehat{s} \models_k \alpha$ *and* $\widehat{\mathcal{M}}, \widehat{s} \models_k \beta$,
- $\widehat{\mathcal{M}}, \widehat{s} \models_k \textbf{EX}\alpha$ *iff* $k > 0$ *and* $(\exists \widehat{\pi} \in \widehat{\Pi}_k(\widehat{s})) \widehat{\mathcal{M}}, \widehat{\pi}(1) \models_k \alpha$,
- $\widehat{\mathcal{M}}, \widehat{s} \models_k \textbf{E}(\alpha \textbf{U}_I \beta)$ *iff* $(\exists \widehat{\pi} \in \widehat{\Pi}_k(\widehat{s}))(\exists 0 \le m \le k)(m \in I$ *and* $\widehat{\mathcal{M}}, \pi(m) \models_k \beta$ *and* $(\forall 0 \le j < m) \widehat{\mathcal{M}}, \widehat{\pi}(j) \models_k \alpha)$,
- $\widehat{\mathcal{M}}, \widehat{s} \models_k \textbf{EG}_I \alpha$ *iff* $(\exists \widehat{\pi} \in \widehat{\Pi}_k(\widehat{s}))((k \ge \textbf{right}(I)$ *and* $(\forall j \in I)$ $\widehat{\mathcal{M}}, \widehat{\pi}(j) \models_k \alpha)$ *or* $(k < \textbf{right}(I)$ *and* $(\exists l \in loop(\widehat{\pi}))(\forall min(\textbf{left}(I), l) \le j < k)$ $\widehat{\mathcal{M}}, \widehat{\pi}(j) \models_k \alpha))$,
- $\widehat{\mathcal{M}}, \widehat{s} \models_k \overline{Y}\alpha$ *iff* $(\exists \widehat{\pi} \in \widehat{\Pi}_k(\widehat{\iota}))(\exists 0 \le j \le k)(\widehat{\mathcal{M}}, \pi(j) \models_k \alpha$ *and* $\widehat{s} \sim \widehat{\pi}(j))$, *where* $\overline{Y} \in \{\overline{K}_i, \overline{D}_\Gamma, \overline{E}_\Gamma, \overline{C}_\Gamma\}$ *and* $\sim \in \{\sim_i, \sim_\Gamma^D, \sim_\Gamma^E, \sim_\Gamma^C\}$.

A RTECTLK formula φ is *valid in an abstract model $\widehat{\mathcal{M}}$ with a bound k* (denoted $\widehat{\mathcal{M}} \models_k \varphi$) iff $\widehat{\mathcal{M}}, \widehat{\iota} \models_k \varphi$, i.e., φ is $k-true$ at the abstract initial state of the abstract model $\widehat{\mathcal{M}}$. The *bounded model checking problem* asks whether $\widehat{\mathcal{M}} \models_k \varphi$.

By straightforward induction on the length of a RTECTLK formula φ we can show that the following lemmas hold.

Lemma 4. *Given are a bound $k \ge 0$, an abstract model $\widehat{\mathcal{M}}$, and a RTECTLK formula φ. Then, the following implication holds: $\widehat{\mathcal{M}}, \widehat{s} \models_k \varphi$ implies $\widehat{\mathcal{M}}, \widehat{s} \models \varphi$, for each $\widehat{s}$ in $\widehat{\mathcal{M}}$.*

Lemma 5. *Given are an abstract model $\widehat{\mathcal{M}}$, a bound $k = |\widehat{\mathcal{M}}|$ (where $|\widehat{\mathcal{M}}|$ denotes the number of states in the abstract model $\widehat{\mathcal{M}}$), and a RTECTLK formula φ. Then, the following implication holds: for each $\widehat{s}$ in $\widehat{\mathcal{M}}$, if $\widehat{\mathcal{M}}, \widehat{s} \models \varphi$, then there exists $k \ge 0$ such that $\widehat{\mathcal{M}}, \widehat{s} \models_k \varphi$.*

The following theorem states that there exists a bound such that bounded semantics is equivalent to the unbounded one, which means that the model checking problem ($\widehat{\mathcal{M}} \models \varphi$) can be reduced to the bounded model checking problem ($\widehat{\mathcal{M}} \models_k \varphi$). Its proof follows from Lemmas 4 and 5.

Theorem 2. *Let $\widehat{\mathcal{M}}$ be an abstract model and φ a RTECTLK formula. Then, the following equivalence holds: $\widehat{\mathcal{M}} \models \varphi$ iff there exists $k \ge 0$ such that $\widehat{\mathcal{M}} \models_k \varphi$.*

The reduction of RTECTLK to the quantifier-free first-order formula allows us to use efficient SMT solvers to perform model checking. A function $\widehat{f}_k$ that gives a bound on the number of k-paths of $\widehat{\mathcal{M}}$, which are sufficient to validate a given RTECTLK formula is defined in [21].

By straightforward induction on the length of a RTECTLK formula φ we can show that φ is k−true in $\widehat{\mathcal{M}}$ if and only if φ is k−true in $\widehat{\mathcal{M}}$ with a number of k−paths reduced to $\widehat{f}_k(\varphi)$.

3.2   The Translation of RTECTLK to the Quantifier-Free First-Order Formulae

Now we present our translation of a RTECTLK formula into a quantifier-free first-order formula. Given are a model $\widehat{\mathcal{M}} = (Act, \widehat{S}, \widehat{\iota}, \widehat{T}, \widehat{V})$, a RTECTLK formula φ, and a bound $k \geq 0$. It is well known that the main idea of the BMC method consists in translating the bounded model checking problem, i.e., $\widehat{\mathcal{M}} \models_k \varphi$, to the problem of checking the satisfiability of the following propositional formula:

$$[\widehat{\mathcal{M}}, \varphi]_k := [\widehat{\mathcal{M}^{\varphi,\widehat{\iota}}}]_k \wedge [\varphi]_{\widehat{\mathcal{M}},k}$$

The formula $[\widehat{\mathcal{M}^{\varphi,\widehat{\iota}}}]_k$ constrains the $f_k(\varphi)$ symbolic k-paths to be valid k-paths of $\widehat{\mathcal{M}}$, while the formula $[\varphi]_{\widehat{\mathcal{M}},k}$ encodes a number of constraints that must be satisfied on these sets of k-paths for φ to be satisfied. Once this translation is defined, checking satisfiability of a RTECTLK formula can be done by means of a SMT-solver.

Let $i \in \mathcal{A} \cup \{Ev\}$. In order to define the formula $[\widehat{\mathcal{M}}, \varphi]_k$ we proceed as follows. We assume that each abstract global state $\widehat{s} \in \widehat{S}$ of $\widehat{\mathcal{M}}$ is represented by a valuation of a *symbolic global state* $\overline{\mathbf{w}} = ((u_1, v_1), \ldots, (u_n, v_n), (u_{Ev}, v_{Ev}))$ that consists of *symbolic local states* and each symbolic local state w_i is a pair (u_i, v_i) of individual variables ranging over the natural numbers, in which the first element represents a location of the agent i, and the second represents the clocks valuation. Each joint action $a \in Act$ is represented by a valuation of a *symbolic action* $\overline{\mathbf{a}} = (a_1, \ldots, a_n, a_{Ev})$ that consists of *symbolic local actions* and each symbolic local action $\widetilde{a}_i$ is an individual variable ranging over the natural numbers.

In order to define the formula $[\widehat{\mathcal{M}}, \varphi]_k$ we proceed as follows. A finite sequence $(\overline{\mathbf{w}}_0, \ldots, \overline{\mathbf{w}}_k)$ of *symbolic states* is called a *symbolic k-path*. Since, in general, we may need to consider more than one symbolic k-path, we introduce a notion of the j-th symbolic k-path, which is denoted by $(\overline{\mathbf{w}}_{0,j}, \ldots, \overline{\mathbf{w}}_{k,j})$, where $\overline{\mathbf{w}}_{i,j}$ are *symbolic states* for $0 \leq j < f_k(\varphi)$ and $0 \leq i \leq k$. Note that the exact number of necessary symbolic k-paths depends on the checked formula φ, and it can be calculated by means of the function f_k [21]. We define the following quantifier-free first-order formulae:

- $I_{\widehat{s}}(\overline{\mathbf{w}})$ - it encodes the abstract global state $\widehat{s}$ of the abstract model $\widehat{\mathcal{M}}$;
- $H_i(w_i, w'_i)$ - it encodes equality of two local states, such that $w_i = w'_i$ for $i \in \mathcal{A} \cup \{Ev\}$;
- $T_i(w_i, (\widetilde{a}, \delta), w'_i)$ - it encodes the local evolution function of agent i;

- $\mathcal{A}(\overline{\mathbf{a}})$ - it encodes that each symbolic local action a_i of $\overline{\mathbf{a}}$ has to be executed by each agent in which it appears;
- $\mathcal{T}(\overline{\mathbf{w}}, (\overline{\mathbf{a}}, \delta), \overline{\mathbf{w}}') := \mathcal{A}(\overline{\mathbf{a}}) \wedge \bigwedge_{i \in \mathcal{A} \cup \{Ev\}} \mathcal{T}_i(w_i, (\overline{\mathbf{a}}, \delta), w_i')$;
- Let π_j denote the j-th *symbolic k-path*, i.e. the sequence of symbolic transitions. $\overline{\mathbf{w}}_{0,j} \xrightarrow{\overline{\mathbf{a}}_{1,j}, \delta_{1,j}} \overline{\mathbf{w}}_{1,j} \xrightarrow{\overline{\mathbf{a}}_{2,j}, \delta_{2,j}} \cdots \xrightarrow{\overline{\mathbf{a}}_{k,j}, \delta_{k,j}} \overline{\mathbf{w}}_{k,j}$

Thus, given the above, we can define the formula $[\widehat{\mathcal{M}^{\varphi,\iota}}]_k$ as follows:

$$[\widehat{\mathcal{M}^{\varphi,\iota}}]_k := \bigvee_{s \in \widehat{\iota}} I_s(\overline{\mathbf{w}}_{0,0}) \wedge \overset{\widehat{f_k}(\varphi)}{\bigvee_{j=1}} \overline{\mathbf{w}}_{0,0} = \overline{\mathbf{w}}_{0,j} \wedge \overset{\widehat{f_k}(\varphi)}{\underset{j=1}{\bigwedge}} \overset{k-1}{\underset{i=0}{\bigwedge}} \mathcal{T}(\overline{\mathbf{w}}_{i,j}, (\overline{\mathbf{a}}_{i,j}, \delta_{i,j}), \overline{\mathbf{w}}_{i+1,j})$$

where $\overline{\mathbf{w}}_{i,j}$ and $\overline{\mathbf{a}}_{i,j}$ are, respectively, symbolic states, symbolic actions for $0 \le i \le k$ and $1 \le j \le f_k(\varphi)$.

The formula $[\varphi]_{\mathcal{M},k}$ encodes the bounded semantics of the RTECTLK formula φ, and it is defined on the same sets of individual variables as the formula $[\mathcal{M}^{\varphi,\iota}]_k$. Moreover, it uses the auxiliary quantifier-free first-order formulae defined in [20].

Furthermore, following [20], our formula $[\varphi]_{\mathcal{M},k}$ uses the following auxiliary functions $g_l, g_r, g_\mu, h_k^U, h_k^G$ which were introduced in [23], and which allow us to divide the set $A \subseteq F_k(\varphi) = \{j \in \mathbb{N} \mid 1 \le j \le f_k(\varphi)\}$ into subsets necessary for translating the sub-formulae of φ.

Definition 3 (Translation of RTECTLK Formulae). *Let φ be a RTECTLK formula, and $k \ge 0$ a bound. We define inductively the translation of φ over path number $n \in F_k(\varphi)$ starting at symbolic state $\overline{\mathbf{w}}_{m,n}$ as shown below.*

- $[\mathbf{EX}\alpha]_k^{[m,n,A]} :=$ *(1)* $\overline{\mathbf{w}}_{m,n} = \overline{\mathbf{w}}_{0,min(A)} \wedge [\alpha]_k^{[1,min(A),g_s(A)]}$, if $k > 0$
         (2) **false**, otherwise,

- $[\mathbf{E}(\alpha\mathbf{U_I}\beta)]_k^{[m,n,A]} := \overline{\mathbf{w}}_{m,n} = \overline{\mathbf{w}}_{0,min(A)} \wedge \bigvee_{i=0}^{k}([\beta]_k^{[i,min(A),h_U(A,k,f_k(\beta))(k)]}$
         $\wedge In(i,\mathbf{I}) \wedge \bigwedge_{j=0}^{i-1}[\alpha]_k^{[j,\,min(A),h_U(A,k,f_k(\beta))(j)]})$,

- $[\mathbf{EG_I}\alpha]_k^{[m,n,A]} :=$ $\overline{\mathbf{w}}_{m,n} = \overline{\mathbf{w}}_{0,min(A)} \wedge$
         (1) $\bigwedge_{j=\mathbf{left(I)}}^{\mathbf{right(I)}} [\alpha]_k^{[j,min(A),h_G(A,k)(j)]}$, if $\mathbf{right(I)} \le k$
         (2) $\bigvee_{l=0}^{k-1}(\overline{\mathbf{w}}_{k,min(A)} = \overline{\mathbf{w}}_{l,min(A)}$
         $\wedge \bigwedge_{j=min(\mathbf{left(I)},l)}^{k-1}[\alpha]_k^{[j,min(A),h_G(A,k)(j)]})$, otherwise,

- $[\overline{K}_i\alpha]_k^{[m,n,A]} :=$ $I_\iota(\overline{\mathbf{w}}_{0,min(A)}) \wedge \bigvee_{j=0}^{k}([\alpha]_k^{[j,min(A),g_s(A)]}$
         $\wedge H_i(\overline{\mathbf{w}}_{m,n}, \overline{\mathbf{w}}_{j,min(A)}))$

- $[\overline{D}_\Gamma\alpha]_k^{[m,n,A]} :=$ $I_\iota(\overline{\mathbf{w}}_{0,min(A)}) \wedge \bigvee_{j=0}^{k}([\alpha]_k^{[j,min(A),g_s(A)]}$
         $\wedge \bigwedge_{i \in \Gamma} H_i(\overline{\mathbf{w}}_{m,n}, \overline{\mathbf{w}}_{j,min(A)}))$,

- $[\overline{E}_\Gamma\alpha]_k^{[m,n,A]} :=$ $I_\iota(\overline{\mathbf{w}}_{0,min(A)}) \wedge \bigvee_{j=0}^{k}([\alpha]_k^{[j,min(A),g_s(A)]}$
         $\wedge \bigvee_{i \in \Gamma} H_i(\overline{\mathbf{w}}_{m,n}, \overline{\mathbf{w}}_{j,min(A)}))$,

- $[\overline{C}_\Gamma\alpha]_k^{[m,n,A]} :=$ $[\bigvee_{j=1}^{k}(\overline{E}_\Gamma)^j\alpha]_k^{[m,n,A]}$.

The theorem below states the correctness and the completeness of the presented translation. It can be proven by induction on the structure of the given RTECTLK formula.

Theorem 3. *Let $\widehat{\mathcal{M}}$ be an abstract model, and φ a RTECTLK formula. For every $k \in \mathbb{N}$, $\widehat{\mathcal{M}} \models_k \varphi$ if, and only if, the quantifier-free first-order formula $[\widehat{\mathcal{M}}, \varphi]_k$ is satisfiable.*

4   Experimental Results

In this section we experimentally evaluate the performance of our SMT-based BMC encoding for RTECTLK over the TIS semantics. We have conducted the experiments using two benchmarks that are no yet widely used in the multi-agent community: the timed generic pipeline paradigm (TGPP) TIS model [22] and the timed train controller system (TTCS) TIS model [22]. We would like to point out that both benchmarks are very useful and scalable examples.

TGPP. The abstract model of TGPP involves $n+2$ agents: Producer producing data within the certain time interval ($[a, b]$) or being inactive, Consumer receiving data within the certain time interval ($[c, d]$) or being inactive within the certain time interval ($[g, h]$), a chain of n intermediate Nodes which can be ready for receiving data within the certain time interval ($[c, d]$), processing data within the certain time interval ($[e, f]$) or sending data, and the environment Ev. The weights are used to adjust the cost properties of Producer, Consumer, and of the intermediate Nodes.

Each agent of the scenario can be modelled by considering its local states, the local actions, the local protocol, the local evolution function, the local weight function, the local clocks, the clock constraints, the invariants, and the local valuation function. Figure 1 shows the local states, the possible actions, and the protocol, the clock constraints, invariants and weights for each agent. Null actions are omitted in the figure. For environment, we shall consider just one local state: $L_{Ev} = \{\cdot\}$. The set of actions for Ev is $Act_{Ev} = \{\epsilon_{Ev}\}$. The local protocols of Ev is the following: $P_{Ev}(\cdot) = Act_{Ev}$. The set of clocks of Ev is empty, and the invariant function is $\mathcal{I}_{Ev}(\cdot) = \{\emptyset\}$.

Given Fig. 1, the local evolution functions of TGPP are straightforward to infer. Moreover, we assume the following set of propositional variables: $\mathcal{AP} = \{ProdReady, ProdSend, ConsReady, ConsFree\}$ with the following definitions of local valuation functions: $\widehat{\mathcal{V}}_P(ProdReady) = \{ProdReady\}$, $\widehat{\mathcal{V}}_P(ProdSend) = \{ProdSend\}$; $\widehat{\mathcal{V}}_C(ConsReady) = \{ConsReady\}$, $\widehat{\mathcal{V}}_C(ConsFree) = \{ConsFree\}$.

Let $Act = Act_P \times \prod_{i=1}^{n} Act_{N_i} \times Act_C \times Act_{Ev}$, with $Act_P = \{Produce, Send_1, \epsilon_P\}$, $Act_C = \{Start_{n+1}, Consume, Send_{n+1}, \epsilon_C\}$, $Act_{N_i} = \{Start_i, Send_i, Send_{i+1}, Proc_i, \epsilon_{N_i}\}$, and $Act_{Ev} = \{\epsilon_{Ev}\}$ defines the set of joint actions for the scenario. For $\tilde{a} \in Act$ let $act_P(\tilde{a})$ denotes an action of Producer, $act_C(\tilde{a})$ denotes an action of Consumer, $act_{N_i}(\tilde{a})$ denotes an action of Node i,

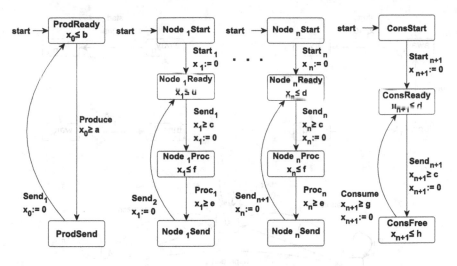

Fig. 1. The TGPP system

and $act_{Ev}(\widetilde{a})$ denotes an action of environment Ev. We assume the following local evolution functions:

- $t_P(ProdReady, \cdot, x_0 \geq a, \emptyset, \widetilde{a}) = ProdSend$, if $act_P(\widetilde{a}) = Produce$;
- $t_P(ProdSend, \cdot, true, \{x_0\}, \widetilde{a}) = ProdReady$, if $act_P(\widetilde{a}) = Send_1$ and $act_{N_i}(\widetilde{a}) = Send_1$;
- $t_C(ConsStart, \cdot, true, \{x_{n+1}\}, \widetilde{a}) = ConsReady$, if $act_C(\widetilde{a}) = Start_{n+1}$;
- $t_C(ConsReady, \cdot, x_{n+1} \geq c, \{x_{n+1}\}, \widetilde{a}) = ConsFree$, if $act_C(\widetilde{a}) = Send_{n+1}$ and $act_{N_n}(\widetilde{a}) = Send_{n+1}$;
- $t_C(ConsFree, \cdot, x_{n+1} \geq g, \{x_{n+1}\}, \widetilde{a}) = ConsReady$, if $act_C(\widetilde{a}) = Consume$.

The set of all the global states $\widehat{S}$ for the scenario is defined as the product $(L_P \times \mathbb{D}_P^{|\mathbb{X}_P|}) \times \prod_{i=1}^{n}(L_{N_i} \times \mathbb{D}_{N_i}^{|\mathbb{X}_{N_i}|}) \times (L_C \times \mathbb{D}_{LC}^{|\mathbb{X}_{LC}|}) \times L_{Ev}$. The set of the initial states is defined as $\widehat{\iota} = \{s^0\}$, where $s^0 = ((ProdReady, 0), (Node_1Start, 0), \ldots, (Node_nStart, 0), (ConsStart, 0), (\cdot))$.

The specifications we consider are as follows:

- $\varphi_1 = \mathbf{EF}_{[0,\infty)}(ProdSend \wedge \mathbf{EG}_{[a,\infty)}\overline{K}_C\overline{K}_P(Received))$, where $a = 2n + 1$ and $n \geq 1$ – states that it is not true that if Producer produces a product, then ultimately in a or more steps, Consumer knows that Producer does not know that Consumer has the product.
- $\varphi_2 = \mathbf{EF}_{[0,\infty)}\overline{K}_P(ProdSend \wedge \mathbf{EF}_{[0,4)}(Received))$ – expresses that it is not true that Producer knows that if he produces a product, then always within the next three steps later Consumer does not have the product.
- $\varphi_3 = \mathbf{EF}_{[0,\infty)}\overline{K}_P(ProdSend \wedge \mathbf{EF}_{[n,n+4)}(Received))$ – states that it is not true that Producer knows that if he produces a product, then always within interval $[n, n + 4)$ Consumer does not have the product.

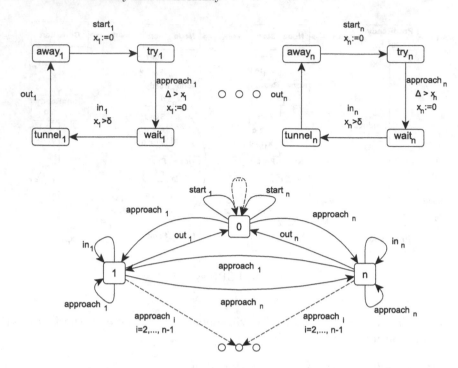

Fig. 2. The TTCS system

TTCS. The TTCS consists of n (for $n \geq 2$) trains $T_1, \ldots, T_n$, each one using its own circular track for travelling in one direction and containing its own clock x_i, together with controller C used to coordinate the access of trains to the tunnel through all trains have to pass at certain point, and the environment Ev. There is only one track in the tunnel, so trains arriving from each direction cannot use it in this same time. There are signals on both sides of the tunnel, which can be either red or green. All trains notify the controller when they request entry to the tunnel or when they leave the tunnel. The controller controls the colour of the displayed signal, and the behaviour of the scenario depends on the values δ and Δ ($\Delta > \delta + 3$ makes it incorrect - the mutual exclusion does not hold) (Fig. 2).

Controller C has $n + 1$ states, denoting that all trains are away (state 0), and the numbers of trains, i.e., $1, \ldots, n$. Controller C is initially at state 0. The action $Start_i$ of train T_i denotes the passage from state away to the state where the train wishes to obtain access to the tunnel. This is allowed only if controller C is in state 0. Similarly, train T_i synchronises with controller C on action $approach_i$, which denotes setting C to state i, as well as out_i, which denotes setting C to state 0. Finally, action in_i denotes the entering of train T_i into the tunnel. For environment, we shall consider just one local state: $L_{Ev} = \{\cdot\}$. The set of actions for Ev is $Act_{Ev} = \{\epsilon_{Ev}\}$. The local protocols of Ev is the following: $P_{Ev}(\cdot) = Act_{Ev}$. The set of clocks of Ev is empty, and the invariant function is $\mathcal{I}_{Ev}(\cdot) = \{\emptyset\}$.

The set of all the global states $\widehat{S}$ for the scenario is defined as the product $\prod_{i=1}^{n}(L_{T_i} \times \mathbb{D}_{T_i}^{|\mathbb{X}_{T_i}|}) \times (L_C \times \mathbb{D}_{L_C}^{|\mathbb{X}_{L_C}|}) \times L_{Ev}$. The set of the initial states is defined as $\widehat{\iota} = \{s^0\}$, where $s^0 = (away_1, 0), \dots, (away_n, 0), (0, 0), (\cdot)$.

Moreover, we assume the following set of propositional variables: $\mathcal{AP} = \{tunnel_1, \dots, tunnel_n\}$ with the following definition of local valuation functions for $i \in \{1, \dots, n\}$: $\widehat{\mathcal{V}}_{T_i}(tunnel_i) = \{tunnel_i\}$.

Let $Act = \prod_{i=1}^{n} Act_{T_i} \times Act_C \times Act_{Ev}$, with $Act_C = \{start_1, \dots, start_n, approach_1, \dots, approach_n, in_1, \dots, in_n, out_1, \dots, out_n\}$, $Act_{T_i} = \{start_1, \dots, start_n, approach_1, \dots, approach_n, in_1, \dots, in_n, out_1, \dots, out_n\}$, and $Act_{Ev} = \{\epsilon_{Ev}\}$ defines the set of joint actions for the scenario. For $\widetilde{a} \in Act$ let $act_{T_i}(\widetilde{a})$ denotes an action of $Train_i$, $act_C(\widetilde{a})$ denotes an action of Controller, and $act_{Ev}(\widetilde{a})$ denotes an action of environment Ev.

We assume the following local evolution functions for $i \in \{1, \dots, n\}$: $t_{T_i}(away_i, \cdot, true, \{x_i\}, \widetilde{a}) = try_i$, if $act_{T_i}(\widetilde{a}) = start_i$ and $act_C(\widetilde{a}) = start_i$; $t_{T_i}(try_i, \cdot, \Delta > x_i, \{x_i\}, \widetilde{a}) = wait_i$, if $act_{T_i}(\widetilde{a}) = approach_i$ and $act_C(\widetilde{a}) = approach_i$; $t_{T_i}(wait_i, \cdot, x_i > 6, \{\emptyset\}, \widetilde{a}) = tunnel_i$, if $act_{T_i}(\widetilde{a}) = in_i$ and $act_C(\widetilde{a}) = in_i$; $t_{T_i}(tunnel_i, \cdot, true, \{\emptyset\}, \widetilde{a}) = away_i$, if $act_{T_i}(\widetilde{a}) = out_i$ and $act_C(\widetilde{a}) = out_i$.

The specifications we consider are as follows:

- $\varphi_4 = \mathbf{EF}_{[0,\infty)}(\overline{\mathbf{K}}_{Train_1}(InTunnel_1 \wedge \mathbf{EG}_{[2,\infty)}(\neg InTunnel_1)))$ – states that it is not true that it is always the case that agent Train 1 knows that whenever he is in the tunnel, it will be in the tunnel once again within a bounded period of steps, i.e., within n steps for $n \geq 2$.
- $\varphi_5 = \mathbf{EF}_{[0,\infty)}(InTunnel_1 \wedge \overline{\mathbf{K}}_{Train_1}(\mathbf{EG}_{[1,n+2)}(\bigwedge_{i=1}^{n}(\neg InTunnel_i))))$ – expresses that it is not true that it is always the case that if Train 1 is in the tunnel, then he knows that either he or other train will be in the tunnel during the next n + 1 steps.

All the above formulae are true in the model for TTCS.

4.1   Performance Evaluation

We have performed our experiments on a computer equipped with I7-3770 processor, 32 GB of RAM, and the operating system Linux with the kernel 4.5.1. Our SMT-based and SAT-based BMC algorithms are implemented as standalone programs written in the programming language C++. We used the state of the art SMT-solver Z3 [16] (https://github.com/Z3Prover). All the benchmarks together with instructions on how to reproduce our experimental results can be found at the web page http://tinyurl.com/smt4tis-rtectlk.

TGPP. The number of considered k-paths for the formula φ_1 is equal to 10 for $n = 1$ and $4 \cdot (n + 1)$ for $n > 1$; for the formula φ_2 is equal to 6 for $n = 1$ and $4 \cdot n$ for $n > 1$; for the formula φ_3 is equal to 6 for $n = 1$, $3 \cdot n$, if n is an even number, and $3 \cdot n$ if n is an odd number.

From Fig. 3 one can observe that the SMT-BMC is able to verify the formula φ_1 for TGPP with 20 nodes, the formula φ_2 for TGPP with 20 nodes, and the formula φ_3 for TGPP with 8 nodes,

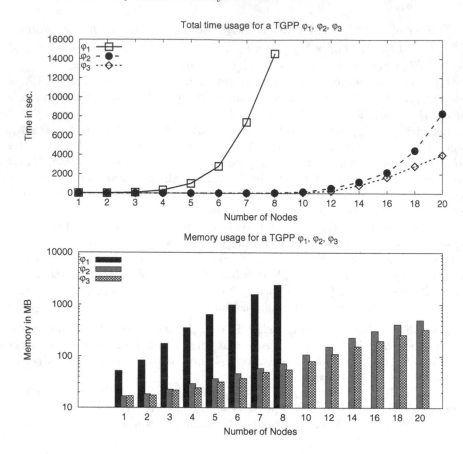

Fig. 3. TGPP with n nodes.

TTCS. The number of considered k-paths for both the formulae is equal to 7.

From Fig. 4 one can observe that the SMT-BMC is able to verify the formulae φ_4 and the formulae φ_5 for TTCS with 550 trains.

4.2 Performance Evaluation Summary

The experimental results show that the SMT-BMC is sensitive to scaling up the size of the benchmarks. As one can see from the line charts in Figs. 3 and 4 showing the total time and the memory consumption for all the tested properties, the experimental results confirm that our new SMT-based BMC for TIS and for RTECTLK is promising.

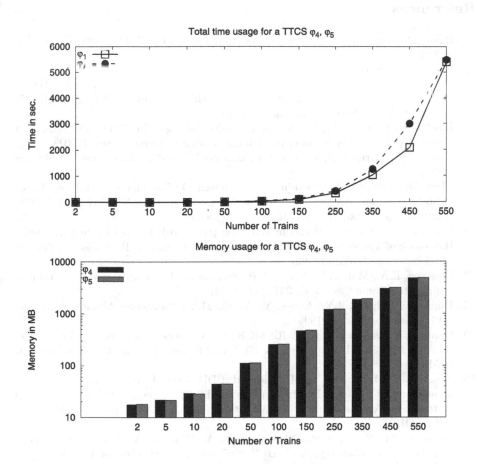

Fig. 4. TTCS with n trains.

5   Conclusions

We have proposed the SMT-based BMC verification method for model checking RTECTLK properties interpreted over the timed interpreted systems. We
have provided a preliminary experimental results. The experimental results show
that the SMT-based BMC method is worth of interest. We would like to use
other SMT-solvers in our implementations and compare experimental results.
The BMC for RTECTLK and for TISs may also be performed by means of
Ordered Binary Diagrams (OBDD) and SAT. This will be explored in the future.

The module will be added to the model checker VerICS [11].

References

1. Baier, C., Katoen, J.-P.: Principles of Model Checking. MIT Press, Cambridge (2008)
2. Barrett, C., Sebastiani, R., Seshia, S., Tinelli, C.: Satisfiability modulo theories (chap. 26). In: Biere, A., Heule, M.J.H., van Maaren, H., Walsh, T. (eds.) Handbook of Satisfiability. Frontiers in Artificial Intelligence and Applications, vol. 185, pp. 825–885. IOS Press, Amsterdam (2009)
3. Blackburn, P., de Rijke, M., Venema, Y.: Modal logic. In: Cambridge Tracts in Theoretical Computer Science, vol. 53. Cambridge University Press (2001)
4. Clarke, E.M., Grumberg, O., Peled, D.A.: Model Checking. MIT Press, Cambridge (1999)
5. Clarke, E., Kroning, D., Ouaknine, J., Strichman, O.: Completeness and complexity of bounded model checking. In: Steffen, B., Levi, G. (eds.) VMCAI 2004. LNCS, vol. 2937, pp. 85–96. Springer, Heidelberg (2004)
6. Emerson, E.A.: Temporal and modal logic (chap. 16). In: van Leeuwen, J. (ed.) Handbook of Theoretical Computer Science, vol. B, pp. 996–1071. Elsevier Science Publishers, Amsterdam (1990)
7. Emerson, E.A., Mok, A.K., Sistla, A.P., Srinivasan, J.: Quantitative temporal reasoning. Real-Time Syst. 4(4), 331–352 (1992)
8. Fagin, R., Halpern, J.Y., Moses, Y., Vardi, M.Y.: Reasoning About Knowledge. MIT Press, Cambridge (1995)
9. Gammie, P., van der Meyden, R.: MCK: model checking the logic of knowledge. In: Alur, R., Peled, D.A. (eds.) CAV 2004. LNCS, vol. 3114, pp. 479–483. Springer, Heidelberg (2004)
10. Jones, A.V., Lomuscio, A.: Distributed BDD-based BMC for the verification of multi-agent systems. In: Proceedings of the 9th International Conference on Autonomous Agents and Multiagent Systems (AAMAS 2010), pp. 675–682. IFAAMAS (2010)
11. Kacprzak, M., Nabialek, W., Niewiadomski, A., Penczek, W., Pólrola, A., Szreter, M., Woźna, B., Zbrzezny, A.: VerICS 2007 - a model checker for knowledge and real-time. Fundamenta Informaticae 85(1–4), 313–328 (2008)
12. Levesque, H.: A Logic of implicit and explicit belief. In: Proceedings of the 6th National Conference of the AAAI, pp. 198–202. Morgan Kaufman, Palo Alto (1984)
13. Lomuscio, A., Qu, H., Raimondi, F.: MCMAS: a model checker for the verification of multi-agent systems. In: Bouajjani, A., Maler, O. (eds.) CAV 2009. LNCS, vol. 5643, pp. 682–688. Springer, Heidelberg (2009)
14. Lomuscio, A., Sergot, M.: Deontic interpreted systems. Stud. Logica. 75(1), 63–92 (2003)
15. Męski, A., Penczek, W., Szreter, M., Woźna-Szcześniak, B., Zbrzezny, A.: BDD-versus SAT-based bounded model checking for the existential fragment of linear temporal logic with knowledge: algorithms and their performance. Auton. Agents and Multi-agent Syst. 28(4), 558–604 (2014)
16. de Moura, L., Bjørner, N.S.: Z3: An efficient SMT solver. In: Ramakrishnan, C.R., Rehof, J. (eds.) TACAS 2008. LNCS, vol. 4963, pp. 337–340. Springer, Heidelberg (2008)
17. Peled, D.: All from one, one for all: on model checking using representatives. In: Courcoubetis, C. (ed.) CAV 1993. LNCS, vol. 697, pp. 409–423. Springer, Heidelberg (1993)

18. Penczek, W., Lomuscio, A.: Verifying epistemic properties of multi-agent systems via bounded model checking. Fundamenta Informaticae **55**(2), 167–185 (2003)
19. Wooldridge, M.: An Introduction to Multi-agent Systems, 2nd edn. Wiley, Hoboken (2009)
20. Woźna Szcześniak, B · SAT-based bounded model checking for weighted deontic interpreted systems. In: Correia, L., Reis, L.P., Cascalho, J. (eds.) EPIA 2013. LNCS, vol. 8154, pp. 444–455. Springer, Heidelberg (2013)
21. Woźna-Szcześniak, B., Zbrzezny, A., Zbrzezny, A.: The BMC method for the existential part of RTCTLK and interleaved interpreted systems. In: Antunes, L., Pinto, H.S. (eds.) EPIA 2011. LNCS, vol. 7026, pp. 551–565. Springer, Heidelberg (2011)
22. Woźna-Szcześniak, B., Zbrzezny, A.: Checking EMTLK properties of timed interpreted systems via bounded model checking. Studia Logica, 1–38 (2015)
23. Zbrzezny, A.: Improving the translation from ECTL to SAT. Fundamenta Informaticae **85**(1–4), 513–531 (2008)

Balancing Rationality and Utility in Logic-Based Argumentation with Classical Logic Sentences and Belief Contraction

Ryuta Arisaka$^{(\boxtimes)}$ and Ken Satoh

National Institute of Informatics, Tokyo, Japan
ryutaarisaka@gmail.com, ksatoh@nii.ac.jp

Abstract. Compared to abstract argumentation theory which encapsulates the exact nature of arguments, logic-based argumentation is more specific and represents arguments in formal logic. One significant advantage of logic-based argumentation over abstract argumentation is that it can directly benefit from logical properties such as logical consistency, promoting adherence of an argumentation framework to rational principles. On the other hand, a logical argumentation framework based on classical logic has been also reported of its less-than-desirable utility. In this work we show a way of enhancing utility without sacrificing so much of rationality. We propose a rational argumentation framework with just classical logic sentences and a belief contraction operation. Despite its minimalistic appearance, this framework can characterise attack strengths, allowing us to facilitate coalition profitability and formability semantics we previously defined for abstract argumentation.

1 Introduction

Logic-based argumentation specialises Dung's abstract argumentation theory [8], representing arguments in formal logic. One significant advantage of logic-based argumentation over abstract argumentation is that it can directly benefit from logical properties such as logical consistency of the underlying formal logic. It promotes adherence of an argumentation framework to rational principles. There are studies (e.g. [2,5,10,15]) in this direction that identify logically desirable properties in argumentation frameworks.

It may appear trivial to attain such logical rigour among arguments and attacks at first sight. If we just assume that all arguments in an argumentation framework are classical logic sentences, any conflict between them could be just logical inconsistency. However, the use of logical inconsistency causes attack relation R to be necessarily symmetric, attacks meanwhile become necessarily cyclic, which was reported to restrict expressiveness of an argumentation framework [6]. A few approaches were proposed to bar the uniform symmetry. One could add a preference relation [12] to eliminate some of the members of R. One may also consider dividing an argument into its supports and its conclusion, facilitating differentiation of attacks. For instance, there is the rebutting

© Springer International Publishing Switzerland 2016
M. Baldoni et al. (Eds.): PRIMA 2016, LNAI 9862, pp. 168–180, 2016.
DOI: 10.1007/978-3-319-44832-9_10

where a conclusion of an argument attacks a conclusion of another argument, and there is the undercutting where a conclusion of an argument attacks a support of another argument. One may make use of both strict and defeasible rules, which is a popular approach in defeasible reasoning.

Either of them could reduce logical rigour, however. The preference relation, while powerful, does not elucidate the origin of the preference. The division or, to be more precise, the assumption that an argument is clear-cuttingly dividable into supports and a conclusion, too, is a source of logical incoherence. Consider a dialogue:

A(1): You finish your homework today.
B: No, dad. I still have one week. I will do it this weekend.
A(2): No arguing. You must listen to me.

Suppose $P_{1,2,3,4}$ are the following propositions: P_1: **B** finish homework today.; P_2: **B** still has one week.; P_3: **B** will do homework this weekend.; and P_4: **B** must listen to **A**. Suppose that (X, F) stands for an argument having its supports X, a set of sentences, and its conclusion F, a sentence. A possible encoding of the three arguments **A**(1), **B** and **A**(2) is then: $(\emptyset, P_1)$, $(\{P_2, P_3\}, \neg P_1)$, and $(\{P_4\}, \neg\neg P_1)$. Assume that each conclusion follows logically from their supports. The problem is that it is not the unique encoding, since $(\emptyset, P_1)$, $(\{P_2\}, \neg P_1 \wedge P_3)$, $(\{\neg\neg P_1\}, P_4)$ is also plausible. Again, assume that each conclusion follows logically from their supports. It is usually not possible to totally demarcate supports and conclusions when arguments are obtained from natural expressions like shown above.

1.1   Contribution

In this work we show a way of enhancing utility without sacrificing so much of rationality by utilising a contraction operation from belief revision theories [1,7,13]. A contraction operation is informally an operation to rationally - as well as minimally - change a particular set of beliefs when existing beliefs are removed from it. A belief is often a formal sentence. We consider a rational argumentation framework $(\Gamma, \div)$ where Γ is a set of classical logic sentences, and $\div$, used for belief contraction, is a binary operation defined on a pair of the power set of the set of formal sentences. This framework as we will show has fair expressiveness despite its minimalistic appearance. The key observation is that $\div$ can be used to know attack strengths, in particular whether an attack is defeating or non-defeating. If we assume the concept of conflict-eliminability [3]: arguments can be grouped together so long as they do not defeat each other, then symmetric attacks are no longer such a big issue, for they do not imply symmetric defeats. We will show that our rational argumentation framework is expressive enough to represent certain features of coalition formation, specifically coalition profitability and formability semantics we described for abstract argumentation [3]. Though we pass the details to Sect. 2, this result - that coalition profitability and formability semantics can be just as well characterised in the rational framework as in abstract framework - is quite nice in light of gathering interests in "argument strength", to which this winter will incidentally dedicate a workshop.[1] Out of the key discussions expected in the venue, our work should offer insights into the following three questions.

1. Which factors influence the strength of an argument?
2. Can weaker arguments defeat and/or defend stronger arguments?
3. How do formal and informal approaches to argument strength relate?

In the rest, we will: go through preliminary materials (in Sect. 2); develop our rational argumentation frameworks (in Sect. 3); and characterise coalition profitability and formability semantics as well as detail relation to abstract argumentation (in Sect. 4), before drawing conclusions with related work.

2   Preliminaries

2.1   Abstract Argumentation Frameworks for Coalition Profitability and Formability

We recall abstract coalition profitability and formability we previously discussed [3]. Let $\mathbb{N}$ be the class of natural numbers including 0, let $\mathcal{A}$ be the set of abstract entities representing arguments, and let $\mathcal{S}$ be $\mathcal{A} \times \mathbb{N}$. We denote each element of $\mathbb{N}$ by i, j, k, m or n with or without a subscript, each element of $\mathcal{A}$ by a with or without a subscript, and each element of $\mathcal{S}$ by s with or without a subscript. We assume a projection operator π which is defined on ordered sets Σ and which is such that $\pi(n, \Sigma)$ is: {n-th element of Σ} if $n \leq |\Sigma|$; and undefined, otherwise. For any $s \in \mathcal{S}$, we call $\pi(1, s)$ the argument identity of s and call $\pi(2, s)$ the argument capacity of s. We assume that an argumentation framework is a (S, R) for $S \subseteq \mathcal{S}$ and $R : 2^{\mathcal{S}} \times \mathcal{S} \rightharpoonup \mathbb{N}$ such that it satisfies all the following conditions. In the rest, a relation G (not the specific symbol G but any relation) being defined for something, say X (likewise, not the specific symbol X, but some entity on which G is defined), is synonymous to $G(X)$ being defined.

1. S is a finite set [Finite arguments].
2. For any $(a, n) \in S$, it holds that $n > 0$ [Positive argument capacity].
3. For any $(a, n) \in S$, there is no $m \neq n$ such that $(a, m) \in S$ [Unique argument identity].
4. R is undefined for $(\emptyset, s)$ for any $s \in \mathcal{S}$ [Attack coherence].
5. For any $S_1 \subseteq S$ and for any $s \in S$, if R is defined for (S_1, s), then R is defined for any (S_2, s) for $\emptyset \subset S_2 \subseteq S_1$. [Quasi-closure by subset relation].
6. For any $S_1, S_2 \subseteq S$ and for any $s \in S$, if R is defined both for (S_1, s) and for (S_2, s), then R is defined also for $(S_1 \cup S_2, s)$ [Closure by set union].
7. For any $S_1 \subseteq S$ and for any $s \in S$ such that R is defined for (S_1, s), it holds that $R(S_1, s) > 0$ [Attack with a positive strength].

---

[1] http://homepages.ruhr-uni-bochum.de/defeasible-reasoning/
Argument-Strength-2016.html.

8. For any $(a, n), (a, m) \in S$ such that $n \leq m$, if $R(S_1, s)$ - for some $s \in S$ and for some $S_1 \subseteq_{\text{fin}} S$ such that $(a, n) \in S_1$ - is defined, then $R(S_2, s)$ for $S_2 = (S_1 \backslash (a, n)) \cup (a, m)$ is defined, which is furthermore such that $R(S_1, s) \leq R(S_2, s)$ [Attack monotonicity 1 (source)].
9. For any $S_1, S_2 \subseteq S \subseteq_{\text{fin}} S$ and for any $s \in S$, if R is defined for (S_1, s), (S_2, s) and $(S_1 \cap S_2, s)$, then $R(S_1 \cap S_2, s) \leq R(S_i, s)$ for both $i = 1$ and $i = 2$ [Attack monotonicity 2 (source)].
10. For any $(a, n), (a, m) \in S$ such that $n \leq m$, it holds that if R is defined for $(S_1, (a, n))$ for some $S_1 \subseteq_{\text{fin}} S$ such that $S_1 \cap \bigcup_{l \in \mathbb{N}} \{(a, l)\} = \emptyset$, then it is defined for $(S_1, (a, m))$, and, moreover, $R(S_1, (a, n)) \leq R(S_1, (a, m))$ [Attack monotonicity 3 (target)].
11. R is undefined for (S_1, s) if $S_1 \subseteq_{\text{fin}} S$ and $s \in S_1$ [No self attacks].

Here and everywhere we may use and to emphasize truth-value comparisons. The expression '$S_1 \subseteq_{\text{fin}} S$ and $s \in S_1$' is basically: 'it is the case that $S_1 \subseteq_{\text{fin}} S$ and it is also the case that $s \in S_1$'.

The first three conditions are for $\pi(1, (S, R))$. The finiteness condition is assumed in many practical situations. The third condition enforces that each argument identified with an argument identity appears once in S. The second condition reflects an assumption that an argument capacity is proportional to meaningfulness of an argument, the greater the more meaningful, and 0 meaningless and not to be considered. Although the capacity is an abstract entity, it can be simplistically the number of sub-arguments of the argument : in the earlier example with $\mathbf{A}(1)$, $\mathbf{B}$ and $\mathbf{A}(2)$, we could give 1 to $\mathbf{A}(1)$, 2 to $\mathbf{B}$, and 2 to $\mathbf{A}(2)$. The remaining conditions are for $\pi(2, (S, R))$. We visualise important points about them with a drawing. We assume that R is defined for $(\{s_1\}, s_2)$ if there is an arrow from s_1 into s_2.

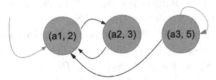

There are five arrows. Among them, two are red, and they are not permitted in this argumentation framework. The red arrow to the left of $(a_1, 2)$ signifies that an attack would be possible without any attacking argument, which [Attack coherence] prohibits. The other red arrow indicates that there may be an argument that attacks itself. Such an argument should not be taken seriously. [No self attacks] prevents it from appearing in the argumentation framework. [Closure by set union] is perhaps intuitive enough. [Quasi-closure by subset relation] precludes the following situation: a group of arguments attacks some argument, but no subgroups of the group attack it. These two conditions may not be so adequate when a group of arguments collectively mean more (or less) than when they are taken individually [14]. We do not deal with this problem of argument accrual. The three attack monotonicity conditions reflect the following observations. Suppose $R(S_1, s)$ is defined for some $S_1 \subseteq S$ and an argument $s \in S$. Now, let us increase argument capacity of some argument $s_1 \in S_1$ into $s_1' \in S$

so that we have $S_2 = (S_1 \backslash \{s_1\}) \cup \{s_1'\}$. An argument with a greater capacity is considered more meaningful, having a greater impact on attacking other arguments. For instance, if we regard the capacity of an argument representative of the number of sub-arguments of the argument, it says more with a greater capacity. Consequently:

1. If R is defined for (S_1, s) for some $S_1 \subseteq S$ and any $s \in S$, then if the capacity of some argument $s_1 \in S_1$ increases into $s_1' \in S$, then, all else unchanged, the attack strength of $S_1' = (S_1 \backslash \{s_1\}) \cup \{s_1'\}$ on s should not be weaker, and, of course, S_1' should still be attacking s.
2. Also, if R is defined for (S_1, s) then if R is also defined for (S_2, s) such that $S_1 \subseteq S_2$, then the attack by S_2 on s should not be weaker than by S_1 on s.

Also, if R is defined for (S_1, s) for any $S_1 \subseteq S$ and any $s \in S$, and if the argument capacity of s increases into $s' \in S$, then the attack strength of S_1 on s' should not be weaker than that of S_1 on s, for an argument with a large argument capacity has more materials for other arguments to attack.

Attacks and Conflict-Eliminable Sets. Assume an abstract argumentation framework (S, R). We say that $S_1 \subseteq S$ attacks $s \in S$ iff there exists $S_2 \subseteq S_1$ such that R is defined for (S_2, s). We say that $S_1 \subseteq S$ defeats $s \in S$ iff S_1 attacks s and there exists $S_2 \subseteq S_1$ such that $R(S_2, s) \geq \pi(2, s)$. We define Attacker : $2^S \rightarrow 2^S$ to be such that $\mathsf{Attacker}(S_1) = \{s \in S \mid \text{there exists } s_1 \in S_1 \text{ such that } s \text{ attacks } s_1.\}$. We say that $S_1 \subseteq S$ is conflict-eliminable iff there exists no $s \in S_1$ such that S_1 defeats s.

A conflict-eliminable set is associated with its intrinsic arguments. Let $\alpha : 2^S \rightharpoonup 2^S$ be such that it is defined for $S_1 \subseteq S$ iff S_1 is conflict-eliminable. If α is defined for $S_1 \subseteq S$, then we define that $\alpha(S_1) = \{(\pi(1, s), n) \mid s \in S_1 \text{ and } n = \pi(2, s) - V^{\max}(S_1, s)\}$ where $V^{\max}(S_1, s)$ is either 0 in case S_1 does not attack s, or else $R(S_2, s)$ for some $S_2 \subseteq S_1$ such that (1) R is defined for (S_2, s); and (2) if R is defined for (S_x, s) for $S_x \subseteq S_1$, then $R(S_x, s) \leq R(S_2, s)$. We say that $\alpha(S_1)$ are intrinsic arguments of S_1 if α is defined for S_1.

A conflict-eliminable set of arguments has its own view of (S, R). Let $\mathsf{Del}_R(S, S_x)$ be $\{(S_y, s) \mid s \in S_x \text{ and } S_y \subseteq S_x \text{ and } R(S_y, s) \text{ is defined.}\}$, which is the set of attack relations within S_x. Now, let S_1 be a subset of S. If α is defined for S_1, then we say that $((S \backslash S_1) \cup \alpha(S_1), R \backslash \mathsf{Del}(S, S_1))$ is S_1's view of S, which we denote by $\mathsf{View}_R(S, S_1)$.

Conflict-Eliminable Sets' Attacks and Admissibility. We say that $S_1 \subseteq S$ c-attacks $s \in S$ iff α is defined for S_1 and there exists some $S_2 \subseteq \alpha(S_1)$ such that $\pi(2, \mathsf{View}_R(S, S_1))$ is defined for (S_2, s). We say that $S_1 \subseteq S$ c-defeats $s \in S$ iff S_1 c-attacks s and $\pi(2, \mathsf{View}_R(S, S_1))(\alpha(S_1), s) \geq \pi(2, s)$. These notions are similar to attacks and defeats, but are from the point of view of a conflict-eliminable set of arguments. Hence, if α is defined for $S_1 \subseteq S$, then for any $s \in S$, $\alpha(S_1)$ does not c-attack s, as can be straightforwardly verified. We say that $S_1 \subseteq S$ is c-admissible iff α is defined for S_1 and if $S_2 \subseteq \pi(1, \text{View}_R(S, S_1))$ attacks $s \in S_1$ and if $S_x \subseteq S_2$ is such that $R(S_x, s)$ is defined, then there exists some $S_3 \subseteq \alpha(S_1)$ such that S_3 c-defeats some $s_x \in S_x$. We say that $S_1 \subseteq S$ is c-preferred iff S_1 is c-admissible and there exists no $S_1 \subset S_y \subseteq S$ such that S_y is c-admissible. Now, in order that a conflict-eliminable set S_1 be coherent in its attacks, it must only attack external arguments with its intrinsic arguments. In comparison, attacks into S_1 are not bound by the restriction: an external argument can attack the conflict-eliminable set S_1 by attacking any $s_1 \in S_1$. Let $S_1 \subseteq S$ be such that $\alpha(S_1)$ is defined. We say that a conflict-eliminable set S_1 is one-directionally attacked iff there exists $S_x \subseteq \pi(1, \text{View}_R(S, S_1))$ such that S_x attacks $s \in S_1$ and S_1 does not c-attack any $s_x \in S_x$.

Coalition Profitability and Formability Semantics. We say that S_2 is in at least as good a state as S_1 is, of which we state $S_1 \preceq S_2$, iff α is defined both for S_1 and S_2 and any of the three conditions below is satisfied: (1) S_2 is c-admissible; (2) S_1 is one-directionally attacked; or (3) neither S_1 nor S_2 is c-admissible or one-directionally attacked. We say that coalition is permitted between $S_1, S_2 \subseteq S$ iff $S_1 \cap S_2 = \emptyset$ and α is defined for $S_1 \cup S_2$. We define profitability relation $\lhd : 2^S \times 2^S$ to be such that $S_1 \lhd S_2$ satisfies three axioms below.

1. $S_1 \subseteq S_2$ (larger set).
   Explanation: A larger set is a better set.
2. $S_1 \preceq S_2$ (better state).
   Explanation: A set that is in a better state is a better set.
3. $|\{s \in \text{Attacker}(S_1) \mid S_1 \text{ does not c-defeat } s \text{ and } s \notin S_1\}| \geq$
   $|\{s \in \text{Attacker}(S_1) \mid S_2 \text{ does not c-defeat } s \text{ and } s \notin S_2\}|$
   (fewer attackers).
   Explanation: A set that is attacked by a fewer number of attackers is better.

We say that S_2 is at least as profitable for S_1 as S_1 is for itself iff $S_1 \lhd S_2$. By profitability discontinuation theorem [3], satisfaction of the three conditions: (1) $S_1 \lhd S_2$; (2) $S_1 \lhd S_3$; and (3) $S_2 \subseteq S_3$, does not guarantee $S_2 \lhd S_3$.

Suppose we denote by $\text{Max}(S_1)$ the set of all $S_x \subseteq S$ that satisfy the conditions: (1) $S_1 \lhd S_x$; and (2) if $S_x \subset S_y \subseteq S$, then it is not the case that $S_1 \lhd S_y$. Then, if S_1 forms a coalition with S_2 satisfying $S_1 \lhd S_1 \cup S_2$, $\text{Max}(S_1) \backslash \text{Max}(S_1 \cup S_2)$ is no longer reachable from $S_1 \cup S_2$. Then suppose that some $S_x \in \text{Max}(S_1)$ is a maximal element in $\text{Max}(S_1)$ under some criteria, it may become unreachable from $S_1 \cup S_2$ by $\lhd$, depending on which conflict-eliminable set S_2 is. From S_1, if such maximal S_x is to be formed potentially incrementally: first with some $S_y \subseteq (S_x \backslash S_1)$ such to obtain $S_1 \lhd S_1 \cup S_y$; then with some $S_z \subseteq ((S_x \backslash S_1) \backslash S_y)$ such to obtain $S_1 \cup S_y \lhd S_1 \cup S_y \cup S_z$, and so on, it is clear that S_y, S_z and so on should be such that $S_x \in \text{Max}(S_1 \cup S_y)$, $S_x \in \text{Max}(S_1 \cup S_y \cup S_z)$, and so on. We shall define a stronger relation: $\lhd_m$, which is such that if $S_1 \lhd_m S_2$, then there exists some $S_a \in \text{Max}(S_2)$ which is a maximal element of $\text{Max}(S_1)$. Formally, let $\leq_l, \leq_b, \leq_f : 2^S \times 2^S$ be such that they satisfy all the following:

1. $S_1 \leq_l S_2$ iff $|S_1| \leq |S_2|$.
2. $S_1 \leq_b S_2$ iff S_2 is at least as good by (better state) as S_1.
3. $S_1 \leq_f S_2$ iff S_2 is at least as good by (fewer attackers) as S_1.

and let $S_1 <_\beta S_2$ for each $\beta \in \{l, b, f\}$ hold just when $S_1 \leq_\beta S_2$ but not $S_2 \leq_\beta S_1$. Then we define $\unlhd_m : 2^S \times 2^S$ to be such that if $S_1 \unlhd_m S_2$, then both of the following conditions satisfy:

1. $S_1 \unlhd S_2$.
2. Some $S_x \in \mathsf{Max}(S_2)$ is such that, for all $S_y \in \mathsf{Max}(S_1)$, if $S_x <_\beta S_y$ for some $\beta \in \{l, b, f\}$, then there exists $\gamma \in (\{l, b, f\} \backslash \beta)$ such that $S_y <_\gamma S_x$.

The second condition is giving a definition to maximality of an element in $\mathsf{Max}(S)$. We have four coalition formability semantics as follows.

$$W(S_1) = \{S_2 \subseteq S \mid S_1 \unlhd S_1 \cup S_2 \text{ or } S_2 \unlhd S_1 \cup S_2\}.$$
$$M(S_1) = \{S_2 \subseteq S \mid S_1 \unlhd S_1 \cup S_2 \text{ and } S_2 \unlhd S_1 \cup S_2\}.$$
$$\mathsf{WS}(S_1) = \{S_2 \subseteq S \mid S_1 \unlhd_m S_1 \cup S_2 \text{ or } S_2 \unlhd_m S_1 \cup S_2\}.$$
$$S(S_1) = \{S_2 \subseteq S \mid S_1 \unlhd_m S_1 \cup S_2 \text{ and } S_2 \unlhd_m S_1 \cup S_2\}.$$

Here and everywhere the semantics of classical logic disjunction is assumed for or. Assume three utility postulates:

  I Coalition is good when it is profitable at least to one party.
  II Coalition is good when it is profitable to both parties.
III Coalition is good when maximal potential future profits are expected from it.

W (, M, WS, S) respects I (, II, I + III, II + III).

2.2 Rational Contraction

We assume propositional logic. Our languages consist of: (1) a fixed number of logical symbols: $\top, \bot, \wedge, \vee, \neg$, as well as parentheses and brackets; and (2) a finite number of propositional variables, each of which is referred to by p with or without a subscript. We denote each language by $\mathbf{K}$ with or without a subscript, but dedicate $\mathbf{K}_0$ to the language having the largest number of propositional variables. We denote the class of sentences constructable in each $\mathbf{K}$ by $\mathcal{P}_{\mathbf{K}}$, and refer to a sentence by F with or without a subscript. We define $\mathsf{L} : 2^{\mathcal{P}_{\mathbf{K}_0}} \to 2^{\mathcal{P}_{\mathbf{K}_0}}$ to be such that $F \in \mathsf{L}(\{F_1, F_2, \ldots\})$ iff F is a logical consequence of a finite subset of $\{F_1, F_2, \ldots\}$. We say that a set of sentences Γ is consistent iff $\mathsf{L}(\Gamma) \neq \mathcal{P}_{\mathbf{K}_0}$. Among three common binary operations: expansion, contraction and revision [1,9] in belief revision theories, we will require just contraction $\div$ which minimally removes some set of sentences off a larger set of sentences. This operator satisfies the following axioms.

1. $\mathsf{L}(\Gamma_1) \div \Gamma_2 = \mathsf{L}(\mathsf{L}(\Gamma_1) \div \Gamma_2)$ (Closure).
2. $\mathsf{L}(\Gamma_1) \div \Gamma_2 \subseteq \mathsf{L}(\Gamma_1)$ (Inclusion).

3. $L(\Gamma_1) \div \Gamma_2 = L(\Gamma_1) \div \Gamma_3$ if $L(\Gamma_2) = L(\Gamma_3)$ (Extensionality).
4. $L(\Gamma_1) \div \Gamma_2 = L(\Gamma_1)$ if, for each $F \in \Gamma_2$, either $L(\{F\}) = L(\{\top\})$ or else $F \notin L(\Gamma_1)$ (Vacuity).
5. For each $F \in \Gamma_2$, $F \notin L(\Gamma_1) \div \Gamma_2$ if $L(\{F\}) \neq L(\{\top\})$ (Success).
6. $L(\Gamma_1) \subseteq (L(\Gamma_1) \div \Gamma_2) \cup \Gamma_2$ (Recovery).

The condition (Vacuity) says firstly that no tautological sentence is removed, and secondly that it is always a sentence in $L(\Gamma_1)$ that is to be removed. The condition (Recovery) ensures a minimal change of $L(\Gamma_1)$.

3   Rational Argumentation Frameworks

Our rational argumentation framework is a tuple $(\Gamma, \div)$ where Γ is a finite non-empty set of sentences.

Definition 1 (Coherence). We say that $(\Gamma, \div)$ is coherent iff (1) no $F \in \Gamma$ is such that $L(\{F\}) = L(\{\top\})$ or that $L(\{F\}) = \mathcal{P}_{K_0}$ and (2) no $F_1, F_2 \in \Gamma$ are such that $L(\{F_1\}) = L(\{F_2\})$.

A coherent rational argumentation framework $(\Gamma, \div)$ will be assumed in the rest. It is clear from the above definition that no $F \in \Gamma$ is a tautology which is a vacuous argument or an inconsistent sentence which is not to be taken seriously. Now, it is certainly possible to define conflict-freeness in a set of arguments: let Γ_1 be a non-empty subset of Γ, then Γ_1 is conflict-free iff $L(\{F_1\} \cup \{F_2\}) \neq \mathcal{P}_{K_0}$ for all $F_1, F_2 \in \Gamma_1$.[2] This notion, however, gives away very useful information of relative strength of attacks. We will instead rely upon conflict-eliminability.

Definition 2 (Opposition Force). Let $O : 2^{\mathcal{P}_{K_0}} \times \mathcal{P}_{K_0} \to 2^{\mathcal{P}_{K_0}}$ be such that $O(\Gamma_1, F_2) = \{F_1 \in \Gamma_1 \mid F_2 \in \Gamma \text{ and } L(\{F_1, F_2\}) = \mathcal{P}_{K_0} \text{ and } \Gamma_1 \subseteq \Gamma\}$. We say that $O(\Gamma_1, F_2)$ is the opposition force in Γ_1 against $F_2 \in \Gamma$.

$O(\Gamma_1, F_2)$ may be empty. We denote $\{\neg F \mid F \in O(\Gamma_1, F_2)\}$ by $O^-(\Gamma_1, F_2)$.

Example 1. Suppose a set of sentences:$\{F_1, F_2, \neg F_1 \wedge \neg F_2\}$. We have O $(\{F_1, F_2\}, \neg F_1 \wedge \neg F_2) = \{F_1, F_2\}$. Then, $O^-(\{F_1, F_2\}, \neg F_1 \wedge \neg F_2) = \{\neg F_1, \neg F_2\}$.

Definition 3 (Attacks and Defeats). For $F \in \mathcal{P}_{K_0}$, let $\mathsf{Lang}(F)$ be the smallest language $\mathbf{K}$ that recognises F. We say that $\Gamma_1 \subseteq \Gamma$ attacks $F \in \Gamma$ iff $O(\Gamma_1, F) \neq \emptyset$. We say that $\Gamma_1 \subseteq \Gamma$ defeats $F \in \Gamma$ iff Γ_1 attacks F and $(L(\{F\}) \div O^-(\Gamma_1, F)) \cap \mathcal{P}_{\mathsf{Lang}(F)} = L(\{\top\}) \cap \mathcal{P}_{\mathsf{Lang}(F)}$.

Example 2. Suppose $\{p_1, \neg p_1 \wedge p_2\}$ where p_1 and p_2 are propositional variables. Both $O(\{p_1\}, \neg p_1 \wedge p_2)$ and $O(\{\neg p_1 \wedge p_2\}, p_1)$ are non-empty, and so each element of the set is attacking the other. However, while $(L(\{p_1\}) \div \{p_1 \vee \neg p_2\}) \cap \mathcal{P}_{\mathsf{Lang}(p_1)} = L(\{\top\}) \cap \mathcal{P}_{\mathsf{Lang}(p_1)}$, $(L(\{\neg p_1 \wedge p_2\}) \div \{\neg p_1\}) \cap \mathcal{P}_{\mathsf{Lang}(\neg p_1 \wedge p_2)} \neq L(\{\top\}) \cap \mathcal{P}_{\mathsf{Lang}(\neg p_1 \wedge p_2)}$, as it contains p_2 for instance. Hence, $\{\neg p_1 \wedge p_2\}$ defeats p_1, but $\{p_1\}$ does not defeat $\neg p_1 \wedge p_2$.

---

[2] In this paper, we will focus on pairwise logical inconsistency only.

Some explanations concerning '$(\mathsf{L}(\{F\}) \div \mathsf{O}^-(\Gamma_1, F)) \cap \mathcal{P}_{\mathbf{K_0}}$' in the above definition may be helpful. Notice in the left operand, i.e. '$(\mathsf{L}(\{F\}) \div \mathsf{O}^-(\Gamma_1, F))$', that we require '$\mathsf{L}(\{F\})$' instead of $\{F\}$. If, say, F is some propositional variable p_1, then $\mathsf{L}(\{F\})$ contains $p_1 \vee p_3, p_1 \vee p_4, \ldots$. Suppose $\mathsf{O}^-(\Gamma_1, F) = \{p_1\}$, then certainly $p_1 \notin \mathsf{L}(\{p_1\}) \div \{p_1\}$, but it may be that some of $p_1 \vee p_3, p_1 \vee p_4, \ldots$ are in $\mathsf{L}(\{p_1\}) \div \{p_1\}$, even though $p_3, p_4, \ldots$ is not in $\mathsf{Lang}(F)$. The set intersection ensures that the result of belief contraction is relevant to $\mathsf{Lang}(F)$.

Definition 4 (Conflict-Eliminable Sets). We say that $\Gamma_1 \subseteq \Gamma$ is conflict-eliminable iff Γ_1 does not defeat any $F \in \Gamma_1$.

The following notion will come in handy. We assume that the length of a sentence is proportional to the number of symbols occurring in the sentence.

Definition 5 (Minimal Support). Let Γ_1 be such that $\Gamma_1 = \mathsf{L}(\Gamma_1)$. We say that F_1 is a support of Γ_1 iff $\Gamma_1 = \mathsf{L}(\{F_1\})$. We say that F_1 is a minimal support of Γ_1 iff there exists no support F_2 of Γ_1 that is shorter than F_1 in length. We denote some minimal support of $\Gamma_1 = \mathsf{L}(\Gamma_1)$ by $\mathsf{minS}(\Gamma_1)$. We define that $\mathsf{minS}(\Gamma_1) = \mathsf{minS}(\Gamma_2)$ if $\Gamma_1 = \mathsf{L}(\Gamma_2)$. For later convenience, we shall assume that $F = \mathsf{minS}(\mathsf{L}(\{F\}))$ for a coherent rational framework $(\Gamma, \div)$ and for any $F \in \Gamma$.

Proposition 1 (Existence of a Minimal Support). *Let F_1 be a member of Γ. Then, if $\Gamma_2 = \mathsf{L}(\{F_1\}) \div \Gamma_1$ for some $\Gamma_1 \subseteq \Gamma$, there exists some F_2 such that $F_2 = \mathsf{minS}(\Gamma_2)$.*

Proof. Γ in the assumed rational argumentation framework is finite. Also a sentence is necessarily of a finite length. □

The purpose of minS is linked closely to our need of referring to a contracted argument. Let us be specific. Suppose a non-defeating attack of $\{p_1\}$ on $\neg p_1 \wedge \neg p_2$. We have $\mathsf{L}(\{\neg p_1 \wedge \neg p_2\}) \div \{\neg p_1\}$ which is nominally an infinite set not as easily treated as a sentence. However, it is actually sufficient if we have $\neg p_2$ for the representation of the infinite set, since $\mathsf{L}(\{\neg p_1 \wedge \neg p_2\}) \div \{\neg p_1\} = \mathsf{L}(\{\neg p_2\})$. With minS, we have $\neg p_2 = \mathsf{minS}(\mathsf{L}(\{\neg p_1 \wedge \neg p_2\}) \div \{\neg p_1\})$. Generally, $\mathsf{minS}(\mathsf{L}(\{F\}) \div \{F_1\})$ is minimal information (as a sentence) about $\mathsf{L}(\{F\}) \div \{F_1\}$ we need.

Definition 6 (Intrinsic Arguments). Let $\Gamma_1 \subseteq \Gamma$ be a conflict-eliminable set. We define intrinsic arguments of Γ_1, denoted $\Gamma_1^\star$ with a super-script $\star$, to be $\{F \in \Gamma_1 \mid \mathsf{O}(\Gamma_1, F) = \emptyset\} \cup \{F_1 \mid F \in \Gamma_1 \text{ and } \mathsf{O}(\Gamma_1, F) \neq \emptyset \text{ and } F_1 = \mathsf{minS}(\mathsf{L}(\{F\}) \div \mathsf{O}^-(\Gamma_1, F))\}$.

Intrinsic arguments of a set of arguments are those sentences that are left after all non-defeating attacks have weakened their targets.

Example 3. Suppose $\Gamma_1 = \{p_1 \wedge \neg p_2, \neg p_1 \wedge p_3, p_4\}$, and suppose that each propositional letter is distinct. $\Gamma_1^\star$ is: $\{\neg p_2, p_3, p_4\}$.

Proposition 2 (No Conflicts). *Let $\Gamma_1 \subseteq \Gamma$ be a conflict-eliminable set. Then $\mathsf{L}(\{F_1\} \cup \{F_2\}) \neq \mathcal{P}_{\mathbf{K_0}}$ for any $F_1, F_2 \in \Gamma_1^\star$.*

Characterisation of Attacks by a Conflict-Eliminable Set. As we stated in Sect. 2, there is an asymmetry in attacks to and from a conflict-eliminable set. While arguments outside it could attack any argument in the conflict-eliminable set, the conflict-eliminable set of arguments may attack the external arguments at most by its intrinsic arguments. We define this coalition attack and then admissible/preferred coalition sets.

Definition 7 (C-Opposition Force). Let $O_C : 2^{\mathcal{P}_{K_0}} \times \mathcal{P}_{K_0} \to 2^{\mathcal{P}_{K_0}}$ be such that $O_C(\Gamma_1, F_2)$ is: empty if Γ_1 is not conflict-eliminable; or else $\{F_1 \in \Gamma_1^\star \mid \Gamma_1 \subseteq \Gamma$ and $F_2 \in \Gamma$ and $\mathsf{L}(\{F_1\} \cup \{F_2\}) = \mathcal{P}_{K_0}\}$. We say that $O_C(\Gamma_1, F_2)$ is the c-opposition force in Γ_1 against $F_2 \in \Gamma$.

We denote $\{\neg F \mid F \in O_C(\Gamma_1, F_2)\}$ by $O_C^-(\Gamma_1, F_2)$.

Definition 8 (C-Attacks and c-Defeats). We say that $\Gamma_1 \subseteq \Gamma$ c-attacks $F \in \Gamma$ iff $O_C(\Gamma_1, F) \neq \emptyset$. We say that $\Gamma_1 \subseteq \Gamma$ c-defeats $F \in \Gamma$ iff Γ_1 c-attacks F and $(\mathsf{L}(\{F\}) \div O_C^-(\Gamma_1, F)) \cap \mathsf{Lang}(F) = \mathsf{L}(\{\top\}) \cap \mathsf{Lang}(F)$.

Proposition 3 (No c-Self Attacks). *Let $\Gamma_1 \subseteq \Gamma$ be conflict-eliminable, and let F be a member of $\Gamma_1^\star$. Then $O_C(\Gamma_1, F) = \emptyset$.*

Proof. Obvious by the definition of c-opposition force and by Proposition 2. □

Definition 9 (One-Directional Attacks). Assume that Γ_1 is a conflict-eliminable set. We say that Γ_1 is one-directionally attacked by $F \in \Gamma \backslash \Gamma_1$ iff $O_C(\Gamma_1, F) = \emptyset$ and there exists some $F_1 \in \Gamma_1$ such that $\{F\}$ attacks F_1.

Example 4. Suppose $\Gamma = \{p_1 \wedge \neg p_2, \neg p_1 \wedge p_3, p_4, p_1\}$. $\Gamma_1 = \{p_1 \wedge \neg p_2, \neg p_1 \wedge p_3, p_4\}$ is a conflict-eliminable set. And p_1 is the only external argument to the set. Because $\Gamma_1^\star = \{\neg p_2, p_3, p_4\}$, it is not c-attacking p_1. But p_1 is (c-)attacking $\neg p_1 \wedge p_3$ in the set.

Definition 10 (C-Acceptance). We say that $\Gamma_1 \subseteq \Gamma$ c-accepts $F \in \Gamma$ iff Γ_1 does not defeat F and if $O(\Gamma \backslash \Gamma_1, F) \neq \emptyset$, then Γ_1 c-defeats each $F_1 \in O(\Gamma \backslash \Gamma_1, F)$.

Definition 11 (C-Admissible and c-Preferred Sets). We say that $\Gamma_1 \subseteq \Gamma$ is c-admissible iff Γ_1 is conflict-eliminable and Γ_1 c-accepts all its members. We say that a c-admissible set $\Gamma_1 \subseteq \Gamma$ is also a c-preferred set iff there exists no $\Gamma_1 \subset \Gamma_2 \subseteq \Gamma$ such that Γ_2 is c-admissible.

4   Logic-Based Coalition Profitability and Formability

Let us adapt some of the notations in Sect. 2. We define $\mathsf{Attacker}(\Gamma_1)$ to be $\{F \in \Gamma \mid$ there exists some $F_1 \in \Gamma_1$ such that F attacks $F_1.\}$. We say that coalition is approved between $\Gamma_1 \subseteq \Gamma$ and $\Gamma_2 \subseteq \Gamma$ iff $\Gamma_1 \cap \Gamma_2 = \emptyset$ and $\Gamma_1 \cup \Gamma_2$ is conflict-eliminable. We define $\preceq : 2^{\mathcal{P}_{K_0}} \times 2^{\mathcal{P}_{K_0}}$ to be such that $\Gamma_1 \preceq \Gamma_2$ iff Γ_1 and Γ_2 are conflict-eliminable and any of the three conditions: (1) Γ_2 is c-admissible; (2) Γ_1 is one-directionally attacked; or (3) neither Γ_1 nor Γ_2 is c-admissible or one-directionally attacked, satisfies. We define $\trianglelefteq : 2^{\mathcal{P}_{K_0}} \times 2^{\mathcal{P}_{K_0}}$ to be such that $\Gamma_1 \trianglelefteq \Gamma_2$ satisfies the following three conditions.

1. If $\Gamma_1 \trianglelefteq \Gamma_2$, then $\Gamma_1 \subseteq \Gamma_2$ (inclusion).
2. If $\Gamma_1 \trianglelefteq \Gamma_2$, then $\Gamma_1 \preceq \Gamma_2$ (better state).
3. $|\{F \in \mathsf{Attacker}(\Gamma_1) \mid \Gamma_1 \text{ does not c-defeat } F \text{ and } F \notin \Gamma_1\}| \geq$
   $|\{F \in \mathsf{Attacker}(\Gamma_1) \mid \Gamma_2 \text{ does not c-defeat } F \text{ and } F \notin \Gamma_2\}|$
   (fewer attackers).

The meaning is the same as in abstract setting: if $\Gamma_1 \trianglelefteq \Gamma_2$ then Γ_2 is at least as profitable for Γ_1 as Γ_1 is for itself. We denote by $\mathsf{Max}(\Gamma_1)$ the set of all $\Gamma_x \subseteq \Gamma$ where $\Gamma_1 \trianglelefteq \Gamma_x$ and if $\Gamma_x \subset \Gamma_y \subseteq \Gamma$, then not $\Gamma_1 \trianglelefteq \Gamma_y$. Let $\leq_l, \leq_b, \leq_f : 2^{\mathcal{P}\kappa_0} \times 2^{\mathcal{P}\kappa_0}$ be such that they satisfy the following three conditions:

1. $\Gamma_1 \leq_l \Gamma_2$ iff $|\Gamma_1| \leq |\Gamma_2|$.
2. $\Gamma_1 \leq_b \Gamma_2$ iff Γ_2 is at least as good by (better state) as Γ_1.
3. $\Gamma_1 \leq_f \Gamma_2$ iff Γ_2 is at least as good by (fewer attackers) as Γ_1.

We write $\Gamma_1 <_\beta \Gamma_2$ for each $\beta \in \{l, b, f\}$ just when $\Gamma_1 \leq_\beta \Gamma_2$ and not $\Gamma_2 \leq_\beta \Gamma_1$. We define $\trianglelefteq_m : 2^{\mathcal{P}} \times 2^{\mathcal{P}}$ to be such that if $\Gamma_1 \trianglelefteq_m \Gamma_2$, then:

1. $\Gamma_1 \trianglelefteq \Gamma_2$.
2. Some $\Gamma_x \in \mathsf{Max}(\Gamma_2)$ is such that, for all $\Gamma_y \in \mathsf{Max}(\Gamma_1)$, if $\Gamma_x \leq_\beta \Gamma_y$ for some $\beta \in \{l, b, f\}$, then there exists $\gamma \in (\{l, b, f\} \backslash \beta)$ such that $\Gamma_y <_\gamma \Gamma_x$.

The four coalition formability semantics in this logic-based argumentation are as follows.

$$\mathsf{W}(\Gamma_1) = \{\Gamma_2 \subseteq \Gamma \mid \Gamma_1 \trianglelefteq \Gamma_1 \cup \Gamma_2 \text{ or } \Gamma_2 \trianglelefteq \Gamma_1 \cup \Gamma_2\}.$$
$$\mathsf{M}(\Gamma_1) = \{\Gamma_2 \subseteq \Gamma \mid \Gamma_1 \trianglelefteq \Gamma_1 \cup \Gamma_2 \text{ and } \Gamma_2 \trianglelefteq \Gamma_1 \cup \Gamma_2\}.$$
$$\mathsf{WS}(\Gamma_1) = \{\Gamma_2 \subseteq \Gamma \mid \Gamma_1 \trianglelefteq_m \Gamma_1 \cup \Gamma_2 \text{ or } \Gamma_2 \trianglelefteq_m \Gamma_1 \cup \Gamma_2\}.$$
$$\mathsf{S}(\Gamma_1) = \{\Gamma_2 \subseteq \Gamma \mid \Gamma_1 \trianglelefteq_m \Gamma_1 \cup \Gamma_2 \text{ and } \Gamma_2 \trianglelefteq_m \Gamma_1 \cup \Gamma_2\}.$$

4.1 The Relation Between Abstract and Logic-Based Argumentation Frameworks

There is a good reason behind the close correlation between the semantics in Sect. 2 and those for our rational argumentation frameworks. Let $\varpi : \mathcal{P}\kappa_0 \to (\mathbb{N} \cup \{\infty\})$ be such that:

1. $\varpi(F) = \infty$ if $\mathsf{L}(\{F\}) = \mathsf{L}(\{\bot\})$.
2. $\varpi(F) = 0$ if $\mathsf{L}(\{F\}) = \mathsf{L}(\{\top\})$.
3. $\varpi(F_1) \leq \varpi(F_2)$ if $\mathsf{L}(\{F_1\}) \subseteq \mathsf{L}(\{F_2\})$.

Let $\kappa : 2^{\mathcal{P}\kappa_0} \times \{\div\} \to 2^S \times \{R\}$ be such that:

1. κ is defined for $(\Gamma, \div)$ iff Γ is finite.
2. Let $\tau : 2^{\mathcal{P}\kappa_0} \to 2^{2^{\mathcal{P}\kappa_0}}$ be such that: $\tau(\{F\}) = \{F_1 \mid \mathsf{L}(\{F_1\}) \subseteq \mathsf{L}(\{F\}) \text{ and } F_1 = \min\mathsf{S}(\mathsf{L}(\mathsf{L}(\{F_1\}) \cap \mathsf{Lang}(F))) \neq \top\}$; and $\tau(\Gamma) = \{\{\tau(F)\} \mid F \in \Gamma\}$. Assume that $\tau(\Gamma)$ is an ordered set in the rest. If κ is defined for $(\Gamma, \div)$, then $\pi(1, \kappa((\Gamma, \div)))$ maps one-to-one to $\tau(\pi(1, (\Gamma, \div)))$ in the following way: for any sentence F in the n-th set of $\tau(\pi(1, (\Gamma, \div)))$ there is $(a_n, \varpi(F))$ in $\pi(1, \kappa((\Gamma, \div)))$. For each $s \in \pi(1, \kappa((\Gamma, \div)))$, we refer to the corresponding sentence in $\tau(\pi(1, (\Gamma, \div)))$ by $\rho(s)$.

3. If κ is defined for $(\Gamma, \div)$, then $\pi(2, \kappa(\Gamma, \div))$ - that is, R - is defined for any (S, s) as long as: (1) $S' = S \cup \{s\}$ is a subset of $\pi(1, \kappa(\Gamma, \div))$ such that $\pi(1, (a_i, n_i)) \neq \pi(1, (a_j, n_j))$ for any $(a_i, n_i), (a_j, n_j) \in S \cup \{s\}$; and (2) for each $s_1 \in S$, $\mathsf{L}(\{\rho(s_1)\} \cup \rho(s)) = \mathcal{P}_{\mathbf{K_0}}$. Further, for each such (S, s), we define $R(S, s)$ to be: $\pi(\rho(s))$ if $\bigcup_{s_1 \in S}\{\rho(s_1)\}$ defeats $\rho(s)$; and $\varpi(\rho(s)) - \varpi(\min\mathsf{S}(\mathsf{L}(\{\rho(s)\}) \div \bigcup_{s_1 \in S}\{\neg \rho(s_1)\}))$, otherwise.

Perhpas no further explanations are needed for κ and ρ. We mention that τ obtains from Γ the set of all the formulas which are some $F \in \Gamma$, or some F_1 which is logically weaker than some $F_2 \in \Gamma$ and which is a member of $\mathsf{Lang}(F_2)$.

Theorem 1 (Embedding). *For any coherent rational argumentation framework* $(\Gamma, \div)$, $\kappa((\Gamma, \div))$ *is an argumentation framework as defined in Sect. 2.*

Proof. [Finite arguments] holds trivially. [Positive argument capacity] and [No self attacks] hold because a coherent rational framework does not contain a tautology or an inconsistent sentence. [Unique argument identity] holds by the way ϖ is defined. [Attack coherence] holds trivially. [Quasi-closure by subset relation] and [Closure by set union] hold by the way $\pi(2, \kappa(\Gamma, \div))$ is defined. [Attack with a positive strength] holds by the way $\pi(2, \kappa(\Gamma, \div))$ is defined. Note that a contracted argument maps into a smaller integer. The three monotonicity conditions hold by the way $\kappa(\Gamma, \div)$ and $(\Gamma, \div)$ are related. $\qquad\square$

5 Conclusion

We showed how the abstract coalition profitability and formability semantics as mentioned in Sect. 2 may be defined in a minimalistic rational argumentation framework. Theorem 1 implies that the definition of the abstract argumentation framework, i.e. the 11 conditions in 2.1 [3], are logically grounded. Our rational framework is rational, provided that (1) representations of arguments in formal logic and (2) belief contraction are rational. The minimality of assumptions directly leads to minimality of logical incoherence.

Related Work. Instantiation of abstract argumentation with formal logic [2, 4, 10, 11, 15] is a fairly natural idea. Yet it is an important study to be undertaken if the knowledge of abstract argumentation is to be applied in practice. Dung's abstract argumentation can be misused; adequate postulates will prevent the misuse. In the above-mentioned works an argument is divided into supports and a conclusion. We showed a way of attaining fair expressiveness in the absence of the insulation by utilising belief contraction. We believe the work by Gabbay and Garcez [10] to be the most relevant work to ours. They, too, observe shifts in attack strength. Compared to [10], we are focusing: on more static pictures of logic-based argumentation as our work does not step through sequences of attacks; on minimal argumentation; and on the relation between logic-based and abstract argumentation for coalition semantics.

Acknowledgement. We thank reviewers for very helpful comments.

References

1. Alchourrón, C.E., Gärdenfors, P., Makinson, D.: On the logic of theory change: partial meet contraction and revision functions. J. Symb. logic **50**, 510–530 (1985)
2. Amgoud, L., Besnard, P.: Bridging the gap between abstract argumentation systems and logic. In: Godo, L., Pugliese, A. (eds.) SUM 2009. LNCS, vol. 5785, pp. 12–27. Springer, Heidelberg (2009)
3. Arisaka, R., Satoh, K.: Coalition Formability Semantics with Conflict-Eliminable Sets of Arguments. arXiv e-prints:1605.00495 (2016)
4. Caminada, M., Amgoud, L.: An axiomatic account of formal argumentation. In: AAAI, pp. 608–613 (2005)
5. Caminada, M., Amgoud, L.: On the evaluation of argumentation formalisms. Artif. Intell. **171**(5–6), 286–310 (2007)
6. Coste-Marquis, S., Devred, C., Marquis, P.: Symmetric argumentation frameworks. In: Godo, L. (ed.) ECSQARU 2005. LNCS (LNAI), vol. 3571, pp. 317–328. Springer, Heidelberg (2005)
7. Darwiche, A., Pearl, J.: On the logic of iterated belief revision. Artif. Intell. **89**, 1–29 (1997)
8. Dung, P.M.: On the acceptability of arguments and its fundamental role in non-monotonic reasoning, logic programming, and n-person games. Artif. Intell. **77**(2), 321–357 (1995)
9. Fuhrmann, A., Hansson, S.O.: A survey of multiple contractions. Logic Lang. Inf. **3**(1), 39–75 (1997)
10. Gabbay, D.M., D'Avila Garcez, A.S.: Logical modes of attack in argumentation networks. Stud. Logica. **93**(2), 199–230 (2009)
11. Gorogiannis, N., Hunter, A.: Instantiating abstract argumentation with classical logic arguments: postulates and properties. Artif. Intell. **175**(9–10), 1479–1497 (2011)
12. Kaci, S., van der Torre, L., Weydert, E.: Acyclic argumentation: attack = conflict + preference. In: ECAI, pp. 725–726 (2006)
13. Katsuno, H., Mendelzon, A.O.: Propositional knowledge base revision and minimal change. Artif. Intell. **52**(3), 263–294 (1991)
14. Prakken, H.: A study of accrual of arguments, with applications to evidential reasoning. In: ICAIL, pp. 85–94 (2005)
15. Prakken, H., Sartor, G.: Argument-based extended logic programming with defeasible priorities. J. Appl. Non-class. Logics **7**, 25–75 (1997)

Individually Rational Strategy-Proof Social Choice with Exogenous Indifference Sets

Mingyu Guo[1], Yuko Sakurai[2]([✉]), Taiki Todo[2], and Makoto Yokoo[2]

[1] The University of Adelaide, Adelaide, Australia
mingyu.guo@adelaide.edu.au
[2] Kyushu University, Fukuoka, Japan
{ysakurai,todo,yokoo}@inf.kyushu-u.ac.jp

Abstract. We consider a social choice problem where individual rationality is required. The status quo belongs to the outcome space, and the selected alternative must be weakly better than the status quo for everybody. If the mechanism designer has no knowledge of the alternatives, we obtain a negative result: any individually rational (IR) and strategy-proof (SP) mechanism can choose at most one alternative (besides the status quo), regardless of the preferences. To overcome this negative result, we consider a domain where the alternatives have a known structure, i.e., an agent is indifferent between the status quo and a subset of the outcomes. This set is exogenously given and public information. This assumption is natural if the social choice involves the participation of agents. For example, consider a group of people organizing a trip where participation is voluntary. We can assume each agent is indifferent between the trip plans in which she does not participate and the status quo (i.e., no trip). In this setting, we obtain more positive results: we develop a class of mechanisms called Approve and Choose mechanisms, which are IR and SP, and can choose multiple alternatives as well as the status quo.

1 Introduction

Social choice theory, which is a primary research field in micro-economics, studies the design and analysis of mechanisms/rules for collective decision making. Recently, due to the growing needs for agent technology in terms of complex information systems, various studies on social choice theory have been conducted in artificial intelligence and multi-agent systems [1,4,10].

We consider *individually rational* (IR) and *strategy-proof* (SP) mechanisms for social choice settings where the *status quo* belongs to the outcome space. Agents submit their preference orders over all outcomes including the status quo. By IR, the selected outcome must be weakly better than the status quo for everybody. IR also implies that the agents have veto power over the alternatives; if an agent declares that one alternative is worse than the status quo, it cannot be chosen. Analyzing veto power for a social choice function is an important problem in social choice literature [3,12].

© Springer International Publishing Switzerland 2016
M. Baldoni et al. (Eds.): PRIMA 2016, LNAI 9862, pp. 181–196, 2016.
DOI: 10.1007/978-3-319-44832-9_11

Unfortunately, we derive a negative result for general settings. If a mechanism is IR and SP, it must choose one particular alternative x in advance and choose between the status quo and x based on the agent preferences. Even if there exist many alternatives as well as the status quo, all but one will never be chosen, regardless of the agents' preferences. This is highly restrictive.

In light of the above negative result, we introduce a domain where the alternatives have a known structure. This allows us to design IR and SP mechanisms that can determine an outcome among multiple alternatives besides the status quo. We assume that for each agent, a set of alternatives, which are equivalent to the status quo for her (called the *indifference set*), is exogenously given. This information is public. For each agent, we call a choice that is not in her indifference set a standard alternative. An alternative is called a *multiagent choice* if multiple agents regard it as a standard alternative. We show that when the number of agents is n, any IR and SP mechanism can determine an outcome among at most $n-1$ multiagent choices. Furthermore, we develop a new class of IR and SP mechanisms called *Approve and Choose* (AC) mechanisms that can choose up to $n-1$ multiagent choices.

When there exist only two agents (agent 1 and 2), the AC mechanism first chooses a set of alternatives $X(f)$ in some way independently from their declarations. We assume $X(f)$ includes the status quo and exactly one multiagent choice x^*; other alternatives $X(f) \backslash x^*$ are standard alternatives only to agent 1. The mechanism first ask agent 2 whether x^* is acceptable, i.e., x^* is better than the status quo. If x^* is acceptable, then agent 1 selects her most preferred alternative from $X(f)$. Otherwise, she selects her most preferred alternative from $X(f) \backslash \{x^*\}$. It is clear that this mechanism is SP and IR. This idea can be generalized to n-agent cases.

We also show the modified AC mechanisms so that the mechanisms can be applied to settings with *quasi-linear utilities*. For such settings, we show that there exist AC mechanisms that simultaneously guarantee individual rationality, strategy-proofness, and *strong budget-balancedness*.

These assumptions we apply in this paper are appropriate in many application domains. For example, assume a travel agency is arranging a group trip. Each alternative can be associated with a different venue and a different set of participants. We can assume that each person is indifferent among tours in which she does not participate. The travel agency can choose one alternative using the AC mechanism. Similarly, consider a programming contest organized by crowdsourcing. Each alternative (a project's candidate) can be associated to a different goal and a different set of programmers. It is reasonable to assume that a programmer is indifferent about the projects she is not involved in. Furthermore, when deciding the location of a facility in one of two relatively remote cities R_1 and R_2, R_1's residents care about the exact location of the facility when it is located in R_1, but they can be indifferent about the exact location when it is located in R_2 since it is already far away.

2   Related Works

We introduce several recent works in social choice theory related to this paper.

Faltings [6] proposed SP and budget-balanced mechanisms that work by sacrificing efficiency for quasi-linear utility settings. Lu and Boutilier considered the multi-winner social choice problem when voter preference profiles are incomplete using the notation of the minimax regret and proposed a greedy algorithm to determine a robust slate of options. However, these models do not assume the existence of the status quo. If we apply these mechanisms in our setting, we cannot guarantee IR.

Sato [13] used an idea called exogenous indifference classes that closely resembles our indifference set. Such indifference classes of agent preferences are exogenously given. He focused on set A of alternatives that every agent strictly ranks, and showed that strategy-proofness implies a dictatorship when $|A| \geq 3$. Since our newly developed mechanism deliberately chooses alternatives utilizing public information so that $|A| \leq 2$ holds, it is SP and non-dictatorial.

Barberá and Ehlers [2] also considered indifferences in agent preferences in voting situations and clarified the necessary and sufficient condition for the majority rule to be quasi-transitive. In this sense, their analysis is quite different from ours; we focused on strategy-proofness.

Darmann et al. [5] addressed a group activity selection problem among agents, where an agent's utility of an activity can depend on the number of participants. Our model is more general; the utility can depend on other factors, e.g., who are going to participate.

Guo et al. [9] proposed the optimal shifted Groves mechanism, which is IR, SP, and non-deficit, and minimizes the worst-case efficiency loss when choosing an outcome from a finite set including the status quo in a quasi-linear domain. To be precise, they require that there exists at least one alternative for which the total valuation of the agents is nonnegative, which is more lenient than requiring the status quo. They assume that every agent's valuation for every outcome is bounded and the bounds are public information. We use a different model in which the set of alternatives over which each agent is indifferent is public information.

3   Preliminaries

A social choice problem is defined by tuple $(N, X, q, \succ)$. $N = \{1, 2, \ldots, n\}$ is a set of agents, and X is a finite set of alternatives. We assume $n \geq 2$. Otherwise, choosing one alternative is easy; the agent can only choose her favorite alternative. Alternative $q \in X$ is called the status quo. $\succ = (\succ_i)_{i \in N} \in \mathcal{P}^n$ is a profile of agent preferences over X. Here, $\mathcal{P}$ is the set of all possible preference relations for an agent. For any pair of alternatives, $x, x' \in X$, $x \succ_i x'$ means agent i strictly prefers x over x'. We assume each $\succ_i$ is transitive, complete, and anti-symmetric. Let N_{-i} denote $N \setminus \{i\}$.

A social choice function (or a mechanism) selects one of the alternatives given in the preference profile of the agents.

Definition 1 (Social Choice Function). *A social choice function is a function* $f : \mathcal{P}^n \to X$.

Let $X(f)$ denote $\{x \in X : \exists \succ \in \mathcal{P}^n \text{ s.t. } f(\succ) = x\}$, where $X(f) \subseteq X$ is the set of all the alternatives, each of which has a chance to be selected.

Next, we introduce several desirable properties of a social choice function.

Definition 2 (Individual Rationality). *We say social choice function f is individually rational (IR) if for all $i \in N$ and for all $\succ \in \mathcal{P}^n$, $f(\succ) \succ_i q$ or $f(\succ) = q$ holds.*

Individual rationality means that the selected alternative must be at least as good as the status quo. Note that we do not assume that the status quo is the worst alternative for each agent; an agent may prefer the status quo over alternative x.

Definition 3 (Strategy-Proofness). *We say social choice function f is strategy-proof (SP), if for all $i \in N$, for all pairs of $\succ, \succ' \in \mathcal{P}^n$ such that $\succ_j = \succ'_j$ for any $j \in N_{-i}$, $f(\succ) \succ_i f(\succ')$ or $f(\succ) = f(\succ')$ holds.*

We assume $\succ_i$ is the private information of agent i. Thus, the outcome is calculated based on declared preferences. If f is not SP, an agent has an incentive to misreport her preference.

4   Impossibility for General Cases

We show a negative result for general cases. The only mechanism that satisfies desirable properties can choose at most one alternative besides the status quo.

Theorem 1. *If f is IR and SP, then $|X(f)| \leq 2$ holds, i.e., f can choose at most two alternatives.*

Proof. From the Gibbard-Satterthwaite theorem [7,14], any SP mechanism must be dictatorial if the number of alternatives is more than or equal to 3. However, a dictatorial mechanism does not satisfy IR. Thus, $|X(f)|$ is at most 2.

It is clear that $q \in X(f)$ must hold as long as f satisfies IR. If a mechanism is IR and SP, then it is either trivial (always chooses q) or it chooses between q and one particular alternative x, which is selected in some way (perhaps in arbitrarily) independently from the agent declarations. The mechanism chooses x if all agents prefer it over q. Otherwise, it chooses q.

5   Social Choice with Exogenous Indifference Sets (SC-EI)

To overcome the negative result obtained in the previous section, we consider a domain where the alternatives have a publicly known structure: a *Social Choice with Exogenous Indifference sets* problem (SC-EI).

An SC-EI is defined by a tuple $(N, X, q, \succ, Q)$. The meanings of $N, X, q, \succ$ are identical to the social choice problem defined in the previous section. Here $Q = (Q_i)_{i \in N}$ is a profile of the indifference sets. Each $Q_i \subseteq X$ represents the set of alternatives that are equivalent to q for agent i where for any $x \in Q_i$, $x \sim_i q$ holds. We assume $\sim_i$ is reflective, transitive and symmetric. We assume $q \in Q_i$ holds for each $i \in N$. We also assume the preference of each agent is strict except for the elements of Q_i, i.e., for any $x \in X \backslash Q_i$ and $x' \in X$, where $x \neq x'$, either $x \succ_i x'$ or $x' \succ_i x$ holds.[1] We denote $x \succeq_i x'$ when $x \succ_i x'$ or $x \sim_i x'$ holds. We say x is indifferent to agent i (with q) if $x \in Q_i$. x is also a standard alternative for agent i if $x \in X \backslash Q_i$.

We assume Q is public information and develop a mechanism that exploits this information. Assuming Q is public is reasonable if each alternative is relevant to only a subset of agents, e.g., an agent is indifferent between alternative trip plans in which she does not participate.

Let us show a concrete example and an informal description about how a mechanism can utilize Q.

Example 1. Consider the following case.

- $N = \{1, 2, 3\}$, i.e., three agents.
- $X = \{x_1, x_2, x_3, x_4, x_5, q\}$, i.e., six alternatives including the status quo. Here, we assume these alternatives are possible trip plans, where x_1 is a plan that all agents go to Thailand, x_2 is a plan that all agents go to Singapore, x_3 is a plan that only agents 1 and 2 go to Thailand, x_4 is a plan that only agents 1 and 3 go to Singapore, and x_5 is a plan that only agent 1 goes to Thailand.
- $Q_1 = \{q\}, Q_2 = \{x_4, x_5, q\}, Q_3 = \{x_3, x_5, q\}$, i.e., each agent considers any trip that she does not participate in as an element of her indifference set.

If Q is not public knowledge, as shown in the previous section, when $|X(f)| = 2$, mechanism f first chooses one alternative x within $\{x_1, \ldots, x_5\}$ in some way, e.g., arbitrary. Then, the mechanism asks each agent whether she approves it, i.e., whether she prefers x over q. If all the agents approve x, then it is chosen. Otherwise, q is chosen.

When Q is public, instead of choosing one alternative, the mechanism can choose two, say, x_3 and x_4. Here, since $x_3 \in Q_3$, it can select x_3 without the approval of agent 3; it is public knowledge that she is indifferent between x_3 and q. The mechanism asks agent 2 whether she approves x_3. Also, it asks agent 3 whether she approves x_4. Let $\widehat{X}$ denote the set of approved alternatives. Then, the mechanism lets agent 1 choose her most preferred alternative within $\widehat{X} \cup \{x_5, q\}$. Clearly, $X(f) = \{x_3, x_4, x_5, q\}$. Thus, $|X(f)|$ becomes strictly more than 2.

We next introduce several criteria to evaluate social choice functions. For alternative $x \in X$, let $S(x)$ denote $\{i \in N : x \notin Q_i\}$, i.e., the set of all agents

---

[1] This assumption is required to obtain Maskin monotonicity [11], which is a powerful tool to show various properties of a mechanism.

who consider x a standard alternative. In Example 1, $S(x_1) = S(x_2) = \{1, 2, 3\}$, $S(x_3) = \{1, 2\}$, $S(x_4) = \{1, 3\}$, and $S(x_5) = \{1\}$.

Definition 4 (Multiagent Choice). *We say alternative x is a multiagent choice if $|S(x)| \geq 2$. Also, we say x is a multiagent choice of mechanism f if x is a multiagent choice and $x \in X(f)$ holds. Let $M \subseteq X$ denote the set of all multiagent choices in X and let $M(f)$ denote $X(f) \cap M$, i.e., the set of all multiagent choices with a chance to be selected by mechanism f. We call $M(f)$ the possible multiagent choices of mechanism f.*

In Example 1, x_1, x_2, x_3, and x_4 are multiagent choices. Also, for the mechanism described in Example 1, $M(f) = \{x_3, x_4\}$. Let $X_i(f)$ denote $X(f) \backslash Q_i$ and let $M_i(f)$ denote $M(f) \cap X_i(f)$.

In the trip organizing example, a multiagent choice is a trip involving more than one agent. It is natural to assume that a social choice function is better if it can choose more multiagent choices. In the general setting, we showed that at most one alternative besides the status quo can be chosen as long as mechanism f is IR and SP. Thus, the number of possible multiagent choices of f is at most 1. In an SC-EI, the number of possible multiagent choices can be increased, e.g., in Example 1, $|M(f)| = 2$. In the next section, we show that the number of possible multiagent choices is bounded, i.e., at most $n - 1$.

From the above definition, for x to be a multiagent choice, $|S(x)| \geq 2$ is sufficient; it does not care whether $|S(x)| = 2$ or $|S(x)| = n$. In the trip organizing example, it is reasonable to assume that a trip plan with more participants is desirable. Thus, let us introduce another criterion that takes into account the quantity of agents who consider an alternative to be standard.

Definition 5 (Agent Count). *For subset of multiagent choices $M' \subseteq M$, we call $C(M') = \sum_{x \in M'} |S(x)|$ its agent count. We also call $C(M(f))$ the agent count of mechanism f.*

In Example 1, $C(M(f)) = |\{1, 2\}| + |\{1, 3\}| = 4$. This value means the cumulative total number of participating agents of trips that involve multiple agents.

In general settings, the agent count is at most n, since there exists at most one multiagent choice. In an SC-EI, the number of multiagent count can be increased, e.g., in Example 1, $C(M(f)) = 4$. In the next section, we show that $C(M(f))$ is bounded, i.e., at most $2(n - 1)$.

6   Properties of SC-EI

We show the bounds of the size of the possible multiagent choices and the agent count of an IR and SP mechanism. Let us introduce another assumption called weak non-bossiness. Let $L(x, \succ_i) = \{y \in X : x \succeq_i y\}$. $L(x, \succ_i)$ is called agent i's *weak lower contour set* for alternative x. In words, the lower contour set of x of agent i means a set of alternatives that are less preferred than or equal to x for i.

Definition 6 (Weak Non-bossiness). *We say social choice function f is weakly non-bossy (WNB) if for any $i \in N$ and any $\succ, \succ' \in \mathcal{P}^n$ s.t. for all $j \in N_{-i}$, $\succ_j = \succ'_j$ and $L(x, \succ_i) \subseteq L(x, \succ'_i)$ hold, $f(\succ) = x \in Q_i$ implies $f(\succ') = x$.*

Weak non-bossiness means that if alternative x is chosen for preference profile $\succ$ and x is in agent i's indifference set, for preference profile $\succ'$ in which only agent i's preference is changed such that x is not considered worse, x is also chosen. Note that Q_i is public information and agent i cannot report a preference that is inconsistent with it. Thus, since x is not considered worse, all of the elements in Q_i are not considered worse.

Standard non-bossiness, which was introduced by [15], means that by changing an agent's preference relation, she cannot change the outcome for the other agents without affecting her own outcome. Here, we use a weaker definition of non-bossiness; by changing agent i's preference in a restricted manner, i cannot change the outcome from one alternative in Q_i to another alternative in it. If an agent could do this, then she could change the outcome for the other agents without affecting her own outcome.

The following theorem holds:

Theorem 2. *Assume social choice function f is IR, SP and WNB. Then, the size of its possible multiagent choices, i.e., $|M(f)|$ is at most $n-1$ and its agent count, i.e., $C(M(f))$ is at most $2(n-1)$.*

To prove this theorem, we utilize a property called Maskin monotonicity [11].

Definition 7 (Maskin Monotonicity). *Social choice function f is Maskin Monotonic (MM) if for all $\succ, \succ' \in \mathcal{P}^n$, $f(\succ) = x$ and $L(x, \succ_i) \subseteq L(x, \succ'_i)$ for all $i \in N$ imply $f(\succ') = x$.*

In words, social choice function f is MM if alternative x, which is chosen for preference profile $\succ$ is also chosen for preference profile $\succ'$, where x is not considered worse for all agents. When the agents have strict preferences over X, strategy-proofness implies Maskin monotonicity [11]. On the other hand, in our model where agent i considers all alternatives in Q_i indifferent, strategy-proofness does not imply Maskin monotonicity. However, if we assume weak non-bossiness, strategy-proofness does imply Maskin monotonicity, and the following proposition holds.

Proposition 1. *If social choice function f is SP and WNB, then it satisfies Maskin monotonicity.*

Proof. To show that strategy-proofness and weak non-bossiness imply Maskin monotonicity, assume that $f(\succ) = x$. It is sufficient to show $f(\succ') = x$ when $\succ'$ satisfies $\succ_j = \succ'_j$ for any agent $j \in N_{-i}$ as well as $L(x, \succ_i) \subseteq L(x, \succ'_i)$ holds. Consider the following three cases:

case (1) $x \sim_i f(\succ')$: either $f(\succ') = x$ or $x \in Q_i$ holds. If $f(\succ') = x$, we are done. If $x \in Q_i$, we obtain $f(\succ') = x$ by weak non-bossiness.

case (2) $f(\succ') \succ_i x$: agent i has an incentive to declare $\succ_i'$ if her true preference is $\succ_i$. This fact violates the assumption that f is SP.

case (3) $x \succ_i f(\succ')$: we obtain $x \succ_i' f(\succ')$ from assumption $L(x, \succ_i) \subseteq L(x, \succ_i')$. Thus, agent i has an incentive to declare $\succ_i$ when her true preference is $\succ_i'$. This fact violates the assumption that f is SP.

As a result, $f(\succ) = f(\succ')$ holds. Thus, strategy-proofness and weak nonbossiness imply Maskin monotonicity.

For $x, x' \in X$, x dominates x' if $x \succeq_i x'$ holds for all $i \in N$ and there exists at least one agent $j \in N$ such that $x \succ_j x'$ holds.

The following proposition holds.

Proposition 2. *Assume that social choice function f is IR, SP, and WNB. When there exists alternative $x' \in X(f)$ that dominates alternative $x \in X(f)$ for $\succ$, $f(\succ) \neq x$ holds. In particular, if there exists alternative $x \in X(f)$ that dominates q, we have $f(\succ) \neq q$.*

Proof. For the sake of contradiction, we assume that there exists $\succ \in \mathcal{P}^n$ s.t. x' dominates x and $f(\succ) = x$. From $f(\succ) = x$ and individual rationality, for all $i \in S(x)$, $x \succ_i q$ holds. Also, from the assumption that x' dominates x, for all $i \in S(x') \cap S(x)$, $x' \succ_i x \succ_i q$ holds. Also, since we assume $x' \in X(f)$, there exists $\succ' \in \mathcal{P}^n$ s.t. $f(\succ') = x'$. From individual rationality, for all $i \in S(x')$, $x' \succ_i' q$ holds. Here, we consider $\succ''$ that satisfies the following conditions:

- If $i \in S(x) \cap S(x')$, $x' \succ_i'' x \succ_i'' q$.
- If $i \in S(x') \backslash S(x)$, $x' \succ_i'' q$ and $x \sim_i'' q$.
- For all $x'' \neq x, x'$, for all $i \in S(x'')$, $q \succ_i'' x''$.

$L(x, \succ_i) \subseteq L(x, \succ_i'')$ holds. Thus, from Maskin monotonicity, $f(\succ'') = x$ must hold. On the other hand, $L(x, \succ_i') \subseteq L(x, \succ_i'')$ holds for all $i \in N$. Thus, from Maskin monotonicity, $f(\succ'') = x'$ must hold. This is a contradiction.

Next, we introduce the classification of agents.

Definition 8 (Agent Types).

Decider: *Agent i is a decider if $|X_i(f)| \geq 2$ and $|M_i(f)| \geq 1$ hold, where at least two possible alternatives of mechanism f are her standard alternatives and at least one is a multiagent choice.*

Approver: *Agent i is an approver if $X_i(f) = M_i(f)$ and $|X_i(f)| = 1$ hold, i.e., exactly one possible alternative of mechanism f is her standard alternative and also a multiagent choice.*

Solitary: *Agent i is solitary if $|M_i(f)| = 0$ holds, where no possible multiagent choice of mechanism f is her standard alternative. There might exist alternative x such that $S(x) = \{i\}$ holds.*

In Example 1, agent 1 is a decider since $X_1(f) = \{x_3, x_4, x_5\}$, and x_3 and x_4 are multiagent choices. Agent 2 and 3 are approvers since $X_2(f) = M_2(f) = \{x_3\}$ and $X_3(f) = M_3(f) = \{x_4\}$.

The next proposition implies that if alternative $x \in X(f)$ is a multiagent choice, then there exists at most one decider who considers x her standard alternative. In Example 1, $X(f)$ includes two multiagent choices, i.e., x_3 and x_4. For both, only agent 1 is the decider of these alternatives.

Proposition 3. *Assume that agents $i, j \in N$ ($i \neq j$) are deciders. If there exists SP, IR, and WNB social choice function f, $X_i(f) \cap X_j(f) = \emptyset$ holds.*

Proof. For the sake of contradiction, we assume that agents 1 and 2 are deciders and $X_1(f) \cap X_2(f) \neq \emptyset$ holds. Consider the following two cases.

case (i) $|X_1(f) \cap X_2(f)| \geq 2$: Without loss of generality, assume $x, x' \in X_1(f) \cap X_2(f)$ ($x \neq x'$), $x \succ_1 x' \succ_1 q$ for agent 1, $x' \succ_2 x \succ_2 q$ for agent 2, and for any $x'' \in X \setminus \{x, x', q\}$, there exists agent $i \in S(x'')$ whose preference is $q \succ_i x''$. From individual rationality, $f(\succ) \neq x''$ holds. Furthermore, assume $x, x' \succeq_i q$ holds for any agent $i \in N \setminus \{1, 2\}$. Also, from Proposition 2, $f(\succ) \neq q$ holds. Without loss of generality, assume $f(\succ) = x$. Then, agent 2 has an incentive to declare $x' \succ_2' q \succ_2' x$ when her true preference is $\succ_2$. This is because when agent 2 declares $\succ_2'$, the social choice becomes x'. This contradicts our assumption that f is SP.

case (ii) $|X_1(f) \cap X_2(f)| = 1$: Without loss of generality, assume $x \in X_1(f) \cap X_2(f), x' \in X_1(f) \cap Q_2$, and $x'' \in Q_1 \cap X_2(f)$. We consider the following five cases of preferences for agents 1 and 2. For each case, we assume that for any $x''' \notin \{x, x', x'', q\}$, there exists agent $i \in S(x''')$ whose preference is $q \succ_i x'''$. We also assume $x, x', x'' \succeq_i q$ for agent $i \in N \setminus \{1, 2\}$. From individual rationality and Proposition 2, $f(\succ) \in \{x, x', x'', q\}$.

(1) agent 1: $x' \succ_1 q \sim_1 x'' \succ_1 x$,
   agent 2: $x \succ_2 q \sim_2 x' \succ_2 x''$
(2) agent 1: $x' \succ_1 x \succ_1 q \sim_1 x''$,
   agent 2: $x \succ_2 q \sim_2 x' \succ_2 x''$
(3) agent 1: $x \succ_1 x' \succ_1 q \sim_1 x''$,
   agent 2: $x \succ_2 x'' \succ_2 q \sim_2 x'$
(4) agent 1: $x' \succ_1 x \succ_1 q \sim_1 x''$,
   agent 2: $x \succ_2 x'' \succ_2 q \sim_2 x'$
(5) agent 1: $x' \succ_1 x \succ_1 q \sim_1 x''$,
   agent 2: $x'' \succ_2 x \succ_2 q \sim_2 x'$

We show the social choice for each case.

(1) From individual rationality and Proposition 2, we have $f(\succ) = x'$.
(2) From (1) and Maskin monotonicity, $f(\succ) = x'$ holds (*).
(3) From Proposition 2, we have $f(\succ) = x$ (**).

(4) We have $f(\succ) = x'$ from the following three reasons: (a) If $f(\succ) = x$, it is contrary to strategy-proofness for agent 2 from (*). (b) If $f(\succ) = x''$, it is contrary to (**) from MM. (c) From Proposition 2, $f(\succ) \neq q$.

(5) From (4) and MM, $f(\succ) = x'$ holds. However, we can create four cases by replacing x' with x'', and agent 1 with agent 2 in cases from (1) to (4), which we call (1') to (4'). For example, in (1'), we set $x \succ_1 q \sim_1 x'' \succ_1 x'$ for agent 1 and $x'' \succ_2 q \sim_2 x' \succ_2 x$ for agent 2. Although $f(\succ) = x'$ has to continue holding in case (5), from (1') to (4'), we obtain $f(\succ) = x''$ in case (5). This is a contradiction.

Now, we are ready to prove Theorem 2.

Proof (Proof of Theorem 2). From Proposition 3, the number of deciders who consider each multiagent choice $x \in M(f)$ their standard alternative is at most one. Since there exists at least one approver for each $x \in M(f)$, we obtain $|M(f)| \leq n$. If $|M(f)| = n$, the number of approvers is n. However, this implies that the number of deciders is 0 and violates the assumption that there are n multiagent choices, since each alternative is a standard alternative only for a single approver. Thus, we derive $|M(f)| \leq n - 1$.

Next, we examine the agent count. If there exists no decider, then the agent count is at most n, where all approvers consider a single multiagent choice as their standard choice. If there exists at least one decider, then the agent count is at most the sum of the number of approvers and multiagent choices. This number is maximized when a single decider considers all $n - 1$ multiagent choices as her standard alternative, and each multiagent choice is considered a standard alternative by a single approver. In such a case, the agent count is $2(n - 1)$.

7 AC Mechanisms

We propose a class of IR, SP, and WNB social choice functions (mechanisms) that is optimal in terms of possible multiagent choices and agent count. We call such mechanisms *Approve and Choose (AC) mechanisms*. For presentation purposes, we first show the AC mechanism for 2 agents.

Mechanism 1 (AC Mechanism for 2 Agents). *We assume that there exist agents 1 and 2. Mechanism f chooses one decider and one approver in some way (which can be arbitrary) independently from the agents' declarations. Here, let assume agent 1 is a decider and agent 2 is an approver. $X(f)$ consists of $\{x^*\} \cup Y$. It determines alternative x^* as a multiagent choice which is a standard alternative for both agent 1 and 2, in some way independently from the agents' declarations. Thus, $x^* \in X_1(f) \cap X_2(f)$ holds. Also, it chooses set of alternatives $Y = \{q\} \cup \{x \in X_1(f) : |S(x)| = 1\}$, where Y contains q and all the alternatives are standard alternatives only to agent 1 in some way independently from the agents' declarations.*

1. *Agent* 2 *approves* x^* *if she prefers* x^* *over* q. *Otherwise, she vetoes* x^*.
2. *Agent* 1 *selects the best alternative according to agent* 2*'s decision:*
   - *If agent* 2 *approves* x^*, *then agent* 1 *selects the most preferred alternative in* $\{x^*\} \cup Y$.
   - *Otherwise, agent* 1 *selects the most preferred alternative in* Y.

We generalize this procedure from 2 agents to n agents. First, the mechanism chooses one decider in some way independently from the agents' declarations. Here, we assume agent 1 is a decider. The mechanism then determines a set X^* of multiagent choices in some way independently from the agents' declarations, such that for each $x^* \in X^*$, agent 1 is the decider and a subset of N_{-1} is approvers. Here, each approver has exactly one alternative in X^* and this choice is her standard alternative. In Example 1, the mechanism chooses X^* as $\{x_3, x_4\}$. For x_3, agent 1 is the decider and agent 2 is the approver. For x_4, agent 1 is the decider and agent 3 is the approver.

Also, the mechanism independently selects set of alternatives $Y = \{q\} \cup \{x \in X_1(f) : |S(x)| = 1\}$ from the agents' declarations. In Example 1, the mechanism chooses Y as $\{x_5, q\}$ and asks each approver in turn whether she approves of her multiagent choice. Let $\widehat{X}^* \subseteq X^*$ denote the set of alternatives that are approved by all own approvers. Then, the decider selects her most preferred alternative among $\widehat{X}^* \cup Y$.

In Example 1, assume $x_3 \succ_1 x_4 \succ_1 x_5 \succ_1 q$, $x_3 \succ_2 q$, and $x_4 \succ_3 q$. Then, x_3 and x_4 are approved by agents 2 and 3, respectively. Thus, $\widehat{X}^* = \{x_3, x_4\}$. Then, agent 1 chooses x_3 from $\widehat{X}^* \cup Y = \{x_3, x_4, x_5, q\}$. If the preference of agent 1 is $x_5 \succ_1 x_4 \succ_1 x_3 \succ_1 q$, then she chooses x_5.

The following theorem illustrates the property of the AC mechanism.

Theorem 3. *Any AC mechanism* f *is IR, SP, and WNB. Also,* $X(f) = X^* \cup Y$. *Furthermore, an instance of the AC mechanisms is optimal in terms of the number of multiagent choices and the agent count.*

Proof. Due to space limitations, we show the proof for the two agent case. Generalizing to the n agent case is rather straightforward (although verbose).

We first show that the AC mechanism is SP. For agent 2 (an approver), if she vetoes x^* even though $x^* \succ_2 q$, the social choice results in her indifference set. If she approves x^*, x^* might be selected. Thus, agent 2 has no incentive to misreport her preference. Agent 1 (a decider) does not have any incentive to misreport her preference, since she can select the best alternative from a set that is determined independently from her declaration. Next we show that the AC mechanism is IR. Obviously, it selects an alternative that is not worse than q as long as the agents truthfully declare their preferences. Then we show that the AC mechanism guarantees weak non-bossiness. Assume agent 1 chooses $y \in Y$ (which is in Q_2) when agent 2 approves x^*. Then if she vetoes x^* by declaring that she prefers y over x^*, agent 1 still chooses y. For agent 1, q is the only alternative in Q_1 that can be selected. If agent 1 chooses q, then under any preference of agent 1 in which q is not considered worse, q is also selected. x^*

can be chosen when both agents deem x^* best. Also, $x \in Y$ can be chosen if agent 1 deems x the best.

Finally, by selecting each multiagent choice so that it is considered a standard alternative by exactly one approver, the number of multiagent choices becomes $n - 1$. The agent count becomes $2(n - 1)$. From Theorem 2, this instance of AC mechanisms is optimal in terms of the number of multiagent choices and the agent count.

Since the agent count is bounded and there exists at most one decider for each alternative, there exists a tradeoff between the numbers of multiagent choices $|M(f)|$ and agents who consider $x \in M(f)$ their standard alternative $|S(x)|$; if $|S(x)|$ becomes large, $|M(f)|$ should become small. As shown in the proof of Theorem 3, $|M(f)|$ is maximized when $|S(x)| = 2$ holds for all $x \in M(f)$.

Unfortunately, the AC mechanism does not characterize all SP, IR, and WNB mechanisms, since we can consider the following (seemingly less attractive) mechanisms.

A Mechanism with Multiple Deciders: From Proposition 3, multiple deciders should not consider the same multiagent choice as their standard alternative. Assume agents are partitioned into several groups that are serialized. Each group contains exactly one decider and the approvers who consider the multiagent choices of the decider as standard alternatives. For the first group, we apply the above procedure of Mechanism 1. When the first group chooses q, the mechanism proceeds to the second group, and so on.

A Mechanism with No Decider: Assume all agents are solitary and serialized. The first agent is asked to choose her most preferred alternative. If her choice is q, the mechanism proceeds to the next agent, and so on.

8   AC Mechanism for Quasi-Linear Utilities

We can extend the idea of AC mechanisms and apply them to the cases where each agent's utility is quasi-linear.

An SC-EI problem in quasi-linear utilities is defined by a tuple (N, X, q, v, Q). The meanings of $N, X, q,$ and Q are basically identical to SC-EI. Here, $v = (v_i)_{i \in N} \in V^n$ is a profile of the valuation functions, where V is the set of all possible valuation functions for an agent. Each valuation function $v_i : X \to \mathbb{R}$ returns the valuation of each alternative. We assume $v_i(x) = 0$ if $x \in Q_i$ holds. Mechanism $f = (g, p)$ consists of allocation function $g : V^n \to X$ and payment function $p : V^n \to \mathbb{R}^n$. When the declared profile of the valuation functions is $\widehat{v}$, the utility of agent i is defined as: $v_i(g(\widehat{v})) + p_i(\widehat{v})$, i.e., a quasi-linear utility function.

We require that the mechanism does not lose or earn money.

Definition 9 (Budget-Balanced). *A mechanism is strongly budget-balanced (SBB) if for any profile of valuations $v \in V^n$, $\sum_{i \in N} p_i(v) = 0$ holds.*

We say a mechanism is *weakly budget-balanced* (WBB) if for any profile of valuations $v \in V^n$, $\sum_{i \in N} p_i(v) \leq 0$ holds. The family of Groves mechanisms is a well-known representative class of efficient and SP social choice functions [8]. In our problem setting, agents can have a negative valuation for an allocation/choice. In such a setting, an instance of Groves mechanisms can satisfy IR, but not WBB. Another instance of Groves mechanisms can satisfy WBB, but not IR. Actually, no instance of a Groves mechanism is simultaneously IR and WBB [9]. We show that the modified AC mechanism guarantees SP, IR, and SBB.

Note that we do not require that WNB be a necessary condition in this section. Since an agent can affect the outcome through payments, it is common that a mechanism does not satisfy non-bossiness. For example, the Groves mechanisms do not satisfy non-bossiness.

8.1   Class of AC Mechanisms

In this section, we propose a class of AC mechanisms for quasi-linear utilities.

Mechanism 2 (AC Mechanism for Quasi-Linear Utilities)

1. *The mechanism selects one agent as a decider. WLOG, we assume agent 1 is the decider.*
2. *It chooses X^* and Y similar to an AC mechanism. In more detail, it selects X^* of multiagent choices such that for $x^* \in X^*$, agent 1 is a decider and subset N_{-1} is approvers. Each approver has exactly one standard alternative in X^*. It also independently chooses a set of alternatives $Y = \{q\} \cup \{x \in X_1(f) \colon |S(x)| = 1\}$.*
3. *Each approver j declares her (not necessarily true) valuation (denoted as $\widehat{v}_j$).*
4. *For each approver j of alternative x, her threshold price $p_j(\widehat{v})$ is determined. It can depend on the declaration of other approvers, but it must be independent from her own declaration.*
5. *$x \in X^*$ remains valid if $\widehat{v}_j(x) \geq p_j(\widehat{v})$ holds for each approver j of x. Let $\widehat{X}^* \subseteq X^*$ denote a set of valid alternatives. We also require that for each valid alternative $x \in \widehat{X}^*$ and for each approver j of x, $p_j(\widehat{v})$ is determined independently from the declarations of the approvers of other valid alternatives. In other words, if $p_j(\widehat{v})$ depends on $\widehat{v}_k$, then the alternative related to agent k is not approved.*
6. *For each $x \in \widehat{X}^*$, $r(x) = \sum_{j \in S(x), j \neq 1} p_j(\widehat{v})$.*
7. *Agent 1 (decider) chooses her most preferred alternative within $\widehat{X}^* \cup Y$. When $x \in \widehat{X}^*$ is chosen, agent 1 receives $r(x)$, and each approver j of x pays $p_j(\widehat{v})$. If agent 1 chooses $x \in Y$, no agent pays/receives anything.*

The following theorem illustrates the properties of the AC mechanism for quasi-linear utilities.

Theorem 4. *The AC mechanism for quasi-linear utilities is SP, IR, and SBB.*

Proof. We first show that the AC mechanism is SP. Agent 1 can choose her most preferred alternative in a fixed set. The set and the corresponding payments are determined independently from her own declaration. Thus, agent 1 has no incentive to misreport her valuation. For each approver j, her threshold price of the alternative related to agent j is determined independently from her own declaration. Also, her own declaration affects the payment of other valid alternatives only when her alternative is not approved. Thus, agent j has not incentive to misreport her valuation.

The AC mechanism is IR, since each approver accepts an alternative only if she can pay a threshold price. Also, the decider always has an option to choose q. Obviously, it satisfies SBB, since the sum of approvers' payments is transferred to the decider.

8.2   Instances of AC Mechanisms

We introduce the instances of AC mechanisms for quasi-linear utilities. The first is called a *fixed price mechanism*, in which a common fixed threshold price is used. To achieve good efficiency, the fixed threshold price must be determined appropriately. To do this, we need precise prior knowledge about the distribution of agent valuations. On the other hand, the second, which is called a *minimum-value $k + 1$-st price mechanism*, is more flexible; the threshold price is determined based on the valuations of other agents.

Mechanism 3 (Fixed Price Mechanism (FPM)). *For all $x \in X^*$ and for all approvers, we set constant c as a threshold price. Each alternative $x \in X^*$ remains valid if $\hat{v}_i(x) \geq c$ holds for each approver. If $x \in X^*$ is chosen, the decider receives $(|S(x)| - 1) \times c$. Clearly, each threshold price of an approver is determined independently from all the approver declarations, including her own declaration.*

Here, we show an example how our FPM works.

Example 2. Consider the same situation as Example 1, but each agent has a valuation for an alternative. We assume that each agent has a profile of valuation functions for $(x_1, x_2, x_3, x_4, x_5, q)$:

- agent 1 : $v_1 = (-200, -100, 20, 250, 100, 0)$
- agent 2 : $v_2 = (250, 200, 150, 0, 0, 0)$
- agent 3 : $v_3 = (100, 100, 0, 50, 0, 0)$

Let's assume that agent 1 is selected as a decider. In this example, the mechanism selects $X^* = \{x_3, x_4\}$ and $Y = \{x_5, q\}$. It also determines a threshold price 100 for approvers. When each approver wants to travel with agent 1 by paying this threshold price, say, her valuation is not less than 100, she approves this offer. For x_3, agent 2 is an approver and for x_4, agent 3 is an approver. In this case, only agent 2 approves the offer, i.e., $\hat{X}^* = \{x_3\}$. Thus, agent 1 selects her most preferred alternative from $Y \cup \hat{X}^* = \{x_3, x_5, q\}$. For agent 1, when she selects x_3, her utility becomes $20 - (-100) = 120$ by receiving 100. On the other hand, if she selects x_5, her utility is 100. As a result, agent 1 selects x_3 and agents 1 and 2 are going to travel in Thailand.

Mechanism 4 (Minimum-Value $k + 1$-st Price Mechanism (MPM)). *For each alternative $x \in X^*$, let $t(u)$ be the minimum of $v_j(x)$ for all approvers of x. Sort X^* in decreasing order of $t(x)$. Top $k \leq |X^*| - 1$ alternatives remain valid and constitute $\widehat{X}^*$. Let x^{k+1} denote the $k + 1$-st alternative. For each valid alternative x, $p_j(\widehat{v})$ is determined to be $t(x^{k+1})$. We can assume the threshold price of an invalid alternative is equal to $t(x^k)$. It is clear that the threshold price of each approver is determined independently from her own declaration. Also, the threshold price of each approved alternative is determined independently from the declarations of the other approvers of valid alternatives.*

In the last of this section, we show an example of MPM.

Example 3. Consider the situation described in Example 2.

The mechanism selects $X^* = \{x_3, x_4\}$ as the same as above. We assume that each agent truthfully declares her valuation functions. Thus, we have decreasing order of $t(x)$: $150 > 50$. As a result, agent 2 is going to pay 50 for agent 1. If agent 1 selects x_3, her utility becomes $20 + 50 = 70$. However, for agent 1, her best alternative is x_5, since her utility is 100 by selecting x_5. As a result, agent 1 is going to travel in Thailand alone.

9   Conclusion

We investigated the IR and SP social choice functions for settings where the agents need to choose from a set of alternatives including status quo q. We first showed a negative result, i.e., IR and SP mechanism can choose at most one alternative besides q. To overcome this negative result, we introduced the SC-EI setting, where the indifference set of each agent is publicly known. We developed a class of IR and SP mechanisms that work in this setting called Approve and Choose (AC) mechanisms, which can be optimal in terms of possible multiagent choices/agent counts.

Our future work will extend the AC mechanisms in a setting with monetary transfers and experimentally evaluate our mechanisms in various application domains.

Acknowledgements. This work was partially supported by JSPS KAKENHI Grant Numbers 24220003 and 15H02751, and JSPS Program for Advancing Strategic International Networks to Accelerate the Circulation of Talented Researchers.

References

1. Bachrach, Y., Elkind, E., Faliszewski, P.: Coalitional voting manipulation: a game-theoretic perspective. In: Proceedings of the 22nd International Joint Conference on Artificial Intelligence (IJCAI 2011), pp. 49–54 (2011)
2. Barberá, S., Ehlers, L.: Free triples, large indifference classes and the majority rule. Soc. Choice Welf. **37**(4), 559–574 (2011)
3. Blau, J.H., Deb, R.: Social decision functions and the veto. Econometrica **45**(4), 871–897 (1977)
4. Brandt, F., Geist, C.: Finding strategyproof social choice functions via SAT solving. In: Proceedings of the 14th International Conference on Autonomous Agents and Multi-agent Systems (AAMAS 2014), pp. 1193–1200 (2014)
5. Darmann, A., Elkind, E., Kurz, S., Lang, J., Schauer, J., Woeginger, G.: Group activity selection problem. In: Goldberg, P.W. (ed.) WINE 2012. LNCS, vol. 7695, pp. 156–169. Springer, Heidelberg (2012)
6. Faltings, B.V.: A budget-balanced, incentive-compatible scheme for social choice. In: Faratin, P., Rodríguez-Aguilar, J.-A. (eds.) AMEC 2004. LNCS (LNAI), vol. 3435, pp. 30–43. Springer, Heidelberg (2006)
7. Gibbard, A.: Manipulation of voting schemes: a general result. Econometrica **41**(4), 587–601 (1973)
8. Groves, T.: Incentives in teams. Econometrica **41**(4), 617–631 (1973)
9. Guo, M., Shen, H., Todo, T., Sakurai, Y., Yokoo, M.: Social decision with minimal efficiency loss: an automated mechanism design approach. In: Proceedings of the 15th International Conference on Autonomous Agents and Multi-Agent Systems (AAMAS 2015), pp. 347–355 (2015)
10. Lu, T., Boutilier, C.: Multi-winner social choice with incomplete preferences. In: Proceedings of the 23rd International Joint Conference on Artificial Intelligence (IJCAI 2013), pp. 263–270 (2013)
11. Maskin, E.: Nash equilibrium and welfare optimality. Rev. Econ. Stud. **66**(1), 23–38 (1999)
12. Peleg, B.: Consistent voting systems. Econometrica **46**(1), 153–161 (1978)
13. Sato, S.: Strategy-proof social choice with exogenous indifference classes. Math. Soc. Sci. **57**(1), 48–57 (2009)
14. Satterthwaite, M.A.: Strategy-proofness and arrow's conditions: existence and correspondence theorems for voting procedures and social welfare functions. J. Econ. Theory **10**, 187–217 (1975)
15. Satterthwaite, M.A., Sonnenschein, H.F.: Strategy-proof allocation mechanisms at differentiable points. Rev. Econ. Stud. **48**(4), 587–597 (1981)

Offer Evaluation and Trade-Off Making in Automated Negotiation Based on Intuitionistic Fuzzy Constraints

Jieyu Zhan and Xudong Luo[✉]

Institute of Logic and Cognition, Department of Philosophy,
Sun Yat-sen University, Guangzhou 510275, China
luoxd3@mail.sysu.edu.cn

Abstract. In automated negotiation, one of crucial problems is how a negotiating agent evaluates the acceptability of an offer. Most models mainly use two kinds of evaluation methods: (i) linear utility functions that depend on issues, and (ii) nonlinear utility functions that depend on crisp constraints. However, in real life, it is hard for human users to input so much and so accurate information that these evaluation methods require. To this end, this paper proposes a new approach for offer evaluation where human users are allowed to input indeterminate information. More specifically, we propose a framework of prioritised intuitionistic fuzzy constraint satisfaction problems for modelling agent's goals. Moreover, we take both satisfaction degree and dissatisfaction degree into consideration when calculating an agent's acceptability of an offer. Finally, we discuss how to make trade-offs via similarity measure based on intuitionistic fuzzy criteria functions.

Keywords: Multi-issue automated negotiation · Intuitionistic fuzzy set · Fuzzy constraint satisfaction · Similarity · Trade-off

1 Introduction

Negotiation is a process in which several parties exchange information to reach an agreement [6,12]. With the development of electronic commerce and intelligent technologies, automated negotiation has attracted lots of attention from various research areas, especially computer science and management science [3,5,12,19]. Thus, many negotiating agents have been designed for maximising individual expected utility or social expected utility, finding equilibria, reducing negotiation time, and so on.

With the rapid growth of B2C and C2C markets, automated bilateral negotiation of multi-issue increasingly becomes more applicable and has great potential in real life. In automated negotiation systems for business, one of crucial problems is how to evaluate the acceptability of an offer during the course of a negotiation. The most common method is weighted average utility functions of multi-issue, which is regarded as a linear method. This method has a strong

© Springer International Publishing Switzerland 2016
M. Baldoni et al. (Eds.): PRIMA 2016, LNAI 9862, pp. 197–215, 2016.
DOI: 10.1007/978-3-319-44832-9_12

assumption that issues are independent of each other. However, in real life, often issues under negotiation are interdependent [13]. So, some researchers [8,11,13] propose the method of nonlinear utility functions that depend on constraints, *i.e.*, an agent's utility of multi-issue is defined as the sum of the utility for the constraints that offers need to satisfy.

However, this method also has some drawbacks. For example, in order to evaluate an offer more accurately, users have to estimate precise satisfaction degrees of U constraints with different values of issues. Nevertheless, somehow it is unpractical for human users to input so much and so accurate information. Moreover, it is hard to explain intuitively why the sum of the utilities for all the constraints is used to get the total utility. Hence, today how to represent human users' information properly and model human users' evaluation of an offer remains an open problem.

Thus, in this paper, we propose a new approach for offering evaluation during the course of a negotiation. Specifically, we evaluate an offer through three steps: (i) characterising agent's goals via prioritised intuitionistic fuzzy constraints, which framework is proposed in this paper; (ii) calculating the overall satisfaction degree and overall dissatisfaction degree of an offer according to the constraints; and (iii) calculating an agent's acceptability of an offer by integrating both overall satisfaction degree and dissatisfaction degree of the offer.

The main contributions of this paper are as follows. First, we propose a framework of prioritised intuitionistic fuzzy constraint satisfaction. Second, we construct a negotiating agent equipped with our new offer evaluation method based on the framework. Finally, we give an approach to generate an offer by making trade-offs between offers, which are evaluated using our method.

The rest of this paper is organised as follows. Section 2 recaps the basic concepts and notations of fuzzy set theory and constraint satisfaction problems. Section 3 proposes the framework of prioritised intuitionistic fuzzy constraint satisfaction problem. Section 4 presents a formal model of offer evaluation. Section 5 illustrates our model with two cases. Section 6 proposes a way of making trade-off in a negotiation. Section 7 discusses the related work. Finally, Sect. 8 concludes the paper with future work.

2   Preliminaries

In this section, we recap some necessary concepts and notations in fuzzy set [25], intuitionistic fuzzy set [2], constraint satisfaction problems [14], fuzzy constraint satisfaction problems [24], and prioritised fuzzy constraint satisfaction problems [18].

We start with the definitions of fuzzy set and intuitionistic fuzzy set.

Definition 1. *Let U be a nonempty set. A fuzzy set A on U is defined by function $\mu_A : U \to [0,1]$, called a membership function of fuzzy set A, and $\forall u \in U$, $\mu_A(u)$ is the membership degree of u in fuzzy set A.*

Definition 2. *Let U be a nonempty set. An intuitionistic fuzzy set A on U is defined by mappings $\mu_A : U \rightarrow [0,1]$ and $\gamma_A : U \rightarrow [0,1]$, which are called a membership function and a non-membership function of intuitionistic fuzzy set A, respectively; $\forall u \in U$, $\mu_A(u)$ and $\gamma_A(u)$ are called the membership degree and non-membership degree of u in intuitionistic fuzzy set A, respectively; and $\forall u \in U, 0 \leqslant \mu_A(u) + \gamma_A(u) \leqslant 1$. Let $\pi_A(u) = 1 - \mu_A(u) - \gamma_A(u)$, called the indeterminacy or hesitation degree of u in intuitionistic fuzzy set A, which reflects the lack of sufficient knowledge for judging whether or not x belongs to intuitionistic fuzzy set A.*

For example, the linguistic term *old-men* can be regarded as an intuitionistic fuzzy set. For a 60-year-old man, let $\mu_{old\text{-}men}(60) = 0.6, \gamma_{old\text{-}men}(60) = 0.3$, then $\pi_{old\text{-}men}(60) = 1 - \mu_{old\text{-}men}(60) - \gamma_{old\text{-}men}(60) = 0.1$. It can be interpreted as the degree to which the 60-year-old man is an old man is 0.6; the degree to which the he is not an old man is 0.3; and the degree to which we hesitate to say he is old or not is 0.1.

The following definitions are about the framework of constraint satisfaction problems:

Definition 3. *A constraint satisfaction problem (CSP) is a 3-tuple (X, D, C), where:*

(1) $X = \{x_i \mid i = 1, \cdots, n\}$ is a finite set of variables.
(2) $D = \{d_i \mid i = 1, \cdots, n\}$ is the set of domains. Each domain d_i is a finite set containing the possible values for variable x_i in X.
(3) $C = \{c_i \mid c_i \subseteq \prod_{x_j \in var(c_i)} d_j, i = 1, \cdots, m\}$ is a set of constraints. Here $var(c_i)$ denotes the set of variables of constraint c_i:

$$var(c_i) = \{x_1', \cdots, x_{k_{c_i}}'\} \subseteq X \tag{1}$$

Definition 4. *A label of a variable x is an assignment of a value to the variable, denoted as v_x. A compound label $v_{X'}$ of all variables in set $X' = \{x_1', \cdots, x_{k_m}'\} \subseteq X$ is a simultaneous assignment of values to all variables in set X':*

$$v_{X'} = (v_{x_1'}, \cdots, v_{x_m'}). \tag{2}$$

Definition 5. *In a CSP (X, D, C), the characteristic function of $c_i \in C$,*

$$\mu_{c_i} : \left(\prod_{x_j \in var(c_i)} d_j \right) \rightarrow \{0,1\}, \tag{3}$$

is defined as:

$$\mu_{c_i}(v_{var(c_i)}) = \begin{cases} 1 & if v_{var(c_i)} \in c_i, \\ 0 & otherwise. \end{cases} \tag{4}$$

A solution to a CSP (X, D, C) is a compound label $v_X = (v_{x_1}, \cdots, v_{x_n})$ of all variables in X such that:

$$\min\{\mu_{c_i}(v_{var(c_i)}) \mid c_i \in C\} = 1. \tag{5}$$

$\mu_{c_i}(v_{var(c_i)}) = 1$ means a constraint c_i is absolutely satisfied with a compound label $v_{var(c_i)}$, while $\mu_{c_i}(v_{var(c_i)}) = 0$ means the complete violation of the constraint c_i over the compound label. However, this formulation is too rigid for dealing with problems in which the satisfaction degree of a constraint is not a simple zero-one matter. Thus, the notion of fuzzy CSP is introduced in [24] as follows:

Definition 6. *A fuzzy constraint satisfaction problem (FCSP) is a 3-tuple* (X, D, C^F), *where* X *and* D *are the same as those in Definition 3, and* C^f *is a set of fuzzy constraints:*

$$C^F = \left\{ c_i^F \mid \mu_{c_i^F} : \left(\prod_{x_j \in var(c_i^F)} d_j \right) \to [0,1], i = 1, \cdots, m \right\}, \tag{6}$$

where $var(c_i^F)$ *denotes the set of variables of* c_i^F.

In an FCSP defined above, each constraint has no priority (*i.e.*, importance), or say, all constraints have the same level of priority. However, this is not always the case in practice. Thus, the prioritised FCSPs has been introduced as follows [18]:

Definition 7. *A prioritised fuzzy constraint satisfaction problem (PFCSP) is a 4-tuple* (X, D, C^F, ρ), *where* (X, D, C^F) *is a FCSP, and* $\rho : C^F \to [0, \infty)$ *is a priority function. Given a compound label* v_X *of all variables in* X, *its overall satisfaction degree is given by:*

$$\alpha_\rho(v_X) = \min \left\{ \left(\frac{\rho(c^F)}{\rho_{max}} \right) \diamond \mu_{c^F}(v_{var(c^F)}) \mid c^F \in C^F \right\}, \tag{7}$$

where

$$\rho_{max} = \max \left\{ \rho(c^F) \mid c^F \in C^F \right\}, \tag{8}$$

and operator $\diamond : [0,1] \times [0,1] \to [0,1]$, *called a priority operator, satisfies:*

(i) $\forall a_1, a_2, a_2' \in [0,1], a_2 \leqslant a_2' \Rightarrow a_1 \diamond a_2 \leqslant a_1 \diamond a_2';$
(ii) $\forall a_1, a_1', a_2 \in [0,1], a_1 \leqslant a_1' \Rightarrow a_1 \diamond a_2 \geqslant a_1' \diamond a_2;$
(iii) $\forall a \in [0,1], 1 \diamond a = a;$ *and*
(iv) $\forall a \in [0,1], 0 \diamond a = 1.$

A solution to a PFCSP (X, D, C^F, ρ) *is a compound label* v_X *of all variables in* X *such that:*

$$\alpha_\rho(v_X) \geqslant \tau, \tag{9}$$

where $\tau \in [0,1]$ *is a predetermined value, called the solution threshold of the PFCSP.*

Intuitively, the solution threshold τ means that if the overall satisfaction degree of a compound label is not less than the threshold, the label is acceptable as a solution; otherwise, it is not.

3 Intuitionistic FCSP and Prioritised Intuitionistic FCSP

In an FCSP or a PFCSP, each fuzzy constraint is associated with a satisfaction degree for each compound label. However, because of insufficient information or knowledge of decision makers in some scenarios (especially, negotiation), a constraint may need to be associated with not only satisfaction degree, but also dissatisfaction degree and indeterminacy. Hence, we propose a framework of intuitionistic fuzzy constraint satisfaction problems (IFCSPs) and then a framework of prioritised IFCSPs as follows:

Definition 8. *An intuitionistic fuzzy constraint satisfaction problem (IFCSP) is a 3-tuple (X, D, C^{IF}), where X and D are the same as those in Definition 3, and C^{IF} is a set of intuitionistic fuzzy constraints:*

$$C^{IF} = \left\{ c_i^{IF} \mid \mu_{c_i^{IF}} : \left(\prod_{x_j \in var(c_i^{IF})} d_j \right) \to [0,1], \gamma_{c_i^{IF}} : \left(\prod_{x_j \in var(c_i^{IF})} d_j \right) \to [0,1], i = 1, \cdots, m \right\},$$

$$(10)$$

where $var(c_i^{IF})$ denotes the set of variables of c_i^{IF}, and $\forall v_{var(c^{IF})}$, $\mu_{c_i^{IF}}(v_{var(c^{IF})}) + \gamma_{c_i^{IF}}(v_{var(c^{IF})}) \leqslant 1$.

Definition 9. *Let (X, D, C^{IF}) be an IFCSP. Then a prioritised intuitionistic fuzzy constraint satisfaction problem (PIFCSP) is a 4-tuple (X, D, C^{IF}, ρ), where $\rho : C^{IF} \to [0, \infty)$ is a priority function. Given a compound label v_X of all variables in X, its overall satisfaction degree is given by:*

$$\alpha_\rho(v_X) = \min \left\{ \left(\frac{\rho(c^{IF})}{\rho_{max}} \right) \diamond \mu_{c^{IF}}(v_{var(c^{IF})}) \mid c^{IF} \in C^{IF} \right\}, \qquad (11)$$

and its overall dissatisfaction degree is given by:

$$\beta_\rho(v_X) = \max \left\{ \left(\frac{\rho(c^{IF})}{\rho_{max}} \right) \bullet \gamma_{c^{IF}}(v_{var(c^{IF})}) \mid c^{IF} \in C^{IF} \right\}, \qquad (12)$$

where

$$\rho_{max} = \max \left\{ \rho(c^{IF}) \mid c^{IF} \in C^{IF} \right\}, \qquad (13)$$

and operator $\diamond : [0,1] \times [0,1] \to [0,1]$, called a priority operator of satisfaction, satisfies the properties that a priority operator in Definition 7 satisfies, and operator $\bullet : [0,1] \times [0,1] \to [0,1]$, called a priority operator of dissatisfaction, satisfies:

(i) $\forall a_1, a_2, a_2' \in [0,1], a_2 \leqslant a_2' \Rightarrow a_1 \bullet a_2 \leqslant a_1 \bullet a_2'$;
(ii) $\forall a_1, a_1', a_2 \in [0,1], a_1 \leqslant a_1' \Rightarrow a_1 \bullet a_2 \leqslant a_1' \bullet a_2$;
(iii) $\forall a \in [0,1], 1 \bullet a = a$; and
(iv) $\forall a \in [0,1], 0 \bullet a = 0$.

The definition of operator ◆ is intuitive. Property (i) reflects the intuition that if the dissatisfaction degree for an constraint is higher, the constraint does more contribution to the overall dissatisfaction degree. Property (ii) reflects the intuition that if a constraint is less important, the constraint has a minor effect on the overall dissatisfaction degree. Property (iii) reflects the intuition that if a constraint is the most important, its dissatisfaction degree can be totally considered when evaluating the overall dissatisfaction degree. Property (iv) reflects the intuition that if a constraint is the least important, its dissatisfaction degree cannot make any impact when evaluating the overall dissatisfaction degree.

Definition 10. *A solution to a PIFCSP* (X, D, C^{IF}, ρ) *is a compound label* v_X *of all variables in* X *such that:*

$$(\alpha_\rho(v_X) \geqslant \tau) \wedge (\beta_\rho(v_X) \leqslant \epsilon), \tag{14}$$

where $\tau \in [0, 1]$ *and* $\epsilon \in [0, 1]$ *are predetermined values, called the solution thresholds of the PIFCSP.*

Intuitively, the solution threshold τ and ϵ means that if the overall satisfaction degree of a compound label is not less than satisfaction threshold τ and not greater than dissatisfaction threshold ϵ, then the label is acceptable as a solution; otherwise, it is not.

4   Offer Evaluation

This section presents a method of offer evaluation during the course of a negotiation.

Firstly, we present the model of our negotiating agent as follows:

Definition 11. *A negotiating agent is 9-tuple* $(X, D, G, A, S, \rho, \zeta, H, W)$, *where:*

(i) $X = \{x_i \mid i = 1, \cdots, n\}$ *is the issue set in negotiation and* x_i *represents an issue.*

(ii) $D = \{d_i \mid i = 1, \cdots, n\}$ *is the set of domains. Each domain* d_i *is a set containing the possible values for issue* x_i *in* X.

(iii) $G = \{g_i \mid i = 1, \cdots, m\}$ *is the set of goals of the agent, which is represented by a set of intuitionistic fuzzy constraints. That is,*

$$G = \left\{ g_i \mid \mu_{g_i} : \left(\prod_{x_j \in var(g_i)} d_j \right) \rightarrow [0, 1], \gamma_{g_i} : \left(\prod_{x_j \in var(g_i)} d_j \right) \rightarrow [0, 1], i = 1, \cdots, m \right\}, \tag{15}$$

(iv) A *is an acceptability function of the agent.*

(v) S *represents the negotiation strategy of the agent.*[1]

---

[1] The negotiation strategy is an important component of an negotiating agent. However, in this paper, the main purpose is to propose a new way of offer evaluation, rather than constructing negotiation strategies. So, we will not detail the strategies in the subsequent part of this paper.

(vi) $\rho : g_i \to [0, \infty)$ *is a priority function, and* $\rho(g_i)$ *represents the importance of the goal* g_i *of the agent.*

(vii) $\zeta \in [0, 1]$ *is the acceptability threshold which the opponent's offer must surpass to be acceptable to the agent.*

(viii) $H = \{h_i \mid i = 1, \cdots, n\}$ *is the set of criterion evaluations, in which* h_i *means a criterion evaluation on an issue, and* μ_h *and* γ_h *represent the degrees that a value meet, and does not meet the criterion, respectively.* $\forall v_{x_i} \in d_i,\ \mu_h(v_{x_i}) \in [0, 1],\ \gamma_h(v_{x_i}) \in [0, 1],\ and\ \mu_h(v_{x_i}) + \gamma_h(v_{x_i}) \leqslant 1.$

(ix) $W = \{w_i \mid i = 1, \cdots, n\}$ *is a set of weights of issues and* $\sum_{x_i \in X_i} w_{x_i} = 1.$

Then we give the definition of an offer as follows:

Definition 12. *Agent* a*'s offer is an assignment of values to all the issues in issue set* X *with the following structure:*

$$o_a = (v_{x_1}, \cdots, v_{x_n}), \tag{16}$$

where $v_{x_i} \in d_i.$

Now we are at the position to discuss the offer evaluation. The acceptability of an offer to an agent should be determined by several factors: the overall satisfaction degree, the overall dissatisfaction degree and the indeterminacy in a real situation. Formally, we have:

Definition 13. *Let* O *be the set of all possible offers. An acceptability function of agent* a*, denoted as* $A_a : O \to [0, 1]$*, is given by:*

$$A_a(o) = \alpha_\rho(o) \odot \beta_\rho(o), \tag{17}$$

where the overall satisfaction degree α_ρ *for offer* o *is given by formula (11), overall dissatisfaction degree* β_ρ *for offer* o *is given by formula (12), and operator* $\odot : [0, 1] \times [0, 1] \to [0, 1]$ *satisfies:*

(i) $\forall a_1, a_2, a_2' \in [0, 1],\ a_2 \leqslant a_2' \Rightarrow a_1 \odot a_2 \geqslant a_1 \odot a_2';$

(ii) $\forall a_1, a_1', a_2 \in [0, 1],\ a_1 \leqslant a_1' \Rightarrow a_1 \odot a_2 \leqslant a_1' \odot a_2;$

(iii) $\forall a_1, a_2, a_1', a_2' \in [0, 1],\ a_1 - a_2 = a_1' - a_2' > 0,\ 1 - a_1 - a_2 \leqslant 1 - a_1' - a_2'$
$\Rightarrow a_1 \odot a_2 \leqslant a_1 \odot a_2';$

(iv) $\forall a_1, a_2, a_1', a_2' \in [0, 1],\ a_1 - a_2 = a_1' - a_2' < 0,\ 1 - a_1 - a_2 \leqslant 1 - a_1' - a_2'$
$\Rightarrow a_1 \odot a_2 \geqslant a_1 \odot a_2';$

(v) $1 \odot 0 = 1;$ *and*

(vi) $0 \odot 1 = 0.$

The above definition is intuitive. Property (i) reflects the intuition that the higher the overall dissatisfaction degree for an offer is, the lower the acceptability of the offer is. Property (ii) reflects the intuition that the higher the overall satisfaction degree for an offer is, the higher the acceptability of the offer is. Property (iii) reflects the intuition that for an offer, if the difference between the overall satisfaction degree and the overall dissatisfaction degree is greater than zero, then the higher the indeterminacy degree is, the higher the acceptability of the offer is. Property (iv) reflects the intuition that for an offer, if the difference between the overall satisfaction degree and the overall dissatisfaction degree is less than zero, then the higher the indeterminacy degree is, the lower the acceptability is. Property (v) reflects the intuition that for an offer, if the overall satisfaction degree of an offer is the highest and the overall dissatisfaction is the lowest, then the acceptability of the offer is the highest. Property (vi) reflects the intuition that for an offer, if the overall satisfaction degree of an offer is the lowest and the overall dissatisfaction is the highest, then the acceptability is the lowest.

Now we give three specific operators ◇, ◆ and ⊙ in Definitions 9 and 13.

Theorem 1. *Operator* $\diamond : [0,1] \times [0,1] \rightarrow [0,1]$, *defined as follows, satisfies the properties listed in Definition 7:*

$$a_1 \diamond a_2 = a_1 \times (a_2 - 1) + 1. \tag{18}$$

Proof. We prove that formula (18) satisfies the properties of operator ◇, listed in Definition 7, as follows:

(1) If $a_2 \leqslant a_2'$, then $a_1 \times (a_2 - 1) + 1 \leqslant a_1 \times (a_2' - 1) + 1$. Hence, $a_1 \diamond a_2 \leqslant a_1 \diamond a_2'$.
(2) If $a_1 \leqslant a_1'$, then $a_1 \times (a_2 - 1) + 1 \geqslant a_1' \times (a_2 - 1) + 1$. Hence, $a_1 \diamond a_2 \geqslant a_1' \diamond a_2$.
(3) $\forall a \in [0,1]$, $1 \diamond a = 1 \times (a - 1) + 1 = a$.
(4) $\forall a \in [0,1]$, $0 \diamond a = 0 \times (a - 1) + 1 = 1$.   □

Theorem 2. *Operator* $\blacklozenge : [0,1] \times [0,1] \rightarrow [0,1]$, *defined as follows, satisfies the properties listed in Definition 9:*

$$a_1 \blacklozenge a_2 = a_1 \times a_2. \tag{19}$$

Proof. We prove that formula (19) satisfies the properties of operator ◆, listed in Definition 9, as follows:

(1) If $a_2 \leqslant a_2'$, then $a_1 \times a_2 \leqslant a_1 \times a_2'$. Hence, $a_1 \blacklozenge a_2 \leqslant a_1 \blacklozenge a_2'$.
(2) If $a_1 \leqslant a_1'$, then $a_1 \times a_2 \leqslant a_1' \times a_2$. Hence, $a_1 \blacklozenge a_2 \leqslant a_1' \blacklozenge a_2$.
(3) $\forall a \in [0,1]$, $1 \blacklozenge a = 1 \times a = a$.
(4) $\forall a \in [0,1]$, $0 \blacklozenge a = 0 \times a = 0$.   □

Theorem 3. *Operator* $\odot : [0,1] \times [0,1] \rightarrow [0,1]$, *defined as follows, satisfies the properties listed in Definition 13:*

$$a_1 \odot a_2 = \frac{(a_1 - a_2)(2 - a_1 - a_2) + 1}{2}. \tag{20}$$

Proof. We prove that formula (20) satisfies the properties of operator ⊙, listed in Definition 13. Consider the two transformations of formulas as follows:

$$a_1 \odot a_2 = \frac{(a_1 - a_2)(2 - a_1 - a_2) + 1}{2} = \frac{(a_2 - 1)^2 - (a_1 - 1)^2 + 1}{2},$$

$$a_1 \odot a_2 = \frac{(a_1 - a_2)(2 - a_1 - a_2) + 1}{2} = \frac{(a_1 - a_2)(1 + a_3) + 1}{2}.$$

Table 1. Goals of the agent and their priorities in example one

g_1	The distance should be about 1 km	$\rho(g_1) = 0.7$
g_2	The price should be no more than 200 pounds per month	$\rho(g_2) = 0.5$
g_3	The size should be no less than 30 m^2	$\rho(g_3) = 0.3$
g_4	The rental-period should be about 6 months	$\rho(g_4) = 0.1$

where $a_3 = 1 - a_1 - a_2$. Thus:

(1) If $a_2 \leqslant a_2'$, then $(a_2 - 1)^2 \geqslant (a_2' - 1)^2$. Thus, $\frac{(a_2-1)^2-(a_1-1)^2+1}{2} \geqslant$ $\frac{(a_2'-1)^2-(a_1-1)^2+1}{2}$. Hence, $a_1 \odot a_2 \geqslant a_1 \odot a_2'$.

(2) If $a_1 \leqslant a_1'$, then $(a_1 - 1)^2 \geqslant (a_1' - 1)^2$. Thus, $\frac{(a_2-1)^2-(a_1-1)^2+1}{2} \leqslant$ $\frac{(a_2'-1)^2-(a_1-1)^2+1}{2}$. Hence, $a_1 \odot a_2 \leqslant a_1' \odot a_2$.

(3) If $a_1 - a_2 = a_1' - a_2' > 0$, $1 - a_1 - a_2 \leqslant 1 - a_1' - a_2'$, then $a_3 \leqslant a_3'$ and $(a_1-a_2)(1+a_3) \leqslant (a_1'-a_2')(1+a_3')$. Thus, $\frac{(a_1-a_2)(1+a_3)+1}{2} \leqslant \frac{(a_1'-a_2')(1+a_3')+1}{2}$. So, $a_1 \odot a_2 \leqslant a_1 \odot a_2'$.

(4) If $a_1 - a_2 = a_1' - a_2' < 0$, $1 - a_1 - a_2 \leqslant 1 - a_1' - a_2'$, then $a_3 \leqslant a_3'$ and $(a_1-a_2)(1+a_3) \geqslant (a_1'-a_2')(1+a_3')$. Thus, $\frac{(a_1-a_2)(1+a_3)+1}{2} \geqslant \frac{(a_1'-a_2')(1+a_3')+1}{2}$. So, $a_1 \odot a_2 \geqslant a_1 \odot a_2'$.

(5) $1 \odot 0 = \frac{(1-0)(2-1-0)+1}{2} = 1$.

(6) $0 \odot 1 = \frac{(0-1)(2-0-1)+1}{2} = 0$. □

5 Case Study

In this section, we illustrate our agent's offer evaluation method in a negotiation for accommodation renting. To make it easier to follow, in the first example, we will illustrate a special kind of buyer agent who has four goals but every goal involves one issue only. That is, these issues are independent of each other. However, our model can also deal with the goals that include more than one issue. So, in the second example, we give an agent which goals depend on interdependent issues.

5.1 Example One

Suppose a visiting student who is going to spend one year studying abroad will rent an accommodation near the university. We use a buyer agent to negotiate on behalf of the student. Suppose the agent takes four issues into consideration: distance (x_1), price (x_2), size (x_3), and rental-period (x_4) of the accommodation, and their domains are: $d_1 = [0,5]$(km), $d_2 = [200,500]$(pounds per month), $d_3 = [10,30]$(m^2), and $d_4 = [1,12]$(month), respectively.

The goals of the agent is represented in Table 1 and Figs. 1, 2, 3 and 4. The goals can be regarded as intuitionistic fuzzy constraints and different value

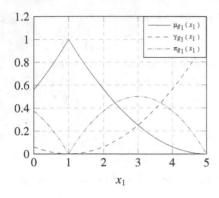

Fig. 1. Intuitionistic fuzzy constraint g_1

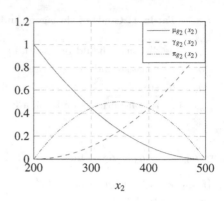

Fig. 2. Intuitionistic fuzzy constraint g_2

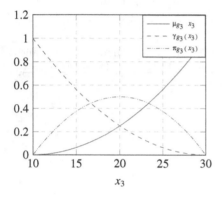

Fig. 3. Intuitionistic fuzzy constraint g_3

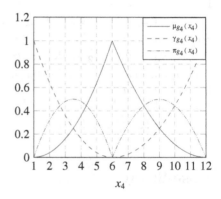

Fig. 4. Intuitionistic fuzzy constraint g_4

assignments to all relevant variables (*i.e.*, negotiation issues) will gain different membership degrees and nonmembership degrees, which represent the satisfaction degrees and dissatisfaction degrees of the goals, respectively. For example, in Fig. 1, the solid line indicates how the satisfaction degree of g_1 changes with distance; the dashed line shows how the dissatisfaction degree of g_1 changes with distance; and the dash-dotted line represent how the hesitation degree of g_1 changes with distance.

Suppose the student prefers to living near the university, where he can walk to the university quickly but he reluctantly lives too close to the university because he thinks walking is a good excise and fun, so he need enjoy a little bit. As a result, he feels that 1 Km is the ideal distance and 5 Km means absolutely too far, so he sets $\mu_{g_1}(1) = 1$, $\gamma_{g_1}(1) = 0$, $\mu_{g_1}(5) = 0$, and $\gamma_{g_1}(5) = 1$. However, he is not exactly sure whether or not $3\,\mathrm{Km}$ is suitable, so he sets a high hesitation degree of $x_1 = 3$ in g_1. On the basis of the analysis above, we can see that intuitionistic fuzzy sets are appropriate to represent the uncertain knowledge about negotiation goals. Similarly, we can understand Figs. 2, 3 and 4.

Now we see how the agent evaluates an offer according to our PIFCSP-based model. Suppose the agent receives an offer $o = (1.5, 250, 20, 6)$, which means an accommodation that is $1.5\,\mathrm{km}$ away from the university, costs 250 pounds per month, has the size of 20 m^2 and needs to be rented for at least 6 months. Firstly, we calculate the overall satisfaction degree of the offer. By formula (11) along with operator (18), we have:

$$\alpha_\rho(o) = \min\left\{(\mu_{g_1}(1.5) - 1)\frac{\rho(g_1)}{\rho_{\max}} + 1, (\mu_{g_2}(250) - 1)\frac{\rho(g_2)}{\rho_{\max}} + 1,\right.$$
$$\left.(\mu_{g_3}(20) - 1)\frac{\rho(g_3)}{\rho_{\max}} + 1, \mu_{g_4}(6)\frac{\rho(g_4)}{\rho_{\max}}\right\}$$
$$= \min\left\{(0.77 - 1)\frac{0.7}{0.7} + 1, (0.69 - 1)\frac{0.5}{0.7} + 1,\right.$$
$$\left.(0.25 - 1)\frac{0.3}{0.7} + 1, (1 - 1)\frac{0.1}{0.7} + 1\right\}$$
$$= \min\{0.77, 0.78, 0.68, 1\}$$
$$= 0.68.$$

Secondly, we calculate the overall dissatisfaction degree of the offer. By formula (12) along with operator (19), we have:

$$\beta_\rho(o) = \max\left\{\gamma_{g_1}(1.5)\frac{\rho(g_1)}{\rho_{\max}}, \gamma_{g_2}(250)\frac{\rho(g_2)}{\rho_{\max}}, \gamma_{g_3}(20)\frac{\rho(g_3)}{\rho_{\max}}, \gamma_{g_4}(6)\frac{\rho(g_4)}{\rho_{\max}}\right\}$$
$$= \max\left\{0.02 \times \frac{0.7}{0.7}, 0.03 \times \frac{0.5}{0.7}, 0.25 \times \frac{0.3}{0.7}, 0 \times \frac{0.1}{0.7}\right\}$$
$$= \max\{0.02, 0.02, 0.11, 0\}$$
$$= 0.11.$$

Finally, we calculate the acceptability of offer o. By formula (13) along with operator (20), we have:

$$A(o) = \alpha_\rho(o) \odot \beta_\rho(o)$$
$$= 0.68 \odot 0.11$$
$$= \frac{(0.68 - 0.11)(2 - 0.68 - 0.11) + 1}{2}$$
$$= 0.84.$$

Suppose the agent's acceptability threshold ζ is 0.6. Then the value of the acceptability of offer o is greater than the acceptability threshold. Therefore, the agent will accept offer $o = (1.5, 250, 20, 6)$.

Table 2. Goals of the agent and their priorities in example two

g'_1	The distance should be closed to the university and the price should be no more than 200 pounds per month	$\rho(g'_1) = 0.6$
g'_2	The size should be about 10 m^2 or the rental-period should be about 12 months	$\rho(g'_2) = 0.4$

5.2   Example Two

Suppose another buyer is in the similar situation, but has different goals. This buyer also takes four issues into consideration: distance (x_1), price (x_2), size (x_3), and rental-period (x_4). However, the buyer thinks that distance and price, size and rental-period are interdependent issues. The buyer demands the shortest distance away from the university together with price as low as possible, but does not mind the room size (*i.e.,* the size does not influence the satisfaction degree directly). However, after the buyer heard that smaller accommodation is easer to rent, the size becomes able to change the influence that the rental-period makes on the satisfaction degree. The buyer also prefers to a longer rental-period for convenience. Specifically, the goals of the buyer are shown in Table 2 and Figs. 5 and 6, where

$$\mu_{g'_1}(x_1, x_2) = \left(\frac{(x_1 - 5)(x_2 - 500)}{5 \times 300} \right)^2,$$

$$\gamma_{g'_1}(x_1, x_2) = \left(\frac{x_1(x_2 - 200)}{5 \times 300} \right)^2,$$

$$\mu_{g'_2}(x_3, x_4) = \sqrt{\frac{x_3 - 10}{20}} \times \left(\left(\frac{x_4 - 1}{11} \right)^2 - 1 \right) + 1,$$

$$\gamma_{g'_2}(x_3, x_4) = - \left(\frac{x_3 - 10}{20} \right)^2 \times \left(\sqrt{\frac{x_4 - 1}{11}} - 1 \right).$$

The functions above are just special cases that satisfy the buyer's demands in this example. Hence, a human user can choose the functions in the negotiating agent model that appropriately depicts their demands.

In Fig. 5, the surface indicates the satisfaction degree of the goal g'_1, which is effected by the assignment of values to the issues of distance and price, while the mesh indicates the dissatisfaction degree of the goal g'_1, and we can understand Fig. 6 similarly. We can see that both figures represent well the buyer's intuition about the relations between issues and their influence of satisfaction.

Next, we see how this new agent evaluates the same offer: $o = (1.5, 250, 20, 6)$. Firstly, we calculate the overall satisfaction degree of the offer. By formula (11) along with operator (18), we have:

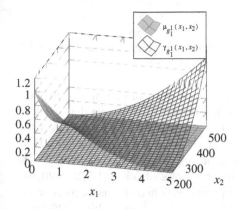

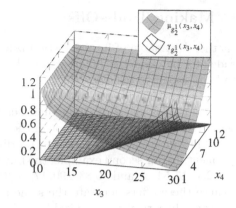

Fig. 5. Intuitionistic fuzzy constraint g_1'

Fig. 6. Intuitionistic fuzzy constraint g_2'

$$\alpha_\rho(o) = \min\left\{(\mu_{g_1'}(1.5, 250) - 1)\frac{\rho(g_1')}{\rho_{\max}} + 1, (\mu_{g_2'}(20, 6) - 1)\frac{\rho(g_2')}{\rho_{\max}} + 1\right\}$$

$$= \min\left\{(0.3403 - 1)\frac{0.6}{0.6} + 1, (0.4390 - 1)\frac{0.4}{0.6} + 1\right\}$$

$$= \min\{0.3403, 0.626\}$$

$$= 0.3403.$$

Secondly, we calculate the overall dissatisfaction degree of the offer. By formula (12) along with operator (19), we have:

$$\beta_\rho(o) = \max\left\{\gamma_{g_1'}(1.5, 250)\frac{\rho(g_1')}{\rho_{\max}}, \gamma_{g_2'}(20, 6)\frac{\rho(g_2')}{\rho_{\max}}\right\}$$

$$= \max\left\{0.0025 \times \frac{0.6}{0.6}, 0.0815 \times \frac{0.4}{0.6}\right\}$$

$$= \max\{0.0025, 0.0543\}$$

$$= 0.0543.$$

Finally, we calculate the acceptability of offer o. By formula (13) along with operator (20), we have:

$$A(o) = \alpha_\rho(o) \odot \beta_\rho(o)$$

$$= 0.3403 \odot 0.0543$$

$$= \frac{(0.3403 - 0.0543)(2 - 0.3403 - 0.0543) + 1}{2}$$

$$= 0.7296.$$

Suppose the new agent's acceptability threshold ζ is 0.6, then the value of the acceptability of offer o is greater than the acceptability threshold. Therefore, this new agent will also accept offer $o = (1.5, 250, 20, 6)$.

6 Making Trade-Offs

Another advantage of intuitionistic fuzzy constraints is that it is easy to model trade-offs between the different possible values for issues in a negotiation. A trade-off means a behavior that an agent lowers its value on some negotiation issues, while demands more on the other issues [7,16,17]. For example, a negotiating agent may choose an immediate service with lower quality or a delayed service with a higher quality. Although the two choices are undifferentiated in total utility for an agent, it may result in a different total utility for the negotiation opponent. In our second example, the buyer agent regards offers $(0.83, 290, 20, 6)$, $(1.5, 250, 17.54, 3)$ and $(0.83, 290, 17.54, 3)$ as trade-offs of offer $(1.5, 250, 20, 6)$, because these offers generate the same acceptability. Then it has become very important how to choose a suitable trade-off offer among all available candidates of trade-offs as a counter-offer. In this section, we will give a way to make this kind of trade-offs.

To choose the most suitable offer when making trade-offs, a negotiating agent should evaluate to what extent the new offer will be accepted by its opponent. If a negotiating agent can know the preference information about offers of its opponent, then it is easy to choose one that the opponent prefers the most. However, in negotiation normally parties are reluctant to reveal too much about their information. Thus, an alternative method is to generate an offer similar to the opponent's last proposal [7]. Thus, firstly we give the definition of similarity between two values as follows:

Definition 14. *Give a domain d_i of issue x_i in X, a similarity between two values $v_{x_i,1}, v_{x_i,2} \in d_i$ is defined as:*

$$
S_{x_i}(v_{x_i,1}, v_{x_i,2}) = 1 - \sqrt{\frac{(\mu_{h_i}(v_{x_i,1}) - \mu_{h_i}(v_{x_i,1}))^2 + (\gamma_{h_i}(v_{x_i,1}) - \gamma_{h_i}(v_{x_i,1}))^2}{2}},
\tag{21}
$$

where h_i means a criterion evaluation on an issue, and μ_{h_i} and γ_{h_i} represent the degrees that a value meet, and does not meet the criterion, respectively.

A criterion in Definition 14 describes a feature of an issue. For example, for the issue price, *low price* can be regarded as a criterion to distinguish different levels of price. More specifically, $\mu_{low\text{-}price}(100) = 0.6$ and $\gamma_{low\text{-}price}(100) = 0.2$ can be interpreted as the degree to which 100 pounds is a low price is 0.6, and the degree to which the money is not a low price is 0.2 for an agent in a certain situation, respectively.

Now, based on the above definition, we give the definition of similarity between two offers as follows:

Definition 15. *Given issue set $X = \{x_i \mid i = 1, \cdots, n\}$ and the domains set $D = \{d_i \mid i = 1, \cdots, n\}$, a similarity between two offers $o_1 = (v_{x_1,1}, \cdots, v_{x_n,1})$ and $o_2 = (v_{x_1,2}, \cdots, v_{x_n,2})$ is defined as*

$$
S_X(o_1, o_2) = \sum_{x_i \in X} w_{x_i} S_{x_i}(v_{x_i,1}, v_{x_i,2}),
\tag{22}
$$

where $(w_{x_i}, \cdots, w_{x_n})$ is a set of appropriate weights, representing the importance of issues in the computation of similarity, $\sum_{x_i \in X_i} w_{x_i} = 1$, and S_{x_i} is given by formula (21).

In order to make good use of trade-offs, the agent should propose an offer that not only has the same acceptability as the agent's previous offer, but also is the most similar to the opponent's proposal since this can increase the chance for getting it accepted [7]. To illustrate the modelling of similarity between offers and how to use it to making trade-offs, consider the second example in the last section. Given $o_1 = (0.83, 290, 20, 6)$, $o_2 = (1.5, 250, 17.54, 3)$ and $o_3 = (0.83, 290, 17.54, 3)$, by the acceptability calculation formula (13), we know these three offers have the same acceptability as offer $(1.5, 250, 20, 6)$. Suppose the opponent gives offer $o = (2, 300, 25, 3)$ in the previous round, then which one among the above three offers is the best offer for the agent to propose? We use the similarity between offers to solve this problem.

Similarity for distance, price, size and rental-period will each be based on criteria: *short distance (sd)*, *low price (lp)*, *small size (ss)*, and *short time (st)*, respectively. These will also be modelled as follows:

$$\begin{cases} \mu_{sd}(v_{x_1}) = \frac{1}{25}(v_{x_1})^2 & \text{if } v_{x_1} \in [0,5], \\ \gamma_{sd}(v_{x_1}) = \frac{1}{25}(v_{x_1} - 5)^2 & \text{if } v_{x_1} \in [0,5]. \end{cases} \begin{cases} \mu_{lp}(v_{x_2}) = \frac{1}{300^2}(v_{x_2} - 200)^2, & \text{if } v_{x_2} \in [200,500], \\ \gamma_{lp}(v_{x_2}) = \frac{1}{300^2}(v_{x_2} - 500)^2, & \text{if } v_{x_2} \in [200,500]. \end{cases}$$

$$\begin{cases} \mu_{ss}(v_{x_3}) = \frac{1}{20^2}(v_{x_3} - 10), & \text{if } v_{x_1} \in [10,30], \\ \gamma_{ss}(v_{x_3}) = \frac{1}{20^2}(v_{x_3} - 30)^2 2, & \text{if } v_{x_1} \in [10,30]. \end{cases} \begin{cases} \mu_{st}(v_{x_4}) = \frac{1}{11^2}(v_{x_4} - 1)^2, & \text{if } v_{x_4} \in [1,12], \\ \gamma_{st}(v_{x_4}) = \frac{1}{11^2}(v_{x_4} - 12)^2, & \text{if } v_{x_4} \in [1,12]. \end{cases}$$

Finally, we assume the following weights: $w_{x_1} = 0.25$, $w_{x_2} = 0.25$, $w_{x_3} = 0.25$, and $w_{x_4} = 0.25$.

By formula (21), we have:

$$S_{x_1}(0.83, 2) = 1 - \sqrt{\frac{(\mu_{sd}(0.83) - \mu_{sd}(2))^2 + (\gamma_{sd}(0.83) - \gamma_{sd}(2))^2}{2}} = 0.74,$$

$$S_{x_2}(290, 300) = 1 - \sqrt{\frac{(\mu_{lp}(290) - \mu_{lp}(300))^2 + (\gamma_{lp}(290) - \gamma_{lp}(300))^2}{2}} = 0.96,$$

$$S_{x_3}(20, 25) = 1 - \sqrt{\frac{(\mu_{ss}(20) - \mu_{ss}(25))^2 + (\gamma_{ss}(20) - \gamma_{ss}(25))^2}{2}} = 0.74,$$

$$S_{x_4}(6, 3) = 1 - \sqrt{\frac{(\mu_{st}(6) - \mu_{st}(3))^2 + (\gamma_{st}(6) - \gamma_{st}(3))^2}{2}} = 0.71.$$

Then, by formula (22), we have:

$$S_X(o_1, o) = 0.25 \times 0.74 + 0.25 \times 0.96 + 0.25 \times 0.74 + 0.25 \times 0.71 = 0.7875.$$

Similarly, we can obtain $S_X(o_2, o) = 0.8325$, $S_X(o_3, o) = 0.8300$. Because $S_X(o_2, o) > S_X(o_3, o) > S_X(o_1, o)$, it is better for the agent to choose o_2 as a counter-offer in the next negotiation round.

7   Related Work

In this section, we discuss the related work to confirm the contributions of this paper. More specifically, we will mainly examine the work related to offer evaluation and the work of fuzzy approach based automated negotiation models.

Many bilateral multi-issue negotiation models have been developed and several methods for offer evaluation are also proposed in different settings. Some of them are based on linear utility functions of issues, some of them are based on constraints upon interdependent issues, and so on. The work closest to ours is that of Luo et al. [17], which proposes a fuzzy constraint based model in semi-competitive negotiation environments. In their model, prioritised fuzzy constraints are used to represent a buyer's requirements on offers and the evaluation of an offer is regards as a prioritised fuzzy constraint satisfaction problem. However, their method just considers the satisfaction degree and neglects the hesitation of human users when they judge an offer is satisfactory or not. Rather, by using intuitionistic fuzzy constraints as negotiating agents' goals, our model does not suffer the problem. Moreover, their agent makes trade-offs just based on the agent's constraints, however, our agent does this by considering not only the acceptability of an offer, but also the similarity with the opponent's offer.

Ito et al. [11] consider negotiating agents with nonlinear utility functions, which is defined in terms of constraints based on interdependent issues. That is, when an offer falls within the region of a constraint, the constraint has a value and the value should be added into the utility of the offer. They propose a bidding-based negotiation protocol to deal with a negotiation of this kind. Later, in [9], Hadfi and Ito provide a hyper-graphical representation for nonlinear utility spaces by adopting a modular decomposition of the issues and the constraints, which can reduce the complexity based on power-law topologies. Compared to the above studies, our model has the following advantages: (i) we handle the importance of different constraints in the offer evaluation, but they did not; (ii) we distinguish different levels of satisfaction and dissatisfaction of constraints, rather they only represent whether or not a constraint is totally satisfied; and (iii) we also consider the hesitation situation where human users have no accurate understanding about the satisfaction of constraints, while their work did not.

Zhan et al. [26] propose two offer evaluation methods for the case where the utilities of policies are not represented by precise numbers. The first one is used to model humans? reasoning about how to calculate concessional utilities from uncertain preference information based on fuzzy reasoning, while the second one is used to measure similarity between an offer and the ideal state based on a prioritised consistency degree. Although the ideal state of an offer could be regarded as a special goal, there is a strong assumption that issues are independent. However, our model in this paper can be applied to the case of interdependent issues. Moreover, in their method, the evaluation criteria are fixed and the ideal state of one issue is a criterion. However, our method can evaluate the same offer through different perspectives. For example, when buying a product, some people are used to evaluating an offer from two independent criteria, price and delivery time, and integrate two evaluation results finally.

Rather, some people are inclined to evaluate an offer through only one criterion, because they think the price and the delivery time are interdependent. In
our negotiating agent proposed in this paper, prioritised intuitionistic fuzzy constraints are suitable to depict different users' perspectives. In addition, we give
an approach of making trade-offs when using our agent models, but they do not.

Some researchers also studied offer acceptance conditions in automated negotiation. For example, in the work of [4], Baarslag et al. systematically classify
some common generic conditions of offer acceptance, which are mainly based
on the criteria related to the utility generated by agent's previous offer or next
offer and so on. Moreover, they propose new acceptance conditions, combined
acceptance conditions, based on the idea that split the negotiation into different
intervals of time and apply different conditions to each interval. However, what
we focus on in this paper is the evaluation of offers, i.e., how the acceptability
of an offer is calculated, rather than offer acceptance conditions. Moreover, in
their model, the agents' preferences are modelled by means of a utility function,
while ours are represented by prioritised intuitionistic fuzzy constraints.

Fuzzy constraints are also applied in some e-markets systems. For example,
Le et al. [15] develop a relaxation strategy with fuzzy constraints to select a
potential power supplier through a broker. In their model, they use prioritised
fuzzy constraints to present trade-offs between the different possible values of
attributes. Different from their application of fuzzy constraints, one of our contributions is that we extend the framework of prioritised fuzzy constraints [18,24]
to the one of prioritised intuitionistic fuzzy constraints, which can represent
not only the degrees of satisfaction and dissatisfaction, but also the hesitation
degree. So, our method can deal with both human user's language fuzziness and
uncertain information, which they cannot do well.

In addition to fuzzy constraints, argumentation is also a popular approach
to model proposals in automated negotiation. Argumentation-based negotiation
frameworks enable agents to not only exchange offers, but also justify their proposals and persuade the opponents, which may affect the preference of the opponent and change their decisions [10,23]. For example, Mbarki et al. [22] propose
an argumentative negotiating agent equipped with two negotiation strategies,
concession strategies and acceptance strategies, and distinguish different agent
types according to their strategies. They also use constraints to analyse the
agent's satisfaction. Marey et al. [21] apply Shannon entropy to measure the
certainty index of the negotiation dialogue games and give both the goodness
metric and fairness metric to measure how good and how fair the agents are in
a negotiation, respectively. Marey et al. [20] propose new measures of agents'
uncertainty about the exchanged arguments in a negotiation dialogue game.
Similar to our work of offer evaluation, Amgoud and Vesic [1] propose a formal
analysis of the outcomes in argumentation-based negotiations and give two kinds
of optimal solutions.

8   Conclusion

This paper studied how to evaluate offers in bilateral multi-issue negotiations. Firstly, we proposed the framework of prioritised intuitionistic fuzzy constraint satisfaction. Secondly, we introduced a negotiating agent model which goals are represented as intuitionistic fuzzy constraints, and thus, the evaluation of an offer is regards as a prioritised fuzzy constraint satisfaction problem. So, our method of offer evaluation takes into account two aspects of evaluation of the same criterion, *i.e.*, the degree of satisfaction and the degree of dissatisfaction. In addition, we gave two examples of buyer agents in an accommodation renting scenario to illustrate how our model works and showed that our method can also be applied to both the cases of independent and interdependent multi-issues. Finally, we gave a way to make trade-offs via calculating similarity to the opponent's offers based on intuitionistic fuzzy criterion.

Acknowledgments. This research is supported by the Bairen Plan of Sun Yat-sen University and the National Fund of Social Science (No. 13BZX066).

References

1. Amgoud, L., Vesic, S.: A formal analysis of the outcomes of argumentation-based negotiations. In: Proceedings of the 10th International Conference on Autonomous Agents and Multiagent Systems, pp. 1237–1238 (2011)
2. Atanassov, K.T.: Intuitionistic fuzzy sets. Fuzzy Sets Syst. **20**(1), 87–96 (1986)
3. Baarslag, T., Fujita, K., Gerding, E.H., Hindriks, K., Ito, T., Jennings, N.R., Jonker, C., Kraus, S., Lin, R., Robu, V., et al.: Evaluating practical negotiating agents: results and analysis of the 2011 international competition. Artif. Intell. **198**, 73–103 (2013)
4. Baarslag, T., Hindriks, K., Jonker, C.: Acceptance conditions in automated negotiation. In: Ito, T., Zhang, M., Robu, V., Matsuo, T. (eds.) Complex Automated Negotiations: Theories, Models, and Software Competitions. SCI, vol. 435, pp. 95–111. Springer, Heidelberg (2012)
5. Cao, M., Luo, X., Luo, X.R., Dai, X.: Automated negotiation for e-commerce decision making: a goal deliberated agent architecture for multi-strategy selection. Decis. Support Syst. **73**, 1–14 (2015)
6. Davis, R., Smith, R.G.: Negotiation as a metaphor for distributed problem solving. Artif. Intell. **20**(1), 63–109 (1983)
7. Faratin, P., Sierra, C., Jennings, N.R.: Using similarity criteria to make issue trade-offs in automated negotiations. Artif. Intell. **142**(2), 205–237 (2002)
8. Fujita, K., Ito, T., Klein, M.: Efficient issue-grouping approach for multiple interdependent issues negotiation between exaggerator agents. Decis. Support Syst. **60**, 10–17 (2014)
9. Hadfi, R., Ito, T.: On the complexity of utility hypergraphs. In: Fukuta, N., Ito, T., Zhang, M., Fujita, K., Robu, V. (eds.) Recent Advances in Agent-based Complex Automated Negotiation. SCI, vol. 638, pp. 89–105. Springer, Heidelberg (2016)
10. Hadidi, N., Dimopoulos, Y., Moraitis, P.: Argumentative alternating offers. In: Proceedings of the 9th International Conference on Autonomous Agents and Multiagent Systems, pp. 441–448 (2010)

11. Ito, T., Hattori, H., Klein, M., Multi-issue negotiation protocol for agents: exploring nonlinear utility spaces. In: Proceedings of the 20th International Joint Conference on Artificial Intelligence, pp. 1347–1352 (2007)
12. Jennings, N.R., Faratin, P., Lomuscio, A.R., Parsons, S., Wooldridge, M.J., Sierra, C.: Automated negotiation: prospects, methods and challenges. Group Decis. Negot. **10**(2), 199–215 (2001)
13. Klein, M., Faratin, P., Sayama, H., Bar-Yam, Y.: Negotiating complex contracts. Group Decis. Negot. **12**(2), 111–125 (2003)
14. Kumar, V.: Algorithms for constraint-satisfaction problems: a survey. AI Mag. **13**(1), 32 (1992)
15. Le, D.T., Zhang, M., Ren, F.: A relaxation strategy with fuzzy constraints for supplier selection in a power market. In: Bai, Q., Ren, F., Zhang, M., Ito, T., Tang, X. (eds.) Smart Modeling Simulation for Complex Systems: Practice and Theory. SCI, vol. 564, pp. 83–97. Springer, Heidelberg (2015)
16. Luo, X., Jennings, N.R., Shadbolt, N.: Acquiring user tradeoff strategies and preferences for negotiating agents: a default-then-adjust method. Int. J. Hum.-Comput. Stud. **64**(4), 304–321 (2006)
17. Luo, X., Jennings, N.R., Shadbolt, N., Leung, H.-F., Lee, J.H.-M.: A fuzzy constraint based model for bilateral, multi-issue negotiations in semi-competitive environments. Artif. Intell. **148**(1), 53–102 (2003)
18. Luo, X., Lee, J.H.-M., Leung, H.-F., Jennings, N.R.: Prioritised fuzzy constraint satisfaction problems: axioms, instantiation and validation. Fuzzy Sets Syst. **136**(2), 151–188 (2003)
19. Luo, X., Miao, C., Jennings, N.R., He, M., Shen, Z., Zhang, M.: KEMNAD: a knowledge engineering methodology for negotiating agent development. Comput. Intell. **28**(1), 51–105 (2012)
20. Marey, O., Bentahar, J., Dssouli, R., Mbarki, M.: Measuring and analyzing agents uncertainty in argumentation-based negotiation dialogue games. Expert Syst. Appl. **41**(2), 306–320 (2014)
21. Marey, O., Bentahar, J., En-Nouaary, A.: On the measurement of negotiation dialogue games. In: Proceedings of the International Conference on Intelligent Software Methodologies, Tools and Techniques, pp. 223–244 (2009)
22. Mbarki, M., Marey, O., Bentahar, J., Sultan, K.: Agent types and adaptive negotiation strategies in argumentation-based negotiation. In: Proceedings of the 26th International Conference on Tools with Artificial Intelligence, pp. 485–492 (2014)
23. Rahwan, I., Ramchurn, S.D., Jennings, N.R., Mcburney, P., Parsons, S., Sonenberg, L.: Argumentation-based negotiation. Knowl. Eng. Rev. **18**(04), 343–375 (2003)
24. Ruttkay, Z.: Fuzzy constraint satisfaction. In: Proceedings of the Third IEEE Conference on Fuzzy Systems, pp. 1263–1268 (1994)
25. Zadeh, L.A.: Information and control. Fuzzy Sets **8**(3), 338–353 (1965)
26. Zhan, J., Zhang, M., Ren, F., Luo, X.: A negotiation-based model for policy generation. In: Proceedings of the 8th International Workshop on Agent-Based Complex Automated Negotiation, pp. 50–57 (2015)

Analyzing Topics and Trends
in the PRIMA Literature

Hoa Khanh Dam[✉] and Aditya Ghose

School of Computing and Information Technology, University of Wollongong,
Wollongong, NSW 2522, Australia
{hoa,aditya}@uow.edu.au

Abstract. This study investigates the content of the literature published in the proceedings of the International Conference on Principles and Practices of Multi-Agent Systems (PRIMA). Our study is based on a corpus of the 611 papers published in eighteen PRIMA proceedings from 1998 (when the conference started) to 2015. We have developed an unsupervised topic model, using Latent Dirichlet Allocation (LDA), over the PRIMA corpus of papers to analyze popular topics in the literature published at PRIMA in the past eighteen years. We have also analyzed historical trends and examine the strength of each topic over time.

1 Introduction

Since the 1980s, agent technology has attracted an increasing amount of interest from the research and business communities. As a result, several international forums were established for researchers and industry practitioners to meet and share their work in the areas of autonomous agents and multi-agent systems. To promote further interactions for the agent community in the Asia Pacific region, the Pacific Rim International Workshop on Multi-Agents (PRIMA) was introduced in 1998. The PRIMA series were held every year since then. In 2009, PRIMA became a full-fledged international conference, namely International Conference on Principle and Practice of Multi-Agent Systems[1]. PRIMA has now emerged as one of the reputable forum for researchers, developers, and industry leaders who are interested agent technology and its practices.

Over the past 18 years, a large number of papers have been published in PRIMA, creating a rich literature for the research and practice of multi-agent systems. This published literature provides an opportunity to understand the history and the current state of multi-agent research within the PRIMA community. Analyzing this literature produce insights regarding the motivation, the development of ideas and progress, and the current problems and questions that are relevant to the PRIMA community. Such a study also helps us understand how the research landscape of multi-agent systems in general has changed and shifted focus over the past 18 years.

---

[1] The conference's abbreviation is still PRIMA.

© Springer International Publishing Switzerland 2016
M. Baldoni et al. (Eds.): PRIMA 2016, LNAI 9862, pp. 216–229, 2016.
DOI: 10.1007/978-3-319-44832-9_13

Studying the history of an entire scientific field or community is however challenging due to the substantial amount of time and effort needed for collecting, processing, and analyzing the data. Most of existing work leverage quantitative methods which are based on publication citations (e.g. scientometrics and bibliometrics [6, 7, 12, 14]). Since those studies look only into citation-related phenomena, they cannot provide insights to the actual content of the published literature. Manual content analysis however is not suitable for large, field-wide studies since the amount of manual effort required does not scale with the substantial data.

Advances in machine learning and natural language processing provides us with a number of useful techniques which are able to automatically summarize and extract meaning from textual data. For example, the topic model approach [1,4,18] has the ability to find the underlying latent topics, or groups of related words that are commonly used in a collection of documents. This can be done in an automatic, unsupervised manner, which is suitable for studying large amounts of data such as the PRIMA literature.

In this paper, we propose a method to understand the historical and current trends in the papers published in PRIMA since 1998 until 2015. Using the topic modeling approach, we aim to answer the following research questions:

- *RQ1: What are the popular topics published in PRIMA?*
  Multi-agent system research is a large and diverse field. There are many sub-fields such as logic and reasoning, engineering multi-agent systems, agent-based modeling and simulation, collaboration and coordination, human-agent interaction, decentralized paradigms, and applications of multi-agent systems. Within each of these sub-fields, there are a wide range of topics. For example, the logic and reasoning sub-field includes topics such as logics of agency, logics of multi-agent systems, norms, argumentation, computational game theory, and multi-agent learning. Hence, answering this question help us identify which topics are the most interested in the PRIMA community. This insight would be useful for both new and existing members of the community in submitting their contribution.
- *RQ2: What are the temporal trends of topics over time?*
  This question seeks to examine the historical trends of the popularity of topics in PRIMA. Specifically, we aim to determine which topics have risen and faded over the years. The trend analysis also helps in reasoning about the rise or fall of certain topics in the PRIMA community. The identification of topic trends can help researchers identify prominent research areas and proceed with further incremental research on those areas.

The paper is organized is as follows. In the next section, we will discuss our methodology for studying the history of PRIMA literature. We then present our findings in Sect. 3. Section 4 serves to discuss related work before we conclude and outline our future work in Sect. 5.

2   Methodology

In this section, we will discuss how we collected, processed and analyzed the data.

2.1   Dataset

PRIMA has been held every year since its inception in 1998 as workshop (PRIMA has become an international conference since 2009). All of the proceedings of the 18 editions (from 1998 to 2015) were published with Springer. Table 1 shows the number of papers and pages published in the PRIMA proceedings at each year. We included both full and short papers published in the proceedings. During the first six years of PRIMA, the number of papers published in the PRIMA proceedings were small (13–17 papers). There was a significant increase in 2006 when the number of papers peaked at 98. After that year, the number of papers fluctuated around 40 (although there was an exception in 2012 with only 16 papers published in the proceedings).

Table 1. PRIMA proceedings from 1998 – 2015

Year	# Papers	# Pages	Year	# Papers	# Pages
1998	13	184	2007	49	478
1999	16	242	2008	44	404
2000	13	181	2009	52	656
2001	16	236	2010	33	474
2002	15	219	2011	42	531
2003	17	213	2012	16	242
2004	24	328	2013	43	533
2005	31	407	2014	36	462
2006	98	824	2015	53	703
Total	611 papers containing 7,317 pages				

In total, we collected 611 papers which contain 7,317 pages in PDF format. This collection forms the *PRIMA corpus* used for our study. In the next subsection, we will discuss how these papers were preprocessed to extract the textual data.

2.2   Preprocessing

We used Apache PDFBox[2] to extract the text from the PDF version of each paper in our dataset. The extracted text includes the title, abstract and the

---

[2] https://pdfbox.apache.org.

main content of the paper. The reference list at the end of a paper was filtered out since it does not really reflect the actual content of the paper. In addition, the non-content materials such as the name of the conference, publisher, and editors were also removed.

Textual preprocessing were also performed to remove common English language stop words (such as "a", "the", "it", etc.), remove all hyphons (i e treating hyphenated words as individual words, remove all whitespaces, remove numbers, and remove punctuation.

2.3   Topic Modeling

The preprocessing procedure provided us with a set of words contained in each paper. The unique words from all of the papers in our PRIMA corpus form the *vocabulary* of the model. We used the popular Latent Dirichlet Allocation (LDA) [5] technique for building a probabilistic topic model over our corpus of PRIMA papers. Topic modeling automatically extract *topics* from a corpus of text documents. A topic here refers to a group of words that co-occur *frequently* in the documents of the corpus. The words in a topic are therefore *semantically* related.

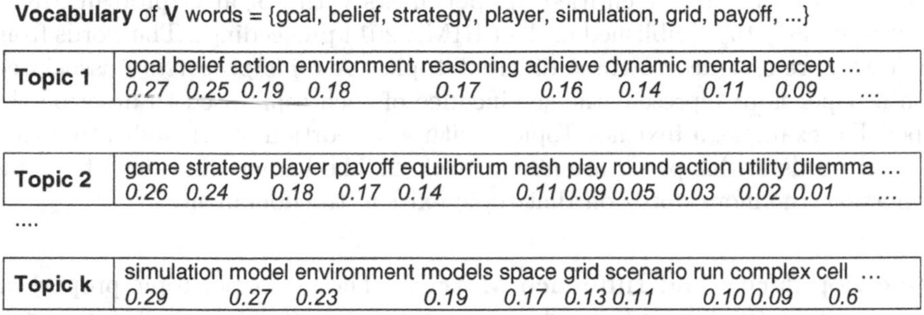

Vocabulary of **V** words = {goal, belief, strategy, player, simulation, grid, payoff, ...}

Topic 1	goal belief action environment reasoning achieve dynamic mental percept ...
	0.27 0.25 0.19 0.18 0.17 0.16 0.14 0.11 0.09 ...

Topic 2	game strategy player payoff equilibrium nash play round action utility dilemma ...
	0.26 0.24 0.18 0.17 0.14 0.11 0.09 0.05 0.03 0.02 0.01 ...

.....

Topic k	simulation model environment models space grid scenario run complex cell ...
	0.29 0.27 0.23 0.19 0.17 0.13 0.11 0.10 0.09 0.6

Fig. 1. Topic and word selection

A topic is described using a number of different words drawn from the vocabulary. Each word in the vocabulary has a different weight (reflecting its frequency) in describing a given topic. For example, Topic 1 in Fig. 1 is described by words such as goals, belief, action, environment, reasoning, achieve, dynamic, mental, and percepts. Each word in a topic has a different frequency usage (or weight), indicating the probability that the word is used to describe the topic. For example, when a word is drawn from Topic 1, there is a 27 % chance of drawing the word "goal" and a 25 % chance of drawing the word "belief" (see Fig. 1).

A paper is comprised of various combination of these topics. Hence, each paper went through the topic assignment process where each word in the paper was assigned to a topic which contains it. For example, Fig. 2 shows a text

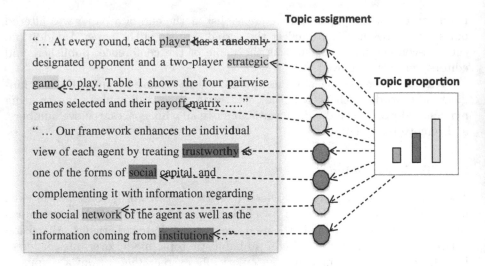

Fig. 2. An example of topic assignment and proportion

extracted from the paper entitled "Experiments with Social Capital in Multi-agent Systems" [15]) published in the PRIMA 2014 proceedings. The words from this text were assigned to three different topics. A *topic proportion* associated with a paper is to represent the significance of each topic used to describe the paper. For example, a text has Topic 2 with a proportion of 0.1, indicating that 10 % all words in this paper are about Topic 2. The higher the value of a topic proportion, the more words on that topic exist in the document.

Topic Popularity and Influence Metrics. The per-paper topic proportion for paper d is denoted as θ_d, and we use it to compute the popularity metric of a topic. Specifically, if the topic proportion of a given topic is high among a number of papers, this topic is regarded as popular [18]. We use $\theta(d, z)$ to denote the proportion of topic z in paper d (noting that $0 \leq \theta(d, z) \leq 1$). We define the overall popularity of a topic z across all papers as:

$$popularity(z) = \frac{1}{|D|} \sum_{d \in D} \theta(d, z)$$

where D is the entire set of all papers in our dataset. The popularity metric measures the proportion of papers that contain the topic z. This metric allows us to measure the relative popularity of a topic across all the papers.

We are also interested in examining temporal trends in the PRIMA literature over time. The basic LDA, however, does not explicitly model how the usage of a topic changes over time. There have been several extensions to the basic LDA to model such temporal relationships. For example, the Dynamic Topic Model [3] represents time as a discrete Markov process, where topics evolve according to a normal distribution. This model therefore discourages fast fluctuation in the topics over time by giving high penalties to abrupt changes from year to year. Another extension is the Topics Over Time Model (TOT) [20] which represents time as a continuous beta distribution and assumes that each document selects its own time stamp. Although the TOT model does not penalize on abrupt changes (as done in the Dynamic Topic Model), it is still relatively inflexible due to its constraint that a topic evolution will not have multiple rises and falls during the corpus history.

Since both of these models impose constraints on the time periods, we adapted the model proposed in [10] by doing post hoc calculation of temporal trends. Specifically, we apply LDA to the entire collection of PRIMA papers at the same time, and then perform post hoc calculations based on the observed probability of each topic in a given year. We define the *influence* metric $influence(z, y)$ of a topic z in year y as below:

$$influence(z, y) = \frac{1}{|D(y)|} \sum_{d \in D(y)} \theta(d, z)$$

where $D(y)$ is the set of all papers in year y. The influence metric measures the relative proportion of papers related to a topic compared to the other topics in a given year.

We use the influence metric to analyze the temporal trends of topics. Specifically, we use the Cox Stuart trend test [8] to determine if each topic's influence metric is significantly (i.e. using the standard 95 % confidence level) *increasing* or *decreasing* over time. The Cox Stuart trend test computes the differences between the earlier observations and the later observations to assess whether there is an increasing or decreasing trend. The magnitudes of the differences are used to determine if the trend is statistically significant using the standard 95 % confidence level (i.e. p-value ≤ 0.05). The Cox-Stuart test is very robust for the trend analysis and it is thus applicable to a wide variety of situations to understand the evolution of observations.

LDA Implementation. There is a number of user-specified parameters in LDA. The most important one is the number of topics K which dictates the granularity of the extracted topics. Smaller values of K will lead to coarser grained, more general topics. On the other hand, large values of K will result in finer-grained, more detailed topics. Previous studies (e.g. [19]) have demonstrated that there is no single value of K suitable in all domains and all data. Our study looks for topics of medium granularity which not only are distinct from each other but also cover the broad trends in the PRIMA literature. After a number of experiments with different values, we set K to 100 which meet our requirements.

We used MALLET 2.0.7 [13], an implementation of LDA. MALLET implements the Gibbs sampling algorithm [9]. We ran MALLET for 1000 Gibbs sampling iterations to stablize the Gibbs sampling algorithm. We also chosen the option for hyperparameter optimization every 20 iterations, which allows the model to better fit the data by allowing some topics to be more prominent than others.

3   Results

In this section, we present the results of applying our research methodology on the PRIMA dataset.

3.1   RQ1: What Are the Popular Topics Published in PRIMA?

A range of words are commonly used in research paper such as section, figure, abstract, etc. Those words form a number of topics that have very high popular score. Thus, we exclude those topics from our consideration. Tables 2, 3, 4, and 5 list the top 40 topics (based on their popularity score) discovered by our methodology from the PRIMA collection of papers. For each topic, we also list the top ten most frequent words in the tables. Note that we hand-assigned the name for each topic. According to our study, the top three most popular topics in PRIMA literature is "Distributed Constraint Optimization", "Computational Game Theory" and "Negotiation". In order to distinguish these three topics, we present here 50 of the strongly weighted words:

– **Distributed Constraint Optimization:** *algorithm problem solution algorithms optimal problems function search approach set distributed solutions graph step time results find local number functions global solving solve optimization space approaches large constraints procedure required size min cost complexity finding good update computed result feasible compute quality total computation improve end figure heuristic computational techniques*
– **Computational Game Theory:** *game strategy player strategies players risk games payoff equilibrium nash play round action payoffs actions pure mixed utility chooses choose theory repeated outcome matrix dilemma fuzzy choosing rep rational strategic multi-agent prisoner profile playing set rounds expected making equilibria function response fig outcomes decision-making dominant decision behavioral shown opponent infinitely*
– **Negotiation:** *negotiation utility offer strategy issues agreement strategies negotiations opponent offers functions negotiating preferences search issue bids space concession proposed bid negotiate accept based multi-issue automated time opponents scenarios region reach agreements utilities protocol bilateral preference proposal deadline contract constraints agent function point anac mediator figure scenario stage outcomes contracts reached*

Table 2. Top 1–10 topics

ID	Topic name	Top 10 LDA words
61	Distributed Constraint Optimization	Algorithm problem solution optimal function search approach set distributed graph
83	Computational game theory	Game strategy player risk game payoff equilibrium nash play round
15	Negotiation	Negotiation utility offer strategy issues agreement opponent offers functions negotiating
22	Web search	Web information query search user documents retrieval results document pages
44	MAS development	Mas development software methodology engineering process requirements models tool system
71	Human-agent interaction	User interface human people application personal mind module home his/her
99	Agent communication	Message protocol interaction messages protocols communication acl fipa send language
25	Multi-agent reasoning	Action state system behaviour transition internal set rules model systems
73	BDI architecture	Plan agent plans intention intentions action execution bdi goal actions
53	Ubiquitous computing	Sensor context ubiquitous environment sensors service manager sensing situation devices

The five papers with the highest weights for the topic "Distributed Constraint Optimization" include:

- Tan, Zhang, Xing, Zhang, Wang. An Improved Multi-agent Approach for Solving Large Traveling Salesman Problem (PRIMA 2006).
- Smith, Sen, Mailler. Adaptive and Non-adaptive Distribution Functions for DSA (PRIMA 2010).
- Wack, Okimoto, Clement, Inoue. Local Search Based Approximate Algorithm for Multi-Objective DCOPs (PRIMA 2014).
- Hirayama, Hanada, Ueda, Yokoo, Iwasaki. Computing a Payoff Division in the Least Core for MC-nets Coalitional Games (PRIMA 2014).
- Duc, Dinh, Xuan. On the Pheromone Update Rules of Ant Colony Optimization Approaches for the Job Shop Scheduling Problem (PRIMA 2008).

Table 3. Top 11–20 topics

ID	Topic name	Top 10 LDA words
35	Ontology for agents	Ontology semantic concepts knowledge concept language temporal ontologies reasoning object
50	Agent programming	Goal goals belief action agent beliefs actions rules base programs
27	Service-oriented computing	Service services web composition provider execution model providers client requests
67	Simulation	Simulation model simulations environment models space grid scenarios simulator behaviors
78	Social network	Network networks nodes node degree cluster links distribution social neighbors
70	Pervasive computing	Node nodes tree number strategy path memory graph message routing
69	Task scheduling and allocation	Task tasks scheduling allocation time subtasks multiagent subtask quality schedule
36	Traffic applications	Traffic road vehicle vehicles route simulation congestion simulator driving data
88	Argumentation	Argumentation argument arguments knowledge dialogue justified logic base dialectical issue
56	Modelling system dynamics	Parameter parameters error estimation values variables estimated equation equations variable

Some of the papers with the highest weights for the topic "Computational Game Theory" include:

- Lam, Leung. Risk Strategies and Risk Strategy Equilibrium in Agent Interactions Modeled as Normal Repeated 2 2 Risk Games (PRIMA 2005)
- Lam, Leung. Existence of Risk Strategy Equilibrium in Games Having No Pure Strategy Nash Equilibrium (PRIMA 2007).
- Lam, Leung. Formalizing Risk Strategies and Risk Strategy Equilibrium in Agent Interactions Modeled as Infinitely Repeated Games (PRIMA 2006).
- Wu, Soo. A Fuzzy Game Theoretic Approach to Multi-Agent Coordination (PRIMA 1998).
- Zhang, Liu. A Momentum-Based Approach to Learning Nash Equilibria (PRIMA 2006).

The five papers with the highest weights for the topic "Negotiation" are:

- Lopez-Carmona, Marsa-Maestre, Hoz, Velasco. NegoExplorer: A Region-Based Recursive Approach to Bilateral Multi-attribute Negotiation (PRIMA 2009)

Table 4. Top 21 – 30 topics

ID	Topic name	Top LDA words
14	Auctioning	Auction bid auctions price bidding bidder mechanism protocol bids auctioneer
29	Artificial evolution	Social model level cognitive behaviour individual people individuals simulation population
96	Business processes	Process interaction processes activities management business individual knowledge events activity
89	Institutions and organizations	Role roles organization organizational mas organizations adaptive dynamic dynamics interaction
32	Distributed constraint satisfaction	Constraint constraints variables problem problems message dcop distributed variable messages
48	Models of emotions	Emotion emotional emotions facial expressions switching human expression pause face
43	Recommender systems	Recommendation users tag user tags items filtering collaborative data document
21	Mechanism design	Price buyer seller market buyers profit sellers demand agents adaptive
28	Agent-based modeling	Model data gama simulation emergent models building agent-based environment agents
37	Logics	Logic worlds world preference belief judgment rule modal object aggregation

- Al-Jaljouli, Abawajy. Negotiation Strategy for Mobile Agent-Based e-Negotiation (PRIMA 2010)
- Fujita. Compromising Adjustment Based on Conflict Mode for Multi-times Bilateral Closed Nonlinear Negotiations (PRIMA 2014).
- Morii, Ito. Agent as Strategy in Multiple-Issue Negotiation Competition and Analysis of Result (PRIMA 2013).
- Baarslag, Hindriks, Jonker. Towards a Quantitative Concession-Based Classification Method of Negotiation Strategies (PRIMA 2011).

The majority of the top 40 topics are related to the theory and principle of multi-agent systems such as constraint optimization, reasoning, BDI architecture, argumentation and logic. However, our findings also show the popularity of some application-oriented topics such as robotics, ubiquitous computing, service-oriented computing, traffic applications, business processes, and recommender systems.

Table 5. Top 31 – 40 topics

ID	Topic name	Top LDA words
49	Learning	Learning reward learn action figure reinforcement state function case learned
92	Resource allocation	Resource resources allocation utility protocol process agents optimal time rational
77	Security	Security key scheme secret certificate server message authentication secure communication
93	Mobile agents	Mobile control message location component messages distributed network light move migration
17	Autonomous systems	Collision avoidance moving direction target area goal path position distance obstacle
10	Social grouping	Group agents groups members leader partition enforcement behaviour abstraction individual
41	Defeasible logics	Rules rule defeasible logic literal theory process business literals compliance
84	Robotics	Robot robots motion discomfort hours mine dynamic mission phase navigation
80	Coalition formation	Coalition coalitions core coalitional games formation representation agents structure payoff
3	Coordination	Coordination agents planning strategy execution tasks mechanisms task strategies goals

3.2   RQ2: What Are the Temporal Trends of Topics over Time?

In order to understand which topics have risen and declined in the past 18 years at PRIMA, we have performed the Cox Stuart trend test on the influence metric of each topic. Table 6 shows the results of the test on the top 40 popular topics. We have found that 10 topics have an increasing trend, 26 have a constant trend (i.e., neither increasing nor decreasing to a significant degree; p-value > 0.05), and 4 have a decreasing trend. Among the top three popular topics, our findings suggest that the distributed constraint optimization topic has an increasing trend (p-value = 0.02), while computational game theory decreases and negotiation increases, but not statistically significant.

There are some interesting insights drawn from the result. We observed that application-oriented topics such as simulation, pervasive computing, traffic application and modelling system dynamics have significantly increased. This can be explained by the fact that PRIMA strongly encourages papers reporting on the development of prototype and deployed agent systems, and experiments demonstrating agent system capabilities. Classical topics such as distributed constraint satisfaction and optimization have also significantly increased, which may be due to a strong sub-community within PRIMA on these topics. Among the popular theoretical topics, only defeasible logics and social grouping enjoy an significant

Table 6. Topic trend using the Cox Stuart trend test

ID	Trend	p-value	ID	Trend	p-value
61	Increasing	0.02	14	Decreasing	0.25
83	Decreasing	0.09	29	Increasing	0.002
15	Increasing	0.09	06	Decreasing	0.25
22	Decreasing	0.02	89	Increasing	0.5
44	Increasing	0.25	32	Increasing	0.02
71	Decreasing	0.002	48	Increasing	0.5
99	Decreasing	0.002	43	Decreasing	0.5
25	Decreasing	0.05	21	Decreasing	0.09
73	Decreasing	0.25	28	Increasing	0.02
53	Increasing	0.25	37	Increasing	0.02
35	Decreasing	0.5	49	Decreasing	0.25
50	Increasing	0.09	92	Decreasing	0.25
27	Decreasing	0.5	77	Decreasing	0.25
67	Increasing	0.002	93	Decreasing	0.5
78	Increasing	0.25	17	Increasing	0.09
70	Increasing	0.02	10	Increasing	0.02
69	Decreasing	0.25	41	Increasing	0.02
36	Increasing	0.02	84	Increasing	0.5
88	Decreasing	0.5	80	Increasing	0.25
56	Increasing	0.02	3	Decreasing	0.25

increase in popularity. On the other hand, traditional topics such as agent communication and multi-agent reasoning have declined over the years. Web search and human-agent interaction was used to be a trendy topic in the late 1990s and early 2000s, but they have also significantly declined.

4   Related Work

To the best of our knowledge, our work is the first which studies the literature of PRIMA using topic models. The topic modeling approach has been used to analyze the history and trends in other research areas. For example, the work by Hall *et al* [10] also uses LDA to study historical trends in the field of Computational Linguistics. Their work discovers several trends in that field such as the general increase in applications and the steady decline in semantics. They also studied three major conferences in the field to identify discover convergence and diversity over time in topic coverage. The use of topic models to extract latent topics from research papers have also been applied to study other research fields (e.g. [11]). Topic modeling has also been used in [16] to extract topics from the Google Books Ngram Corpus and link them with historic periods and events.

Previous work in scientometrics and bibliometrics (e.g. [6,7,12,14]) use publication citations to study the impact and trends within a scientific field. Such studies only focus on citation-related phenomena, and thus they do not uncover the actual content of the published literature. Recent work have started combining both topic modeling (i.e. content analysis) with citation-based analysis. For example, the work in [17] uses topic modeling to generate the popular topics from the papers published at the International Symposium on Empirical Software Engineering and Measurement (ESEM). They also used citation analysis to understand the citation distribution of papers published in ESEM. The work in [2] uses not only topic modeling but also other metadata about a publication such as authors affiliations, publication venue, and publication year as a rich descriptor for topics in the literature of statistics. Their analysis discovered the existence of certain popular topics, explained by different descriptors, and identify patterns of citations generated from those topics.

5   Conclusions and Future Work

In this paper, we have described a methodology using topic modeling to identify popular topics and their trends in the history of PRIMA literature. According to our findings, topics that are commonly seen at PRIMA include distributed constraint optimization, computational game theory, and negotiation. We have also found that a number of topics such as agent communication, multi-agent reasoning, human-agent interaction and web search have declined over time. On the other hand, application-oriented topics such as simulation, pervasive computing, traffic applications and modelling system dynamics become more prominent at PRIMA. This suggests that PRIMA recently aims to attract papers reporting how agents are applied in practice.

To the best of our knowledge, our work is the first in analyzing the PRIMA literature and the multi-agent research literature in general using topic modeling. We plan to extend our study to papers published at other major agent-related venues such as the International Conference on Autonomous Agents and Multi-Agent Systems (AAMAS) and the Journal of Autonomous Agents and Multi-Agent Systems (JAAMAS). This large-scale study will cover the entire field of multi-agent system research. Studying the the synergies and differences between different agent communities is also part of our future work. Finally, our future study will combine topic modeling with authorship and citation analysis to understand the impact of topics and authors.

References

1. Anthes, G.: Topic models vs. unstructured data. Commun. ACM **53**(12), 16–18 (2010)
2. Battisti, F., Ferrara, A., Salini, S.: A decade of research in statistics: a topic model approach. Scientometrics **103**(2), 413–433 (2015)

3. Blei, D.M., Lafferty, J.D.: Dynamic topic models. In: Proceedings of the 23rd International Conference on Machine Learning, ICML 2006, pp. 113–120. ACM, New York (2006)
4. Blei, D.M., Lafferty, J.D.: Topic models, pp. 71–94. CRC Press (2009)
5. Blei, D.M., Ng, A.Y., Jordan, M.I.: Latent dirichlet allocation. J. Mach. Learn. Res. 3, 993, 1022 (2003)
6. Börner, K., Chen, C., Boyack, K.W.: Visualizing knowledge domains. Ann. Rev. Inf. Sci. Technol. **37**(1), 179–255 (2003)
7. Chen, C.: Citespace II: detecting and visualizing emerging trends and transient patterns in scientific literature. J. Am. Soc. Inf. Sci. Technol. **57**(3), 359–377 (2006)
8. Cox, A.S.D.R.: Some quick sign tests for trend in location and dispersion. Biometrika **42**(1/2), 80–95 (1955)
9. Geman, S., Geman, D.: Stochastic relaxation, Gibbs distributions, and the Bayesian restoration of images. IEEE Trans. Pattern Anal. Mach. Intell. **6**(6), 721–741 (1984)
10. Hall, D., Jurafsky, D., Manning, C.D.: Studying the history of ideas using topic models. In: Proceedings of the Conference on Empirical Methods in Natural Language Processing, EMNLP 2008, pp. 363–371. Association for Computational Linguistics, Stroudsburg (2008)
11. Liu, P., Jameel, S., Lam, W., Ma, B., Meng, H.M.: Topic modeling for conference analytics. In: INTERSPEECH 2015, 16th Annual Conference of the International Speech Communication Association, Dresden, Germany, 6–10 September 2015, pp. 707–711 (2015)
12. Mann, G.S., Mimno, D., McCallum, A.: Bibliometric impact measures leveraging topic analysis. In: Proceedings of the 6th ACM/IEEE-CS Joint Conference on Digital Libraries, JCDL 2006, pp. 65–74. ACM, New York (2006)
13. McCallum, A.K.: MALLET: a machine learning for language toolkit (2002). http://mallet.cs.umass.edu
14. Neff, M.W., Corley, E.A.: 35 years and 160, 000 articles: a bibliometric exploration of the evolution of ecology. Scientometrics **80**(3), 657–682 (2009)
15. Petruzzi, P.E., Busquets, D., Pitt, J.: Experiments with social capital in multiagent systems. In: Dam, H.K., Pitt, J., Xu, Y., Governatori, G., Ito, T. (eds.) PRIMA 2014. LNCS, vol. 8861, pp. 18–33. Springer, Heidelberg (2014)
16. Popa, T., Rebedea, T., Chiru, C.: Detecting and describing historical periods in a large corpora. In: 26th IEEE International Conference on Tools with Artificial Intelligence, ICTAI 2014, Limassol, Cyprus, 10–12 November 2014, pp. 764–770 (2014)
17. Raulamo-Jurvanen, P., Mäntylä, M.V., Garousi, V.: Citation, topic analysis of the ESEM papers. In: 2015 ACM/IEEE International Symposium on Empirical Software Engineering and Measurement, ESEM 2015, Beijing, China, 22–23 October 2015, pp. 136–139 (2015)
18. Steyvers, M., Griffiths, T.: Latent semantic analysis: a road to meaning. In: Chapter Probabilistic Topic Models. Lawrence Erlbaum (2007)
19. Wallach, H.M., Murray, I., Salakhutdinov, R., Mimno, D.: Evaluation methods for topic models. In: Proceedings of the 26th Annual International Conference on Machine Learning, ICML 2009, pp. 1105–1112. ACM, New York (2009)
20. Wang, X., McCallum, A.: Topics over time: a non-Markov continuous-time model of topical trends. In: Proceedings of the 12th ACM SIGKDD International Conference on Knowledge Discovery and Data Mining, KDD 2006, pp. 424–433. ACM, New York (2006)

Sequence Semantics for Normative Agents

Guido Governatori[1]([✉]), Francesco Olivieri[2],
Erica Calardo[3], Antonino Rotolo[3], and Matteo Cristani[2]

[1] Data61, CSIRO, Spring Hill, QLD, Australia
guido.governatori@data61.csiro.au
[2] University of Verona, Verona, Italy
[3] University of Bologna, Bologna, Italy

Abstract. We proposed a novel framework for the representation of
goals and other mental-like attitudes in terms of degree of expected
outcomes, where an outcome is an order of possible alternatives. The
sequences of alternatives is modelled by a non-classical (substructural)
operator. In this paper we provide a modal logic based axiomatisation of
the intuition they propose, and we discuss some variants (in particular for
the notion of social intention, intentions that are compliant with norms).
Given that the outcome operator is substructural, we first propose a
novel sequence semantics (a generalisation of possible world semantics)
to model the outcome operator, and we prove that the axiomatisation is
sound and complete with respect to the new semantics.

1 Introduction and Background

Normative Multi-Agent Systems (NorMAS) proved a powerful abstraction for
the modelling of socio-technical systems [1]. A normative agent integrates two
components: a rational agent component, often inspired by the well known BDI
agent architecture, and the normative component to model the norms the agent
is subject to.

The BDI architecture is a prominent approach to model rational agents. As
is well-known, BDI agents are means-ends reasoners equipped with: (i) Desires,
Goals, Intentions (or Tasks); (ii) a description of the current state of the environment (Beliefs); (iii) Actions. The key tenet of this architecture is that the agent's
behaviour is the outcome of a rational balance among different mental states.

The framework we developed in [9] considers goals, desires, and intentions
as facets of the same phenomenon (all of them being goal-like attitudes): the
notion of *outcome*, which is simply something an agent would like or is expected
to achieve. An advantage of the proposed framework is that it allows agents to
compute different degrees of motivational attitudes, and degrees of commitment
that take into account other factors, such as beliefs and norms.

A. Rotolo—Supported by EU H2020 research and innovation programme under the
Marie Sklodowska-Curie grant agreement No. 690974 for the project *MIREL: MIning
and REasoning with Legal texts*.

M. Baldoni et al. (Eds.): PRIMA 2016, LNAI 9862, pp. 230–246, 2016.
DOI: 10.1007/978-3-319-44832-9_14

While different schemas for generating and filtering agents' outcomes are possible, the authors of [9] restricted themselves to schemas where they adopted the following principles:

- When an agent faces alternative outcomes in a given context, these outcomes are ranked in preference orderings,
- Mental attitudes are obtained from *outcomes*, which are ranked,
- Beliefs prevail over conflicting motivational attitudes, thus avoiding various cases of wishful thinking [3,10];
- Norms and obligations are used to filter social motivational states (*social intentions*) and compliant agents [3,6].

The motivational and deliberative components of agents are generated from preference orderings among outcomes. As done in other research areas (e.g., rational choice theory), we move with the idea that agents have preferences and choose which ones to attain the least of in given situations based on such preferences. Preferences involve outcomes and are explicitly represented in the syntax of the language for reasoning about agents, thus following the logical paradigm initially proposed in [2,5] for the representation of preferences as explicit orders (sequences) of logical formulae and inference mechanisms to reason about them.

The combination of an agent's mental attitudes with the factuality of the world defines her deliberative process, i.e., the objectives she decides to pursue. The agent may give up some of them to comply with the norms, if required. Indeed, many contexts may prevent the agent from achieving all of her objectives; the agent must then understand which objectives are mutually compatible with each other and choose which ones to attain the least of in given situations by ranking them in a preference ordering.

Consider, for instance, the following scenario. Alice is thinking what to do on Saturday afternoon. She has three alternatives: (i) she can visit John; (ii) she can visit her parents who live close to John's place; or (iii) she can watch a movie at home. The alternative she likes the most is visiting John, while watching a movie is the least preferred. If John is not at home, there is no point for Alice to visit him. In this case, paying a visit to her parents becomes the "next best" option. Also, if visiting her parents is not possible, she settles for the last choice, that of staying home and watching a movie.

Suppose that Alice knows that John is actually away for the weekend. Since the most preferred option is no longer available, she decides to opt for the now best option, namely visiting her parents.

To represent the scenario above, we need to capture the preferences about her alternatives, and her beliefs about the world. To model preferences among several options, we build a sequence of alternatives that are preferred when the previous choices are no longer feasible. Normally, each set of alternatives is the result of a specific context determining under which conditions (premises) such a sequence of alternatives is considered.

Accordingly, we can represent Alice's alternatives with the notation

$$Saturday \rightarrow (visit\_John \odot visit\_parents \odot watch\_movie)$$

where the ⊙ operator is used to encode the preference of the agent over alternative outcomes. In this case *visit_John* is the most preferred outcome, *visit_parents* is the second best outcome (we can see it as the plan B of the agent), and *watch_movie* is the least of the acceptable outcome for a Saturday afternoon. Notice that *do_home_chores* is not an "acceptable" outcome for Alice.

This intuition resembles the notion of contrary-to-duty obligations presented by [5], where a norm is represented by an expression like

$$drive\_car \rightarrow (\neg damage \otimes compensate \otimes foreclosure)$$

where the symbol "⊗" separates the alternatives. In this case, each element of the chain is the reparative obligation that shall come in force in case the immediate predecessor in the chain has been violated. Thus, the meaning of the formula above is that, if an agent drives a car, then she has the obligation not to cause any damage to others; if this happens, she is obliged to compensate; if she fails to compensate, there is an obligation of foreclosure.

In both examples, the sequences express a preference ordering among alternatives. Accordingly, *watch_movie* and *foreclosure* are the last (and least) acceptable situations. Notice that while Alice's alternatives come from a mental and a (inner) deliberation process, the use of ⊗ describes situations of compliance with regards the environment the agent is situated in, and as such is up to the agent to comply with them, or not. Whilst both operators can be said to express preferences, who those preferences belong to differ: in the ⊙ case, it is the agent's preferences, while in the ⊗ case, it could be argued to be the stated preference of the institution/norms. These are not necessarily the same, as there are a number of instances in the real world of organisations breaking laws knowing that they will be fined: the institution prefers compliance over the fine, but the organisation may prefer paying the fine over complying with the law.

Example 1. Alice settled for visit her parents who live downtown, but the downtown part where they live is a traffic area restricted to residents and parking for not resident is forbidden on weekends. Alice would prefer to take her car to visit her parent to take public transports. The scenario can be represented by the formulas:

$$visit\_parents \rightarrow (parking\_downtown \odot public\_transport \odot pay\_fine) \quad (1)$$

$$weekend \rightarrow (\neg parking\_downtown \otimes pay\_fine) \quad (2)$$

In this case Alice has to balance her preference for driving her car to visit her parents and the prohibition to park downtown. But then she prefers to take a bus instead of paying a parking fine.

In the rest of the section, we shall illustrate the principles and intuitions relating sequences of alternatives (that is, outcome rules), beliefs, obligations, and how to use them to characterise different types of goal-like attitudes and degrees of commitment to outcomes: *desires*, *goals*, *intentions*, and *social intentions*.

Desires as Acceptable Outcomes. Desires are acceptable outcomes independently of whether they are compatible with other expected or acceptable outcomes. Let us contextualise the previous example to better explain the notion of desire by considering the following setting.

Example 2. Consider the following formulae:

$$Saturday \tag{3}$$

$$John\_sick \tag{4}$$

$$Saturday \rightarrow (visit\_John \odot visit\_parents \odot watch\_movie) \tag{5}$$

$$John\_sick \rightarrow (\neg visit\_John \odot short\_visit). \tag{6}$$

The agent has both *visit_John* and its opposite as acceptable outcomes.

Goals as Preferred Outcomes. We consider a *goal as the preferred desire in a chain.*

In the situation described by Example 2, *visit_parents* and *short_visit* are the goals we can obtain: a desire is a goal only if it is compatible with other desires.

1.1   Two Degrees of Commitment: Intentions and Social Intentions

The next issue is to clarify which are the acceptable outcomes for an agent to commit to. Naturally, if the agent values some outcomes more than others, she should strive for the best, in other words, for the most preferred outcomes (goals).

Consider a formula $b_1 \odot b_2 \odot b_3$. Let us examine a first case where the agent should commit to the outcome she values the most, that is b_1. But what if the agent *believes* that b_1 cannot be achieved in the environment where she is currently situated in, or she knows that $\neg b_1$ holds? Committing to b_1 would result in a waste of the agent's resources; rationally, she should target the next best outcome b_2. Accordingly, the agent derives b_2 as her *intention. An intention is an acceptable outcome which does not conflict with the beliefs describing the environment.*

Suppose now that b_2 is *forbidden,* and that the agent is social (a social agent is an agent not knowingly committing to anything that is forbidden [6]). Once again, the agent has to lower her expectation and settle for b_3, which is one of her *social intentions. A social intention is an intention which does not violate any norm.*

1.2   The Contribution of This Paper

The above notions have been formalised by [9] in the context of Defeasible Logic. That model was motivated by computational concerns: the proposed logic for agents' desires, goals, and intentions has in fact linear complexity. However, the approach was only proof-theoretic whereas no semantic model-theoretic analysis of the operators $\otimes$ and $\odot$ has been provided. In this paper, we work on the combination of these operators in the context of classical propositional logic and fill the gap by defining a suitable possible-world semantics for them. Such semantics is a sequence-based non-normal one extending and generalising neighbourhood models for classical modal logics.

The layout of the paper is as follows: Sect. 2 presents the language of our logic; Sect. 3 discusses some axiom schemata governing the behaviour and the interactions of the various operators; Sect. 4 describes an account of the semantics for the logic while Sect. 5 offers some relevant completeness results. Some conclusions end the paper.

2   Language

The language consists of a countable set of atomic formulae. Well-formed-formulae are then defined using the typical Boolean connectives, the n-ary connectives $\otimes$ and $\odot$, and the modal (deontic) operators O for obligation, B for beliefs, D for desires, G for goals, I for intentions, and SI for social intentions. The intended reading of $\otimes$ is that it encodes a sequence of obligations where, each obligation is meant to compensate the violation of the previous obligation. The intuition behind $\odot$ is to model ordered lists of preferred outcomes.

Let $\mathcal{L}$ be a language consisting of a countable set of propositional letters $Prop = \{p_1, p_2, \ldots\}$, the propositional constant $\bot$, round brackets, the boolean connective $\rightarrow$, the unary operators O, B, D, G, I, and SI, the set of n-ary operators $\otimes^n$ for $n \in \mathbb{N}^+$ and the set of n-ary operators $\odot^n$ for $n \in \mathbb{N}^+$.

Definition 1 (Well Formed Formulae). *Well formed formulae (wffs) are defined as follows:*

- *Any propositional letter $p \in Prop$ and $\bot$ are wffs;*
- *If a and b are wffs, then $a \rightarrow b$ is a wff;*
- *If a is a wff and no operator $\otimes^m$, $\odot^m$, O, B, D, G, I, and SI occurs in a, then Oa, Ba, Da, Ga, Ia, and SIa are a wff;*
- *If $a_1, \ldots, a_n$ are wffs and no operator $\otimes^m$, $\odot^m$, O, B, D, G, I, and SI occurs in any of them, then $a_1 \otimes^n \cdots \otimes^n a_n$ and $a_1 \odot^n \cdots \odot^n a_n$ are wffs, where $n \in \mathbb{N}^+$;[1]*
- *Nothing else is a wff.*

We use WFF to denote the set of well formed formulae.

Other Boolean operators are defined in the standard way, in particular $\neg a =_{def} a \rightarrow \bot$ and $\top =_{def} \bot \rightarrow \bot$.

We say that any formula $a_1 \otimes \cdots \otimes a_n$ is an $\otimes$-*chain*, while $a_1 \odot \cdots \odot a_n$ is an $\odot$-*chain*; also the negation of an $\otimes$-*chain* (resp. $\odot$-chain) is an $\otimes$-*chain* (resp. $\odot$-chain). The formation rules allow us to have $\otimes$-chain and $\odot$-chain of any (finite) length, and the arity of the operator is equal to number of elements in the chain; we hence drop the index m from $\otimes^m$ and $\odot^m$. Moreover, we use the prefix notation $\bigotimes_{i=j}^{n} a_i$ for $a_j \odot \cdots \odot a_n$ and $\bigodot_{i=j}^{n} a_i$ for $a_j \odot \cdots \odot a_n$.

---

[1] We use the prefix forms $\otimes^1 a$ and $\oplus^1 a$ for the case of $n = 1$.

In addition, we use the following notation: $\bigotimes_{i=j}^{n} a_i \otimes b \otimes \bigotimes_{k=l}^{m} c_k$, where $j, l \in \{0, 1\}$. The "a" part and "c" part are optional, i.e., they are empty when $j = 0$ or $l = 0$, respectively. Otherwise the expression stands for the following chain of $n+1+m$ elements: $a_1 \otimes \cdots \otimes a_n \otimes b \otimes c_1 \otimes \cdots \otimes c_m$. The same reasoning holds for $\bigodot_{i=1}^{n} a_i \odot b \odot \bigodot_{k=l}^{m} c_k$.

3 Axiomatisation for Norms, Beliefs and Outcomes

The aim of this section is to discuss the intuitions behind some principles governing the behaviour and the interactions of the various operators. These principles are captured by axioms or inference rules.

3.1 Basic Axioms and Inference Rules

In this paper, we assume classical propositional logic, CPC, as the underlying logic. The first principle is that of syntax independence or, in other terms, that the operators are closed under logical equivalence. To this end, all the logics have the following inference rules:

$$\frac{a \equiv b}{\Box a \equiv \Box b} \tag{$\Box$-RE}$$

with $\Box \in \{\mathsf{O}, \mathsf{B}, \mathsf{D}, \mathsf{G}, \mathsf{I}, \mathsf{SI}\}$.

$$\frac{\bigwedge_{i=1}^{n} (a_i \equiv b_i)}{\bigotimes_{i=1}^{n} a_i \equiv \bigotimes_{i=1}^{n} b_i} \otimes\text{-RE} \qquad \frac{\bigwedge_{i=1}^{n} (a_i \equiv b_i)}{\bigodot_{i=1}^{n} a_i \equiv \bigodot_{i=1}^{n} b_i} \odot\text{-RE} \qquad (\otimes \text{ and } \odot\text{-RE})$$

Consider the $\otimes$ chain $a \otimes b \otimes a \otimes c$. The meaning of the chain above is that a is obligatory, but if a is violated (meaning that $\neg a$ holds) then b is obligatory. If also b is violated, then a becomes obligatory. But we already know that we will incur in the violation of it, since $\neg a$ holds. We thus have the obligation of c. However, this is what we want to obtain from the $\otimes$-chain: $a \otimes b \otimes c$.

Now, consider the $\odot$-chain $a \odot b \odot a \odot c$. The intuitive reading is that a should be the most preferred outcome, while b is the second best in case a is not possible to achieve. However, if also b is not attainable, then a should be the agent's third best choice. Nevertheless, we have already established that this is not possible, and we thus have c as the following preferred outcome.

The above example shows that duplications of formulas in $\otimes$-chains and $\odot$-chains do not contribute to the meaning of the chains themselves. This motivates us to adopt the following axioms to remove (resp., introduce) an element from (to) a chain if an equivalent formula occurs on the left of it.

$$\bigotimes_{i=1}^{n} a_i \equiv \bigotimes_{i=1}^{k-1} a_i \otimes \bigotimes_{i=k+1}^{n} a_i \text{ where } a_j \equiv a_k, \ j < k \qquad (\otimes\text{-contraction})$$

$$\bigodot_{i=1}^{n} a_i \equiv \bigodot_{i=1}^{k-1} a_i \odot \bigodot_{i=k+1}^{n} a_i \text{ where } a_j \equiv a_k, \ j < k \qquad (\odot\text{-contraction})$$

Given that we use classical propositional logic as the underlying logic, it is not possible that an $\otimes$-chain ($\odot$-chain) and its negation hold at the same time. What about when $\otimes$-chains like $a \otimes b \otimes c$ and $\neg(a \otimes b)$ hold. In this case, the first chain states that a is obligatory and its violation is compensated by b, which in turn is itself obligatory and it is compensated by c. The second expression states that 'either it is not the case that a is obligatory, but if it is so, then its violation is not compensated by b'. Accordingly, the combination of the two expressions should result in a contradiction (a similar argument can be made for $\odot$-chains). To ensure this, we must assume the following axioms that allow us to derive, given a chain, all its sub-chains with the same initial element(s).

$$a_1 \otimes \cdots \otimes a_n \rightarrow a_1 \otimes \cdots \otimes a_{n-1}, \ n \geq 2 \qquad (\otimes\text{-shortening})$$

$$a_1 \odot \cdots \odot a_n \rightarrow a_1 \odot \cdots \odot a_{n-1}, \ n \geq 2 \qquad (\odot\text{-shortening})$$

If Alice prefers to visit John to visit her parents to watch a movie to spend her Saturday afternoon she prefer to visit John to visit her parents. Thus, we can derive

$$visit\_John \odot visit\_parents$$

from

$$visit\_John \odot visit\_parents \odot watch\_movie.$$

3.2 Axioms for Obligations and Mental Attitudes

In the previous section we proposed the basic axioms for a logic of norms and goals. In this section, we address the relationships between $\otimes$, $\odot$, obligations, beliefs and mental attitudes;

In this paper we assume that the description of the environment in which an agent is situated is given by a set of propositional formulas. The agent is rational in the sense that the agent is able to reason with the formulas using classical propositional logic as the underlying logic. We further assume that the provided description of the environment is truthful and the agent knows it. Accordingly, we do not have to introduce a further modal operator to describe the knowledge of an agent. The second principle of rationality for the agents is that they do not form self-inconsistent beliefs and goal-like mental attitudes, and similarly for the norms (obligations) they are subject to. Namely, we assume that all unary modal operators are internally consistent. Internal consistency of beliefs, obligations, and goal-like mental attitudes is expressed by the following axiom:

$$\neg \Box \bot \qquad (\bot\text{-}\Box)$$

with $\Box = \{\mathsf{O}, \mathsf{B}, \mathsf{D}, \mathsf{G}, \mathsf{I}, \mathsf{SI}\}$.

Similarly, rational agents are expected to avoid conflictual beliefs and individual mental-attitudes (but desires), and there are no norms that make something obligatory and forbidden at the same time. This property is called external consistency and it is modelled by the following axiom:

$$\Box a \rightarrow \neg \Box \neg a \qquad (\mathbf{D})$$

with $\Box = \{B, O, G, I, SI\}$. As we discussed in [9] we do not assume this external consistency for desires. Thus Da and $D\neg a$ is consistent within our framework. For example, Alice may desire to visit Bob while, at the same time and for other reasons, she might not to. Visiting Bob and not visiting him are two possible outcomes for Alice deliberation, and she can use other information to determine what course of action she commits to. Hence, it is rational for her to derive that she has both desires (they are two acceptable and viable outcomes).

In addition the agent can have a set of beliefs of how the environment is (for example, about what is not given by the explicit description of the environment or can be inferred from it using classical propositional logic). Thus, to represent the agent belief we use the B operator. B is axiomatised as a normal KD45 operator, with the standard axioms for positive and negative introspections (Axioms 4 and 5). Accordingly the axioms for B are:

$$Ba \rightarrow BBa \tag{4}$$

$$\neg B\neg a \rightarrow B\neg B\neg a \tag{5}$$

$$B(a \rightarrow b) \rightarrow (Ba \rightarrow Bb) \tag{K}$$

$$B\top \tag{N}$$

For the other modal operators, we establish that they are regular, namely, that the following inference $\Box$-RR holds for them

$$\frac{a_1 \wedge \cdots \wedge a_n \rightarrow b}{\Box a_1 \wedge \cdots \wedge \Box a_n \rightarrow \Box b} \tag{$\Box$-RR}$$

for $\Box \in \{O, D, G, I, SI\}$. As explained in [6] $\Box$-RR allows us to model, for example, the notion of intentionality: Suppose that an agent knows that $a_1 \wedge \cdots \wedge a_n \rightarrow b$ (or in other terms, that the implication is a property of the environment in which the agent is situated). This means, that in the given environment, b is an unavoidable consequence of $a_1, \ldots, a_n$. Therefore, if the agents intend all the a_is, i.e., Ia_i, then the agent knows that in case she is successful in achieving all the a_is, then she will bring about b, thus committing herself to the a_is indirectly commits herself to b as well. Thus, $\Box$-RR allows us to derive Ib.

We can now move to the analysis of the axioms relating norms ($\otimes$-chains) and obligations. In this paper we follow the analysis proposed in [8] for the relationships between norms and obligations. Thus the first axiom we consider is:

$$a_1 \otimes \cdots \otimes a_n \rightarrow Oa_1 \tag{$\otimes$-O}$$

For instance, given the "*driving_car*" example above, we can obtain the first element as the current obligation ($O\neg damage$). Furthermore, we say that if the first element does not hold, we can infer the obligation of the second element. For example

$$a_1 \otimes \cdots \otimes a_n \wedge \neg a_1 \to Oa_2. \tag{7}$$

In this occasion (always referring to the "*driving_car*" example), we actually did cause soma damage, thus the new obligation in force is to compensate for it ($O compensate$).

Moreover, we argued that we can repeat the same procedure. This leads us to generalise (7) for the axiom that expresses the detachment principle for $\otimes$-chains and factual statements about the opposites of the first k elements of an $\otimes$-chain.

$$a_1 \otimes \cdots \otimes a_n \wedge \bigwedge_{i=1}^{k<n} \neg a_i \to Oa_{k+1} \qquad \text{(O-detachment)}$$

For alternative axiomatisation of the relationships between obligations and norms see [8].

As stated before, desires are expected or acceptable outcomes, independently of whether they are compatible with other expected or acceptable outcomes. As such, given an $\odot$-chain, we consider each element to be desired by the agent since she has expressed a preference order on such a chain and she thus considers all of them to be acceptable. This is expressed by the following axiom.

$$a_1 \odot \cdots \odot a_n \to Da_i, \text{ with } 1 \leq i \leq n \qquad \text{($\odot$-D)}$$

According to this axioms, given the preference of Alice her "desires", i.e., the outcomes that she considers acceptable are *visit_John*, *visit_parents* and *watch_movie*, but she has no desire to her household chores.

Given an $\odot$-chain, a goal represents what should be the most preferred outcome for the agent, provided that the agent does not have the opposite desire.

$$a_1 \odot \cdots \odot a_n \wedge \neg D \neg a_1 \to Ga_1 \qquad \text{($\odot$-G$_1$)}$$

Again, if an agent has opposite desires then, given an $\odot$-chain, the goal is the first element such that the agent does not desire the opposite. By rationality, if for each element of such a chain, the agent has expressed an opposite desire, then any element of the chain cannot represent a goal.

$$a_1 \odot \cdots \odot a_n \wedge \bigwedge_{i=1}^{k<n} D \neg a_i \wedge \neg D \neg a_{k+1} \to Ga_{k+1} \qquad \text{($\odot$-G-gen)}$$

An intention is the first mental attitude where the agent compares her outcomes (her preferred courses of action) with the environment she is operating in. Indeed, given an $\odot$-chain, it may be the case that neither of the first, say, four outcomes are attainable because facts of the environment (or her own beliefs) state that the opposites of such four outcomes actually hold. (For instance, a_1 may be that the agent would like travel to California, but she beliefs that her current funds would not cover the whole trip.) Consequently, intentions represent the first level of real commitment of the agent.

Our agents are not omniscient, they may lack the knowledge of certain facts of the world: an agent's belief represents the fact that she has reasons to accept a certain statement to be true without having the evidence that it is so. Using her competence/knowledge, she forms an opinion (a belief) of how the environment she is situated in is, or might be. Consequently, she can use her beliefs or the knowledge she possesses about the environment to determine to what outcomes she commits to, depending on her risk attitude. The outcomes she commits to are her intentions.

The axiom hereafter tries to capture many facets of the agent's level of commitment, represented by the three different αs combined with the four different βs (in fact, the β_5 alternative of *wishful thinker* has been introduced for completeness sake only).

$$a_1 \odot \cdots \odot a_n \wedge \left\{ \begin{array}{l} \alpha_1 = \bigwedge_{i=1}^{k<n} \neg a_i \\ \alpha_2 = \bigwedge_{i=1}^{k<n} B \neg a_i \\ \alpha_3 = \bigwedge_{i=1}^{k<n} \neg a_i \vee B \neg a_i \end{array} \right\} \wedge \left\{ \begin{array}{l} \beta_1 = B a_{k+1} \\ \beta_2 = \neg B \neg a_{k+1} \\ \beta_3 = B a_{k+1} \vee \neg B \neg a_{k+1} \\ \beta_4 = a_{k+1} \\ \beta_5 = \neg a_{k+1} \end{array} \right\} \rightarrow I a_{k+1}.$$

(1)

A few comments are in order. In alternative α_1 we have the strongest commitment for the agent (some sort of *omniscient/librairian* agent). In our example, this case model the situation that Alice knows that John is not at home, so she cannot visit him so she will not form the intention to visit him. In here, we use the term omniscient not in the perspective/meaning of a know-it-all agent, but to stress out the fact that the agent does not relies on her own beliefs but she needs to verify the falsity of a statement to proceed in the $\odot$-chain about what things really are (she has the burden of proof). This can be view as the most burdensome among our alternatives.

Alternative α_2 is the more 'introspective' one (or more *cautious*): the agent is not interested in how things truly are and her decision process relies only upon what she believes in. It can be described as a more cautious approach because the agent discards a possible outcome based only on her own beliefs, which can be false. For instance, if $w \models a$ and $w \models B \neg a$, then the agent should derive $I a$ (even if an oracle would forecast her eventual failure).

Alternative α_3 can be called as the 'good enough' alternative: if the agent has not the capabilities to verify a certain statement, she 'trusts' in her own beliefs.

Alternative β_1 is 'risk-adverse': the agent's decision is based upon on her beliefs only about the truthfulness of the outcome she will try to achieve.

On the contrary, alternative β_2 is a 'risk-taking' position, given that the agent looks at whether the opposite outcome holds. Based on her competence/experience, she has evidence that the opposite actually does not hold, and she thus tries to achieve that particular outcome.

The alternative-sequence $\alpha_3 \wedge \beta_3$ is the most pragmatic one: the agent takes neither a risk-taking, nor a risk-adverse position.

β_4 represents a non-risk taking position (a *win-win* situation): the agent knows that such an outcome actually holds in the environment she is situated in and then it is feasible to achieve (in our running Alice example, she is already at John's place).

Alternative β_5 is a typical case of *wishful thinker* (the agent knows she will fail).

A social intention is an intention that is permitted within the legal system the agent is operating in.

$$\frac{\mathsf{I}a \land \neg\mathsf{O}\neg a}{\mathsf{S}\mathsf{I}a} \tag{8}$$

Naturally, in the decision process to decide whether an outcome may be a social intention, the agent uses the $\odot$-chains. Therefore, to state that an element in an $\odot$-chain is a social intention (say a_{k+1}), it must satisfy the following requirements: (1) every element before a_{k+1} is not an intention or the opposite obligation holds, (2) a_{k+1} is actually an intention, and (3) the opposite obligation $(\mathsf{O}\neg a_{k+1})$ does not hold. This is expressed by the following axiom.

$$a_1 \odot \cdots \odot a_n \land \left(\bigwedge_{i=1}^{k<n} \neg\mathsf{I}a_i \lor \mathsf{O}\neg a_i \right) \land \mathsf{I}a_{k+1} \land \neg\mathsf{O}\neg a_{k+1} \to \mathsf{S}\mathsf{I}a_{k+1}. \tag{SI}$$

To illustrate this axioms consider again Example 1. From (2) we have $\mathsf{O}\neg parking\_downtown$, and there is no norm to prevent her to take public transports, so $\neg\mathsf{O}\neg public\_transports$. She does not want to get a parking ticket, so she decided not to take her care, so she does not form the intention to park downtown, thus her next preference is to take public transport, that is $\mathsf{I}public\_transports$. Thus this intention is also a social intention, i.e., we have $\mathsf{S}\mathsf{I}public\_transports$.

In the final part of this paper, we shall prove soundness and completeness results for a system S containing the schemata presented above.

Definition 2. *Let* S *be a logical system extending the Classical Propositional Calculus (*CPC*), containing the axiom schemata* ($\otimes$-**contraction**), ($\odot$-**contraction**), ($\otimes$-**shortening**), ($\odot$-**shortening**), (**K**), ($\bot$-$\Box$), (**D**), (**4**), (**5**), (**N**), ($\otimes$-O), (O-**detachment**), ($\odot$-D), ($\odot$-G_1), ($\odot$-G-*gen*), (I), *and closed under the following rules:* ($\Box$-RE), ($\otimes$ *and* $\odot$-RE) *and* ($\Box$-RR).

4   Sequence Semantics

Sequence semantics is an extension of neighbourhood semantics. The extension is twofold: (1) we introduce a second neighbourhood like function, and (2) the new function generates a set of sequences of sets of possible worlds instead of set of sets of possible worlds. This extension allows us to provide a clean semantic representation of $\otimes$- and $\odot$-chains.

The sequence semantics addresses the problem identified in [7] for possible world semantics for deontic logic for compensatory obligations. A compensatory obligation is a sub-class of a contrary-to-duty obligation, where the violation of the primary obligation is compensated by the fulfilment of the secondary obligation. Compensatory obligations can be modelled by $\otimes$-chains. As we have already discussed $a \otimes b$ means that a is obligatory, but its violation is compensated by b, or in other terms it is obligatory to do b to compensate the violation of the obligation of a. Thus, a situation where a does not hold (or $\neg a$ holds) and b holds is still deemed as a "legal" situation. Accordingly, when we use a "standard" possible world semantics, there is a deontically accessible world where $\neg a$ holds, but this implies, according the usual evaluation conditions for permission (something is permitted, if there is a deontically accessible world where it holds), that $\neg a$ is permitted. However, we have the norm modelling the compensatory obligation that states that a is obligatory (and if it were not, then there would be no need for b to compensate for the violation, since, there would be no violation of the obligation of a). The sequence semantics solves this problem by establishing that to have an obligation, we must have a norm generating the obligation (where a norm is represented by an $\otimes$-chain), and not simply that something is obligatory because it holds in all the deontically accessible worlds. Similarly, when we consider mental-attitudes, an agent forms a mental attitude because the agent has an outcome in mind (where, as we have argued, an outcome is a gradation of alternative objectives).

Before introducing the semantics, we give some technical definitions for operation of *s-zipping*, i.e., the operation that removes repetitions or redundancies occurring in sequences of sets of worlds. This operation is required to capture the intuition described by the $\otimes$- and $\odot$-contraction axioms.

Definition 3. *Given a set of possible worlds W, let $X = \langle X_1, \ldots, X_n \rangle$ be such that $X_i \in 2^W$ $(1 \leq i \leq n)$. A sequence of sets Y is s-zipped from X iff Y is obtained from X by applying the following operation: for $1 \leq k \leq n$, if $X_j = X_k$ and $j < k$, delete X_k from the sequence.*

Definition 4. *A set S of sequences of sets of possible worlds is closed downward s-zipping iff if $X \in S$, then (i) for all Y such that X is s-zipped from Y, $Y \in S$; and (ii) for all Z such that Z is s-zipped from X, $Z \in S$.*

Closure under s-zipping essentially determines classes of equivalences for $\otimes$-chain and $\odot$-chain based on Axioms ($\otimes$-**contraction**) and ($\odot$-**contraction**).

Definition 5. *A sequence frame is a structure*

$$\mathcal{F} = \langle W, \mathcal{C}^O, \mathcal{C}^{out}, \mathcal{N}^O, \mathcal{N}^B, \mathcal{N}^D, \mathcal{N}^G, \mathcal{N}^I, \mathcal{N}^{SI} \rangle,$$

where

- W *is a non empty set of possible worlds;*
- $\mathcal{C}^O$ *and $\mathcal{C}^{out}$ are two functions with signature $W \mapsto 2^{(2^W)^n}$, such that for every world $w \in W$, for every $X \in \mathcal{C}_w^O$, and $Y \in \mathcal{C}_w^{out}$ X and Y are closed under s-zipping;*
- $\mathcal{N}^O$, $\mathcal{N}^B$, $\mathcal{N}^D$, $\mathcal{N}^G$, $\mathcal{N}^I$, *and $\mathcal{N}^{SI}$ are functions with Signature $W \mapsto 2^{2^W}$.*

As we have already said the sequence semantics is an extension and generalisation of neighbourhood semantics. Here the $\mathcal{N}$ functions are just instances of the standard neighbourhood function that associates sets of propositions (a proposition can be represented by the set of possible world where the proposition holds) to possible worlds. Thus, for example, $\mathcal{N}_w^{\mathsf{B}}$ denotes the set of propositions that an agent believes at w. The $\mathcal{C}$ functions are generalisations of the $\mathcal{N}$ functions. Instead of a set of propositions, each of these functions associates a set of sequences of propositions to each possible worlds. Each of such sequences describes an order over the propositions in it (with respect to a possible world). Thus, $\mathcal{C}_w^{\mathsf{out}}$ gives the semantic representation of the preferences of the agents at w; similarly, $\mathcal{C}^{\mathsf{O}}$ models the norms in force in a particular possible world.

Definition 6. *A sequence model is a structure* $\mathcal{M} = \langle \mathcal{F}, V \rangle$, *where*

- $\mathcal{F}$ *is a bi-sequence frame, and*
- V *is a valuation function,* $V \colon Prop \mapsto 2^W$

Given a model $\mathcal{M} = \langle \mathcal{F}, V \rangle$, *let* $\|a\|_V := \{w \mid \models_w^V a\}$.

Definition 7. *The valuation function for a sequence model is a follows:*

- *usual for atoms and boolean conditions,*
- $\models_w^V a_1 \otimes \cdots \otimes a_n$ *iff* $\langle \|a_1\|_V, \ldots, \|a_n\|_V \rangle \in \mathcal{C}_w^{\mathsf{O}}$,
- $\models_w^V \odot \cdots \odot a_n$ *iff* $\langle \|a_1\|_V, \ldots, \|a_n\|_V \rangle \in \mathcal{C}_w^{\mathsf{out}}$,
- $\models_w^V \Box a$ *iff* $\|a\|_V \in \mathcal{N}_w^{\Box}$, *where* $\Box = \{\mathsf{O}, \mathsf{B}, \mathsf{D}, \mathsf{G}, \mathsf{I}, \mathsf{SI}\}$.

The definition above allows us to characterise a minimal logic satisfying ($\Box$-RE), ($\otimes$ and $\odot$-RE), ($\otimes$-**contraction**) and ($\odot$-**contraction**) [8].

Definition 8. *A neighbourhood function* $\mathcal{N}$ *is*

- *supplemented if* $X \cap Y \in \mathcal{N}$, *then* $X \in \mathcal{N}$ *and* $Y \in \mathcal{N}$;
- *closed under the intersection if* $X \in \mathcal{N}$ *and* $Y \in \mathcal{N}$, *then* $X \cap Y \in \mathcal{N}$;
- *contains the unit if* $W \in \mathcal{N}$.

A neighbourhood function is a filter *if it is supplemented, closed under intersection and contains the unit. A neighbourhood function is a* quasi-filter *if it is supplemented and closed under intersection.*

The definition below gives the conditions of the frames for the various axioms.

Definition 9. *A sequence model for* S, *as defined in 2, is a structure* $\mathcal{M} = \langle \mathcal{F}, v \rangle$ *satisfying the following conditions:*

(K) and (N): $\mathcal{N}_w^{\mathsf{B}}$ *is a filter.*
($\bot$-$\Box$): $\emptyset \notin \mathcal{N}_w^{\Box}$, *for* $\Box \in \{\mathsf{O}, \mathsf{B}, \mathsf{D}, \mathsf{G}, \mathsf{I}, \mathsf{SI}\}$.
(D): *If* $X \in \mathcal{N}_w^{\Box}$, *then* $-X \notin \mathcal{N}_w^{\Box}$, *for* $\Box \in \{\mathsf{O}, \mathsf{B}, \mathsf{G}, \mathsf{I}, \mathsf{SI}\}$.
(4): *If* $X \in \mathcal{N}_w^{\mathsf{B}}$, *then* $\{x \in W : X \in \mathcal{N}_x^{\mathsf{B}} \in \mathcal{N}_w^{\mathsf{B}}\}$.
(5): *If* $X \notin \mathcal{N}_w^{\mathsf{B}}$, *then* $\{x \in W : X \notin \mathcal{N}_x^{\mathsf{B}} \in \mathcal{N}_w^{\mathsf{B}}\}$.
($\Box$-RR): $\mathcal{N}_w^{\Box}$, *for* $\Box \in \{\mathsf{O}, \mathsf{D}, \mathsf{G}, \mathsf{I}, \mathsf{SI}\}$, *is a quasi-filter.*

($\otimes$-**shortening**) **and** ($\odot$-**shortening**): *If* $\langle X_1, \ldots, X_n \rangle \in \mathcal{C}_w^x$, *then, for* $x \in \{O, \text{out}\}$, $\langle X_1, \ldots, X_{n-1} \rangle \in \mathcal{C}_w^x$.

($\otimes$-**O**): *If* $\langle X_1, \ldots, X_n \rangle \in \mathcal{C}_w^O$, *then* $X_1 \in \mathcal{N}_w^O$.

(**O-detachment**) *If* $\langle X_1, \ldots, X_n \rangle \in \mathcal{C}_w^O$ *and* $w \notin X_i$ *for* $1 \leq i \leq k$ *and* $k < n$, *then* $X_{k+1} \in \mathcal{N}_w^O$.

($\odot$-**D**): *If* $\langle X_1, \ldots, X_n \rangle \in \mathcal{C}_w^{\text{out}}$, *then* $X_i \in \mathcal{N}_w^D$, *with* $1 \leq i \leq n$.

($\odot$-**G$_1$**): *If* $\langle X_1, \ldots, X_n \rangle \in \mathcal{C}_w^{\text{out}}$ *and* $-X_1 \notin \mathcal{N}_w^D$, $X_1 \in \mathcal{N}_w^G$.

($\odot$-**G-gen**): *If* $\langle X_1, \ldots, X_n \rangle \in \mathcal{C}_w^{\text{out}}$ *and, for* $1 \leq i \leq k$ *and* $k < n$, $-X_i \in \mathcal{N}_w^D$ *and* $-X_{k+1} \notin \mathcal{N}_w^D$, *then* $X_{k+1} \in \mathcal{N}_w^G$.

(**I**): *If* $\langle X_1, \ldots, X_n \rangle \in \mathcal{C}_w^{\text{out}}$ *and, for* $1 \leq i \leq k$ *and* $k < n$,
either

α_1: $w \notin X_i$;

α_2: $-X_i \in \mathcal{N}^B$;

α_3: $w \notin X_i$ *or* $-X_i \in \mathcal{N}^B$

and either

β_1: $X_{k+1} \in \mathcal{N}^B$;

β_2: $-X_{k+1} \notin \mathcal{N}^B$;

β_3: $X_{k+1} \in \mathcal{N}^B$ *or* $-X_{k+1} \notin \mathcal{N}^B$;

β_4: $w \in X_{k+1}$;

β_5: $w \notin X_{k+1}$,

then $X_{k+1} \in \mathcal{N}_w^I$.

(**SI**): *If* $\langle X_1, \ldots, X_n \rangle \in \mathcal{C}_w^{\text{out}}$ *and for* $1 \leq i \leq k$ *and* $k < n$, $X_i \notin \mathcal{N}_w^I$ *or* $\neg X_i \in \mathcal{N}_w^O$, $X_{k+1} \in \mathcal{N}_w^I$, *and* $-X_{k+1} \notin \mathcal{N}_w^O$, *then* $X_{k+1} \in \mathcal{N}_w^{SI}$.

A few comments are in order. The conditions for axioms (**K**), (**D**), (**4**), (**5**), (**N**) and ($\bot$-$\square$) and the inference rule ($\square$-**RR**) are the standard conditions for such axioms in neighbourhood semantics (see [4]). The conditions for the remaining axioms exploit the strong correspondence between propositions and truth sets that allows for a semantic rewriting of the axioms. Axioms ($\otimes$-**shortening**), ($\odot$-**shortening**), ($\otimes$-**O**) and (**O-detachment**) where first proposed by [8] for the use of the sequence semantics for logics to model norms and obligations.

5   Soundness and Completeness

In this section we study the soundness and completeness of the logics defined in Sect. 3. Completeness is based on adaptation of the standard Lindenbaum's construction for modal (deontic) neighbourhood semantics (see [4]).

Definition 10 ($\mathcal{L}$-maximality). *A set w is $\mathcal{L}$-maximal iff for any formula a of $\mathcal{L}$, either $a \in w$, or $\neg a \in w$.*

Lemma 1 (Lindenbaum's Lemma). *Any S-consistent set w of formulae in the language $\mathcal{L}$ can be extended to a S-consistent $\mathcal{L}$-maximal set w^+.*

Proof. Let $a_1, a_2, \ldots$ be an enumeration of all the possible formulae in $\mathcal{L}$.

- $w_0 := w$;

- $w_{n+1} = w_n \cup \{a_n\}$ if its closure under the axioms and rules of S is consistent, $w \cup \{\neg a_n\}$ otherwise;
- $w^+ = \bigcup_{n \geq 0} w_n$.

The construction of a sequence canonical model is as follows.

Definition 11 (S-Canonical Models). *A sequence canonical model*

$$\mathcal{M} = \langle W, \mathcal{C}^O, \mathcal{C}^{out}, \mathcal{N}^O, \mathcal{N}^B, \mathcal{N}^D, \mathcal{N}^G, \mathcal{N}^I, \mathcal{N}^{SI}, V \rangle$$

for the system S *is defined as follows:*

1. W *is the set of all the* $\mathcal{L}$-*maximal consistent sets.*
2. *For any propositional letter* $p \in Prop$, $\|p\|_V := |p|_L$, *where*

$$|p|_L := \{w \in W \mid p \in w\}.$$

3. *Let* $\mathcal{C}^O := \bigcup_{w \in W} \mathcal{C}_w^O$, *where, for each* $w \in W$,

$$\mathcal{C}_w^O := \{\langle \|a_1\|_V, \ldots, \|a_n\|_V \rangle \mid \bigotimes_{i=1}^{n} a_i \in w\},$$

where each a_i *is a meta-variable for a Boolean formula.*
4. *Let* $\mathcal{C}^{out} := \bigcup_{w \in W} \mathcal{C}_w^{out}$, *where, for each* $w \in W$,

$$\mathcal{C}_w^{out} := \{\langle \|a_1\|_V, \ldots, \|a_n\|_V \rangle \mid \bigodot_{i=1}^{n} a_i \in w\},$$

where each a_i *is a meta-variable for a Boolean formula.*
5. *Let* $\mathcal{N}^\square := \bigcup_{w \in W} \mathcal{N}_w^\square$ *where for each world* w,

$$\mathcal{N}_w^\square := \{\|a_i\|_V \mid \square a_i \in w\},$$

where $\square \in \{O, B, D, G, I, SI\}$.

Lemma 2 (Truth Lemma for Canonical Sequence Models). *If* $\mathcal{M} = \langle W, \mathcal{C}^O, \mathcal{C}^{out}, \mathcal{N}^O, \mathcal{N}^B, \mathcal{N}^D, \mathcal{N}^G, \mathcal{N}^I, \mathcal{N}^{SI}, V \rangle$ *is canonical for* S, *then for any* $w \in W$ *and for any formula* A, $A \in w$ *iff* $\models_w^V A$.

Proof. Given the construction of the canonical model, this proof is easy and can be given by induction on the length of an expression A. We consider only some relevant cases.

Assume A has the form $a_1 \otimes \cdots \otimes a_n$. If $A \in w$, by definition of canonical model, then there is a sequence $\langle \|a_1\|_V, \ldots, \|a_n\|_V \rangle \in \mathcal{C}_w^O$. Following from the semantic clauses given to evaluate $\otimes$-formulae, it holds that $\models_w^V a_1 \otimes \ldots \otimes a_n$. For the opposite direction, assume that $\models_w^V a_1 \otimes \ldots \otimes a_n$. By definition, there is $\mathcal{C}_w$ which contains an ordered j-tuple $\langle \|a_1\|_V, \ldots, \|a_n\|_V \rangle$ and by construction $a_1 \otimes \ldots \otimes a_n \in w$. Clearly the same argument holds in the case of operator $\odot$.

If, on the other hand, A has the form $\square b$, where $\square \in \{O, B, D, G, I, SI\}$, and $\square b \in w$, then $\|b\|_V \in \mathcal{N}_w^\square$ by construction, and by definition $\models_w^V \square b$. Conversely, if $\models_w^V \square b$, then $\|b\|_V \in \mathcal{N}_w^\square$ and, by construction of $\mathcal{N}^\square$, $\square b \in w$.

It is easy to verify that the canonical model exists, it is not empty, and it is a sequence semantics model.

Consider any formula $A \notin S$; $\{\neg A\}$ is consistent and it can be extended to a maximal set w such that for some canonical model, $w \in W$. By Lemma 2, $\nvDash_w^V A$.

Corollary 1. *The system S is sound and complete with respect to the class of bi-sequence frames.*

Lemma 3. *The canonical model for S enjoys all the properties listed in Definition 9.*

Proof. For the cases for ($\Box$-RE), (**K**), (**N**), ($\bot$-$\Box$), (**D**), (**4**) and (**5**), see [4]. The proofs for the cases for ($\otimes$ and $\odot$-RE), ($\otimes$-**contraction**), ($\odot$-**contraction**), ($\otimes$-**shortening**), ($\odot$-**shortening**), ($\otimes$-**O**) and (**O-detachment**) are given in [8].

The proof of the remaining cases is rather straightforward and it follows the structure of the axioms involved.

($\odot$-D) Assume $\langle X_1, \ldots, X_n \rangle \in \mathcal{C}_w^{\text{out}}$. Then, by construction of the canonical model, for $1 \leq i \leq n$, it holds that $X_i = \|a_i\|_V$ and $a_1 \odot \cdots \odot a_n \in w$. Thus $\mathsf{D}a_i \in w$ for $1 \leq i \leq n$ by ($\odot$-D), hence $X_i \in \mathcal{N}_w^{\mathsf{D}}$, with $1 \leq i \leq n$.

($\odot$-G_1) Assume $\langle X_1, \ldots, X_n \rangle \in \mathcal{C}_w^{\text{out}}$ and $\neg X_1 \notin \mathcal{N}_w^{\mathsf{D}}$. Then, by construction, $a_1 \odot \cdots \odot a_n \wedge \neg \mathsf{D}\neg a_1 \in w$, where for $1 \leq i \leq n$, $X_i = \|a_i\|_V$. By ($\odot$-G_1), $\mathsf{G}a_1 \in w$ and $X_1 \in \mathcal{N}_w^{\mathsf{G}}$.

($\odot$-G-gen) Suppose $\langle X_1, \ldots, X_n \rangle \in \mathcal{C}_w^{\text{out}}$ and, for $1 \leq i \leq k$ and $k < n$, $\neg X_i \in \mathcal{N}_w^{\mathsf{D}}$ and $\neg X_{k+1} \notin \mathcal{N}_w^{\mathsf{D}}$, then $a_1 \odot \cdots \odot a_n \wedge \bigwedge_{i=1}^{k<n} \mathsf{D}\neg a_i \wedge \neg \mathsf{D}\neg a_{k+1} \in w$ by construction of the canonical model. By ($\odot$-G-gen), $\mathsf{G}a_{k+1} \in w$ and $X_{k+1} \in \mathcal{N}_w^{\mathsf{G}}$.

(I) Assume $\langle X_1, \ldots, X_n \rangle \in \mathcal{C}_w^{\text{out}}$ and, for $1 \leq i \leq k$ and $k < n$, α_1: $w \notin X_i$ and β_1: $X_{k+1} \in \mathcal{N}^{\mathsf{B}}$. Then $a_1 \odot \cdots \odot a_n \wedge \bigwedge_{i=1}^{k<n} \neg a_i \wedge \mathsf{B}a_{k+1} \in w$. Hence, by (I), $\mathsf{I}a_{k+1} \in w$ and $X_{k+1} \in \mathcal{N}_w^{\mathsf{I}}$. The proof for the other cases is similar.

(SI) Suppose $\langle X_1, \ldots, X_n \rangle \in \mathcal{C}_w^{\text{out}}$ and for $1 \leq i \leq k$ and $k < n$, $X_i \notin \mathcal{N}_w^{\mathsf{I}}$ or $\neg X_i \in \mathcal{N}_w^{\mathsf{O}}$, $X_{k+1} \in \mathcal{N}_w^{\mathsf{I}}$, and $\neg X_{k+1} \notin \mathcal{N}_w^{\mathsf{O}}$. Then, by construction of the canonical model, $a_1 \odot \cdots \odot a_n \wedge \left(\bigwedge_{i=1}^{k<n} \neg \mathsf{I}a_i \vee \mathsf{O}\neg a_i \right) \wedge \mathsf{I}a_{k+1} \wedge \neg \mathsf{O}\neg a_{k+1} \in w$. By (SI) and modus ponens, $\mathsf{SI}a_{k+1} \in w$ and thus $X_{k+1} \in \mathcal{N}_w^{\mathsf{SI}}$.

6 Conclusions

This paper offered a semantic study of the $\otimes$ and $\odot$ operators originally introduced in [5] to model deontic reasoning and contrary-to-duty obligations. We showed that a suitable axiomatisation was able to capture characteristics in the context of multi-modal logics the unified framework by [9] for agents' motivational and deliberative components where goals, desires, and intentions are *different facets* of the *same phenomenon*, all of them being goal-like attitudes. In particular, we proved that $\otimes$- and $\odot$ expressions can be characterised in a class of structures extending neighbourhood frames with sequences of sets of worlds.

We argued that both the formalism, and the semantics can be employed, with some adjustments, to grasp various forms of reasoning about BDI-like agents.

A number of open research issues are left for future work. The logic of [9] investigates how to characterise different degrees and types of goal-like mental attitudes of agents. These works assume defeasible logic as the underlying logic and they are restricted to literals. However, they show that the extension of defeasible logic obtained from adding $\otimes$ and $\odot$ are still computationally feasible. The natural question is to see how to use the sequence semantics we have presented in this paper to capture the different intuitions of $\otimes$ and $\odot$ discussed in the above mentioned work. In addition we plan to explore decidability questions using, for example, the filtration methods. The fact that neighbourhoods contain sequences of sets of worlds instead of sets is not expected to make the task significantly harder than the one in standard neighbourhood semantics for modal logics.

Second, we expect to enrich the language and allow for nesting of $\otimes$- and $\odot$-expressions, thus having formulae like $a \otimes \neg(b \otimes c) \otimes d$. We argued in [5] that the meaning of those formulae is not clear in deontic reasoning. However, a semantic analysis of them in the sequence semantics can clarify the issue. Indeed, in the current language we can evaluate in any world w formulae like $\neg(a \otimes b)$.

References

1. Andrighetto, G., Governatori, G., Noriega, P., van der Torre, L.W.N. (eds.) Normative Multi-agent Systems. Dagstuhl Follow-Ups, vol. 4. Schloss Dagstuhl - Leibniz-Zentrum fuer Informatik (2013)
2. Brewka, G., Benferhat, S., Le Berre, D.: Qualitative choice logic. Artif. Intell. **157**(1–2), 203–237 (2004)
3. Broersen, J., Dastani, M., Hulstijn, J., van der Torre, L.: Goal generation in the BOID architecture. Cogn. Sci. Q. **2**(3–4), 428–447 (2002)
4. Chellas, B.F.: Modal Logic, An Introduction. Cambridge University Press, Cambridge (1980)
5. Governatori, G., Rotolo, A.: Logic of violations: a Gentzen system for reasoning with contrary-to-duty obligations. Australas. J. Logic **4**, 193–215 (2006)
6. Governatori, G., Rotolo, A.: BIO logical agents: norms, beliefs, intentions in defeasible logic. Auton. Agent. Multi-agent Syst. **17**(1), 36–69 (2008)
7. Governatori, G.: Thou shalt is not you will. In: Atkinson, K. (ed.) Proceedings of the Fifteenth International Conference on Artificial Intelligence and Law, pp. 63–68. ACM, New York (2015)
8. Governatori, G., Olivieri, F., Calardo, E., Rotolo, A.: Sequence semantics for norms and obligations. In: Proceedings Deontic Logic and Normative Systems, pp. 93–108. College Publications (2016)
9. Governatori, G., Olivieri, F., Scannapieco, S., Rotolo, A., Cristani, M.: The rational behind the concept of goal. Theory Pract. Logic Program. **16**(3), 296–324 (2016)
10. Thomason, R.H.: Desires, defaults: a framework for planning with inferred goals. In: Cohn, A.G., Giunchiglia, F., Selman, B. (eds.) KR2000. Morgan Kaufmann, San Francisco (2000)

Revenue Maximizing Markets
for Zero-Day Exploits

Mingyu Guo[1]($\boxtimes$), Hideaki Hata[2], and Ali Babar[1]

[1] School of Computer Science, University of Adelaide, Adelaide, Australia
{mingyu.guo,ali.babar}@adelaide.edu.au
[2] Graduate School of Information Science,
Nara Institute of Science Technology, Ikoma, Japan
hata@is.naist.jp

Abstract. Markets for zero-day exploits (software vulnerabilities unknown to the vendor) have a long history and a growing popularity. We study these markets from a revenue-maximizing mechanism design perspective. We first propose a theoretical model for zero-day exploits markets. In our model, one exploit is being sold to multiple buyers. There are two kinds of buyers, which we call the defenders and the offenders. The defenders are buyers who buy vulnerabilities in order to fix them (*e.g.*, software vendors). The offenders, on the other hand, are buyers who intend to utilize the exploits (*e.g.*, national security agencies and police). Our model is more than a single-item auction. First, an exploit is a piece of information, so one exploit can be sold to multiple buyers. Second, buyers have externalities. If one defender wins, then the exploit becomes worthless to the offenders. Third, if we disclose the details of the exploit to the buyers before the auction, then they may leave with the information without paying. On the other hand, if we do not disclose the details, then it is difficult for the buyers to come up with their private valuations. Considering the above, our proposed mechanism discloses the details of the exploit to all offenders before the auction. The offenders then pay to delay the exploit being disclosed to the defenders.

Keywords: Revenue maximization · Mechanism design · Security economics · Bug bounty

1 Introduction

A zero-day exploit refers to a software vulnerability that has not been disclosed to the public, and is unknown to the software vendor. Information of new vulnerabilities gives cyber attackers free passes to attacking targets, while the vulnerabilities remain undetected. The trading of zero-day exploits has a long history, and selling them by security researchers as "legitimate source of income" is a recent trend [5].

Zero-day exploits markets are not necessarily black markets where the buyers are potential cyber criminals. Software vendors buy exploits via bug bounty

© Springer International Publishing Switzerland 2016
M. Baldoni et al. (Eds.): PRIMA 2016, LNAI 9862, pp. 247–260, 2016.
DOI: 10.1007/978-3-319-44832-9_15

reward programs. National security agencies and police also buy exploits. It is widely reported that government agencies utilize zero-day exploits to track criminals or for other national security reasons. Financial industry companies buy exploits to prevent attacks (once an exploit method is known, these companies can then carry out counter measures to prevent attacks). There are legitimate venture capital backed security companies whose business model is to sell exploits for profit. For example, ZeroDium is a zero-day acquisition firm, which buys high-risk vulnerabilities with premium rewards, then resells them to mostly government clients [6]. Another similar company is Vupen, who offers a subscription service for its clients, providing vulnerability data and exploits for zero days and other bugs [6].

Greenberg presented a price list of zero-day exploit sale, ranging from $5,000–$30,000 to $100,000–$250,000 [8]. These prices are so high because it is generally difficult for the software vendor to independently discover these vulnerabilities [2], hence the exploits are expected to be alive for long periods of time.

In this paper, we study markets for zero-day exploits from a revenue-maximizing mechanism design perspective. Our contributions are:

- We present a theoretical mechanism design model for zero-day exploits markets. We identify the unique features of zero-day exploits markets. First, an exploit is a piece of information, so one exploit can be sold to multiple buyers. Second, buyers have externalities. We divide the buyers into two types: the offenders and the defenders. Once a defender "wins" an exploit, the exploit becomes worthless for the offenders. Third, if we disclose the details of the exploit to the buyers before the auction, then they may leave with the information without paying. On the other hand, if we do not disclose the details, then it is difficult for the buyers to come up with their private valuations.
- We propose the *straight-forward (SF)* mechanism property, which requires that the mechanism discloses the full details of the exploit to the offenders before they submit their bids. In Proposition 1, we show that for the purpose of designing revenue-maximizing mechanisms, if SP, IR, and SF are required, then it is without loss of generality to focus on mechanisms that "divide" the time frame into two regions. Such a mechanism would disclose the full details of the exploit to all offenders, and then based on the reports from both the offenders and the defenders, pick an ending time. Before the ending time, the exploit is alive. Once it reaches the ending time, the exploit is revealed to the defenders, which renders it worthless. The offenders bid to keep the exploit alive, while the defenders bid to close the exploit earlier. Our model is similar to both the *cake-cutting* problem [3,4] and the *single facility location* problem [7,13].
- For a simplified single-parameter model, where every agent's type is characterized by a single parameter instead of a valuation function over time. We modify and apply Myerson's classic technique for designing optimal single-item auction [12] to our problem of dividing a continuous region. We derive an optimal mechanism that maximizes the expected revenue for the single-parameter model.

- For the general model, we adopt the computationally feasible automated mechanism design approach [9]: instead of optimizing over all mechanisms, we focus on a family of parameterized mechanisms, and tune the parameters in order to obtain a good mechanism. We focus on the AMA mechanisms used for designing revenue-maximizing combinatorial auctions [10,11]. To identify a good AMA mechanism, we propose a technique that combines both optimization and heuristics. We show via numerical experiments that our technique produces good revenue expectation: when applied to a single-parameter model (our technique does not require the single-parameter model), our technique achieves nearly 80 % of the optimal revenue (one reason we test our technique in a single-parameter model is that we are able to calculate the optimal revenue for comparison).

2 Model Description

In this section, we present our mechanism design model for zero-day exploits markets. Our aim is to create a model with minimal assumptions, and draw a parallel between our model and existing classic mechanism design models.

There is one exploit being sold to multiple game-theoretically strategic buyers. The seller is also the mechanism designer, who wants to maximize her revenue (e.g., the seller is a security company that sells exploits for profit[1]).

Assumption 1. The set of all buyers consists of two types of buyers: the defenders and the offenders.

- A defender is a buyer who buys exploits in order to fix them. Given a specific exploit, usually there is only one defender. For example, suppose the exploit attacks the Chrome browser, then Google is the defender, who would, for example, buy the exploit via its bug bounty reward program. Our model allows multiple defenders, but we assume that as soon as one defender gets hold of an exploit, the exploit gets immediately fixed, therefore rendering it worthless. That is, if one defender receives information about an exploit, then all defenders benefit from it.
- An offender is a buyer who intends to utilize the exploit.

Based on the above assumption, we cannot sell an exploit to an offensive buyer after we sell it to any defensive buyer.

Assumption 2. One exploit is sold over a time frame $[0, 1]$. 0 represents the moment the exploit is ready for sale. 1 represents the exploit's end of life (e.g., it could be the end of life of the affected software, or the release of a major service pack).

A mechanism outcome is represented by $(t_1, t_2, \ldots, t_n)$, where t_i is the moment the exploit is disclosed to buyer i. We assume that all defenders receive the information at the same time, denoted by t_{end} (if one defender receives the

---

[1] Example such companies include ZeroDium and Vupen [6].

information, then the exploit is fixed right away). It is also without loss of generality to assume that if i is an offensive buyer, then $t_i \in [0, t_{end}]$ (receiving the information after t_{end} is equivalent to receiving it exactly at t_{end} – from this point on, the exploit is worthless).

Buyer i's type is characterized by a nonnegative function $v_i(t)$. If i is an offensive buyer who receives the exploit at t_i and the exploit gets fixed at t_{end}, then i's valuation equals $\int_{t_i}^{t_{end}} v_i(t)dt$. Similarly, if i is a defensive buyer, then her valuation equals $\int_{t_{end}}^{1} v_i(t)dt$. Basically, the offenders wish to keep the exploit alive for as long as possible, while the defenders wish to fix the exploit as early as possible.

A mechanism takes as input the valuation functions ($v_i(t)$ for $i = 1, 2, \ldots, n$), and produces an outcome $(t_1, t_2, \ldots, t_n)$ and a payment vector $(p_1, p_2, \ldots, p_n)$, where p_i is the amount i pays under the mechanism. A buyer's utility equals her valuation minus her payment. We focus on mechanisms that are strategy-proof and individually rational.

Definition 1. Strategy-proof (SP): *For every buyer i, by reporting $v_i(t)$ truthfully, her utility is maximized.*

Definition 2. Individually rational (IR): *For every buyer i, by reporting $v_i(t)$ truthfully, her utility is nonnegative.*

Besides SP and IR, we introduce another mechanism property specifically for zero-day exploits markets.

One thing we have been ignoring is that an exploit is a piece of information. As a result, if we disclose the exploit's details to the buyers beforehand, then they may simply walk away with the information for free. If we do not describe what we are selling, then it is difficult for the buyers to come up with their valuation functions.

Assumption 3. We assume that there are two ways for the seller to describe an exploit: either describe the full details, or describe what can be achieved with the exploit (*e.g.*, with this exploit, anyone can seize full control of a Windows 7 system remotely).

- We assume that it is safe for the seller to disclose what can be achieved with the exploit. That is, the buyers will not be able to derive "how it is done" from "what can be achieved".
- If the seller only discloses what can be achieved, then it is difficult for an offensive buyer to determine whether the exploit is new, or something she already knows. It is therefore difficult for the offensive players to come up with their valuation functions in this kind of situation. They may come up with expected valuation functions (by estimating how likely the exploit is new), but this may then lead to regret after the auction.
- We assume that the defenders are able to come up with private valuation functions just based on what can be achieved. This is because all zero-day

exploits are by definition unknown to the defenders. This assumption is consistent with practise. For bug bounty programs, vulnerabilities are generally classified into different levels of severities, and vendors pay depending on these classification [1]. For example, Google Chrome provides guidelines to classify vulnerabilities into critical, high, medium, and low severities, and pay accordingly [14].

The above assumptions lead to the following mechanism property:

Definition 3. Straight-forward (SF): *A mechanism is straight-forward if the mechanism reveals the full details of the exploit to the offensive buyers, before asking for their valuation functions.*

It should be noted that SF does not require that the exploit details be revealed to the defenders before they bid. If the seller does this, then the defenders would simply fix the exploit and bid $v_i(t) \equiv 0$. Due to IR, the defenders can get away without paying.

Offenders are revealed the details before they bid, but they cannot simply bid $v_i(t) \equiv 0$ to get away without paying. Our mechanisms' key idea is to use the defenders as "threat". That is, if the offenders bid too low, then we disclose the exploit to the defenders earlier, which renders the exploit worthless. Essentially, the offenders need to pay to keep the exploit alive (the more they pay, the longer the exploit remains alive).

From now on, we focus on mechanisms that are SP, SF, and IR. We present the following characterization result:

Proposition 1. *Let M be a mechanism that is strategy-proof, individually rational, and straight-forward.*

We can easily construct M′ based on M, so that M′ is also strategy-proof, individually rational, and straight-forward. M′ and M have the same revenue for all type profiles. M′ takes the following form:

- *At time 0, the seller reveals the exploit in full details to all offenders, and reveals what can be achieved with the exploit to all defenders.*
- *Collect valuation functions from the buyers.*
- *Pick an outcome and a payment vector based on the reports. It should be noted that it is sufficient to represent the outcome using just t_{end}, which is when the exploit gets fixed.*

The above proposition implies that for the purpose of design revenue-maximizing mechanisms, it is without loss of generality to focus on mechanisms with the above form.

Proof. Given M, we modify it and construct $M′$ as follows: for all i that is an offender, we move t_i to 0. For all i that is a defender, we do not change t_i. For every type profile, we keep M's payment vector. That is, $M′$ has the same revenue for every type profile. $M′$ is obviously SF.

Now we show M' is still SP and IR. It is easy to see that the defenders' valuations are not changed, so M' is still SP and IR for the defenders. Offenders' valuations are changed. For offender i, originally under M, she receives the information at time t_i. Under M', she receives the information at time 0. It should be noted that because M is SF, that means t_i is not dependent on i's own report. Therefore, the valuation increase for i, which equals $\int_0^{t_i} v_i(t)dt$, is independent of i's own report. Hence, this increase of valuation does not change i's strategy. M' is still SP and IR for the offenders as well.

3   Comparing Against Classic Models

To summarize our model, there are two types of agents (offenders and defenders). Agent i's type is characterized by her valuation function $v_i(t)$. The outcome $t_{end}(v_1, v_2, \ldots, v_n) \in [0, 1]$ is chosen based on the type profile. The exploit is active between $[0, t_{end}]$, during which period all offenders can utilize the exploit. The exploit becomes worthless from t_{end}. High bids (high valuation functions) from the offenders would push t_{end} toward 1, while high bids from the defenders would push t_{end} toward 0.

Our model is very similar to both the *cake-cutting* problem and the *single facility location* problem.

Cake-cutting: The time frame $[0, 1]$ can be viewed as the cake. t_{end} cuts the cake into two halves. The agents' types are also characterized by valuation functions instead of single values. On the other hand, there are also differences. For one thing, our model is more like *group* cake cutting, as both sides involve multiple agents. Secondly, the offenders are bound to the left-hand side ($[0, t_{end}]$) while the defenders are bound to the right-hand side ($[t_{end}, 1]$).

Single facility location: t_{end} can also be viewed as the position of the facility in a single facility location problem. The defenders are all positioned at 0, so they prefer t_{end} to be closer to 0 (which enlarges the interval $[t_{end}, 1]$). The offenders are all positioned at 1, so they prefer t_{end} to be closer to 1 (which enlarges the interval $[0, t_{end}]$).

Unfortunately, most cake-cutting and facility location literatures focus on money-free settings, so previous results do not apply to our problem of revenue maximizing mechanism design.

4   Optimal Single-Parameter Mechanism

In this section, we study a simplified single-parameter model, and derive an optimal mechanism that maximizes the expected revenue. Results in this section are based on Myerson's technique on optimal single item auction, which is modified to work for our problem.

Assumption 4. Single-parameter model (we need this assumption only in this section): Agent i's valuation function $v_i(t)$ is characterized by a single parameter $\theta_i \in [0, \infty)$:
$$v_i(t) = \theta_i c_i(t)$$

Here, $c_i(t)$ is a publicly known nonnegative function. That is, i's type is characterized by a single parameter θ_i.

For example, consider an offender i, if $c_i(t)$ represents the number of users i may attack using the exploit at time t, and θ_i is agent i's valuation for attacking one user over one unit of time, then we have $v_i(t) = \theta_i c_i(t)$. (For defenders, it'd be saving instead of attacking.)

For the single-parameter model, a mechanism is characterized by functions t_{end} and p. $t_{end}(\theta_1, \theta_2, \ldots, \theta_n)$ determines the outcome. $p(\theta_1, \theta_2, \ldots, \theta_n)$ determines the payment vector. Actually, for mechanisms that are SP and IR, p is completely determined by the allocation function t_{end}.

Fixing θ_{-i} and drop it from the notation, when agent i reports θ_i, we denote the outcome by $t_{end}(\theta_i)$.

Proposition 2. *If i is an offender, then we define*

$$x_i(\theta_i) = \int_0^{t_{end}(\theta_i)} c_i(t)dt$$

If i is a defender, then we define

$$x_i(\theta_i) = \int_{t_{end}(\theta_i)}^1 c_i(t)dt$$

A mechanism is SP and IR if and only if for all i, $x_i(\theta_i)$ is nondecreasing in θ_i, and agent i's payment equals exactly

$$\theta_i x_i(\theta_i) - \int_0^{\theta_i} x_i(z)dz$$

Proof. Suppose $x_i(\theta_i)$ is nondecreasing in θ_i and i pays according to the above expression. By reporting θ_i, i's utility equals

$$\theta_i x_i(\theta_i) - \theta_i x_i(\theta_i) + \int_0^{\theta_i} x_i(z)dz = \int_0^{\theta_i} x_i(z)dz \geq 0.$$

The above implies IR. We then show SP. By reporting θ_i', i's utility equals

$$\theta_i x_i(\theta_i') - \theta_i' x_i(\theta_i') + \int_0^{\theta_i'} x_i(z)dz.$$

We subtract the above from i's utility when reporting truthfully, the difference equals

$$\int_0^{\theta_i} x_i(z)dz - \theta_i x_i(\theta_i') + \theta_i' x_i(\theta_i') - \int_0^{\theta_i'} x_i(z)dz.$$

If $\theta_i > \theta_i'$, then the above equals

$$\int_{\theta_i'}^{\theta_i} x_i(z)dz - (\theta_i - \theta_i')x_i(\theta_i') \geq \int_{\theta_i'}^{\theta_i} x_i(\theta_i')dz - (\theta_i - \theta_i')x_i(\theta_i')$$

The right-hand side equals 0. Hence, under-reporting is never beneficial. Similarly, we can show over-reporting is never beneficial.

For the other direction, suppose the mechanism under discussion is SP and IR. We use $p_i(\theta_i)$ to represent i's payment. By SP, we have

$$\theta_i x_i(\theta_i) - p_i(\theta_i) \geq \theta_i x_i(\theta_i') - p_i(\theta_i')$$

$$\theta_i' x_i(\theta_i') - p_i(\theta_i') \geq \theta_i' x_i(\theta_i) - p_i(\theta_i)$$

Combining these two inequalities, we get

$$(\theta_i - \theta_i') x_i(\theta_i) \geq (\theta_i - \theta_i') x_i(\theta_i').$$

Therefore, x_i must be nondecreasing.

By reporting θ_i', i's utility equals $\theta_i x_i(\theta_i') - p_i(\theta_i')$. This is maximized when $\theta_i' = \theta_i$. Also, θ_i is arbitrary. We have $z x_i'(z) = p_i'(z)$. Integrating both sides from 0 to θ_i, we get that i's payment must be as described in the proposition.

For agent i, we assume θ_i is drawn independently from 0 to an upper bound H_i, according to a probability density function f_i (and cumulative density function F_i). Agent i's virtual valuation $\phi_i(\theta_i)$ is defined as

$$\phi_i(\theta_i) = \theta_i - \frac{1 - F_i(\theta_i)}{f_i(\theta_i)}$$

We need the *monotone hazard rate condition*: the virtual valuation functions are nondecreasing (which is generally true for common distributions).

Given the payment characterization result, the expected payment from agent i equals $E_{\theta_i}(\phi_i(\theta_i) x_i(\theta_i))$. That is, given a type profile, to maximize revenue, we pick t_{end} to maximize $\sum_i(\phi_i(\theta_i) x_i(\theta_i))$. This decides how to pick the outcome.

The last step is a new step on top of Myerson's technique, which is required for our problem. For our model, x_i is not necessarily bounded between 0 and 1 (for single-item auction, the proportion won by an agent is between 0 and 1). Also, the sum of the x_i is not necessarily bounded above by 1 (for single-item auction, the total proportion allocated is at most 1). Without these bounds, picking the x_i becomes more difficult. Fortunately, for our model, an outcome is characterized by a single value, so we simply run a single dimensional optimization. It should be noted that when an agent increases her bid, her virtual valuation also increases according to the monotone hazard rate condition. This leads to higher value for x_i under our model. That is, the above rule for picking an outcome ensures that the x_i are monotone.

The payments are then calculated according to the payment characterization result. The resulting mechanism maximizes the expected revenue.

5   General Model and Randomized Mechanisms

In this section, we return to the original model where an agent's type is characterized by a valuation function instead of a single parameter.

To design revenue-maximizing mechanisms for the general model, we adopt the computationally feasible automated mechanism design approach [9]. That is, instead of optimizing over all mechanisms (which is too difficult), we focus on a family of parameterized mechanisms, and tune the parameters in order to obtain a good mechanism. We focus on the AMA mechanisms used for designing revenue-maximizing combinatorial auctions [10, 11]. To identify an AMA mechanism with high revenue, we propose a technique that combines both optimization and heuristic methods.

The family of AMA mechanisms includes the VCG mechanism as a special case. For our model, the VCG mechanism works as follows:

- Pick an outcome t^*_{end}, which maximizes the agents' total valuation. We denote the set of offenders by O and the set of defenders by D. For an offender $i \in O$, her valuation for outcome t equals $V_i(t) = \int_0^t v_i(z)dz$. For a defender $i \in D$, her valuation for outcome t equals $V_i(t) = \int_t^1 v_i(z)dz$.

$$t^*_{end} = \arg \max_{t \in [0,1]} \left\{ \sum_i V_i(t) \right\}$$

- Then agent i pays how much her presence hurts the other agents. That is, agent i pays

$$\max_{t \in [0,1]} \left\{ \sum_{j \neq i} V_j(t) \right\} - \sum_{j \neq i} V_j(t^*_{end})$$

The AMA mechanisms generalize the VCG mechanisms by assigning a positive coefficient μ_i to each agent. The AMA mechanisms also assign an "adjustment term" $\lambda(o)$ for each outcome o, where λ can be any arbitrary function. For our model, the AMA mechanisms work as follows (different μ_i and λ correspond to different AMA mechanisms):

- Pick an outcome t^*_{end}, which maximizes the agents' total valuation, considering the μ_i and the function λ.

$$t^*_{end} = \arg \max_{t \in [0,1]} \left\{ \sum_i \mu_i V_i(t) + \lambda(t) \right\}$$

- Then agent i pays how much her presence hurts the other agents, again, considering the μ_i and the function λ. Agent i pays

$$\frac{1}{\mu_i} \left(\max_{t \in [0,1]} \left\{ \sum_{j \neq i} \mu_j V_j(t) + \lambda(t) \right\} - \sum_{j \neq i} \mu_j V_j(t^*_{end}) - \lambda(t^*_{end}) \right)$$

The idea behind the AMA mechanisms is that by assigning larger coefficients to the weaker agents (agents who most likely lose according to the prior distribution), it increases competition, therefore increases revenue. Also, if an outcome o is frequently chosen and the agents have high surplus on this outcome, then by assigning a negative $\lambda(o)$, the agents may be forced to pay more for this outcome.

All AMA mechanisms are SP and IR. Since we disclose the full details of the exploit to all offenders in the beginning, SF is always guaranteed.

So far, we have only considered deterministic mechanisms. t^*_{end} refers to a particular moment. Between $[0, t_{end}]$, the exploit is 100 % alive, while between $[t_{end}, 1]$, the exploit is 100 % dead (already fixed). We could generalize the outcome space by allowing randomized mechanisms. A randomized mechanism's outcome is not just a single value. Instead, the outcome is characterized by a function $\alpha(t)$ over time. For any moment t, $\alpha(t)$ represents the probability that the exploit is still alive at this moment. α's values must be between 0 and 1, and it needs to nonincreasing. The new outcome space includes all deterministic outcomes. For example, the deterministic outcome t^*_{end} is simply

$$\alpha(t) = \begin{cases} 1, t \leq t^*_{end} \\ 0, t > t^*_{end} \end{cases}$$

Allowing randomized mechanisms potentially increases the optimal expected revenue. For example, if one offender has extremely high valuation with very low probability, then under a randomized mechanism, the mechanism could threat to disclose the exploit with a low probability (say, 1 %), unless the agent pays a buck load of money. If the agent doesn't have high valuation, which is most of the time, then she wouldn't pay. Since the seller is only disclosing the exploit with 1 % probability, this does not change the expected revenue too much. But if the agent does have high valuation, then the mechanism could earn way more from this agent.

A valid outcome function maps the time frame $[0, 1]$ to values between 1 and 0, and are nonincreasing. Let A be the outcome space. It should be noted that A does not have to contain all valid outcome functions. Allowing randomization, the AMA mechanisms have the following form:

– Pick an outcome function $\alpha \in A$, which maximizes the agents' total valuation, considering the μ_i and the function λ.
  For an offender $i \in O$, her valuation for outcome function α equals $V_i(\alpha) = \int_0^1 \alpha(z)v_i(z)dz$.
  For a defender $i \in D$, her valuation for outcome function α equals $V_i(\alpha) = \int_0^1 (1 - \alpha(z))v_i(z)dz$.

$$\alpha^* = \arg\max_{\alpha \in A}\{\sum_i \mu_i V_i(\alpha) + \lambda(\alpha)\}$$

– Then agent i pays how much her presence hurts the other agents, again, considering the μ_i and the function λ. Agent i pays

$$\frac{1}{\mu_i}\left(\max_{\alpha \in A}\{\sum_{j \neq i} \mu_j V_j(\alpha) + \lambda(\alpha)\} - \sum_{j \neq i} \mu_j V_j(\alpha^*) - \lambda(\alpha^*)\right)$$

We need to pick the μ_i and λ that correspond to high expected revenue. It is infeasible to numerically try all μ_i values and all λ functions. As a result, we adopt a heuristic method for picking the μ_i and λ.

First, we restrict the outcome space A to functions of the following form:

$$\alpha(t) = \begin{cases} \beta_1, \, t \leq \beta_2 \\ 0, \quad t > \beta_2 \end{cases}$$

Here, both β_1 and β_2 are values between 0 and 1. All functions in A are characterized by these two parameters. We denote the outcome function characterized by β_1 and β_2 by α_{β_1,β_2}. The idea is that instead of making the exploit $100\,\%$ alive from the beginning, we may simply kill the exploit right from the beginning with probability $(1 - \beta_1)$.

We choose the following λ, where ζ is a parameter of the mechanism:

$$\lambda(\alpha_{\beta_1,\beta_2}) = \zeta(1 - \beta_1) * \beta_2$$

What we are doing is that we reward outcomes that kill the exploit (with high probabilities) right from the beginning (making these outcomes easier to get chosen under AMA). As a result, if the offenders would like to keep the exploit alive with high probability from the beginning, they have to pay more. Previously, for deterministic mechanisms, the exploit is alive $100\,\%$ from the beginning. After the adjustments here, the agents need to pay to achieve high probability from the beginning.

Once we focus our attention on λ of the above form. An AMA mechanism is characterized by n parameters: the μ_i (except for μ_1, since it is without loss of generality to set $\mu_1 = 1$) and ζ. For small number of agents, we are able to numerically optimize over these parameters and obtain an AMA mechanism with good expected revenue.

6   Example and Simulation

In this section, we present an example mechanism design scenario, and simulate our proposed mechanisms' performances.

To make the examples more accessible, we consider a simple single-parameter setting involving just one offender (agent 1) and one defender (agent 2).

For single-parameter settings, an agent's valuation function $v_i(t)$ equals $\theta_i c_i(t)$, where $c_i(t)$ describes the pattern of this agent's valuation over time. For the offender, we assume $c_1(t) = 1 - t$. That is, the offender has higher valuation for the exploit earlier on, and her valuation drops to 0 at the end of the time frame. For the defender, we assume $c_2(t) = 1$. That is, the defender's valuation for the exploit does not change over time.

In order to make our example and simulation more realistic, we assume the exploit is a vulnerability of the Chrome browser. According to [8], an exploit that attacks the Chrome browser sells between $80k$ and $200k$ for offensive clients (USD). According to Google's official bug bounty reward program for the Chrome browser [14], a serious exploit is priced between $0.5k$ and $15k$. That is, for a defender, we expect the total valuation to be from this range.

The valuation of agent 1 (the offender) for the exploit for the whole time frame equals $\theta_1 \int_0^1 (1 - t)dt = \theta_1/2$. So we assume θ_1 is drawn from a uniform distribution $U(160, 400)$. The valuation of agent 2 (the defender) for the exploit for the whole time frame equals $\theta_2 \int_0^1 1 dt = \theta_2$. So we assume θ_2 is drawn from a uniform distribution $U(0.5, 15)$.

Optimal single-parameter mechanism: Agent 1's virtual valuation equals

$$\phi_1(\theta_1) = \theta_1 - \frac{1 - \frac{\theta_1 - 160}{240}}{1/240} = 2\theta_1 - 400$$

Agent 2's virtual valuation equals Similarly, agent 2's virtual valuation equals $\phi_2(\theta_2) = 2\theta_2 - 15$. Both are monotone as required.

Given a type profile, to maximize revenue, we pick t_{end} to maximize

$$\sum_i (\phi_i(\theta_i) x_i(\theta_i)),$$

where $x_1(\theta_1) = \int_0^{t_{end}} (1 - t) dt = t_{end} - \frac{t_{end}^2}{2}$ and $x_2(\theta_2) = \int_{t_{end}}^1 dt = 1 - t_{end}$. That is, we pick t_{end} to maximize

$$(2\theta_1 - 400)(t_{end} - \frac{t_{end}^2}{2}) + (2\theta_2 - 15)(1 - t_{end})$$

For example, if $\theta_1 = 300$ and $\theta_2 = 10$, $t_{end} = 0.975$.

Based on the payment characterization result, agent 1 pays 102.4 and agent 2 pays 0.2188. Considering all type profiles, the expected total revenue equals 79.20.

AMA mechanism: As mentioned earlier, we focus on AMA mechanisms that are characterized by 2 parameters: μ_2 and ζ. For each pair of parameters, we can simulate the expected revenue. After optimization, we choose $\mu_2 = 13$ and $\zeta = 31$. For this pair, the expected revenue is 63.53. This value is nearly 80 % of the optimal revenue (79.20). Also, we cannot achieve such good result without the heuristic term. If we set $\zeta = 0$, then the obtained revenue is 52.63. We believe this example demonstrates the usefulness of our AMA and heuristic-based technique.

VCG mechanism: The VCG mechanism is the AMA mechanism with $\mu 2 = 1$ and $\zeta = 0$. Under VCG, the expected revenue is merely 7.667.

7   Conclusion

In this paper, we study markets for zero-day exploits from a revenue-maximizing mechanism design perspective. We proposed a theoretical mechanism design model for zero-day exploits markets. By requiring a new mechanism property called straight-forwardness, we also showed that for the purpose of designing revenue-maximizing mechanisms, it is without loss of generality to focus on mechanisms that "divide" the time frame into two regions, which makes our model similar to both the cake-cutting problem and the single facility location problem.

We first considered a simplified single-parameter model, where every agent's type is characterized by a single parameter. With necessary modification and extension at the last step, we were able to apply Myerson's classic technique for designing optimal single-item auction to our model and derived the optimal mechanism for single-parameter models.

For the general model, we adopted the computationally feasible automated mechanism design approach. We focused on the AMA mechanisms. To identify an AMA mechanism with high revenue, we proposed a technique that combines both optimization and heuristics. Numerical experiments demonstrated that our AMA and heuristic-based technique performs well.

References

1. Algarni, A.M., Malaiya, Y.K.: Software vulnerability markets: discoverers and buyers. Int. J. Comput. Electr. Autom. Control Inf. Eng. **8**(3), 71–81 (2014)
2. Bilge, L., Dumitras, T.: Before we knew it: an empirical study of zero-day attacks in the real world. In: Proceedings of 2012 ACM Conference on Computer and Communications Security, CCS 2012, pp. 833–844. ACM, New York (2012). http://doi.acm.org/10.1145/2382196.2382284
3. Brams, S.J., Jones, M.A., Klamler, C.: Better ways to cut a cake - revisited. In: Brams, S., Pruhs, K., Woeginger, G. (eds.) Fair Division. No. 07261 in Dagstuhl Seminar Proceedings, Internationales Begegnungs- und Forschungszentrum für Informatik (IBFI), Schloss Dagstuhl, Germany, Dagstuhl, Germany (2007)
4. Chen, Y., Lai, J., Parkes, D., Procaccia, A.: Truth, justice, and cake cutting. In: Proceedings of the National Conference on Artificial Intelligence (AAAI), Atlanta, GA, USA (2010)
5. Egelman, S., Herley, C., van Oorschot, P.C.: Markets for zero-day exploits: ethics and implications. In: Proceedings of 2013 Workshop on New Security Paradigms Workshop, NSPW 2013, pp. 41–46. ACM, NewYork (2013). http://doi.acm.org/10.1145/2535813.2535818
6. Fisher, D.: Vupen founder launches new zero-day acquisition firm zerodium, 24 July 2015. https://threatpost.com/vupen-launches-new-zero-day-acquisition-firm-zerodium/113933/
7. Goemans, M., Skutella, M.: Cooperative facility location games. J. Algorithms **50**, 194–214 (2004). Early version: SODA 2000, 76–85
8. Greenberg, A.: Shopping for zero-days: a price list for hackers' secret software exploits, 23 March 2012. http://www.forbes.com/sites/andygreenberg/2012/03/23/shopping-for-zero-days-an-price-list-for-hackers-secret-software-exploits/
9. Guo, M., Conitzer, V.: Computationally feasible automated mechanism design: general approach and case studies. In: Proceedings of the National Conference on Artificial Intelligence (AAAI), Atlanta, GA, USA, pp. 1676–1679 (2010). Nectar Track
10. Likhodedov, A., Sandholm, T.: Methods for boosting revenue in combinatorial auctions. In: Proceedings of the National Conference on Artificial Intelligence (AAAI), San Jose, CA, USA, pp. 232–237 (2004)
11. Likhodedov, A., Sandholm, T.: Approximating revenue-maximizing combinatorial auctions. In: Proceedings of the National Conference on Artificial Intelligence (AAAI), Pittsburgh, PA, USA (2005)

12. Myerson, R.: Optimal auction design. Math. Oper. Res. **6**, 58–73 (1981)
13. Procaccia, A.D., Tennenholtz, M.: Approximate mechanism design without money. In: Proceedings of the ACM Conference on Electronic Commerce (EC), Stanford, CA, USA, pp. 177–186 (2009)
14. Projects, T.C.: Severity guidelines for security issues (2015). https://www.chromium.org/developers/severity-guidelines. Accessed 15 Sept 2015

Distant Group Responsibility in Multi-agent Systems

Vahid Yazdanpanah[1][(✉)] and Mehdi Dastani[2]

[1] University of Twente, Enschede, The Netherlands
v.yazdanpanah@utwente.nl
[2] Utrecht University, Utrecht, The Netherlands
m.m.dastani@uu.nl

Abstract. In this paper, we introduce a specific form of graded group responsibility called "distant responsibility" and provides a formal analysis for this concept in multi-agent settings. This concept of responsibility is formalized in concurrent structures based on the power of agent groups in such structures. A group of agents is called responsible for a state of affairs by a number of collective decision steps if there exists a strategy for the agent group to preclude the specified state of affairs in the given number of steps. Otherwise, the group is partially responsible based on its maximum contribution to fully responsible groups. We argue that the notion of distant responsibility is applicable as a managerial decision support tool for allocation of limited resources in multi-agent organizations.

1 Introduction

The emergence of autonomous agents and multi-agent systems requires formal models to represent and reason about the responsibility of agents and agent groups for the outcome of their actions (See [15]). Such models allow to identify agent groups that are responsible for some realised state of affairs, or to support designing agent-based systems with formally specified responsibility for the involved agent groups. Studies in philosophy, e.g., [5,10], and artificial intelligence, e.g., [6,8,11], discuss various aspects of responsibility. Philosophical studies such as [5,10] have focused on the moral and ontological aspect of responsibility while in artificial intelligence, we encounter formalisations for the grade of responsibility [8], for responsibility in organisational settings [11], and for coalitional responsibility [6].

The concept of responsibility also has various dimensions such as individual or group responsibility and backward-looking or forward-looking responsibility. In particular some studies, e.g., [5,8], merely focus on individuals and attribution of responsibility to single agents; while group responsibility is addressed in works that also consider agent groups and ascribe responsibility to a collective of agents, e.g., [6,14]. The second dimension, i.e., backward/forward -looking responsibility, takes into account if the state of affairs is already realized and we are reasoning about it while we are looking back to the past (backward-looking), or whether

© Springer International Publishing Switzerland 2016
M. Baldoni et al. (Eds.): PRIMA 2016, LNAI 9862, pp. 261–278, 2016.
DOI: 10.1007/978-3-319-44832-9_16

the state of affairs that we are reasoning about might eventually take place in the future (forward-looking) [17]. For instance, in [5,8] their responsibility notion is backward-looking, in [6] the focus is on forward-looking responsibility, and in [11], the authors provide notions for both, the forward and backward-looking responsibility.

Existing formal approaches to responsibility focus on either the responsibility of individual agents or one-shot encounters. For example, in [5] the responsibility of an individual agent for a specific state of affairs is explained in terms of the causal relation between the available actions of the involved agents and the resultant outcome, while in [6], a coalition/group is responsible only for the state of affairs that it could preclude by means of its available actions in a one-shot encounter. These approaches, however, do not account for some important and intuitive subtleties of this concept as practised in realistic scenarios such as in political or organisation domains. For instance, in political discourse a party that could avoid the approval of a bill, even via a sequence of interactions, is often seen to be responsible for the bill. Note that the approval of the bill could be formulated as preclusion of its disapproval. In further sections of this paper, we provide a concrete example, i.e., a furnace scenario, via which the nuances of the notion that we have in mind will be displayed.

This paper investigates the general problem of whether and to which extent an arbitrary group of agents is responsible for a state of affairs given the abilities of the involved agents. We aim at addressing this problem by proposing the novel concept of *distant responsibility* that captures the capacity of an agent group to influence the realisation of a state of affairs by a number of collective decision steps. Accordingly, an agent group is responsible for a given state of affairs when it has a collective strategy to avoid the state of affairs by a number of collective decision steps. We differentiate between agent groups that are only able to avoid the state of affairs and those who can maintain their avoidance.

Inspired by [6], we focus on power-based responsibility[1] and formally define an agent group to be responsible for a state of affairs by a number of collective decision steps when it is a minimal group and has the potential to avoid the state of affairs. We deem that it is reasonable to attribute responsibility for a state of affairs to a minimal group whenever the realization of the state of affairs is not possible without the allowance of that agent group. However, we believe that it is not reasonable to attribute any degree of responsibility to a group (for a given state of affairs) that is able to avoid the state of affairs but has imperfect knowledge about its ability. Hence, we assume that all the involved agents have perfect knowledge of the multi-agent system. The concept of distant responsibility is forward-looking in the sense of [17] and not limited to one-shot encounters as it focuses on the potential power of agent groups in a multi-agent setting. Moreover, it allows the assignment of responsibility to arbitrary groups of agents, albeit to a certain quantified degree.

---

[1] Other aspects of the concept of responsibility, such as intention of agent groups and their commitment to strategies, are orthogonal to our approach in this paper.

The rest of this paper is organized as follows. Section 2 provides a power-based analysis of the concept of responsibility. Section 3 presents models and preliminary notions for our formalization. In Sects. 4 and 5, we give our definitions for the concept of distant responsibility, introduce formulations for degrees of distant responsibility, and analyse their properties. In Sects. 6 and 7, we provide some discussion of responsibility and related work, respectively. Finally, concluding remarks is presented in Sect. 8.

2   Power-Based Responsibility

Imagine a furnace situated in an industrial firm. The well-functioning of the furnace depends on the actions of the agents a_1, a_2, and a_3 who work on the furnace. They are able to bring units of *fuel* from an illimitable bunker (one unit at a time), make a *spark*, or have a *rest*. While the furnace is active, providing at least two units of fuel is necessary to keep it active. When more than one worker choose to have a rest (or to spark), the furnace is deactivated yet burns out all its available fuel. To activate the furnace, three units of fuel must be provided followed by a spark. We assume that the spark must be provided after (and not simultaneous with) the realization of three units of fuel. The furnace is capable of holding maximum three units of fuel and extras will overflow to the bunker. We write f, s, and r for bringing *fuel*, providing *spark*, and having *rest*, respectively. E.g., while the furnace is inactive and empty, if a_1 and a_2 choose to perform f, and a_3 does s, the furnace will remain inactive. In this case, at least two more rounds are needed to activate the furnace: one to provide a unit of fuel and one to make a spark. In the rest of this paper, we consider the inactivity of the furnace as the (to be avoided) state of affairs.

Responsible Groups by Distance: Let us assume that the furnace is inactive and empty. Attributing responsibility to the groups of agents that are able to preclude the inactivity of the furnace (i.e., the state of affairs) by means of their collective strategy, introduced at [6], suggests that all nonempty groups are responsible for the state of affairs, but in different number of steps. E.g., the group a_2a_3 can provide three units of fuel in at least two rounds and then make a spark in order to activate the furnace. Therefore, we see that responsible agent groups can be characterized by the minimum number of steps they need to be a minimal group that possesses the preclusive power over the state of affairs. E.g., assuming inactive and empty furnace, a_1 is a minimal group that is able to preclude the inactivity in at least four steps, a_1a_2 is a minimal group that is able to do the same in at least three steps, and $a_1a_2a_3$ is a minimal group that is responsible for the state of affairs in two steps. Note that $a_1a_2a_3$ is not responsible in three steps due to the minimality condition because any of its two member subsets, i.e., a_1a_2, a_1a_3, and a_2a_3, are responsible in three steps. We see that the preclusive power of a group, together with the minimality and the length of the collective strategy, are sufficient elements to characterize the notion of *distant group responsibility*. The rationale behind this concept of group responsibility is that in real scenarios (e.g., from the industrial and political context) it enables the beneficiary parties (e.g., managers and lobbyists) to balance and decide how to invest their limited resources in the agent groups involved in the multi-agent system (e.g., investing on minimum number of agents with least number of interactions).

Two Types of Responsibility: We distinguish agent groups that are able to preclude a state of affairs in some steps, *responsible groups*, from those that are able to maintain their preclusion as well, *strictly responsible groups*. E.g., assuming inactive and empty furnace, singleton groups could preclude the inactivity in at least four steps, but they are not able to maintain their preclusion afterwards. Instead, two-member groups are able to preclude the inactivity in at least three steps and maintain their preclusion afterwards. We call the latter agent groups with maintenance ability *strictly responsible* groups for the state of affairs. This distinction can be meaningful for a manager who aims at keeping the furnace active (and not only activating it). In this case, we believe that it is reasonable to allocate relatively larger investment in the groups that are able to preclude the inactivity and maintain it in comparison to those that are only able to activate the furnace.

Responsibility Degrees: The proposed notions of responsibility can be used to assign a *responsibility degree* to groups. Consider the furnace in the inactive and empty state. Although singleton groups cannot preclude the inactivity in three steps, they contribute to the groups a_1a_2, a_1a_3, and a_2a_3 that enjoy such a preclusive power in three steps. Based on this observation and in continuation of the notion of *structural degree of responsibility* in [22], we assign a responsibility degree in some given d steps to any group that shares member(s) with responsible groups in d steps. This degree reflects the maximum contribution of the group in question to the groups that possess a strategy towards preclusion of the state of affairs in the given number of steps. E.g., a_1 contributes to a_1a_2 and a_1a_3, but not to a_2a_3. If we shift to two steps, two member groups have a larger share in $a_1a_2a_3$ (which has a two step preclusion power) than any singleton group. Thus, the proportion of contribution of a group to responsible groups is the key element in the formulation of our responsibility degree. Such a gradation provides a measure that enables the reasoner to make quantitative distinction among non-responsible groups for a state of affairs.

3   Models and Preliminary Notions

We use *Concurrent Structures* to model the behaviour of multi-agent systems [3].

Definition 1 (Concurrent Structure). *A concurrent structure is a tuple $M = (N, Q, Act, d, o)$, where $N = \{a_1, ..., a_k\}$ is a set of agents, Q is a non-empty finite set of states with typical element $q \in Q$, Act is a non-empty finite set of atomic actions, $d : N \times Q \to \mathcal{P}(Act)$ is the function that determines the actions available to any agent $a \in N$ in state $q \in Q$, and o is a deterministic and partial transition function that assigns a state $q' = o(q, \bar{\alpha})$ to a state $q \in Q$ and* action profile $\bar{\alpha} = \langle \alpha_1, ..., \alpha_k \rangle \in d(a_1, q) \times \ldots \times d(a_k, q)$. We use $d_a(q)$ instead of $d(a, q)$, and $d(q)$ instead of $d(a_1, q) \times \ldots \times d(a_k, q)$.

For the sake of readability, we use N (Q, Act, etc.) to denote the set of agents (states, actions, etc.) in M, without explicitly referring to a concurrent structure M. A *path* in M is an infinite sequence $\lambda = q_0, q_1, ...$ of states such that $q_i \in Q$ ($i \geq 0$) and there is a transition between each q_i, q_{i+1}. For a path λ, $\lambda[i] = q_i$ denotes the ith state ($i \geq 0$) of λ and $\Lambda(q)$ denotes the set of all paths that start in q. A perfect information (memoryless) *strategy* of agent a is a function $s_a : Q \rightarrow Act$ such that $s_a(q) \in d_a(q)$. Set of such functions will be denoted by Σ_a. A collective strategy s_C for a group $C \subseteq N$ is a tuple of individual strategies for all agents $a \in C$. The *outcome* of strategy s_C in state $q \in Q$ is defined as the set of all paths that may result from execution of s_C: $out(q, s_C) = \{\lambda \in \Lambda(q) \mid \forall i \in \mathbb{N}_0 \ \exists \bar{\alpha} = \langle \alpha_1, ..., \alpha_k \rangle \in d(\lambda[i]) \ \forall a \in C$ $(\alpha_a = s_C^a(\lambda[i]) \wedge o(\lambda[i], \bar{\alpha}) = \lambda[i+1])\}$, where s_C^a denotes the individual strategy of agent a in the collective strategy s_A. A *state of affairs* refers to a set $S \subseteq Q$ and $\bar{S}$ denotes the set $Q \setminus S$.

Our multi-agent furnace scenario is modelled as the concurrent structure $M = (N, Q, Act, d, o)$, where $N = \{a_1, a_2, a_3\}$, $Q = \{q_0, ..., q_4\}$, $Act = \{f, s, r\}$, $d_a(q) = Act$ for all $a \in N$ and $q \in Q$ (Fig. 1). The inactivity of the furnace, considered as the state of affairs $S = \{q_0, q_1, q_2, q_3\}$.

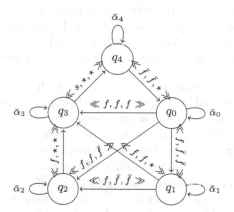

Fig. 1. State q_4 is the only state where the furnace is active. In $q_i \in \{q_0, q_1, q_2, q_3\}$ the furnace is inactive with i unit(s) of fuel. For convenience $\bar{f}$ denotes either s or r, and $\ll f, \bar{f}, \bar{f} \gg$ denotes the set of action profiles involving one single action f, i.e., $\{\langle f, \bar{f}, \bar{f} \rangle, \langle \bar{f}, f, \bar{f} \rangle, \langle \bar{f}, \bar{f}, f \rangle \mid \bar{f} \in \{s, r\}\}$ (similar for others). Moreover, $\bar{\alpha}_i$ denotes any unspecified action profile in $q_i \in Q$ and $\star \in Act$ denotes any available action. The outcome function is as displayed by the accessibility relation in the figure, e.g., $o(q_0, \ll f, f, f \gg) = q_3$ is illustrated by the arrow from q_0 to q_3.

In the following definitions, we omit $M = (N, Q, Act, d, o)$ as it is clear from the context that we are always focused on a given multi-agent system. Thus, references to elements of M should be seen as elements of a given concurrent structure M that is modelling the multi-agent system. For instance, we simply write (the set of states) Q instead of Q *in* M.

Definition 2 (Ability to achieve/maintain). *Let $q \in Q$ and $S \subseteq Q$ a state of affairs. Group $C \subseteq N$ can q-achieve S in $d \in \mathbb{N}_1$ steps iff there is $s_C \in \Sigma_C$ such that $\lambda[d] \in S$ for all $\lambda \in out(q, s_C)$ and C cannot q-achieve S in $d' < d$ steps. Moreover, group $C \subseteq N$ can q-maintain S in $d \in \mathbb{N}_1$ steps iff there is $s_C \in \Sigma_C$ such that $\lambda[i] \in S$ for all $\lambda \in out(q, s_C)$ and $i \geq d$, and C cannot q-maintain S in $d' < d$ steps.*

Assuming inactive and empty furnace (from now state q_0), groups $a_1 a_2$, $a_1 a_3$, and $a_2 a_3$ can activate the furnace in three steps but not less. These groups can also q_0-maintain the activity of the furnace in three steps. However, group $a_1 a_2 a_3$ can q_0-maintain the activity by two steps. Note that a group that can q-achieve/maintain S in d steps cannot do so in $d' < d$. Also, a group C might be able to q-achieve S in d steps by a strategy while it can q-maintain S in $d' \geq d$ steps by means of a different strategy.

Proposition 1 (Maintain implies achieve). *For $q \in Q$, if $C \subseteq N$ can q-maintain $S \subseteq Q$ in d steps, then C can q-achieve S in $d' \leq d$ steps.*

Proof. The ability to q-maintain S in d steps necessitates the existence of a collective strategy s_C that guarantees that among all the paths in $out(q, s_C)$, from state $\lambda[d]$ on, all states are a member of S (Definition 2). Hence, achieving S in d steps is guaranteed. As C may have another strategy s'_C that could guarantee S in $d' < d$ steps, C can q-achieve S in $d' \leq d$ steps.

Note that the ability to achieve does not imply the ability to maintain. So, the other way does not hold in general. The next property shows that adding new members to a group that is able to achieve/maintain a state of affairs, preserves both of the abilities. This would be in correspondence with *monotonicity of power* in [12]. In other words, adding new members to an agent group does not have any negative influence on the ability of the group to achieve/maintain a state of affairs from a given source state and in a specific number of steps. In the following, whenever it is clear from the context, we may omit the phrase "from a given source state and in a specific number of steps".

Proposition 2 (Preservation of abilities). *For $q \in Q$, if $C \subseteq N$ can q-achieve/maintain $S \subseteq Q$ in d steps, then C' can q-achieve/maintain S in $d' \leq d$ steps for $C \subseteq C' \subseteq N$.*

Proof. C has a strategy s_C to q-achieve/maintain S in d steps, regardless of the actions of agents in $N \setminus C$. So, either the group $C' \supseteq C$ has a different strategy $s_{C'}$ to q-achieve/maintain S in $d' < d$ steps or the subgroup $C \subseteq C'$ can execute the former strategy s_C and q-achieve/maintain S in d steps while agents in $C' \setminus C$ are executing an arbitrary action. So, in both cases the claim is justified.

4 Distant Group Responsibility

The concept of *distant* responsibility that we have in mind is *forward-looking*, *local*, and *minimal*. Our approach is forward-looking in the sense of [17] as we merely appraise the potential of groups to avoid a state of affairs and consider that the state of affairs cannot be realized without the group's allowance. However, this does not suggest that a responsible group necessarily practices its preclusive power and prevents the state of affairs. Secondly, our responsibility notion is local in the sense that the preclusive power of groups is considered with respect to a given state and not globally in the whole multi-agent system. Hence, a group that is responsible for a state of affairs from the current state in some given number of steps, might be non-responsible for the same state of affairs from another state in the given number of steps. Finally, a responsible group for a state of affairs in a given number of steps is minimal in the sense that the group is a smallest possible group that has the power to avoid the state of affairs in the given number of steps. In the following definition we omit concurrent structure $M = (N, Q, Act, d, o)$ as we assume it is clear from the context.

Definition 3 (Distant responsibility). *For $q \in Q$, group $C \subseteq N$ is q-responsible for $S \subseteq Q$ in $d \in \mathbb{N}_1$ steps iff C is a minimal group that can q-achieve $\bar{S}$ in d steps. The set of all q-responsible groups C for S in d steps is denoted by $\delta(q, d, S)$.*

Definition 3 allows two distinct groups being q-responsible for one and the same state of affairs by the same or even different number of steps. According to the following proposition, any two distinct responsible groups for one and the same state of affairs in the same number of steps could not be a subgroup of each other.

Proposition 3 (Incomparability). *For $q \in Q$, let $C \neq C'$ be two distinct q-responsible groups from N for $S \subseteq Q$ in d steps. Then, $C \not\subseteq C'$ and $C' \not\subseteq C$.*

Proof. Suppose either $C \subset C'$ or $C' \subset C$. The former case contradicts with the minimality of C' as a q-responsible for S in d steps and the latter contradicts with the minimality of C as a q-responsible for S in d steps.

Due to the minimality, we have the following corollary of Proposition 3.

Corollary 1. *For $q \in Q$, if $C \subseteq N$ is q-responsible for $S \subseteq Q$ in d steps, then for $C' \subseteq N$ neither $C' \subset C$ nor $C' \supset C$ are q-responsible for S in d steps.*

In case a group is responsible for a state of affairs in d steps, it would not be responsible by any number of steps other than d. So, in case of existence, this distance has the uniqueness property.

Proposition 4 (Responsibility distance). *For $q \in Q$, if $C \subseteq N$ is q-responsible for $S \subseteq Q$ in d and d' steps, then $d = d'$.*

Proof. Suppose the contrary. According to Definition 3, C is a minimal group that can q-achieve $\bar{S}$ in both d and d' steps with either $d < d'$ or $d > d'$. Both cases contradict the final part of Definition 2 which states that a group that can q-achieve S in d steps cannot q-achieve S in $d' < d$ steps.

4.1   Strictly Responsible Groups by Distance

A group that, in addition to having the power to preclude the realization of a state of affairs in a certain number of steps, has the power to maintain the preclusion afterwards is called *strictly responsible group*. E.g., groups a_1, a_2, and a_3 in our furnace scenario are able to preclude the inactivity in four steps, but they are unable to maintain their preclusion. In contrast, groups a_1a_2, a_1a_3, a_2a_3, and $a_1a_2a_3$ are able to preclude the inactivity in three steps and maintain their preclusion afterwards.

Definition 4 (Strict responsibility). *For $q \in Q$, group $C \subseteq N$ is strictly q-responsible for $S \subseteq Q$ in $d \in \mathbb{N}_1$ steps iff C is a minimal group that can q-maintain $\bar{S}$ in d steps. The set of all strictly q-responsible groups C for S in d steps is denoted by $\sigma(q, d, S)$.*

Intuitively, this notion attributes the responsibility for a state of affairs S to a group of agents that can preclude S in some steps, has control on holding the preclusion of the state of affairs, and all its members are necessary for this performance.

Example 1 (Responsible Groups). Following our furnace scenario and using Definitions 3 and 4, we have $\delta(q_0, 4, S) = \{a_1, a_2, a_3\}$, $\delta(q_0, 3, S) = \{a_1a_2, a_1a_3, a_2a_3\}$, $\delta(q_0, 2, S) = \{a_1a_2a_3\}$, $\sigma(q_0, 3, S) = \{a_1a_2, a_1a_3, a_2a_3\}$ and $\sigma(q_0, 2, S) = \{a_1a_2a_3\}$. We note that singleton groups, i.e., a_1, a_2, and a_3, are not able to maintain their preclusion of inactivity. Hence, they are q_0-responsible for the inactivity of the furnace in 4 steps but are not strictly q_0-responsible for such a state of affairs in any number of steps. This is due to their inability, i.e., lack of sufficient members, to keep the furnace active while it is activated.

Although all strictly responsible groups possess the combined ability of precluding the state of affairs and maintaining their preclusion in some steps, due to the minimality concern, it is not necessary that a strictly responsible group be also a responsible group by a distance.

Proposition 5 (Two forms of responsibility). *For $q \in Q$, if $C \subseteq N$ is strictly q-responsible for $S \subseteq Q$ in d steps, C is not necessarily a distantly q-responsible group for S.*

Proof. We provide a counter example. Consider $S = \{q_0, q_1, q_3\}$ as the state of affairs in the furnace scenario. Then, $a_1a_2a_3$ is strictly q_0-responsible for S in 1 step as it is a minimal group that can q_0-achieve $q_2 \in \bar{S}$ in 1 step from q_0 (by selecting action profiles $\langle f, f, \bar{f} \rangle$) and stay in q_2 for ever (by selecting action profile $\langle \bar{f}, \bar{f}, \bar{f} \rangle$). Note that due to the minimality condition the set of q_0-responsible groups for S in 1 step contains only a_1a_2, a_1a_3, and a_2a_3.

4.2   Responsibility for Contingent Situations

We circumscribe the set of states of affairs by excluding two classes of *impossible* and *necessary* states of affairs and introducing our *contingency* postulate. To demonstrate the rationale behind this, consider again the furnace scenario. In this scenario, precluding $S = \{q_0, q_1, q_2, q_3\}$ from the state q_0 in 1 step is not possible. In other words, S is a necessity in 1 step and precluding it in 1 step is seen as an impossibility. In contrast, precluding the state of affairs $S' = \{q_4\}$ in 1 step from q_0 is a necessity as there always exists a strategy (e.g., $s_\varnothing \in \Sigma_\varnothing$) that succeeds in preclusion of S' in 1 step. This is due to the fact that for all possible $s_N \in \Sigma_N$ it holds that $\lambda[1] \in \bar{S}'$ for all $\lambda \in out(q_0, s_N)$. Thus, S' is an impossibility in 1 step and its avoidance in 1 step is inherently necessary. We believe that in either of the cases, attributing responsibility to any group $C \in N$ is not a meaningful imputation because in both cases the achievement or avoidance of the state of affairs does not depend on the agents' actions.

Definition 5 (Contingency postulate). *For $q \in Q$, a state of affairs $S \subseteq Q$ is q-contingent in $d \in \mathbb{N}_1$ steps iff N can q-achieve $\bar{S}$ in $d' \leq d$ steps and $\varnothing$ cannot q-achieve $\bar{S}$ in $d'' \leq d$ steps.*

By excluding necessities, we omit all states of affairs S that are not avoidable in d steps. So, any q-contingent state of affairs S in d steps would be avoidable by N in d steps or less, and moreover, S should not be an impossibility in d steps or less (i.e., $\bar{S}$ should not be a necessity, and thus achievable by the empty group, in d steps or less). In the following proposition, we show that for any contingent state of affairs, there exists at least a (minimal) non-empty group that is responsible for it in at most $d \in \mathbb{N}_1$ steps. This matches the intuition that when a state of affairs S is reachable but not necessary within some rounds of collective actions, at least one group of involved agents must be able to preclude it. Hence, in case S occurs, its occurrence took place by means of allowance of such a group.

Proposition 6 (Existence of responsible group). *For $q \in Q$, if $S \subseteq Q$ is q-contingent in d steps, there exists a non-empty q-responsible group $C \subseteq N$ for S in $d' \leq d$ steps.*

Proof. According to Definition 5, for any q-contingent S in d steps, we have that N can q-achieve $\bar{S}$ in $d' \leq d$ steps. So, if N is a minimal group that can q-achieve $\bar{S}$ in d' steps, based on Definition 3, $C = N$ would be q-responsible for S in $d' \leq d$ steps. Otherwise, via exclusion of excess members, we reach a minimal subgroup $C \subset N$ that is q-responsible for S in $d' \leq d$ steps. Note that according to the second condition for q-contingency of S (Definition 5), C could not be empty. Thus, a nonempty group $C \subseteq N$ would be q-responsible for S in $d' \leq d$ steps.

5   Degrees of Distant Responsibility

We attributed the distant responsibility for a state of affairs to agent groups that can preclude the state of affairs by a given number of steps. Thus, a group that only misses one member (in comparison to a responsible group by distance) will be simply considered as a non-responsible group. However, in realistic scenarios, parties with interests in preclusion of a state of affairs are often prepared to invest their limited resources even in such non-responsible groups of agents, albeit proportional to the contribution they can have in the responsible groups. We therefore formulate the degree of responsibility with respect to the contributory share of agent groups in responsible groups.

5.1   Two Responsibility Degrees

Consider again the furnace scenario. For a manager who wants to activate the furnace with the least number of actions (from state q_0), it would be reasonable to invest more resources on two member groups than in singleton groups, although none are q_0-responsible for the inactivity of the furnace in 2 steps. So, despite the fact that two member groups are not able to preclude the inactivity in 2 steps, they have larger contribution than singleton groups to the group $a_1a_2a_3$ which is the q_0-responsible group in 2 steps. Note that the inactivity could not be avoided by shorter distances from q_0. We apply the methodology of [22] for formulating the notion of *structural degree of responsibility* and deem that attributing a degree of responsibility that reflects the grade of preclusive power of agent groups would be a reasonable notion for gradation of distant responsibility. Note again that we omit the repetition of M in the following as it is clear from the context that we are focused on a given multi-agent system.

Definition 6 (Degrees of responsibility). *For $q \in Q$, the degree of q-responsibility of $C \subseteq N$ for $S \subseteq Q$ in $d \in \mathbb{N}_1$ steps defined as $\mathcal{DRD}(C, q, d, S) = \max_{\hat{C} \in \delta(q,d,S)} (\{i \mid i = 1 - \frac{|\hat{C} \backslash C|}{|\hat{C}|}\})$. In case $\delta(q, d, S) = \varnothing$, $\mathcal{DRD}(C, q, d, S)$ is undefined. Moreover, the degree of strict q-responsibility of C for S in $d \in \mathbb{N}_1$ steps is defined as $\mathcal{DSD}(C, q, d, S) = \max_{\hat{C} \in \sigma(q,d,S)} (\{i \mid i = 1 - \frac{|\hat{C} \backslash C|}{|\hat{C}|}\})$. In case $\sigma(q, d, S) = \varnothing$, $\mathcal{DSD}(C, q, d, S)$ is undefined.*

Note that the degrees are bounded in the range of $[0, 1]$: degree 1 is assigned to the responsible groups and degree 0 is assigned to the groups that have no contribution to the responsible groups. It should be noted that attribution of distant responsibility (degrees) to non-contingent states of affairs is not meaningful. According to the following proposition, the addition of new members to a group could not have negative influence on the responsibility degrees. This is in accordance with the concept of *monotonicity of power* [12].

Proposition 7 (Monotonicity of degrees). *Let $q \in Q$, $d \in \mathbb{N}_1$ and $C \subseteq C' \subseteq N$. We have that $\mathcal{DRD}(C, q, d, S) \leq \mathcal{DRD}(C', q, d, S)$ and $\mathcal{DSD}(C, q, d, S) \leq \mathcal{DSD}(C', q, d, S)$.*

Proof. Based on Definition 6, both degrees of responsibility reflect the maximum contribution of C to all responsible groups. This leads to a degree in range of

$[0,1]$ for C. So, all elements in $C' \setminus C$ are either influential in increasing the share of C' in a responsible group by distance or have no influence. Hence, the two degrees might only increase after absorption of some new members.

According to the next proposition, responsible groups by a distance for a given state of affairs and their supergroups, have the full degree of responsibility equal to one, for the state of affairs by the specified distance.

Proposition 8 (Full degrees of responsibility). *For $q \in Q$, let $C \subseteq N$ be a q-responsible group for $S \subseteq Q$ in $d \in \mathbb{N}_1$ steps. Then, for all $C' \supseteq C$, $\mathcal{DRD}(C', q, d, S) = \mathcal{DRD}(C, q, d, S) = 1$. Analogously, for a strictly q-responsible group C for S in $d \in \mathbb{N}_1$ steps, for all $C' \supseteq C$ we have that $\mathcal{DSD}(C', q, d, S) = \mathcal{DSD}(C, q, d, S) = 1$.*

Proof. Based on Definition 6, the degree of (strict) responsibility of a responsible group C in d steps is equal to 1. This is due to fact that C has the maximum possible contribution to C itself. As value of 1 is the maximum possible value for both degrees and according to the monotonicity of degrees (Proposition 7), all super-groups of responsible groups by distance will be assigned with responsibility degree 1.

Example 2 (Responsibility Degrees). According to Definition 3, for the furnace scenario we have $\delta(q_0, d, S) = \varnothing$ for $d \leq 1$ and $d \geq 5$ such that $\mathcal{DRD}(C, q_0, d, S)$ is undefined for all groups C when $d \leq 1$ or $d \geq 5$. For all singleton groups $A \in \{a_1, a_2, a_3\}$, $\mathcal{DRD}(A, q_0, 2, S) = 1/3$, $\mathcal{DRD}(A, q_0, 3, S) = 1/2$, and $\mathcal{DRD}(A, q_0, 4, S) = 1$. Moreover, for two member groups $B \in \{a_1 a_2, a_1 a_3, a_2 a_3\}$, $\mathcal{DRD}(B, q_0, 2, S) = 2/3$ and $\mathcal{DRD}(B, q_0, 3, S) = \mathcal{DRD}(B, q_0, 4, S) = 1$. Finally, we have $\mathcal{DRD}(a_1 a_2 a_3, q_0, d, S) = 1$ and $\mathcal{DRD}(\varnothing, q_0, d, S) = 0$ for all $d \in \{2, 3, 4\}$. When we move to strict degrees of q_0-responsibility for S, for $d \leq 1$ and $d \geq 4$, $\sigma(q_0, d, S) = \varnothing$. Accordingly, for any group C, $\mathcal{DSD}(C, q_0, d, S)$ is undefined for all $d \leq 1$ and $d \geq 4$. We have $\sigma(q_0, 2, S) = \{a_1 a_2 a_3\}$ and $\sigma(q_0, 3, S) = \{a_1 a_2, a_1 a_3, a_2 a_3\}$. So, in distances 2 and 3, for all singleton groups $A \in \{a_1, a_2, a_3\}$, $\mathcal{DSD}(A, q_0, 2, S) = 1/3$ and $\mathcal{DSD}(A, q_0, 3, S) = 1/2$. Furthermore, for all two member groups $B \in \{a_1 a_2, a_1 a_3, a_2 a_3\}$, $\mathcal{DSD}(B, q_0, 2, S) = 2/3$ and $\mathcal{DSD}(B, q_0, 3, S) = 1$. Finally, we have $\mathcal{DSD}(a_1 a_2 a_3, q_0, d, S) = 1$ and $\mathcal{DRD}(\varnothing, q_0, d, S) = 0$ for $d \in \{2, 3\}$.

The next proposition illustrates a case in which a singleton group exclusively possesses the preclusive power over a state of affairs; hence, is the unique (strictly) responsible group for the state of affairs from a given source state in a specific number of steps. The existence of such a *dictator* agent, polarizes the space of (strict) responsibility degrees of all the possible groups for the state of affairs in the specified distance.

Proposition 9 (Polarizing dictatorship). *For $q \in Q$, let $\hat{C} \subseteq N$ be a unique singleton q-responsible group for $S \subseteq Q$ in $d \in \mathbb{N}_1$ steps. Then, for any arbitrary $C \subseteq N$, $\mathcal{DRD}(C, q, d, S) \in \{0, 1\}$ such that $\mathcal{DRD}(C \in I, q, d, S) = 1$ and $\mathcal{DRD}(C \in O, q, d, S) = 0$ where $I = \{C \subseteq N \mid C \supseteq \hat{C}\}$ and $O = \{C \subseteq N \mid$*

$C \not\supseteq \hat{C}\}$. Moreover, for $q \in Q$, let $\hat{C} \subseteq N$ be a unique singleton strictly q-responsible group for $S \subseteq Q$ in $d \in \mathbb{N}_1$ steps. Then, for any arbitrary $C \subseteq N$, $\mathcal{DSD}(C, q, d, S) \in \{0,1\}$ such that $\mathcal{DSD}(C \in I, q, d, S) = 1$ and $\mathcal{DSD}(C \in O, q, d, S) = 0$ where $I = \{C \subseteq N \mid C \supseteq \hat{C}\}$ and $O = \{C \subseteq N \mid C \not\supseteq \hat{C}\}$.

Proof. For any arbitrary $C \subseteq N$, we have that either $C \in I$ or $C \in O$. Based on Proposition 8, for all the supersets of a q-responsible group for a state of affairs in a given number of steps, the degree of q-responsibility is equal to one (for the same state of affairs and in the specified number of steps). So, for all the groups C in $I = \{C \subseteq N \mid C \supseteq \hat{C}\}$, we have that $\mathcal{DRD}(C \in I, q, d, S) = 1$. Moreover, in case a group C does not include the dictator $\hat{C}$, there exists no other q-responsible group to contribute to. Therefore, the degree of q-responsibility for all the groups C in $O = \{C \subseteq N \mid C \not\supseteq \hat{C}\}$ would be equal to zero. By an analogous line of proof, we will have the second part of the proposition for the degree of strict q-responsibility of any arbitrary $C \subseteq N$.

This proposition illustrates that in existence of a uniquely responsible agent, responsibility becomes an all-or-nothing concept. Hence, any arbitrary agent group will be either responsible for the state of affairs (from a source state and in a given number of steps) or non-responsible. I.e., no agent group will be *partially* responsible. This is due to the aggregation of preclusive power in a unique agent.

5.2   Responsibility Degrees for Collaborative Situations

In this section we focus on a specific class of states of affairs, called *collaborative states of affairs*. The realization of a collaborative state of affairs in a given number of steps depends on all agents in the multi-agent system. For these states of affairs, the grand coalition N is the unique (strictly) q-responsible group for some d steps. For instance, in the furnace scenario, the grand coalition $a_1 a_2 a_3$ is the only (strictly) q_0-responsible group for the inactivity of the furnace in 2 steps.

Definition 7 (Collaborative situations). *For $q \in Q$, a state of affairs $S \subseteq Q$ is q-collaborative in $d \in \mathbb{N}_1$ steps iff $\delta(q, d, S) = \{N\}$. Moreover, a state of affairs S is strictly q-collaborative in $d \in \mathbb{N}_1$ steps iff $\sigma(q, d, S) = \{N\}$.*

The following lemma focuses on degrees of distance responsibility for collaborative situations and illustrates the proportionality of degrees to the group size.

Lemma 1 (Proportionality). *For $q \in Q$, if $S \subseteq Q$ is a q-collaborative state of affairs in $d \in \mathbb{N}_1$ steps then for any $C \subseteq N$ we have that $\mathcal{DRD}(C, q, d, S) = \frac{|C|}{|N|}$. Moreover, If S is a strictly q-collaborative state of affairs in $d \in \mathbb{N}_1$ steps then for any $C \subseteq N$ we have that $\mathcal{DSD}(C, q, d, S) = \frac{|C|}{|N|}$.*

Proof. First, we note that $N = \{a_1, \ldots, a_k\}$. Based on Definition 7, grand coalition N is the unique q-responsible group for S in d steps, i.e., $\delta(q, d, S) = \{N\}$. Hence, for any group $C \subseteq N$ the degree of q-responsibility for S in d steps (Definition 6) can be reformulated as $\mathcal{DRD}(C, q, d, S) = 1 - \frac{|N \setminus C|}{|N|}$ which is equal to $\frac{|C|}{|N|}$. Proof of the second claim follows the same line of reasoning in which the assumption that $\sigma(q, d, S) = \{N\}$ implies that $\mathcal{DSD}(C, q, d, S) = \frac{|C|}{|N|}$ for any $C \subseteq N$.

Based on this lemma, in case the grand coalition N is the unique (strictly) responsible group for a specific state of affairs S in d steps, for any group $C \subseteq N$, the degree of (strict) q-responsibility for S in d steps is directly proportional to the size of C. For a collaborative state of affairs the two functions of responsibility degree, i.e., degree of responsibility by distance and degree of strict responsibility by distance, are both additive and scalable.

Proposition 10 (Semilinearity). *For $q \in Q$, if $S \subseteq Q$ is a q-collaborative state of affairs in $d \in \mathbb{N}_1$ steps then (1.1) for $C, C' \subseteq N$ such that $C \cap C' = \varnothing$ we have that $\mathcal{DRD}(C \cup C', q, d, S) = \mathcal{DRD}(C, q, d, S) + \mathcal{DRD}(C', q, d, S)$ and (1.2) for $a \in \mathbb{Q}_{\geq 0}$ and $C, C' \subseteq N$ such that $|C'| = a.|C|$ we have that $\mathcal{DRD}(C', q, d, S) = a.\mathcal{DRD}(C, q, d, S)$. Moreover, If S is a strictly q-collaborative state of affairs in $d \in \mathbb{N}_1$ steps then (2.1) for $C, C' \subseteq N$ such that $C \cap C' = \varnothing$ we have that $\mathcal{DSD}(C \cup C', q, d, S) = \mathcal{DSD}(C, q, d, S) + \mathcal{DSD}(C', q, d, S)$ and (2.2) for $a \in \mathbb{Q}_{\geq 0}$ and $C, C' \subseteq N$ such that $|C'| = a.|C|$ we have that $\mathcal{DSD}(C', q, d, S) = a.\mathcal{DSD}(C, q, d, S)$.*

Proof. "(1.1 and 2.1) Additivity": According to Lemma 1, as $\delta(q, d, S) = \{N\}$ we have that $\mathcal{DRD}(C \cup C', q, d, S) = \frac{|C \cup C'|}{k=|N|}$. Considering that $C \cap C' = \varnothing$ we can reformulate it as $\frac{|C|}{k} + \frac{|C'|}{k}$ which is equal to $\mathcal{DRD}(C, q, d, S) + \mathcal{DRD}(C', q, d, S)$. An analogous line of proof shows that if $\sigma(q, d, S) = \{N\}$ it holds that $\mathcal{DSD}(C \cup C', q, d, S) = \mathcal{DSD}(C, q, d, S) + \mathcal{DSD}(C', q, d, S)$. Additionally, we can also entail that for any arbitrary group C and partition $P = \{C_1, \ldots, C_n\}$ of C, we have $\sum_{i=1}^{n} \mathcal{DRD}(C_i, q, d, S) = \mathcal{DRD}(C, q, d, S)$ if $\delta(q, d, S) = \{N\}$. Moreover, $\sum_{i=1}^{n} \mathcal{DSD}(C_i, q, d, S) = \mathcal{DSD}(C, q, d, S)$ if $\sigma(q, d, S) = \{N\}$. "(1.2 and 2.2) Scaling behaviour": Based on Lemma 1 and the assumption that $|C'| = a.|C|$, we have that $\mathcal{DRD}(C', q, d, S) = \frac{|C'|}{k=|N|} = a.\frac{|C|}{k=|N|}$ which is equal to $a.\mathcal{DRD}(C, q, d, S)$. Analogously for Part 2.2.

6 Discussion

Although the concept of responsibility is extensively studied in philosophy and AI, there is no consensus on a general (in)formal definition or about semantics for this concept. We believe this is due to various dimensions of responsibility such as causality, knowledge, intentionality, morality, etc. As a result, various studies have focused on different dimensions of responsibility (see Sect. 1). In this work, we focused on the *power dimension* of responsibility ignoring other dimensions such as knowledge dimension. Hereby, we discuss the relation between these two concepts, i.e., power and knowledge, and our notion of responsibility. We are aware that our formal exposition of responsibility ignores various dimensions of this concept. This is by purpose as our concern is to investigate the power dimension of responsibility. We believe that formalizing this dimension captures some (but not all) intuitive subtleties of responsibility and can be applied in some real-world scenarios such as strategic planning, reasoning in political context, and design of resource sharing mechanisms in multi-agent systems as we will explain later in this section. Note that focusing on a specific dimension of a phenomenon such as responsibility is a common practice. E.g., Chokler and Halpern [8] focus merely on causal aspect of responsibility ignoring other issues.

As framed by [16], *"power is a capacity or potential"* which might remain unexercised. If a group of agents is able to preclude a state of affairs, it is not justified to entail that they will necessarily do so. We do not claim that a group is responsible if collective actions take place. Conversely, we consider forward-looking responsibility (in sense of [17]). Roughly speaking, possessing power does not imply that the group necessarily exercise its power. As we only analyze possibilities, groups that possess collective strategies towards a preclusion are not committed to execute it (see [1] for an in-detail analysis and an ATL-based formalization of group strategies that come without (or with) commitment). Our analysis applies before the coalition formation process and considers the possibilities of potential groups/coalitions. Our notion of responsibility is formulated by assuming that agents have perfect knowledge about the system. By means of emphasizing our approach to formulating responsibility in terms of *power* and our *perfect knowledge* assumption, a possible misunderstanding of our forward-looking notion of group responsibility can be pointed out. This is to apply our notions in scenarios from legal domain. We believe that in assessing culpability, it is the case that the reasoning is about an already realized state of affairs (in past), where backward-looking responsibility is applicable. Moreover, we follow [8] and believe that for attribution of liability, blameworthiness, and in principles such as *contributory negligence* in the legal domain, level of knowledge of agents plays a significant role. Therefore, responsibility notions that take into account the imperfect knowledge are applicable while we consider perfect knowledge. Moreover, we remind that our conception of responsibility is free of any moral overtone.

Our notion of distant responsibility can be applied to design and analyse task-allocation mechanisms and resource-sharing protocols in multi-agent systems. As argued in [13], a task-decomposition procedure that takes the potentials of involved agent groups into account can enhance the applicability of the task-allocation mechanisms. Consider a decision-maker who is faced with a complex task (e.g., to avoid the inactivation of an industrial furnace) and is able to compute the degrees of distant responsibility of all the possible agent groups in the system for various combinations of sub-tasks. This simply enables the decision-maker to allocate each sub-task to an agent group with highest degree of distant responsibility in the least number of steps. In the ideal cases where for each sub-task a fully responsible group does exist, this task allocation mechanism guarantees the fulfillment of the complex task. And in other cases, it is guaranteed that each sub-task is allocated to the most capable agent group.

Concerning the resource allocation process, sharing resources among agent groups and applying justifiable methods for resource allocation could be challenging (see [7]). Based on degrees of responsibility of agent groups for (un-)desired states of affairs in a given distances, the decision maker(s) can categorize the agent groups that are influential for realization of a state of affairs concerning the cost of the groups (e.g., the group size) or the quality of group's available strategy regarding the state of affairs (e.g., length of the strategy). We see that such a categorization establishes a justifiable base for prioritizing the agent groups for resource allocation. Our proposed framework could also be applied to decide whether a specific resource assignment (in a given multi-agent system) ensures that a state of affairs is avoidable. For such a purpose, we can model a certain scenario in our framework where we specify the resource assignment in terms of available actions for each agent in each state (the d function in the concurrent structure). Then the avoidability of a given state of affairs could be verified based on our notion of distant responsibility. For instance, if for all states $q \in Q$ there exists at least one q-responsible group for the given state of affairs in one step, we can verify that the specified resource assignment guarantees the avoidability of S in one step. Applying the concept of responsibility for verifying system specifications is an already exploited methodology (see [8,9]).

The other domain in which we see applicability for the notion of distant responsibility is in analysis of industrial supply chain and specifically as a method for ascribing *extended product responsibility* in Life-Cycle Assessment (LCA). The so called *extended product responsibility* mainly concerns the extent of responsibility of involved actors in the business and industry sector, e.g., producer, middle-customer, and consumer, for the environmental consequences of the whole life-cycle of a product (see [21]). We deem that in case (for instance) the producer and a set of customers have a joint strategy to avoid the incidence of an undesired environmental situation, e.g., release of a specific amount of a hazardous gas, they are responsible for such a situation (distant responsibility) while each of the involved agents/groups in such a responsible group are partially responsible (degree of distant responsibility).

7   Related Work

The proposed notions of responsibility are closely related to the forward-looking notions in [6]. More precisely, the notion of (weakly) q-responsible in [6] is identical to distant responsibility in 1 step. Another study that investigates both backward- and forward-looking responsibility is [11]. They formalize forward-looking responsibility in terms of the set of organizational plans that define the agents' obligations. Our work is also related to studies such as [19,20] that provide qualitative degrees for the concept of responsibility in comparison to our quantitative degrees.

One noticeable work that defines a qualitative degree of responsibility is [8] which has a causality-based approach. They build their graded notion of responsibility on the critically degree of a setting regarding an already materialized event in the past (backward-looking) while our notions are power-based and regard the eventualities in the future. However, one main similarity between our approach and [8] is that both the studies provide a quantitative degree of responsibility while most works on the concept of responsibility, either introduce qualitative degrees of responsibility, e.g., crucial or necessary coalitions in [6], or basically conceptualize responsibility as an all-or-nothing notion and refuse to grade it.

Two other studies that focus on aspects of responsibility that we ignored in our conception are [5,14]. In [5], an agent is *morally* responsible for an outcome in case all the three conditions: agency, causal relevancy, and avoidance opportunity are fulfilled. Besides their main focus on *moral* responsibility (in comparison to our power-based responsibility), our approach to formulating the concept of responsibility is distinguishable from their study regarding the three following aspects. Firstly, their notion is merely focused on a single agent while we address agent groups. Secondly, in their formalization, causal relations play the main role while we base our notions on strategic abilities of agents. And thirdly, they claim that attribution of responsibility requires both (1) the causal relation between actions of the agent and the realized outcome and (2) the avoidance opportunity for the agent in question; while we consider the forward-looking precluding power, a sufficient condition. In [14], STIT logic is used to provide a logical analysis of the concept of responsibility and attribution of responsibility. There are three main differentiating points between our study and their approach. Firstly, they investigate the relation between responsibility and attribution emotions, e.g., moral disapproval, where we focus on possibilities of potential agent groups. Secondly, their study regards already materialized state of affairs and formulate backward-looking responsibility; while we have a forward-looking approach. And finally, they consider different "time of choice" and regard the level of knowledge of agents about the choice of other agents while we have local notions for each state of the multi-agent system and assume the perfect knowledge of agents on available actions for each agent and possible state transitions in the system.

Our conception of *distant responsibility* investigates whether an agent group has the strategic power to influence the materialization of a situation. So, we briefly compare our approach with the Banzhaf index [4] and the Shapley-Shubik index [18] as the two well-established power indices. Firstly, in our conception, we consider agent groups while both the indices are focused on the power of an individual agent. Secondly, in the formulation of our degree of distant responsibility we follow the methodology of [22] and regard the maximum contribution of agent groups (to a responsible group) where Banzhaf has a probabilistic approach. Finally, our focus is merely on the preclusive power (in sense of [16]) of agent groups while both the Banzhaf measure and the Shapley-Shubik index consider the ability of agents to determine the final outcome which we see more related to the combined ability to be able to both preclude and provide a situation.

8   Conclusion and Future Work

We proposed various notions of group responsibility and for each notion explained how the degree of the responsibilities for arbitrary groups of agents can be determined. The presented notions allows one to analyse and reason about the potential of an arbitrary group of agents and differentiate between agent groups with respect to their (1) responsibility attribution, (2) type of responsibility, and (3) degree of responsibility. Our notions are motivated by intuitive and desirable properties, e.g., an agent group which only misses one member to become responsible for a state of affairs receives a higher responsibility degree than one that misses more members. The presented notions of responsibility are forward-looking and local in the sense that they capture the potential of agent groups regarding the realization of a given state of affairs within the current state.

Although the attribution of *responsibility* and the *degree of responsibility* are addressed in this paper, the question about supremacy order among *responsible* groups (by the same distance) or within the set of *partially responsible* groups (with similar degrees) is a domain-specific question that could be answered with respect to characteristics of the application domain. Hence, we are aiming to enhance our *responsibility notions* by an additional *cost function* that regards the balancing between two parameters: *group size* and *responsibility distance*. This extended *responsibility framework* could provide a ranking among the set of (partially) responsible groups of agents and be used as an analysis tool for reasoning in collective decision making scenarios such as multi-step election scenarios in political domain or in analysing the dynamics of system behaviour and process executions in multitasking computer systems. We believe that our approach in formalizing the forward-looking responsibility in terms of power, is also applicable in conceptualizing the backward-looking responsibility and related notions such as *blameworthiness* and *accountability*. However, following [8,11], we see that for these concepts and in particular for the concept of *blame*, one prerequisite is to allow the variety in *knowledge* of the involved agents in the multi-agent system and to consider the epistemic state of agents. Finally, we aim to enrich our responsibility framework by providing logical characterization of the proposed notions in the coalitional logic with quantification [2].

References

1. Ågotnes, T., Goranko, V., Jamroga, W.: Alternating-time temporal logics with irrevocable strategies. In: Proceedings of the 11th Conference on Theoretical Aspects of Rationality and Knowledge, pp. 15–24. ACM (2007)
2. Ågotnes, T., van der Hoek, W., Wooldridge, M.: Quantified coalition logic. Synthese **165**(2), 269–294 (2008). http://dx.doi.org/10.1007/s11229-008-9363-1
3. Alur, R., Henzinger, T.A., Kupferman, O.: Alternating-time temporal logic. J. ACM **49**(5), 672–713 (2002). http://doi.acm.org/10.1145/585265.585270
4. Banzhaf, J.F.: Weighted voting doesn't work: a mathematical analysis. Rutgers L. Rev. **19**, 317 (1964)

5. Braham, M., Van Hees, M.: An anatomy of moral responsibility. Mind **121**(483), 601–634 (2012)
6. Bulling, N., Dastani, M.: Coalitional responsibility in strategic settings. In: Leite, J., Son, T.C., Torroni, P., van der Torre, L., Woltran, S. (eds.) CLIMA XIV 2013. LNCS, vol. 8143, pp. 172–189. Springer, Heidelberg (2013)
7. Chevaleyre, Y., Dunne, P.E., Endriss, U., Lang, J., Lemaître, M., Maudet, N., Padget, J.A., Phelps, S., Rodríguez-Aguilar, J.A., Sousa, P.: Issues in multiagent resource allocation. Informatica **30**(1), 3–31 (2006). Slovenia
8. Chockler, H., Halpern, J.Y.: Responsibility and blame: a structural-model approach. J. Artif. Intell. Res. (JAIR) **22**, 93–115 (2004). http://dx.doi.org/10.1613/jair.1391
9. Chockler, H., Halpern, J.Y., Kupferman, O.: What causes a system to satisfy a specification? ACM Trans. Comput. Logic (TOCL) **9**(3), 20 (2008)
10. Fischer, J.M., Ravizza, M.: Responsibility and Control: A Theory of Moral Responsibility. Cambridge University Press, Cambridge (2000)
11. Grossi, D., Royakkers, L.M.M., Dignum, F.: Organizational structure and responsibility. Artif. Intell. Law **15**(3), 223–249 (2007). http://dx.doi.org/10.1007/s10506-007-9054-0
12. Holler, M.J., Napel, S.: Monotonicity of power and power measures. Theor. Decis. **56**(1–2), 93–111 (2004)
13. Kuhn, N., Müller, H.J., Müller, J.P.: Task decomposition in dynamic agent societies. In: International Symposium on Autonomous Decentralized Systems, Proceedings, ISADS 1993, pp. 165–171. IEEE (1993)
14. Lorini, E., Longin, D., Mayor, E.: A logical analysis of responsibility attribution: emotions, individuals and collectives. J. Log. Comput. **24**(6), 1313–1339 (2014). http://dx.doi.org/10.1093/logcom/ext072
15. Matthias, A.: The responsibility gap: ascribing responsibility for the actions of learning automata. Ethics Inf. Technol. **6**(3), 175–183 (2004)
16. Miller, N.R.: Power in game forms. In: Holler, M.J. (ed.) Power, Voting, and Voting Power, pp. 33–51. Springer, Heidelberg (1982)
17. van de Poel, I.: The relation between forward-looking and backward-looking responsibility. In: Vincent, N.A., van de Poel, I., van den Hoven, J. (eds.) Moral Responsibility, Library of Ethics and Applied Philosophy, vol. 27, pp. 37–52. Springer, Netherlands (2011)
18. Shapley, L.S., Shubik, M.: A method for evaluating the distribution of power in a committee system. Am. Polit. Sci. Rev. **48**(03), 787–792 (1954)
19. Shaver, K.: The Attribution of Blame: Causality, Responsibility, and Blameworthiness. Springer Science & Business Media, New York (2012)
20. Sulzer, J.L.: Attribution of responsibility as a function of the structure, quality, and intensity of the event. Ph.D. thesis, University of Florida (1965)
21. White, A.L., Stoughton, M., Feng, L.: Servicizing: The Quiet Transition to Extended Product Responsibility. Tellus Institute, Boston, p. 97 (1999)
22. Yazdanpanah, V., Dastani, M.: Quantified degrees of group responsibility. In: COIN@ AAMAS 2015, p. 205 (2015)

Competitive VCG Redistribution Mechanism for Public Project Problem

Mingyu Guo[(⊠)]

School of Computer Science, University of Adelaide, Adelaide, Australia
mingyu.guo@adelaide.edu.au

Abstract. The VCG mechanism has many nice properties, and can be applied to a wide range of social decision problems. One problem of the VCG mechanism is that even though it is efficient, its social welfare (agents' total utility considering payments) can be low due to high VCG payments. VCG redistribution mechanisms aim to resolve this by redistributing the VCG payments back to the agents. Competitive VCG redistribution mechanisms have been found for various resource allocation settings. However, there has been almost no success outside of the scope of allocation problems. This paper focuses on another fundamental model - the public project problem. In Naroditskiy et al. 2012, it was conjectured that competitive VCG redistribution mechanisms exist for the public project problem, and one competitive mechanism was proposed for the case of three agents (unfortunately, both the mechanism and the techniques behind it do not generalize to cases with more agents). In this paper, we propose a competitive mechanism for general numbers of agents, relying on new techniques.

Keywords: VCG redistribution mechanisms · Dominant strategy implementation · Groves mechanisms · Public good provision

1 Introduction

The VCG mechanism [2,3,15] (referring specifically to the Clarke mechanism) has many nice properties. It is *efficient*, *strategy-proof*, and *weakly budget-balanced (non-deficit)*. It is a general mechanism that can be applied to many different social decision problems.

One problem of the VCG mechanism is that even though it is efficient[1], its social welfare[2] can be low due to high VCG payments. As a result, the VCG mechanism is not suitable for scenarios where we want to maximize the social welfare. One example scenario is that a group of agents may need to allocate among themselves some shared resources (*e.g.*, airlines unsharing take-off/landing slots).

---

[1] The VCG mechanism always picks the outcome that maximizes the agents' total valuation.

[2] By social welfare, we mean the agents' total utility: total valuation minus total payment.

© Springer International Publishing Switzerland 2016
M. Baldoni et al. (Eds.): PRIMA 2016, LNAI 9862, pp. 279–294, 2016.
DOI: 10.1007/978-3-319-44832-9_17

Another example scenario is that a group of agents may need to decide among themselves whether or not to build a public project (*e.g.*, community library) that can be accessed by everyone.

In light of the above drawback of the VCG mechanism, the VCG redistribution mechanisms were proposed [1]. These mechanisms would allocate according to the VCG mechanism, but then on top of the VCG payments, the agents also receive *back* some redistribution payments, therefore increasing the social welfare. An agent's redistribution must not depend on her own type, which is to ensure that the redistribution process does not change the agents' incentives. After incorporating redistribution, the overall mechanism remains efficient and strategy-proof (as the original VCG mechanism is efficient and strategy-proof, plus that the agents' incentives do not change). The problem of VCG redistribution mechanism design is essentially designing how to redistribute the VCG payments back to the agents *as much as possible without redistributing too much*. We cannot redistribute too much because if we redistribute more than the total VCG payment, then the mechanism is no longer weakly budget-balanced. In summary, VCG redistribution mechanisms are non-deficit Groves mechanisms.

Formally, given a social decision problem, let the outcome space be O and the number of agents be n. We use Θ_i to denote agent i's type space. For $o \in O$ and $\theta_i \in \Theta_i$, we use $u(\theta_i, o)$ to denote agent i's valuation for outcome o when her type is θ_i.

The VCG mechanism picks the following optimal outcome:

$$o^* = \arg\max_{o \in O} \sum_i u(\theta_i, o)$$

Agent i's VCG payment equals how much her presence hurts the other agents:

$$\max_{o \in O} \sum_{j \neq i} u(\theta_j, o) - \sum_{j \neq i} u(\theta_j, o^*)$$

A VCG redistribution mechanism is characterized by a list of redistribution functions r_i, where $r_i(\theta_{-i})$ represents agent i's redistribution (positive means receiving money). We notice that agent i's redistribution $r_i(\theta_{-i})$ does not depend on agent i's own type, which ensures strategy-proofness and efficiency. To ensure weakly budget balance, we require that the total redistribution $\sum_i r_i(\theta_{-i})$ is at most the total VCG payment.

Moulin [13] proposed the following performance evaluation criterion for VCG redistribution mechanisms. A mechanism's worst-case efficiency ratio is defined as the worst-case ratio (over all type profiles) between the achieved social welfare and the optimal social welfare. The optimal social welfare is the same as the maximum total valuation, which can be achieved by the (omniscient/omnipotent) *first-best* mechanism.

The achieved social welfare of a VCG redistribution mechanism equals

$$\sum_i u(\theta_i, o^*) - \sum_i (\max_{o \in O} \sum_{j \neq i} u(\theta_j, o) - \sum_{j \neq i} u(\theta_j, o^*)) + \sum_i r_i(\theta_{-i})$$

The three terms in the above expression represent the "achieved total valuation under VCG", "the agents' total VCG payment", and "the agents' total redistribution", respectively.

The worst-case efficiency ratio is then (θ represents the type profile):

$$\min_{\theta} \frac{n \sum_i u(\theta_i, o^1) - \sum_i \max_{o \in O} \sum_{j \neq i} u(\theta_j, o) + \sum_i r_i(\theta_{-i})}{\sum_i u(\theta_i, o^*)} \tag{1}$$

The worst-case efficiency ratio is between 0 and 1. Higher ratios correspond to better worst-case performance in terms of social welfare. The original VCG mechanism (not redistributing anything) typically has a worst-case efficiency ratio of 0, or approaching 0 asymptotically, which we will elaborate more later on. In this paper, we study *competitive VCG redistribution mechanisms*.

Definition 1. *A VCG redistribution mechanism is* **competitive** *if its worst-case efficiency ratio is bounded below by a positive constant.*

That is, a VCG redistribution mechanism is competitive if it guarantees a constant fraction of the optimal social welfare in the worst case.

There has been a lot of success on designing competitive VCG redistribution mechanisms in *resource allocation settings*. Actually, a lot of the proposed mechanisms are not only competitive, but also proven to be optimal (you cannot find other mechanisms with higher worst-case efficiency ratios). For example, for multi-unit auctions with unit demand, Moulin [13] identified a competitive mechanism with the optimal ratio. For the slightly more general setting of multi-unit auctions with nonincreasing marginal values, an almost identical result (under a slightly different objective) was independently proposed by Guo and Conitzer [7]. Gujar and Narahari [4] conjectured that the mechanism proposed in Moulin [13] and Guo and Conitzer [7] can be further generalized to heterogeneous item auctions with unit demand. The conjecture was confirmed by Guo [6]. There has also been work on competitive VCG redistribution mechanisms that are not optimal. Guo [5] proposed competitive VCG redistribution mechanisms for combinatorial auctions with gross substitutes valuations.

Despite the success in resource allocation settings, no competitive VCG redistribution mechanisms were identified outside of the scope of resource allocation. The only exception is Naroditskiy et al. [14], where the authors studied the public project problem. The authors derived an upper bound on the worst-case efficiency ratio for the public project setting. The authors also proposed one mechanism whose worst-case efficiency ratio matches the upper bound when there are exactly three agents. Unfortunately, the proposed mechanism and its underlying techniques do not generalize to more than three agents. The authors also proposed a few heuristic-based redistribution mechanisms that seem to perform well based on numerical simulation (unfortunately, the numerical simulation can only handle up to six agents[3]).

---

[3] Even for n between 4 and 6, there is no guarantee of worst-case performance, because the worst-case is simulated via sampling, which may not be extensive enough.

Guo et al. [9] also studied redistribution for the public project problem. Most results are not directly related to this paper, because the authors there focused on inefficient partitioning-based mechanisms instead of VCG redistribution mechanisms. However, there is one result that is relevant, which is that the original VCG mechanism has a worst-case efficiency ratio of $1/n$ for the public project problem. That is, the original VCG mechanism is not competitive.

In summary, outside of the scope of resource allocation, there are no known competitive VCG redistribution mechanisms. This paper continues the study of public project problem, and proposes the first competitive VCG redistribution mechanism outside of the scope of resource allocation.

2   Model Description

We study the public project problem, which is a classic problem well studied in both computer science and economics [8–12,14].

There are n agents who need to decide among themselves whether or not to build a public project that can be accessed by everyone (e.g., a bridge). The cost of the project is C. We assume the cost is already there in the beginning, e.g., the government has bestowed C to the community, and the community needs to decide what to do with it. There are two outcomes: (1) build the public project; (2) not build and divide the money evenly (everyone receives C/n). Without loss of generality, we assume $C = 1$.

We use θ_i to represent agent i's valuation for the public project, so an agent's valuation is θ_i if the decision is to build, and her valuation is $1/n$ if the decision is to not build (divide money instead). Without loss of generality [14], we assume θ_i is in $[0, 1]$.

The VCG mechanism chooses to build if and only if the total valuation of the project exceeds the cost. That is, we build if and only if $\sum_i \theta_i \geq 1$. The agents' total valuation under VCG is then $\max\{\sum_i \theta_i, 1\}$. If the VCG decision is to build, then agent i's VCG payment equals $\max\{\sum_{j \neq i} \theta_j, \frac{n-1}{n}\} - \sum_{j \neq i} \theta_j$. If the VCG decision is not to build, then agent i's VCG payment equals $\max\{\sum_{j \neq i} \theta_j, \frac{n-1}{n}\} - \frac{n-1}{n}$. The agents' total VCG payment equals

$$\sum_i \max\{\sum_{j \neq i} \theta_j, \frac{n-1}{n}\} - (n-1)\max\{\sum_i \theta_i, 1\}$$

Based on Expression 1, if we use the r_i to represent the redistribution functions, then the worst-case efficiency ratio equals:

$$\min_\theta \frac{n\max\{\sum_i \theta_i, 1\} - \sum_i \max\{\sum_{j \neq i} \theta_j, \frac{n-1}{n}\} + \sum_i r_i(\theta_{-i})}{\max\{\sum_i \theta_i, 1\}} \tag{2}$$

Our task is to design the r_i so that the above ratio is bounded below by a positive constant.

Based on Expression 2, it is easy to see that the VCG mechanism's worst-case efficiency ratio is at most $1/n$. For example, let us consider the profile where $\theta_1 = 1$ and $\theta_i = 0$ for $i > 1$. Expression 2 simplifies to

$$\frac{n - (n - 1) - \frac{n-1}{n}}{1} = \frac{1}{n}$$

3 Intuition and Result

Ideally, we want the total redistribution to be as close as possible to the total VCG payment. There are n agents, so it is a reasonable heuristic to try to make sure that every agent's redistribution is as close as possible to $1/n$ times the total VCG payment. The Cavallo mechanism [1] is somewhat based on this idea. The Cavallo mechanism has found a lot of success in the resource allocation settings. It is competitive in all the resource allocation settings mentioned earlier.[4]

We use $VCG(\theta_i, \theta_{-i})$ to represent the total VCG payment. Under Cavallo's mechanism, $r_i(\theta_{-i})$ is defined as

$$\frac{\min_{\theta_i'} VCG(\theta_i', \theta_{-i})}{n}$$

It should be noted that based on the above definition, an agent's redistribution is independent of her own type, and the total redistribution is never more than the total VCG payment.

Unfortunately, the Cavallo mechanism is not competitive for the public project problem, because it never redistributes anything. No matter what is θ_{-i}, we can always find θ_i' so that $VCG(\theta_i', \theta_{-i})$ equals 0.[5]

We notice that for all the resource allocation settings mentioned earlier, we have[6]

$$\min_{\theta_i'} VCG(\theta_i', \theta_{-i}) = VCG(\theta_{-i})$$

$VCG(\theta_{-i})$ represents the total VCG payment when agent i is removed from the system. Given that redistributing to every agent $VCG(\theta_{-i})/n$ resulted in competitive mechanisms for resource allocation settings, what if we do the same for the public project problem?

In the public project setting, if we remove agent i, then there are $n-1$ agents left, who choose between building the project and receiving $1/(n-1)$ each. If we redistribute every agent $VCG(\theta_{-i})/n$, then we have

$$r_i(\theta_{-i}) = \frac{VCG(\theta_{-i})}{n} = \frac{\sum_{j \neq i} \max\{\sum_{k \neq i,j} \theta_k, \frac{n-2}{n-1}\} - (n-2)\max\{\sum_{k \neq i} \theta_k, 1\}}{n}$$

---

[4] We do need the minor assumption that the number of agents is large compared to the number of items.

[5] If $\sum_{j \neq i} \theta_j \geq \frac{n-1}{n}$, then pick $\theta_i' = 1$. Otherwise, pick $\theta_i' = 0$.

[6] This is called revenue monotonicity.

We numerically simulated the above redistribution functions and were not satisfied with its performance (if it does not even work well numerically, then there is no point investing time trying to prove that it has good worst-case performance). Fortunately, after trials and errors (based on both manual analysis and numerical simulation), we noticed that if we make two minor technical adjustments, we are able to obtain much better redistribution functions. We replace the denominator n by $n-1$, and we replace $\frac{n-2}{n-1}$ by $\frac{n-1}{n}$. At the end, we have

$$r_i(\theta_{-i}) = \frac{\sum_{j \neq i} \max\{\sum_{k \neq i,j} \theta_k, \frac{n-1}{n}\} - (n-2) \max\{\sum_{k \neq i} \theta_k, 1\}}{n-1} \tag{3}$$

We (partly) used numerical simulation to reach the above starting point. We then **mathematically prove** that we can build a competitive VCG redistribution mechanism based on the above functions.

Let θ be a type profile, we define $Diff(\theta)$ as

$$\sum_i r_i(\theta_{-i}) - VCG(\theta)$$

$Diff(\theta)$ represents the difference between the amount redistributed and the total VCG payment. It turns out that we can bound $Diff(\theta)$ as follows:

Proposition 1.
$$\forall \theta, L(n) \leq Diff(\theta) \leq U(n)$$

$$U(n) = \frac{1}{n-1} + \frac{n-1}{4n} + \frac{4(n+1)^3}{27n(n-1)^2}$$

$$L(n) = \min\{\frac{1}{n-1} - \frac{1}{n} - \frac{(n-1)^2}{4n^2}, \frac{1}{n-1} + \frac{1}{2n} - \frac{1}{2}\} - \frac{n-2}{n(n-1)}$$

Theorem 1. *We define $r_i'(\theta_{-i})$ to be $r_i(\theta_{-i}) - U(n)/n$.*
(r_i is defined according to Eq. 3. $U(n)$ is defined according to Proposition 1.)
If we redistribute according the r_i', then the corresponding VCG redistribution mechanism is competitive.
When n goes to infinity, the worst-case efficiency ratio approaches 0.102.

4   Proof of Proposition 1

For presentation purposes, we introduce the following notation:

- For all i, $X_i = \sum_{j \neq i} \theta_j$ (the sum of the types other than i's own type).
- $X = \sum_i \theta_i = \frac{\sum_i X_i}{n-1}$ (the sum of all the types).

Using the new notation, we have $Diff(\theta)$ equals

$$(n-1)\max\{X,1\} + \frac{1}{n-1}\sum_i\sum_{j\neq i}\max\{X_i + X_j - X, \frac{n-1}{n}\}$$

$$- \sum_i \max\{X_i, \frac{n-1}{n}\} - \frac{n-2}{n-1}\sum_i \max\{X_i, 1\} \tag{1}$$

We use $E(X_1, X_2, \ldots, X_n)$ to denote Expression 4. We use the short form E when there is no ambiguity. The set of all possible values of the X_i must be a subset of:

$$\Lambda = \{(X_1, X_2, \ldots, X_n) | \forall i, 0 \leq X_i \leq X = \frac{\sum_i X_i}{n-1}\}$$

$Diff(\theta)$ is bounded above by $\max_\Lambda E$. Next, we show how to calculate (an upper bound of) $\max_\Lambda E$.

Proposition 2. *Let $(X_1, X_2, \ldots, X_n)$ be an arbitrary element of Λ. $X = \frac{\sum_i X_i}{n-1}$. Two coordinates X_i and X_j are said to be* **from the same band** *if*

- *$0 \leq X_i, X_j \leq \min\{\frac{n-1}{n}, X\}$, or*
- *$\frac{n-1}{n} \leq X_i, X_j \leq \min\{1, X\}$, or*
- *$1 \leq X_i, X_j \leq X$.*

Let X_i and X_j be two coordinates from the same band. Without loss of generality, we assume $X_i \leq X_j$. We use $(X_i, X_j, \ldots)$ to denote the original element $(X_1, X_2, \ldots, X_n)$ from Λ. We use $(X_i - \epsilon, X_j + \epsilon, \ldots)$ to denote the new element where X_i is replaced by $X_i - \epsilon$ and X_j is replaced by $X_j + \epsilon$ ($\epsilon \geq 0$).
If $X_i - \epsilon$ and $X_j + \epsilon$ are still from the same band, then

- *$(X_i - \epsilon, X_j + \epsilon, \ldots)$ is still an element of Λ.*
- *$E(X_i, X_j, \ldots) \leq E(X_i - \epsilon, X_j + \epsilon, \ldots)$.*

In words, if two coordinates X_i and X_j are from the same band, then by "pushing their values apart within their band", the resulting element is still in Λ, and the resulting new value of E does not decrease.

4.1   Upper Bound of E

Our goal is to calculate $\max_\Lambda E$. We recall that Λ is defined as

$$\Lambda = \{(X_1, X_2, \ldots, X_n) | \forall i, 0 \leq X_i \leq X = \frac{\sum_i X_i}{n-1}\}$$

We notice that Λ is the union of the following three sets:

$$\Lambda_1 = \{(X_1, X_2, \ldots, X_n) | \forall i, 0 \leq X_i \leq X = \frac{\sum_i X_i}{n-1}, X \leq \frac{n-1}{n}\}$$

$$\Lambda_2 = \{(X_1, X_2, \ldots, X_n) | \forall i, 0 \leq X_i \leq X = \frac{\sum_i X_i}{n-1}, \frac{n-1}{n} \leq X \leq 1\}$$

$$\Lambda_3 = \{(X_1, X_2, \ldots, X_n) | \forall i, 0 \leq X_i \leq X = \frac{\sum_i X_i}{n-1}, 1 \leq X\}$$

We certainly have

$$\max_\Lambda E = \max\{\max_{\Lambda_1} E, \max_{\Lambda_2} E, \max_{\Lambda_3} E\}$$

Value of $\max_{\Lambda_1} E$. We first analyze $\max_{\Lambda_1} E$. Let $(X_1^*, X_2^*, \ldots, X_n^*)$ be an element in Λ_1 that maximizes E. Let $X^* = \frac{\sum_i X_i^*}{n-1}$. Since $(X_1^*, X_2^*, \ldots, X_n^*) \in \Lambda_1$, $X^* \leq \frac{n-1}{n}$. By symmetry, it is without loss of generality to assume that $X_1^* \leq X_2^* \leq \cdots \leq X_n^*$.

$E(X_1^*, X_2^*, \ldots, X_n^*)$ simplifies to

$$(n-1) + \frac{1}{n-1} \sum_i \sum_{j \neq i} \max\{X_i^* + X_j^* - X^*, \frac{n-1}{n}\}$$

$$-\sum_i \frac{n-1}{n} - \frac{n-2}{n-1} \sum_i 1$$

Since $X_i^* + X_j^* - X^* \leq X^* \leq \frac{n-1}{n}$, the above further simplifies to

$$(n-1) + \frac{1}{n-1} \sum_i \sum_{j \neq i} \frac{n-1}{n} - (n-1) - \frac{n-2}{n-1} n = \frac{1}{n-1}$$

That is, $\max_{\Lambda_1} E = \frac{1}{n-1}$.

Value of $\max_{\Lambda_2} E$. We now analyze $\max_{\Lambda_2} E$. Let $(X_1^*, X_2^*, \ldots, X_n^*)$ be an element in Λ_2 that maximizes E. Let $X^* = \frac{\sum_i X_i^*}{n-1}$. Since $(X_1^*, X_2^*, \ldots, X_n^*) \in \Lambda_2$, $\leq \frac{n-1}{n} \leq X^* \leq 1$. By symmetry, it is without loss of generality to assume that $X_1^* \leq X_2^* \leq \cdots \leq X_n^*$.

Since $\frac{n-1}{n} \leq X^* \leq 1$, the X_i^* fall into two possible bands. They are $[0, \frac{n-1}{n}]$ and $[\frac{n-1}{n}, X^*]$. (One band may be empty.) By Proposition 2, it is without loss of generality to assume that there exists at most one X_i^* that is in $(0, \frac{n-1}{n})$, and there exists at most one X_j^* that is in $(\frac{n-1}{n}, X^*)$. Hence, it is without loss of generality to assume that $(X_1^*, X_2^*, \ldots, X_n^*)$ has the following form:

$$(0, 0, \ldots, 0, [u], \frac{n-1}{n}, \frac{n-1}{n}, \ldots, \frac{n-1}{n}, [v], X^*, X^*, \ldots, X^*)$$

In the above, $[u]$ represents that there is at most one value u in $(0, \frac{n-1}{n})$, and $[v]$ represents that there is at most one value v in $(\frac{n-1}{n}, X^*)$.

- Case 1: There does not exist one value v that is within $(\frac{n-1}{n}, X^*)$. That is, $(X_1^*, X_2^*, \ldots, X_n^*)$ has the following form:

$$(0, 0, \ldots, 0, [u], \frac{n-1}{n}, \frac{n-1}{n}, \ldots, \frac{n-1}{n}, X^*, X^*, \ldots, X^*)$$

Let p be the number of X^*. $E(X_1^*, X_2^*, \ldots, X_n^*)$ simplifies to

$$(n-1) + \frac{1}{n-1} \sum_i \sum_{j \neq i} \frac{n-1}{n} + \frac{1}{n-1} p(p-1)(X^* - \frac{n-1}{n})$$

$$-(n-p)\frac{n-1}{n} - pX^* - \frac{n-2}{n-1}n$$

We notice that the above expression is linear in X^* and it is nonincreasing in X^*. To maximize it, we let $X^* = \frac{n-1}{n}$. The expression simplifies to

$$(n-1) + \frac{1}{n-1} \sum_i \sum_{j \neq i} \frac{n-1}{n} - n\frac{n-1}{n} - \frac{n-2}{n-1}n = \frac{1}{n-1}$$

- Case 2: There does exist one value v that is in $(\frac{n-1}{n}, X^*)$. That is, $(X_1^*, X_2^*, \ldots, X_n^*)$ has the following form:

$$(0, 0, \ldots, 0, [u], \frac{n-1}{n}, \frac{n-1}{n}, \ldots, \frac{n-1}{n}, v, X^*, X^*, \ldots, X^*)$$

Let p be the number of X^*. $E(X_1^*, X_2^*, \ldots, X_n^*)$ simplifies to

$$(n-1) + \frac{1}{n-1} \sum_i \sum_{j \neq i} \frac{n-1}{n} + \frac{1}{n-1} 2p(v - \frac{n-1}{n}) + \frac{1}{n-1} p(p-1)(X^* - \frac{n-1}{n})$$

$$- (n-p-1)\frac{n-1}{n} - v - pX^* - \frac{n-2}{n-1}n \qquad (5)$$

Expression 5 is linear in v. We know $\frac{n-1}{n} \leq v \leq X^*$. Therefore, by replacing v by either $\frac{n-1}{n}$ or X^*, we obtain an upper bound on Expression 5. Replace v by $\frac{n-1}{n}$: Expression 5 becomes

$$(n-1) + \frac{1}{n-1} \sum_i \sum_{j \neq i} \frac{n-1}{n} + \frac{1}{n-1} p(p-1)(X^* - \frac{n-1}{n})$$

$$-(n-p)\frac{n-1}{n} - pX^* - \frac{n-2}{n-1}n$$

Just like Case 1, the above is nonincreasing in X^*. When $X^* = \frac{n-1}{n}$ (minimized), it equals $\frac{1}{n-1}$.
Replace v by X^*: Expression 5 becomes

$$(n-1) + \frac{1}{n-1} \sum_i \sum_{j \neq i} \frac{n-1}{n} + \frac{1}{n-1} p(p+1)(X^* - \frac{n-1}{n})$$

$$-(n-p-1)\frac{n-1}{n} - (p+1)X^* - \frac{n-2}{n-1}n$$

Again, the above is nonincreasing in X^*. When $X^* = \frac{n-1}{n}$ (minimized), it equals $\frac{1}{n-1}$.

In conclusion, $\max_{\Lambda_2} E = \frac{1}{n-1}$.

Value of $\max_{\Lambda_3} E$. We now analyze $\max_{\Lambda_3} E$. Let $(X_1^*, X_2^*, \ldots, X_n^*)$ be an element in Λ_3 that maximizes E. Let $X^* = \frac{\sum_i X_i^*}{n-1}$. Since $(X_1^*, X_2^*, \ldots, X_n^*) \in \Lambda_3$, $X^* \geq 1$. By symmetry, it is without loss of generality to assume that $X_1^* \leq X_2^* \leq \cdots \leq X_n^*$.

Since $1 \leq X^*$, the X_i^* fall into three possible bands. They are $[0, \frac{n-1}{n}]$, $[\frac{n-1}{n}, 1]$, and $[1, X^*]$. (Some bands may be empty.) By Proposition 2, it is without loss of generality to assume that there exists at most one value in each of the following three intervals: $(0, \frac{n-1}{n})$, $(\frac{n-1}{n}, 1)$, and $(1, X^*)$. That is, $(X_1^*, X_2^*, \ldots, X_n^*)$ has the following form:

$$(0, 0, \ldots, 0, [u], \frac{n-1}{n}, \frac{n-1}{n}, \ldots, \frac{n-1}{n}, [v], 1, 1, \ldots, 1, [w], X^*, X^*, \ldots, X^*)$$

In the above, $[u]$ represents that there is at most one value u in $(0, \frac{n-1}{n})$, $[v]$ represents that there is at most one value v in $(\frac{n-1}{n}, 1)$, and $[w]$ represents that there is at most one value w in $(1, X^*)$.

Proposition 3. *Let $(X_1, X_2, \ldots, X_n)$ be an arbitrary element of Λ_3. We use $(X_1', X_2', \ldots, X_n')$ to denote the following new element*

$$\left(\max\{X_1, \frac{n-1}{n}\}, \max\{X_2, \frac{n-1}{n}\}, \ldots, \max\{X_n, \frac{n-1}{n}\} \right)$$

– $(X_1', X_2', \ldots, X_n')$ is still an element of Λ_3.
– $E(X_1, X_2, \ldots, X_n) \leq E(X_1', X_2', \ldots, X_n')$.

By Proposition 3, we can further assume that $X_i^* \geq \frac{n-1}{n}$ for all i. That is, $(X_1^*, X_2^*, \ldots, X_n^*)$ has the following form:

$$(\frac{n-1}{n}, \frac{n-1}{n}, \ldots, \frac{n-1}{n}, [v], 1, 1, \ldots, 1, [w], X^*, X^*, \ldots, X^*)$$

In the above, $[v]$ represents that there is at most one value v in $(\frac{n-1}{n}, 1)$, and $[w]$ represents that there is at most one value w in $(1, X^*)$.

Proposition 4. *Let $(X_1, X_2, \ldots, X_n)$ be an element of Λ_3 with the following form*

$$(\frac{n-1}{n}, \frac{n-1}{n}, \ldots, \frac{n-1}{n}, [v], 1, 1, \ldots, 1, [w], X, X, \ldots, X)$$

In the above, $[v]$ represents that there is at most one value v in $(\frac{n-1}{n}, 1)$, and $[w]$ represents that there is at most one value w in $(1, X^*)$.
We use $(X_1', X_2', \ldots, X_n')$ to denote the following new element

$$(\max\{X_1, 1\}, \max\{X_2, 1\}, \ldots, \max\{X_n, 1\})$$

If $X_n \geq 1$, then

– $(X_1', X_2', \ldots, X_n')$ is still an element of Λ_3.
– $E(X_1, X_2, \ldots, X_n) \leq E(X_1', X_2', \ldots, X_n') + \frac{4(n+1)^3}{27n(n-1)^2}$.

Proof. We first prove that $(X'_1, X'_2, \ldots, X'_n)$ is still an element of Λ_3. By definition, $X = \frac{\sum_i X_i}{n-1} \geq 1$. We use X' to denote $\frac{\sum_i X'_i}{n-1}$. Certainly, $X' \geq X \geq 1$. Since $X \geq 1$ and $X \geq X_i$ for all i, we have $X' \geq X \geq X'_i = \max\{X_i, 1\} \geq 0$ for all i. Hence $(X'_1, X'_2, \ldots, X'_n)$ is still in Λ_3.

Next, we compare $E(X'_1, X'_2, \ldots, X'_n)$ and $E(X'_1, X'_2, \ldots, X'_n)$ under the assumption that $X_n \geq 1$.

If all the X_i are at least 1, then $E(X'_1, X'_2, \ldots, X'_n)$ equals $E(X_1, X_2, \ldots, X_n)$.

Next, we consider scenarios in which at least some X_i are less than 1. Let p be the highest index of X_i so that $X_p < 1$. Let $\Delta = X' - X$. Since $X_n \geq 1$, $\Delta = \frac{\sum_{i<n}(X'_i - X_i)}{n-1} \leq \frac{(n-1)\frac{1}{n}}{n-1} = \frac{1}{n}$. $E(X'_1, X'_2, \ldots, X'_n) - E(X_1, X_2, \ldots, X_n)$ simplifies to[7]

$$(n-1)\Delta + \frac{1}{n-1}\sum_i\sum_{j\neq i}\left(\max\{X'_i + X'_j - X', \frac{n-1}{n}\}\right.$$

$$\left. - \max\{X_i + X_j - X, \frac{n-1}{n}\}\right) - (n-1)\Delta$$

$$= \frac{1}{n-1}\sum_i\sum_{j\neq i}\left(\max\{X'_i + X'_j - X', \frac{n-1}{n}\} - \max\{X_i + X_j - X, \frac{n-1}{n}\}\right)$$

If $i < p$, then $X_i = \frac{n-1}{n}$. In this case, we have $X'_i + X'_j \geq (X_i + \frac{1}{n}) + X_j$. We also have $\Delta = X' - X \leq \frac{1}{n}$. Therefore, if $i < p$,

$$\max\{X'_i + X'_j - X', \frac{n-1}{n}\} - \max\{X_i + X_j - X, \frac{n-1}{n}\} \geq 0$$

Similarly, if $j < p$, we also have the above.

If $i \geq p$ and $j \geq p$, we have $X'_i + X'_j \geq X_i + X_j$. We also have $\Delta = X' - X = \frac{\sum_{i \leq p}(X'_i - X_i)}{n-1} \leq \frac{p}{n(n-1)}$. Therefore, if $i \geq p$ and $j \geq p$,

$$\max\{X'_i + X'_j - X', \frac{n-1}{n}\} - \max\{X_i + X_j - X, \frac{n-1}{n}\} \geq -\frac{p}{n(n-1)}$$

Based on the above,

$$E(X'_1, X'_2, \ldots, X'_n) - E(X_1, X_2, \ldots, X_n)$$

$$= \frac{1}{n-1}\sum_i\sum_{j\neq i}\left(\max\{X'_i + X'_j - X', \frac{n-1}{n}\} - \max\{X_i + X_j - X, \frac{n-1}{n}\}\right)$$

$$\geq \frac{1}{n-1}\sum_{i \geq p}\sum_{j \geq p, j \neq i}\left(\max\{X'_i + X'_j - X', \frac{n-1}{n}\} - \max\{X_i + X_j - X, \frac{n-1}{n}\}\right)$$

$$\geq \frac{1}{n-1}(n-p+1)(n-p)(-\frac{p}{n(n-1)})$$

---

[7] The fourth term of E stays the same.

$$\geq -\frac{1}{n(n-1)^2}(n-p+1)^2p$$

$$\frac{\partial(n-p+1)^2p}{\partial p} = (1+n-p)(1+n-3p)$$

Since $0 \leq p \leq n$, the maximum of $(n-p+1)^2p$ can only happen when $p = 0$, $p = n$, or $p = \frac{n+1}{3}$. Hence,

$$(n-p+1)^2p \leq \max\{0, n, \frac{4(n+1)^3}{27}\} = \frac{4(n+1)^3}{27}$$

Therefore,

$$E(X_1', X_2', \ldots, X_n') - E(X_1, X_2, \ldots, X_n) \geq -\frac{4(n+1)^3}{27n(n-1)^2}$$

Proposition 4 can help us further simplify the optimization problem. However, for it to apply, we need $X_n \geq 1$. If $X_n < 1$, then $(X_1^*, X_2^*, \ldots, X_n^*)$ has the following form:

$$(\frac{n-1}{n}, \frac{n-1}{n}, \ldots, \frac{n-1}{n}, [v])$$

E simplifies to

$$(n-1)X^* + \frac{1}{n-1}\sum_i\sum_{j\neq i}\frac{n-1}{n} - (n-1)X^* - \frac{n-2}{n-1}\sum_i 1 = \frac{1}{n-1}$$

We then consider cases where $X_n \geq 1$. Here, Proposition 4 does apply. Proposition 4 basically says that we can focus on the following form, and the resulting maximum plus $\frac{4(n+1)^3}{27n(n-1)^2}$ must be higher than or equal to the actual maximum.

$$(1, 1, \ldots, 1, [w], X^*, X^*, \ldots, X^*)$$

In the above, $[w]$ represents that there is at most one value w in $(1, X^*)$.
We allow w to be equal to 1 or X^*. The above form simplifies to

$$(1, 1, \ldots, 1, w, X^*, X^*, \ldots, X^*)$$

Let p be the number of 1s. To simplify E, we need to consider three separate cases:

- Case $1 + 1 - X^* \geq \frac{n-1}{n}$: E simplifies to[8]

$$\frac{1}{n-1}\sum_i\sum_{j\neq i}(X_i^* + X_j^* - X^*) - \frac{n-2}{n-1}(n-1)X^*$$

$$= \frac{1}{n-1}(2(n-1)^2X^* - n(n-1)X^*) - \frac{n-2}{n-1}(n-1)X^*$$

$$= (2(n-1)X^* - nX^*) - (n-2)X^* = 0$$

---

[8] Term one and three cancel out.

- Case $1 + 1 - X^* < \frac{n-1}{n}$ and $1 + w - X^* \geq \frac{n-1}{n}$: E simplifies to

$$\frac{1}{n-1}\sum_i \sum_{j\neq i}(X_i^* + X_j^* - X^*) + \frac{1}{n-1}p(p-1)(\frac{n-1}{n} - 1 - 1 + X^*) - \frac{n-2}{n-1}(n-1)X^*$$

$$= \frac{1}{n-1}\mu(\mu-1)(\frac{n-1}{n} - 1 \quad 1 + X^*)$$

If $p = 0$ or 1, then the above expression is 0.
We then consider $p \geq 2$. To maximize the above, we want X^* to be as large as possible.

$$X^* = \frac{\sum_i X_i^*}{n-1} = \frac{p + w + (n-p-1)X^*}{n-1} \leq \frac{p + (n-p)X^*}{n-1}$$

$$(n-1)X^* \leq p + (n-p)X^*$$

$$(p-1)X^* \leq p$$

$$X^* \leq \frac{p}{p-1}$$

Hence, E is at most

$$\frac{1}{n-1}p(p-1)(\frac{n-1}{n} - 2 + \frac{p}{p-1})$$

$$= \frac{1}{n(n-1)}(-p^2 + p(n+1))$$

This expression is maximized when $p = \frac{n+1}{2}$. Hence,

$$E \leq \frac{(n+1)^2}{4n(n-1)} = \frac{1}{n-1} + \frac{n-1}{4n}$$

- Case $1 + w - X^* < \frac{n-1}{n}$: E simplifies to

$$\frac{1}{n-1}p(p-1)(\frac{n-1}{n} - 1 - 1 + X^*) + \frac{1}{n-1}2p(\frac{n-1}{n} - 1 - w + X^*)$$

If $p = 0$, then the above expression equals 0. We then consider $p \geq 1$. Since $X^* = \frac{\sum_i X_i^*}{n-1}$, we have $(n-1)X^* = p + w + (n-p-1)X^*$. That is, $X^* = \frac{p+w}{p}$. E is then

$$\frac{1}{n-1}p(p-1)(\frac{n-1}{n} - 1 + \frac{w}{p}) + \frac{1}{n-1}2p(\frac{n-1}{n} - w + \frac{w}{p})$$

The above expression is linear in w and w's coefficient equals

$$\frac{1}{n-1}(p-1) - \frac{1}{n-1}2p + \frac{1}{n-1}2 = \frac{1}{n-1}(1-p) \leq 0$$

To maximize the above expression, we let $w = 1$. E now equals

$$\frac{1}{n-1}p(p-1)(\frac{-1}{n} + \frac{1}{p}) + \frac{1}{n-1}2p(\frac{-1}{n} + \frac{1}{p})$$

$$= \frac{1}{n(n-1)}(-p^2 + p(n-1) + n)$$

The above expression is maximized when $p = \frac{n-1}{2}$. Hence, E is at most

$$\frac{1}{n(n-1)}(\frac{(n-1)^2}{4} + n) = \frac{n-1}{4n} + \frac{1}{n-1}$$

In conclusion, $\max_{\Lambda_3} E \leq \frac{1}{n-1} + \frac{n-1}{4n} + \frac{4(n+1)^3}{27n(n-1)^2}$.

Summary on the upper bound of E

$$\max_\Lambda E = \max\{\max_{\Lambda_1} E, \max_{\Lambda_2} E, \max_{\Lambda_3} E\}$$

$$\leq \frac{1}{n-1} + \frac{n-1}{4n} + \frac{4(n+1)^3}{27n(n-1)^2}$$

When n approaches infinity, this upper bound approaches $\frac{1}{4} + \frac{4}{27} \approx 0.398$.

4.2   Lower Bound of E

The process of finding a lower bound of E is similar.

$$\min_\Lambda E = \min\{\min_{\Lambda_1} E, \min_{\Lambda_2} E, \min_{\Lambda_3} E\}$$

Due to space constraint, we omit the details. We first show that if $X < 1$, then there must exist one $X_i < \frac{n-1}{n}$. Increasing X_i will never increase E. Therefore, as long as $X < 1$, we can push up values that are less than $\frac{n-1}{n}$ among the X_i. If all the X_i are at least $\frac{n-1}{n}$, then $X \geq 1$. In summary, when it comes to calculating the minimum value. It is without loss of generality to only consider Λ_3. That is,

$$\min_\Lambda E = \min_{\Lambda_3} E$$

Value of $\min_{\Lambda_3} E$. We now analyze $\min_{\Lambda_3} E$. Let $(X_1^*, X_2^*, \ldots, X_n^*)$ be an element in Λ_3 that minimizes E. Let $X^* = \frac{\sum_i X_i^*}{n-1}$. Since $(X_1^*, X_2^*, \ldots, X_n^*) \in \Lambda_3$, $X^* \geq 1$. By symmetry, it is without loss of generality to assume that $X_1^* \leq X_2^* \leq \ldots \leq X_n^*$.

Since $1 \leq X^*$, the X_i^* fall into three possible bands. They are $[0, \frac{n-1}{n}]$, $[\frac{n-1}{n}, 1]$, and $[1, X^*]$. (Some bands may be empty.) By Proposition 2, it is without loss of generality to assume that values inside the same band are all identical. Hence, it is without loss of generality to assume that $(X_1^*, X_2^*, \ldots, X_n^*)$ has the following form:

$$(u, u, \ldots, u, v, v, \ldots, v, w, w, \ldots, w)$$

Here, $0 \leq u \leq \frac{n-1}{n}$, $\frac{n-1}{n} \leq v \leq 1$, and $1 \leq w \leq X^*$.

We have

$$\min_{\Lambda} E = \min_{\Lambda_9} E \geq \min\{\frac{1}{n-1} - \frac{1}{n} - \frac{(n-1)^2}{4n^2}, \frac{1}{n-1} + \frac{1}{2n} - \frac{1}{2}\} - \frac{n-2}{n(n-1)}$$

When n approaches infinity, this lower bound approaches $-\frac{1}{2} = -0.5$.

5 Proof of Theorem 1

If we redistribute according to the r'_i, then the corresponding VCG redistribution mechanism must be non-deficit for the following reason (based on Proposition 1):

$$\sum_i r'_i(\theta_{-i}) = \sum_i r_i(\theta_{-i}) - U(n) \leq VCG(\theta)$$

The achieved social welfare equals

$$\max\{\sum_i \theta_i, 1\} - VCG(\theta) + \sum_i r'_i(\theta_{-i})$$

$$= \max\{\sum_i \theta_i, 1\} - VCG(\theta) + \sum_i r_i(\theta_{-i}) - U(n)$$

$$\geq \max\{\sum_i \theta_i, 1\} + L(n) - U(n)$$

The worst-case efficiency ratio is then at least

$$\min_\theta \frac{\max\{\sum_i \theta_i, 1\} + L(n) - U(n)}{\max\{\sum_i \theta_i, 1\}} = 1 + \min_\theta \frac{L(n) - U(n)}{\max\{\sum_i \theta_i, 1\}} \geq 1 + L(n) - U(n)$$

$$(6)$$

We have the analytical forms of $L(n)$ and $U(n)$. When n goes to infinity, $1 + L(n) - U(n) = 1 - 0.5 - 0.398 = 0.102$. Actually, it is easy to verify that $1 + L(n) - U(n)$ is bounded below by a positive constant if $n > 10$. For $n \leq 10$, based on the proof of Proposition 1, we know that the profiles that maximize/minimize E can only take a few specific forms. By numerically going over these forms (since $n \leq 10$, it is computationally easy to do so), we can find the numerical values of $\max_\Lambda E$ and $\min_\Lambda E$ for $n \leq 10$. Given a specific $n \leq 10$, we use the numerical values to replace $U(n)$ and $L(n)$ in Eq. 6, which actually shows that the worst-case efficiency ratio is always bounded below by a positive constant.

6 Conclusion

In this paper, we proposed the first competitive VCG redistribution mechanism outside of the scope of resource allocation. The proposed mechanism is efficient, strategy-proof, non-deficit, and its social welfare is guaranteed to be at least a constant fraction of the optimal social welfare.

References

1. Cavallo, R.: Optimal decision-making with minimal waste: strategyproof redistribution of VCG payments. In: Proceedings of the International Conference on Autonomous Agents and Multi-agent Systems (AAMAS), pp. 882–889, Hakodate, Japan (2006)
2. Clarke, E.H.: Multipart pricing of public goods. Publ. Choice **11**, 17–33 (1971)
3. Groves, T.: Incentives in teams. Econometrica **41**, 617–631 (1973)
4. Gujar, S., Yadati, N.: Redistribution of VCG payments in assignment of heterogeneous objects. In: Papadimitriou, C., Zhang, S. (eds.) WINE 2008. LNCS, vol. 5385, pp. 438–445. Springer, Heidelberg (2008)
5. Guo, M.: VCG redistribution with gross substitutes. In: Proceedings of the National Conference on Artificial Intelligence (AAAI), San Francisco, CA, USA (2011)
6. Guo, M.: Worst-case optimal redistribution of VCG payments in heterogeneous-item auctions with unit demand. In: Proceedings of the Eleventh International Joint Conference on Autonomous Agents and Multi-Agent Systems (AAMAS), Valencia, Spain (2012)
7. Guo, M., Conitzer, V.: Worst-case optimal redistribution of VCG payments in multi-unit auctions. Games Econ. Behav. **67**(1), 69–98 (2009)
8. Guo, M., Markakis, E., Apt, K.R., Conitzer, V.: Undominated groves mechanisms. J. Artif. Intell. Res. **46**, 129–163 (2013)
9. Guo, M., Naroditskiy, V., Conitzer, V., Greenwald, A., Jennings, N.R.: Budget-balanced and nearly efficient randomized mechanisms: public goods and beyond. In: Chen, N., Elkind, E., Koutsoupias, E. (eds.) Internet and Network Economics. LNCS, vol. 7090, pp. 158–169. Springer, Heidelberg (2011)
10. Mas-Colell, A., Whinston, M., Green, J.R.: Microeconomic Theory. Oxford University Press, Oxford (1995)
11. Moore, J.: General Equilibrium and Welfare Economics: An Introduction. Springer, Berlin (2006)
12. Moulin, H.: Characterizations of the pivotal mechanism. J. Publ. Econ. **31**(1), 53–78 (1986)
13. Moulin, H.: Almost budget-balanced VCG mechanisms to assign multiple objects. J. Econ. Theory **144**(1), 96–119 (2009)
14. Naroditskiy, V., Guo, M., Dufton, L., Polukarov, M., Jennings, N.R.: Redistribution of VCG payments in public project problems. In: Goldberg, P.W. (ed.) WINE 2012. LNCS, vol. 7695, pp. 323–336. Springer, Heidelberg (2012)
15. Vickrey, W.: Counterspeculation, auctions, and competitive sealed tenders. J. Finance **16**, 8–37 (1961)

Coalition Structure Formation Using Anytime Dynamic Programming

Narayan Changder[1(✉)], Animesh Dutta[1], and Aditya K. Ghose[2]

[1] National Institute of Technology, Durgapur, West Bengal, India
narayan.changder@gmail.com, animeshnit@gmail.com
[2] University of Wollongong, Wollongong, NSW 2522, Australia
aditya@uow.edu.au

Abstract. The optimal coalition structure generation is an important problem in multi-agent systems that remains difficult to solve. This paper presents a novel anytime dynamic programming algorithm to compute the optimal coalition structure. The proposed algorithm can be interrupted, and upon interruption, uses heuristic to select the largest valued coalition from each subproblem of size x and picks the rest of the unassigned agent from other subproblem of size $n - x$, where n is the total number of agents. We compared the performance of our algorithm against the only existing proposal in the literature for the optimal coalition structure problem that uses anytime dynamic programming using 9 distinct datasets (each corresponding to a different distribution). The empirical evaluation shows that our algorithm always generates better or, at least, as good a solution as the previous anytime dynamic programming algorithm.

Keywords: Multi agent system · Optimization · Coalition formation

1 Introduction

The optimal coalition structure generation is an interesting research problem in Multi-Agent Systems (MAS). This problem is interesting to MAS community due to its important applications and its computational challenges. The problem is challenging because of exponential growth of coalition structures when number of agents grows linearly. It is proved that optimal coalition structure generation problem is **NP-** complete [15]. Agents cooperate on issues of their common interest. Given a set of autonomous agents and a value to each subset of agents. One of the main challenges is to create disjoint groups of autonomous agents that cooperate in order to achieve their individual goal or to maximize the total payoff of the system. This complex research process is known as *Coalition Structure Formation* (CSF) process.

Coalition Structure Formation is important in many real world applications such as in e-commerce, customers can form a group/coalition to buy some product in bulk and can get a price discounts for bulk purchasing [18]. In distributed

M. Baldoni et al. (Eds.): PRIMA 2016, LNAI 9862, pp. 295–309, 2016.
DOI: 10.1007/978-3-319-44832-9_18

sensor network, sensors are grouped to make a coalition and work together to track targets of interest [2]. Several delivery companies may agree together and can form coalition to make profit by reducing the transportation costs [14]. To determine an optimal way in which agents must co-operate to get the maximum payoff from the system is a computationally hard problem. In simplest terms, a coalition is a group of agents with a common interest who agree to work together towards a common goal. A cooperative game is best choice to model such a scenario. Here, cooperative game is defined by n agents (or players), where the set of agents is denoted as $A = \{a_1, a_2, \ldots, a_n\}$. Any non empty subset of A is called as coalition, where value of each coalition C is given by a characteristic function $v(.)$. Furthermore, a collection of pairwise disjoint coalitions is called a "*coalition structure*" provided that all the agents are present in coalition structure. Formally, this complex procedure of coalition structure formation is defined as follows:

Definition 1. *Given a set of agents $A = \{a_1, a_2, \ldots, a_n\}$, a Coalition Structure (CS) over A is a partitioning of the agents into different coalitions $\{C_1, C_2, \ldots, C_k\}$, where k is called size of coalition structure i.e. $k = |CS|$. Such that it satisfies the following constraints:*

1. $C_j \neq \emptyset$, $j = \{1, 2, \ldots, k\}$
2. $C_i \cap C_j = \emptyset$ for all $i \neq j$ and
3. $\bigcup_{i=1}^{k} C_i = A$

For example, in a multi-agent system consisting of three agents $A = \{a_1, a_2, a_3\}$, we have total seven possible coalitions:

$$\{\{a_1\}, \{a_2\}, \{a_3\}, \{a_1, a_2\}, \{a_1, a_3\}, \{a_2, a_3\}, \{a_1, a_2, a_3\}\}$$

The set of all coalitions structures over A is denoted as Π^A

$$\Pi^A = \{\{a_1\}, \{a_2, a_3\}\}, \{\{a_3\}, \{a_1, a_2\}\}, \{\{a_2\}, \{a_1, a_3\}\}\{\{a_1\}, \{a_2\}, \{a_3\}\},$$
$$\{\{a_1, a_2, a_3\}\}$$

Now it is observed that the optimal coalition structure and complete partition of a set of agents are same. We are now ready to state our optimization problem formally.

Definition 2. *The value of any coalition structure CS is defined by*

$$V(CS) = \sum_{C_i \in CS} (v(C_i))$$

Generally, the goal of the coalition structure formation problem is to find the coalition structure which maximizes social welfare by finding an optimal coalition structure $CS^* \in \Pi^A$.

$$CS^* = arg\ max_{CS \in \Pi^A} V(CS)$$

The number of coalition structure increases exponentially as the number of participating agent increases linearly (for example, using 25 agents, there are total 4638590332330743949 coalition structures). The total number of coalition structure for n agents is also known as n^{th} Bell number and denoted as $\mathfrak{B}_n$ [5], satisfies $\alpha n^{n/2} \leq \mathfrak{B}_n \leq n^n$ for some positive constant α. Hence, we can not directly enumerate all the coalition structure in polynomial time

In Multi-agent systems there are often time limits to get the solution of the problem, and after deadline is over the result becomes useless. The applicability of coalition structure formation problem in multi-agent settings with hard time constraint requires that the result must comes before the time limit is over.

There are two popular techniques available for coalition structure formation including dynamic programming [19] and anytime search algorithms [8,12,13,16]. The advantage of dynamic programming is that it gives optimal result without enumerating all the coalition structures. However, the biggest disadvantage is that it needs to be run to completion to provide optimal solution. Hence, this method is not a good choice when the time required to produce optimal solution is larger than the time available to the agents. In multi-agent settings without hard time limits, dynamic programming algorithm is efficient to solve many real life problem instances. However, in other circumstances with strict deadline and short execution time, we need an alternative approaches.

Against the research aims outlined above, this paper makes the following contributions to the coalition structure formation problem.

- We proposed anytime dynamic programming algorithm for coalition structure formation. Our anytime dynamic programming is an extension of basic dynamic programming [19] for coalition structure formation.
- Anytime dynamic programming needs a good heuristic to solve the problem. The proposed algorithm uses an inexpensive greedy approach to choose a good answer from the remaining possible solutions. The experimental result shows that our greedy strategy works well.
- We compared our algorithm empirically with the existing anytime dynamic program [16] for 9 different data distributions and result shows that our algorithm occasionally fails to produce good result for certain data distributions but for most of the distribution it always generates better or, at least, as good solution as previous algorithm [16]. We experiments our algorithm for 16 agents and averaged the runtime over 40 runs for each experiment.

Our anytime dynamic programming is a shifted paradigm of traditional dynamic programming for coalition structure formation problem. To help the reader for understanding how our anytime dynamic programming algorithm works, we explain the traditional dynamic programming algorithm [19] followed by our novel anytime dynamic programming algorithm to compute the optimal coalition structure.

2 The DP Algorithm

The first dynamic program to solve coalition structure formulation problem is proposed by Yin Yeh [19]. The approach used is shown in Algorithm 1.

Algorithm 1. Dynamic Programming algorithm

Input: Set of all possible non- empty subsets of n agents $(2^n - 1)$. The value of any coalition C is $v(C)$. If no $v(C)$ is specified then $v(C) = 0$
Output: Optimal coalition structure $CS^*(n)$
 1: **for** $i = 1$ to n **do**
 2:    **for** $C \subseteq A$, where $|C| = i$ **do**   ▷ A is set of n agents
 3:       $V_t(C) \leftarrow v(C)$
 4:       $P_t(C) \leftarrow \{C\}$
 5:       **for** $C' \subset C$ **do**   ▷ for every possible way of splitting C into two halves
 6:           **if** $V_t(C') + V_t(C \setminus C') > v(C)$ **then**
 7:               $V_t(C) \leftarrow V_t(C') + V_t(C \setminus C')$
 8:               $P_t(C) \leftarrow \{C', C \setminus C'\}$
 9:           **end if**
10:       **end for**
11:    **end for**
12: **end for**
13: $CS^* \leftarrow \{A\}$
14: **for** $C \in CS^*$ **do**
15:    **if** $P_t(C) \neq \{C\}$ **then**
16:       $CS^* \leftarrow (CS^*/C, P_t(C))$
17:       Go to line 14 and start with the new CS^*
18:    **end if**
19: **end for**
20: Return $CS^*(n)$

The way dynamic programming works is by manipulating two tables — partition table $P_t[C]$ and value table $V_t[C]$. For example in Table 1, $C = \{1, 2\}$, in this case $P_t[C] = P_t[\{1, 2\}] = \{1\}\{2\}$ and $V_t[C] = V_t[\{1, 2\}] = 70$. For any coalition $C \subseteq A$ it calculates value of $P_t[C]$ and $V_t[C]$ as follows. First, coalition C is split into two halves in all possible ways and computes the highest welfare with the original welfare $v(C)$ of coalition C. If it finds best splitting which gives highest welfare, stores the splitting into $P_t[C]$ otherwise stores coalition C into $P_t[C]$ without splitting[1] coalition C. Suppose coalition C split into two coalitions as $\{C', C''\}$ then it is evaluated as $V_t[C'] + V_t[C'']$. In other words it check

$$v(C) < V_t[C'] + V_t[C'']$$

Note that $v(C)$ is the original input values to all coalitions whereas $V_t[C']$ and $V_t[C'']$ is previously computed value of coalition C' and C''. To compute $V_t[C]$ the algorithm must first evaluates all the $V_t[\ ]$ values of the subsets of C. Below Table 1 shows an example how to compute P_t and V_t with 4 agents $A = \{1, 2, 3, 4\}$

---

[1] If the coalition contains single agent, we do not need to split it anymore.

Table 1. Example of DP program with 4 agents

Size	C	v(C)	All splitting by DP	P_t	V_t
1	{1}	30	$v[\{1\}] = 30$	{1}	30
	{1}	40	$v[\{2\}] = 40$	{2}	40
	{3}	25	$v[\{0\}] = 25$	{3}	25
	{4}	45	$v[\{4\}] = 45$	{4}	15
2	{1,2}	50	$v[\{1,2\}] = 50, v\{1\} + v\{2\} = 70$	{1}{2}	70
	{1,3}	60	$v[\{1,3\}] = 60, v\{1\} + v\{3\} = 55$	{1,3}	60
	{1,4}	80	$v[\{1,4\}] = 80, v\{1\} + v\{4\} = 75$	{1,4}	80
	{2,3}	55	$v[\{2,3\}] = 55, v\{2\} + v\{3\} = 65$	{2}{3}	65
	{2,4}	70	$v[\{2,4\}] = 70, v\{2\} + v\{4\} = 85$	{2}{4}	85
	{3,4}	80	$v[\{3,4\}] = 80, v\{3\} + v\{4\} = 70$	{3,4}	80
3	{1,2,3}	90	$v[\{1,2,3\}] = 90, v\{1\} + v\{2,3\} = 95$	{2}{1,3}	100
			$v\{2\} + v\{1,3\} = 100, v\{3\} + v\{1,2\} = 95$		
	{1,2,4}	120	$v[\{1,2,4\}] = 120, v\{1\} + v\{2,4\} = 115$	{1,2,4}	120
			$v\{2\} + v\{1,4\} = 110, v\{4\} + v\{1,2\} = 115$		
	{1,3,4}	100	$v[\{1,3,4\}] = 100, v\{1\} + v\{3,4\} = 110$	{1}{3,4}	110
			$v\{3\} + v\{1,4\} = 105, v\{4\} + v\{1,3\} = 105$		
	{2,3,4}	115	$v[\{2,3,4\}] = 115, v\{2\} + v\{3,4\} = 120$	{2}{3,4}	120
			$v\{3\} + v\{2,4\} = 110, v\{4\} + v\{2,3\} = 110$		
4	{1,2,3,4}	140	$v[\{1,2,3,4\}] = 140, v\{1\} + v\{2,3,4\} = 150$	{1}{2,3,4}	150
			$v\{2\} + v\{1,3,4\} = 150, v\{3\} + v\{1,2,4\} = 145$		
			$v\{4\} + v\{1,2,3\} = 145, v\{1,2\} + v\{3,4\} = 120$		
			$v\{1,3\} + v\{2,4\} = 145, v\{1,4\} + v\{2,3\} = 145$		

To compute the value V_t for coalition of size x, algorithm need to calculates V_t values for all the coalition of size $1, 2, \ldots, x - 1$. Whenever the algorithm determines all the entries of P_t and V_t the optimal coalition structure CS^* can be computed recursively as shown in Table 1. Algorithm looks for grand coalition structure $\{1, 2, 3, 4\}$ and checks it is more beneficial to split $\{1, 2, 3, 4\}$ into $\{1\}$ and $\{2, 3, 4\}$. Similarly by looking at coalition $\{2, 3, 4\}$ algorithm finds it is more beneficial to split $\{2, 3, 4\}$ into $\{2\}$ and $\{3, 4\}$. As a result, the optimal solution is $\{\{1\}, \{2\}, \{3, 4\}\}$. The running time of algorithm is calculated as follows. there are total $\binom{n}{k}$ coalition of size k over the n agents and each of them requires $O(2^k)$ time

$$\sum_{k=1}^{n} \binom{n}{k} O(2^k)$$

According to the binomial theorem, we have

$$(x + y)^n = \sum_{k=0}^{n} \binom{n}{k} x^{n-k} y^k$$

Now, take $x = 1$ and $y = 2$

$$(1+2)^n = \sum_{k=0}^{n} \binom{n}{k} x^{n-k} y^k$$

Hence we get bound as:

$$\sum_{k=1}^{n} \binom{n}{k} O(2^k) = O(3^n)$$

Having described how DP operates, we will now describes how to get a good solution after DP completes k^{th} iteration.

3   Anytime Dynamic Programming

An anytime algorithm is an algorithm that can return a valid solution to a problem even if it is interrupted at any time before it ends. Our algorithm uses two heuristics.

1. At runtime it calculates coalition structures by greedily adding all the singleton coalition i.e. $\{(a_1), (a_2), \ldots (a_n)\}$ and grand coalition $\{(a_1, a_2, a_3, \ldots, a_n)\}$, then it selects better of two as initial solution.
2. After algorithm completes k^{th} iteration[2], it chooses all the largest valued coalition from each of the subproblem of sizes $n, n-1, n-2 \ldots 3, 2, 1$[3] and rest of the unassigned agent/agents are picked from the subproblem of sizes $0, 1, 2, \ldots, n-3, n-2, n-1$. Note that whatever be the coalition of sizes $1, 2, \ldots k$, it has already been stored in optimal way. The intuition behind this greedy strategy is as follows: Since the algorithm is stopped before the completion, for example, if it stops after k^{th} iteration and it might be the case that there is some large valued coalition in rest of the coalition with sizes $k+1, k+2, \ldots n$

Now, the DP algorithm starts and it solves all the incremental subproblems of size $1, 2, \ldots k$. If run to completion, it returns optimal solution. If the algorithm stops prematurely, the better of the initial solution and current iterative solution using above heuristic is returned. The pseudo-code of algorithm is given in Algorithm 2. The algorithm works as follows: In line 1, algorithm creates an initial solution using grand coalition and singleton coalitions, then it picks one amongst them which gives maximum social welfare. The algorithm chooses singleton coalition because it is not clear about the relationships among agents. If the domain happens to be super-additive, the optimal coalition structure is obviously grand coalition.

---

[2] After k^{th} iteration algorithm solves all the subproblem of size $1, 2, \ldots, k$.
[3] We pick the largest valued coalition of size n, because if $C_{max} = n$, then it contains optimal solution.

Algorithm 2. Anytime Dynamic Programming algorithm

Input: Set of all possible non-empty subsets of n agents ($2^n - 1$). The value of any coalition C is $v(C)$. If no $v(C)$ is specified then $v(C) = 0$ and C_{max} is the maximum number of iteration

Output: Good coalition structure $CS^*(n)$

1: $CS^*_{initial} \leftarrow \max[\sum_{i=1}^{n} v(a_i), v(a_1, a_2, \ldots, a_n)]$ ▷ Calculate initial solution by using grand coalition and singleton coalitions.

2: **for** $i = 1$ to C_{max} **do**

3:     **for** $C \subseteq A$, where $|C| = i$ **do**   ▷ A is set of n agents

4:         $V_t(C) \leftarrow v(C)$

5:         $P_t(C) \leftarrow \{C\}$

6:         **for** $C' \subset C$ **do**   ▷ for every possible way of splitting C into two halves

7:             **if** $V_t(C') + V_t(C \setminus C') > v(C)$ **then**

8:                 $V_t(C) \leftarrow V_t(C') + V_t(C \setminus C')$

9:                 $P_t(C) \leftarrow \{C', C \setminus C'\}$

10:             **end if**

11:         **end for**

12:     **end for**

13: **end for**

14: Maximum $\leftarrow 0$

15: **for** $i = n$ to 1 **do**   ▷ Heuristic is used to pick largest valued coalition for each subproblem

16:     $X \leftarrow C | \max_{C \in C^i}(V_t(C))$ ▷ C^i is the coalitions of size i

17:     $Y \leftarrow U \setminus X^a$ ▷ U is the set of all agents and Y is the unassigned agents belongs to coalition of sizes $n - i$.

18:     $\text{Temp}_{value} \leftarrow V_t(X) + V_t(Y)$ ▷ for any coalition $C \in \{X, Y\}$, if $|C| > C_{max}$, then it uses $v(C)$ value.

19:     **if** $\text{Temp}_{value} > Maximum$ **then**

20:         $Maximum \leftarrow \text{Temp}_{value}$

21:         $CS_{Temp} \leftarrow \{X, Y\}$

22:     **end if**

23: **end for**

24: $CS^*(n) \leftarrow$ Best of $CS^*_{initial}$ and CS_{Temp}

---

[a] Each time X is considered, Y is the complement.

Line 2–13 is same as dynamic programming. C_{max} is the iteration limit of proposed algorithm. The incremental subproblem of size 1 to C_{max} are solved exactly with dynamic programming. After the iteration limit C_{max} reached, all the coalition of size 1 to C_{max} are already solved and results are stored in table P_t and V_t. Note that if $C_{max} = n$, it will return optimal solution.

Line 15–18 is used for greedy heuristic after the iteration limit C_{max} is reached. The heuristic used here is to pick up the largest valued coalition with size $n, n - 1, n - 2, \ldots, 1$ and pick the rest of the unassigned agents with sizes $0, 1, 2, \ldots n - 1$[4]

---

[4] If size of coalition X is 0 then the value of the coalition $X = 0$.

Line 19–22 is to keep track of highest valued coalition structure found till now.

Line 24 compares the best of initial solution and the solution using greedy approach used after the iteration limit C_{max}.

Example 1. *Consider the example used in Table 2. Suppose that the iteration limit $C_{max} = 2$. All the coalition of size $1, \ldots 2$ are solved and stored in the table after the iteration limit $C_{max} = 2$ is reached.*

At first the algorithm creates initial solution as follows:

$$CS^*_{initial} = \text{Max}\{\underbrace{\{v(1,2,3,4)\}}_{\text{Value}=140}, \underbrace{\{v(1) + v(2) + v(3) + v(4)\}}_{\text{value}=30+40+25+45=140}\}$$

Table 2. Example of DP program with 4 agents with $C_{max} = 2$

Size	C	v(C)	All splitting by DP	P_t	V_t
1	{1}	30	$v[\{1\}] = 30$	{1}	30
	{2}	40	$v[\{2\}] = 40$	{2}	40
	{3}	25	$v[\{3\}] = 25$	{3}	25
	{4}	45	$v[\{4\}] = 45$	{4}	45
2	{1,2}	50	$v[\{1,2\}] = 50, v\{1\} + v\{2\} = 70$	{1}{2}	70
	{1,3}	60	$v[\{1,3\}] = 60, v\{1\} + v\{3\} = 55$	{1,3}	60
	{1,4}	80	$v[\{1,4\}] = 80, v\{1\} + v\{4\} = 75$	{1,4}	80
	{2,3}	55	$v[\{2,3\}] = 55, v\{2\} + v\{3\} = 65$	{2}{3}	65
	{2,4}	70	$v[\{2,4\}] = 70, v\{2\} + v\{4\} = 85$	{2}{4}	85
	{3,4}	80	$v[\{3,4\}] = 80, v\{3\} + v\{4\} = 70$	{3,4}	80
3	{1,2,3}	90			
	{1,2,4}	120			
	{1,3,4}	100			
	{2,3,4}	115			
4	{1,2,3,4}	140			

Hence, our initial solution $CS^*_{initial}$ is any of them because they gives same value.

Next, algorithm picks the maximum valued coalition with sizes 4 and it is the grand coalition $\{1, 2, 3, 4\}$ with value 140.

Now, algorithm picks the maximum valued coalition of size 3, which is the coalition $\{1, 2, 4\}$ with value 120. Then algorithm chooses the rest of unassigned agent from coalition of size 1, which is the coalition $\{3\}$ with value 25. Total value of coalition structure $\{1, 2, 4\}\{3\}$ is $120 + 25 = 145$.

Next, maximum valued coalition $\{2, 4\}$ of size 2 is picked up and rest of unassigned agents is picked up from coalition of size 2. Total value of coalition structure is $\{2, 4\}\{1, 3\}$ is $85 + 60 = 145$.

At last maximum valued coalition $\{4\}$ of size 1 is picked up and rest of unassigned agents form coalition of size 3 is picked up. Total coalition value is $\{4\}\{1,2,3\} = 45 + 90 = 135$.

Now, compare initial solution $CS^*_{initial}$ with present greedy solution and finds that the maximum value it given is 145 with coalition structure $\{2,4\}\{1,3\}$. The final coalition structure is $\{2\}\{4\}\{1,3\}$ because we see that $\{2,4\}$ is stored as $\{2\}\{4\}$. Note that algorithm could also choose $\{1,2,4\}\{3\}$ as final coalition structure because it also gives value 145.

4   Anytime Property of Proposed Algorithm

The anytime property is also satisfied by proposed algorithm

i) **Monotonicity**— the quality of the result is a nondecreasing function of computation time. In general proposed algorithm is monotonic.

   Proof— The algorithm is clearly monotonic. Suppose we have n agents in the system. For this scenario we have problem sizes of $1, 2, \ldots, n$. With problem size i, all the coalition contains i number agents. Suppose, maximum valued coalition in problem size i is M_i. Let algorithm interrupted after k^{th} iteration. Now, all the coalition of sizes $1, 2, \ldots k$ are already solved. In this case the maximum valued coalition structure is computed as follows:

$$max_{\forall i \in [1,2,\ldots,k,k+1,\ldots n]}\{v(M_i) + v(U \setminus M_i)\}$$

   where U is the set of all agents. The largest valued coalition in problem size k is M_k. If maximum valued coalition structure contains any of the coalition with problem sizes $1, 2 \ldots, k$, then in $(k+1)^{th}$ iteration this value must be the same as the value generated in k^{th} iteration or greater because the values generated in $(k+1)^{th}$ iteration is depends on the values generated in $1, 2, \ldots, k$ iteration.

ii) **Preemptability**— the algorithm can be suspended and resumed with minimal overhead. Proposed algorithm is clearly preempt-able. After the iteration limit is reached, algorithm needs to check the largest valued coalition from each subproblem of size x, where $x \in [1, n]$ and fetch the remaining unassigned agents from subproblem of sizes $n - x$, where n is the total number of agents. This procedure takes $O(n)$ time.

5   Evaluating Proposed Algorithm

In this section we describe the environment on which algorithms have been tested.

5.1   Experimental Setup

To calculate the time performance, we repeat each experiment 40 times and averaged the runtime. The algorithms are implemented in Python (Version:3.4), compiled in IDE Pycharm, and the experiments were run on a Intel(R) Core(TM) i5-4690 CPU, running at 3.50 GHz under Windows 7 operating system (64 bit).

5.2   Dataset Generation

The **NP**-complete problems are intractable but there is no conclusive proof. We cannot deny the possibility that **NP**-complete problem is solvable in polynomial time. Intractable in the sense that there is no polynomial time algorithm for that problem which gives correct result. That means every algorithm for coalition structure formation is imperfect because we know this is an **NP**-complete problem. One way to validate or compare imperfect algorithm for **NP** hard combinatorial optimization problem is to run them on typical problem instances and see how often they fail. The word imperfect means that there is some input for which the algorithm fails to give the correct result. Any imperfect algorithm is usefull if they do not fail too often. With this in mind, we compare proposed algorithm with existing anytime dynamic programming [16] using different value distributions. Specifically, we consider the following distributions.

  i) **Uniform**— as studied by Larson and Sandholm [6]: for all coalition $C \in 2^A - 1$, $v(C) \sim U(a, b)$, where $a = 0$ and $b = |C|$

 ii) **Modified Uniform**— as proposed by Service and Adams [17]. The value of each coalition C is drawn uniformly $v(C) \sim U(a, b)$, where $a = 0$ and $b = 10 \times |C|.$, next a random number r is generated $r \sim U(0, 50)$ and is added to the coalition value $v(C)$ with probability 0.2.

 iii) **Normal**— as studied by Rahwan et al. [12] every coalition value is drawn from $v(C) \sim N(\mu, \sigma^2)$, where $\mu = 10 \times |C|$ and $\sigma = 0.1$

 iv) **Modified Normal**— as proposed by Rahwan et al. [10]. The value of each coalition C is first drawn $v(C) \sim N(a, b)$, where $a = 10 \times |C|$ and $b = 0.01$, next a random number r is generated $r \sim U(0, 50)$ and is added to the coalition value $v(C)$ with probability 0.2.

  v) **Beta** — The value of each coalition C is drawn as $v(C) \sim |C| \times$ Beta (α, β), where $\alpha = \beta = 0.5$.

 vi) **Gamma**— The value of each coalition C is drawn as $v(C) \sim |C| \times$ Gamma (x, θ), where $x = \theta = 2$

 vii) **Agent-based Uniform**— as proposed by Rahwan et al. [10], each of the agent a_i is assigned a random power $p_i \sim U(0, 10)$, reflecting its average performance over all coalitions. Then for all coalition C in which agent a_i appears, the actual power of a_i in C is determined as $p_i^C \sim U(0, 2 \times p_i)$ and the coalition value is calculated as the sum of all the members power in that coalition. That is, $\forall C$, $v(C) = \sum_{a_i \in C} p_i^C$.

viii) **Agent-Based Normal**— as proposed by Tomasz Michalakn et al. [7], each of the agent a_i is assigned a random power $p_i \sim N(10, 0.01)$. Then for all coalition C in which agent a_i appears, the actual power of a_i in C is determined as $p_i^C \sim N(p_i, 0.01)$ and the coalition value is calculated as the sum of all the member's power in that coalition. That is, $\forall C$, $v(C) = \sum_{a_i \in C} p_i^C$.

 ix) **Normally Distributed Coalition Structures (NDSC)**— as proposed by Rahwan et al. [13], value of each coalition C is drawn as $v(C) \sim N(\mu, \sigma^2)$, where $\mu = |C|$ and $\sigma = \sqrt{|C|}$.

In the comparison graph shown in Figs. 1 and 2, we call our algorithm as PADP (Proposed Anytime Dynamic Programming) and the algorithm proposed by Service and Adams [16] is denoted as ADP (anytime dynamic programming).

6 Performance

In order to evaluate the proposed algorithm we implemented it in the Python programming (Version: 3.4) language and tested the behavior of coalition structure formation problem. As our benchmark we use the algorithm presented in [16]. We selects algorithm in [16] because according to our knowledge, it is the only available coalition structure formation algorithm using anytime dynamic programming. Here we present experimental results on the behaviors of PADP and ADP [16], considering in particular solution quality and runtime performances. We tested both the algorithms for 16 agents and compare it with the increasing iteration limit of basic dynamic programming. For each of the above distributions, we plotted the termination times of both algorithms for each iteration with 16 agents. Here, time is measured in seconds, and plotted on a log scale and similarly solution is also plotted on a log scale. Figure 1 shows the resulting performances of both algorithms with respect to solution obtained. The results show that if proposed algorithm is interrupted before running to completion, it may still return a solution with relatively high quality than the algorithm proposed by Service and Adams [16]. Specifically, we find that.

i) Except Normal and Agent based normal distribution our proposed algorithm always produces better solution as compared to previous algorithm [16]. The results are shown in Fig. 1a, 1b, 1e, 1f, 1g, 1i.
ii) With Normal and Agent based normal distribution (shown in Fig. 1c, 1h) both algorithm performances are same in terms of solution quality, because of the fact that, under these distribution, the optimal solution mainly consisted of the singleton coalitions.
iii) With Modified Uniform, Normal, Beta and Agent-based Normal distributions,(shown in Fig. 1b, 1c, 1e, 1i) PADP takes very less time to produce near optimal solution.
iv) With Modified Normal distribution, PADP fails to produce better result for first $n/2$ iterations, after that it always produce better result than ADP.

In terms of runtime, results show that the proposed algorithm runs little bit faster for first few iterations and after that both algorithms running time is same. The runtime comparison is given in Fig. 2.

7 Related Work

The current research work on coalition structure formation can be classified into three categories [8].

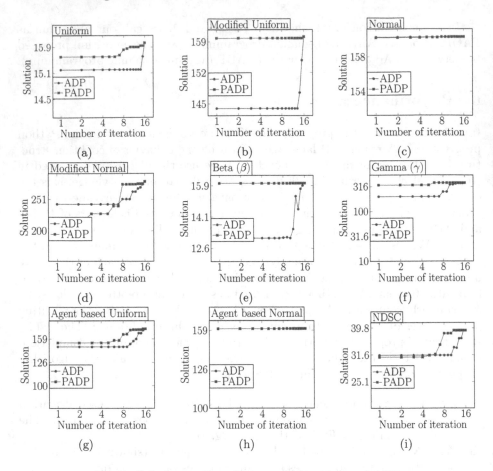

Fig. 1. Solution quality of proposed algorithm and ADP

1. **Anytime algorithms**— It permits premature termination (i.e., before the optimal solution has been found) but at the same time it provides guarantees on the quality of the solution. One of the disadvantage of anytime algorithm in coalition formation mechanism is that they all requires, in the worst case to check all coalition structures. Hence, time required is $O(n^n)$.

2. **Design-to-time algorithms**— This type of algorithm guarantees to return an optimal solution but to do so, it must run on completion. That is they can not produce intermediate result like anytime algorithms.

3. **Heuristics algorithms**—This type of algorithm sacrifices quality guarantees of solution for speed. The main drawback of this type algorithm is that it is impossible to verify the quality of generated solution.

The optimal coalition structure can be generated by using dynamic programming algorithm [19] in $O(3^n)$ time, however it is impractical for moderate size of inputs.

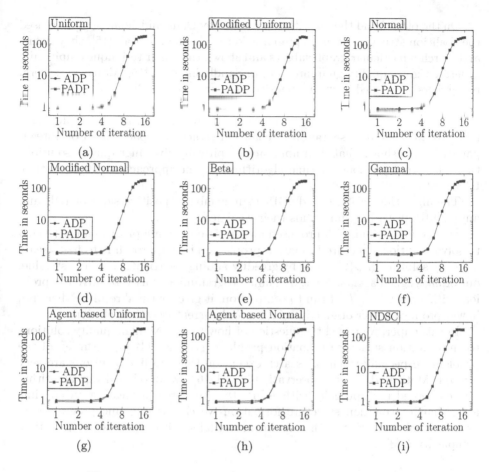

Fig. 2. Time performance of proposed algorithm and ADP

The state-of-the-art *Improved Dynamic Programming* (IDP) [9] algorithm is improved version of [19] it is improved by Rahwan and Jennings [9] to enhance the usability of dynamic programming. Their approach is not to evaluate some unnecessary splitting. The author shows that their approach is empirically faster and uses less memory, but still worst case runtime is $O(3^n)$. The main drawback of this approach is it does not have anytime properties.

Due to the high complexity of dynamic programming many researchers are developing anytime algorithm which allow quality suboptimal solution very faster. Many anytime coalition structure formation algorithm operates on the space of all coalition structures, between $\omega(n^n)$ to $O(n^n)$ [15]. Sandholm et al. [15] proposes first anytime algorithm for coalition structure formation problem. They proved that to provide a bound on the quality of the solution algorithm needs to check at-least 2^{n-1} coalition structures. Their approach uses coalition structure graph, where nodes in the graph are coalition structures and edges between nodes are splitting(or mergers) of coalition structure.

On the other hand the algorithm proposed by Dang and Jenning [3] also used the coalition structure graph representation as Sandholm et al. [15], they define and search a particular graph subsets and shown that their technique empirically generate tighter quality guarantee's than Sandholm et al. [15]. Moreover, several researchers developed anytime algorithms that searches the space of coalition structure graph in different ways [3,8,13].

Rahwan and Jennings [13] have not used coalition structure graph. They use a totally new representation of coalition structures space based on integer partitions and shown that their approach empirically gives high quality solutions than any other previous anytime algorithms. Their approach is called anytime IP algorithm.

The algorithm in [8], called IDP-IP, it combines positive sides of IDP and anytime IP algorithm and avoids their weakness.

Service and Adams [16] proposed an anytime dynamic programming (ADP) to solve coalition structure formation problem. Their approach is to first create a greedy solution in $O(2^n)$ time by greedily adding the coalition of largest value, out of unassigned agents. Next, dynamic programming is used to solve the problem with sizes $1, 2, \ldots k$. If run to completion, it gives optimal result. Otherwise, it will produce better of greedy solution and current iterative solution.

In this paper, we raised the question of how to achieve high quality solutions to the coalition structure formation problem (see e.g. [11] for a survey of the problem), especially when the search execution times to find solutions are very limited. Motivated by the observations in [1,16], we developed our algorithm and compared it empirically with ADP [16]. In search of creating an anytime algorithm for coalition structure formation we choose dynamic programming as basic tool because it is the algorithm available with lowest worst case time complexity $O(3^n)$.

8   Conclusion

Coalition structure formation is a computationally hard, combinatorial problem in multi-agent systems. This work represents a new anytime dynamic programming for solving coalition structure formation and has been compared with previous anytime dynamic programming algorithm [16]. The backbone of both algorithms are dynamic programming but they used different heuristics to get the solution.

Both the algorithm use preprocessing to make a greedy solution before dynamic program starts. The preprocessing phase of ADP [16] runs in $O(2^n)$ and the preprocessing phase of our proposed algorithm runs in $O(n)$. In most of the input distribution, proposed algorithm performs well than ADP [16].

Acknowledgments. This research work is funded by Visvesvaraya PhD scheme of DeitY (Department of Electronics & Information Technology), Govt. of India.

References

1. Boddy, M.S.: Anytime problem solving using dynamic programming. In: AAAI, pp. 738–743 (1991)
2. Dang, V.D., Dash, R.K., Rogers, A., Jennings, N.R.: Overlapping coalition formation for efficient data fusion in multi sensor networks. In: AAAI, vol. 6, pp. 635–640 (2006)
3. Dang, V.D., Jennings, N.R.: Generating coalition structures with finite bound from the optimal guarantees. In: Proceedings of the Third International Joint Conference on Autonomous Agents and Multiagent Systems, vol. 2, pp. 564–571. IEEE Computer Society (2004)
4. Kahan, J.P., Rapoport, A.: Theories of Coalition Formation. Psychology Press, Palo Altom (2014)
5. Kreher, D.L., Stinson, D.R.: Combinatorial Algorithms: Generation, Enumeration, and Search, vol. 7. CRC Press, Boca Raton (1998)
6. Larson, K.S., Sandholm, T.W.: Anytime coalition structure generation: an average case study. J. Exp. Theoret. Artif. Intell. **12**(1), 23–42 (2000)
7. Michalak, T., Rahwan, T., Elkind, E., Wooldridge, M., Jennings, N.R.: A hybrid exact algorithm for complete set partitioning. Artif. Intell. **230**, 14–50 (2015)
8. Rahwan, T., Jennings, N.R.: Coalition structure generation: dynamic programming meets anytime optimization. In: AAAI, vol. 8, pp. 156–161 (2008)
9. Rahwan, T., Jennings, N.R.: An improved dynamic programming algorithm for coalition structure generation. In: Proceedings of the 7th International Joint Conference on Autonomous Agents and Multiagent Systems, vol. 3, pp. 1417–1420. International Foundation for Autonomous Agents and Multiagent Systems (2008)
10. Rahwan, T., Michalak, T., Jennings, N.R.: A hybrid algorithm for coalition structure generation (2012)
11. Rahwan, T., Michalak, T.P., Wooldridge, M., Jennings, N.R.: Coalition structure generation: a survey. Artif. Intell. **229**, 139–174 (2015)
12. Rahwan, T., Ramchurn, S.D., Dang, V.D., Giovannucci, A., Jennings, N.R.: Anytime optimal coalition structure generation. In: AAAI, vol. 7, pp. 1184–1190 (2007)
13. Rahwan, T., Ramchurn, S.D., Jennings, N.R., Giovannucci, A.: An anytime algorithm for optimal coalition structure generation. J. Artif. Intell. Res. **34**, 521–567 (2009)
14. Sandhlom, T.W., Lesser, V.R.: Coalitions among computationally bounded agents. Artif. Intell. **94**(1), 99–137 (1997)
15. Sandholm, T., Larson, K., Andersson, M., Shehory, O., Tohmé, F.: Coalition structure generation with worst case guarantees. Artif. Intell. **111**(1), 209–238 (1999)
16. Service, T.C., Adams, J.A.:Anytime dynamic programming for coalition structure generation. In: Proceedings of the 9th International Conference on AutonomousAgents and Multiagent Systems, vol. 1, pp. 1411–1412. International Foundation for Autonomous Agents and Multiagent Systems (2010)
17. Service, T.C., Adams, J.A.: Approximate coalition structure generation. In: Twenty-Fourth AAAI Conference on Artificial Intelligence (2010)
18. Tsvetovat, M., Sycara, K.: Customer coalitions in the electronic marketplace. In: Proceedings of the Fourth International Conference on Autonomous Agents, pp. 263–264. ACM (2000)
19. Yun Yeh, D.: A dynamic programming approach to the complete set partitioning problem. BIT Numer. Math. **26**(4), 467–474 (1986)

Early Innovation Short Papers

Demand Response Integration Through Agent-Based Coordination of Consumers in Virtual Power Plants

Anders Clausen[(✉)], Aisha Umair, Zheng Ma, and Bo Nørregaard Jørgensen

University of Southern Denmark, Odense, Denmark
{ancla,aiu,zma,bnj}@mmmi.sdu.dk

Abstract. The transition towards an electricity grid based on renewable energy production induces fluctuation in electricity generation. This challenges the existing electricity grid design, where generation is expected to follow demand for electricity. In this paper, we propose a multi-agent based Virtual Power Plant design that is able to balance the demand of energy-intensive, industrial loads with the supply situation in the electricity grid. The proposed Virtual Power Plant design uses a novel inter-agent, multi-objective, multi-issue negotiation mechanism, to coordinate the electricity demands of industrial loads. Coordination happens in response to Demand Response events, while considering local objectives in the industrial domain. We illustrate the applicability of our approach on a Virtual Power Plant scenario with three simulated greenhouses. The results suggest that the proposed design is able to coordinate the electricity demands of industrial loads, in compliance with external Demand Response events.

1 Introduction

The transition towards an electricity production based on renewable energy, challenges the electricity infrastructure. Maintaining a balance between supply and demand is crucial, and fluctuations from electricity production must be handled. To this end, consumer participation in Demand Response (DR) programs offers a cheap and carbon friendly solution [3]. In DR programs, consumers are offered incentive, in the form of variable electricity prices or direct payments, to change their consumption pattern [7]. To overcome capacity constraints on DR markets, the coordinated actions of multiple consumers can be exposed through a Virtual Power Plant (VPP) [9].

Literature contain numerous proposals for VPP designs. In general, these approaches can be categorized either as centralized- or distributed approaches. Centralized approaches such as the ones proposed by Ruiz et al. [11], Binding et al. [1] and Molderink et al. [8] rely on direct load control of consumers, which scales poorly for larger virtual power plants. Further, this deprives consumers of their autonomy. To overcome these limitations, distributed approaches coordinate consumers represented as autonomous agents. Kok et al. [5], Kulasekara et al. [6],

© Springer International Publishing Switzerland 2016
M. Baldoni et al. (Eds.): PRIMA 2016, LNAI 9862, pp. 313–322, 2016.
DOI: 10.1007/978-3-319-44832-9_19

Zhang et al. [13] and Ramchurn et al. [10] contains examples of such approaches. But to our knowledge, existing literature does not account for the fact, that consumers are often complex entities, with several objectives negotiating over several issues. Under these circumstances, several local objectives must be pursued by each consumer while adhering to global requirements presented by DR events.

To this end, we propose a multi-agent based VPP design, which uses a novel inter-agent multi-objective multi-issue (MOMI) negotiation mechanism to achieve a group objective among self-interested agents. Agents represent complex consumer domains, and the group objective is defined by DR events received by a VPP entity. The design has been implemented in a software application used to simulate a VPP containing three greenhouses, which are coordinated towards various DR events. The results show that the electricity consumption of the greenhouses can be coordinated in accordance with received DR events, without violating their production requirements, when sufficient flexibility is available in the greenhouses.

The remainder of the paper is organized as follows. In Sect. 2 we present the proposed multi-agent based VPP design. This is followed by a description of a VPP scenario in Sect. 3. Section 4 describes experimental results and finally Sect. 5 draws conclusions.

2   Model for an Multi-agent Based VPP

We propose a multi-agent based VPP design, in which the complex nature of consumer domains is recognized. The design consists of an Aggregator-agent who negotiates with a number of Load-agents. The purpose of the negotiation is to agree on an electricity profile for each of the Load-agents. The electricity profile describes planned consumption (or, production) for a consumer domain across a VPP-specific period of time. When combined, the electricity profiles of all consumer domains should adhere to requests for DR services received as DR events. In this context, the Aggregator-agent is a coordinating entity that receives DR events, and the Load-agents represent consumer domains. The Aggregator-agent may form bilateral negotiations with Load-agents. When this happens, the Load-agent will provide an electricity demand profile to the Aggregator-agent. The Aggregator-agent initiates negotiation with the Load-agents by calculating electricity allocation profiles. These form a combined electricity profile that adheres to the received DR event. Further, the allocations for each Load-agent is as close to the electricity demand profiles as possible. The Aggregator-agent will then inform the Load-agents of the suggestions for electricity allocation profiles, and Load-agents will respond with a revised electricity demand profile. This process is repeated until the Aggregator-agent and Load-agents reach consensus on allocation - or the negotiation reaches a specified time-limit.

The agent decision logic is modeled as a multi-objective, multi-issue (MOMI) negotiation using a genetic algorithm (GA). Agents may have several objectives and address several issues, and the GA will query each objective with suggestions for issue values. This can be perceived as a mediator-based negotiation, where the GA assumes a man-in-the-middle position towards a set of objectives, represented by concerns, who negotiate over a set of issues. The mediator proposes values for issues, in the form of *contracts*, to the concerns. Each concern defines a cost function, which will yield a cost as a function of a contract and a *target vector.* This cost describes the degree to which a proposed contract adheres to the objective represented by the concern, at the time of the proposal. The use of cost functions means that concerns will seek to reduce the distance between a contract and its target vector. Here, the concern may select a subset of values from the contract and manipulate them, in order to make them comparable to its target vector. This means that the mediator has incomplete information: The mediator has knowledge of the concerns and - after querying - the cost they associate with a specific contract. It does not have knowledge of the cost function of the concern or the value of its target vector. The use of a GA means that contract proposals will initially be random within limits defined by the issues. The mediator will create a vector for each contract containing costs for each concern. Using the Pareto criteria, the mediator then creates and evolves a Pareto set of contract proposals based on their cost vectors. Evolution happens through genetic operations (crossover and mutation) on the contracts. The evolution of the Pareto set continues, until a time-limit, or a given number of evolutions, is reached. This concludes local optimization and enables the mediator to select a contract from the Pareto set, in order to provide a proposal in the inter-agent negotiation. To this end, mediators use concern's priority: A concern's priority is given by a value of either 0, 1 or 2. The lower the value, the higher the priority. These priorities are used to classify mission critical Domain Concerns (DCs) in priority 0, Representation Concerns (RCs) in priority 1, and non-mission critical DCs in priority 2. DCs are used by the agent to represent local objectives where RCs represent objectives of agents, with which it is negotiating. The concept is illustrated in Fig. 1.

A selection criteria based on maximizing social benefit [4] is then used recursively on the priority groups to select the best contract. This means that all contracts from priority 0 that yield the same social benefit, are evaluated for all concerns in priority 1 and so on. The priority based selection scheme will guarantee the selection of a contract, that satisfies concerns with a higher priority before it considers concerns with lower priority. After selecting a contract, a mediator will update target vectors of all RCs representing its agent.

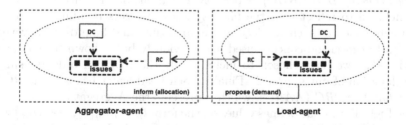

Fig. 1. Concept of bilateral negotiation between agents in agent decision logic

This initiates the next round of inter-agent negotiation, and the process continues until a final number of negotiation rounds is reached or the allocated time for inter-agent negotiation expires. This design enures, that agents may mutually influence each other without violating mission-critical, local objectives. This design enables a differentiation between DCs and RCs: The mediator can prioritize local objectives over objectives, which represent external agents. This is necessary to avoid a self-enforcing feedback loop between an opponent agent and its RCs, during inter-agent negotiation. In agent terminology, this ensures that agents act truthful, and not based on external bias. Once the inter-agent negotiation terminates, the Pareto set in each agent contains one or more contracts, with maximum social benefit for both mission-critical DCs and RCs, *iff* there are no conflicts between the Aggregator-agent and Load-agents. However, in case of a conflict, no such contract exist. To solve this conflict, a choice can be made to prioritize the Aggregator-agent, in order to guarantee compliance with DR events, or to prioritize Load-agents, to ensure successful operation of consumer domains (or compromises in between these extremes). This topic is outside the scope of this paper.

3   Case Study

In our case study, we have created a VPP using the design presented in section Sect. 2. The VPP is implemented with a single Aggregator-agent and four Load-agents who simulate consumers. These consumers resemble commercial greenhouse growers, who play an important role in the production of ornamental pot plants and vegetables in Northern Europe. These are ideal candidates for VPPs, as they constitute complex process domains, where maintaining an optimal growth climate for plants requires intensive energy use and continuous supervision of different climate parameters such as CO_2 levels, temperature and humidity.

3.1   Load-Agent Decision Logic

Each Load-agent has been configured with a single issue, namely the Light Plan-issue. Further, each Load-agent has a mission-critical *Production DC (PDC)* at priority 0, which reflects production needs, as well as a non-mission critical *Energy Reducing DC* (ERDC) at priority 2. Various other concerns could have been included to reflect that the photosynthesis process is influenced by various climate concerns such as CO_2, air temperature, and humidity. However, as the MOMI negotiation concept used has previously been shown to handle such scenarios [12], we have chosen to include only the PDC, in order to simplify the explanation of our approach. Finally, each Load-agent has a single RC, the *Aggregator Agent RC (AARC)*, which represents the Aggregator-agent.

The Light Plan-issue defines values on the form $l_n = [l_{1,n}, l_{2,n}, \cdots, l_{t,n}]$ where n is the Load-agent. This means that each contract in the Load-agent will contain a vector with values on this form. The values of elements in this vector depend on the nature of the Load-agent - or rather, the load that the issue represents in the Load-agent. For simplicity, loads are assumed to be either on or off in the following, yielding $l_{x,n} \in \{0, 1\}$, which means that this value maps to the state of the actuator - not its consumption.

The PLM reflects the need for artificial growth light to the plants. Specifically, the target vector of the PDC represents the amount of photo-synthetically active radiation (PAR) in MolSqrMeter, required to achieve the production goal. In this case then, the target vector is a scalar defined as $g_n \in \mathbb{R}$.

The contribution from artificial growth light varies across the day. That is, the contribution is marginal when the sun shines whereas the contribution is significant in hours with cloudy weather - or after sunset/before sunrise. To this end, the PDC is supplied with a *coefficient vector* defined as $v_n = [v_{1,n}, v_{2,n}, \cdots, v_{t,n}]$ where $v_{x,n} in \mathbb{R}$. The coefficient vector represents the estimated amount of photosynthesis obtained from artificial light in each hour. This is used by the PDC to calculate the PAR contribution for a given contract C as $h_n = \sum_i^t (v_{i,n} * l_{i,n})$, where $l_n \in C$. The PDC then returns a cost, q_n, defined by the absolute difference between g_n and h_n, $q_n = |g_n - h_n|$. The coefficient vector changes over time as a result of the underlying estimates changing. This means that the nature of the cost space created as a function of contracts and the PDC target vector, changes over time. This again means that the relation between the PDC and other concerns changes over time, as this relation is forged solely based on costs returned by concerns to contracts. Hence, no assumption about relations between concerns can be made.

The AARC compares suggestions for allocations made by the VPP towards contracts suggested by the mediator in the Load-agent. Each AARC has a target vector $f_n = [f_{1,n}, f_{2,n}, \cdots, f_{t,n}]$, which is the current electricity allocation made in the Aggregator-agent for that particular Load-agent. This means, that the target vector of the AARC changes as the inter-agent negotiation progresses. As the Load Plan-issues represents an actuator, the task of the AARC is to convert actuation values into an electricity consumption, which can be compared towards its target vector. The AARC maps off-hours to a consumption of 0 MWh and on-hours to a consumption of 1 MWh. The 1 MWh then corresponds to the installed effect of the lamps in the greenhouse, in which the Load-agent reside. Essentially, this means that the AARC has a coefficient vector of 1's, which are multiplied on value suggestions for the Light Plan-issue. Had the installed effect been different, this would be reflected by the coefficient vector of the AARC. Multiplying the coefficient vector of the AARC with values for the Light Plan-issue, yields a vector $d_n = [d_{1,n}, d_{2,n}, \cdots, d_{t,n}]$. The AARC calculates the cost, q_n of a contract as the absolute difference of each element in f_n and d_n, - $q_n = \sum_i^t |f_{i,n} - d_{i,n}|$.

The ERDC is included to have Load-agents generate baselines, which adhere to the assumption of being energy efficient. The cost function of ERDC returns a value, which corresponds to the sum of elements in l_n, defined as $q_n = \sum_i^t l_{i,n}$, which means that use of more artificial light returns a higher cost. Implementing the ERDC as a non-mission critical DC means that the Load-agent will favor adhering to requests of the Aggregator-agent over achieving energy efficiency.

3.2 Aggregator-Agent Decision Logic

The Aggregator-agent contains three Electricity Allocation-issues, which represent allocations for Load-agents as well as seven concerns: one mission critical Load Management DC (*LMDC*) which represents DR events in the MOMI negotiation, and two Load Agent RCs (*LARCs*) for each Load-agent. The logic behind using two RCs for each Load-agent is that allocations of electricity do not attribute the same contribution to the Load-agent, if it is moved from one slot to another. By having two RCs representing a single Load-agent, a distinction between temporal allocation of electricity and the amount of electricity allocated can be made. This means that a profile, in which electricity allocation has been shifted, is preferred over one, in which the electricity allocation has been reduced. If the Load-agent was represented by only one RC in the Aggregator-agent, a profile which time shifts an allocation would yield a higher cost, than one which simply reduces the allocation made to the Load-agent.

Values for the Electricity Allocation-issues represent hourly electricity allocation, for each of the Load-agents across a day. The issue values are defined as vectors, on the form $e_n = [e_{1,n}, e_{2,n}, \cdots, e_{t,n}]$, where t is the number of slots, n is the Load-agent, to which the allocation maps and $e_{x,n} in \{0, 1\}$ is the allocation size. The definition of the values that $e_{x,n}$ can take on depends on the minimum and maximum consumption of the industrial process as well as the steps in which the consumption of a given process can be regulated.

The LMDC enables the VPP to offer Load Management (LM) actions towards external parties. LM encompass the actions load shedding, valley filling and load shifting [2]. In peak clipping, load is reduced in one slot of an electricity profile, as opposed to valley filling, in which load is increased in a slot. Finally, load shifting is a combination of these actions, where load is moved from one slot to one (or several) other(s). The LMDC negotiates over the summarized value of all Electricity Allocation-issues, defined as $y = \sum_n^t e_n$, to ensure that the combined allocation adheres to incoming DR events. It has a target vector $p = [p_1, p_2, \cdots, p_t]$ which is defined by the DR event. That is, the DR event contains a target vector for the LMDC. As the Aggregator-agent has knowledge of the electricity profile of each Load-agent, before starting negotiation with these, it is fair to assume, that the Aggregator-agent can propagate this as an aggregated baseline electricity profile to an external party. This enables external parties to create DR events with target vectors as altered versions of the initial, aggregated baseline electricity profile of the VPP. The cost function of the LMDC returns a value, which corresponds to the absolute difference of each element in y and p, formally defined as $q_n = \sum_i^t |y_i - p_i|$.

The concern $\text{LARC}_{\text{time}}$ negotiates over the Electricity Allocation-issue, representing allocation for its Load-agent. Each $\text{LARC}_{\text{time}}$ has a target vector $d_n = [d_{1,n}, d_{2,n}, \cdots, d_{t,n}]$, which represents the electricity demand profile of the Load-agent. The value of this vector changes over time, as the inter-agent negotiation progresses. Again, this is due to the bilateral negotiation between the Aggregator-agent and the Load-agent. The cost function of each $\text{LARC}_{\text{time}}$ returns a value, which corresponds to the absolute difference of each element in

e_n and d_n, defined as $q_n = \sum_i^t |e_{i,n} - d_{i,n}|$. The concern LARC$_{sum}$ works in a similar way, except this concern is solely concerned with the amount of electricity allocation - and not the time at which it is allocated. The cost function of each LARC$_{sum}$ returns a value, which corresponds to absolute difference of the accumulated values of elements in e_n and d_n, defined as $q_n = |\sum_i^t e_{i,n} - \sum_i^t d_{i,n}|$.

4   Experiments and Results

We consider 4 sets of experiments based on the scenario in Sect. 3. The first experiment serves as a baseline case, to validate that Load-agents will be allocated their requested demand, in case of no DR event. The three subsequent experiments map to each of the LM actions described in Sect. 3. Each of the PDCs were given a target vector of 400 MolSqrMeter. This number reflects that each Load-agent needs to reach a certain light sum, in order to achieve the required plant growth. Each PDC x is assigned a coefficient vector v_x as shown in (1), (2), and (3), which varies between the Load-agents, to reflect varying conditions in each of the domains. For the purpose of illustration, the coefficients vectors share the property that they yield a single optimal schedule with respect to energy efficiency, in order to reach the goal of 400 MolSqrMeter.

$$v_1 = [25\ 0\ 25\ 25\ 25\ 25\ 50\ 50\ 50\ 100\ 50\ 25\ 50\ 25\ 25\ 25\ 25\ 25\ 25\ 50\ 25\ 25\ 25\ 25]\quad(1)$$

$$v_2 = [25\ 0\ 25\ 25\ 25\ 25\ 25\ 25\ 25\ 50\ 100\ 50\ 50\ 50\ 25\ 50\ 50\ 25\ 25\ 25\ 25\ 25\ 25]\quad(2)$$

$$v_3 = [25\ 0\ 25\ 25\ 50\ 50\ 25\ 25\ 50\ 100\ 50\ 50\ 25\ 25\ 25\ 25\ 25\ 25\ 50\ 25\ 25\ 25\ 25\ 25]\quad(3)$$

The most energy efficient schedules for the Load-agents are used as baselines, which are shown in (4),(5) and (6) and the aggregated baseline profile of the three Load-agents is shown in (7). In a real-life scenario, the baseline would be deducted live, as this knowledge is present in the target vectors of the LARC's in the VPP.

$$d_1 = [0\ 0\ 0\ 0\ 0\ 0\ 1\ 1\ 1\ 1\ 0\ 1\ 0\ 0\ 0\ 0\ 0\ 1\ 0\ 0\ 0\ 0]\quad(4)$$

$$d_2 = [0\ 0\ 0\ 0\ 0\ 0\ 0\ 0\ 0\ 1\ 1\ 1\ 1\ 0\ 1\ 1\ 0\ 0\ 0\ 0\ 0\ 0]\quad(5)$$

$$d_3 = [0\ 0\ 0\ 0\ 1\ 1\ 0\ 0\ 1\ 1\ 1\ 0\ 0\ 0\ 0\ 0\ 1\ 0\ 0\ 0\ 0\ 0]\quad(6)$$

$$d_{agg} = [0\ 0\ 0\ 0\ 1\ 1\ 1\ 1\ 2\ 2\ 3\ 2\ 2\ 1\ 1\ 0\ 1\ 1\ 1\ 0\ 0\ 0\ 0]\quad(7)$$

To simulate DR events, three target vectors were created for the LMDC, based on the aggregated baseline profile in (7). These can be seen in (9), (10) and (11) respectively. The baseline target vector shown in (8) is equal to d_{agg}, as we want each Load-agent to be provided with the most energy efficient allocation, in case of no LM request. The subsequent target vectors were defined by altering the baseline goal according to the LM actions peak clipping, load shifting and valley filling. Obviously, the target vector of the LMDC is defined by the DR event in a real life setting.

$$p_{baseline} = [0\ 0\ 0\ 0\ 1\ 1\ 1\ 1\ 2\ 2\ 3\ 2\ 2\ 1\ 1\ 0\ 1\ 1\ 1\ 0\ 0\ 0\ 0]\quad(8)$$

$$p_{peak\_clip} = [0\ 0\ 0\ 0\ 1\ 1\ 1\ 1\ 2\ 2\ 2\ 2\ 2\ 1\ 1\ 0\ 1\ 1\ 1\ 0\ 0\ 0\ 0]\quad(9)$$

$$p_{valley\_fill} = [0\ 0\ 0\ 0\ 1\ 1\ 1\ 1\ 2\ 2\ 3\ 2\ 2\ 1\ 1\ 1\ 1\ 1\ 1\ 0\ 0\ 0\ 0] \qquad (10)$$

$$p_{load\_shift} = [0\ 0\ 0\ 0\ 1\ 1\ 1\ 1\ 2\ 2\ 2\ 2\ 2\ 1\ 1\ 1\ 1\ 1\ 1\ 1\ 0\ 0\ 0] \qquad (11)$$

Each experiment was executed with a generation limit of 500, which was empirically found to ensure convergence in the local negotiation. Each experiment was repeated 30 times to remove influence of randomness from the GA, as recommended by [14]. In order for the design of the proposed mechanism to be successful, the experiments should show that adherence to incoming DR events is made with minimal impact on the Load-agents. That is, each Load-agent should be allocated their demand - or as close to it as possible. When the correct amount of allocation is available (in case of a load shift), no conflict should exist between Load-agents and the Aggregator-agent.

The results of the baseline experiment is shown in Fig. 2. Here we see that the aggregated demand profile corresponds to the one in (7). Figure 3 shows the result of a peak clipping experiment, in which the LMDC in the Aggregator-agent will enforce a peak clipping request of 1 MW. To do so, a single Load-agent must be forced to compromise its electricity demand by 1 MW. As can be seen, one Load-agent is allocated 1 MW less than it demands in slot 11. This leads to an inter-agent negotiation conflict as expected. The Load-agent, which is being forced to compromise, is observed to change over the 30 experiments. However, the aggregated profiles remain the same for all experiments. In the valley filling experiment, a single Load-agent must increase its consumption. As in the peak clipping experiments, this leads to a conflict, as it forces one of the Load-agents to exceed the goal of its PDC in time slot 16. The results are shown in Fig. 4. Again, the Load-agent selected for an increase varies throughout the experiments. Lastly, Fig. 5 shows

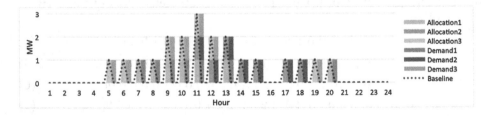

Fig. 2. Result of baseline experiment. Numbers behind legend map to Load-agents

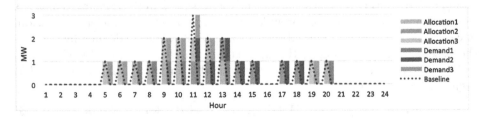

Fig. 3. Result of peak clipping experiment. Numbers behind legend map to Load-agents

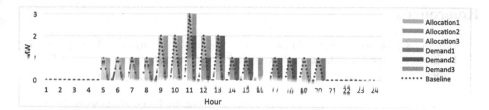

Fig. 4. Result of valley filling experiment. Numbers behind legend map to Load-agents

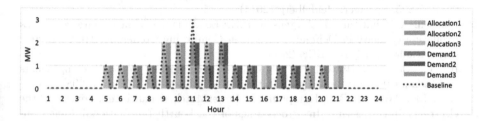

Fig. 5. Result of load shifting experiment. Numbers behind legend map to Load-agents

the results of the load shifting experiment, where a Load-agent must shift its consumption. We observed that the aggregated load is shifted as expected, increasing its consumption in slots 16 and 21 in return for a reduction in slot 11. An important note here is, that the Load-agent making a shift, is compensated in a way, which ensures that it reaches its production goal. In a real-life scenario this could mean, that the Aggregator-agent would first have to shed load, and then gradually increase compensation, until the conflict is solved.

5 Conclusion

Flexibility in electricity consumption on the consumer side can help to maintain balance between supply and demand, in electricity grids with high penetration of wind- and solar power. In this paper, we propose a multi-agent based design of a VPP that is able to integrate energy-intensive industrial loads in DR programs. We propose a novel inter-agent multi-objective multi-issue (MOMI) negotiation mechanism to coordinate the individual electricity consumption of several industrial loads towards received DR events. In this way, a VPP may expose an aggregated load profile which conforms to electricity market requirements. Our design handles DR events by performing LM in the form of peak clipping, valley filling, and load shifting on aggregates of industrial loads. We illustrate how the proposed design will adhere to DR events, without violating production requirements of the industrial domains, in cases where sufficient electricity is available. Further we show, how allocation of electricity follows demand from the industrial domains, to the best degree possible. Based on the present proof of concept, we plan to extend the model to handle conflicts which can arise in cases of insufficient electricity.

References

1. Binding, C., Gantenbein, D., Jansen, B., Sundström, O., Andersen, P.B., Marra, F., Poulsen, B., Træholt, C.: Electric vehicle fleet integration in the Danish EDISON project-a virtual power plant on the island of Bornholm. In: IEEE PES General Meeting, pp. 1–8. IEEE (2010)
2. Clausen, A., Demazeau, Y., Jørgensen, B.N.: An agent-based framework for aggregation of manageable distributed energy resources. In: Corchado, J.M., Bajo, J., Kozlak, J., Pawlewski, P., Molina, J.M., Gaudou, B., Julian, V., Unland, R., Lopes, F., Hallenborg, K., García Teodoro, P. (eds.) PAAMS 2014. CCIS, vol. 430, pp. 214–225. Springer, Heidelberg (2014)
3. Clausen, A., Ghatikar, G., Jorgensen, B.N.: Load management of data centers as regulation capacity in Denmark. In: Green Computing Conference (IGCC), 2014 International, pp. 1–10. IEEE (2014)
4. Ito, T., Klein, M., Hattori, H.: A multi-issue negotiation protocol among agents with nonlinear utility functions. Multiagent Grid Syst. 4(1), 67–83 (2008)
5. Kok, J.K., Warmer, C.J., Kamphuis, I.: PowerMatcher: multiagent control in the electricity infrastructure. In: Proceedings of the Fourth International Joint Conference on Autonomous Agents and Multiagent Systems, pp. 75–82. ACM (2005)
6. Kulasekara, A., Hemapala, K., Gopura, R.: Dual layered architecture for multi agent based islanding and load management for microgrids. J. Power Energy Eng. 3(05), 29 (2015)
7. Lee, M., Aslam, O., Foster, B., Kathan, D., Kwok, J., Medearis, L., Palmer, R., Sporborg, P., Tita, M.: Assessment of demand response and advanced metering. Technical report. Federal Energy Regulatory Commission (2013)
8. Molderink, A., Bakker, V., Bosman, M.G., Hurink, J.L., Smit, G.J.: Management and control of domestic smart grid technology. IEEE Trans. Smart Grid 1(2), 109–119 (2010)
9. Pudjianto, D., Ramsay, C., Strbac, G.: Virtual power plant and system integration of distributed energy resources. Renew. Power Gener. IET 1(1), 10–16 (2007)
10. Ramchurn, S.D., Vytelingum, P., Rogers, A., Jennings, N.: Agent-based control for decentralised demand side management in the smart grid. In: The 10th International Conference on Autonomous Agents and Multiagent Systems-Volume 1, pp. 5–12. International Foundation for Autonomous Agents and Multiagent Systems (2011)
11. Ruiz, N., Cobelo, I., Oyarzabal, J.: A direct load control model for virtual power plant management. IEEE Trans. Power Syst. 24(2), 959–966 (2009)
12. Rytter, M., Sørensen, J., Jørgensen, B., Körner, O.: Advanced model-based greenhouse climate control using multi-objective optimization. IV Int. Symp. Models Plant Growth Environ. Control Farm Manag. Prot. Cultivation 957, 29–35 (2012)
13. Zhang, M., Ye, D., Bai, Q., Sutanto, D., Muttaqi, K.: A hybrid multi-agent framework for load management in power grid systems. In: Bai, Q., Fukuta, N. (eds.) Advances in Practical Multi-agent Systems. SCI, vol. 325, pp. 129–143. Springer, Heidelberg (2010)
14. Zitzler, E., Thiele, L.: Multiobjective evolutionary algorithms: a comparative case study and the strength Pareto approach. IEEE Trans. Evol. Comput. 3(4), 257–271 (1999)

A Multi Agent System for Understanding the Impact of Technology Transfer Offices in Green-IT

Christina Herzog[1,2], Jean-Marc Pierson[1]([⊠]), and Laurent Lefèvre[3]

[1] IRIT, University Paul Sabatier Toulouse 3, Toulouse, France
{herzog,pierson}@irit.fr
[2] EfficIT, Toulouse, France
[3] INRIA-Lyon, ENS-Lyon, Lyon, France
laurent.lefevre@ens-lyon.fr

Abstract. We present a multi agent system simulating the complex interplay between the actors of innovation involved in the development of technology transfer for Green IT. We focus on the role and the influence of technology transfer offices on the individual objectives of each other actor (researchers, research facilities, companies). We analyse also their impact on several parameters, including sustainability.

1 Introduction

Technology Transfer Offices (TTO) have been promoted in many research centers and universities as a mean for accelerating the adoption of research in the industry. While it seems obvious that these dedicated offices might have a positive role on the effective transfer, we did not see any computerized model of their impact. It would be too ambitious to analyse it through the wide spectrum of science, hence we focus on Green IT, the part of Information Technologies interested in environmental aspects, besides social and economical ones.

In the last decade, research on energy savings in IT has become important for both industry and academics. Several studies conducted by international organisations warn about the steady increase of energy consumption in various fields such as Datacentres, Cloud Computing [12], raising concerns on economic, social and ecological aspects. In laboratories techniques have been developed and show promising results in terms of energy consumption reduction. Unfortunately, the transfer (or even the knowledge) of these techniques to industries is limited. To understand the (positive or negative) impact of the presence of TTO on Green IT development, we analyse it through a simulation conducted with a multi agent system (MAS). The MAS helps to define the different actors involved in the technology transfer (including researchers, companies, funding agencies), and to observe the evolution of their objectives when parameters of the simulation evolves (external funding, company policies, ...). Previously we proposed [13] the concept of a generic multi agent system for technology transfer, where we observed the evolution of the actors objectives. In this work we design the implementation of this MAS and its extension to integrate TTO.

© Springer International Publishing Switzerland 2016
M. Baldoni et al. (Eds.): PRIMA 2016, LNAI 9862, pp. 323–332, 2016.
DOI: 10.1007/978-3-319-44832-9_20

The main contributions of this research work are:

- An agent based model of technology transfer between researchers, companies, TTO and its implementation;
- An analysis of the TTO's presence and its impact on individual objectives of actors and on the overall objective of sustainability.

The article is organized in the following way: We present in Sect. 2 the multi agent system including the description of the selected actors and their links, the sustainability concept in Sect. 3 and the implementation of the model with NetLogo in Sect. 4. We present simulation results in Sect. 5 before state of the art in Sect. 6, and we conclude in Sect. 7.

2   Multi Agent System for Technology Transfer

In [13] we have conceptualized a MAS for modeling the relationships between innovation actors in terms of technology transfer. The MAS has been built from a literature review and a detailed analysis of 80 responses to a survey sent to colleagues in the field of Green IT field. Their motivations and their links in the context of a transfer from research facilities to industry (and vice versa) were analyzed. The main players in the technology transfer, their general goals and their means of action were extracted and detailed.

In this paper, we detail the implementation of the MAS, focusing on researchers, research facilities, companies and TTO, together with their links. The full system adds funding agencies, standardization bodies, lobbying groups, governments and business angels in [1]. This simplified presentation highlights the keys for the transfer and is not exhaustive. Note finally that only the activities of the actors in direction of Green IT have been taken into account (leaving aside individual non related goals).

2.1   Researchers, Research Facilities and Companies

First concerned by technology transfer, they produce knowledge through publications that they seek to increase, and by building up projects with companies through their research institute. In the scope of this work, their primary goal is the number of publications where publications are related to their connections they create at conferences and/or collaborative projects, and the financial budget of their research centre. More links leads to more opportunities for publications. Researchers may be permanent or non-permanent. Non-permanent researchers (PhD candidate, PostDoc, ...) are supervised by permanent (and their number is limited by the number of permanent researchers) and have a limited contract duration.

The researchers are grouped in research facilities. Research facilities contribute to the technology transfer by giving incentives to researchers for publications. However they have their own objective (their reputation) that pushes them to build external contracts: collaborative projects (in a consortium) or direct cooperations with companies. The research facility's reputation is computed as the moving average (within a sliding window of 3 years) of its researchers' publications together with its contracts. Research facilities hire non permanent researchers within contracts.

Companies look to increase their profits by taking a competitive difference. Their goal is to increase their share in the market and therefore to increase their turnover. Participation in collaborative projects increase leadership when the project is successful, but requires initial investment that might be lost. They hire new employees to participate in projects. They dedicate a portion of their sales to research and development.

2.2   Technology Transfer Offices

Technology Transfer Offices (for instance SATT-Technology Transfer Anonymous Society- in France, PSB in Austria) are structures associated with research facilities, intended to facilitate and accelerate technology transfer. Their goal is to increase their turnover (and therefore that of their public shareholders) taking part in the implementation of contracts. In return they provide a permanent support and address book helping research facilities and businesses to contract better. While a contract between a research facility and a company lasts for a limited duration, the existing link through a TTO lasts beyond the duration of the contract. Also, the chances of finding a market for a research is higher when a TTO exists, increasing the chances of contracts for the associated research facility. In this work we will investigate in particular the impact of their presence on the goals of each of the other actors, but also on a general goal for improving society's sustainability.

3   The Concept of Sustainability

A presented in [14], sustainability is a concept defined by the conjunction of three factors: environmental, social and economic. In a simplified way, an actor of a system improves its sustainability if at least one of these increases when the others do not decrease. As an example, in the field of Green IT, a more recent material often uses less electricity for the same computing power, but at the same time its production, transport, the recycling of the older equipment, all have a negative impact on the environment [15]. The SPI (Sustainability Performance Indicator) for each actor has 3 factors, weighted at 33 % each: ecological, societal, economical. Each factor is itself dependent on several elements weighted differently. Full details of our proposal for the calculation can be retrieved in [1].

The ecological factor is reflected by (i) the awareness of green IT solutions by the actor and (ii) by its efforts in terms of Reduce, Reuse and Recycle, typically during collaborative projects.

The social factor shows the actor's role in society: (i) green employment represents the employees recruited to work on (green IT) contracts. Employment is an important aspect for social evolution in a society. (ii) the society's knowledge on IT consumption. Reports like [12] help develop this, and is based on studying the publications from researchers and press releases from companies. (iii) Rethink is the ability of an actor to rethink its green IT in terms of strategy. For instance, a company with more contacts can rethink its strategy better, while a researcher has more freedom of thoughts when not involved in contracts. (iv) the actor's image in society is dependent on its communication strategy, mainly based on contracts and publications. (v) the influence of an actor on the standardization organizations. Big companies have more influence in organizations like ISO or IEC than individuals.

Finally, the economic factor is valued by: (i) the economic impact of green solutions. It tracks the successful contracts, meaning ones that generated benefits. (ii) the turnover representing the richness of each actor. (iii) the attractiveness of an actor for investors is an important factor for the economic dimension since it allows companies, TTO and research facilities to grow their turnover, indirectly increasing their R&D efforts.

All these values evolve with actors' actions and time. For instance, the awareness of Green IT solutions increases with the number of publications and contracts and decreases as time passes.

4   Implementation of the Multi Agent System

4.1   Netlogo as a Multi Agent System Framework

We implemented a multi agent system with NetLogo 5.3.1 [2]. NetLogo simulates the evolution and interaction of agents in complex systems. NetLogo was created in 1999 by U. Wilenski, and is regularly updated (last version in 2015) [3]. It is used in many scientific fields: social science, economics, commercial distribution, biology, modeling complex behaviorrs in a population, etc. In NetLogo we used the agents turtles, links and observers. The turtles represent the actors in our world, the links are their connections. Observers collect the information used for statistics. Each agent operates independently in discrete time-steps.

4.2   Representation of the Actors and Their Evolution

Each agent has its own attributes, those values change with interaction and time. A researcher may be permanent or not. If they are not permanent, they are associated with a contract those duration is given (ttl for time-to-live). It may be extended in case of successful collaborations. Researchers are members of a research facility. This is represented by a link between them (see Sect. 4.3).

As explained earlier, the primary goal for a researcher (as seen in this work) is to publish and therefore should have an attribute reflecting this. However, this attribute is shared with other actors, like all the attributes given here: each actor is active in the system at different regular intervals (action_period). Contracts and publications are stored, as well as the interests of one actor for 3 technologies (cloud, virtualization and cooling) having potential for energy reduction.

These interests are used to compute a compatibility between actors when trying to collaborate (euclidian distance is used).

Research facilities have a turnover (richness), an amount dedicated to green research, a reputation (sliding value over 3 years), and its active research contracts at any point in time (used for linking the contracts with the non permanent researchers). If a TTO is attached to this research facility, a link is set up (see Sect. 4.3).

The TTO have a turnover, the number of transactions they were involved in and the percentage they take on every contract. Finally, the companies have a turnover and a R&D budget, and a number of employees in R&D. Funding agencies were modeled simply by regularly launching funds to initiate projects.

Once the actors defined, their evolution is controlled by algorithms called every time step. In our model, a time step (ticks in NetLogo) is equal to one day. The algorithm for a researcher is given in Algorithm 1.

Algorithm 1. Evolution of a researcher agent

1: **if** not permanent **then** $ttl = ttl - 1$
2: **if** $ttl \leq 0$ **then** die
3: e = research facility employing the researcher
4: newpublication $= 0$
5: **for all** regular-neighbor **do**
6:     $money = funding\_research$ of e
7:     **if** random-float $1.0 < (0.20 * 1/90)$ and $money > 1000$ **then**
8:         $newpublication = newpublication + 1$
9:         ask e [$funding\_research = funding\_research - 1000$]
10: publication $=$ publication $+$ newpublication
11: ask my-regular-links [**if** random-float $1 \leq 1/180$ **then** die]
12: **if** count regular-neighbors $<$ max_link_per_researcher **then**
13:     $bonus = P(e)$
14:     **if** random-float $1 \leq (1 / 90) + bonus$ **then**
15:         r = random 100
16:         **if** $r < 50$ **then** p $=$ partner-choice
17:         **else if** $r < 75$ **then** p $=$ tto-choice
18:         **else** p $=$ one-of find-neighbors-of-neighbors
19:         make-link p"regular"

Each day, if it is not a permanent, its ttl is reduced (line 1). If it becomes zero, this researcher is removed from the system (line 2). Then, for each of its regular neighbors (loop in lines 5 to 9, definition of regular neighbors in Sect. 4.3), and if the research facility employing this researcher has sufficient funds dedicated to research (1000 in this case), then there is a probability of publishing with a neighbor (on average every 3 months with a probability of 20 % -acceptance rate-). In this case, the research centre funds (1000) the publication (line 9). The number of publications by the researcher is updated (line 10). Contacts with neighbors can disappear (line 11, on average every 6 months), but also appear (lines 12 to 20). When a maximum of neighbors is not reached (line 12, this value is set to 10 in our experiments), a new contact might be established (a minimum of 3 months, line 14). As a function of the employer's performance, a bonus for creating new links is given (line 13): If a research facility has some contracts and/or is rich (high turnover), the bonus is increased and the new contacts are built more often. When a contact is built up, the question is with who should this researcher be linked: A survey we conducted within the Green IT community [1] has shown that new contacts are established 50 % randomly with other researchers and businesses, favoring the compatibility of interests (line 16, function partner-choice). 25 % come from the social network (line 18, function find-neighbors-of-neighbors). TTO helps to establish new contacts in 25 % of the cases (especially with companies, line 17, function tto-choice).

The algorithm for a research facility is the following (details omitted by lack of space): First it updates its interests (average of those of its researchers) and its reputation. If the budget is critical, the research facility finishes the contract of some non-permanent researchers, and then it pays the remaining ones. Then, it will act depending on its action period. If the budget is comfortable, it will hire a non-permanent (for one year, to a maximum of 4 times more non-permanents than permanents) and it will dedicate an incentive as a percentage of its turnover to research. Finally, it tries to launch a collaborative project. These are projects that will create technology transfer, based on their success.

The algorithm for the project creation is too long to be detailed here: a research facility seeks to form a consortium (between 3 and 6 partners) according to its own links, links of its researchers and those of its TTO, if existing. The other research facilities and companies can be partners if all their permanent researchers are not already in projects. If the project is accepted (20 % chances), research facilities and companies receive a share of the funding (a 50 % fraction of what is taken as overhead costs), they hire non-permanents during the project (maximum 36 months, depending on the share received), and companies invest what they receive. For all research facilities where TTO are present, these TTO take a percentage of the share (20 % in the experiments). Finally, links (project, see Sect. 4.3) are created between all partners.

For a company, the algorithm is quite similar to that of a research facility except that it tries to create a direct partnership with only one research facility (links partnership). The algorithm of TTO's evolution is simple. If it is time to act, it transfers a back-percentage amount to its research facility (a percentage of its turnover).

4.3   Representation of Links and Their Evolution

We have defined 5 kind of links: (i) regular: contacts between researchers (from research facilities and companies); (ii) project: relationship between a research facility and a project consortium; (iii) partnership: contract between a company and a research facility; (iv) belongto: link between a research facility and its researchers; (v) ttolink: link between a research facility and its TTO.

The project and partnership links refers the collaboration's characteristics. Each link has its own attributes. For such link, the attributes are: original investment for companies, strength of collaboration linked to the compatibility between the partners of the link, number of contracts and turnover generated by the link, lifetime of the link, number of researchers in the research facility and company sides involved in this link, and finally the contract number.

Like all agents, links evolve at every time steps. For non-permanent links, the lifetime is reduced by one at each time step. When the lifetime is zero, if it is a project, it is finished and the permanent researchers of each partner of the consortium are available for new contracts. As a function of conversion rate (conversion is success-or failure of a project), it gains a profit up to 4 times the initial cumulative investment. This represents the success of a project and reflects the patents that may arise from the project. If it is a partnership, the principle is the same as for project except that only one company and one research facility are involved. Moreover the partnership will be extended for one year if it was generating a benefit (favoring the efficient partnerships, also controlled by conversion rate). Other links disappear.

5   Experiments

5.1   Methodology and Objectives of Experiments

The proposed multi agent system is complex (about 2000 lines of code), and has a large number of parameters. We varied its main parameters in extensive experiments. We give here the results of a representative subset showing the impact of the TTO presence, the others can be found in [1]: number of TTO, number of companies, back_percentage rates (the percentage a TTO returns to its research facility). When not specified otherwise, back_percentage rates is set to 30 % in the experiments. The action_period for research facilities is set randomly (uniform) between 3 and 9 months, while for companies it is between 1 and 2 years, and for TTO it is between 1 and 3 months.

We compare the results on the objectives of each actor and on the SPI value. In the selected experiments we selected the following indicators:

- publications: the sum of the publications of the permanent researchers
- reputation: the mean reputation of the research facilities
- SPI: the mean value of the SPI value of research facilities and companies

The studied system simulates 10 research centres, 50 permanent researchers. We vary the number of TTO (from 0 to 10, i.e. with 10 all research centers have a TTO) and companies (from 10 to 50). Larger experiments were conducted but did not give more lessons while significantly increasing the simulation time. Each experiment simulates 3640 days (10 years). We present boxplot values for 50 experiments with the same parameters.

5.2 Results

Fig. 1(a) shows the impact of the number of TTO (x-axis, from 0 to 10) on the publications of the researchers. In this graph we see that the number of publications increases with the number of TTO. This exhibits the positive influence of TTO on the work of individual researchers. It increases also with the number of companies, whatever the number of TTO. This is expected since more companies means more potential contacts for researchers, leading to more publications. In Fig. 1(b), we studied the direct influence of TTO on the research facilities they are attached to: on the left the reputation of research facilities without TTO, on the right with TTO. One can observe that, the reputation for research facilities with TTO is higher than the one for research facilities without TTO, whatever the number of TTO and companies.

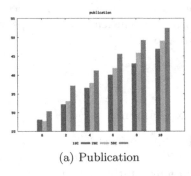
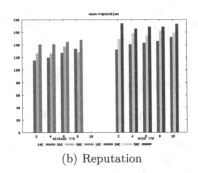

(a) Publication   (b) Reputation

Fig. 1. (a) Mean publications of permanent researchers, as a function of number of TTO (0 to 10) and companies (10, 20 and 50 companies). (b) Mean reputation of research facilities, as a function of TTO and companies numbers. (left: research facilities without TTO, right: research facilities with TTO)

Figure 2(a) shows SPI value. Here also the values are quite insensitive to the TTO number. This indicates that the influence of TTO on companies and sustainability is not important in our simulation. Finally in Fig. 2(b) we show the mean reputation of research facilities as a function of the back_percentage experiment with 4 TTO and 20 Companies. We observe again the positive influence of TTO on research facilities, but the influence of back_percentage is negligible, indicating that the presence of the TTO is more important that the percentage it returns (see also in parallel Fig. 1(b)).

6   Related Work

Few studies have focused on modeling technology transfer and links between the actors. A review article [5] is interested in multi agent systems for the diffusion of innovation. Although the setting is a different (towards marketing and customer

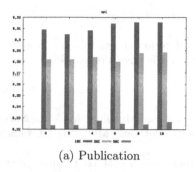

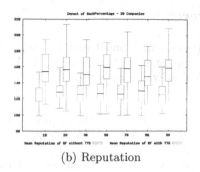

(a) Publication   (b) Reputation

Fig. 2. (a) SPI value, as a function of TTO and companies numbers. (b) Mean reputation of research facilities, without (red) and with (blue) TTO, as a function of back_percentage. (Color figure online)

targeting), it sheds much light. Social network's dominance in the adoption of innovation is highlighted [6]. The spread in social networks has received much attention in recent years [7–10]. Actors dissemination (individuals, groups, organizations), a broadcast medium (diffusion environment, strong and weak links between actors, the network structure), and the content to be broadcast are the three elements of the diffusion. This distribution is described as the collective behavior of a group of social actors interacting on social networks [11]. Technology transfer is a kind of diffusion in a social network, which has inspired our model of linkages between actors. In the case of a competition for a market, two types of diffusion models are identified [16,17]: the threshold models where agents adopt if enough neighbors have, and cascade models where the probability of adoption increases with the number of neighbors who have adopted. In our case, the cascade model was implemented. The closest work to ours is that of Ning and Quing [4] which presents a multi agent model for technology transfer. Their model has two kinds of agents (universities and industry), and 4 states, 'doing nothing' to 'active part in a collaboration'. The transfer is modeled between 0 and 100 for each agent. Their results show that the key to a good transfer cost is to seek information (distance between agents) and the probability of finding a partner. The study is limited, omitting financing and turnover to influence direction.

7   Conclusion

In this paper we analyzed the positive or negative influence of the TTO on the individual objectives of other actors in the technology transfer. We shown that they have a positive role in helping to create contacts between the actors. The ultimate goal of this work is to give a tool to understand the springs of technology transfer in Green IT. Note in passing that the methodology and models developed can be extended to other areas. The next step will be to modify the model so that the actors' behaviors is influenced by their SPI value.

References

1. Herzog, C.: Contribution to the modeling of technological transfer in green IT using multi-agent-systems. Ph.D. University of Toulouse, France, November 2015
2. Wilensky, U.: NetLogo itself (1999). http://ccl.northwestern.edu/netlogo/. NetLogo - Center for Connected Learning and Computer-Based Modeling, Northwestern University, Evanston, IL
3. Wilensky, U., Rand, W.: Introduction to Agent-Based Modeling. Modeling Natural, Social, and Engineered Complex System with NetLogo. MIT Press, Cambridge (2015)
4. Ning, M., Qiang, L.: Influence of information search cost on technology transfer based on multi-agent system. In: 16th International Conference on Industrial Engineering and Engineering Management, IE&EM, pp. 443–447 (2009)
5. Kiesling, E., Günther, M., Stummer, C., Wakolbinger, L.M.: Agent-based simulation of innovation diffusion: a review. Cent. Eur. J. Oper. Res. 20(2), 183–230 (2012). doi:10.1007/s10100-011-0210-y
6. Kuandykov, L., Sokolov, M.: Impact of social neighbourhood on diffusion of innovation S-curve. Decis. Support Syst. 48, 531–535 (2010)
7. Jiangs, Y., Jiang, J.C.: Diffusion in social networks: a multiagent perspective. IEEE Trans. Syst. Man Cybern. 45(2), 198–213 (2015)
8. Xu, S., Lu, W., Xu, L.: Push-and pull-based epidemic spreading in networks: thresholds and deeper insights. ACM Trans. Autonom. Adapt. Syst. 7(3), 32 (2012)
9. Valente, T.: Social network thresholds in the diffusion of innovations. Soc. Netw. 18(1), 69–89 (1996)
10. Jiang, Y.: Concurrent collectives strategy diffusion of multiagents: the spatial model and case study. IEEE Trans. Syst. Man Cybern. C Appl. Rev. 39(4), 448–458 (2009)
11. Jiang, Y., Jiang, J.: Understanding social networks from a multiagent perspective. IEEE Trans. Parallel Distrib. Syst. 25(10), 2743–2759 (2014)
12. Cook, G., Dowdall, T., Pomerantz, D., Wang, Y.: Clicking clean: how companies are creating the green internet. Technical report, Greenpeace, April 2014
13. Herzog, C., Pierson, J.M., Lefèvre, L.: Modelling technology transfer in green IT with multi agent system. In: International Conference on Leadership, Innovation and Entrepreneurship, Dubai. Springer, Heidelberg, April 2016
14. Costanza, Robert, Patten, Bernard C.: Defining and predicting sustainability. Ecol. Econ. 15(3), 193–196 (1995)
15. Hilty, L.: Information technology and sustainability. In: Essays on the Relationship between ICT and Sustainable Development, pp. 35–43 (2008). ISBN: 9783837019704
16. Libai, B., Muller, E., Peres, R.: Decomposing the value of word-of-mouth seeding programs: acceleration versus expansion. J. Market. Res. 50(2), 161–176 (2013)
17. Kempe, D., Kleinberg, J., Tardos, E.: Maximizing the spread of influence through a social network. In: Proceedings of the Ninth ACM SIGKDD International Conference on Knowledge Discovery and Data Mining, KDD 2003, NY, USA, pp. 137–146 (2003)

Modeling Organizational and Institutional Aspects in Renewable and Natural Resources Management Context

Islem Hènane[1(✉)], Sameh Hadouaj[2], Khaled Ghedira[3], and Ali Ferchichi[4]

[1] National School of Computer Sciences, Manouba University, Manouba, Tunisia
islemhenane@yahoo.fr
[2] Faculty of Economics and Management, Carthage University, Nabeul, Tunisia
hadouaj@yahoo.fr
[3] Higher Institute of Management, Tunis University, Tunis, Tunisia
khaled.ghedira@isg.rnu.tn
[4] National Agronomic Institute, Carthage University, Carthage, Tunisia
ferchichi.ali@ira.rnrt.tn
[5] Higher Colleges of Technology, Abu Dhabi, United Arab Emirates

Abstract. Since 1990, there has been a striking increase in using multi-agent systems to study renewable resources management systems. The ultimate objective is to contribute to decisions support on resources management. The adopted strategic decisions are always joined with access to resources norms. However, the defined norms are statics and suppose that all agents are not autonomous and always obey to the underlying norms which do not reflect reality. In previous work, we proposed ML-MA [1], a multi-level multi-agent architecture to support renewable resources management systems modeling. In this work, we focus on the integration of normative aspects in our architecture. Our approach is illustrated using "Ouled Chehida" case study from Tunisian pastoral context.

Keywords: Multi-agent modeling · Complex system · Multi-level architecture · Organizational modeling · Norms · Environment · Normative agent · Simulation · Renewable resources management · Tunisian pastoral system modeling

1 Introduction

Multi-agent systems are widely used to study renewable resources management problematic [2]. Such formalism has proven its effectiveness to deal with properties of cognition, decision making and micro and macro dynamics explanation. However, we pointed out two main weaknesses of most developed models: (1) the "complexity" of such systems still not well explicitly handled as developed models are often based on hypothesis or limited on some parts of the problem and (2) the lack of institutional aspects. In fact, models do not usually consider norms of access to resources or suppose that all agents obey to the established norms. To deal with the first issue, we proposed in previous work ML-MA, a multi-level multi-agent architecture for renewable and natural resources management systems modeling [1]. ML-MA guarantees results accuracy, ensures modeling simplicity and supports collaborations between experts from

© Springer International Publishing Switzerland 2016
M. Baldoni et al. (Eds.): PRIMA 2016, LNAI 9862, pp. 333–343, 2016.
DOI: 10.1007/978-3-319-44832-9_21

different domains. The challenge at this stage is to enrich ML-MA with organizational and institutional aspects. We illustrate our approach with "Ouled Chehida" case study from the Tunisian pastoral context. The rest of this paper is organized as follows. Section 2 presents a state of the art of institutional and organizational aspects modeling in renewable resources management context. Section 3 deals with institutional and organizational aspects integration in ML-MA architecture. Section 4 illustrates our contributions with "Ouled Chehida" case study. Finally, we state our concluding remarks and give some avenues for future works.

2   Norms in Multi-agent Models for Renewable Resources Management

In recent years, the concepts "organization", "institution" and "norms" have become a key issue in multi-agent systems community. "Organization" refers to agents groups and communities structures. Organizational concepts encompass "roles", "groups", "tasks", etc. [3]. The concept "Institution" regroups norms governing agents' behavior. Norms are obligations, prohibitions and permissions that regulate the community agents' behavior [4]. In renewable resources management context, institutional aspects have been mostly absent. In fact, some models aim explanatory objectives, they focus on resources dynamic in response to stakeholders' interactions [2]. Others (mainly participative approach) [5] are always used as basis of negotiation and concerts to define future strategies and/or norms of access to resources. However, it is always assumed that all agents will obey to norms, which is not the case in reality. In fact, stakeholders have different goals (social, economic) and constraints urging them to behave differently. Introducing institutional aspects in this context is needful to reflect the real world interactions thereby resources dynamic. The question that rises at this stage is "What organizational model to adopt and how to integrate norms?"

In [6], Ferber identifies three classes of multi-agent systems: (1) purely communicative, (2) purely situated and (3) communicative and situated. Most organizational meta-models and institutional architectures are developed to deal with the first class of multi-agent systems according to Ferber classification (ISLANDER [7], AGR [3], OMNI [8]). However, in renewable resources management context, the physical environment plays a crucial role. It supports agents' displacements and encapsulates resources. Agents may also interact with the environment and with each other's. Such systems belong to the third class as defined by Ferber. To take into account social environment as well as physical one, Ferber et al. propose the organizational meta-model AGRE [9] which is an extension of AGR [3] supporting the physical environment. It is based on three main concepts: (1) *"Agent"*, (2) *"Space"* and (3) *"Mode"* However, AGRE lacks explicit specifications of institutional aspects (powers, obligations, permissions). To this end, AGREEN model has been developed [10]. It takes into account social and physical environment and describes explicitly institutional aspects. In renewable and natural resources management context, different granularity levels are involved. Resources are almost physically distributed or closely linked to the physical space such as land use. With reference to AGREEN meta-model, controlling access to resources is performed by agents. In that case, increasing the control degree requires a great number of 'Controller agents' and several interactions which affects time and memory use. Moreover, norms are static. The developed architecture does not support norms change over time. Mechanisms of norms establishment and modification are not explicitly presented. At this stage, the challenge is (1) to adapt ML-MA architecture previously developed for support norms establishment, execution and control and (2) to adapt AGREEN model to take into account these institutional deficiencies as well the multi-level modeling as evoked in ML-MA.

3 ML-MA: Organizational and Institutional Aspects Integration

3.1 System Architecture

ML-MA includes two modules: Risk management and Operative module (Fig. 1).

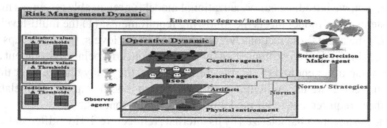

Fig. 1. Global system architecture

Risk Management Module. It controls the system evolution using a battery of indicators, defines strategies and establishes norms. It includes two types of agents: (1) Strategic Decision Maker agent and (2) Observer agents. Observer agents calculate indicators values, compare them with thresholds and relate the emergency degree to the Strategic Decision Maker agent. The latter makes decisions by adopting strategic actions (e.g. reforestation) and/or defining norms (e.g. preventing pasture). It defines for each norm established: (1) its application constraints, (2) temporal scope (beginning, duration), (3) spatial scope, (4) the concerned type of agents and (5) its application tools (positive sanctions e.g. subsidy, negative sanction e.g. pay consumption).

Operative Dynamic. It concerns intra-layer and inter-layers interactions and supports norms control and execution. Layers identification is exposed in details in [11].

Intra and Inter-layers Interactions. Each layer i is a multi-agent system characterized by the triplet $<A_i, I_i, E_i>$ (agents, interactions and environment of i layer). It evolves according to its spatial and temporal scales. However, agents may interact with other layers. Interactions concern mainly exploitation. As layers evolve in different temporal and spatial scales, coherence should be guaranteed in terms of time, space and scope (see [11] for more details). For this purpose, we define for each agent type a set of *views* defining temporal and spatial scales in which agents may evolve. When a resource layer receives an activation from an agent, it creates its spatial-temporal decomposition or aggregation according to the agent current view forming the *interaction-view*. Using *interaction-views* allow different levels of analysis and system comprehension. If the lowest levels are validated and the macro-level dynamic is deduced from micro simulations, it is possible to use *interaction-views* with macro temporal and spatial scales.

Norms Control and Execution. We consider that access to resources norms are controlled by the physical environment encapsulating resources. This fact allows control distribution and makes benefits in terms of agents involved in the simulation, interactions and memory allocation mainly when the control scope and/or intensity are important. Agents are endowed with a normative architecture supporting autonomous behavior with regards to the objectives and the environment perception.

3.2 Organizational Model for Renewable Resources Management Systems

In this section, we introduce our organizational model for renewable resources management systems. This model meets the following requirements: (1) the multi-level architecture, (2) the agents' interactions with higher and lower levels, (3) the encapsulation of resources in physical environment, (4) norms may concern social environment as well as physical environment and (5) norms are not statics, they may change over time. As outlined in Sect. 2, we use AGREEN model and enrich it with concepts and relations to support these requirements. Our model is based on four concepts:

Agent. An agent is characterized by its internal architecture, its identifier and its type. The agent type Ta is a tuple <Ita, Aa*, V*> where Ita is the agent type identifier, Aa* is the set of attributes and V* is the set of views. A view V is a tuple <Iva, S, T, Sc*> where Iva is the view identifier, S is the spatial scale, T is the temporal scale and Sc* is the set of operations taking into account the spatial and temporal scale. This concept complies with the second requirement through the *"view"* component.

Space. As defined in AGREEN, the space is the environment of agents' interactions. We define "Social Space" to take into account social interactions (e.g. Community) and "Physical Space" to take into account spatial interactions and resources exploitation (e.g. course). The concept "Space" complies with the first requirement. The concept "Social Space" is a tuple <Iss, Tss, I*> where Iss is the social space identifier, Tss is the social space type, and I* is the set of interactions means (for example communication protocols). The social space type is a tuple <Isst, IT*> where Isst is the social space type identifier and IT* is the set of interactions types. The concept "Physical Space" is a tuple <Ips, Ipsp, Tps, O*, R*> where Ips is the physical space unique identifier, Ipsp is the unique identifier of its parent, Tps is the physical space type, O* is the set of objects and R* is the set of resources. The physical space type is a tuple <Ipst, Ipstp, OT*, RT*> where Ipst is the physical space type identifier, Ipstp is its parent identifier, OT* is the set of objects type, RT* is the set of resources type.

The concept "Resource" is a tuple <Ir, Tr, Ar*> where Ir is the resource identifier, Tr is its type and Ar* is the set of attributes. The resource type concept is a tuple <Irt, Vr*> where Irt is the resource type identifier and Vr* is the set of resource views. The resource view Vr is a tuple <Ivr, Sr, Tr, Scr*> where Ivr is the resource view identifier, Sr is the resource spatial scale, Tr is the resource temporal scale and Scr* is the set of operations taking into account the spatial and temporal scales. The concept "Resource" ensures the third requirement. The concept "Object" is a tuple ‹Io, To, Ao*› where Io is the object identifier, To is the object type, Ao* is the set of attributes characterizing an object. Objects can be tools or infrastructure.

Interaction-View. This concept (e.g. plot of land) ensures agents interactions with their environment. The interaction-view concept is a tuple <Ii, Ia, Ips, Iva> where Ii is the interaction-view identifier, Ia is the agent identifier, Ips is the physical space identifier and Iva is the agent view identifier. This concept ensures the second requirement.

Norms. This concept (e.g. exclosure) is a tuple <In, Ia, Is, nT> where In is the norm identifier, Ia is the agent identifier, Is is the space identifier and Tn is the norm type. The norm type Tn is a tuple <Tni, Ta*, Ts*, C*, A*, Ts> where Tni is the norm type identifier, Ta* is the set of agent types concerned, Ts* is the set of space types concerned, C* is the set of conditions of the norm appliance, A* is the set of the norm application tools (award, sanction) and Ts is the time scope of the norm. This concept complies with the fourth and fifth requirements.

Figure 2 gives a simplified description of our organizational model involving the concepts just mentioned. In the next section, we illustrate our approach with "Ouled Chehida" case study from Tunisian pastoral context.

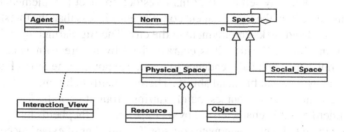

Fig. 2. Simplified UML representation of the organizational model

4   Application: Modeling Normative Aspects in Pastoral Resources Management Context: "Ouled Chehida" Case Study

Our study is carried out on "Ouled Chehida" pastoral region located in the south east of "Tataouine" city in south of Tunisia. This region faces several challenges (desertification, poverty, livestock reduction). Such system involves tightly interrelated variables (ecologic, economic, and social), several interactions between different stakeholders and different granularity levels. Using ML-MA approach, we have identified three main layers (see [11] for more details): (1) Ecological dynamic, (2) Livestock dynamic and (3) Local population. The ecological dynamic has been modeled and validated [11]. We have also integrated the livestock dynamic using the model proposed in [12].

In the following, we focus on modeling and simulation of the "Local population" level. We study the impact of institutional aspects on some system indicators.

4.1 Multi-agent Modeling and Simulation of the "Local Population" Layer

Risk Management Dynamic. We identify two indicators to reflect the situation of the local population: (1) Household income (in the following we use "complementation need" to validate our model) and (2) Confrontation. We define an Observer agent which calculates the values of these indicators and relates degree of emergency to the Strategic Decision Maker agent. The latter makes decisions which may be strategic action and/or norms of access to resources. It may change dynamically the adopted norms according to a set of objectives and the data collected by Observer agents.

Operative Dynamic. *Intra and inter-layers interactions.* Our model includes: (1) Farmer agent, (2) Big Farmer agent, (3) Small Farmer agent and (4) Shepherd agent. The Farmer agent is the herd owner. It is characterized by its attachment to the residence point and its complacency. The latter attribute depends on financial situation as:

$$C(t) = (T(t) - S(t))/ T(t) \tag{1}$$

- $C(t)$, $T(t)$: the Farmer agent complacency at the time step t, Turnover at time step t
- $S(t)$: the Farmer agent spending, mainly composed of complementation needs

The Farmer agent may sell a part of his livestock to meet complementation needs (decapitalization). When the Farmer agent complacency is less than the threshold to quit C_q, it sells his herd and seeks employment in the city. The Big Farmer agent inherits the Farmer agent attributes. Besides, it is characterized by its great financial ability, an important complacency and independence to residence points. The Small Farmer agent is characterized by its weak financial ability. Thereby, herds belonging to Small Farmer agents pasture in non-distant courses mainly during drought period.

The Shepherd agent is characterized by its experience. Shepherds had good experience allowing them to identify adequate courses. The number of experienced shepherds is in continuous decline due to the settlement. The Shepherd agent displacement depends on climate conditions. In rainy year, the displacement depends on seasons. In spring, it can move to the farthest courses of residence and water points. The watering frequency is less than once per month. In summer, watering frequency is every two days; it cannot pasture his herd within a radius greater than 5 km from the water point. In autumn, it may conduct exploratory visits of courses. Winter is the time of farrowing. In dry years, the pasture is limited to courses near water points and complementation points of sale. The Shepherd agent selects the pasture course monthly. The latter creates its decomposition (if not yet decomposed) on plots of land (*interaction-view*) to consider herds displacement and exploitation.

Norms Control and Execution. Norms control is ensured by courses and plots of land encapsulating norms according to the control rate. The Shepherd agent perceives norms and decides to adopt them or not. We endow it with abilities to choose between desires and obligations. The BDI (Belief, Desire, Intention) architecture [13] has been widely used to deal with agents' internal decision process. Broersen et al. [14] proposed the BOID (Belief, Obligation, Intention, Desire) architecture as an extension of BDI taking into account obligations. Four types of agents are identified: (1) Realistic (believes overrule all other components), (2) Simple-minded (prior intentions overrule desires and obligations), (3) Selfish (Desires overrule obligations) and (4) Social (Obligations overrule desires). The authors proposed the ordering function ρ corresponding to the agent type. ρ defines the consideration order of the different components rules. Rules are affected a unique value of ρ. The one with the lowest value is executed first. In this work, we consider realistic agents which can be selfish or social. According to the authors reasoning, ρ verifies the following assertions: (1) Social: $\rho(b)<\rho(o)<\rho(d)$ (belief, o: obligation, d: desire) or (2) Selfish: $\rho(b)<\rho(d)<\rho(o)$. In this work, we consider that agents may progress from selfish to social behavior dynamically. That is the corresponding ordering function is not steady and may vary over time. In their study of the Tunisian pastoral system, Nefzaoui et al. [15] affirm that norms adoption depends on the confidence on norms application and the sensitization efficiency. Based on this study, we express the confidence on norm as follows:

$$\text{Nor\_conf} = ((\text{awa/sub}) + (\text{sanc/viol})) - ((\text{aw/sub}) * (\text{sanc/viol})) \tag{2}$$

- Nor_conf: confidence on norms (Nor_conf $\in [0,1]$)
- awa: the number of obtained awards if norms have been respected
- sub, viol: the number of submissions to the norm, the number of norm violations
- sanc: the number of undergone sanctions if norms have been violated

The sensitization efficiency is calculated as follows:

$$\text{Eff}_{t+1} = \begin{cases} \text{Eff}_0 & t = 0 \\ \text{Eff}_t * (1 + sra) & t > 0 \end{cases} (t \in IN) \tag{3}$$

- Eff_{t+1}: the sensitization efficiency at the moment $t + 1$ ($\text{Eff}_t \in [0, 1]$)
- Eff_t, sra: the sensitization efficiency at the moment t, the sensitization rate

The order of rules execution is defined using the following expressions:

$$\rho_{t+1}(o) = \min\left(T, \left(1 - \left((\text{Eff}_t + \text{Nor\_conf}_t) - (\text{Eff}_t * \text{Nor\_conf}_t)\right)\right)\right) \tag{4}$$

$$\rho_{t+1}(d) = \min\left(T, \left((\text{Eff}_t + \text{Nor\_conf}_t) - (\text{Eff}_t * \text{Nor\_conf}_t)\right)\right) \tag{5}$$

- ρ_{t+1} (o): obligations order at the moment $t + 1$ ($t \in IN$) ($\rho_{t+1}(o)\epsilon[0, 1]$)
- ρ_{t+1} (d): desires order at the moment $t + 1$ ($t \in IN$) ($\rho_{t+1}(d)\epsilon[0, 1]$)
- T: Threshold of switching between desires adoption and obligations

If the Shepherd agent adopts a selfish behavior, it tries to maximize its profits. Its behavior depends on the frequency of previous sanctions, the sanction value and the gain of norms violation.

4.2 Experiments

In this section, we study the impact of institutional parameters on some established indicators. We use GAMA platform [16] to implement our framework. GAMA is characterized by its ability to support a large number of agents and using complex GIS data. We feed our simulations with GIS layers (pedology, soil occupation, water points, residence points), climate data (wind, precipitation, temperature) economic data (complementation cost, meat cost). In the following, we concentrate mainly on parameters concerning the "Local Population layer". We exploit estimations gathered from studies carried out on the "Ouled Chehida" region: (1) Herds number: 110, (2) Mean size of herd: 270, (3) Percentage of big farmers: 3 %, (4) Percentage of experimented shepherds: 80 %.

Witness Scenario. Let's try to reproduce the real pastoral dynamic over the study period (1990–2000). At this stage, we do not consider normative aspects. Figure 3a shows that the vegetation cover has dropped in the beginning of the simulation and remained in decline due to resources unavailability and overexploitation. The complementation need is in continuous increase. According to Fig. 3b, the complementation need per head is about 39 kg (vs. 49 kg total need) which ties with reality. In fact, Bourbouze [17] confirms that pasture activity is no more able to cover more that 20 % of the livestock needs. Socially, Fig. 3c shows that confrontation is in continued increase. Confrontation rises when two or more herds are in the same course while biomass does not cover the total herds' needs. It depends on year type (drought, rainy), resources availability and seasons. That is why the histogram is fluctuating.

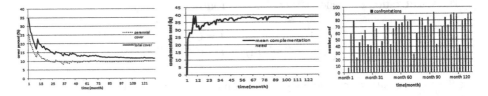

Fig. 3. Evolution of: (a) Vegetation cover, (b) Complementation need and (c) Confrontation

Scenario 2. Let's consider the following norms defined by the Strategic Decision Maker agent: (1) "After each season, plots of land which have been grazed are blocked in the next season; otherwise a penalty is assigned to the incorrect Shepherd agents.", and (2) "During pasture activity, Shepherd agents are forbidden to make their herds grazing in a plot of land where other Shepherd agents are presents if the available biomass does not cover the total herds needs or does not respect sustainability." Plots of land verifying constraints of norms application encapsulate the underlying norms. Plots of land controlling norms execution are randomly distributed according to the control rate. We carry out our simulation using the normative parameters: (1) Sensitization rate: 0, (2) Control rate (the percentage of controlled plots of land): 50 %, (3) Sanction: the herd total need.

Figure 4a shows that the obedience probability has increased during the simulation. However, complete obedience has not been reached. This is due to the fact that some Shepherd agents continue to violate norms without being penalized (control rate = 0.5). Compared to the witness scenario, we notice economic, social and ecologic betterments. In fact, there is a diminution of the mean of complementation needs (Fig. 4b), a concrete reduction of confrontation (Fig. 4c) and an increase of vegetation cover (Fig. 4d). We notice that full norms adoption has not been reached. This is possible, but after several iterations which is not realistic. In fact, we simulate human cognitive behavior and the emergence of full adoption is desired swiftly. We note also that this scenario fulfillment is delicate in realty. In fact, ensuring such value of control rate (0.5) requires the commitment of several staff and equipment.

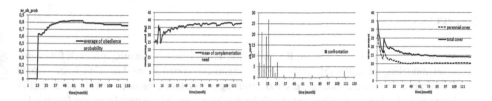

Fig. 4. (a) Norms adoption (b) complementation needs (c) Confrontation and (d) Cover change

Scenario 3. Let's proceed to normative parameters variation: (1) Sensitization rate: 0.15, (2) Control rate: 20 % and (3) Sanction: herd total need.

Shepherd agents are sensitized periodically. Once a Shepherd agent becomes social (adopt norms), it begins to sensitize its acquaintances. Figure 5a shows the obedience probability evolution. Compared to the second scenario, we conclude the importance of sensitization, especially among Shepherd agents, in maintaining maximum norms adoption. Results assert social (Fig. 5c) (reduction of confrontation intensity and frequency) and ecological (Fig. 5d) betterments (increase of vegetation cover).

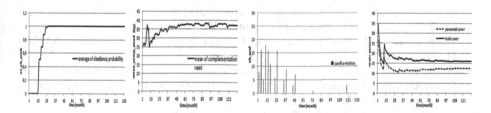

Fig. 5. (a) Norms adoption (b) Complementation needs (c) Confrontation (d) Cover change

However, we notice that the need of complementation has increased compared to the previous scenario (Fig. 5b). In fact, Shepherd agents are sometimes blocked especially in dry seasons and years. They have to wait for subsidy as reward for norms respects. These assertions lead us to study the adequacy of such strategies. So, the Strategic Decision Maker agent defines new strategies according to objectives priorities and preferences. We will focus on the strategic decision process in future works.

5   Conclusion and Perspectives

We enriched ML-MA architecture with organizational and institutional aspects. We opted for the adaptation of AGREEN meta-model (to take into account organizational aspects pursuant to ML-MA requirements) and BOID architecture (to model agents' internal decision process). We illustrated our approach with "Ouled Chehida" case study. Results showed that introducing normative aspects (sensitization, confidence) may prompt the objectives achievement. However, as noticed, some sub-objectives may be adversely affected or relatively achieved. Therefore, it is necessary to define the appropriate strategies. In future works, we intend to develop our decision support system to define adequate strategies in long and short terms.

References

1. Hènane, I., Hadouaj, S., Ghédira, K., Ferchichi, A.: Towards a generic approach for multi-level modeling of renewable resources management systems. In: The 13th International Conference on Autonomous Agents and Multi-agent Systems, Paris, pp. 1471–1472 (2014)
2. Epstein, J.M., Axtell, R.: Growing Artificial Societies: Social Science From the Bottom Up (Complex Adaptive Systems). The MIT Press, Cambridge (1996)
3. Ferber, J., Gutknecht, O., Michel, F.: From agents to organizations: an organizational view of multi-agent systems. In: Giorgini, P., Müller, J.P., Odell, J.J. (eds.) AOSE 2003. LNCS, vol. 2935, pp. 214–230. Springer, Heidelberg (2004)
4. Hollander, C., Wu, A.: The current state of normative agent-based systems. J. Artif. Soc. Soc. Simul. **14** (2011)
5. Guyot, P., Drogoul, A.: Multi-agent based participatory simulations on various scales. In: Ishida, T., Gasser, L., Nakashima, H. (eds.) MMAS 2005. LNCS (LNAI), vol. 3446, pp. 149–160. Springer, Heidelberg (2005)
6. Ferber, J.: Multi-agent Systems: An Introduction to Distributed Artificial Intelligence. Addison-Wesley, Great Britain (1999)
7. Esteva, M., Rodriguez-Aguilar, J.-A., Sierra, C., Garcia, P., Arcos, J.-L.: On the formal specification of electronic institutions. In: Sierra, C., Dignum, F.P. (eds.) AgentLink 2000. LNCS (LNAI), vol. 1991, pp. 126–147. Springer, Heidelberg (2001)
8. Vazquez-Salceda, J., Dignum, V., Dignum, F.: Organizing multiagent systems. J. AAMAS **11**, 307–360 (2005)
9. Ferber, J., Michel, F., Baez, J.: AGRE: integrating environments with organizations. In: Weyns, D., Van Dyke Parunak, H., Michel, F. (eds.) E4MAS 2004. LNCS (LNAI), vol. 3374, pp. 48–56. Springer, Heidelberg (2005)
10. Baez-Barranco, J.A., Stratulat, T., Ferber, J.: A unified model for physical and social environment. In: Weyns, D., Parunak, H.V.D., Michel, F. (eds.) E4MAS 2006. LNCS, vol. 4389, pp. 41–50. Springer, Heidelberg (2006)
11. Hènane, I., Hadouaj, S., Ghedira, K.: ML-MA: multi-level multi-agents modeling to simulate renewable resources management systems application on pastoral system "Ouled Chehida" case study. In: 13th European Conference on Multi-agent Systems (2015)
12. Henane, I., Said, L.B., Hadouaj, S., Ragged, N.: Multi-agent based simulation of animal food selective behavior in a pastoral system. In: Jędrzejowicz, P., Nguyen, N.T., Howlet, R.J., Jain, L.C. (eds.) KES-AMSTA 2010, Part I. LNCS, vol. 6070, pp. 283–292. Springer, Heidelberg (2010)

13. Bratman, M.: Intentions, Plans and Practical Reason. Cambridge University Press, Cambridge (1987)
14. Broersen, J., Dastani, M., Hulstijn, J., Huang, Z., Van der Torre, L.: The BOID architecture: conflicts between beliefs, obligations, intentions and desires. In: 5th International Conference on Autonomous Agent, New York, pp. 9–16 (2011)
15. Nefzaoui, A., El Hanzi, K., El Mourid, M.: Autonomisation des Ruraux Pauvres et Volatilité Des Politiques De Développement en Tunisie. ICARDA Aleppo, Syria (2009)
16. Taillandier, P., Vo, D.-A., Amouroux, E., Drogoul, A.: GAMA: a simulation platform that integrates geographical information data, agent-based modeling and multi-scale control. In: Desai, N., Liu, A., Winikoff, M. (eds.) PRIMA 2010. LNCS, vol. 7057, pp. 242–258. Springer, Heidelberg (2012)
17. Bourbouze, A.: Pastoralism in the Maghreb: the silent revolution. Fourrages **161**, 3–21 (2000)

Generalising Social Structure Using Interval Type-2 Fuzzy Sets

Christopher K. Frantz[1]([✉]), Bastin Tony Roy Savarimuthu[2], Martin K. Purvis[2], and Mariusz Nowostawski[3]

[1] College of Enterprise and Development, Otago Polytechnic, Dunedin, New Zealand
christopher.frantz@op.ac.nz
[2] Department of Information Science, University of Otago, Dunedin, New Zealand
{tony.savarimuthu,martin.purvis}@otago.ac.nz
[3] Faculty of Computer Science and Media Technology,
Norwegian University of Science and Technology, Gjøvik, Norway
mariusz.nowostawski@hig.no

Abstract. To understand the operation of the informal social sphere in human or artificial societies, we need to be able to identify their existing behavioural conventions (institutions). This includes the contextualisation of seemingly objective facts with subjective assessments, especially when attempting to capture their meaning in the context of the analysed society. An example for this is numeric information that abstractly expresses attributes such as wealth, but only gains meaning in its societal context. In this work we present a conceptual approach that combines clustering techniques and Interval Type-2 Fuzzy Sets to extract structural information from aggregated subjective micro-level observations. A central objective, beyond the aggregation of information, is to facilitate the analysis on multiple levels of social organisation. We introduce the proposed mechanism and discuss its application potential.

1 Introduction

The seamless interaction of software agents within open environments (i.e. in environments in which actors can join and leave over time) requires the ability to observe and identify behavioural patterns in order to adapt and interpret behaviours that are unknown (i.e. have not been formally encoded at design time) or can change over time. In addition to identifying complex social behaviours, such as composite actions and social interaction patterns, both of which are fundamental characteristics of institutions [12], individuals require the ability to infer information about the social structure of the observed social environment, such as relevant demographic information.

In this work we propose a generic process that allows the generalisation of social structure from observational information. We achieve this by aggregating subjectively categorised micro-level observations on arbitrary level of social organisation, and use Interval Type-2 Fuzzy Sets (IT2FS) to identify patterns of category allocations across ordinally-scaled dimensions.

© Springer International Publishing Switzerland 2016
M. Baldoni et al. (Eds.): PRIMA 2016, LNAI 9862, pp. 344–354, 2016.
DOI: 10.1007/978-3-319-44832-9_22

In Sect. 2 we outline the motivation for the proposed approach, briefly identify related research fields and existing work. This is followed by a brief introduction to IT2FS in Sect. 3. In Sect. 4 we introduce the essential contribution that consists of a staged use of clustering techniques in addition to IT2FS. Finally, in Sect. 5, we summarise and discuss application areas for our contribution, but also identify further potential for future work.

2   Motivation and Related Work

When humans interact in new environments, they rely on previous experience to guide their actions. However, to capture the social meaning of actions or interaction patterns (and thus inform their action choice appropriately), they also develop an understanding of the social roles, order and dynamics, in short: the social structure of the social environment they are acting in. Learning about social structure implies a generalisation process in order to make the acquired knowledge transferable to unknown situations and environments. Inferring structural information from observation involves several challenges that apply to humans as much as to artificial entities:

- Bounded rationality [15] – Individuals have a limited ability to keep track of the characteristics of all observed individuals, an aspect that challenges the inference of social structure in open systems.
- Incomplete information – Specific social attributes, such as age, may not be accessible for all observed individuals.
- Locality of observations – Individuals do not have a global view, but are constrained to the observation of their specific social environment.

To deal with those challenges, humans rely on abstraction mechanisms that permit the categorisation of observations (e.g. aggregating individual observations into age groups), while operating subconsciously without relying on the individual's explicit mental attention. Following this rationale, individuals continuously invoke some notion of stereotyping or labelling based on 'implicit social cognition' [6] that aims at categorising observation traces by their structural components. The intrinsic operation further includes the consideration of individuals' biases (e.g. attitudes, self-esteem, previous experience) and situational involvement. Those priming influences shape the interpretation and internalisation of observation traces – making it both product of a situational assessment and subjective influence factor for future assessments at the same time. As a response to personal experiences as well as objectives, individuals can invoke subjective social comparison processes [3] that reflect the relative position or role in a social environment (e.g. allocating oneself in a specific age group), as opposed to capturing a comprehensive objectified picture.

While computational capabilities seemingly permit artificial agents to overcome the challenge of bounded rationality, retaining full information permanently is inefficient, both in terms memory consumption and computational efficiency, especially if attributes change, have only temporary relevance, or require frequent computing. Similar to humans, artificial entities face the challenges of operating on incomplete and local information when attempting to infer social structure.

In this work we propose an initial approach that models stereotyping processes in a generic fashion using Fuzzy Sets [16], or, more specifically, Interval Type-2 Fuzzy Sets (IT2FS) [17], as the underlying technique. Fuzzy sets represent a natural conceptual fit for the problem of *quantifying ordinal categories for given dimensions* (e.g. Age: 'young', 'middle-aged', 'old'), and are able to *capture the blurry boundaries between those categories*. Moreover, beyond serving as a compatible conceptual mapping for specific category definitions, fuzzy sets can be comprised of multiple individual observations, making them a tool for the analysis of observations on arbitrary levels of aggregation, thus facilitating the identification of social structures on various levels of social organisation, such as micro, meso and macro level. As such, fuzzy sets complement imperfect subjective categorisation processes with analytical facilities to allow the objective characterisation of their aggregated outcomes.

The proposed approach sits at the intersection of norm synthesis, a subfield of normative multi-agent systems, and the social-scientific application of fuzzy sets. Work on norm synthesis include centralised, hybrid, and decentralised approaches. Morales et al. [11] propose a centralised norm synthesiser that monitors agents' behaviours in a traffic scenario and infers and imposes rules at runtime. An alternative hybrid approach by Riveret et al. [14] marries bottom-up norm inference and top-down enforcement in which individual agents play stochastic games and individually nominate a preferred normative strategy based on observed strategy outcomes, which are then put forth as motions, voted on and implemented based on a collective social choice mechanism. Frantz et al. [5] use a decentralised approach in which agents infer generalise behavioural patterns and structural information based on observation and present those in human-readable form using a generic norm representation.

We will highlight related work in the area of fuzzy sets after introducing the underlying concept in more detail in the following Sect. 3.

3 Interval Type-2 Fuzzy Sets

An essential novel aspect in this work is the use of Interval Type-2 Fuzzy Sets (IT2FS) to facilitate the generalisation and synthesis of non-categorical attributes. Zadeh [16] introduced fuzzy sets as a mechanism to represent uncertain information, the complexity of which he deemed to be in inherent conflict with precision. Instead of unambiguously classifying information as members of well-defined (crisp) sets (as exemplified in Fig. 1a), fuzzy sets remove the assumption of unambiguous set associations and instead emphasise a continuous *degree of membership* (with boundaries 0 and 1), reflecting the certainty with which a value is a member of the corresponding fuzzy set (as shown in Fig. 1b). This flexibility qualifies fuzzy sets for the use in a wide range of application domains involving classification problems that are characterised by the complexity of

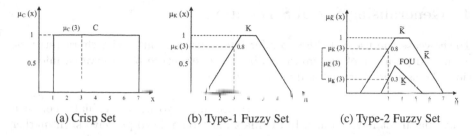

(a) Crisp Set   (b) Type-1 Fuzzy Set   (c) Type-2 Fuzzy Set

Fig. 1. Examples for crisp, Type-1, and Type-2 fuzzy sets

input data. Examples of those include micro-controllers [9] and image processing [1], but also social-scientific aspects, such as modelling personality traits [13] or establishing a fuzzy measure of social relationships [7].

Referring to the examples shown in Fig. 1, crisp sets (Fig. 1a) are characterised by their unambiguous association of input values (here: 3 of the dimension x) with a given set (here: C), with a degree of membership ($\mu_C(3)$) of 1. For the (Type-1) Fuzzy Set K (as shown in Fig. 1b) the degree of membership ($\mu_K(3)$) is 0.8.

However, an essential problem associated with Type-1 Fuzzy Sets (T1FS) is the conception of uncertainty as a discrete value, i.e. the representation assumes 'certainty about the uncertainty', here expressed as the degree of membership. A possible solution to this problem is to represent the degree of membership as a fuzzy value itself, making it a recursive problem reflected in Type-n Fuzzy Sets [17] (with n reflecting the order). In this work we concentrate on an interval-based representation of fuzzy sets, specifically Interval Type-2 Fuzzy Sets. In this concept second-order uncertainty is expressed as a *Footprint of Uncertainty* (FOU) that is delimited by an *upper membership function* (UMF) and *lower membership function* (LMF). Consequently, the degree of membership for a specific input value is represented as an interval itself. For the exemplified Type-2 Fuzzy Set $\widetilde{K}$ in Fig. 1c the degree of membership for the input value 3 is $\mu_{\widetilde{K}}(3)$ = [0.3, 0.8], determined by the input value's intersections with UMF ($\overline{K}$) and LMF ($\underline{K}$).

More than reflecting a philosophically more accurate representation of uncertainty, the use of IT2FS lends itself well for the representation of systems in which the global state is an emergent property of its constituents' interactions. This enables the inspection on multiple levels of analysis, with the emerging FOU being an essential construct to quantify aspects such as social coherence – an aspect that we exploit in this work. To our knowledge IT2FS have found limited application for the purpose of social modelling, with the exception being their use to quantify the concept of normative alignment [4].

4   Generalising Social Structure

To showcase the use of IT2FS to infer information about social characteristics, we introduce a set of assumptions about the structure of observable information. We assume that each individual carries attributes or markers of numerical (or at least ordinally-scaled) nature, such as their specific age. The corresponding attribute (e.g. 'age') must furthermore apply to all individuals, i.e. each individual must have an age. Individuals must be able to perceive such marker instance values, either based on public display or some form of inference on the part of the observing individual (e.g. gauging another individual's age relative to oneself). Individuals reduce cognitive load (see Sect. 2) by allocating their observations in ordinally-scaled categories of given dimensions (such as the categories 'low', 'medium', and 'high' for the dimension 'wealth'). These categories are then expressed as value intervals. Following the motivation of this work, intervals are shaped by the individuals' experiences, with interval centre values bearing higher certainty values than boundary values.[1] However, the proposed generalisation approach is agnostic about the origin of those value intervals.

The devised process exploits the strength of IT2FS to systematically combine individual varying value ranges on arbitrary levels of aggregation. However, to apply IT2FS generation to social systems, we need to take the potential conflicting analytical objectives of both into account. The IT2FS generation process (which we explore in more detail at a later stage) aims to produce a *coherent single membership function* that describes a category of interest while attempting to produce a minimal FOU (i.e. minimising uncertainty about the fuzzy set boundaries) by applying statistical corrections in order to isolate (presumed) irrelevant data or outliers as shown in Fig. 2 (individual input intervals are represented in grey colour; the bold red trace reflects the UMF; the green trace represents the LMF). However, social systems exhibit, if not promote, *broad stratification or even polarisation of observed characteristics* (as seen for the clustered intervals on the far left in Fig. 2) such as individual or social markers, attitudes, and opinions. Coercing those into a uniform macro-level construct in order to increase coherence (by filtering outliers, etc.) would prevent the comprehensive representation of the existing social landscape and limits explorative analysis, and thus rendering the application of the otherwise appropriate mechanism questionable.

We thus devise preliminary steps that adapt the use of fuzzy sets for the purpose of social systems by preempting MF generation with steps for both supervised and unsupervised identification of relevant social clusters. The complete process involves

– the collection of individuals' interpretations of categories for given dimensions, i.e. the numeric intervals describing specific categories (e.g. low, medium, high) within given dimensions (e.g. wealth),

---

[1] For example, 'low wealth' could comprise the interval 0 to 50 ([0, 50]), medium wealth [50, 100], and anything above 100 considered as 'high wealth'. The membership of boundary values (e.g. 50) with specific sets is of lower certainty than interval centres values (e.g. 75).

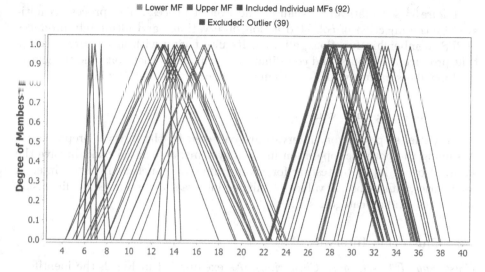

Fig. 2. Exemplified operation of MF generation on widely-spread input intervals

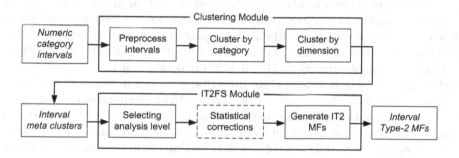

Fig. 3. Process overview

- the identification of interval clusters for given categories (intra-category clustering),
- the clustering of interval clusters across all categories within a given dimension (inter-category clustering), and finally,
- the generation of the IT2FS.

We conceive two mechanisms to group this functionality, with the first three steps being managed by the *Clustering Module*, and the remaining ones by the *IT2FS Module*.

Figure 3[2] schematically visualises the overall process. The process is initiated by the injection of collected action observations, and ultimately produces IT2FS membership functions, allowing its interfacing with agent architectures that produce the inputs, and coordination mechanisms that consume the generated membership functions (e.g. to model collective decision-making).

4.1 Collecting Intervals

As an initial step, category intervals are collected by the interval preprocessor. Assuming the potential operation in open systems, associated tasks involve the sanitisation of input by testing for invalid intervals (such as inverted interval boundaries, infinite or null values). Sanitised intervals are organised by dimension and corresponding categories.

4.2 Clustering Intervals

Clustering (Intra-category Clustering). As exemplified in Fig. 2, the identification of a unique set of intervals based on conventional statistical operations cannot accommodate widely-spread input intervals. Instead, we apply density-based clustering in order to identify grouped intervals that may be indicative for a shared conceptual understanding of a given term, i.e. the varying conceptions of 'low wealth' between different individuals (intra-category clustering). To allow the unsupervised identification of clusters we rely on the DBSCAN [2] algorithm that operates on the principle of identifying core points that have at least a specified number of neighbouring points ($minPts$) within a maximum permissible distance ε. For clustering operations explored in the experimental evaluation we consider three as the minimum number of members ($minPts$) to constitute a cluster. As distance metric for intervals we use specified minimal range intersections of intervals, with 0 indicating complete overlap of interval ranges (i.e. either identical interval ranges or one range encompassing the other), and 1 indicating no interval overlap. A distance or ε value of 0.3 would thus imply a minimum proportional overlap of 0.7 to consider two intervals clustered.

Meta-Clustering (Inter-category Clustering). The clustering of intervals occurs independently for individual categories in order to characterise varying interpretations for specific categories (e.g. 'low wealth'). However, the individual categories (e.g. 'low', 'medium', 'high') of a given dimension (e.g. 'wealth') do not exist in isolation if we want to characterise social clusters based on their conceptual understanding. We thus perform a meta-clustering operation to integrate the understanding across all category clusters as indicated in Fig. 4. Exemplified interval clusters are identified by colour; the horizontal lines highlight the cross-category relationships.

---

[2] Grouped boxes indicate system components along with elementary processing steps, whereas individual boxes with italicised labels signify processing artefacts such as inputs (e.g. intervals) and outputs (e.g. membership functions). Dashed boxes indicate the optional nature of the operation (e.g. statistical correction).

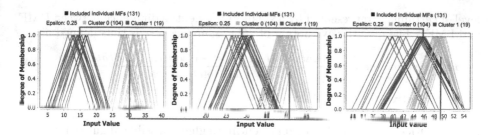

Fig. 4. Meta-clustering across categories

The meta-clustering step is based on the assumption that all *individuals hold conceptions across all categories* of a given domain. However, that does *not* imply that individuals with similar conceptions within a given category need to maintain those across all categories of a given dimension. To facilitate the identification of inter-category clusters, each interval iv maintains a reference to the originating individual iv_{orig}. In an effort to reduce the number of meta clusters (for larger number of clusters), we devise an optional algorithm. As a first step, all possible cluster combinations across all categories are identified. Following this the proportional intersection of individuals linked to the clustered intervals (relative to the mean size of combined clusters) is determined (with $\{iv, \ldots\}$ as individual category clusters):

$$x_{combination} = \frac{count(\cap\,(\{iv_{orig},\ldots\}_1,\ldots,\{iv_{orig},\ldots\}_k))}{\mu(count(\{iv,\ldots\}_1),\ldots,count(\{iv,\ldots\}_k))} \tag{1}$$

The combination with the *largest proportional intersection* for each cluster is the most representative meta cluster for a given individual cluster.

4.3 Membership Function Generation

The identified meta clusters provide an overview of the presumed social structure based on the differentiated generalised interpretation of conceptual dimensions, but do not make the individual clusters analytically accessible. Here we invoke Interval Type-2 Fuzzy Sets as introduced in Sect. 3. The essential purpose of IT2FS is to transform the clustered intervals into a uniform representation that generalises the certainty with which a given input value for a dimension is associated with a category.

Levels of Analysis. The process of generalising IT2FS is challenged by the trade-off between representativeness (*quantity* of represented intervals) for the entire category – represented by the UMF – and the IT2FS's *quality*, i.e. its ability to extract a shared understanding of the proximate intervals by introducing some level of certainty – represented by a small FOU (i.e. the difference between UMF and LMF). The quantitative notion of *Representativeness* is thus defined as

$$Representativeness := \frac{count(totalIntervals) - count(excludedIntervals)}{count(totalIntervals)} \quad (2)$$

The qualitative notion of *Alignment* is expressed as the relative difference in area under the LMF relative to the area captured by the UMF (with a value of 1, i.e. identical LMF and UMF, representing highest possible alignment):

$$Alignment := \frac{LMF}{UMF} \quad (3)$$

From a sociological perspective this corresponds to the differentiation into macro- and meso-level analysis (with individual intervals reflecting the micro level). Macro-level analysis thus considers all input intervals for a given category, whereas meso-level analysis concentrates on individual clusters. The selection of meso-level clusters depends on the analytical objectives (e.g. the focus on majority or minority groups), such as the selection of *largest, smallest,* most *central* or most *extremal* clusters.

Statistical Corrections. In addition to the coarse-grained trade-off based on ana-lytical levels, individual clusters can be refined by statistical corrections inspired by Liu and Mendel [8] to remove noise, emphasise central cluster regions, and enforce at least a minimal aligned understanding. Corresponding non-parametric corrections include

– the filtering of intervals that lie outside a given factor of the interquartile ranges, (to emphasise central intervals), and
– the filtering of non-overlapping intervals (to ensure the establishment of a LMF).

Generating Membership Functions. At this stage the intervals have been selected based on analytical strategy and potential further statistical corrections. As indi-cated at the beginning of this section, we assume that the individual intervals themselves express conceptual understanding of varying certainty, with (full) cer-tainty at interval centres and (in our case linearly) decreasing certainty towards the interval boundaries (e.g. because of overlapping interval regions or dynami-cally changing boundary values).

Based on the input intervals, the UMF $\overline{\mu_S(x)}$ (for an IT2FS S) is determined as the highest degree of membership for each input x, and LMF $\mu_S(x)$ as lowest degree of membership for each input x (see Sect. 3). The corresponding FOU is then determined as the area between UMF and LMF [10], or union of differences between UMF and LMF membership degrees across all values in X, expressed as:

$$FOU(S) = \bigcup_{x \in X} [\mu_S(x),\ \overline{\mu_S(x)}] \quad (4)$$

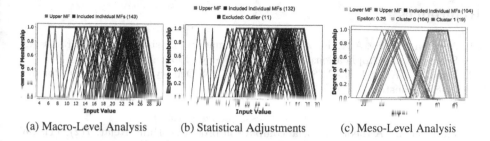

(a) Macro-Level Analysis   (b) Statistical Adjustments   (c) Meso-Level Analysis

Fig. 5. Configuring IT2FS generation

Figure 5 visualises the effects of analysis levels on the generated membership function, with macro-level selection shown in Fig. 5a, statistical adjustments to macro-level selection shown in Fig. 5b (exclusion of intervals outside 1.5 * interquartile range), and the selection of a specific cluster for MF generation in Fig. 5c.

The established IT2FSs provide an integrated representation of the chosen intervals with respect to the previously introduced metrics, and furthermore generalise the shared understanding of a given term. This allows the invocation with analytical tools to determine an associated term for a given input across the considered input intervals.

5   Summary, Discussion and Outlook

In this work we have outlined an approach to extract general information about social structures from micro-level observations. This includes the initial identification of category clusters and the subsequent generation of IT2FS membership functions. The presented approach is generic and makes few assumptions about the underlying individuals, which include their *ability to represent observations in a uniform structural representation* and the *ability to subjectively categorise numeric variables*. It lends itself well for autonomous unsupervised operation (only required parameters: granularity of clustering (see Subsect. 4.2); choice of desired analysis level and eventual statistical corrections (see Subsect. 4.3)). Alternatively, as done in our example, the mechanism can be applied to inspect emerging social clusters and inform a supervised analysis by modifying the configuration (e.g. analysis level) at runtime.

Currently, the proposed approach operates non-intrusively and is only used for analytical purposes. Individual agents neither require awareness nor are they directly affected by their operation. However, looking at future work, the use of fuzzy sets is not constrained to analytical purposes. IT2FS provide a helpful metaphor to instil a computationally accessible mechanism that allows individuals to compare and evaluate their own and others' conceptual understandings. Beyond this, IT2FS can be used to inject notions of computational social choice (such as majority-based decision-making), closing the feedback loop between micro-level entities and emergent meso- or macro-level phenomena.

References

1. Acharya, T., Ray, A.K.: Fuzzy set theory in image processing. In: Image Processing: Principles and Applications, pp. 209–226. Wiley, Hoboken (2005)
2. Ester, M., Kriegel, H.-P., Sander, J., Xu, X.: A Density-based algorithm for discovering clusters in large spatial databases with noise. In: Simoudis, E., Han, J., Fayyad, U. (eds.) Second International Conference on Knowledge Discovery and Data Mining, pp. 226–231. AAAI Press, Portland (1996)
3. Festinger, L.: A theory of social comparison processes. Hum. Relat. **7**(2), 117–140 (1954)
4. Frantz, C., Purvis, M.K., Savarimuthu, B.T.R., Nowostawski, M.: Analysing the dynamics of norm evolution using interval type-2 fuzzy sets. In: WI-IAT 2014 Proceedings of the 2014 IEEE/WIC/ACM International Joint Conferences on Web Intelligence (WI) and Intelligent Agent Technologies (IAT), vol. 3, pp. 230–237 (2014)
5. Frantz, C.K., Purvis, M.K., Savarimuthu, B.T.R., Nowostawski, M.: Modelling dynamic normative understanding in agent societies. Scalable Comput.: Pract. Experience **16**(4), 355–378 (2015)
6. Greenwald, A.G., Banaji, M.R., Rudman, L.A., Farnham, S.D., Nosek, B.A., Mellott, D.S.: A unified theory of implicit attitudes, stereotypes, self-esteem, and self-concept. Psychol. Rev. **109**(1), 3–25 (2002)
7. Hassan, S., Salgado, M., Pavón, J.: Friendship dynamics: modelling social relationships through a fuzzy agent-based simulation. Discrete Dyn. Nat. Soc. **2011**, Article ID 765640, 19 p (2011)
8. Liu, F., Mendel, J.M.: Encoding words into interval Type-2 fuzzy sets using an interval approach. IEEE Trans. Fuzzy Syst. **16**(6), 1503–1521 (2008)
9. Long, Z., Yuanc, Y., Long, W.: Designing fuzzy controllers with variable universes of discourse using input-output data. Eng. Appl. Artif. Intell. **36**, 215–221 (2014)
10. Mendel, J., John, R., Liu, F.: Interval Type-2 fuzzy logic systems made simple. IEEE Trans. Fuzzy Syst. **14**(6), 808–821 (2006)
11. Morales, J., López-Sánchez, M., Rodriguez-Aguilar, J.A., Vasconcelos, W., Wooldridge, M.: Online automated synthesis of compact normative systems. ACM Trans. Auton. Adapt. Syst. **10**(1), 2:1–2:33 (2015)
12. North, D.C.: Institutions, Institutional Change, and Economic Performance. Cambridge University Press, New York (1990)
13. Ören, T., Ghasem-Aghaee, N.: Personality representation processable in fuzzy logic for human behavior simulation. In: Proceedings of the 2003 Summer Computer Simulation Conference, Montreal, Canada, July 20–24, pp. 11–18. SCS, San Diego (2003)
14. Riveret, R., Artikis, A., Busquets, D., Pitt, J.: Self-governance by transfiguration: from learning to prescriptions. In: Cariani, F., Grossi, D., Meheus, J., Parent, X. (eds.) DEON 2014. LNCS, vol. 8554, pp. 177–191. Springer, Heidelberg (2014)
15. Simon, H.A.: A behavioral model of rational choice. Q. J. Econ. **69**(1), 99–118 (1955)
16. Zadeh, L.A.: Fuzzy sets. Inf. Control **8**(3), 338–353 (1965)
17. Zadeh, L.A.: The concept of a linguistic variable and its application to approximate reasoning - I. Inf. Sci. **8**(3), 199–249 (1975)

Argumentation Versus Optimization
for Supervised Acceptability Learning

Hiroyuki Kido$^{(\boxtimes)}$

The University of Tokyo, 7-3-1 Hongo, Bunkyo-ku, Tokyo 113 8656, Japan
kido@sys.t.u-tokyo.ac.jp

Abstract. This paper deals with the question of how one should predict agent's psychological opinions regarding acceptability statuses of
arguments. We give a formalization of argumentation-based acceptability
learning (ABAL) by introducing argument-based reasoning into supervised learning. A baseline classifier is defined based on an optimization
method of graph-based semi-supervised learning with dissimilarity network where neighbor nodes represent arguments attacking each other,
and therefore, the optimization method adjusts them to have different
acceptability statuses. A detailed comparison between ABAL instantiated with a decision tree and naive Bayes, and the optimization method
is made using each of 29 examinees' psychological opinions regarding
acceptability statuses of 22 arguments extracted from an online discussion forum. We demonstrate that ABAL with the leave-one-out cross-
validation method shows better learning performance than the optimization method in most criteria under the restricted conditions that the
number of training examples is small and a test set is used to select the
best models of both methods.

Keywords: Argumentation · Acceptability learning · Graph-based
semi-supervised learning · Abstract argumentation framework · Acceptability semantics

1 Introduction

Argumentation is a human verbal, social and rational activity seen in various situations. e.g., scientific conferences, judicial contests, domestic quarrels, Twitter,
and so on. Much work has been done to understand and organize argumentation theory both informally and formally. Today, argumentation is recognized as
a promising approach for wicked, or ill-defined, problems of which one cannot
easily get a complete view, and as communication and computation mechanisms
for networked software agents. One of the most influential work in the study of
formal argumentation is Dung's theory of abstract argumentation [1] that refor-
mulates consequences of various nonmonotonic reasoning, e.g., Reiter's default
logic and Pollock's defeasible reasoning. After his work, argumentation in artificial intelligence has witnessed quite some research on argumentation frameworks
[2–6] and acceptability semantics [7–11], where argumentation frameworks give

© Springer International Publishing Switzerland 2016
M. Baldoni et al. (Eds.): PRIMA 2016, LNAI 9862, pp. 355–365, 2016.
DOI: 10.1007/978-3-319-44832-9_23

a description of inconsistent, uncertain, subjective and distributed knowledge, and acceptability semantics defines consequence notions from such knowledge. In the context of multi-agent systems, they have provided self-interested agents with the ability to conduct persuasion, negotiation and deliberation.

In this context, acceptability semantics studies the question of which set of arguments (i.e., belief) agents *should rationally* accept. Meanwhile, they do not aim to answer the question of which set of arguments agents *actually and psychologically* accept. This observation motivates us to have the research question, *"How should one predict agent's actual opinions regarding acceptability statuses of the arguments?"* This question is not easy to answer in terms of acceptability semantics because agents see arguments as acceptable based on the contents described in the arguments, whereas acceptability semantics sees arguments as acceptable based on an attack relation existing between arguments. We think, however, that acceptability semantics is still useful to predict agent's actual opinions regarding acceptability statuses of arguments. This comes from our hypothesis that agents are likely to have the same opinion on acceptability statuses of two arguments when acceptability semantics characterizes them as being in the same position.

In this paper, we deal with *acceptability learning*, that is a cross-disciplinary research agenda between argumentation and machine learning. We define argumentation-based acceptability learning (ABAL) in the form of supervised learning and an optimization method along the idea of graph-based semi-supervised learning. Intuitively, ABAL uses extensions, i.e., rational sets of arguments, defined by acceptability semantics to characterize arguments and arguments with the same characteristics are classified into the same acceptability status. On the other hand, the optimization method propagates acceptability statuses to neighbors so that they have different statuses. Data used in our experiment are an abstract argumentation framework with 22 arguments extracted from an online discussion forum, and 29 examinees' opinions on acceptability statuses of the individual 22 arguments. We carry out performance analysis using decision-tree and naive-Bayes classifiers for ABAL and a quadratic cost function for the optimization method both using leave-one-out cross-validation (LOOCV) method with machine learning common criteria. The key result is that ABAL shows better performance than the optimization method in most criteria under the restricted conditions that the number of training examples is small and a test set is used to select the best models of both methods.

The contributions of this paper are as follows. First, we give a formal definition of ABAL (see Sect. 3.1). Second, we formalize an optimization method for acceptability learning in the form of graph-based semi-supervised learning (see Sect. 3.2). Third, we compare learning performance of argumentation-based and optimization-based methods in the context of acceptability learning, and show that, under some restricted conditions, the argumentation-based method gives better performance than the optimization-based method (see Sect. 4).

2   Motivating Example

Before giving a motivating example of acceptability learning, we outline preliminary notions of abstract argumentation. Dung's acceptability semantics is
defined on an abstract argumentation framework $AF = (Arg, Att)$ where Arg is
a set of arguments and $Att \subseteq Arg \times Arg$ is a binary relation on Arg. $(a,b) \in Att$
means "a attacks b." Suppose $a \in Arg$ and $S \subseteq Arg$. S attacks a iff some member
of S attacks a. S is conflict-free iff S attacks none of its members. S defends a iff
S is conflict-free and S attacks all arguments attacking a. A characteristic func-
tion $F : Pow(Arg) \rightarrow Pow(Arg)$ is defined as $F(S) = \{a | S \; defends \; a\}$ where
$Pow(Arg)$ is the power set of Arg. Given AF, Dung's acceptability semantics
defines four kinds of rational sets, called extensions, of arguments. S is a complete extension iff S is a fixed point of F. S is a grounded extension iff it is
the minimum complete extension with respect to set inclusion. S is a preferred
extension iff it is a maximal complete extension with respect to set inclusion.
S is a stable extension iff it is a complete extension attacking all members in
$Arg \setminus S$.

Now consider the abstract argumentation framework $AF = (\{a, \; b, \; c, \; d, \; e, \;
f\}, \; \{(a,b), \; (b,a), \; (b,c), \; (c,b), \; (a,d), \; (d,a), \; (d,e), \; (e,d), \; (e,f), \; (f,e)\})$ shown
in Fig. 1 where each node represents an argument and each edge represents an
attack relation between arguments. Consider an agent who observes only arguments b, c, e, and f, and states the opinions that the agent accepts b, c, and
e, but does not accept f. The opinions are represented by the node labels in
Fig. 1 where white means "acceptable" whereas black "unacceptable." Now, the
question here is whether arguments a and d are acceptable to the agent, or
not. Our hypothesis is that the agent accepts argument a, but does not accept
argument d. This is because we think that an agent is likely to have the same
opinion about acceptability status of arguments when they are defended by the
same extension(s), i.e., characterized similarly by the acceptability semantics. In
the above-mentioned example, AF has 5 preferred extensions $\{b,d,f\}$, $\{c,d,f\}$,
$\{a,c,f\}$, $\{a,c,e\}$ and $\{b,e\}$, and accepted arguments b, c, and e can be characterized as being a member of $\{a,c,e\}$ or $\{b,e\}$. These two extensions are represented
by the surrounding dotted lines in Fig. 1. This means that these arguments have
the same property that they are defended by at least one of these extensions.

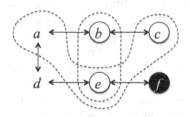

Fig. 1. Abstract argumentation framework AF (directed graph), agent's actual and
psychological opinions (labels), and two preferred extensions (surrounding dotted lines).

Table 1. Input examples of argumentation-based acceptability learning.

Argument x	Membership relation of x		Opinion on x
	with respect to $\{a, c, e\}$	with respect to $\{b, e\}$	
b	0	1	*acceptable*
c	1	0	*acceptable*
e	1	1	*acceptable*
f	0	0	*unacceptable*

In other words, the opinions conform to the rule that, for all arguments x, the agent accepts x iff x is in extensions $\{a, c, e\}$ or $\{b, e\}$. As a result, this generalized rule gives the prediction that argument a is acceptable whereas argument d is unacceptable.

In this paper, we introduce *argument-based acceptability learning* (ABAL) in the form of supervised learning. In the above-mentioned example, ABAL assumes the example data shown in Table 1 where the leftmost column shows arguments with opinions (i.e., labels), the rightmost shows the opinions, and the center shows truth values, 1 (True) or 0 (False), of membership relations between each argument and each extension. Figure 2 shows an output decision-tree obtained by applying some decision tree algorithm to the data shown in Table 1. Each node (except leaf) of the tree represents a question, each branch an answer to the question, and each leaf a decision. For example, the tree classifies argument b into an acceptable argument in accordance with the following steps: b goes down to the right branch from the root because it is not in $\{a, c, e\}$, and it goes down to the left branch because it is in $\{b, e\}$. It is observed that the tree classifies all labeled arguments correctly, and moreover, classifies unobserved argument a (resp. d) into acceptable (resp. unacceptable) argument.

3   Two Approaches for Acceptability Learning

3.1   Argumentation-Based Method

A supervised learning is a subfield of machine learning where some input and output pairs of an unknown target function are available when trying to find an approximated function of the unknown target function. More formally, given a training set of N example input-output pairs $(\boldsymbol{x}_1, y_1)$, $(\boldsymbol{x}_2, y_2)$, $\cdots$, $(\boldsymbol{x}_N, y_N)$, where each y_i was generated by an unknown function $y = f(\boldsymbol{x})$, the problem of supervised learning is to discover a function h that approximates the true function f. Our idea is to see individual arguments in an abstract argumentation framework as examples of supervised learning, and characterize them using extensions defined by the acceptability semantics.

Definition 1 (Argumentation-based acceptability learning). *Let* a_1, $a_2, ..., a_N$ *be arguments and* $E_1, E_2, ..., E_M$ *be extensions of an abstract argumentation framework. The problem of argument-based acceptability learning is described as follows:*

Given. *A training set of N example input-output pairs* $(x_1, y_1), (x_2, y_2), ...,$ (x_N, y_N) *where, for all $i (1 \leq i \leq N)$, $r_i = (r_i^j)_{j=1}^M$ is a sequence of membership degrees of a_i with respect to E_j, and $y_i \in S$ is an acceptability status of a_i generated by an unknown function $y = f(x)$.*
Find. *A function h that approximates the true function f.*

In Table 1, the membership degrees correspond to the truth values of membership relations between arguments and extensions. The following definition extends this by taking into account the number of minimal subsets of extensions that defend arguments.

Definition 2 (Membership degree). *Let a be an argument and E be an extension of an abstract argumentation framework. A membership degree of a with respect to E is the number of minimal subsets $S \subseteq E$ such that $a \in F(S)$.*

Example 1. The membership degree of a with respect to extension $\{a, c, e\}$ is 2 because $a \in F(\{a\})$ and $a \in F(\{c, e\})$, but 0 with respect to $\{b, e\}$ because $a \notin F(\{b, e\})$.

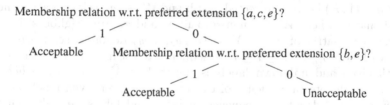

Fig. 2. Output decision tree of argument-based acceptability learning.

Different agents would generally take different credulous and skeptical attitudes about opinions on acceptability statuses of arguments. From the viewpoint of supervised learning, we want to characterize arguments using only extensions that are fit to agent's individual attitudes. We consider a partition of the power set of extensions that is used to define possible attributes or features of supervised acceptability learning. Let $(\mathscr{E}, \subseteq)$ denote a partially ordered set where $\mathscr{E}$ is a set of extensions of an abstract argumentation framework and $\subseteq$ is the set inclusion relation. For $\mathscr{S} \subseteq \mathscr{E}$ and $E \in \mathscr{E}$, $\mathscr{S}$ is called a *strict down-set* of E iff, for all extensions $F \in \mathscr{E}$, if $F \subset E$ then $F \in \mathscr{S}$. We use notation $D(E)$ to represent the strict down-set of extension E, and $D(\mathscr{S})$ to represent the strict down-set of all extensions $E \in \mathscr{S}$, i.e., $D(\mathscr{S}) = \bigcup_{E \in \mathscr{S}} D(E)$. $D^i(\mathscr{S})$ denotes i-time iteration of operator D where $D^0(\mathscr{S}) = \mathscr{S}$ and $D^{i+1}(\mathscr{S}) = D(D^i(\mathscr{S}))$. The notation $\max \mathscr{S}$ denotes the set of maximal elements of $\mathscr{S}$.

Definition 3 (Attribute set). *Let $\mathscr{C}$ be a set of complete extensions. i-th attitude set is defined by* $\max D^{i-1}(\mathscr{C})$.

$\mathscr{A} = \{\max D^0(\mathscr{C}), \max D^1(\mathscr{C}), \cdots, \max D^{n-1}(\mathscr{C})\}$ is the set of n attribute sets where $\max D^0(\mathscr{C}) = \mathscr{P}$ and $\max D^{n-1}(\mathscr{C}) = \mathscr{G}$. Note that $\mathscr{A}$ is a partition of $(\mathscr{C}, \subseteq)$, i.e., $\emptyset \notin \mathscr{A}$, $\bigcup_{i=1}^{n} \max D^{i-1}(\mathscr{C}) = \mathscr{C}$, and, for all $E, F \in \mathscr{A}$, if $E \neq F$ then $E \cap F = \emptyset$. Moreover, for all $E, F \in \mathscr{E}$, if $E \subset F$ then there are $i, j (i < j)$ such that $F \in \max D^i(\mathscr{C})$ and $E \in \max D^j(\mathscr{C})$. Therefore, for all i, if $E, F \in \max D^i(\mathscr{C})$ then $E \not\subset F$, i.e., $\max D^i(\mathscr{C})$ is an antichain, for all i.

Example 2. AF shown in Fig. 1 has the partition consisting of the four attribute sets: $\{\{b, e\}, \{a, c, e\}, \{b, d, f\}, \{a, c, f\}, \{c, d, f\}\}$ $(= \max D^0(\mathscr{C}))$, $\{\{e\}, \{b\}, \{a, c\}, \{d, f\}, \{c, f\}\}$ $(= \max D^1(\mathscr{C}))$, $\{\{c\}, \{f\}\}$ $(= \max D^2(\mathscr{C}))$, and $\{\emptyset\}$ $(= \max D^3(\mathscr{C}))$.

3.2 Optimization-Based Method

Graph-based semi-supervised learning relies on the idea that labels of unlabeled nodes are predicted from labels of their neighbor nodes based on the structural information of the graph. It assumes an undirected graph with some labeled nodes where each labeled or unlabeled node represents a data point and each edge represents a relationship, e.g., similarity, between data points. This subsection focuses on a *quadratic criterion optimization* used in graph-based semi-supervised learning and gives a modification to deal with acceptability learning.

Let $g = (V, E)$ be an undirected graph and W be an weight matrix encoding node similarity where $W_{i,j}$ is non-zero iff x_i and x_j are neighbors, i.e., W is an adjacency matrix of g. Let $Y_l = (y_1, y_2, ..., y_l)$ denote a sequence of given or known labels y_i, for $1 \leq i \leq l$. A sequence of estimated or predicted labels on both given and unknown labels is denoted by $\hat{Y} = (\hat{Y}_l, \hat{Y}_u)$ where $\hat{Y}_l = (\hat{y}_1, \hat{y}_2, ..., \hat{y}_l)$ denotes a sequence of estimated labels on given labels and $\hat{Y}_u = (\hat{y}_{l+1}, \hat{y}_{l+2}, ..., \hat{y}_n)$ denotes a sequence of estimated labels on unknown labels. Consistency between the estimated labeling and given labeling can be measured by the following term [12].

$$C_1(\hat{Y}_l) = \sum_{i=1}^{l} (\hat{y}_i - y_i)^2 = ||\hat{Y}_l - Y_l||^2 \qquad (1)$$

Minimization of term (1) makes predicted labels consistent with initial labels. On the other hand, neighbor nodes are assumed to have the same labeling in similarity graphs. It is often called the smoothness (or manifold) assumption. Now, let $L = D - W$ denote the un-normalized graph Laplacian where D is a diagonal matrix of g defined as $D_{i,i} = \sum_j W_{j,j}$. Consistency between estimated neighbor labeling can be measured by the following penalty term [12].

$$C_2(\hat{Y}) = \frac{1}{2} \sum_{i,j=1}^{n} W_{i,j}(\hat{y}_i - \hat{y}_j)^2 = \frac{1}{2} \left(2 \sum_{i=1}^{n} \hat{y}_i^2 \sum_{j=1}^{n} W_{i,j} - 2 \sum_{i,j=1}^{n} W_{i,j} \hat{y}_i \hat{y}_j \right) = \hat{Y}^{\mathrm{T}} L \hat{Y} \qquad (2)$$

Minimization of term (2) makes predicted labels of neighbors same. A regularization term is also assumed to make predicted labels as simple as possible. Thus, terms (1) and (2) with the regularization term and an additional balancing terms give us the following quadratic cost function for similarity graphs [12].

$$C(\hat{Y}) = ||\hat{Y}_l - Y_l||^2 + \mu \hat{Y}^T L \hat{Y} + \mu_\epsilon ||\hat{Y}||^2 \tag{3}$$

On the other hand, we want to deal with an abstract argumentation framework where edges represent a symmetric attack relation between arguments. So, what is expected in acceptability learning is a quadratic cost function that is minimized when predicted labels, i.e., acceptability statuses, are consistent with given labels, but neighbors of predicted labels are different. We thus make a revision on (2) and (3) and obtain the following terms where $M = D + W$.

$$C_2'(\hat{Y}) = \frac{1}{2} \sum_{i,j=1}^{n} W_{i,j} (\hat{y}_i + \hat{y}_j)^2 = \hat{Y}^T M \hat{Y} \tag{4}$$

$$C'(\hat{Y}) = ||\hat{Y}_l - Y_l||^2 + \mu \hat{Y}^T M \hat{Y} + \mu_\epsilon ||\hat{Y}||^2 \tag{5}$$

Our goal is to minimize (5). Let S denote an $(n \times n)$ diagonal matrix S where $S_{i,i} = 1$ iff $i \in \{1, 2, ..., l\}$. The first and the second derivatives of the function are given as follows.

$$\frac{1}{2} \frac{\partial C'(\hat{Y})}{\partial \hat{Y}} = S(\hat{Y} - Y) + \mu M \hat{Y} + \mu\varepsilon \hat{Y} = (S + \mu M + \mu\varepsilon I)\hat{Y} - SY \tag{6}$$

$$\frac{1}{2} \frac{\partial^2 C'(\hat{Y})}{\partial^2 \hat{Y}} = S + \mu M + \mu\varepsilon I \tag{7}$$

The second derivative is a positive definite matrix when $\varepsilon > 0$. This ensures that the cost is minimized when the first derivative is set to 0, i.e.,

$$\hat{Y} = (S + \mu M + \mu\varepsilon I)^{-1} SY. \tag{8}$$

4   Experimental Analysis

SYNCLON [13] is an online discussion forum that provides users opportunities to argue on various issues with others to explore valid beliefs. It is equipped with a function by which users can make it explicit an role of their utterances. Such role can be an attack against, support for, or supplement to a preceding utterance. We focused on argument on active euthanasia that actually took place in SYN-CLON and manually extracted 22 arguments and an attack relation between them where the attack relation is assumed to be symmetric. We conducted an online questionnaire using Google Forms where 29 people (12 workers and 17 university students) were asked to look at the abstract argumentation framework and choose either "acceptable" or "unacceptable" to express their psychological opinions about acceptability statuses of the individual 22 arguments. Figure 3

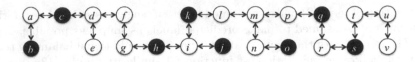

Fig. 3. Abstract argumentation framework with labeled arguments representing a certain agent's opinions on acceptability statuses of individual arguments.

shows the abstract argumentation framework with a certain examinee's opinions where a white argument represents his/her acceptance and black unacceptance.

We use ASPARTIX [14] to calculate extensions of the abstract argumentation framework. It gave 11028 complete extensions, denoted by set $\mathscr{C}$, 354 preferred extensions, denoted by set $\mathscr{P}$ (and the same stable extensions, denoted by set $\mathscr{S}$), and one grounded extension, denoted by set $\mathscr{G}$. Note that these extensions depend only on its graphical structure of the abstract argumentation framework without depending on people's opinions on arguments. Our Python program

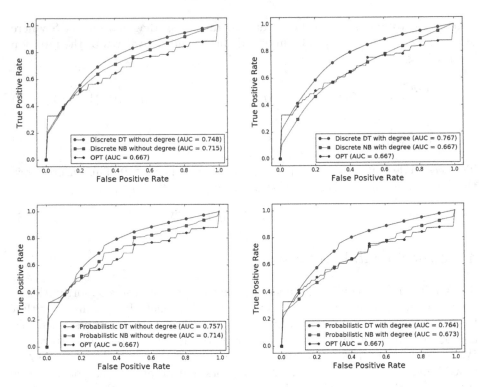

Fig. 4. Average ROC curves of DT (decision trees), multinomial NB (naive Bayes), and OPT (optimization). The upper two graphs show discrete methods, while the lower ones probabilistic. The left two graphs show a membership relation, while the right ones a membership degree.

Table 2. Performance summary of discrete decision tree, discrete naive bayes, and optimization.

Criteria	Optimization-based method	Argumentation-based method			
		Decision-tree		Naive-bayes	
		Without degree	With degree	Without degree	With degree
Accuracy	0.522	0.791	**0.800**	0.751	0.760
Precision	0.810	0.841	0.843	0.836	0.801
Recall	0.458	0.973	0.971	**0.979**	0.909
F_1	0.542	0.838	**0.845**	0.827	0.827
AUC	0.668	0.760	**0.761**	0.716	0.667

calculating all attribute sets gave the partition $\{\mathscr{A}_i \subseteq \mathscr{C} | 1 \leq i \leq 11\}$ of $\mathscr{C}$ where $|\mathscr{A}_1| = 354$, $|\mathscr{A}_2| = 1361$, $|\mathscr{A}_3| = 2480$, $|\mathscr{A}_4| = 2802$, $|\mathscr{A}_5| = 2163$, $|\mathscr{A}_6| = 1191$, $|\mathscr{A}_7| = 481$, $|\mathscr{A}_8| = 149$, $|\mathscr{A}_9| = 38$, $|\mathscr{A}_{10}| = 8$, and $|\mathscr{A}_{11}| = 1$. Note that every two sets are disjoint, the union of all sets are $\mathscr{C}$. Moreover, $\mathscr{A}_1 = \mathscr{P}$ and $\mathscr{A}_{11} = \mathscr{G}$.

We use the *leave-one-out cross-validation* (LOOCV) method for the evaluation of learning performance. In LOOCV, each of 21 arguments of the abstract argumentation framework is used to generate an approximated function, i.e., classifier, and it is used to predict an acceptability status of the remaining one argument. LOOCV fits parameters of the classifier to the training examples during this process. 22 times iteration of this process yields predicted acceptability statuses of all 22 arguments. We instantiate ABAL using decision-tree and naive-Bayes classifiers. Decision trees are parameterized by a tree-depth ranging from 1 to 5, the number of examples per leaf ranging from 1 to 5, and an attribute set ranging from $\mathscr{A}_1$ to $\mathscr{A}_{11}$. Naive-Bayes are parameterized only by an attribute set. The optimization-based methods are parameterized by μ and ε shown in Eq. (8) ranging from 0.2 to 1.0 and from 0.02 to 0.10, respectively. These whole processes are iterated 10 times to get the average evaluation scores.

Figure 4 shows the average ROC curves of decision-tree classification, multinomial naive-Bayes classification, and optimization-based methods. The graphs show that ABAL results in better learning performance than the optimization methods regardless of consideration of a degree of membership and probability. Table 2 shows learning performance of discrete decision-tree and naive-Bayes classifications and optimization-based classification, where the best scores of each criterion are highlighted in bold. In general, introduction of membership degree does not give a strong effect on improving learning performance. In fact, it negatively affects on learning performance of naive-Bayes classification although it positively affects on a decision tree classification.

5 Related Work and Discussions

Some research studies [15–17] have already been tackling research issues across argumentation and machine learning. They have a common characteristic that knowledge conveyed by arguments has a crucial role in their problem settings.

Goldberg et al. [18] extend the idea of graph-based semi-supervised classification on a similarity network to deal with a dissimilarity network. Although it enables us to predict unknown labels on dissimilarity network, it does not aim to neither give an interpretation nor generalize underlying rules of how labels are distributed in the network. However, this paper focuses on the issue of how to generalize a rule of agent's psychological opinions regarding acceptability status of arguments merely by addressing the attack relation existing between arguments, without referring to knowledge conveyed by arguments.

A preliminary idea of acceptability learning is presented in the research [19]. It, however, does not lay a foundation of argument-based acceptability learning in the form of supervised learning. Moreover, it deals with no technique to improve learning performance. On the other hand, the formal definition of ABAL in this paper allows us to use other types of argumentation frameworks, acceptability semantics and classification algorithms. Moreover, this paper gives an attribute set improving learning performance under the restricted condition that a test set is used for model selection.

6   Conclusions and Future Work

This paper proposed argumentation-based acceptability learning (ABAL) taking into account a membership degree, and gave its decision-tree and naive-Bayes representations. We defined optimization-based acceptability learning along the idea of graph-based semi-supervised learning. Our small-scale experiment showed that argumentation-based method resulted in better performance than optimization-based one in most criteria. We are planning to have more large-scale experiments with a lot of arguments to handle model selection using not a test set, but a cross-validation set.

Acknowledgments. This work has been conducted as a part of "Research Initiative on Advanced Software Engineering in 2015" supported by Software Reliability Enhancement Center (SEC), Information Technology Promotion Agency Japan (IPA).

References

1. Dung, P.M.: On the acceptability of arguments and its fundamental role in non-monotonic reasoning, logic programming, and n-person games. Artif. Intell. **77**, 321–357 (1995)
2. Cayrol, C., Lagasquie-Schiex, M.C.: On the acceptability of arguments in bipolar argumentation frameworks. In: Godo, L. (ed.) ECSQARU 2005. LNCS (LNAI), vol. 3571, pp. 378–389. Springer, Heidelberg (2005)
3. Amgoud, L.: Repairing preference-based argumentation frameworks. In: Proceedings of the 21st International Joint Conference on Artificial Intelligence, pp. 665–670 (2009)
4. Bench-Capon, T.J.M.: Value-based argumentation frameworks. In: Proceedings of the 9th International Workshop on Non-Monotonic Reasoning, pp. 443–454 (2002)

5. Modgil, S., Luck, M.: Argumentation based resolution of conflicts between desires and normative goals. In: Rahwan, I., Moraitis, P. (eds.) ArgMAS 2008. LNCS, vol. 5384, pp. 19–36. Springer, Heidelberg (2009)
6. Leite, J., Martins, J.: Social abstract argumentation. In: Proceedings of the 22nd international joint conference on Artificial Intelligence, pp. 2287–2292 (2011)
7. Verheij, B.: Two approaches to dialectical argumentation,: admissible sets and argumentation stages. In: Proceedings of the 8th Dutch Conference on Artificial Intelligence, pp. 357–368 (1996)
8. Caminada, M.: Semi-stable semantics. In: Proceedings of the 1st International Conference on Computational Models of Argument, pp. 121–130 (2006)
9. Dung, P.M., Mancarella, P., Toni, F.: A dialectic procedure for sceptical, assumption-based argumentation. In: Proceedings of the 1st International Conference on Computational Models of Argument, pp. 145–156 (2006)
10. Baroni, P., Giacomin, M., Guida, G.: SCC-recursiveness: a general schema for argumentation semantics. Artif. Intell. 168(1–2), 162–210 (2005)
11. Coste-Marquis,S., Devred, C., Marquis, P. : Prudent semantics for argumentation frameworks. In: Proceedings of the 17th International Conference on Tools with Artificial Intelligence, pp. 568–572 (2005)
12. Chapelle, O., Schölkopf, B., Zien, A.: Semi-Supervised Learning. The MIT Press, Cambridge (2010)
13. SYNCLON: Synclon$_\beta^3$ (2013). http://synclon3.com/
14. Egly, U., Gaggl, S., Woltran, S.: Aspartix: implementing argumentation frameworks using answer-set programming. In: Proceedings of the Twenty-Fourth International Conference on Logic Programming, pp. 734–738 (2008)
15. Amgoud, L., Serrurier, M.: Agents that argue and explain classifications. Auton. Agents Multi-Agent Syst. 16(2), 187–209 (2008)
16. Možina, M., Žabkar, J., Bratko, I.: Argument based machine learning. Artif. Intell. 171(10–15), 922–937 (2007)
17. Gao, Y., Toni, F.: Argumentation-based reinforcement learning for robocup soccer takeaway (extended abstract). In: Proceedings of the 13th International Conference on Autonomous Agents and Multiagent Systems, pp. 1411–1422 (2014)
18. Goldberg, A.B.: Dissimilarity in graph-based semisupervised classification. In: Proceedings of the 11th International Conference on Artificial Intelligence and Statistics (2007)
19. Kido, H.: Learning argument acceptability from abstract argumentation frameworks. In: Proceedings of the 2nd International Workshop on Argument for Agreement and Assurance, pp. 40–53 (2015)

Towards Better Crisis Management in Support Services Organizations Using Fine Grained Agent Based Simulation

Vivek Balaraman[✉], Harshal Hayatnagarkar, Meghendra Singh,
and Mayuri Duggirala

Human Centric Systems, TCS Research, 54-B Hadapsar Industrial Estate, Pune, India
{vivek.balaraman,h.hayatnagarkar2,meghendra.singh,
mayuri.duggirala}@tcs.com

Abstract. Critical support service operations have to run 24 × 7 and 365 days a year. Support operations therefore do contingency planning to continue operations during a crisis. In this paper we explore the use of fine-grained agent-based simulation models, which factor in human-behavioral dimensions such as stress, as a means to do better people planning for such situations. We believe the use of this approach may allow support operations managers to do more nuanced planning leading to higher resilience, and quicker return to normalcy. We model a prototypical support operation, which runs into different crisis severity levels, and show for each case, a reasonable size of the crisis team that would be required. We identify two contributions in this paper: First, emergency planning using agent based simulations have mostly focused, naturally, on societal communities such as urban populations. There has not been much attention paid to study crisis responses within support services organizations and our work is an attempt to address this deficit. Second, our use of grounded behavioral elements in our agent models allows us to build complex human behavior into the agents without sacrificing validity.

Keywords: Agent based simulation · Crisis · Business continuity · Disaster resilience · Human behavior modelling

1 Motivation and Past Work

Crisis arising out of natural disasters include events such as earthquakes, floods, fires, droughts etc., while manmade causes include events such as riots, terrorism, wars or the collapse of share markets. The effects of such events have been studied in a wide range of contexts such as in terms of economic impact [1], humanitarian impact (e.g. after an earthquake [2]) and organizational impact where organizational responses and strategies to sudden, disruptive threats are of interest [3]. The focus of the current paper is on the impact of various crisis intensities on a support services organization, and how various mitigation strategies may reduce the impact and help return the organization to business as usual (BAU). Support services organizations provide critical services for clients such as voice-based customer support across a range of industries such as banking and finance, insurance, mortgage, healthcare, etc., as well as non-voice support for back office file processing in several industry domains. Given the criticality of their operations

© Springer International Publishing Switzerland 2016
M. Baldoni et al. (Eds.): PRIMA 2016, LNAI 9862, pp. 366–375, 2016.
DOI: 10.1007/978-3-319-44832-9_24

for the client's business, support services organizations follow stringent processes outlined in the contract between the organization and the client [4]. While most parts of the contract pertain to business as usual (BAU) situations, a vital part is the business continuity plan (BCP) which is "a management process that identifies potential factors that threaten an organization and provides a framework for building resilience and the capability for an effective response" [5, 6]. In this study we use an agent based simulation approach to study strategic decision making during a crisis in a prototypical support services organization. Our goals in this work were two: First, creating a realistic agent based virtual sandbox for organizational crisis-event management planners to design crises strategies. Second, to continue our approach of composing grounded agent behavior models (also described in [7]) applied here to crisis planning and response. Agent based modelling (ABM) has been used to develop frameworks on organization-level responses to crisis events such as floods [8] or explore how crisis response strategies would serve to enhance organizational resilience [9, 10]. A system dynamics model has been used in [11] to explore how organizations are likely to be prone to major disasters due to an accumulation of minor interruptions. A parallel stream of research has focused on development of simulated environments with crisis response as their focus to help test out crisis response strategies in a less expensive but realistic environment [12]. Building on these earlier works, we do granular modelling of an organizational crisis.

2 Model of Crisis Management in Support Services

The support services industry is known for its ability to keep operations going 24 × 7 while meeting stringent performance and service quality requirements even in the presence of challenges such as unexpected spikes in task arrival. Working under such conditions is stressful and affects both individual productivity and the productivity of teams. We have described elsewhere [13] a field study we did in a support services organization to understand the behavioral drivers behind absenteeism and productivity as well as the agent model we built using the findings to help the organization understand the dynamics and implications of the findings. In this section, we describe how we extend that model for business continuity planning (BCP) during a crisis, and how different strategies would lessen the impact and ease a quick return to BAU once the crisis ends.

We now define some terms used in the support services industry: (a) Task arrival rate: Rate at which tasks arrive at the beginning of each day; (b) Backlog: Unfinished tasks for an employee at the end of each work day; (c) Unplanned absenteeism: Unplanned leave taken by an employee; (d) Productivity: Capacity of an employee to do work related tasks per hour; (e) Turn-around-time (TAT): Time duration for a task from its arrival to completion in hours; (f) Bench strength: A pool of employees that is assigned work in case of absenteeism or increased workload, and calculated as percentage of original team size; (g) Crisis team: A pool of employees is formed at a different location than the original team's location, after the onset of the crisis and works only during crises; (h) Recovery time: A metric that quantifies the duration it took the simulated team to reach normal operation after a crisis event.

2.1   The Support Service Process – During BAU and During a Crisis

A support services organization receives work from the client's business environment, which generates the tasks that are dealt with by the services organization. Within the support organization, each task is allocated to the specific team that handle that class of tasks. The task is then added to the work pool for that team. Each task is usually independent of other tasks in the work pool. Given the task pool for a team, tasks may be allocated either by individuals picking up tasks from the task pool or an automatic allocation process. Incomplete tasks for end of each day become the backlog for the next day's operations. The total team size including bench strength is planned keeping in mind the mean time taken for each task and the task volume and its variability. While this is the setup for routine or BAU operation, crisis operations are managed differently (see Fig. 1). Once the crisis starts, the operation is then executed in whole or in part by another team called the 'Crisis Team'. The crisis team may consist of some of the regular team members who have relocated to a new location, an entirely new team at the new location or a mix of both. Some part of the Regular team may also continue work from the original location.

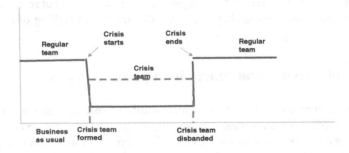

Fig. 1. Crisis situation plan – crisis team and regular team

Once the crisis ends, the Crisis Team is disbanded and the operations resume in full in the original location with only the Regular team. From a BCP perspective the question that a planner may want to understand are: For different levels of crisis intensity, and for the estimated task arrival during the crisis, what should be the size of the Crisis Team such that business is able to return to BAU as soon as possible? Faster the system is able to return to normalcy, better the business resilience.

2.2   Recapitulation of the Behavior Model

We recapitulate the behavior model we discussed in [14] for the convenience of the readers. The model ties together components of work related stressors, total accumulated stress, workplace absenteeism, worker productivity and workload. In the current paper, we use this model to do BCP, which factors in the human dimension. The behavior model (Fig. 2a) consists of a set of relations, each of which ties a behavior variable (such as a stressor) to another behavior variable (such as integrated stress) or to an outcome variable (such as productivity of an individual). Each relation in our model is grounded i.e. it comes from an empirical study or observation.

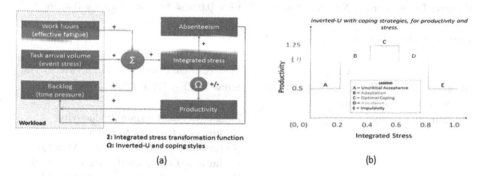

Fig. 2. (a) Behavior model and (b) Impact of coping strategies on productivity (1.0 = 100 %)

Some of the relations are from a field study we conducted at a support services organization, which looked at the behavior factors driving absenteeism and productivity [13]. Other relations are from other sources such as by Silverman [15] who proposed an integrated model of stress combining the Yerkes-Dodson Inverted U model [16] with the Janis-Mann coping taxonomy [17] to calculate values for the outcome variables of interest. Our approach (reported already in [14]) combines relations on stress from Silverman [15] with coping strategies reported in [19]. In this paper we use this model in the context of crisis management which is appropriate given that the relations in the integrated model are more closely aligned to the experience of stress in the support services context than alternative models, such as the JD-R model [20].

Our field study data showed that the three most important stress factors were long work hours, increase in the daily task arrival rate, and accumulated backlog. Silverman's integrated stress model too had three main components – Effective fatigue (EF), Event stress (ES), and Time pressure (TP). Our domain expert felt that these components map well to the stressors in our study as follows: Long work hours = Effective fatigue, Increase in the daily task arrival rate = Event stress, and Accumulated backlog = Time pressure. Each component varies in value between 0 and 1. We assume that all three components are additive and carry equal weightage. We define Integrated Stress as: Integrated Stress = (EF + ES + TP)/3.

Integrated Stress too thus varies between 0 and 1. Integrated Stress feeds into a decision module, which like in PMFServ, combines the Yerkes-Dodson Inverted U with the Janis-Mann Coping Strategy Levels to come up with a value for individual productivity (as given above in Fig. 2(b)). Integrated Stress thus becomes the predictor of productivity of an individual. Thus, (if one refers to Fig. 2(b)) when the agent is in State C the productivity of the agent would be 1.25 times the base productivity and when in State E, the productivity would be half the base productivity. The productivity of the individual feeds into the productivity of the team and which therefore then feeds back into the Workload. The fully composed model is given in Table 1 (fuller details on the model given in [14]).

Table 1. Composed behavior model, adapted from [14]

Relation	Model
Effective Fatigue (EF) ← Number of work hours	EF = 0.01054 * (Work Hours) + 0.4536;
Event stress (ES) ← Volume of task arrival	ES = (Task Arrival Today/2)/Mean Task Arrival
Time pressure (TP) ← Backlog	TP = (Current Backlog/2)/Mean Task Arrival
Integrated stress ← Effective Fatigue, Event stress, and Time pressure	Stress = (EF + ES + TP)/3

Productivity ← Stress	<u>Productivity = **M** * Base Productivity</u>
	If (Stress <= 0.2) then M = 0.5
	If (Stress > 0.2 && <= 0.4) then M = 1.0
	If (Stress > 0.4 && <= 0.6) then M = 1.25
	If (Stress > 0.6 && <= 0.8) then M = 1.0
	If (Stress > 0.8) then M = 0.5

P(Absenteeism) ← Stress	If stress > 0.8 then N(0.1, 0.1)

A question could be on why agent-agent interactions are not being modelled. The reason is that in a lot of the work in support services organization the tasks require just one person and tasks are independent thus requiring fewer interactions among peers. We thus model agent-task interactions and not agent-agent interactions. The agents are autonomous, are driven by the behavior model described above and react to events driven by a combination of their state, the event and the behavior model.

2.3 Crisis Process Model

The behavior model we have described is embedded in all the agents in our agent model. There are 2 sets of agents, one representing the regular team and the second, the agents representing the crisis team Fig. 3.

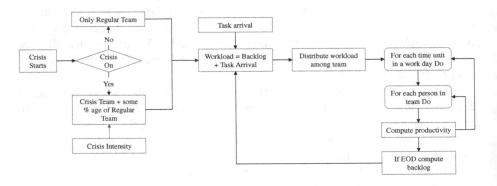

Fig. 3. Process model

Each agent in both teams is driven by the behavior model given in Sect. 2.3. In the wake of a crisis, the BCP should regulate business from regular team to crisis team, within the ambit of a process model. Following flowchart provides such a process model used in our simulation experiments.

2.4 Assumptions

In the simulation models we have discussed here as well as earlier work [13], we have retained only the most necessary environmental, situational and behavioral factors in the models, by making few assumptions. We simulate single support service workgroup within a support services organization. The simulated tasks are associated with only one business process, have the same complexity, and are independent of each other. All members of the regular team have the same base productivity while members of crisis team have 80 % of base productivity of the regular team. We felt this was a valid assumption as regular team members would be more efficient than a new team. All members of the crisis team become available at the start of crisis. All members of regular team become available at the end of the crisis. There is no productivity loss for members of original team who become available for work. Apart from unavailability of people, the crisis does not affect the organization in any other way, for example, infrastructure outage.

3   Experiments and Results

We model three crisis intensities using two dimensions: crisis duration and the percentage of the regular team being unavailable in that duration (see Table 2).

Table 2. The studied crisis scenarios

Intensity	% of regular team unavailable	Start day	Duration
Low	20 %	Day 6	2 days
Moderate	50 %	Day 6	5 days
High	75 %	Day 6	7 days

For each intensity, we varied the crisis team size as a percentage of initial team size from 0 % to 50 %. For each scenario, we had 10 runs. We used GAMA [18] for its powerful model specification language, good visualization capabilities and extensibility.

3.1   Time to Recover from Crises Induced Backlog

Due to the unavailability of a part of the team during a crisis, backlog is accumulated. The accumulated backlog acts as a stressor for the team and leads to lower productivity levels, which causes more backlog resulting in a vicious cycle. It can take many days for the accumulated backlog to reach normal levels and break this vicious cycle. Recovery time can be lessened by increasing the number of team members in the crisis team. In Fig. 4, we show the recovery time for three crisis intensities as described in Table 2, when the crisis team size is increased. We observe that, the simulated team recovers from low intensity crisis on the same day. However, with the increasing crisis intensity from low to moderate to high, the recovery time grows quickly. In fact, even if 50 % of the original team is deployed as crisis team, the recovery time is >0.

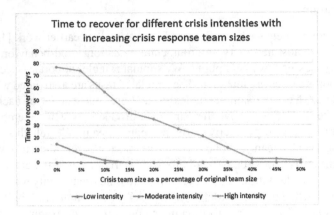

Fig. 4. Recovery time for different crisis intensities and crisis team sizes

3.2 Turn-Around Time

Similar to recovery time, the TAT for each task increases in the event of a crisis because of unavailability of workforce. Figure 5 shows the average TAT achieved by the simulated team as the crisis intensity and the available crisis team size is varied.

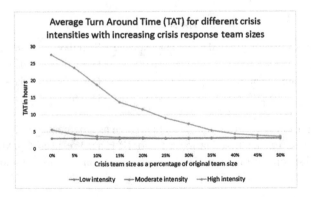

Fig. 5. Turn-around time for different crisis intensities and crisis team sizes

As the crisis intensity increases the TAT increases since more people remain unavailable for work for longer durations, leading to backlog accumulating which leads to an increase in the average TAT. As the crisis team size increases the average TAT reduces. We can see that for a high intensity crisis, a crisis team size of 50 % or more may be required to bring down TAT to BAU levels.

3.3   Time Spent in the Different Stress Coping Levels

Our behavior model predicts the stress coping level occupied by an agent at a point in time, which can be used to explain the results in the previous experiments. Since the backlog induced by a crisis event acts as a stressor for the simulated team the amount of time spent by the team in different coping levels changes when crisis intensity is changed. Since a crisis team acts as a bulwark against crisis induced backlog an increase in the crisis team size naturally leads to lower levels of stress among the individuals in the original team. This lower stress results in the team spending more time in the coping levels of adaptation and optimal coping leading to corresponding higher levels of productivity. Our analysis of time spent by the team in the five coping levels for a *low intensity crisis* and different crisis team sizes showed an insignificant change in the stress related coping behavior of the team as the crisis team size increases. This is primarily because a low intensity crisis event does not cause sufficient accumulation of backlog. However, for *moderate intensity crisis* we found that the stress related coping behavior of the team changes. Figure 6 shows that the change in coping behavior for the team when a high intensity crisis occurs is significantly different from low and moderate intensity crises scenarios. During a high intensity crisis if the crisis team is absent, the team spends a significant amount of time in the *avoidance coping* level. This results in sub optimal performance of the available team, leading to high backlog and TAT. As the size of the crisis team is increased, the overall stress on individual agents in the team is reduced. As the crisis team size reaches 50 % (half of the original team size), the stress related coping behavior becomes similar to that in the case of moderate intensity crisis.

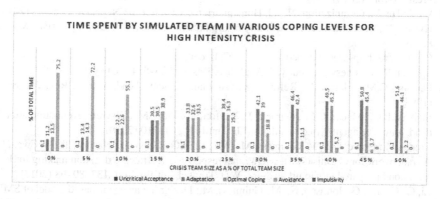

Fig. 6. Amount of time spent in various coping levels for a high intensity crisis.

4   Discussion and Conclusion

As summarized in Table 2, the crisis intensity from low to medium to high is attributed to the number of people unavailable and duration of unavailability. If we call the Impact Factor (IF) of a crisis as the product of these two numbers (and closely related to person-days lost), we see the IF of low, medium and high intensity crises as 0.4, 2.5 and 5.25, respectively. A high intensity crisis thus has more than 12 times the effect of a low intensity crisis. Without a crisis team, the original team takes approximately 80 days to recover from a high intensity crisis. It requires a crisis team 45 percent of the original team size for the operations to reach and maintain BAU during the crisis. A key takeaway from this study is in terms of developing a measure for crisis planning, namely, the Crisis-Team-Factor (CTF), which is a percentage of the original team such that BAU is maintained even during a crisis. Based on the results of the simulation, this would be 45 % of the original team for the high intensity crisis, 15 % for a medium intensity crisis, and same day recovery for a low intensity crisis. If the crisis team size is larger than mandated by the CTF, then it acts as an insurance to deal with more unanticipated workload.

The contributions of our paper are as follows: a fine grained model that embeds human behavioral dynamics, the model is ground in that each relation is based on past research and or studies and finally the creation of a virtual sandbox whose insights can be used for better planning of crisis responses based on what-if scenarios. In future, we intend to include factors like personality traits and emotion to drive agent behavior in an organization. We also intend to study the impact of a team's network structure on behavioral drivers like stress and coping. We believe that the combined influence of these extensions can produce interesting and dynamic agent behavior during crises.

References

1. Guha-Sapir, D., Santos, I.: The Economic Impacts of Natural Disasters. Oxford University Press, Oxford (2013)
2. World Health Organization, Nepal. Humanitarian crisis after the Nepal earthquakes (2015)
3. Hwang, P., Lichtenthal, J.D.: Anatomy of organizational crises. J. Conting. Crisis. Manag. **8**, 129–140 (2000)
4. Call Centre. https://en.wikipedia.org/wiki/Call_centre
5. Speight, P.: Business continuity. J. Appl. Sec. Res. **6**, 529–554 (2011)
6. Pearson, C.M., Clair, J.A.: Reframing crisis management. Acad. Manag. Rev. **23**, 59–76 (1998)
7. Siebers, P.O., Macal, C.M., Garnett, J., Buxton, D., Pidd, M.: Discrete-event simulation is dead, long live agent-based simulation! J. Simul. **4**, 204–210 (2010)
8. Coates, G., Hawe, G.I., McGuinness, M., Wright, N.G., Guan, D., Harries, T., McEwen, L.: A framework for organisational operational response and strategic decision making for long term flood preparedness in urban areas. WIT Trans. Built Environ. **133**, 89–98 (2013)
9. Li, C., Coates, G., Johnson, N., Mc Guinness, M.: Designing an agent-based model of SMEs to assess flood response strategies and resilience. Int. J. Soc. Educ. Econ. Manag. Eng. **9**, 7–12 (2015)
10. Li, C., Coates, G.: Design and development of an agent-based model for business operations faced with flood disruption. Complex Syst.: Fundam. Appl. **90**, 275 (2016)
11. Rudolph, J.W., Repenning, N.P.: Disaster dynamics: understanding the role of quantity in organizational collapse. Adm. Sci. Q. **47**, 1–30 (2002)
12. Balasubramanian, V., Massaguer, D., Mehrotra, S., Venkatasubramanian, N.: DrillSim: a simulation framework for emergency response drills. In: Mehrotra, S., Zeng, D.D., Chen, H., Thuraisingham, B., Wang, F.-Y. (eds.) ISI 2006. LNCS, vol. 3975, pp. 237–248. Springer, Heidelberg (2006)

13. Singh M., Duggirala M., Hayatnagarkar H., Balaraman V.: Multi-agent model of workgroup behavior in an enterprise using a compositional approach. In: Second Modeling Symposium (ModSym), ISEC (2016)
14. Duggirala M., Singh M., Hayatnagarkar H., Patel S., Balaraman V.: Understanding Impact of Stress on Workplace Outcomes Using an Agent Based Simulation, Summer Simulation Multi-Conference (2016, forthcoming)
15. Silverman, B.G.: More Realistic Human Behavior Models for Agents in Virtual World: Emotion, stress, and value ontologies (2001). http://www.seas.upenn.edu/~barryg/TechRpt.pdf
16. Yerkes, R.M., Dodson, J.D.: The relation of strength of stimulus to rapidity of habit-formation. J. Comp. Neurol. Psychol. **18**(5), 459–482 (1908)
17. Janis, I.L., Mann, L.: Decision Making: A Psychological Analysis of Conflict, Choice, and Commitment. Free Press, New York (1977)
18. Grignard, A., Taillandier, P., Gaudou, B., Vo, D.A., Huynh, N.Q., Drogoul, A.: GAMA 1.6: advancing the art of complex agent-based modeling and simulation. In: Boella, G., Elkind, E., Savarimuthu, B.T.R., Dignum, F., Purvis, M.K. (eds.) PRIMA 2013. LNCS, vol. 8291, pp. 117–131. Springer, Heidelberg (2013)
19. Connor-Smith, J.K., Flachsbart, C.: Relations between personality and coping: a meta-analysis. J. Pers. Soc. Psychol. **93**(6), 1080 (2007)
20. Bakker, A.B., Demerouti, E.: The job demands-resources model: state of the art. J. Manag. Psychol. **22**, 309–328 (2007)

Plan Failure Analysis: Formalization and Application in Interactive Planning Through Natural Language Communication

Chitta Baral[1], Tran Cao Son[2(✉)], Michael Gelfond[3], and Arindam Mitra[1]

[1] Department of Computer Science and Engineering, Arizona State University,
Tempe, AZ, USA
[2] Department of Computer Science, New Mexico State University,
Las Cruces, NM, USA
tson@cs.nmsu.edu
[3] Department of Computer Science, Texas Tech University, Lubbock, TX, USA

Abstract. While most robots in human robot interaction scenarios take instructions from humans, the ideal would be that humans and robots collaborate with each other. The Defense Advanced Research Projects Agency Communicating with Computer program proposes the collaborative blocks world scenario as a testbed for this. This scenario requires the human and the computer to communicate through natural language to build structures out of toy blocks. To formulate and address this, we identify two main tasks. The first task, called the *plan failure analysis*, demands the robot to analyze the feasibility of a task and to determine the reasons(s) in case the task is not doable. The second task focuses on the ability of the robot to *understand communications via natural language*. We discuss potential solutions to both problems and present prototypical architecture for the integration of planning failure analysis and natural language communication into an intelligent agent architecture.

Keywords: Human-robot interaction (HRI) · Planning · Plan failure analysis · Natural language communication

1 Introduction

Human-robot interaction is an important field where humans and robots collaborate to achieve tasks. Such interaction is needed, for example, in search and rescue scenarios where the human may direct the robot to do certain tasks and at times the robot may have to make its own plan. Although there has been many works on this topic, there has not been much research on interactive planning where the human and the robot collaborate in making plans. For such interactive planning, the human may communicate to the robot about some goals and the robot may make a plan to achieve them. If planning fails the robot may explain the failure, and the human may use the explanation to make suggestions for

© Springer International Publishing Switzerland 2016
M. Baldoni et al. (Eds.): PRIMA 2016, LNAI 9862, pp. 376–386, 2016.
DOI: 10.1007/978-3-319-44832-9_25

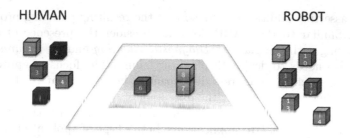

Fig. 1. A blocks world example

overcoming the problem. This interaction may continue until a plan is made and executed. Let us consider an example of such an interactive planning.

Consider the block world domain in Fig. 1 [9]. The robot has its own blocks and the human has some blocks. The two share a table and some other blocks on the table. Suppose that the human communicates to the robot the sentence "*Add another blue stack of the same height!*"

Even if we assume that the robot is able to recognize the color of the blocks, create, and execute plans for constructions of stacks of blocks, such a communication presents several challenges to a robot. Specifically, it requires that the robot is capable of understanding natural language, i.e., it requires that the robot is able to identify that

- the human refers to stacks of only blue blocks;
- the human refers to the height of a stack as the number of blocks on the stack;
- there is a blue stack of the height 2 on the table; and
- it should use its two blue blocks to build a new stack of two blue blocks.

In addition to the above, it is easy to see that the robot cannot accomplish the task in the situation in Fig. 1 if it is limited to the typical actions in the block domain (e.g., pick up, put down, or un/stack blocks) and uses only its own blocks. It is because of its planning process—looking for a plan to create a stack of two blue blocks—fails. *What should the robot do? Can it reply back that it needs an additional blue block? Can it ask for the blue block of the human?* In this paper, we address this task of plan failure analysis.

Previous approaches to dealing with the planning failure problem have been proposed. *Partial satisfaction planning* (PSP) identifies a maximal subset of the goal (or a sub-formula; or a collection of subgoals with a maximal aggregated ultility) that can be satisfied (e.g., [4]). This approach does not take into consideration the fact that some actions/fluents are not considered in the planning process and/or the presence of a human user interacting with the planner. Applications of planning system in the literature such as mixed-initiative (e.g., [1,2,14]) emphasize the need for interaction between a human user and a planning system. However, the human user plays the primary role in the generation of a working plan. *Assumption-based planning* [10] assumes that the planning agent does not have complete information about the world and thus focuses on asserting additional facts so that the resulting planning problem has a solution. Similar to PSP, ABP does not consider the presence of a human user interacting with the planner. *Diagnostic planning* and/or *replanning* (e.g., [5,11,12]) also needs to deal with planning failure. The focus of approaches in this line of research is to address discrepancies between what is observed and what is hypothetically true after the execution of a sequence of actions.

In this paper, we propose an orthogonal approach to deal with planning failure within the context of HRI applications. In this type of applications, the robot understands a basic set of vocabularies for communication with the human user and is actively engaged in dealing with the failure of the planning process. It will identify possible reasons for the failure and possible course of actions for recovering from the failure. To achieve this goal, we formalize the *planning failure analysis problem* and introduce a notion called a *failure analysis* of a planning problem with respect to an extension (Sect. 2). We propose a potential solution for the natural language understanding problem and describe a system that translates communications from a human user into an answer set programming representation (Sect. 3). We discuss how the proposed components can be integrated into an intelligent agent architecture that allows agents to interactively planning with humans through natural language communication (Sect. 4).

2   Planning Failure Analysis: Formalization

A planning problem is specified by a tuple $\mathcal{P} = \langle F, A, I, G \rangle$ where F is a set of fluents (time-dependent Boolean variables), A is a set of actions with their preconditions and (conditional) effects, I describes the initial state, and G describes the goal state. $\langle F, A \rangle$ is often referred to as the domain of the planning problem.

A fluent literal is a fluent f or its negation $\neg f$. A set of fluent literals S is consistent if it does not contain f and its negation $\neg f$. S is complete if for every $f \in F$, either $f \in S$ or $\neg f \in S$. Each *action* $a \in A$ is associated with a consistent set of literals, $pre(a)$, called the precondition of a; and a set $e(a)$ of conditional effects of the form $\varphi \rightarrow \psi$ where φ and ψ are consistent sets of literals. Intuitively, $\varphi \rightarrow \psi$ says that when a is executed in a state satisfying φ then ψ is true in the resulting state.

A *state* is an interpretation of F, i.e., a complete and consistent set of fluent literals. Truth value of a fluent formula in a state is evaluated in the standard way. If φ is true in a state s, we write $s \models \varphi$. A set of fluent literals is viewed as conjunction of literals belonging to it. For an action a and a state s, let $es(a, s) = \bigcup_{\varphi \rightarrow \psi \in e(a), s \models \varphi} \psi$. The semantics of $\mathcal{P}$ is defined by a transition function Φ that maps each pair of a state s and an action a into a state denoted by $\Phi(a, s)$. Formally, $\Phi(a, s)$ is defined as follows: $\Phi(a, s) = s \setminus \overline{es(a, s)} \cup es(a, s)$ if $s \models pre(a)$ where $\overline{es(a, s)} = \{\bar{l} \mid l \in es(a, s)\}$ and for every $f \in F$, $\bar{f} = \neg f$ and $\overline{\neg f} = f$; otherwise, $\Phi(a, s)$ is undefined. This function is extended to define $\Phi^*([a_1, \ldots, a_n], s)$ as (i) $\Phi^*([], s) = s$; and (ii) $\Phi^*([a_1, \ldots, a_n], s) = \Phi(a_n, \Phi^*([a_1, \ldots, a_{n-1}], s))$.

A state is called the initial state of $\mathcal{P}$ if it satisfies I. A plan of length n for G is a sequence of actions $[a_1, \ldots, a_n]$ (or a solution of $\mathcal{P}$) if for every state s_0 satisfying I, $\Phi^*([a_1, \ldots, a_n], s_0)$ is defined and satisfies G.

Example 1. The block domain in Fig. 1—in the view of the robot—can be represented by the planning domain $\langle F_b, A_b \rangle$ with a set of constants[1] denoting the human (h), the robot (r), the set of blocks $Blks = \{b_1, \ldots, b_{14}\}$, $F_b = \{on(B_1, B_2), has(X, B), ontable(B), holding(X, B), clear(B), handempty, color(B, C)\}$ and $A_b = \{pick(B), putdown(B), stack(B_1, B_2), unstack(B_1, B_2), takes(B)\}$ where $X \in \{h, r\}$, C is one of the colors, and $B, B_1, B_2 \in Blks$ are blocks with $B_1 \neq B_2$. Preconditions and effects of actions are defined as usually, e.g., for the action of picking up a block from the table or taking its own block, they are:

- $pre(pick(B)) = \{handempty, ontable(B), clear(B)\}$
- $e(pick(B)) = \{\emptyset \rightarrow \{holding(B), \neg ontable(B), \neg handempty, \neg clear(B)\}\}$
- etc.

We omit the description of other actions for brevity. The planning problem discussed in the first section can be represented by $\mathcal{P}_b = \langle F_b, A_b, I_b, G_b \rangle$ with I_b encodes the configuration in Fig. 1 and G_b be the following formula:

$$\bigvee_{x \neq y \in Blks, \{x,y\} \cap \{b_7, b_8\} = \emptyset} \begin{bmatrix} color(x, blue) \wedge color(y, blue) \wedge \\ ontable(x) \wedge on(y, x) \wedge clear(y) \end{bmatrix}$$

We will now formally define the planning failure analysis problem. The above discussion leads us to the definition.

Definition 1. *Let* $\mathcal{P} = \langle F, A, I, G \rangle$ *be a planning problem. We say that* $\mathcal{P}$ *needs a failure analysis if it has no solution.*

We can easily check that $\mathcal{P}_b$ does not have a solution and thus needs a failure analysis. Realizing that a planning problem needs a failure analysis is identical with checking whether it has a solution or not. As such, the complexity of the problem of identifying whether or not a planning problem needs a failure analysis is the same as that of planning. It is known that the complexity of planning is undecidable in the general case [13]. Under certain assumptions (e.g., finite and deterministic domains), it reduces to PSPACE-complete [6]. For planning problems considered in this paper, if we limit the length of plans then the complexity reduces to NP-complete. We will next focus on answering the question of why the planning process fails and what can one do when the planning problem has no solution. *We start with the assumption that changes can be caused only by actions.* Thus, one way to rectify this problem is to provide additional actions that could be used in creating a plan.

---

[1] Fluents/actions with variables are shorthands for collections of their ground instantiations. The formalization used in this example is a variant of the block world domain representation in planning benchmarks and assumes that each block has a unique color. The goal is simplified to be "build a stack of two blue blocks."

Definition 2. *An extension to a planning problem* $\mathcal{P} = \langle F, A, I, G \rangle$ *is a pair* $(Afs, Acts)$ *where* Afs *is a set of fluents and* $Acts$ *is a set of actions such that* $F \cap Afs = \emptyset$ *and* $A \cap Acts = \emptyset$.

Intuitively, $Acts$ is the set of actions that the planning agent (robot) could execute and Afs could be the set of fluents, which occur in the definition of $Acts$ and do not belong to F. Observe that $Acts$ could change the fluents in F and their definitions could introduce new fluents. It can contain actions that the robot cannot use without permission and/or execute independently. Note that this is different from *planning with preferences*, which considers that the actions are available at the robot's disposal but the robot prefers not to use them.

In our running example, $Acts$ could be the set with a single action *ask_permission* whose precondition is empty (true) and whose effect is that the robot can use the human's blocks in solving the problem[2], i.e., $e(ask\_permission) = \{\{has(h, B)\} \rightarrow \{has(r, B)\} \mid B \in Blks\}$; $Afs = \emptyset$ since every fluent occurring in the definition of *ask_permission* also belongs to F. For later reference, we will denote with $\mathcal{E}_1$ the extension $(\emptyset, \{ask\_permission\})$ to $\mathcal{P}_b$. Notice that this extension can be refined by the extension $\mathcal{E}_2 = (\emptyset, \{ask\_permission(B) \mid B \in Blks\})$ where, for each $b \in Blks$, $ask\_permission(b)$ has the precondition $\{has(h, b)\}$ and an effect $\emptyset \rightarrow \{has(r, b)\}$.

Given an extension $\mathcal{E} = (Afs, Acts)$ to a planning problem $\mathcal{P} = \langle F, A, I, G \rangle$, what could be a failure analysis for $\mathcal{P}$ w.r.t. $\mathcal{E}$? The above discussion suggests that it could be a pair (Af, Ac) with $Af \subseteq Afs$ and $Ac \subseteq Acts$ such that $\mathcal{P}^* = \langle F \cup Af, A \cup Ac, I \cup Af^*, G \rangle$ has a solution where Af^* is an interpretation of the set of fluents Af. By this definition, $\mathcal{E}_1$ is an analysis for $\mathcal{P}_b$ w.r.t. $\mathcal{E}_1$ since $\mathcal{P}^* = \langle F, A \cup \{ask\_permission\}, I, G \rangle$ has a solution. Similarly, we can check that for every $X \subseteq \{ask\_permission(B) \mid B \in Blks\}$ such that $ask\_permission(b_1) \in X$, $(\emptyset, X)$ is an analysis for $\mathcal{P}_b$ w.r.t. $\mathcal{E}_2$.

The above definition appears reasonable for $\mathcal{E}_1$ and $\mathcal{E}_2$. However, it allows the possibility of *wishful analysis* as in the next example. Let us consider the extension $\mathcal{E}_3 = (\{color(b_{10}, blue)\}, \emptyset)$, i.e., the robot wishes that the color of another block in its possession is blue. If we were to use the above definition then $\mathcal{E}_3$ is also an analysis for $\mathcal{P}_b$ w.r.t. $\mathcal{E}_3$. Clearly, this analysis is not practical for $\mathcal{P}_b$ since the robot cannot change the color of a block. On the other hand, $\mathcal{E}_4 = (\{color(b_{10}, blue), paint\_available\}, \{paint\_blue(b_{10}), buy\_paint\})$ where buy_paint causes $paint\_available$ to be true and $paint\_blue(b_{10})$ causes the block 10 to be blue is an extension of $\mathcal{P}_b$ and is itself an analysis for $\mathcal{P}_b$.

Definition 3. *Let* $\mathcal{P} = \langle F, A, I, G \rangle$ *be a planning problem and* $\alpha = [a_1, \ldots, a_n]$ *be one of its solution. We say that a fluent* f *changes its value during the execution of* α, *denoted by* $\pm f \xrightarrow{\alpha} \mp f$, *if there exist some* $1 \leq j < n$ *such that* f *is true (resp. false)* $\Phi^*([a_1, \ldots, a_{j-1}], s_0)$ *and false (resp. true) in* $\Phi^*([a_1, \ldots, a_j], s_0)$.

---

[2] Observe that the action *ask_permission*(.) refers to a communication between the robot and the human user and thus is not included in the initial planning domain of $\mathcal{P}_b$. Furthermore, we assume that the human is collaborative and thus would grant the robot the permission to use his blocks.

If we require that the fluent that are added to the domain change their values in the plans that could be generated, then $\mathcal{E}_3$ cannot be used to provide an analysis for $\mathcal{P}_b$. Observe that there are situations in which wishful analyses might be useful. For example, when the robot does not have complete information about the world (e.g., its sensors are imperfect and the robot know that the information about the initial state can be incorrect, or the robot executes a plan and observes something unexpected). This issue has been investigated in [11] or in the literature on diagnostic planning and/or replanning. As discussed, the focus of the present work is different.

Definition 4. *Let* $\mathcal{E} = (Afs, Acts)$ *be an extension to the planning problem* $\mathcal{P} = \langle F, A, I, G \rangle$. *A pair* (Af, Ac) *such that* $Af \subseteq Afs$ *and* $Ac \subseteq Acts$ *is called a* plan failure analysis *for* $\mathcal{P}$ *w.r.t.* $\mathcal{E}$ *(or an analysis for* $\mathcal{P}$, *for short) if there exists an interpretation* Af^* *of the set of fluents* Af *and* $\mathcal{P}^* = \langle F \cup Af, A \cup Ac, I \cup Af^*, G \rangle$ *has a solution* α *such that* $\pm f \xrightarrow{\alpha} \mp f$ *for every* $f \in Af$.

   When $Af = Ac = \emptyset$, *we say that it is a* no-fault analysis; *otherwise, it is a* non-trivial *analysis*.

By the above definition, we can see that $\mathcal{E}_1$ is an analysis for $\mathcal{P}_b$ w.r.t. $\mathcal{E}_1$ but $\mathcal{E}_3$ is not an analysis for $\mathcal{P}_b$ w.r.t. $\mathcal{E}_3$. Definition 4 characterizes analyses as those that introduce new fluents and actions into the planning problem so that they will be useful in creating a solution for the new planning problem. In general, we prefer analyses that change the planning problem in a minimal way. For example, $(\emptyset, \{ask\_permission(b_1)\})$ could be viewed as better than $(\emptyset, \{ask\_permission(b_1), ask\_permission(b_2)\})$ w.r.t. $\mathcal{E}_2$ as the former asks for less from the human.

Definition 5. *Let* $\mathcal{E} = (Afs, Acts)$ *be an extension to the planning problem* $\mathcal{P} = \langle F, A, I, G \rangle$. *Let* (Af, Ac) *and* (Af', Ac') *be two plan failure analyses for* $\mathcal{P}$ *w.r.t.* $\mathcal{E}$. *We say that* (Af, Ac) *is a* more preferred failure analysis *than* (Af', Ac'), *denoted* $(Af, Ac) \prec (Af', Ac')$, *if* $Ac \subsetneq Ac'$.

   An analysis (Af, Ac) *is said to be a* most preferred analysis *for* $\mathcal{P}$ *w.r.t.* $\mathcal{E}$ *if there exists no other analysis that is more preferred than* (Af, Ac).

By Definition 5, it is easy to see that $(\emptyset, \{ask\_permission(b_1)\})$ is the most preferred failure analysis for $\mathcal{P}_b$ w.r.t $\mathcal{E}_2$. We prove that the relation $\prec$ is a partial order over the set of analyses for a planning problem.

Proposition 1. *For a planning problem* $\mathcal{P} = \langle F, A, I, G \rangle$ *and an extension* $\mathcal{E} = (Afs, Acts)$ *to* $\mathcal{P}$, *the following holds:* (i) $\prec$ *defines a partial ordering over the set of failure analyses for* $\mathcal{P}$ *w.r.t.* $\mathcal{E}$; *and* (ii) *if* $(\emptyset, \emptyset)$ *is an analysis for* $\mathcal{P}$ *then it is the unique most preferred analysis for* $\mathcal{P}$ *w.r.t.* $\mathcal{E}$.

It is reasonable to assume that given a planning problem $\mathcal{P} = \langle F, A, I, G \rangle$ there exists an extension $\mathcal{E}$ to $\mathcal{P}$ that covers all possible failure analyses for $\mathcal{P}$ should it need a failure analysis. For example, the robot in our running example should be able to assume that it can ask the human for permission to use the human's blocks in responding to the command (as in $\mathcal{E}_1$ or $\mathcal{E}_2$); or it has, at its disposal, actions for changing the color of a block (as in $\mathcal{E}_4$); or all of these (as in $\mathcal{E}_1 \cup \mathcal{E}_2 \cup \mathcal{E}_4$). However, the fact that the robot cannot make unreasonable assumptions such as the color of a block could change by itself (as in $\mathcal{E}_3$) should be taken into consideration. Specifying $\mathcal{E}$ is therefore problem-dependent and is out of the scope of this paper. We note that the proposed notion of plan failure analysis has been proposed by in our earlier work [3]. The formalization proposed in this paper only shares Definition 1 with the earlier one.

3   Natural Languge to Answer Set Programming (ASP)

The previous section deals with the planning failure analysis problem, assuming that the robot understands the commands from the human user. Computing planning failure analyses can be done using *logic programming under answer set semantics* [15] and can be implemented similar to the proposal in [3]. For space reason, we omit the discussion on computing planning failure analyses. In this section, we focus on providing this capability to the robot. Specifically, we describe a translation system that represents the communicative signals of a human in machine understandable terms. It is a relatively well-studied problem in Natural Language Processing (NLP) and popularly known as *semantic parsing* [17]. A semantic parser maps natural language sentences to a formal representation language (such as) to allow automated inference and processing. Recently several powerful systems have been developed to build a semantic parser for varied target representations [7,16,18–20,22,23]. In this research, we have trained the NL2KR system [22] for the task of translation.

In NL2KR, the meaning of words and phrases are expressed as λ-calculus [8] expressions. The meaning of a sentence is built from the semantics of constituent words through appropriate λ-calculus applications. The parse tree of

Table 1. A set of human commands and their representation in an intermediate language. NL2KR has been trained on these sentences to translate new sentences similar to these sentences. A small program is written to convert the intermediate formal representation to the syntax of ASP.

Sentence	Meaning
Add another blue stack of the same height.	$\lambda x.\ goal\_cond(x,\ op,\ add) \wedge goal\_cond(x,\ is,\ stack) \wedge goal\_cond(x,\ color,\ blue) \wedge goal\_cond(x,\ height,\ same) \wedge goal\_cond(x,\ type,\ another).$
Take my blocks.	$\lambda x.\ add\_block(has\_robot(x),\ has(human,\ x) \wedge block(x)).$
How about a red stack of the same height as the blue stack?	$\lambda x.\ goal\_cond(x,\ is,\ stack) \wedge goal\_cond(x,\ color,\ red) \wedge goal\_cond(x,\ height,\ same) \wedge goal\_cond(x,\ origin,\ blue) \wedge goal\_cond(x,\ type,\ another).$
Add another stack of the same height as the tallest stack.	$\lambda x.\ goal\_cond(x,\ op,\ add) \wedge goal\_cond(x,\ is,\ stack) \wedge goal\_cond(x,\ height,\ tallest) \wedge goal\_cond(x,\ type,\ another).$

the sentence in Combinatory Categorial Grammar [21] (henceforth CCG) directs how the words are combined to produce the meaning of the sentence. During training NL2KR takes as input: (1) a set of training sentences and their target formal representation, and (2) an initial lexicon or dictionary consisting of some words, their CCG categories and meanings in terms of λ-calculus expressions. It then produces a bigger lexicon that is used in translation. For this work, the training set contained the sentences shown in Table 1. For the translation of a new sentence into the syntax of ASP, the λ-calculus expression of the sentence is first obtained. A small program then adds syntactic sugar to the λ-calculus expression to make it a valid ASP statement.

Consider the sentence "*Take my blocks*" from the Table 1. Let us say that the initial dictionary contains two entries as shown in Table 2. The first entry says that the word "take" with the CCG category "S/NP" has the meaning $\lambda p.\lambda x.\ use(has\_robot(x),\ p\ @x)$. The second entry provides a meaning of the word "blocks" for the category "NP".

Table 2. A sample *initial* dictionary containing two entries.

Word	CCG	Meaning
Take	S/NP	$\lambda p.\lambda x.\ add\_block(has\_robot(x),\ p\ @x)$
Blocks	NP	$\lambda x.\ block(x)$

Given this information, NL2KR then learns the meaning of the unknowns i.e. the phrase "my blocks" and the word "my" in the following way. It first obtains the CCG parse tree (Fig. 2) of the input sentence. A CCG parse tree shows how the words are combined together to characterize the meaning of the sentence. For example, the CCG in Fig. 2 indicates that the determiner (NP/N) "my" takes the noun (N) "blocks" as the input to produce the meaning of the noun phrase (NP) "my blocks".

The verb (S/NP) "take" then scoops the noun phrase (NP) "my blocks" to produce the meaning of the sentence (S) "take my blocks". With the CCG parse tree in hand, NL2KR then uses an operation called "Inverse-λ" to obtain the meaning of the phrase "my blocks" as "$\lambda x.has(human, x) \wedge block(x)$" from the meaning of "take" and "take my blocks". The "Inverse-λ" operator takes two λ-expressions, H (the root node) and G (the left child or the right child) and returns the λ-expression F for the other child such that either $H = G@F$ (when G is the left child) or $H = F@G$ (when G is the right child). Finally, it obtains the meaning of the word "my" $\lambda x8.\lambda x6.has(human, x6) \wedge x8@x6$ by "Inverse-λ" from the meaning of "my blocks" and "blocks" and saves it in the final dictionary for use during the translation of new sentences.

Furthermore, NL2KR uses a operation called "generalization" to handle unknown words. For example, given a new sentence "Use my blocks" NL2KR will generalize the meaning of "use" by the meaning of "take" to translate it

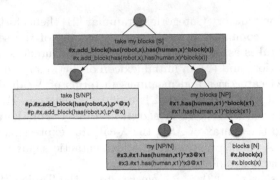

Fig. 2. An augmented CCG parse tree for the sentence "take my blocks" obtained from NL2KR. Each node shows the CCG category, the text description and the λ-expression associated with that node. NL2KR treats '#' as 'λ'.

to "$\lambda x.\ add\_block(has\_robot(x),\ has(human,\ x) \wedge block(x))$". A λ-to-ASP procedure will then convert the λ expression to the desired ASP representation, $add\_block(has\_robot(S) \leftarrow has(human,\ S),\ block(S))$.

4   Discussion

The components described in the previous sections are developed in response to the challenge given in [9]. Since a non-trivial analysis represents a reason for the failure of the planning process, an intelligent agent (robot) working interactively with a human user can use failure analyses to explain to him/her why it fails to achieve the goal. In fact, we envision that the proposed components can be integrated into a general architecture for a robot to interactively working with a human user as in Fig. 3.

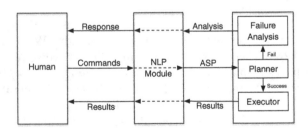

Fig. 3. Schematic integration of planning failure analysis and NLP module into an intelligent agent architecture

We will next discuss additional tasks that are required for an end-to-end implementation of the architecture in Fig. 3. The first task is to compute the plan failure analyses that can be computed using answer set programming.

The second task is related to the planning component of the robot. In general, the planner is supposed to plan for goals of arbitrary formulae over the set of fluents of the planning domain. Yet, it is expected that a communication between the human and the robot would sometimes contain directives that do not belong to the language of the planning domain (e.g., 'same', 'height', 'tallest', 'another', etc.). As demonstrated, our translation system can learn new vocabularies[3] and translates these directives to new statements representing in the language of the planner. We believe that if other state-of-the-art off-the-shelf planning systems (e.g., FF, Fast Downward, etc.) are used, converting the new directives to a formula might be more suitable. How to train our translation system for this task and what is the impact on the performance of the system are two very interesting questions that we leave for future research.

5   Conclusions

We discuss challenges in development of intelligent agents that interact with humans in planning. We introduce the notion of a planning failure analysis for a planning problem given its extension and also show that failure analyses can be computed using ASP and used for generating responses. We describe a translation system that can convert natural language communications to ASP goals. We discuss how the proposed components can be integrated into an overall architecture for developing intelligent agents that interact with human in problem solving and describe additional tasks that need to be completed.

References

1. Ai-Chang, M., Bresina, J., Charest, L., Chase, A., Hsu, J.C.J., Jonsson, A., Kanefsky, B., Morris, P., Rajan, K., Yglesias, J., Chafin, B.G., Dias, W.C., Maldague, P.F.: Mapgen: mixed-initiative planning and scheduling for the Mars Exploration Rover Mission. IEEE Intell. Syst. **19**, 8–12 (2004)
2. Allen, J.F., Ferguson, G.: Human-machine collaborative planning. In: Proceedings of 3rd International Workshop on Planning and Scheduling for Space (2002)
3. Baral, C., Son, T.C.: "Add another blue stack of the same height!": ASP based planning and plan failure analysis. In: Calimeri, F., Ianni, G., Truszczynski, M. (eds.) LPNMR 2015. LNCS, vol. 9345, pp. 127–133. Springer, Heidelberg (2015)
4. Benton, J., Do, M.B., Kambhampati, S.: Anytime heuristic search for partial satisfaction planning. Artif. Intell. **173**(5–6), 562–592 (2009)
5. Brafman, R.I., Shani, G.: Replanning in domains with partial information and sensing actions. J. Artif. Intell. Res. **45**, 565–600 (2012)
6. Bylander, T.: The computational complexity of propositional strips planning. Artif. Intell. **69**(1–2), 165–204 (1994)
7. Chen, D.L., Mooney, R.J.: Learning to interpret natural language navigation instructions from observations (2011)

---

[3] If it cannot deal with a new word, the system should respond by asking for an alternative or about the meaning of the word.

8. Church, A.: An unsolvable problem of elementary number theory. Am. J. Math. **58**(2), 345–363 (1936)
9. DARPA: Communicating with Computers (CwC) (2015)
10. Davis-Mendelow, S., Baier, J.A., McIlraith, S.A.: Assumption-based planning: generating plans and explanations under incomplete knowledge. In: Proceedings of AAAI (2013)
11. De Giacomo, G., Reiter, R., Soutchanski, M.: Execution monitoring of high-level robot programs. In: Principles of Knowledge Representation and Reasoning, pp. 453–465. Morgan Kaufmann Publishers (1998)
12. Erdem, E., Patoglu, V., Saribatur, Z.G.: Integrating hybrid diagnostic reasoning in plan execution monitoring for cognitive factories with multiple robots. In: ICRA (2015)
13. Erol, K., Nau, D., Subrahmanian, V.: Complexity, decidability and undecidability results for domain-independent planning. Artif. Intell. **76**(1–2), 75–88 (1995)
14. Ferguson, G., Allen, J.F.: Trips: An integrated intelligent problem-solving assistant. In: Proceedings of AAAI, pp. 567–572 (1998)
15. Gelfond, M., Lifschitz, V.: Logic programs with classical negation. In: Proceedings of 7th International Conference on Logic Programming, pp. 579–597 (1990)
16. Ge, R., Mooney, R.J.: Learning a compositional semantic parser using an existing syntactic parser. In: JCAMACL and IJCNLP, pp. 611–619. Association for Computational Linguistics (2009)
17. Kate, R.J., Wong, Y.W., Mooney, R.J.: Learning to transform natural to formal languages. In: Proceedings of AAAI 2005 (2005)
18. Kwiatkowski, T., Zettlemoyer, L., Goldwater, S., Steedman, M.: Inducing probabilistic CCG grammars from logical form with higher-order unification. In: EMNLP, pp. 1223–1233. ACL (2010)
19. Kwiatkowski, T., Zettlemoyer, L., Goldwater, S., Steedman, M.: Lexical generalization in CCG grammar induction for semantic parsing. In: EMNLP, pp. 1512–1523. ACL (2011)
20. Mooney, R.J.: Learning for semantic parsing. In: Gelbukh, A. (ed.) CICLing 2007. LNCS, vol. 4394, pp. 311–324. Springer, Heidelberg (2007)
21. Steedman, M.: The Syntactic Process. MIT Press, Cambridge (2000)
22. Vo, N.H., Mitra, A., Baral, C.R.: The NL2KR platform for building natural language translation systems. In: Association for Computational Linguistics (ACL) (2015)
23. Zettlemoyer, L.S., Collins, M.: Online learning of relaxed CCG grammars for parsing to logical form. In: EMNLP-CoNLL, pp. 678–687 (2007)

Automatic Evacuation Management Using a Multi Agent System and Parallel Meta-Heuristic Search

Leonel Aguilar, Maddegedara Lalith(✉), Tsuyoshi Ichimura, and Muneo Hori

Earthquake Research Institute, The University of Tokyo,
Bunkyo, Tokyo 113-0032, Japan
{leaguilar,lalith,ichimura,hori}@eri.u-tokyo.ac.jp

Abstract. An automatic evacuation management system taking advantage of a multi agent based mass evacuation simulator is proposed and prototyped. The aim of this system is to provide a stepping stone in the direction of automated evacuation managing. The proposed system is currently capable of identifying evacuation anomalies, proposing a mitigation strategy and providing feedback for human expert evaluation and query. All the pieces although seamlessly connected are independently developed. This allows their independent improvement and evaluation. This paper provides an overview of the developed automatic evacuation management system and all of its components, a demonstrative example, and discussion of its current limitations and future development direction. The demonstrative example shows increases of more than 10 % in the evacuation throughput by using the proposed system.

1 Introduction

The complexity and scale of mass evacuations provide extensive challenges in their analysis, management and planning. Due to the inability to perform real life drills and the scarcity of these events, researchers and planners have opted to rely on simulations. As the size of the evacuations grow the amount of data generated by the simulators become impractical for human analysis. Methods and techniques need to be developed to process this data and provide useful information for evacuation planners. It is in this context that the usage of an evacuation simulation tool for automatic evacuation management is studied.

Several automatic evacuation management techniques have been proposed. Liu *et al.* assign traffic considering real time data, propose a feedback control system and take advantage of traffic micro simulations [1]. Similarly, Hu *et al.* take advantage of micro simulations and search new paths to handle the overflow of a specific road link [2]. This paper prototypes an automatic evacuation management system using a highly scalable multi agent system based evacuation simulator [3] as a micro simulation tool. The evacuation simulator allows the consideration of environmental details, the heterogeneity of evacuees in large scale simulations and micro scale mixed mode interactions [4]. Furthermore the

© Springer International Publishing Switzerland 2016
M. Baldoni et al. (Eds.): PRIMA 2016, LNAI 9862, pp. 387–396, 2016.
DOI: 10.1007/978-3-319-44832-9_26

search for alternative paths is treated as combinatorial optimization problem, providing ad-hoc routes based on the individual evacuees properties. This combinatorial optimization problem is solved using a genetic algorithm (GA) based parallel meta-heuristic approach. The GA search is enhanced with a heuristic capable of incorporating the time history of the state of the road network.

The proposed automatic evacuation management system consists of 3 modules. The first provides anomaly detection identifying prospective hazardous scenarios, problems with the evacuation, etc. This module would ideally rely on direct user input [5], mobile sensors data [6], urban mobility data projections [7], etc. For demonstrative purposes, in the proposed system a simple module is prototyped. The second module evaluates mitigation strategies and provides the evacuees with alternative evacuation routes through a combinatorial optimization process. The central component of both modules is the evacuation simulator. Finally the third module provides mechanisms to evaluate the system knowledge.

The contribution of this paper is the proposal and prototyping of a system capable of identifying anomalies in an evacuation, providing a mitigation strategy and presenting feedback to human operators to aid their judgement. Furthermore it provides description of a heuristic used to take advantage of time history data condensed from a continuous 2D domain to a graph.

The rest of the paper is structured as follows. Section 2 provides a brief overview of the evacuation simulator and its multi agent system used as the base for the different modules. Section 3 presents an overview of the evacuation management system and details on its main constitutive parts. Section 4 presents a demonstrative example. Section 5 discusses the current limitations of the system and its future development direction. Section 6 concludes this paper.

2   Mass Eavacuation Simulator

The modules proposed for the automatic mitigation system take advantage of a mass evacuation simulator. This section provides a brief overview of the components of this simulator.

The base mass evacuation simulator uses the multi agent system paradigm. The simulator is time step driven and takes efficient advantage of high performance computing infrastructures [8]. Evacuees move in a continuous 2D space. The underlying logic of the agents is left for the implementers to decide based on the relevant features for the evacuation being modeled. Predefined functions are provided to aid the modeling. Details of this workbench relevant to this paper are included below for the sake of completeness.

Conceptually the evacuation simulator is designed as parallel dynamical system for further information please refer to [3]. An agent a is defined as $a = \{f, s\}$, where s represents the agents state (internal and external) and f denotes its local update function. A local update function represents all the logic embedded in the agent, actions, interactions, etc.

2.1   Environment

The environment represents the dynamic context in which the agents are being executed. Evacuees movement happen in a continuous 2D space only limited by the obstacles in the environment. The environment is modeled with a hybrid vector/raster domain, see Fig 1

Details of the surrounding space, obstacles, exits and designated evacuation areas are provided by a grid. The agents are able to discover and perceive the domain through their vision. Additionally, traversable spaces are represented with graph edges. This graph represents the possible knowledge of the agent about the environment. It is the agents' mental map of the undamaged domain and possible traversable routes. By using a hybrid environment the advantages of raster and vector based paradigms are exploited. Details are represented with the grid and complex tasks involving past experiences are executed efficiently with the graph.

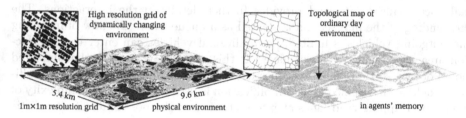

Fig. 1. Hybrid model of grid and graph environments. Grid is dynamically updated, reflecting changes in the environment. The graph is static and represents the path network before the disaster.

2.2   Agents

Agents are used to model evacuees in the simulation. Heterogeneity in the agent's mode of evacuation, characteristics and behaviors is accomplished through the specialization of an agents f and s.

Basic functionality is provided by constitutive functions g. They provide functionality to perform tasks such as path planning, $g^{path\_planning}$, visually identify blocked paths, $g^{is\_path\_blocked}$, navigate, $g^{navigate}$, avoid collisions, g^{coll_av}, etc. [9]. These constitutive functions g are used to create an agent's local update function $f = g^1 \circ g^2 \circ ... \circ g^m$, see Fig. 2.

Although several models of pedestrian evacuees are implemented (visitors, residents, law enforcement) car evacuees are the most relevant for the demonstrative examples of this paper.

Cars navigate by visually identifying openings and obstacles in the environment and using their knowledge about the possible traversable roads in the network. The road lanes are considered as offsets of the center road line.

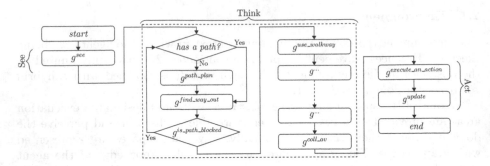

Fig. 2. Local system update function f, and a behavioural specialization example f^τ.

The widths considered for each lane are 2.4 m for multi lane roads and 3 m for single lane roads. Cars are able to manoeuvre inside the road lanes. This is specially critical in single lane roads to avoid obstacles and other agents partially occupying a lane and provides further details in the interactions. The surrounding of the intersection is treated as a queue where the flow of incoming and outgoing vehicles is limited, i.e. additional vehicles can enter the intersection area once enough vehicles have left this evacuation area. In the simplified model of intersections the direct interaction between vehicles through the collision avoidance is disabled. This simplification is used to handle the complexity of several overlapping road lanes at intersections and the possibility of unrealistic deadlocks in them.

3   Automated Evacuation Managment System

It is highly desirable to have a system which will analyze real time data, predict and propose possible means of improving the evacuation. During disasters such as earthquakes and tsunamis the existing communication networks are expected to be disrupted. Furthermore the complexity of evacuations and the existence of unforeseeable issues throughout the evacuation increase the difficulty in the analysis and the proposal of solutions.

It is in this context where the authors envision an automated evacuation management system that would make use of the limited connectivity and servers distributed in the cloud to provide robust advice to authorities and victims in real time. This system requires further advances in the robustness of the communication networks during disasters, accurate forecasts evaluating the possible caveats of evacuation scenarios, etc. By no means the prototyped system fulfils these requirements, but is a stepping stone in that direction.

The proposed system is based on 3 modules (anomaly detection, mitigation search and system knowledge analysis), each developed individually and seamlessly integrated to provide automatic evacuation management, see Fig. 3.

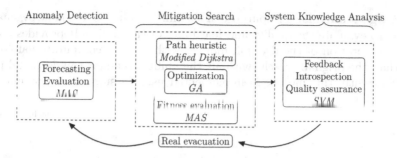

Fig. 3. Automated evacuation management system sketch containing its main components, *MAS* refers to the multi agent system based large scale evacuation simulator, *SVM* refers to a support vector machine used for evaluating the advice provided generated by the mitigation search module, *GA* refers to genetic algorithm the meta-heuristic approach used for the mitigation search.

Anomaly Detection. The anomaly detection module would ideally make use of the existing early warning sensor data, mobile sensors and users feedback. Currently a simple anomaly detection module is implemented. It uses the evacuation simulator to perform Monte Carlo simulations of problem free evacuations. These Monte Carlo simulations are condensed from the continuous 2D simulation to graphs. These graphs provide time dependent average speed thresholds for every road. This anomaly detection module triggers the mitigation search module in case a certain projected road average speed falls below the simulated normal thresholds.

Mitigation Search. The mitigation search module provides evacuation routes to the people affected by the disaster. Providing routes to improve the evacuation is a complex challenge due to the large amount of combinations of possible evacuation paths, the interferences of the traffic in these routes and the heterogeneity of the evacuees. It is important to highlight that the mitigation search needs to define the type of advice it will provide to the evacuees in this case, use the shortest route or use an alternative route. Additionally, for advice on alternative routes the mitigation search module needs to determine which route is better from a large number of candidates.

The proposed solution is based on using a Genetic Algorithm (GA) driven parallel meta-heuristic approach to optimize the proposed routes. The use of a parallel meta-heuristic approach enables the exploitation of high performance computing infrastructure. It uses the evacuation simulator to evaluate the fitness of a given route combination. Furthermore it uses a heuristic with high chances of providing successful routes. This heuristic is formed by utilizing the results of the previous generation in the GA evolution and using a modified Dijkstra Algorithm to find the fastest path, see Sect. 3.2.

Knowledge Analysis. The purpose of the third module is to enable evacuation planners to evaluate the quality and feasibility of the advice. It provides a compact representation of the decision making with a lower computational cost to query than the original search (without the ability to adapt to additional problems). Currently this module is implemented using a support vector machine. As the explored scenarios increase in size it must be considered the usage of techniques that scale better to larger amounts of data, such as artificial neural networks.

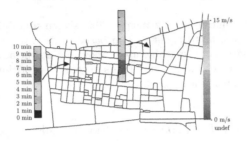

Fig. 4. Time extended graph formed from the graphs condensed from the previous GA generation.

3.1   Time Extended Graph

During the evaluation of a single GA generation fitness (the execution of a simulation) the state of the road network is condensed to the graph every t minutes of simulated time. This information is further gathered in a time extended graph, see Fig. 4. This time extended graph provides a time history of the state of each road. This information coupled with a modified Dijkstra algorithm, see Sect. 3.2, provides the base for the search heuristic that guides the GA based search.

3.2   Modified Dijkstra

The proposed modified Dijkstra algorithm, see Algorithm 1, provides a heuristic to identify good candidate evacuation routes. It assumes that the network state in the previous evacuation would remain constant and finds the *fastest* path under this assumption. It is evident that this assumption differs from the reality, thus it is used only as a heuristic. The quality of the guess provided by the fastest route algorithm is dependent on the differences from the GA generation using this heuristic and its previous GA generation producing the time extended graph.

4   Demonstrative Application

The aim of this paper is to highlight the importance of the development of automated disaster management systems. For this purpose a demonstrative toy example where the difficulty and the complexity of a successful mitigation strategy becomes evident is presented.

Algorithm 1. Fastest route: Modified Dijkstra algorithm.

---

    input : Starting node a, own average speed s_{av}, boolean functor
            `IsADestination()`,boolean functor `IsValid()` instantiated with the
            minimum width required by the agent w_{min} and his known to be
            blocked paths, positive weighted time extended graph $G = (V, E)$ (each
            edge has information about its l-length, w-width, $s(t)$ average crossing
            speed at time t
    output: *path* to destination and its *length*

1 **for** $\forall u \in V$ **do** `time`$(u)= \infty$; `parent`$(u)= -1$; // Initialize shortest time
    to reach every node to ∞ and best node parent to -1-unknown
2 `time`$(a)= 0$;

3 *priority_queue*.`add`$(a,$`time`$(a))$;

4 **while not** *priority_queue*.`empty()` **do**
5     $u = $ *priority_queue*.`top()`;
6   **if** `IsADestination`(u) **then** **break()**;

7   *priority_queue*.`pop()`;
8   **for** $\forall(u,v) \in E$ **do**
            // GetSpeed() Estimates the speed of an agent crossing the
                link (u,v) from u given s_{av} and $s(t)$
9             $dt = l(u,v)/$`GetSpeed`$(u,v,s,$`time`$(u),s_{av})$
10   **if** `time`$(v) > $ `time`$(u)+dt$ **and** `IsValid`(u,v) **then**
11   `distance`$(v)=$`distance`$(u)+l(u,v)$;
12   `time`$(v)=$`time`$(u)+dt$;
13   `parent`$(v)=u$;
14   *priority_queue*.`add`$(v,$`time`$(v))$;

15 **if** `IsADestination`(u) **then** // Extracts the path
16   *length* $= $ `distance`(u);*path*.`pushBack`(u);
17   **while** $u \neq a$ **do** $u = $ `parent`(u); *path*.`pushBack`(u);
18 **return** *path* , *length*

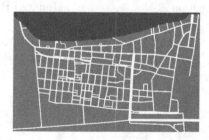

Fig. 5. Evacuation area $(1.5\,\text{km} \times 1\,\text{km})$, white - traversable spaces, gray - untraversable areas, green - evacuation area. (Color figure online)

4.1 Setting

A 1.5 km × 1 km region in a coastal city in Japan is chosen for the demonstrative example. This is a densely populated urban area that was highly affected during the 2011 Great Tohoku Earthquake. The model of the data is automatically extracted from an on-line map service in 1 m × 1 m cell resolution, see Fig. 5. Its flat topography increases the region's vulnerability to tsunami inundation.

For demonstrative purposes only evacuees using vehicles are considered. The objective here is to highlight the need of automatic disaster management tools and not to simulate a realistic evacuation. Even in this simplified example the necessity of the system becomes evident. The synthetic vehicle population is divided in fast and slow evacuees. The means of their speed distributions are initialized to 10 m/s (fast) 5 m/s (slow). The standard deviation is set to 2 m/s. The distributions are truncated outside the 2–20 m/s range. All evacuees are initialized randomly along the roads. The evacuation involves 500 vehicles during 10 min of evacuation. The time resolution for the evacuation is 0.2 s/timestep. All evacuees are assumed to try to reach an evacuation area, green in Fig. 5, from the beginning of the simulation.

4.2 Automatic Managing

The automatic evacuation management is kick-started through the detection of an anomaly. In this example an anomaly is defined as a case where the throughput falls below the acceptable thresholds. For the demonstrative example an evacuation problem is induced in one area as seen in Fig. 6. This problem is then considered in the mitigation search module.

The optimization module uses a genetic algorithm approach enhanced by the search heuristic to find better evacuation routes and guide the search. A mitigation strategy that improves the evacuation throughput in more than 10 % is obtained through the optimization process, see Fig. 7(a).

Finally the third module provides visual feedback and introspection on the advice found through optimization, see Fig. 7(b). This highlights the complexity

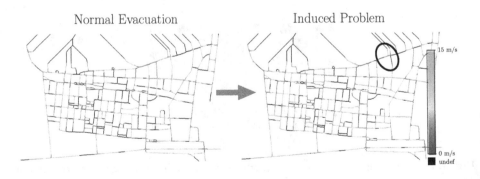

Fig. 6. Induced problem for demonstrative example.

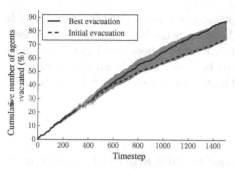

Fig. 7. (a)-left, GA based optimization results. Best throughput found (black), Searched space (gray). (b)-right, Support vector machine based decision introspection, white dots evacuees advised to use alternative roads, black dots evacuees not provided with advice. (Color figure online)

of the successful solution. The third module can be further queried providing alternative routes not only based on the geographical location of the agents but also on their properties. Figure 7(b) shows contiguous agents, differing in their average speed, being provided with different advice. Through further inspection it is discovered that the reason why this happens is that the system avoids to incorporate slow evacuees in fast evacuees flows.

5   Discussion

The proposed system shows that even in a simplified scenario using a simple system the complexity of the successful mitigation measure is quite high, irregular boundaries, contiguous evacuees receiving different type of advice, etc. In its current state this system only serves the purpose of a proof of concept. It highlights its need and points to many areas of improvement. It is currently unfeasible to provide quality results using detailed models fast enough as to provide real time guiding. An alternative to this could be the preprocessing of scenarios. With preprocessed scenarios and using the query capabilities of the knowledge analysis module this task could be improved.

The anomaly detection requires to integrate and take advantage of several information sources. Information sources such as mobile sensor data, user feedback, etc. need to be considered. The evacuation simulator used as the core component of the automatic evacuation mitigation system should be able to provide realistically accurate simulation of evacuations. This would improve the quality of the advice. The game theoretic stability of the strategies should be evaluated and ways to maximize compliance should be researched.

6   Concluding Remarks

A prototype of an automatic evacuation mitigation system has been implemented and its usefulness has been highlighted through a demonstrative application.

Through the combination of GA based optimization and a Dijkstra based search heuristic the evacuation throughput in the demonstrative example is increased in more than 10 %. As the size of the evacuation areas become bigger it becomes unrealistic to expect human controllers to be able to guide an evacuation. In the future work it is needed to evaluate the robustness of the strategies to non-compliance of the advice. Additionally, the evacuation simulator should be further developed to consider the behavioral factors of the evacuation to provide more accurate estimates.

Acknowledgments. This work was supported by JSPS KAKENHI Grant Number 24760359. Parts of the results are obtained using K computer at the RIKEN Advanced Institute for Computational Science.

References

1. Liu, H.X., Ban, J.X., Ma, W., Mirchandani, P.B.: Model reference adaptive control framework for real-time traffic management under emergency evacuation. J. Urban Plan. Dev. **133**, 43–50 (2007)
2. Jihua, H.U., Jiaxian, L., Guoyuan, L.I., Lixiao, G.A.O.: A traffic assignment method of urgent dispersion under road flooding. In: Proceedings of the Transportation Information and Safety Conference (ICTIS), pp. 288–294 (2015)
3. Melgar, L.E.A., Lalith, M., Hori, M., Ichimura, T., Tanaka, S.: A scalable workbench for large urban area simulations, comprised of resources for behavioural models, interactions and dynamic environments. In: Dam, H.K., Pitt, J., Xu, Y., Governatori, G., Ito, T. (eds.) PRIMA 2014. LNCS, vol. 8861, pp. 166–181. Springer, Heidelberg (2014)
4. Leonel, A., Lalith, W., Tsuyoshi, I., Hori, M., Seizo, T.: Mixed mode large urban area tsunami evacuation considering car-pedestrian interactions. J. Jpn. Soc. Civ. Eng. Ser. A2 (Appl. Mech. Pap. vol. 18) **71**, 633–641 (2015)
5. Gunawan, L.T., Fitrianie, S., Yang, C.-K., Brinkman, W.-P., Neerincx, M.A.: TravelThrough: a participatory-based guidance system for traveling through disaster areas. In: CHI 2012: CHI 2012 Extended Abstracts on Human Factors in Computing Systems (2012)
6. Pournaras, E., Nikolic, J., Velasquez, P., Trovati, M., Bessis, N., Helbing, D.: Self-regulatory information sharing in participatory social sensing. Eur. Phys. J. Data Sci. **5**, 14 (2016)
7. Jiang, S., Ferreira Jr., J., Gonzalez, M.C.: Activity-Based Human Mobility Patterns Inferred from Mobile Phone Data: A Case Study of Singapore. ACM KDD UrbComp (2015)
8. Wijerathne, M.L., Melgar, L.A., Hori, M., Ichimura, T., Tanaka, S.: HPC enhanced large urban area evacuation simulations with vision based autonomously navigating multiagents. Procedia Comput. Sci. **18**, 1515–1524 (2013)
9. Melgar, L.E.A., Lakshman, W.M.L., Hori, M., Ichimura, T., Tanaka, S.: On the development of an MAS based evacuation simulation system: autonomous navigation and collision avoidance. In: Boella, G., Elkind, E., Savarimuthu, B.T.R., Dignum, F., Purvis, M.K. (eds.) PRIMA 2013. LNCS, vol. 8291, pp. 388–395. Springer, Heidelberg (2013)

Dialectical Proof Procedures for Probabilistic Abstract Argumentation

Phan Minh Thang$^{(\boxtimes)}$

BUUIC College, Burapha University, Chon Buri, Thailand
thangfm@gmail.com

Abstract. A dialectical proof procedure for computing grounded semantics of probabilistic abstract argumentation is presented based on the notion of probabilistic dispute tree. We also present an algorithm for top-down construction of probabilistic dispute trees.

1 Introduction

It is often necessary to combine normative reasoning with causal and probabilistic reasoning in practical reasoning. For illustration, consider the following example adapted from Dung and Thang (2010) and borrowed from Riveret et al. (2007).

Example 1. John sues Henry for the damage caused to him when he drove off the road to avoid hitting Henry's cow. John's argument is:

> *J: Henry should pay for the damage because Henry is the owner of the cow and the cow caused the accident.*

Henry counter-attacks by stating that,

> H_1: *John was negligent, for evidence at the accident site shows that John was driving fast.*
>
> H_2: *The cow was mad and the madness of the cow should be viewed as a force-majeure.*

John's argument is based on a common norm (or law) that owners are responsible for the damages caused by their animals. Henry's first argument is based on the causal relationship between John's fast driving and the accident. Henry's second argument is based on the legal concept of force-majeure and the probability of the event of a cow getting mad. Can John win the case?

The chance of John winning the case depends on how probable the judge considers Henry's arguments. Suppose the judge dismisses the madness of the cow as improbable, then the probability of Henry's second argument is 0. Therefore the chance for John to win depends on the probability of Henry's first argument. Suppose the judge considers the probability that John was driving fast to be 0.3, then the probability for John's argument to stand is 0.7, and John would win the case. However, if the judge considers the probability of the event "John's driving fast" to be 0.6, then Henry would win the case because the probability for John's argument to stand is 0.4 only. □

© Springer International Publishing Switzerland 2016
M. Baldoni et al. (Eds.): PRIMA 2016, LNAI 9862, pp. 397–406, 2016.
DOI: 10.1007/978-3-319-44832-9_27

The abstract argumentation framework is introduced by Dung (1995). It has been shown that many frameworks for non-monotonic reasoning are instances of abstract argumentation like logic programming, default logic, assumption based argumentation. Many proof theories had been developed for abstract argumentation. Dung and Thang (2010) developed a probabilistic argumentation framework to model applications involving both causal and norm-based reasoning as in the example above. However until now, no proof theory on how to actually compute the result, has been offered. This paper will introduces such a proof theory that could serve as an useful guidance for developing proof theories of instances of probabilistic abstract argumentation frameworks.

The paper is structured as follows. In Sect. 2, a basic background on abstract argumentation framework and dialectical proof procedures for abstract argumentation framework are given. In Sect. 3 a proof procedure for a probabilistic abstract argumentation framework is introduced. The conclusion is in Sect. 4.

2 Background

2.1 Probabilistic Abstract Argumentation Framework

An *abstract argumentation* (AA) framework introduced by Dung (1995) is a pair $\mathcal{F} = (Ar, Att)$, where Ar is a finite set of arguments and Att is a binary relation over Ar representing attacks between arguments, with $(A, B) \in Att$ meaning 'A attacks B'.

Let S be a set of arguments. S *attacks* an argument A if some argument in S attacks A. S attacks a set S' of arguments if S attacks some arguments in S'. S is *conflict-free* iff it does not attack itself. An argument A is *acceptable* with respect to S iff S attacks each argument attacking A. S is *admissible* iff S is conflict-free and each argument in S is acceptable with respect to S. An admissible set S of arguments is called a *complete extension* iff each argument, which is acceptable with respect to S, belongs to S. The semantics of argumentation can also be characterized by a fixpoint theory of the characteristic function $C_{\mathcal{F}}(S) = \{A \in Ar \mid A \text{ is acceptable with respect to } S\}$. As $C_{\mathcal{F}}$ is monotonic, there is a least fixed point. The *grounded extension* of $\mathcal{F}$ is defined as the least fixed point of $C_{\mathcal{F}}$. It is well known that the grounded extension is the least complete extension. An argument A is said to be *groundedly accepted* if it is contained in the grounded extension.

Note 1. For an argument A, $Attack_A$ and $AttackBy_A$ refer to the set of arguments attacking A or attacked by A respectively, i.e. $Attack_A = \{B \mid B \text{ attacks } A\}$, $AttackedBy_A = \{B \mid A \text{ attacks } B\}$

The below definitions of the probability space and the probabilistic abstract argumentation framework are adapted from Definitions 1.1 and 1.2 of Dung and Thang (2010).

Definition 1. *A probability space Π is a pair $(\mathcal{W}, P)$ such that*

1. *$\mathcal{W}$ is a finite set of possible worlds.*
2. *P is a probabilistic distribution over $\mathcal{W}$, i.e. $P: \mathcal{W} \to (0,1]$ s.t.*
   $\sum_{w \in \mathcal{W}} P(w) = 1$.

Definition 2. *A probabilistic abstract argumentation framework (PAA) is a triple $(\mathcal{F}, \Pi, \vdash)$ satisfying the following conditions:*

1. *$\mathcal{F} = (Ar, Att)$ is an abstract argumentation framework.*
2. *$\Pi = (\mathcal{W}, P)$ is a probability space.*
3. *$\vdash \subseteq \mathcal{W} \times Ar$ specifies which arguments are possible with respect to which worlds in Π.*
   We often say that A is possible with respect to w when $w \vdash A$ holds for $w \in \mathcal{W}$ and $A \in Ar$.

The above defined probabilistic abstract argumentation framework is a single-agent version of a more general multiagent probabilistic abstract argumentation framework referred as "Abstract Argumentation framework for Jury-based dispute resolution" (AAJ framework) introduced by Dung and Thang (2010).

Example 2. Example 1 can be represented as a *PAA* framework $(\mathcal{F}, \Pi, \vdash)$ as follows.

- $\mathcal{F} = (Ar, Att)$ with $Ar = \{J, H_1, H_2\}$ and $Att = \{(H_1, J), (H_2, J)\}$
- The worlds in $\mathcal{W}$ are characterized by two events "John was driving fast" (JF) and "the cow was mad" (CM). Therefore $\mathcal{W} = \{w_1, w_2, w_3, w_4\}$ where $w_1 = \{JF, CM\}$, $w_2 = \{JF, \neg CM\}$, $w_3 = \{\neg JF, CM\}$, $w_4 = \{\neg JF, \neg CM\}$.
- Suppose the judge considers the probability of the event JF is 0.6, and the probability of the event CM is 0.1. As the event JF and CM are independent, the probabilities of the possible worlds are calculated as follows $P(w_1) = P(JF) \times P(CM) = 0.06$, $P(w_2) = P(JF) \times P(\neg CM) = 0.54$, $P(w_3) = P(\neg JF) \times P(CM) = 0.04$, $P(w_4) = P(\neg JF) \times P(\neg CM) = 0.36$.
- Because J is an argument based on legal norms, J is possible in all worlds. Hence $w_1 \vdash X$ iff $X \in \{J, H_1, H_2\}$, $w_3 \vdash X$ iff $X \in \{J, H_2\}$, $w_2 \vdash X$ iff $X \in \{J, H_1\}$ and $w_4 \vdash X$ iff $X \in \{J\}$ □

For a world w, the set of arguments possible with respect to w and the attack relation related to them is denoted by $\mathcal{F}_w$.

Definition 3. *Let $(\mathcal{F}, \Pi, \vdash)$ be a PAA framework, with $\mathcal{F} = (Ar, Att)$, $\Pi = (\mathcal{W}, P)$, and let $w \in \mathcal{W}$.*

- *The abstract argumentation framework $\mathcal{F}_w$ is (Ar_w, Att_w) with $Ar_w = \{A \in Ar \mid w \vdash A\}$, $Att_w = Att \cap (Ar_w \times Ar_w)$.*
- *The grounded extension of $\mathcal{F}_w$ is denoted by $\mathcal{G}_w$.*
- *An argument A is said to be groundedly accepted with respect to w iff $A \in \mathcal{G}_w$.*

The probability of an argument A to be accepted with respect the grounded semantic in a probabilistic abstract argumentation framework is defined as the sum of probabilities of worlds in which argument A is groundedly accepted.

Definition 4. *Let* $(\mathcal{F}, \Pi, \vdash)$ *be a PAA framework, with* $\mathcal{F} = (Ar, Att)$, $\Pi = (\mathcal{W}, P)$, *and let* $w \in \mathcal{W}$. *The grounded probability of argument* A *is defined as follows:*

$$Prob_{\mathcal{G}}(A) = \sum_{w \in \mathcal{W}: A \in \mathcal{G}_w} P(w)$$

In Example 2, the abstract argumentation frameworks $\mathcal{F}_{w_1}, \mathcal{F}_{w_2}, \mathcal{F}_{w_3}, \mathcal{F}_{w_4}$ are defined as follows $Ar_{w_1} = \{J, H_1, H_2\}$, $Att_{w_1} = \{(H_1, J), (H_2, J)\}$, $Ar_{w_2} = \{J, H_1\}$, $Att_{w_2} = \{(H_1, J)\}$, $Ar_{w_3} = \{J, H_2\}$, $Att_{w_3} = \{(H_2, J)\}$, $Ar_{w_4} = \{J\}$ and $Att_{w_4} = \emptyset$. Therefore, J is not groundedly accepted in three possible worlds w_1, w_2 and w_3. However, J is groundedly accepted in possible world w_4. Hence the grounded probability of J is $Prob_{\mathcal{G}}(J) = P(w_4) = 0.36$.

2.2   A Dialectical Proof Procedures for (Non Probabilistic) Abstract Argumentation Framework

In a dispute, the proponent starts by putting forward an argument supporting his claim. The opponent and the proponent then alternatively present their arguments attacking the rival's previous arguments. The proponent wins if all presented arguments of the opponent are countered by the proponent and the opponent runs out of arguments.

Note 2. From now, for ease of reference, it is assumed that the proponent is a man and the opponent is a woman.

In the following, we first recall a proof procedure for grounded semantic for non-probabilistic abstract argumentation from Thang et al. (2009).

Given a (non-probabilistic) abstract argumentation $\mathcal{F} = (Ar, Att)$, a dispute derivation specifies a proof procedure to determine whether an argument A is groundedly accepted with respect to $\mathcal{F}$. More formally, a dispute derivation is a sequence of triples $\langle P_i, O_i, PP_i \rangle$, where P_i is a set of arguments presented by the proponent but not yet attacked by the opponent, O_i is a set of arguments presented by the opponent but not yet countered by the proponent, and PP_i is the set of all presented proponent arguments. Arguments in $PP_i \setminus P_i$ are arguments already defended by the proponent until step i. At every step, either the proponent or the opponent makes a move. If the proponent makes a move at step i, he will select an argument B from O_i and attacks B by an argument from $Attack_B$. If the opponent makes a move at step i, she will select an argument C from P_i and attacks C by all arguments from $Attack_C$.

Definition 5. *A* dispute derivation *for an argument A is a sequence of triples* $\langle P_0, O_0, PP_0 \rangle \ldots \langle P_n, O_n, PP_n \rangle$, *where:*

1. *P_i, O_i, and PP_i are sets of arguments*
2. *$P_0 = PP_0 = \{A\}, O_0 = \emptyset$*
3. (a) *Suppose the opponent makes a move at step i and selects an argument $B \in P_i$ for attack, then*
$$P_{i+1} = P_i \setminus \{B\} \qquad O_{i+1} = O_i \cup Attack_B \qquad PP_{i+1} = PP_i$$
   (b) *Suppose the proponent makes a move at step i and selects an argument $B \in O_i$ for attack, then he will select an argument $C \in Attack_B$ and*
$$P_{i+1} = P_i \cup \{C\} \qquad O_{i+1} = O_i \setminus \{B\} \qquad PP_{i+1} = PP_i \cup \{C\}$$

Definition 6. *A* dispute derivation $\langle P_0, O_0, PP_0 \rangle \ldots \langle P_n, O_n, PP_n \rangle$ *is said to be* successful *iff $P_n = O_n = \emptyset$.*

The following theorem says that an argument A is groundedly accepted iff there is a successful dispute derivation for A. It is a slightly different version of Theorem 2 in Thang et al. (2009).

Theorem 1. *An argument A is groundedly accepted with respect to a finite abstract argumentation $\mathcal{F}$ iff there is a successful dispute derivation* $\langle P_0, O_0, PP_0 \rangle \langle P_1, O_1, PP_1 \rangle \ldots \langle P_n, O_n, PP_n \rangle$ *such that*

1. *$P_0 = PP_0 = \{A\}, O_0 = \emptyset$*
2. *$P_n = O_n = \emptyset$*
3. *$A \in PP_n$ and $PP_n \subseteq \mathcal{G_F}$.*

Example 3. Figure 1 shows an abstract argumentation framework $\mathcal{F} = (Ar, Att)$ with $Ar = \{A, B, C, D\}$ and $Att = \{(B, A), (C, A), (D, B), (D, C)\}$. A successful dispute derivation for A is also shown in the Fig. 1 where the selected argument is underlined. □

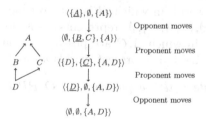

Fig. 1. A successful dispute derivation for A

3 Probabilistic Dispute Trees

Example 4. For an illustration, let us first look at a probabilistic abstract argumentation $(\mathcal{F}, \Pi, \vdash)$ where $\mathcal{F} = (Ar, Att)$ with $Ar = \{A, B, C\}$ and $Att = \{(B, A), (C, B)\}$ (see the left of Fig. 2). $\Pi = (\mathcal{W}, P)$ with $\mathcal{W} = \{w_1, w_2, w_3, w_4\}$ and $P(w_1) = 0.432$, $P(w_2) = 0.108$, $P(w_3) = 0.1$, $P(w_4) = 0.36$. Thus $w_1 \vdash X$ iff $X \in \{A, B, C\}$, $w_2 \vdash X$ iff $X \in \{A, B\}$, $w_3 \vdash X$ iff $X \in \{B, C\}$ and $w_4 \vdash A$.

A dispute between the proponent and the opponent could proceed as follows.

- At the first step, the proponent puts forward argument A.
- At the second step, the opponent attacks argument A by argument B.
- At the third step, the proponent could defend A from the attack of B by either using argument C to counterattack B or pointing out that the opponent's argument B is probabilistic, and there is world in which B is not possible. The proponent can win if the grounded probability of A is over 0.5.

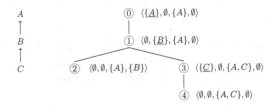

Fig. 2. A probabilistic abstract argumentation framework $\mathcal{F}$ (Left) and the probabilistic dispute tree for argument A (Right)

This dispute can be represented by a sequence of quadruple $\langle P, O, PP, IO \rangle$ where P, O, and PP are like in Definition 5 before, and IO consists of the opponent's arguments characterizing worlds, in which they are not possible. The above dispute can be represented as on the right of Fig. 2. The branch from the root to the leaf node $\langle \emptyset, \emptyset, \{A\}, \{B\} \rangle$ represents a successful dispute derivation with respect to a world, in which B is not possible. The branch from the root to the leaf node $\langle \emptyset, \emptyset, \{A, C\}, \emptyset \rangle$ represents a successful dispute derivation with respect to worlds, in which A, C are possible. In our example, leaf nodes $\langle \emptyset, \emptyset, \{A\}, \{B\} \rangle$, $\langle \emptyset, \emptyset, \{A, C\}, \emptyset \rangle$ represent worlds w_4 and w_1 respectively.

Definition 7. *A dispute state is a quadruple $\langle P, O, PP, IO \rangle$ representing a state of a dispute where*

- *P is a set of arguments presented by the proponent but not yet attacked by the opponent.*
- *O is a set of arguments presented by the opponent but not yet countered by the proponent.*
- *PP is the set of all presented proponent arguments.*
- *IO consists of opponent arguments characterizing worlds, in which they are not possible.*

The probability of every branch of the probabilistic dispute tree in Fig. 2 represents a lower bound of grounded probability of A. It could be quite useful. For example, in civil case, the probability of A only need to be greater than 0.5 for the proponent to win the case represented by A. Thus, it is enough to find a branch (a dispute derivation) which has a probability greater than 0.5. However, in many cases we may have to search the whole probabilistic dispute tree for A to know the sum of all probabilities of branches to greater than 0.5, even though the probability of each of them is smaller than 0.5 (see the above example). This probabilistic dispute tree is constructed formally for A as below.

Definition 8. *A probabilistic dispute tree T for an argument A with respect to a probabilistic abstract argumentation framework is defined as follows:*

1. *Every node of T is labeled by a dispute state.*
2. *The root is a node labeling by the initial dispute state $\langle \{A\}, \emptyset, \{A\}, \emptyset \rangle$.*
3. *At every node labeled by $\langle P, O, PP, IO \rangle$, one argument from either P or O is selected.*
4. *Suppose an argument $B \in P$ is selected at node N labeled by $\langle P, O, PP, IO \rangle$ meaning that the move is an opponent move. Then there is exactly one child of N labeled by a dispute state of the form $\langle P', O', PP', IO' \rangle$ where*
   $$P' = P \setminus \{B\} \qquad\qquad PP' = PP$$
   $$O' = O \cup (Attack_B \setminus IO) \qquad IO' = IO$$
5. *Suppose an argument $B \in O$ is selected at node N labeled by $\langle P, O, PP, IO \rangle$ meaning that the move is a proponent move. Following conditions hold:*
   (a) *Exactly a child of N is labeled by a dispute state of the form $\langle P', O', PP', IO' \rangle$ where*
   $$P' = P \qquad\qquad PP' = PP$$
   $$O' = O \setminus \{B\} \qquad IO' = IO \cup \{B\}$$
   (b) *For each argument C attacking B, there is exactly a child of N labeled by a dispute state of the form $\langle P_C, O_C, PP_C, IO_C \rangle$ where*
   $$P_C = P \cup \{C\} \qquad\qquad PP_C = PP \cup \{C\}$$
   $$O_C = O \setminus \{B\} \qquad IO_C = IO$$
   (c) *There is no other child of N.*
6. *There are no other nodes except those given by rules 1–5 above.*

Definition 9.

- *A successful probabilistic dispute derivation for an argument A is defined as a branch from the top to a leaf node of a probabilistic dispute tree for A.*
- *A dispute state $\langle P, O, PP, IO \rangle$ is said to be final iff $P = O = \emptyset$.*

It is obvious that the last state in a successful probabilistic dispute derivation is always a final state.

Example 5. (Continue Example 4) There are two successful probabilistic dispute derivations for A in Fig. 2. The first one is the branch from the root to the leaf node $\langle \emptyset, \emptyset, \{A\}, \{B\} \rangle$. This dispute is possible with respect to world w_4, in which A is possible but B is not possible. The second one is the branch from the root to the leaf node $\langle \emptyset, \emptyset, \{A, C\}, \emptyset \rangle$. This dispute is possible with respect to world w_1, in which arguments A, C are possible. □

Definition 10. *Let $S = \langle \emptyset, \emptyset, PP, IO \rangle$ be a final state. The probability of S is defined as below*

$$Prob(S) = \sum_{w \in W_S} P(w)$$

where

$$W_S = \{w \mid PP \subseteq Ar_w \text{ and } IO \cap Ar_w = \emptyset\}$$

The probability of a successful derivation $\mathcal{D} = S_0, S_1, \ldots, S_n$ is denoted to be the probability of its final state S_n, i.e. $Prob(\mathcal{D}) = Prob(S_n)$.

Lemma 1. *Given a successful dispute derivation $\mathcal{D}$ for an argument A in a PAA framework $\mathcal{PA}$, the grounded probability of A in $\mathcal{PA}$ is greater or equal $Prob(\mathcal{D})$, i.e.*

$$Prob_\mathcal{G}(A) \geq Prob(\mathcal{D})$$

Proof. (Sketch) Let $\mathcal{D} = S_0, S_1, \ldots, S_n$ where $S_n = \langle \emptyset, \emptyset, PP, IO \rangle$ and $w \in W_{S_n}$. Hence $PP \subseteq Ar_w$ and $IO \cap Ar_w = \emptyset$. It is not difficult to show that $A \in \mathcal{G}_w$. The lemma holds then obviously. □

Definition 11. *Let $\mathcal{T}$ be a probabilistic dispute tree for an argument A in a PAA framework $\mathcal{PA}$ where leaves are labeled by final states $S_1, S_2, \ldots, S_n$. The set $W_\mathcal{T}$ of worlds of $\mathcal{T}$ are defined as below.*

$$W_\mathcal{T} = \bigcup_{i=1}^{n} W_{S_i}$$

The probability of $\mathcal{T}$ is denoted to be the probability of $W_\mathcal{T}$, i.e. $Prob(\mathcal{T}) = Prob(W_\mathcal{T})$

Example 6. (Continue Example 4) There are two final states $S_1 = \langle \emptyset, \emptyset, \{A\}, \{B\} \rangle$ and $S_2 = \langle \emptyset, \emptyset, \{A, C\}, \emptyset \rangle$ in Fig. 2. Thus $W_{S_1} = \{w_4\}$ and $W_{S_2} = \{w_1\}$. Therefore, $W_\mathcal{T} = \{w_1, w_4\}$. Hence $Prob(\mathcal{T}) = Prob(W_\mathcal{T}) = Prob(w_1) + Prob(w_4) = 0.792$. □

The correctness of the notion of probabilistic dispute tree is given in the following theorem.

Theorem 2. *Let A be an argument in a PAA framework $\mathcal{PA}$ and $\mathcal{T}$ be a probabilistic dispute tree for A in $\mathcal{PA}$. Then, the grounded probability of A equals the probability of $\mathcal{T}$, i.e.*

$$Prob_\mathcal{G}(A) = Prob(\mathcal{T})$$

Proof. (Sketch) Let $W_A = \{w \mid A \in \mathcal{G}_w\}$. It is obvious that $Prob_\mathcal{G}(A) = Prob(W_A)$. It is not difficult to see that $W_\mathcal{T} \subseteq W_A$.

It is also not difficult to see that $\forall w \in W_A$ there is a final state $S = \langle \emptyset, \emptyset, PP, IO \rangle$ in $\mathcal{T}$ s.t. $\forall X \in IO : w \not\vdash X$. Therefore, $w \in W_S$. Hence $W_A \subseteq W_\mathcal{T}$. □

A top-down construction of probabilistic dispute tree is defined in the following definition.

Definition 12. *An extended probabilistic dispute derivation for an argument A is a sequence of sets $\mathcal{S}_0 \mathcal{S}_1 \ldots \mathcal{S}_n$, where*

1. $\mathcal{S}_0 = \{ \langle \{A\}, \emptyset, \{A\}, \emptyset \rangle \}$ and $\mathcal{S}_i$ is a set of quadruples $\langle P, O, PP, IO \rangle$,
2. (a) *Suppose the opponent moves at step i by selecting $\delta = \langle P, O, PP, IO \rangle$ from $\mathcal{S}_i$ and an argument $B \in P$. The dispute proceeds as below.*

$$\mathcal{S}_{i+1} = (\mathcal{S}_i \setminus \{ \delta \}) \cup \{ \delta' \}$$

   where $\delta' = \langle P', O', PP', IO' \rangle$ and $P' = P \setminus \{B\}$, $PP' = PP$, $O' = O \cup (Attack_B \setminus IO)$ and $IO' = IO$.

   (b) *Suppose the proponent moves at step i by selecting $\delta = \langle P, O, PP, IO \rangle$ from $\mathcal{S}_i$ and an argument $B \in O$. The dispute proceeds as below.*

$$\mathcal{S}_{i+1} = (\mathcal{S}_i \setminus \{ \delta \}) \cup \{ \delta' \} \cup \mathcal{S}'$$

   where $\delta' = \langle P', O', PP', IO' \rangle$ and $P' = P$, $PP' = PP$, $O' = O \setminus \{B\}$ and $IO' = IO \cup \{B\}$
   $\mathcal{S}' = \{ \delta_C \mid C \in Attack_B \}$ with $\delta_C = \langle P_C, O_C, PP_C, IO_C \rangle$ and
   $P_C = P \cup \{C\}$, $PP_C = PP \cup \{C\}$, $O_C = O \setminus \{B\}$ and $IO_C = IO$

Definition 13. *Let $\mathcal{E}$ be an extended probabilistic dispute derivation $\mathcal{S}_0, \ldots, \mathcal{S}_n$ for an argument A in a PAA framework where $\mathcal{S}_n$ consists of only final states. The set $\mathcal{W}_{\mathcal{E}}$ of worlds of $\mathcal{E}$ is defined as below.*

$$\mathcal{W}_{\mathcal{E}} = \bigcup_{S \in \mathcal{S}_n} \mathcal{W}_S$$

Theorem 3. *Let A be an argument in a PAA framework $\mathcal{PA} = (\mathcal{F}, \Pi, \vdash)$ with $\Pi = (\mathcal{W}, P)$. And let $\mathcal{E}$ be an extended probabilistic dispute derivation for A in $\mathcal{PA}$. Then*

$$Prob_{\mathcal{G}}(A) = \sum_{w \in \mathcal{W}_{\mathcal{E}}} P(w)$$

Example 7. (Continue Example 4) The extended probabilistic dispute derivation for A is $\mathcal{S}_0 \mathcal{S}_1 \ldots \mathcal{S}_3$, where $\mathcal{S}_0 = \{ \langle \{\underline{A}\}, \emptyset, \{A\}, \emptyset \rangle \}$, $\mathcal{S}_1 = \{ \langle \emptyset, \{\underline{B}\}, \{A\}, \emptyset \rangle \}$, $\mathcal{S}_2 = \{ \langle \emptyset, \emptyset, \{A\}, \{B\} \rangle, \langle \{\underline{C}\}, \emptyset, \{A, C\}, \emptyset \rangle \}$, $\mathcal{S}_3 = \{ \langle \emptyset, \emptyset, \{A\}, \{B\} \rangle, \langle \emptyset, \emptyset, \{A, C\}, \emptyset \rangle \}$

The final states $\langle \emptyset, \emptyset, \{A\}, \{B\} \rangle$ and $\langle \emptyset, \emptyset, \{A, C\}, \emptyset \rangle$ represent possible world w_4 and w_1 respectively. Thus $\mathcal{W}_{\mathcal{E}} = \{w_1, w_4\}$. Hence, the grounded probability of A is $P_{\mathcal{E}} = P(w_1) + P(w_4) = 0.792$. $\qquad\square$

4   Conclusions

Until today, there are many frameworks integrating argumentation with probabilistic reasoning. For example, in frameworks proposed by Li et al. (2011), Polberg and Doder (2014), Hunter(2013) and Doder and Woltran (2014), probabilities are associated to individual arguments instead of considering a probability distribution over possible worlds where arguments are possible, as in PAA framework. Hunter and Thimm (2014), Hunter (2014) propose frameworks, that are single agent versions of a more general multiagent probabilistic abstract argumentation introduced by Dung and Thang (2010). Therefore, with slight modification, our proof theories could be applied to their frameworks as well. Poole (1998), Baral et al. (2009) propose probabilistic logic programming frameworks. It could be interesting to see whether their frameworks could be viewed as instances of the probabilistic abstract argumentation framework that has been studying in this paper, and how to apply our proof theories in their frameworks. It is also interesting to see whether our proof theories could be applied for frameworks by Li et al. (2011), Polberg and Doder (2014), Hunter (2013) and Doder and Woltran (2014).

References

Baral, C., Gelfond, M., Rushton, N.: Probabilistic reasoning with answer sets. Theor. Pract. Logic Program. **9**(1), 57–144 (2009)

Doder, D., Woltran, S.: Probabilistic argumentation frameworks – a logical approach. In: Straccia, U., Calì, A. (eds.) SUM 2014. LNCS, vol. 8720, pp. 134–147. Springer, Heidelberg (2014)

Dung, P.M.: On the acceptability of arguments and its fundamental role in non-monotonic reasoning, logic programming and n-person games. AIJ **77**(2), 321–357 (1995)

Dung, P.M., Thang, P.M.: Towards (probabilistic) argumentation for jury-based dispute resolution. In: Proceedings of COMMA, pp. 171–182. IOS Press (2010)

Hunter, A.: A probabilistic approach to modelling uncertain logical arguments. Int. J. Approximate Reasoning **54**(1), 47–81 (2013)

Hunter, A.: Probabilistic qualification of attack in abstract argumentation. Int. J. Approximate Reasoning **55**, 607–638 (2014)

Hunter, A., Thimm, M.: Probabilistic argument graphs for argumentation lotteries. In: Computational Models of Argument (COMMA 2014). IOS Press (2014)

Li, H., Oren, N., Norman, T.: Probabilistic argumentation frameworks. In: Proceedings of the First International Workshop on Theory and Applications of Formal Argumentation (TAFA11) (2011)

Polberg, S., Doder, D.: Probabilistic abstract dialectical frameworks. In: Fermé, E., Leite, J. (eds.) JELIA 2014. LNCS, vol. 8761, pp. 591–599. Springer, Heidelberg (2014)

Poole, D.: Abducing through negation as failure, stable models within independent choice logic. J. Logic Program. **44**(1–3), 5–35 (1998)

Riveret, R., Rotolo, N., Sartor, G., Prakken, H., Roth, B.: Success chances in argument games, a probabilistic approach to legal disputes. In: Proceedings of Jurix (2007)

Thang, P.M., Dung, P.M., Hung, N.D.: Towards a common framework for dialectical proof procedure in abstaract argumentation. J. Logic Comput. **9**(6), 1071–1109 (2009)

Erratum to: PRIMA 2016: Principles and Practice of Multi-Agent Systems

Matteo Baldoni[1]([📧]), Amit K. Chopra[2], Tran Cao Son[3],
Katsutoshi Hirayama[4], and Paolo Torroni[5]

[1] Dipartimento di Informatica, Università degli Studi di Torino, Turin, Italy
baldoni@di.unito.it
[2] Computing and Communications, Lancaster University, Lancaster, UK
[3] Department of Computer Science, New Mexico State University,
Las Cruces, NM, USA
[4] Graduate School of Maritime Sciences, Kobe University, Kobe, Japan
[5] Dept. di Informatica: Sci. e Ingegneria, Universitá di Bologna, Bologna, Italy

Erratum to:
M. Baldoni et al. (Eds.)
PRIMA 2016: Principles and Practice of Multi-Agent Systems
DOI: 10.1007/978-3-319-44832-9

The original version of the cover and title page was revised: The conference title is updated. Title of the conference is updated from PRIMA 2016: Princiles and Practice of Multi-Agent Systems to PRIMA 2016: Principles and Practice of Multi-Agent Systems.

The updated original online version for this book can be found at 10.1007/978-3-319-44832-9

© Springer International Publishing Switzerland 2016
M. Baldoni et al. (Eds.): PRIMA 2016, LNAI 9862, p. E1, 2016.
DOI: 10.1007/978-3-319-44832-9_28

Social Science Extended Abstracts

Summary of "How, When and Where Can Spatial Segregation Induce Opinion Polarization? Two Competing Models"

Paper Under Review as JASSS Fast Track Submission

Thomas Feliciani[1]([✉]), Andreas Flache[1], and Jochem Tolsma[2]

[1] ICS/Department of Sociology,
University of Groningen, Groningen, The Netherlands
[2] ICS/Department of Sociology, Radboud University,
Nijmegen, The Netherlands

The ethnic diversity in western societies is increasing – at the same time, scholars observe a rise in anti-immigrant attitudes and in the support for radical right-wing parties. This fosters scholarly and societal interest in how the spatial segregation of groups affects opinion polarization in a society. Despite much empirical and theoretical research, there is little consensus in the literature on the causal link between the spatial segregation of two groups and the emergence of opinion polarization. We address the segregation-polarization relationship theoretically by framing the puzzle in a formal fashion and adopting a generative approach. We study *how*, *when* and *where* spatial segregation based on a static demographic characteristic leads to the emergence of opinion polarization. We test different causal pathways by explicating alternative micro-level mechanisms (i.e. how) under different initial segregation patterns (i.e. when) and by assessing the extent of opinion polarization between and within demographic groups both at the global and local level (i.e where). For this purpose, we focus on two types of models of opinion formation: models that combine positive with negative influence (hereafter: 'NI') [1, 2] and models of persuasive arguments exchange ('PA') [3, 4], both of which root in classic sociological and psychological theories of polarization processes. We align and compare these two models in a model-to-model analysis, manipulating the degree of agents' spatial segregation by group membership by means of a Schelling-like model of residential segregation [5, 6].

NI models build on classical computational models of social influence, which only assume positive social influence – that is, interacting individuals tend to reduce their opinion differences. NI models add that individuals are not only homophilic, but xenophobic, too: they tend to like similar people and dislike dissimilar ones. In NI models, being exposed to dissimilar others evokes negative influence, defined as the tendency of individuals to adjust their opinions in a way to increase opinion differences to negatively evaluated others. In case of an exogenously imposed segregation of agents by a demographic characteristic, the intuition is that NI model predict that *lack of* group segregation fosters opinion polarization between the groups. The reason is that members of segregated groups have less chance to be exposed to dissimilar others (members of the outgroup), and thus less chances to get negatively influenced and maximize opinion distance to outgroup members.

© Springer International Publishing Switzerland 2016
M. Baldoni et al. (Eds.): PRIMA 2016, LNAI 9862, pp. 409–410, 2016.
DOI: 10.1007/978-3-319-44832-9

Compared to the NI model, the PA model produces the opposite intuition. It combines the homophily principle and the assumption that individuals sharing opinions also share arguments supporting such opinions. Two interacting partners with similar opinions keep on providing each other new arguments supporting their initial tendencies. Previous modeling work showed how this results in their opinions slowly shifting towards the extreme end of the opinion scale they initially leaned to. Assuming that ingroup agents exert a stronger influence than outgroup ones, we expect that the PA model predicts more opinion polarization for increasing levels of spatial segregation. This is because, under conditions of spatial segregation based on a demographic characteristic, agents will be more exposed to their demographic ingroup members and less exposed to demographic outgroup members. This increased exposure to demographic ingroup members will lead to a reinforcement of initial opinion tendencies within a demographic subgroup and to increasing differences between demographic subgroups.

Simulation results show that the NI model does indeed predict a negative relationship between spatial segregation and emerging opinion polarization. Simulations also show a strong alignment of opinions and demographic group membership (that is, ingroup members tend to develop the same opinion, opposite to the opinion of the outgroup).

With regard to the PA model, we find little support for a positive relationship between segregation and polarization. Secondly, the PA model generates less alignment of opinion and group membership, and this alignment is shown to emerge only within individual interaction neighborhoods. Furthermore, we observe that the PA model generates overall less opinion polarization than observed in previous work - the reasons behind this lack of polarization are further analyzed in the paper.

References

1. Macy, M.W., Kitts, J.A., Flache, A., Benard, S.: Polarization in dynamic networks: a hopfield model of emergent structure. In: Dynamic Social Network Modeling and Analysis, pp. 162–173 (2003)
2. Flache, A., Macy, M.W.: Small worlds and cultural polarization. J. Math. Sociol. 35, 146–176 (2011)
3. Mäs, M., Flache, A.: Differentiation without distancing. Explaining bi-polarization of opinions without negative influence. PloS one 8, e74516 (2013)
4. Mäs, M., Flache, A., Takács, K., Jehn, K.A.: In the short term we divide, in the long term we unite: demographic crisscrossing and the effects of faultlines on subgroup polarization. Organ. Sci. 24, 716–736 (2013)
5. Zhang, J.: Residential segregation in an all-integrationist world. J. Econ. Behav. Organ. 54, 533–550 (2004)
6. Schelling, T.C.: Dynamic models of segregation†. J. Math. Sociol. 1, 143–186 (1971)

Can Noise in Behavioral Models Improve Macro-Predictions? An Empirical Test

Michael Mäs[1]([⊠]) and Dirk Helbing[2]

[1] Department of Sociology/ICS, University of Groningen,
Grote Rozenstraat 31, 9712 TG, Groningen, The Netherlands
m.maes@rug.nl
[2] Chair of Computational Social Science, ETH Zurich,
Clausiusstrasse 50, 8092 Zurich, Switzerland

1 Extended Abstract

Assume that you have developed a new explanation for collective uprisings, such as the Arab Spring. Testing your theory with a representative survey, you find that your theory is able to explain 95 percent of individuals' protest behavior. Would you conclude hat your theory explains why, for instance, the Arab spring happened? Would you use this theory to predict future uprisings?

Most social scientists, would consider your theory a great explanation. However, formal models of human collective phenomena suggest that there might be conditions where even this highly accurate micro-theory makes false macro-predictions [1–11]. According to these models, misjudgment or trial-and-error behavior can lead to deviations from individuals' behavioral patterns that micro-theories describe. Under certain conditions even a seemingly negligible amount random deviations can spark a cascade of behavioral changes that fundamentally change the behavior of the collective. These theories assume that deviations are random and, therefore, unpredictable. Nevertheless, criteria of stochastic stability permit to identify the conditions under which deviations lead to system instability [1]. This suggests that including noise in micro-theories can improve macro-predictions.

The potentially critical effects of random deviations have been studied in fields as diverse as physics, chemistry, cognitive science, traffic research, biology, and economics. Most prominent are certainly the effects of random mutations in evolution and the effects of the random movement of particles, or temperature, in gases and liquids [12]. Recently, random deviations have also been studied in theoretical models of social processes [5, 11]. However, the vast majority of social science theory is based on deterministic assumptions [13]. What is more, to date there is no empirical evidence for the macro-effects of micro-deviations.

In two laboratory experiments we tested whether or not micro-deviations can affect the emergence of social norms, a collective outcome that has been studied extensively with games of coordination and anti-coordination in networks. In these games, participants repeatedly decide between several behavioral options and sometimes establish a shared social norm in the sense that all individuals

M. Baldoni et al. (Eds.): PRIMA 2016, LNAI 9862, pp. 411–412, 2016.
DOI: 10.1007/978-3-319-44832-9

coordinate on one behavior. We studied the effects of micro-level deviations on collective coordination, because existing theoretical and experimental research has established a standard theory of individual decision making in these games [4, 5]. With this micro-model, we could derive hypotheses about the conditions under which micro-deviations affect the macro-pattern of coordination.

Experiment 1 had two aims. First, we tested the central notion that deviations matter, studying a social setting where a micro-theory that abstracts from deviations makes very different macro-predictions than the same micro-theory with deviations. Second, we tested whether the theoretical model with deviations accurately identifies the conditions under which deviations matter for macro-outcomes and when macro-outcomes are unaffected by deviations. Experiment 2 challenged the assumption that deviations are random. On the one hand, the prediction that micro-deviations have macro-effects is most surprising when deviations are assumed to occur randomly. On the other hand, we show that sometimes the theoretical assumption that deviations are random leads to very different macro-predictions than assumptions about systematic deviations from the prevalent patterns of individual decision-making. Experiment 2, therefore, empirically tested whether it may be problematic to assume that deviations are always random.

References

1. Foster, D., Young, P.: Stochastic evolutionary game dynamics. Theor. Popul. Biol. **38**(2), 219–232 (1990)
2. Young, H.P.: The dynamics of social innovation. Proc. Natl. Acad. Sci. U.S.A. **108**, 21285–21291 (2011)
3. Binmore, K., Samuelson, L.: Evolutionary drift and equilibrium selection. Rev. Econ. Stud. **66**(2), 363–393 (1999)
4. Montanari, A., Saberi, A.: The spread of innovations in social networks. Proc. Natl. Acad. Sci. U.S.A. **107**(47), 20196–20201 (2010)
5. Young, H.P.: The evolution of conventions. Econometrica **61**(1), 57–84 (1993)
6. Blume, L.E.: The statistical-mechanics of strategic interaction. Games Econ. Behav. **5**(3), 387–424 (1993)
7. Ellison, G.: Learning, local interaction, and coordination. Econometrica **61**(5), 1047–1071 (1993)
8. Kandori, M., Mailath, G.J., Rob, R.: Learning, mutation, and long-run equilibria in games. Econometrica **61**(1), 29–56 (1993)
9. Mäs, M., Flache, A., Helbing, D.: Individualization as driving force of clustering phenomena in humans. PLoS Comput. Biol. **6**(10), e1000959 (2010)
10. McKelvey, R.D., Palfrey, T.R.: Quantal response equilibria for normal-form games. Games Econ, Behav. **10**(1), 6–38 (1995)
11. Pineda, M., Toral, R., Hernandez-Garcia, E.: Noisy continuous-opinion dynamics. J. Stat. Mech.Theory E. P08001 (2009)
12. Nicolis, G., Prigogine, I.: Self-Organizationin Nonequilibrium Systems: from Dissipative Structures to Order Through Fluctuations. Wiley-Interscience, New York (1977)
13. Macy, M., Tsvetkova, M.: The signal importance of noise. Sociol. Methods Res. **44**(2), 306–328 (2015)

Ali Baba and the Thief, Convention Emergence in Games

Xin Sun[✉] and Livio Robaldo[✉]

Faculty of Science, Technology and Communication, University of Luxembourg,
Esch-sur-Alzette, Luxembourg
{xin.sun,livio.robaldo}@uni.lu

Game theoretical study of the emergence of conventions and social norms has been developed by both computer scientists and philosophers [1, 3–5]. In this paper we propose a model that supports the emergence of conventions or social norms which prescribe peaceful behavior via multiagent learning in social networks. In our model, individual agents repeatedly interact with their neighbors in a game called 'Ali Baba and the Thief'. Our results show that conventions prohibiting harmful behaviors, such as "don't rob", can emerge after repeated interactions among agents.

The general methodology for studying the emergence of norms in Alexander [1] is the following:

1. Identify norms with a particular strategy in a two-player game.
2. Use replicator dynamics and multiagent learning to test whether norms emerge as a result of the repeated play of the two-player game.
3. Test norm emergence with different social networks.

Two-player games studied in Alexander [1] includes prisoner's dilemma, stag hunt, cake cutting and ultimatum game. Alexander uses these games to analyze the emergence of norms of cooperation, trust, fair division and retaliation respectively. In this paper, we follow Alexander's general methodology but we study convention emergence in a game which is not explored in Alexander [1].

As a variant of the famous Hawk-Dove game, *Ali Baba and the Thief* is a 2-player game, where each agent has two strategies: Ali Baba and Thief. Each agent has initial utility x. If both agents choose Ali Baba, then their utility does not change. If they both choose Thief, then there will be a fight between them and they are both injured. The resulting utility is 0. If one chooses Ali Baba and the other chooses Thief, then Thief robs Ali Baba and the utility of the one who chooses Thief increases by d and the other one decreases by d, where $0 < d < x$. We call d the amount of robbery. The payoff matrix of this game is shown in Table 1.

We identify conventions prescribing peaceful behavior with the strategy of Ali baba in this game. In our model this game is repeatedly played by a given amount of agents. Each agent adapts its strategy using a learning rule between different rounds of play. In general, we say a convention has emerged in the population if:

© Springer International Publishing Switzerland 2016
M. Baldoni et al. (Eds.): PRIMA 2016, LNAI 9862, pp. 413–415, 2016.
DOI: 10.1007/978-3-319-44832-9

Table 1. Ali Baba and Thief

	Ali Baba	Thief
Ali Baba	x,x	$x-d,x+d$
Thief	$x+d,x-d$	0,0

(1) All agents are choosing and will continue to choose the action prescribed by the convention.

(2) Every agent believes that all agents, who are relevant in its social network, will choose the action prescribed by the convention in the next round.

(3) Every agent believes that all other agents, who are relevant in its social network, believe that it is good if the agent chooses the action prescribed by the convention.

The above three criteria of convention emergence is a reformulation of Lewis' famous analysis of conventions: "Everyone conforms, everyone expects others to conform, and everyone has good reasons to conform because conforming is in each person's best interest when everyone else plans to conform" [2]. In our game, we are interested in the rounds where all agents choose Ali Baba. This can be understood as no agent is willing to be Thief, which shows conventions like "you should not rob" or "don't harm others" have emerged.

We use replicator dynamics and imitate-the-best as rules of learning. No social network is assumed when agents learn using replicator dynamics while lattice model and small world model are used when agents use imitate-the-best.

Table 2. lattice model, critical point, $x = 1000$

Amount of robbery (d)	Probability of norm emergence
428.57142	1
428.57143	0.16

In both lattice model and small world model, our experimental results suggest that there are critical points of convention emergence which are decided by the quotient of the amount of robbery and the initial utility in the Ali baba and the Thief game. When the quotient of the amount of robbery and the initial utility is smaller than the critical point, the probability of convention emergence is high. The probability drops dramatically as long as the quotient is larger than the critical point. In the lattice model, the probability of convention emergence drops quickly as long as the amount of robbery is large than 428.57142.

References

1. McKenzie Alexander, J.: The Structural Evolution of Morality. Cambridge University Press (2007)
2. Lewis, D.: Conventions: A Philosophical Study. Harvard University Press, Cambridge (1969)
3. Savarimuthu, B.T.R., Cranefield, S.: Norm creation, spreading and emergence: a survey of simulation models of norms in multi-agent systems. Multiagent Grid Syst. **7**(1), 21–54 (2011)
4. Shoham, Y., Tennenholtz, M.: On the emergence of social conventions: modeling, analysis, and simulations. Artif. Intell. **94**(1–2), 139–166 (1997)
5. Skyrms, B.: Evolution of the Social Contract. Cambridge University Press (2014)

Author Index